A View
From The Ledge

CREDITS

EDITOR Barbara Huck

ASSOCIATE EDITOR Peter St. John

INDEX Ellinor Schulz, Joan Nicolas

DESIGN Dawn Huck

PREPRESS & PRINTING Friesens, Manitoba, Canada

Library and Archives Canada Cataloguing in Publication

Schulz, Herbert, 1926-
   A view from the ledge: an insider's look at the Schreyer years / Herb Schulz.

Includes bibliographical references and index.
ISBN 1-896150-19-5 (pbk.)

   1. Schreyer, Edward, 1935-. 2. Manitoba--Politics and government--1969-1977. 3.New Democratic Party of Manitoba--History. 4. Manitoba--History--1945-.
I.title.

FC3377.2.S35 2005   971.27'03   C2005-905828-5

Front cover image
The west face of the Manitoba Legislative Building. Peter St. John.

Back cover images
At left, author Herb Schulz, 2005. Joan Nicolas

Background photo: Elated at the prospect of forming Manitoba's first New Democratic Party government, newly-elected NDP cabinet members celebrate with a cheer on June 26, 1969. From left, Al Mackling, Saul Miller, Saul Cherniack, Phillip Petursson, Ben Hanuschak, Ian Turnbull, Russell Doern, Sid Green and Howard Pawley. Winnipeg Tribune Photograph Collection, PC18_4163_2, University of Manitoba Archives and Special Collections.

At right, Premier Ed Schreyer, in a photo taken just before he was elected for the first time in 1969. Gerry Cairns, Winnipeg Free Press.

 Conseil des Arts Canada Council
du Canada for the Arts

Created with the generous
support of the
Manitoba Arts Council/
Conseil des Arts du Manitoba

 CONSEIL DES arts DU MANITOBA
MANITOBA COUNCIL

A View From The Ledge

An Insider's Look at the Schreyer Years

By Herb Schulz

Heartland Associates, Inc.
Winnipeg, Canada

Printed in Manitoba, Canada

TABLE OF CONTENTS

TABLE OF CONTENTS

Introduction

English philosopher and historian John E.E. Dahlberg Acton sagely advised "those who would write history, don't." So I haven't. This is a memoir of experiences and perceptions into which, inevitably and with apologies to Lord Acton, some history may have crept.

From September 1971 to October 1977, I was special assistant to the Premier of Manitoba. As a political appointee, I was expected to be involved in the apparatus and operations of government and concerned with outcomes. From that vantage point, I observed decisions being taken and transmuted through the individual and collective minds of premier, cabinet, caucus, party, and political opposition, forged in the crucible of the legislature into law, and implemented by the bureaucracy. I was high enough in both political and governmental hierarchies to witness, with varying degrees of satisfaction or frustration, the unfolding of public policy, but not high enough to make it. Hence the title.

This work is dedicated to all those who made a historic period in Manitoba possible by being who they were and by the paths their life took and which thus touched mine. Despite my periodic unhappiness with the way some things developed and my abiding belief that much could have been done better, this did not breed the cynicism currently fashionable among many who have never been at the centre of the policy-making apparatus. For me it was both inspiring and humbling to observe rational men and women, in the government or the opposition, making decisions, whether political or personal, they knew would cost them votes, but which they believed to be in the long-term interests of the society that had placed its trust in them.

Some had never heard of Edmund Burke, but knew they owed their community their best judgement, and they drew on conscience and a deep well of personal and community values to stand alone, never sure their rectitude would be rewarded. It is this dedication across the political spectrum described in William Manchester's *American Caesar* that "keeps the ballot the political expression of a free people instead of the charmed tribute of the ignorant to the eloquent." These men and women allowed me to work with them and for that I shall be forever grateful.

This is no hagiography creating amorphous myths of great men and women nor an attempt to be 'politically correct'. I'm hopeful that this work has enough acerbic delineations of character and critical commentary on the political and administrative apparatus of government to satisfy Canadian historian Jack Granatstein, who has accused faceless bureaucrats, obsessed with not offending anyone, of killing Canadian history.

Joseph Conrad wrote in *The Nigger of the Narcissus*, "My task is to make you hear, to feel, to see." What follows is a view of government the public does not often see, of how history is made and of those who make it.

This is also the story of someone who, by a morbid happenstance, was transported to the beating heart of the Manitoba government and became a Forrest Gumpish figure often, by pure coincidence, where the action was. Since this was a time when the province was grinding through revolutionary and historic changes, fate placed me where I could work at changing society and, for a moment in time, to enjoy the illusion that I might succeed.

Some events described are compressed and some dialogues are composites, but a sincere effort has been made to maintain authenticity. There is no 'objective' history. Therefore there is in the following no pretense of being a dispassionate observer; yet I was an observer with more than an historian's interest in events. Since history is essentially in the mind of the writer, different witnesses, with different recollections, perceptions and ideological spectacles, will have seen events differently, and, like the six blind men examining the elephant, "each is partly in the right and each is partly wrong". As the era recedes into folklore and myth, others will have their own versions. This one is mine.

Wayne Boyce / Courtesy of the Schulz family.

Herb Schulz, 1971

Acknowledgements

My deepest gratitude to all those with whom I have had the honour of working during my many years as a political activist and government functionary. I also wish to thank all those who have helped put this publication together: Peter St. John for his encouragement; Barbara Huck for her gentle, but firm, editorial hand and Dawn Huck, who patiently laid out chapter after chapter.

I wish to acknowledge the unstinting assistance of my family, and particularly of my two daughters, Joan Nicolas and Karen Schulz, who contributed their literary, artistic and typing talents. Most of all, I want to thank my wife, Ellinor, for her assistance, but particularly for just being there when I needed her and, with her infinite patience, for encouraging me on the many occasions when it appeared this work would never be completed.

This book is dedicated to all those politicians, past, present and future, at every level of government, who have contributed their time and energy to demonstrate the validity of the proposition enunciated by King Arthur in *Camelot*—that the people can govern themselves.

More particularly, it is dedicated to the former Member of the Manitoba Legislature, former Member of Parliament, former Governor General of Canada, former High Commissioner to Australia, Edward Schreyer, who, as Premier of Manitoba, gave me the opportunity to see democracy in action—from the inside.

Publisher's note: Though Canada officially "went metric" in the late 1960s, the popular conversion came about much more gradually and some measurements, including human height, are still commonly expressed in Imperial measurement. Even twenty-something Canadians regularly speak of friends who are six feet tall, rather than 1.83 metres. Givern the period covered in these pages—1969 to 1977 —the author's use of Imperial measurement, with only a handful of exceptions for measurements such as the voltage or wattage of hydro-electric power, seemed appropriate.

I

So It Begins

Media Vita, In Morte Sumus [1]
   —Roman Proverb

"Hello!"

It had taken a moment for the strident ringing of the telephone to rouse me from my reverie about the problem that had erupted two days earlier. Languidly, I picked up the receiver.

"Yes, Ed here," the voice on the other end said. "What are you doing?"

It took a second or two to realize who "Ed" was.

"Oh—yes—Ed! Oh, just putting in time. Nothing exciting ever happens to me." That was not quite true, but it satisfied the casual attitude to life I had affected for the past several days.

"I have a problem." The serene voice made it hard to believe Ed ever had a problem. "My assistant is ill and the paper-work is up to my ears. Could you to come and help me out until he returns?"

The question was totally unexpected and my heart raced. I had been offered a part-time teaching position at the University of Manitoba. It was not much, but I could not be selective and it was an opportunity to embark on a new career and fulfill a life-long ambition, but now came an offer I had never dreamed of. Temporary perhaps, but the ultimate in job aspirations. And it might be fun to indulge in some nepotism—but then I remembered my problem.

"What's the problem with your assistant?"

"He has cancer. A note of sadness infused the calm voice. "He is scheduled for surgery the day after tomorrow."

---

[1] "In the middle of life we are dying."

Christ! What mordant irony.

"Well Ed, I'm glad you called and I would love to work with you, but I have this problem." I was not ready to utter the words.

"What problem?"

"You are aware I have been prepping for my exams?"

"When do you write?"

"Tomorrow."

"No sweat." The overused expression seemed inappropriate in the mouth of one usually so precise with the language. "Then you can come in Friday."

"Well, as you know, I am to begin teaching at the university next Tuesday." I said the "am to begin" somewhat tentatively, subliminally aware something might intervene.

"That's only one course. It leaves twenty-two hours a day spare time."

I simply could not bring myself to articulate the real problem. Why was Ed being so persistent?

"Well, I may not survive. I'm approaching it with the alacrity of a condemned man approaching the gallows ..."

"There is no record of anyone killed by a university exam. So I can expect you Friday?" It was more assertion than question.

"Well, there is another slight problem." I felt as though refusing to verbalize it would exorcise the spectre. "I hesitate to tell you, but I had a routine check-up last week and ..."

"I am sure your poor, emaciated body will survive the agonies of a routine check-up."

The voice remained calm but with a slight edge, indicating irritation by time wasted in small talk. "Sorry, I must go. My secretary is holding a call. See you Friday A.M."

Oh Jesus! Was there no easy way out? Must it be said? Must the spectre be invoked by speaking its dread name?

"Well Ed, I don't want to delay you, but my friendly sawbones has told me I am to be afflicted with a slight case of surgery."

"When?"

"Perhaps the day after tomorrow."

"What's the problem?"

"Cancer." There it was. I had finally said it aloud to another person. It was finally final. The spectre had won.

THE PREVIOUS FRIDAY I had casually attended my doctor's office. I had protested against visiting doctors since age nine, when I was thrown by a horse and broke my arm. My father drove me town in our rickety Chevrolet touring car, with canvas top flapping and plastic windows rattling in the wind, bumping and grinding over ten miles of rutted back-country trails amid suffocating dust. He stood by while the doctor, a large, aging man with hamlike hands and the disposition of a bear roused from winter hibernation, gently refitted the broken ends of bone under the torn, purpled skin, and splinted the fracture. A nurse, a big horse of a woman, mixed plaster-of-Paris in a tin basin, soaked a strip of bandage in the greyish mess, and spiralled it around my arm. I did not scream—I dared not scream in my father's presence—but the pain was such that I determined to avoid doctors and hospitals in the future.

Our pioneer family relied on home cures. Severe colds meant—after completing my chores—sitting with feet in hot water, wrapped in my father's caracul-wool coat (one of the few items brought from Eastern Europe), eating a raw onion and then almost suffocating under a feather quilt. In the morning I stank like a boar but the cold was gone—no self-respecting germ could survive such barbaric treatment. Bad cuts were treated with the miracle cures of that time—Watkins' Ointment and Iodine, which was tested for potency by how loud the patient screamed when it was poured on an open wound.

But sometimes there was no Iodine. At age twelve, a horse had thrown me onto a barb-wire fence that cut a hole in my cheek large enough to stick my tongue through. There was rust on the fence and I was an hour from home, so I applied the Army treatment my father had taught me—I urinated on my handkerchief and plugged the wound. It left me with nothing but a scar—and the beginning of a feeling of invincibility.

But I was no stranger to doctors and hospitals. At thirteen, I was severely burned in a gasoline fire and spent fourteen months in three separate hospitals. It left me with a crippled arm that took years to rehabilitate, and the left side of my body looking like a patchwork quilt with white swatches of grafted skin interspersed among angry red welts of scar tissue requiring periodic skin grafts. My body rehabilitated itself—a generation later I would have created jobs for several social workers—but was slightly canted to the left by the tension of the inflexible scar tissue, and my left pectoral looked like that of the woman whose breast had been torn off by Jaws. Talk of doctors recalled the agony.

I had graduated in Agriculture at twenty, farmed until age thirty-five, enrolled in first year Arts, earned my master's degree in History with Political Science and Economics minors, and begun doctoral studies. The need to work to make a living interrupted and time passed. At a social function someone had asked what I would be after graduating and before I could formulate some profound reply my wife had smiled beatifically and pronounced: "Senile."

I did not feel senile now while sitting, unclad, legs dangling over the edge of the high cot. I felt good and casually bantered with our family doctor, a short, balding Holocaust survivor, a kindly man with a wrinkled face that made him look older than his mid-fifties, round shouldered as though, like some miniature Atlas, he carried the burdens of the world on his back, and gentle hands.

The doctor's gentle hands were now around my throat. "How long have you had that lump in your throat?" he asked.

"I didn't know I had one."

"You have one."

"Weeell doctor, when I sit here all naked-like and think of that beautiful nurse beyond that door I get a lump in my throat." I said it lightly but with some vague apprehension upon suddenly recalling that my shirt collar had felt very tight lately.

"Its not that kind of a lump. I don't like it."

"Since we appear to be distinguishing between lumps and lumps, what kind of lump do you think this particular lump is?"

"I don't know. I'm sending you to the St. Boniface Clinic for tests. I'm making an appointment for Monday." The nonchalant repartee lost its flavour. It was a beautiful weekend except for the unease in my mind because of the lump in my throat.

At the clinic the middle-aged, bespectacled nurse ordered me to swallow a paper vial of evil-smelling, milky liquid, strip to the waist, and lie on a narrow table. An apparatus on a rail emitted a peculiar crackling sound, like radio static in a thunderstorm, when passing over my throat. The nurse uttered no word; the urgent crackling on the machine brought a slight frown to her forehead but she was too professional to show more than a flicker of emotion. After the process had been repeated several times, I was ordered to dress and leave. The doctor phoned next morning:

"Hello. Doctor Goldstein here. How are you this morning?" He made it sound as though he really cared.

"Fine, considering I am taking my lumps in the throat."

"The lump in your throat is cancer," said the kindly voice. "I'm reserving the first available bed at Victoria Hospital."

My universe suddenly assumed the shape of a huge, gooey tumor growing in and clawing at my throat.

THAT WAS TUESDAY MORNING. It was now Wednesday and when the phone startled me out of my reverie I thought it was the doctor and was terrified; it had taken me a moment to respond. But it was Ed with an offer that ignited my imagination; there was just this one little problem that I had finally articulated and ...

"There seems to be a lot of that going around these days." My brother-in-law's deep, quiet voice pierced the long, palpable silence. "When did you find out?"

"Yesterday."

"How is Ellinor taking it?"

"I haven't told her."

When the doctor had called with the portentous diagnosis, in some deep recesses of my brain rang Seeger's lines:

I have a rendezvous with death,
I shall not fail that rendezvous [2]

At the hospital I ran the gauntlet of receptionists, bookkeepers, nurses and a psychiatrist, with a professional smile and clipboard, asking how I felt about my impending surgery. So how should I feel? Like Hell! Like two barrels of shit! I was poked, primped, prodded, purged and prepared for my rendezvous at dawn with the surgeon's scalpel.

They took me early in the morning, with terrifying efficiency, half-unconscious from the sedative, transferring me quickly from the bed to the white-sheeted gurney, turning toward the elevator, wheeling along the corridor, mind reeling dazedly, moving swifly into the vortex of the kaleidoscope:

Hands and faces floating free,
Doors and floors and many things
That slip beneath the wheels of time,
And change the real to phantasy …

The OR was cool and spartan, two gloved disembodied hands from behind placed a mask over my face; the strong odour of ether pervaded; a sound of a small bell like that tolled by priests at Catholic funerals titillated my auditory senses; I stared into an intense white light; an ethereal Presence beckoned through a diaphanous curtain; unlike Dylan Thomas, I would "go gentle into that good night"; my body was warm and relaxed and floated above:

The sheets; the cool white sheets,
To make love on, or to die upon …

I MOVED THROUGH A LONG WARM phantasmagoric spun cotton-candy tunnel into consciousness, my senses returning one by one. My eyes began opening, feeling heavy as portcullises. I was seeing through a small, undulating, swirling aperture. Then I saw her.

She sat, miniaturized by the aperture through which I saw the world, the light behind her, like an illuminated pieta.

"It's all right dear. Don't talk. I just wanted to be here." I was safe. My wife was beside me. Nothing could hurt me now.

Two days later, while slowly emerging from the fleecy clouds of drugs, an alien object in my neck that felt like a football, my throat lacerated by tubes inserted while I lay helpless on those "cool white sheets", my voice an octave below that of

---

[2] Alan Seeger, "I Have a Rendezvous with Death", 1916.

Paul Robeson, the nurse came. No, it was not a nurse; it was my sister-in-law. Well, same difference. She was an operating room nurse.

"You are a very lucky fellow." The pain seeping through the fog did not validate that opinion. "I am?"

"Yes. We cut your throat open and found a huge, horrible tumor. We excised the tumour and ninety per cent of your thyroid gland, which means you must take supplements for the rest of your life. And you will be adorned with a scar which means wearing turtleneck sweaters or strangers will run from you shouting 'unclean, unclean'."

My befogged mind attempted to cope with the ominous news I would forever be captive of a pill bottle, while wondering what else they had done to me while I lay helpless.

"So that makes me 'a lucky fellow'?"

"Normally when we do surgery in a case like this we send a sample of tissue to the lab for a biopsy, which usually takes two or three days to be returned, and then we base any further procedures on that report. In your case, however, the pathologist happened by coincidence to be right there in the OR during the surgery. His considered opinion was that the tumor was malignant."

MALIGNANT! A giant hand seized my throat. The word pierced me like an arrow. My sister-in-law's voice sounded as though from another dimension.

"The doctor had to decide if he should suture up your neck and risk cutting you open again if the biopsy showed malignancy, or accept the pathologist's diagnosis and do a radical."

"A radical?" I croaked.

"That means removing your larynx and lower jaw". I was sinking back into the long, warm, phantasmagoric spun cotton candy tunnel.

"The doctor decided to sew you up and wait for the biopsy report. It came back an hour ago. Your tumor proved benign."

While she spoke, my emotions looped like a rollercoaster, then stabilized. I had suffered the shocks that flesh falls heir to and survived, and there was nothing more they could do to me.

"In Wellington's words, it was a damn close-fought thing," continued my erudite sister-in-law. She paused: "The reason I said you are a very lucky fellow is because, if your doctor had been younger, or if he did not know you so well personally and knew you need your voice more than you need your penis, he would have removed your larynx."

TWO WEEKS LATER I ANSWERED ED'S CALL for help. I was ensconced in a tiny basement cubicle smelling of stale air and suspended dust, adjacent to the public washroom smelling of urine and disinfectant, and with a steady stream of traffic. A bag of mail was dumped on my small metal desk. Concerns about my inauspicious debut were soon submerged by my work, which settled around me like a well-worn cloak. I was no novice; I had operated a large farm for twelve years and built apartment blocks for eight years, and stumped the province on behalf of farm organizations and politics and fought the Establishment of various organizations, as well as previous governments. By comparison, this job was easy.

And on my first day an incident made me realize that this job, no matter how temporary, could be exciting and rewarding. Needing some information from the minister of Public Works, I went to his office where the dazzling blond secretary explained the minister was busy with someone in his private office and politely asked me to wait in the reception area. A few minutes later a young man entered, gave his name to the secretary, and also sat down to await the minister's pleasure. He was thirtyish, tall and slim with neatly combed blond hair, an Ivy-League-handsome face, and wore a moderately expensive medium-brown suit and carried a slim attaché case. Exuding professional enthusiasm, he quickly initiated a conversation. We did not introduce ourselves but during the conversation he revealed himself to be an architect with a firm specializing in publicly funded projects.

Recollections of publicly funded projects, and their enormous cost overruns, rushed through my mind—the National Arts Centre in Ottawa recently completed for several times the estimated cost—refitting of the ill-fated World War II carrier, *Bonaventure*, for three times the estimated $3,000,000. I smiled at the young man to show I was being half-facetious: "I have a theory about architects who work on publicly funded projects. They never tell the government what the actual cost is going to be because they fear if the price is known the project will not be begun, but they also know that once begun it will be completed no matter what the costs."

"Oh yes, we do that all the time," the young man responded with youthful candour. "For example, there is currently a dispute over what is going to be the actual cost of building the Winnipeg Convention Centre. The government has been told it will cost $15 million." He leaned toward me, voice lowered conspiratorially: "Actually it's going to cost $25 million."

In retrospect, I was proud of how I had disguised my surprise, but subsequent conversation was blotted out as I struggled with what had been said. After a moment I excused myself and left.

I always felt a thrill when entering the executive offices, a sentiment that never diminished during my years at "The Ledge" (the name for the Legislative Building was at first spelled "Leg", with the "g" pronounced as "j", until someone among us with a sense of history and humour remarked that we in government stood on a high "Ledge" from which one day we might be thrown by an angry electorate or voluntarily jump to expunge a personal scandal). The Premier's Office occupied an entire wing of the great Tyndall stone structure.

I opened the heavy partially glassed door into the office of the secretary to the premier. Light streamed through the window, the wall was lined with bookcases and filing cabinets halfway to the beamed ceiling, and behind a desk sat pleasant, phenomenally efficient Rita Goebel, a slim, dark-haired, fortyish woman with an easy smile and an air of quiet control.

To the left a door led into the dark-panelled office of the clerk to the cabinet. The first item seen by those who dared enter was a huge VanDyke painting of King Charles I, unique in English history for being shortened by a head by an obstreperous Parliament. The room was fastidiously tidy and exuded foreboding officiousness as though it had assumed the character of its longtime occupant, Derek Bedson, who in his more sardonic moments, claimed kinship with the luckless monarch whose idealized unlikeness adorned his wall.

Another door led into the nucleus of government, the Premier's Office. Rita ushered me in.

First impressions were of Old World charm and sumptuousness. It was spacious and partially panelled with dark oak wainscotting and then off-white plaster rising to its ceiling sixteen feet above. One wall was lined with books while the opposite wall displayed a large functioning fireplace and an oak door into the premier's private washroom. The massiveness of the exterior wall was interrupted by two large double windows, leaving enough panelled wall between them for photos and plaques. At the far end, along the interior wall, a sound-proof door led into the Cabinet Room.

Eight feet from the exterior wall, in front of the dark-panelled area between two windows, was the premier's desk, a huge, heavy piece of furniture suited to carry the burden of the executive decisions signed upon its surface for more than a half-century. Behind it, on a great leather-covered chair, in a light gray suit, white shirt and blue polka dot tie, determinedly but without the slightest sign of hurry, working his way through two large piles of files on his desk, sat the premier.

"Mr. Premier," (I always addressed my brother-in-law formally when at The Ledge or at governmental or formal functions) "I do not know if this has any significance but I thought you should know." Then I repeated the conversation with the young architect.

The premier gave no sign he had heard, except for a slight pursing of his lips. He sat a moment as though his mind was far away. Then he picked up his inter-office phone: "Rita, would you bring me the agreement we have with the city relative to the cost-sharing of the Convention Centre." He spoke quietly and with almost an air of detachment as though nothing could possibly happen to disturb his composure.

The phone was hardly back in its cradle when Rita walked in and placed a bulky file before him. He flipped through the document and located a sentence reading: "The Government of Manitoba agrees to pay 50% of the cost of construction of the Winnipeg Convention Centre". He reached into his shirt pocket for the 'macho' pen with the nylon nib that wrote large and authoritatively, and added interlineally immediately following that sentence the words: "to a maximum of $7,500,000."

"Refer that to Urban Affairs," the premier remarked laconically as he handed the file back to his secretary, and then turned his attention back to the files on his desk. I had been dismissed.

The ultimate cost of the Convention Centre was approximately $25 million. I had apparently saved the Government of Manitoba almost $5 million on the first day at my temporary job.

And, like Pa in *The Grapes of Wrath*[3], who was suspicious of "service" station operators, always after, whenever I saw a well-dressed, bright-looking young man with a slim briefcase, I wondered who was getting screwed.

"FRANCIS JUST DIED." Tears welled up in the large, brown, vulnerable eyes of the tall, slim, raven-haired, Grecian-featured woman—the lady with the lustrous eyes.

Francis Eady was a slim, fiftyish workaholic with the air of an aristocrat and the sentiments of a coal miner. He had been raised on the traditions of the British Labour Party and become a valuable asset to the executive and organizational structure of the Ontario labour union movement. He came to Manitoba in 1970 to assist the premier, replacing Douglas Rowland who had left to contest the federal riding of Selkirk. He became ill and within several months wasted away to a shadow of his former self in body, but not in spirit. He died hard. Almost to the last day before his death of cancer he came to his office at The Ledge, determined the demons within him would not have the last word.

But they did.

My surgery had left me with a neck one size smaller, a severely attenuated thyroid gland, a necklace-like pattern of scars where my throat had been cut from ear to ear and sutured, and a residue of panic whenever I reflected on the helplessness of a person on an operating table. But I had been, in my sister-in-law's words —"a very lucky fellow".

Francis Eady had not been so lucky; his tumour had been malignant. I immediately inherited his position, his spacious, high-ceilinged office directly across the corridor from the premier's office, a key to the executive washroom, the status attached to working in the executive wing on the second floor of The Ledge, and the office staff of three including the kinetic principal secretary, Dorothy Corney, the lady with the lustrous eyes. Dorothy had a phenomenal store of energy; she could simultaneously answer three phones, read a brief, converse with someone seeking information or an appointment, while under her desk making signals with her feet, alerting me through the open door of my private office, that in the form of an irate citizen, danger was approaching.

By a morbid happenstance, I had arrived near the apex of the government, with automatic access to the premier of the province, and to caucus and cabinet meetings of the government. I would be working for Premier Edward Schreyer,

---

[3] John Steinbeck, *The Grapes of Wrath*, p. 164.

who headed the first social democratic government in the history of the Province of Manitoba. I took the oath of office and was assigned my duties, initially answering mail and calls to the Premier's Office, writing speeches for the premier, and—theoretically—advising him on matters political.

As it developed the premier, who consulted widely and was confident with his own counsel, did not often take my advice, or did so with modification, but people thought he did, and that was to sustain my power and authority for the next seventy-four months.

I was "Special Assistant to the Premier of Manitoba". On such accidents of fate, life turns.

II

The Man For All Reasons

Life is what happens to you while you are making other plans.
—John Lennon

"**A**re you canvassing here?** Who are you?"

Ron McBryde, the tall, athletic social worker who looked like Clark Kent without the Superman suit, was canvassing house to house on the native reserve in the constituency of The Pas. A stranger was canvassing house to house from the opposite direction. When they met and the stranger asked him who he was, and if he was seeking electoral support, he responded aggressively: "I'm Ron McBryde. Yes, I am canvassing. I'm the NDP candidate here. By the way, who the hell are you?"

"Oh, I'm Ed Schreyer, your leader."

It had been that kind of campaign.

On May 22, 1969, Progressive Conservative Premier Walter Weir suddenly dissolved the legislature and called a general election for June 25th, barely leaving the required thirty-five days to E-Day. He had two years left in his mandate and he left on the Order Paper some sixty bills, including such heavies as hydro-electric development on the Nelson River, the flooding of South Indian Lake, labour, public housing, agriculture, business development and the rumour-plagued Churchill Forest Industries pulp and paper plant at The Pas.

It surprised everyone. It shocked the third-place New Democratic Party, which had no money, a central office staff of two and very little organizational capacity. Party leader Russ Paulley was in the hospital, under an oxygen tent, with chronic emphysema. It seemed we were beaten before the battle began. But elections concentrate the mind of the politically active. The organization was taken in hand by its legislative members and some old pros, who had been beaten so often they were inured to defeat but reacted to an election call like a war horse to the smell of gunpowder. They were supplemented by a group of young turks anxious to cut their political teeth, hundreds of volunteers, and party personalities in a host of localities.

Party president Sam Uskiw moved swiftly. A leadership meeting, set for October, was moved forward to June. Sidney Green announced he would seek the leadership. Several days later, Ed Schreyer flew in from Ottawa to announce that so would he.

Green and Schreyer campaigned for the leadership, for election in their respective constituencies, and for the party to form the Government of Manitoba. In what confused both the media and political aficionados, they often drove to meetings in the same car, each spoke of why he should be leader, and then drove home together.

By June 7th, the date of the leadership convention, the two contenders seemed very close in the number of votes they would receive. Green, eschewing his usual impassioned speaking style, was calm and reasoned. Schreyer, who usually spoke in highly reasoned terms and circumlocutorily, spoke directly and with unusual fervour. The labour delegates swung to Schreyer. He was elected NDP leader less than three weeks before election day. Then began a campaign that was energetic, imaginative, inexpensive, uncoordinated, fatiguing, and hugely exciting.

Weir, escorted by crowds of organizers, fans and reporters, conducted a ponderous campaign for retrenchment of government and ascendancy of conservatism and free enterprise capitalism: "I am telling the people of Manitoba that if they would like to have a government that is aimed at development using the free enterprise as a base ... vote Conservative."[1]

Meanwhile, Liberal Leader "Bobby" Bend was "enmeshed in the razzmatazz his workers cooked up for him. The bevy of pretty girls in micro-minis, the recorded message touting 'The Bend Brigade is coming ... are you with us?' hides the man in a cloak of party imagery ... the micro-mini brigade, with their sticky badges, antagonized about half the people in [Grant Park] shopping centre and the other half didn't seem to give a damn. One man mistook Bend for a paint salesman."[2]

By contrast: "Mr. Schreyer arrives in a small plane with a single assistant or in the back of his brother-in-law's car with his attractive wife, Lily, as the only member of his campaign team."[3]

We raced from town to town, unsure of where we were supposed to be or what we were to do when we arrived, but for no discernible reason it all came together. René Toupin, a credit union manager, joined the party after the election

---

[1] *Winnipeg Free Press*, June 21, 1969.

[2] Derek Hodgson, *The Winnipeg Tribune*, June 23, 1969.

[3] Bob Culbert, *op cit.*, June 23, 1969.

call, reluctantly agreed to be a candidate for the constituency of Springfield, and seven weeks later was a cabinet minister. In The Pas, Ron McBryde had not recognized his leader when they met. In Swan River, businessman Alex Filuk was nominated and was on the platform delivering his acceptance speech when someone realized he was not a party member and rushed up to slip a card into his pocket.

The next day, I drove Schreyer from Swan River to Roblin for a 2 P.M. meeting. Shortly after he began speaking, someone tugged at my arm: "There's a phone call for you at the hotel." It was from an old friend, Vincent Polloway, in Dauphin. He was very angry: "Where in hell is Ed?"

"Oh, he is here in Roblin."

"So why in hell is he not here in Dauphin?"

"Because he's here in Roblin."

"But party headquarters in Winnipeg told us he would be here at two o'clock and we have a meeting here of forty or fifty people and it is already after two and Ed is not here."

"But we have over 200 at this meeting and Ed is needed here."

We compromised; he would hold the crowd as long as he could and I would get Ed there as soon as I could.

The meeting ended at 3 P.M. We left for Dauphin.

Schreyer had left Ottawa hurriedly to attend the nominating convention. He had brought one suit, some shirts and socks, one tie, one pair of shoes that he wore throughout the campaign, and no coat. My father loaned him a mackinaw jacket, which he promptly lost. Two years later, I was visited by a friend working on the hydro-electric development on the Nelson River, who gleefully showed me some snapshots he had taken during the campaign. Suddenly my attention was arrested; there, draped over a fence somewhere in Gillam, was my father's mackinaw jacket. I remarked ruefully, "I suppose by now its gone to the great polling booth in the sky."

He was very helpful. "Well yes, but at least it's good to know where it is. We wouldn't want to have it lost or anything."

Schreyer had also left his car in Ottawa, so we used mine. It was a 1968, eight-cylinder Chrysler Newport with 383 horses under the hood and when the pedal hit the metal it cruised at 115 mph. It was sixty miles to Dauphin and I was determined to get there in forty-five minutes. I skidded around a curve with the loose gravel on the highway shoulder spewing in every direction. From the rear seat, where Ed sat making notes, came a sepulchral voice: "Well, Herb, we really don't need to hurry. By now there probably won't be anyone left at the meeting anyway."

"Ed, I'm driving fast just because I like to."

"Oh. Well, okay then. Carry on."

So I drove with one hand on the wheel and one eye on the road while scanning the daily newspaper: "Ed. It states right here in the *Winnipeg Free Press* that the NDP has "a magnificently oiled election machine".

"Well, in that case I'd hate to see the others."

"Oh, by the way Ed. I have some information I've been saving for an apppropriate occasion. The party stalwarts promised if you came back from Ottawa and became leader, they would collect at least $50,000 for the campaign. That is not going to happen."

"Ummmm. Well, with such a short campaign we wouldn't have time to spend it anyway."

At 3:50, almost two hours late, we roared into Dauphin and skidded to a stop in front of the Eighth Avenue Hall in a cloud of dust, expecting to find no one there except the caretaker to collect the rent for the hall. Instead, we were greeted by an exhilarating scene. Some 400 people filled the street from curb to curb, waiting to see this young politician who had caught their imagination, their eyes aglow, as though witnessing the Second Coming.

Reporter Bob Culbert named the phenomenon "Schreyermania" [4]

Returning to Winnipeg very late that night, we crossed the Disraeli Bridge into East Kildonan. On an arch stretching over the bridge the city had hung a huge banner reading W-I-N-N-I-P-E-G. Some party workers had gone up during the night, changed the second "I" to "D", and then blocked out the last two letters. What we saw when we drove up the south ramp was W-I-N N-D-P.

Then there was "The Walk". The party had arranged for Schreyer, his wife Lily, and their two little girls, Lisa, six, and Karmel, four, to take "a walk" during the noon hour. They would begin at the CPR station on Higgins, go south on Main Street to Portage Avenue and west to the Polo Park Shopping Centre. As they passed through each constituency along the route several party members would join them and, hopefully, when they arrived at Polo Park, enough would have joined the parade to attract attention.

Ed was missing. The organizers of the parade were in a frenzy. He was found campaigning with our Flin Flon candidate, Tom Barrow [5], on a northern reserve, dressed in high rubber boots and coveralls. A light plane, carrying his "city" clothes, was sent to fetch him. "The Walk" was delayed as long as possible but then Lily, the two girls and several others set out, with great trepidation, and quickly became noticed.

At Portage and Main, Ed in his suit—the green one—joined them. Smiling and shaking hands, they proceeded westward. The crowd enlarged like a rolling snowball. The media arrived and the news cameras attracted even more attention. By the time they arrived at Polo Park a great throng of people had collected, striding along, Schreyer in the lead, a mass of banners floating over the crowd like the eagles over an advancing Roman legion.

News photos the following day depicted clearly that a new attraction had

---

[4]   *Ibid.*, June 24, 1969.

[5]   Barrow was elected.

hit town—and that this young politician had "arrived".

Much of the impact was sheer bravado and good luck. The four hours of free television exposure during the nominating convention launched the NDP as a serious contender. The enthusiasm of party people, who sensed something different in the air, was contagious.

Legendary Tommy Douglas came to town during the last week of the campaign. He had, in the very rural province of Saskatchewan, headed North America's first socialist government for seventeen years. He was now national leader of the NDP, a member of Parliament, and the revered initiator of what had become national Medicare. He was known to approach governing with the coolness of a field general, never allowing short-term deviations to obscure long-term objectives or tactics to be mistaken for strategy, but he approached politics with the passion of the evangelist. He packed the huge auditorium in Winnipeg and took his audience through the full gamut of emotions as only Tommy could. "International relations," he told the crowd, with reference to the Cold War and the need for international organizations to maintain peace, "is like the American Wild West. If two farmers argued over a cow, they reached for their six-guns. The one who got his gun out first got the cow."

He waited for the laughter to subside. "The other one didn't need the cow." The audience roared.

"Today we have laws. When two farmers argue over ownership of a cow, they hire lawyers." The audience clapped and whistled, believing that had been the punchline. Again the dramatic pause: "The lawyers get the cow."

The audience virtually rolled in the aisles. A moment later, many were blinking back tears as he quoted from William Blake, that otherworldly poet-socialist of 150 years earlier:

> I shall not rest from mental strife,
> Nor shall my sword sleep in my hand;
> Til we have built Jerusalem,
> In this green and pleasant land.[6]

And there were 'the photos'. During the campaign I attended a Conservative meeting in a North End hall. Coming in late, I was forced to sit at the extreme front. Premier Weir was already speaking. From my perspective under the edge of the four-foot high platform, the 230-pound, 5'9" Weir looked wide at the hip and narrow at the shoulder. His suit of silk—the kind that seduces the eye but wrinkles in the closet—appeared to have been slept in. I had a vagrant thought; if a photo of him looking like this were to appear in the newspapers, he would lose the election. The following day, there was the photo on the front page. It seemed almost like sabotage. The cameraman must have crouched on

---

[6] "Jerusalem".

the floor near where I had been sitting, for the camera angle made Weir look like an inverted blimp. Every wrinkle in his shiny black suit was emphasized by the light. It was a killer.

By contrast, during the nominating convention, photographer Gerry Cairns took a candid shot of the photogenic Schreyer. The next day it was in the *Winnipeg Free Press*. It was an unusual, perhaps unique, photo, showing him, head and torso leaning slightly back and to the right, right elbow on the armrest of the chair he sat in, chin resting lightly on the thumb of his right hand, looking to the side which showed an expanse of the whites of his large eyes, gazing serenely into the near distance, half matinee idol and half visionary, a face from central casting topped by dark wavy hair. A picture-perfect shot candidates would kill for.

Ed Schreyer, 1969.

Gerry Cairns / Winnipeg Free Press

Terry Grier (later an NDP member of the Ontario Legislature) had come to act as our media relations person. When he spotted the photo in the newspaper, he exploded, "Get the rights to that photo. Whatever it takes, GET IT." The photo was made into large placards, over the caption: THE MAN FOR ALL REASONS. More than thirty years later it still adorns the walls of some Manitoba homes.

Despite this auspicious beginning, the end was far from certain—sixteen months earlier NDP defector Ross Thatcher and his Liberals had defeated the NDP in Saskatchewan —Canadian socialism's breeding ground—a second time. But it was soon clear we would gain seats and, whether as government or official opposition, we would have more policy-making power than ever before—and power imposes responsibility. We were passing beyond the easy rhetoric of a party forever condemned to the political fringe and we needed to sort out our policies and philosophy.

Since the 1966 election, the hyperactive NDP caucus had promoted a solid base of policies: publicly administered, premium free, universal health insurance;

a publicly owned motor vehicle insurance company; loans to farmers to assist in retention of the family farm; an improved farm crop insurance program; producer controlled farm product marketing boards; transfer of education costs from municipalities to the province; better access to post-secondary education; funding universities; taxation realignment; review of the Nelson River hydro-electric development; control of urban sprawl; reorganization of the City of Winnipeg and its contiguous municipalities; northern economic development; review of the scandal plagued Churchill Forest Industries at The Pas; transparency in the use of the Manitoba Development Fund; establishment of an ombudsman; a consumer protection bureau; an audit department to assure efficiency and accountability in government spending; a program of low rent public housing; senior citizens housing; nursing homes to ease hospital costs; home care and integration of Aboriginal Manitobans into the economic mainstream.

But that left the more nebulous, and delicate, area of political philosphy; how far should the state intrude into the economy on behalf of the socially and economically vulnerable? To what extent should state instruments be used for economic development? What is the optimum relationship between private and public investment and does it vary from one jurisdiction and/or time to another? If the private sector fails to make the investments deemed necessary for balanced economic development, is it more efficient to undertake public investment or to subsidize the private sector? Should farm product marketing boards be voluntary or compulsory? Would abolition of Medicare premiums encourage abuse? Is post-secondary education best encouraged by low tuition fees or student loans? Should the province pay all primary education costs? Do social programs induce sloth? Should welfare be left to municipalities where applicants are known or assumed by the province and standardized? Should migration to cities be left to its natural course or should government intervene with programs to keep people in rural areas? To what extent, and by what means, should government direct social change?

As we raced from town to town, we philosophized. I was the passionate protagonist of causes and a child of the Great Depression, when economic survival depended on collective action through cooperatives or government. Crown corporations were instruments of public policy. "Keynesianism" was the modern version of the Pharoah's dream, which Joseph had interpreted to mean the state should store the surplus of good years to offset shortages in bad years—something any good farmer or businessman should do without needing a justifying philosophy.

As for state action to augment consumer purchasing power, even industrialist mogul Henry Ford, twenty years before Keynes, knew he could not sell cars if he did not pay his workers enough to buy them. Yet the consumer must not be inordinately elevated because without production, there would be no cars to buy. A state administered health care system was not 'state intervention' in the hallowed doctor/patient relationship, but a giant group insurance program including all citizens. Capitalism was a great improvement over earlier systems based on custom and command, but it appeared essentially based on Voltaire's aphorism that:

"The comfort of the rich depends on an adequate supply of poor."

To me, the greatest threat to the health of a modern economy and the peaceable kingdom was a few super-rich and many poor, and this could be ameliorated only by redistributive mechanisms such as taxes or social programs. The creative talents of individuals must not be stifled, but there was no reason why those talents would not respond to the needs of the community (as proven when the nation is threatened), as well as to personal acquisitiveness, and collective prosperity could be achieved more efficaciously by the arm of government than by the "Invisible Hand". Any rational analysis of the operations of a modern industrial economy must include the study of Karl Marx[7] as well as Adam Smith, and whoever did not understand that did not want to. Schreyer, a decade younger, was cool, analytical, cerebral—a utilizer of Reason who believed in a wisdom deeper than the mind:

> It is not wisdom to be merely wise;
> Tis wisdom also to believe the heart.[8]

These notions or beliefs differ for each individual, depending on their education, theology, experience, philosophy and history, both personal and racial. He was philosophically more liberal and politically more astute. The latter came of an observant nature and a decade of political experience at both federal and provincial levels, and the former of being a product of the touching enlightenment notion that among reasonable people, Reason will prevail. He believed people can change their social environment—and themselves—by linking social and economic change in the interests of a better society. But he also knew one needed power to make that better society and was not content to remain in the shadow of political power patronizingly referred to as the "conscience" of Parliament, while other parties borrowed our ideas and implemented them—badly. Neither of us were classical "socialists"; I was as a democratic socialist, while he was a social democrat.

So I often raged during our nocturnal travels between towns: "Ed, what the hell are you doing to our party? You may be a powerful political figure after this election and we must be careful about diluting both our policies and our philosophy. Dilution will occur soon enough as we get nearer to power, so let's not rush it. What is this shit about 'social democracy' that has crept into your vocabulary? Once we were 'socialists', but became 'democratic socialists' to distinguish ourselves from advocates of 'the dictatorship of the proletatiat' and as a compromise between encouraging private aspirations while maintaining the public good of social and economic equity. Now you have invented this bastardized term of 'social democracy'. To you it may be a cute term to relieve people's angst and get us extra votes, but to me it means turning our backs on history."

---

[7] Philosopher George Steiner commented: "To date the world has produced only two philosophies designed to make man more gentle and to more evenly distribute the resources of the earth, Christianity and Communism." CBC interview, September 8, 1992.

[8] George Santayana.

Ed would patiently explain that all the pretty philosophizing would get us no nearer to power so long as the electorate was suspicious of us, and we could never demonstrate what a socially sensitive government could do to—and this had become his mantra—"improve the human condition", unless we became government. "Our society has coined the shibboleth that we should rely on the economy, not government, because the economy is neutral. That is precisely the problem; the economy IS neutral and does not recognize the human misery it causes and which, in the last analysis, can be ameliorated only by government. But we cannot demonstrate that unless we ARE government. So what is the point of using politically loaded terms when we know that, on one hand, it frightens people into fearing that the term 'democratic' is the fig-leaf to hide our 'socialist' determination to nationalize everything in sight[9], while on the other hand, we know we will not do that because the socioeconomic system of which we are a part will not permit it. For most Canadians, the world has moved by a magnitude since the Regina Manifesto. Our working people, our party's main support, are becoming the new bourgeoisie ..."

"So you are saying if we are elected, in terms of effecting fundamental social change, we are beaten before we start ..."

"No," he said. "I am saying 'government is the art of the possible'..." [10] History is strewn with the bloody wreckage of Grand Designs. Probably our greatest tragedies resulted from dogmatic zealots unwilling to compromise on less than the ultimate, imposing a textbook theory on a society unable to accommodate it or unwilling to accept it without coercion."

I could not let that pass. I told him we were not speaking of zealots, but of popularly elected governments, which must sometimes act out of necessity.

He reminded me of Pitt the Younger, prime minister of Britain during the Napoleonic Wars, who said that every evil done by governments has been rationalized as being in the name of necessity. "Our *Weltanschuung* differs from that of previous governments and we will move society, but within the constraints of our historical context and the matrix of our political economy. Our success will depend on how we are seen to be using power."

"To quote Comrade Karl, our task is not to explain the world, but change it."

"And we know where that got us," said Schreyer, "in the Soviet Union. The world Marx experienced needed changing, but I am not of the opinion every social change must be born in pain and bloodshed. It is a truism that power is not vol-untarily surrendered—unless we have a powerful consensus for change. That means explaining in detail the changes we wish to make and the reasons for them, that social change need not be a zero-sum game. All this requires patience and dedication. Even bloody-minded Machiavelli, who urged his prince to do whatever

---

[9] "Canada is 50 to 70% communist controlled, according to *American Opinion*, the official publication of the John Birch Society." Published in *Manitoba Cooperator*, August 29, 1963.

[10] In the 1990s, Israeli Prime Minister Yitzak Rabin (who was later assassinated by a Jewish religious/nationalist zealot) revised this to "Government is the art of the IMpossible."

necessary to enforce his will, wrote that 'making fundamental change is slow work'." [11]

"Ed, the rumors are true. You are nothing but a Liberal."

"I should not need to re-establish my political credentials every time I open my mouth. In any case 'liberal' is one of the most beautiful words in the political lexicon. The liberalism enunciated by Locke and Mill, based on the concept that government rests on the consent of the governed, was a massive improvement over what preceded it. It liberated people from gods, kings and clans, and embodied the aspirations of generations."

Later Ed added, "Socialism, in its North American context, is simply the use of government to do what the private sector cannot or will not do because it is too risky or they lack capital. It comes in various forms. When FDR became president in 1933, the U.S. had fourteen million unemployed, homes and farms were being lost, some 6,000 banks had closed, investment had stopped. Leadership was desperately needed. Roosevelt did not intervene in the economy because he had nothing else to do, but because the free market economy had failed—and for that he was damned as a socialist."

He was quiet for a while and then continued, "The threat today is different. We risk too many benefits of our fast-growing, technology driven economy ending up in the hands of those who own the technology displacing the workers. If that continues Marx will be proven right in predicting capitalism will destroy itself by depriving workers of the income to buy the goods they produce. We must find instrumentalities to harness the genie of technology to the public welfare for purposes of equity and continuity. But that does not mean private enterprise, which is the basis of Western economies, will be replaced. In that sense I am a Kennedy democrat—a social democrat."

It was late at night and we were returning to Winnipeg from a meeting at Minnedosa. As usual I was driving at ninety mph, one finger lightly on the steering wheel, half-pivoted and leaning into the rear seat, half-shouting over the noise of the car: "Dammit Ed, again you have used that bastard expression. Acton was wrong. It is not 'power' that corrupts men, but the lust for power. You are not even elected and already you are equivocating. Ed, you are becoming far too accepting of our economic system. We are engaged in an election campaign and that requires equivocation and modification and accommodation. That doesn't concern me. What troubles me is that you believe what you are saying."

Terry Grier, also in the rear seat, leaned forward and silenced me for the balance of the campaign: "You asshole, why don't you stop this pointless bitching. Ed has thought this through in terms of fundamentals and he knows exactly what he is doing. Can't you understand that we are dealing here with a superior mind?"

Actually, he was much more than that.

---

[11] *Il Principe (The Prince)*, 1513.

III

The Making of a Legend

*He who has never risked going too far will never know how
far he can go.*

—T.S. Eliot

Ted Chudyk was provincial party organizer and 'bagman' for most of the
Schreyer years. Affable and committed, with an independent source of income that
allowed him latitude of thought and action, he roamed Canada, quietly presenting
the party's message, collecting money from supporters or those believing a third
party had a role in a democratic society, and extracting from others reasons why
they could not contribute. His greatest triumph in the latter category was a 1973
letter from the chairman of Gulf Oil Canada, who stated that his company could
not contribute to the NDP because it had "strong elements in Manitoba and
nationally, advocating a 'resources for the people' concept."[1]

The letter was a treasure. It stated precisely the difference between the NDP
and parties that believed the country's resources were the property of extraction
companies, mostly foreign-owned, who came, reaped and vanished, leaving the
taxpayers ghost towns and rehabilitation costs to mark their having passed this way.

In 1974, Ted's father, from Edmonton, visited with him and his wife for a
week at their spacious suburban cottage just north of Winnipeg. Early in the visit,
he made Ted promise to introduce him to "Premier Schreyer" before he returned
home. One evening, while relaxing at home, there was a knock on the door,
followed immediately by the Schreyers, casually dressed in slacks and loafers,
walking in, waving greetings, proceeding to the bar to mix themselves drinks,
and then walking nonchalantly into the living room to be introduced to Ted's
father as "Ed and Lily".

---

[1]   Shepard to Chudyk, March 14, 1973..

After an hour of light conversation they bade their farewells and left. Later, as Ted's father was preparing for bed, he reminded Ted: "Don't forget. I leave the day after tomorrow and you promised to introduce me to Premier Schreyer before I leave."

That was the way it was. They were an unpretentious couple.

After Lily developed a public profile, someone said to me: "Oh! I understand your sister was born in a log cabin." It seems the prevailing myth is still that great figures are born in a log cabin—à la Abraham Lincoln. I was forced, sadly, to admit, "No. Her birth was much more humble. She was born in one of the two grain bins we lived in at the time, one a living room/kitchen and the other a bedroom. We were much too poor to have a log cabin. But we moved into one as soon as we could build it."

We called her "Tiger Lily", not because of her temperament but because of what we saw as her resemblance to that rather extraordinary red-petalled flower that graced the prairies in those days. And like the flower, there on the fertile black loam of that little rural community, we witnessed the development of an extraordinary personality—and we did not even know it.

She grew up fast. Our father believed children, by age five, should contribute to the family income. By the time she began attending school she spoke English and German interchangeably, walked through grain fields as much a six hours a day pulling up mustard stalks, helped her mother plant and harvest the garden and cook for a room full of people, drove the Ford tractor dragging a cultivator or harrows, fetched the milk cows from the pasture and went horseback riding at the faintest excuse. How she loved to ride, her hair and the horse's mane streaming in the wind as they galloped carelessly across the fields. And she developed an uncommon rapport with animals, particularly horses.

One day, walking through the woods to the cow pasture, I heard a voice and quietly moved toward the sound. Lily, not yet six, stood on a tree-stump, imperiously addressing our riding horse: "Frank! Listen to me good when I tell you to go then I want you to go and when I tell you to run I want you to run and when I tell you to stop I want you to stop and do you understand what I mean and when I tell you to stop I want you to go I mean I want you to stop I mean I want you to go when I tell you to go and right now I want you to come over here to this stump so I can get on your back and then I want you to go I mean stop I mean go."

Her words tumbled over each other, but the horse understood. He stood with head bowed, as though apologizing for offending her, then came dutifully to the stump and stood rock still while she mounted. Riding bareback and without even a halter, they galloped away, she steering him by pressing her hand against his neck.

She was effervescent, vivacious, intelligent, friendly and unassuming. Much later, while first lady of Canada, she was walking, casually dressed, on the grounds at the entrance to Rideau Hall, near where the fountain and flower beds and scarlet coated, bearskin-hatted RCMP cadets make a classical backdrop for tourists' photos.

Two middle-aged ladies called to her: "Oh, could we ask you to take a picture of us with our camera while we stand with this officer?" She smilingly accommodated them, chatted long enough to learn they were from Grenfell, Saskatchewan, and went on. There is no report that they committed hari-kari when they learned of her identity—if they ever did.

Aboard a tour boat on the Ottawa River, she was sitting with a group of visiting relatives. As the young male tour guide announced points of interest along the route: This is the French Embassy; that one is the American Embassy. We are now going by the prime minister's residence and so on. Unaware of her presence, he became loquacious as the boat rounded a bend and approached Rideau Hall: "That's where the governor general and his beautiful wife live. They are my personal friends. The place has eighty bedrooms. Two are specially reserved. One is for the queen. The other is for me."

When he completed his pitch, Lily unobtrusively walked over, introduced herself and invited him to join the family for dinner. He looked as if he was having difficulty swallowing something.

But she was no shrinking lily and could be disconcertingly direct. When a group of feminists called upon the premier's wife to discuss the contribution of women to the world, each detailed her own contribution and then asked what she had done. Lily patted her seven-months-pregnant belly and suggested quietly: "Well, I would like to think I am contributing something."

Later, when Ed went to London to receive his appointment as governor general, and the queen invited them to dinner, Lily got into a heated argument about Medicare—with Prince Philip.

Ed was studious, soft-spoken, cerebral, introspective, inner-directed and reserved. His innate shyness sometimes created a public image of coolness and even pomposity. Mordecai Richler wrote of spending a boring hour at dinner in 1970 with Schreyer at the Hotel Fort Garry where the atmosphere was uninviting, the food unappetizing and the young premier "had no presence".[2]

His natural introversion prohibited him from being the glad-handing, backslapping stereotypical politician with the synthetic smile. Worse, he had read Plato's cynical comment that, "politicians are respected and admired not because they are good and wise but because they flatter the people and satisfy their baser desires and instincts," and he was precluded by both his nature and his philosophy from pursuing that practice.

He was not good with small talk on semi-official occasions, but his private persona was humourous, approachable and he had the patience of Job. The key to their attractive but unpretentious ranch-style house at the "Cabbage Patch"—their home three kilometres north of Winnipeg's Perimeter Highway—was lost shortly after they purchased it in 1967, so it was never locked and often they returned

---

[2] Mordecai Richler, *Home Sweet Home, My Canadian Album*, pp. 77-8.

home, sometimes late in the evening, to find visitors, or mendicants, from any-where in the province, whom they would then entertain. Donald Malinowski, NDP MLA from 1969 to 1986, succinctly illustrated: "If one did not know Ed is premier, one would not know Ed is premier." But while perhaps many might not have known what he was, all who met him knew he was something.

Edward Richard Schreyer was born on December 21, 1935, near the small town of Beausejour in east-central Manitoba where his grandparents, among Clifford Sifton's "sheep-skin clad immigrants", German Catholics from Galicia in Central Europe, settled in 1897.

His father arrived in his mother's womb, married a local girl whose parents had come from the same area of the Austro-Hungarian Empire, and they raised a family of five sons and one daughter for whom they had no higher ambitions than that they be honest hard workers and good neighbors. They all became farmers and businessmen except the youngest who, by age twenty-nine, had a Bachelor of Pedagogy, a Bachelor of Education and a Master of Arts, was a second lieutenant in the Canadian Officers Training Corps, had taught International Relations in the Department of Political Science at the University of Manitoba, served seven years in the Manitoba Legislature, and been elected to the House of Commons in Ottawa.

There seemed to be an aura about him. In 1962, as a young MLA, he spoke at an NDP meeting in the suburb of St. James, not a hotbed of socialism, and with only a score of persons present. In the ponderous speech patterns that often bedevilled his delivery and making him sound slightly sanctimonius, he quietly outlined the policies of the NDP and sought to relieve the angst of his audience by explaining Canadian socialism owed more to Methodism than to Marx. My wife and I were not excited by the presentation—until we overheard two elderly women whispering to each other with approval: "Do you hear the vocabulary that young man is using. And just look at him. Isn't he great?"

Suddenly we looked at him through different eyes. His speeches were never banal, and standing there in the effulgence of his youth, slim and straight, dark blue suit, clean features and dark curly hair, he looked like a young god. As was to be demonstrated, he had an understated charisma that resonated far beyond NDP supporters to attract ditch-diggers and glitterati alike.

Frank Syms, cynical veteran of war and politics and *Winnipeg Tribune* reporter (later NDP party president and chairman of the Manitoba Liquor Control Board), walked over to us: "Have you noticed these people are enthralled by Ed? This guy, whether he knows it or not, is premier material."

He almost did not become premier, or even a politician. His talents were first exhibited as a baseball pitcher, and he was offered a contract with a farm team in the United States. At precisely that point, at age twenty-one, that another life crossed his path.

Ironically, it was baseball that led him into politics. He was going home from a local game, dog-dirty from sliding into bases, when, out of curiousity, he entered the Legion Hall where a political meeting was about to begin. Seen by the audience as an "educated" young man, he was pushed to the front of the hall to chair the meeting. There he met the CCF candidate for Springfield in the 1957 federal election, Jake Schulz, his future father-in-law, political mentor and friend, and as Robert Frost so famously put it, he "took the road less travelled by".

Twenty-five years later, he was to pay tribute to that relationship in a moving eulogy, quoting George Bernard Shaw: "Some look at things the way they are and wonder why—others dream of things that never were and ask, why not?"

Referring to the enormous energies expended by the reform-minded Schulz, who knew that great wealth narrowly held is as destructive of a society as cancer is of a body, he concluded with the gentle invocation: *"Ruhe dich, Jakob; du hast es wohl verdient."* [3]

The recording secretary at the meeting that evening was Jake's lithe, flame-haired, nineteen-year-old daughter, Lily. Two years later they were married. Eighteen months before they were wed, at age twenty-two, Ed was elected to the legislature—at the time, the youngest MLA in Canadian history.

He was elected to the Manitoba Legislature in 1958, 1959 and 1962. In 1965, he was elected to the Parliament of Canada—the youngest MP in the country at that time—defeating the man who had defeated his father-in-law, and this was repeated in 1968. In May 1969, the Manitoba election was called. He resigned his seat to return home.

I first met this quiet young man when he was brought to our farm by my sister, who was visiting from Winnipeg. Several months earlier I had been prominently involved in a riot at a Conservative federal election meeting, where eggs and punches were thrown, and I was threatened with arrest and prison after being set up and then blamed. The publicity was used against the CCF, and even months later the memory of it all infuriated me and I raged and cursed in responding to his queries about the incident. It was quickly noticeable that he soaked up the information like a sponge but remained imperturbable, without expression or comment, other than brief questions for elucidation. Clearly, this man did not easily allow anyone to enter the temple of his private thoughts.

Arriving in Winnipeg in May 1969, he announced, almost apologetically, that he would seek the leadership of the Manitoba NDP. The previous October, when challenged by Sid Green, incumbent Russ Paulley had stated he wanted to retain his position until "Eddie" decided to return. Schreyer had been low key, but it was recognized if he became leader the NDP could be a threat to the government.

The *Winnipeg Free Press* editorialized: "Conservative officials believe [they] should call a June election [before Schreyer returns from Ottawa]," and "You can't blame the present government for quaking over the prospect of pitting their head man against Mr. Schreyer." [4]

Premier Weir, a pleasant, pedestrian mortician from the scenic town of

---

[3] German, "Rest yourself Jacob, you have earned it."

Minnedosa—he was called "Minnedosa Fats" because of a resemblance to the Jackie Gleason character in *The Hustler*—was propelled into the premier's chair by the conservative element in the party when the kinetic Duff Roblin, after winning the 1966 election, resigned in August 1967 to seek the leadership of the national Conservative Party. Weir wanted his own mandate to give him flexibility to trump the progressives brought into the caucus by Roblin. Earlier in the year he had won three by-elections—and considerable television time fighting Prime Minister Pierre Elliott Trudeau on the constitution. He felt on his neck the hot breath of the feisty NDP, which had won the Thompson seat in a by-election in January, to bring it to within one seat of the official opposition Liberals. But NDP Leader, Russ Paulley was in hospital and the next NDP convention was scheduled for October. Emboldened by his opponent's disarray, Weir took the advice of the *Winnipeg Free Press* to seize the day. He miscalculated.

As noted earlier, the NDP executive immediately advanced the convention to June 7th, Schreyer immediately resigned his seat in Parliament, and he and Green contested the party leadership. It was a splendid affair with the defining event being four hours of free, wall-to-wall television coverage of the convention in which Manitobans were treated to revealing glimpses of a party bursting with energy and enthusiasm and a group of candidates featuring many who had already proven themselves at every level of politics. And here was an attractive new quadri-lingual (English, French, German, Ukrainian) leader, with broad "ethnic" appeal who, at age thirty-three, had eleven years of political experience in both the Manitoba Legislature and the House of Commons. The NDP seemed "ready to govern".

The NDP that campaigned in Manitoba, unlike the Progressives in 1921, did not suddenly appear in the spring of 1969 like Minerva from the head of Jove. The party was full of what former leader Lloyd Stinson dubbed "political warriors"[5] who, as labour, then CCF, then NDP, had sat on school boards, municipal councils —including the City of Winnipeg—and in the legislature since the 1920s.

With no contributions from banks and corporations, the party had carried its message the only way it could—on foot, from door to door—and that miniature army of canvassers was in place. Party organizers, accustomed to working with little help, found it easy when there was some. Party candidates, having long faced hostile audiences, had developed a confidence in both themselves and their message. Reduced to a splinter in 1958, the party had roared back to within two seats of the second-place Liberals, which had governed from 1922 to 1958. In 1966, they elected eight new members,[6] to become the actual—if not official—opposition in the legislature. All that was needed to galvanize the party machine and attract the floating votes was the injection of a new leader to whom they could attach some sense of resonance and some hope of victory. That was provided by Schreyer.

And the province had undergone a sea change. Liberal Leader Douglas Campbell, after forty-eight years in the legislature, ten as premier, had retired.

---

[4]   May 3, 1969 and May 6, 1969.

Respected by friend and foe (Sid Green described him, at age ninety-six, as "the youngest mind I know") as a gentleman of unimpeachable integrity, he was particularly popular among farmers. Rural areas at night were bright with yard lights like giant candles, lighting up the earth and reflecting off the sky, as farmers celebrated Campbell's Rural Electrification Program. He was replaced by politically uninspiring Robert Bend, who conducted his campaign dressed in cowboy garb and turned his party to the right just when the Western World was turning left. That left him, like those later described by President Reagan's speechwriter, Peggy Noonan, "waiting at the station listening for the whistle of the train that did not stop here anymore."[7]

Rural domination of electoral politics by the conservative and Conservative heartland south of No. 1 Highway bisecting the province, was ending. Veterans of wars in Europe and Korea, perceiving economic prosperity following expenditure of billions of dollars blowing holes in the air, could no longer be beguiled into believing a "balanced budget" was the Eleventh Commandment or that governments are helpless to mitigate economic conditions.

The energetic Roblin administration had demonstrated to farmers, businessmen and students what changes could be wrought by an "interventionist" government and that the credit of the province could be used to initiate economic growth and social change. The economy was growing and the public mood was expansive.

The leaders of the first mass generation of university graduates were seeking problems for which they had solutions, a governmental apparatus in which they could seize "the big levers", and a leader of their own generation and educational level with whom they could identify. A year earlier, Canada had been swept by Trudeaumania and here was another bright, photogenic young man in the "Kennedy" mould. The people of Manitoba were ready to experiment with something new and different. In the context of the ferment within the body politic, Schreyer was the agent of the *Zeitgeist*.

Yet I, for one, never for a moment thought we would win. I predicted twenty -two seats. The electorate and the opinion makers had become accustomed to tolerating the NDP as the "conscience" of politics and encouraged us between elections but, except in Saskatchewan, at the polling booth they invariably returned to the safety of Tweedledum or Tweedledee. We would need to defeat both the opposition Liberals and the governing Conservatives, and it appeared unlikely we could do that to form the only, and only the second,[8] social democratic government in North America.

Both Weir's Conservatives and Bend's Liberals were turning to the right,

---

[5] *Political Warriors*, 1975.

[6] Russell Doern, Sidney Green, Saul Miller, Peter Fox, Sam Uskiw, Ben Hanuschak, Rev. Phillip Petersson, Mike Kawchuk. All except Kawchuk (who was defeated in 1969) became cabinet ministers after the 1969 election.

7 *What I Saw at the Revolution.*

making room for the NDP in its natural constituency, but the Conservatives were campaigning on having provided eleven years of progressive government and were confident of victory, while the Liberals scattered election promises like Johnny Appleseed. Party president Frank Syms quoted H.L. Mencken: "The Liberals are so promising that if they thought voters were cannibals they would promise them missionaries for lunch."

On June 23rd, Schreyer summarized the NDP's economic priorities, including both private sector and public initiatives, and then broadened the scope. His party was constantly accused of having a fixation with the core of Marx: that impetus for social change lies not in the brain but the belly, not in philosophy but in economics; that social relations result from the way men feed themselves, and, having established that, develop a government to protect it and a philosophy to justify it. But the NDP knew that men and women do not live on bread alone—they need ideals to engage their passions.

Schreyer stated his *Leitmotiv*: "We will widen the scope of social justice, strive for equality of condition, and enlarge individual and collective opportunities … We will be guided by our belief that government is an instrument people can use to achieve aims for themselves … and to broaden opportunities for people to be involved in the governing process."

And then, suddenly, it was Election Day!

At 6 P.M. Ed came home to announce, with clear frustration: "We will win twenty-eight seats. We will lose the majority by one seat." The evening of kaleidoscopic images went by with agonizing slowness and frightening swiftness. Three hours later we had twenty-eight seats. The people had followed the fellow who followed the dream. It was:

> Bartlett pears of romance that were honey at the core, and
> Torchlights down the street to the end of the world.[9]

The next day, in the living room of his modest bungalow, I witnessed my brother-in-law metamorphose into the Premier of Manitoba. He was somber, as though sensing the demands of *Realpolitik*. And no one needed to tell me that our relationship would be forever changed.

Then the bargaining began. We had a plurality, but with twenty-eight of the fifty-seven seats, the other parties could coalesce and foreclose our claim to office.[10] Even if the lieutenant governor invited the NDP to form the government, appointing a speaker would leave us only twenty-seven votes and vulnerable to defeat at any time by the combined opposition.

Appointing a Speaker from opposition ranks would leave us with twenty-

---

[8]   The Liberals had defeated the NDP in Saskatchewan in 1964.

[9]   Vachel Lindsay, "Bryan."

[10]   Progressive Conservative 22, Liberal 5, Social Credit 1, Independent 1.

eight seats while reducing theirs to twenty-eight. Gordon Johnson, the soft-spoken war veteran storekeeper from Portage la Prairie, one of five Liberals re-elected, showed interest but then declined. Jake Froese, the squarely built, highly principled leader of the one-member Social Credit Party in the legislature was flattered by the offer, but also declined. And then there was Desjardins.

Laurent Desjardins was like a heavy mass around which, as hypothesized by Einstein, light waves bend. He was 240 pounds of raw emotion, an independent, vitriolic, sensitive, self-confident brawler. He had served in the navy in World War II, established a successful mortician's practice, was an active sports buff and an aggressive hockey player who never hesitated to go into a corner, took no "shit" from anyone, and would argue at any excuse. This "Rabelaisian character", as described by cabinet colleague Russell Doern[11] was also cheerful and witty. At a cabinet meeting, during a tense policy debate when Saul Miller exploded with uncharacteristic emotion, "It doesn't matter how good I may think this policy is, if people don't like it, I will go down," Desjardins pulled a tape measure from his pocket and asked, "Before you do, would you like to buy a pre-arranged funeral?"

During a cabinet meeting, I observed the corpulent 5'9" figure ambling about, eating from a brown paper bag, and suggested, "Larry, considering that belly, rather than eating you should be giving something back." His response was swift: "Not so! I'm losing two pounds a week." When I looked skeptical, he added: "I used to gain four pounds a week and now I am only gaining two."

In the legislature, when he referred to a female MLA as "beautiful" and she objected, on the grounds that this was "anti-feminist", he humbly apologized: "Okay then Mr. Speaker, so she is not beautiful."

He was also a politically shrewd street-fighter. A francophone proud to represent St. Boniface, the largest French community outside Québec, he took seriously his responsibilities to his constituency and culture. He had served on the St. Boniface City Council and hospital board, and was elected to the legislature in 1959 as a Liberal. Shortly before the 1969 election, however, he had expressed unhappiness with the party. When contacted, his response to Schreyer was, no, he would not accept appointment as Speaker; no, he would not join the NDP; no, he would not sit in the NDP caucus except perhaps as a Liberal Democrat; yes, he would support legislation, if he agreed with it.

Would there be a price for his support? No, but we knew his position on the issue of public aid to private and parochial schools. Since Schreyer agreed with that position, there was no need to debate the point. The Peck's bad boy of the legislature was to become the kingmaker.

Desjardins was also approached by both the Conservative and Liberal parties. He was offered public aid to non-public schools plus a major cabinet post in any government either formed. But he had given his word to his friend, Ed Schreyer, and would honour it. The manoeuvring of the Conservatives to remain in office

---

[11] *Wednesdays are Cabinet Days,* 1981.

failed. And the NDP had a functional—if tentative—majority.

The morning after the election the Schreyer home was overrun with well wishers, and media persons gathered to test the young premier-elect. After the press conference, outside the front door, CBC reporter Bob Preston was leaning against the Tyndall stone wall of the patio, a stunned expression on his face as though witnessing the impossible. Staring off into space, he was mumbling repeatedly: "I see no reason why the NDP can't govern. I see no reason why the NDP can't govern." It sounded as though he was attempting to convince himself—and losing the argument.

July 15, 1969, was the kind of idyllic day for which Manitoba summers are famous. The inauguration was a splendid affair. The manicured green lawns at the Legislative Building were a kaleidoscope of hundreds of men in dark suits and women in pastel-shaded summer gowns, picture hats and high heels. On this day of Empyrean magic, the huge, imposing Greco-Roman edifice, surrounded by gardens reminiscent of a many-flowered Camelot, appeared to echo to a different drum as, in the ornate, polished and chandeliered Blue Room, reserved for royal visits and inaugurations, the thirteen ministers, some still half expecting the Wicked Witch to snatch away their prize, were sworn into office.

We "socialist hordes" had captured the Shining City on the Hill.

Hugh Allan, *The Winnipeg Tribune*, June 28, 1969

Just three days after their remarkable election victory, the members of Manitoba's first NDP caucus looked ready to govern. From left, provincial treasurer Frances Thompson, provincial secretary Betty Klein, René Toupin, Harry Shafransky, Howard Pawley, Tom Barrow, Ron McBryde, John Gottfried, Bill Uruski, Bud Boyce, Rev. Donald Malinowski, Joe Borowski, Jean Allard, Ben Hanuschak, Sid Green, Russell Doern, Russ Paulley, Wally Johansson, Ian Turnbull, Cy Gonick, Sam Uskiw, Al Mackling, Phillip Petursson, Peter Fox, provincial vice-president Bill Hutton, executive assistant Doug Rowland, Premier Ed Schreyer and provincial president Frank Syms.

IV

That First Faint Careless Rapture

A great army can capture a city, but to govern it requires a great idea.
—Victor Hugo

"**Hell, we took that leap on June 25th**", said NDP president Frank Syms four days after the inauguration, when Neil Armstrong's historic "giant leap for mankind" on the moon bumped Manitoba's "political revolution" off the front pages. "Now let's legislate some great ideas."

Peter C. Newman, in his critique of the Pearson regime, wrote: "To perform his supreme task a prime minister needs knowledge, power and purpose. Lester Pearson had the knowledge, did not use the power and failed to supply a purpose."[1]

Premier Schreyer was determined the same would not be said of him. On August 14, 1969, barely a month after taking office, the new government went into legislative session. This was necessitated because the Weir government, in its rush to judgement of the electorate while Paulley was in hospital and Schreyer in Ottawa, had neglected to pass its annual spending estimates.

The Winnipeg Tribune heralded the opening of the Twenty-Ninth Legislature with a huge black headline: "NDP GOVERNMENT PROMISES WIDE-RANGING LEGISLATION; AT LEAST 22 BILLS DURING NEW SESSION".

In an exercise rich with pomp and ceremony, while cannons boomed the ritualistic fifteen times and martial music echoed through one of the most impressive legislative buildings in North America, people filled the visitor's gallery and the chamber to standing-room-only capacity.[2] At the appointed moment,

---

[1] *The Distemper of Our Times: Canadian Politics in Translation 1963-68*, p.48.

[2] The opening of the legislature is the only occasion when non-elected persons are allowed in the chamber while it is in session.

Lieutenant Governor Richard Bowles, resplendent in striped trousers, swallow-tailed coat and black top hat, escorted by Premier Schreyer, strode between the twin columns of the military honour guard, who stood smartly at attention in full dress uniform. They ascended the Grand Staircase with its three flights of thirteen steps each, crossed the patterned, mirror-polished marble floor of the magnificent rotunda, which rises from the Pool of the Black Star on giant fluted stone columns with Corinthian capitals to the majestic dome sixty metres above, and entered the opulent, round Legislative Chamber.

The chamber is the inner sanctum of the legislative process and none dare enter without invitation. It exudes nineteenth-century elegance and antique grandeur, and rises from the rich, royal blue carpet, on arches and pillars draped in off-white curtains to the giant domed ceiling skylight. Elected member's desks and chairs, of polished walnut and inlaid ebony, are arranged in a semicircle of three tiers on each side rising like an amphitheatre from the sunken floor between them. At one end are the semi-circular polished brass rails that mark the visitor's gallery high above the chamber; at the other, on a dias five steps above the floor, stands the great high-backed, black leather, throne-like Speaker's chair topped by the Manitoba coat of arms. Above that is the press gallery, from which members of the fourth estate observe and report to the public. And above that is a mural representing Justice, Wisdom and Knowledge, as well as panels bearing the names of the great lawmakers from which modern law draws its inspiration: Confucius, Lycurgus, Alfred, Justinian and Manu. Circling the inside of the dome are representations of the evolution of laws and the basic documents of civil liberty. On either side of the Speaker's chair, in niches, are the burnished bronze figures of Moses and Solon, representing the spiritual and the secular roots of Western law.

Routinely, when the legislature is in session, at the appointed minute, a loud buzzer summons the members to enter and sit, government to the right and Her Majesty's loyal opposition to the left, of the Speaker's chair. The Speaker, in cer-emonial black robe and tri-cornered hat, preceded by the uniformed sergeant-at-arms bearing the mace, walk in slow procession from his office into the chamber. The Speaker proceeds to his chair and the sergeant-at-arms, with military precision, marches to the far end of the polished table on the floor between the member's seats. He turns, faces the Speaker, places the mace, a silver staff surmounted by orb and cross representing the authority of the crown delegated to the legislature, on the table, and snaps to attention. The Manitoba Legislature is ready to make laws.

But on this day—the opening of the new legislature—the exercise was more colourful. The premier went to his place at the middle of the front bench to the right of the Speaker and the lieutenant governor proceeded to the Speaker's chair. He was handed a copy of the Speech from the Throne, prepared by the premier, which he read to the assembly in English. In a significant break with the past (when it had been read by a clerk) the French version was read by the premier.

The brief throne speech outlining the government's program enunciated the basic belief of the New Democratic Party that economic democracy is a pre-requisite of political democracy:[3] "more equitable distribution of necessities for economic well-being will [enable] increasing numbers of people to exercise civil rights and freedom of choice in a more meaningful way. Policy on a wide range of social and economic problems will be submitted [to the] Legislative Assembly."

These included:

- A natural products marketing act to strengthen agriculture
- Stimulation of economic development
- Reduction of regional economic disparities
- Reduction of tax anomalies
- Changes to the Public Schools Act to allow native Manitobans to serve on school boards
- Substantial reduction of health care premiums
- Increased income tax to replace losses from health premium reduction
- A study of high-benefit, low-cost automobile insurance
- To work with Ottawa to establish a Freshwater Fish Marketing Board
- The establishment of a Consumer Protection Bureau
- The establishment of an ombudsman's office
- The establishment of a Manitoba Human Rights Commission
- Legislation for compensation to victims of crime
- The reduction of the age of majority [voting age] from twenty-one to eighteen

Finally, the lieutenant governor intoned the government's mantra: "to work towards greater equality of the human condition." [4]

Press comments were mostly favourable. Marilyn Dill, political reporter for *The Winnipeg Tribune* wrote: "It's the best throne speech I've ever read." CBC national reporter Larry Zolf thought it "an astute speech which will be praised by the Eastern press". Len Earl, who had reported from the legislative press gallery since the 1920s, wrote: "This speech is more direct and blunt in communicating what the government plans than most I've seen." [5]

Gordon Johnston, MLA for Portage la Prairie and Liberal house leader

---

[3.] This was not just "socialist dogma." Famed New York jurist Learned Hand argued that political democracy, to be meaningful, must be accompanied by sufficient economic equality to enable a person to enjoy the attendant individual rights and liberties.

[4.] The throne speech lacked the rhetoric and the cadence, but in substance echoed the spirit of John F. Kennedy's inaugural speech: "Let the word go forth ... the torch has been passed to a new generation."

[5.] Some members of the media, relating to politicians of their own age, became quite friendly—and inquisitive. On one occasion, the premier entered The Ledge and was accompanied to his office by a local reporter. Finding his private secretary out and the door locked, the premier fished into his pockets for the keys, which he often misplaced. Deep in conversation, and not thinking about what he was doing, the reporter pulled a key from his own pocket, unlocked the premier's door—and then became very embarrassed.

commented, "I don't see too much I don't like in the speech." By contrast, former Premier Walter Weir displayed the polar opposite of the government's thinking by complaining the throne speech failed to propose "estate taxes rebates".

The throne speech completed, the lieutenant governor departed. Ben Hanuschak, MLA for Burrows, who during the preceding hour had metamorphosed from slacks, windbreaker and sandals into dark, striped trousers, a swallow-tailed coat and gray ascot, was ceremoniously dragged from his seat to the Speaker's chair by the premier and the leader of the official opposition[6]. With the presiding officer installed and the assembly called to order, the new Government of Manitoba was ready to do business.

How young, fresh-faced, eager and confident they looked, these members of the government caucus! They had been lawyers, farmers, teachers, social workers, school trustees, managers, labourers, miners, preachers, businessmen, mayors and councillors, all now transported into a new and exotic milieu. They represented much of Manitoba's wide racial spectrum, their ranks included the youngest (twenty-seven) and oldest (sixty-seven) members of the legislature, and on the front benches sat the multiracial, multilingual, degree-draped cabinet.

Maclean's wrote: "On July 15, Schreyer was sworn in with a cabinet that read like a battle hymn of the unwashed—four Anglo-Saxons, three Jews, two Ukrainians, one French-Canadian, one Pole, one Icelander, one German [Schreyer]. Never before have minorities of Manitoba been so well represented. And no previous cabinet has been so well educated; there are at least 15 university degrees shared among the NDP ministers."[7]

They might have appeared less eager, and less confident, had they known the nature of the tasks that lay ahead and the toll on their lives that the work of the next eight years would take. They were to find that the pay and perks did not compensate for the pain—that the game was hardly worth the name—unless one had a fire in the belly.

But they DID have a fire in the belly! They were fully aware they were the first social democratic government in Manitoba and the only one in North America. They had been a long time getting here, they had been given an opportunity beyond the dreams of most, and they did not intend that it be squandered.

And there was the premier himself. After the reading of the throne speech, veteran political reporter and Southam News Service chief Charles Lynch remarked it was, "a skilfully worked document showing the quality that Ed Schreyer has exhibited consistently—competence." *New York Times* correspondent Edward Cowan commented on the young man who had exploded from obscurity to prominence: "Premier Schreyer carries himself like a leader, with confidence[8] ... has a

---

[6.] This ritual relates to the days when being Speaker was potentially dangerous, if he dared disagree with the monarch, and also to signify that he (or she) is an officer of the legislature, not the government.

[7.] December 1970.

[8.] *The Winnipeg Tribune,* August 15, 1969.

wide vocabulary … knows government affairs … gives no false starts in his answers."

Indeed, Schreyer seemed to fit into the role and robes of office—business suit or striped trousers and white tie—as though they had been made for him. "He was to the manor born," his colleague Saul Cherniack, said of him. And there were times when he looked like a prince. In May 1974, Princess Margaret and her consort, Lord Snowden, attended the gala centennial of the City of Winnipeg. The premier looked splendid in a dark blue suede suit his wife had purchased for his birthday. During the evening Snowden, a pleasant, friendly and direct man, commented admiringly on the suit and inquired where it had been purchased. Schreyer turned to his wife, who told him.

Snowden took a pen and pad from his pocket and made a note: "I must get myself a suit just like that while I am here. By the way, if I may make bold to ask, what did you pay for it?" The premier's wife told him. Snowden looked stricken: "Oh hell, I can't afford that." He put away his pen and pad.

There was about the premier a quiet, unruffled dignity—reporter Ron Campbell referred to "the cool, magisterial ethos of a Schreyer press conference". He soaked up information as by osmosis and quoted facts and figures that impressed many who would never vote for him. And he had an innate stoicism permitting sublimation of reaction to unpleasantness. At the unveiling of the Louis Riel statue, when the shroud dropped revealing the naked, grotesque monstrosity with distorted body and contorted features, I glanced at the premier. The impulse to scream obscenities was revealed by nothing more than a slight curl of his upper lip.[9]

Like Ulysses, Schreyer appeared to be a part—and the sum—of all he had met and he approached his task with a dedication born of conviction and with a wisdom deeper than learning. As Sorenson wrote of Kennedy: "He wanted to get things done." Schreyer's waking hours were preoccupied with translating theory into effective programs. His desire to create rather than criticize emerged with stark clarity after his electoral defeat (eight and a half years later) when he proved a lacklustre leader of the opposition with no instinct for the jugular—a fact he readily admitted. "I am not temperamentally suited to the role of leader of the opposition."[10]

As premier, however, Schreyer quickly placed the imprimatur of his

---

[9.] Riel has proved as controversial in death as in life. Hanged for high treason in 1885, the Métis wanted him rehabilitated and petitioned the Schreyer government to grant a location and funds for a statue. A committee, including a Métis, chose the design and Marcien Lemay sculpted it. It was intended to symbolize the emotional torment of the unhappy martyr, but the effect was ghoulish. As 'white guilt' developed—the Métis became mythologized—the author of one glowing account of their history began with: "Long before the white man came, the Métis was 'lord of the Plains'," obviously forgetting that, as the issue of mixed-blood relationships, there were no Métis before the white man came. Over time, the statue became an embarrassment and ultimately it was replaced in its place of prominence on the bank of the Assiniboine River directly behind the Legislative Building by a more forceful, middle-class, frock-coated—but moccasined—Bruno Gerussi-type figure, which the government again commissioned and paid for.

[10.] Aside from his uncombative personality, he did not attack the government as fiercely as his caucus thought he should because he believed a new government deserves a period of grace and having been premier for eight years, he knew there were no quick solutions to problems confronting government.

personality and philosophy on the administration of government. He ignored Machiavelli's advice that "a new prince must organize his government anew." The civil service was treated with the respect of professionals for professionals and few personnel changes were made. The special cabinet committees, which reported directly to cabinet were treated as cabinet instruments: Management Committee was slowly infiltrated with NDP supporters and Planning and Priorities Committee, the government's 'think-tank', became an NDP preserve, but the administrative part of government was left virtually intact. Party supporters seeking government jobs were required, like anyone else, to respond to civil service bulletins and submit to requisite examinations.

When there was an investigation, or appraisal, of a program or public investment that had failed, it was not asked WHO but WHAT went wrong, and how it could have been done better. I would rage, demanding that heads roll, but he saw things differently: "If we want civil servants to give candid opinions and burn them when they prove wrong, we will end up talking to ourselves."

Also, aside from his natural timidity in blaming anyone for anything, he intuitively knew that in an operation as large as government, many are involved in the making of a decision—or of a mistake—and that if one was looking for blame there was plenty to go around. And he knew from experience that if a witch hunt begins, there is no predicting how far it will reach.[11]

He never raised his voice and questions were asked, or directions given, with unfailing calm and courtesy. His way of getting the best service from his personal and civil service staff, was to let it appear something was their idea. He seldom gave a direct order. It was usually: "You may want to see if this can be done"; "It might be a good idea to have this matter handled this way." Or, "I am really convinced this matter should be pursued."

But he knew the power of his position and carefully guarded his prerogatives. At a cabinet meeting, when a minister volunteered, "It seems to me the consensus is …", the premier interrupted with asperity: "I [with emphasis] interpret the consensus here." When his wife, one day, referred to herself as "Mrs. Premier", he chided gently, "You are Mrs. Schreyer, not Mrs. Premier."

And he could make tough policy decisions. The board of directors of the new Concordia Hospital came to his office to request construction of an additional floor, while representatives from the Department of Health came to oppose it as unnecessary and wasteful. The hospital's directors lived in the premier's constituency and it would have been easy to use public money to buy votes in an area with the largest concentration of Mennonites in Canada. He listened to the opposing arguments and reflected for a moment, his face imperturbable. Then he announced quietly: "The department has decided, for the reasons stated, that there should be

---

[11.] On five occasions, when I investigated the source of 'leaks' to the media, four were traced to unguarded comments by ministers and the fifth, a document declared CONFIDENTIAL by cabinet, was sent to a newspaper by an MLA and was published. This last incident caused the premier to remark tersely: "It seems the best way to get anything into the papers is to declare it 'confidential'."

no additional floor. The decision stands."

Ted Tulchinsky, associate deputy minister of Health and a hardliner, who was skeptical of the premier's ability to be firm, whispered to me admiringly: "Today I learned what kind of man Schreyer is."

Veteran journalist Charles Lynch expressed surprise that the throne speech contained so little "socialism", but suspected that ugly virus, in the keeping of party ideologues, was kept ready to infect the body politic: "Schreyer's cool competence has won grudging admiration from the business community ... [but] youthful supporters are worried, and carried signs ... imploring him to not let them down." [12]

As the throne speech was being read, and 2,000 persons consumed sandwiches and lemonade on the manicured lawns, rejoicing that their men were in the legislature, groups of young people paraded with placards pleading with Schreyer to not betray their youthful—and socialistic—ideals. Schreyer fully appreciated the duality and the need to maintain a delicate balance between frightening his opponents with 'socialistic' rhetoric and disappointing his supporters with 'non-socialistic' performance. In a speech to the Canadian Learned Societies, he summarized the dilemma: "The media see the most virulent Bolshevism in everything we propose, even if identical proposals have been made by [Liberal and Conservative governments], while the theorists within our own party are prone to detecting nefarious efforts at selling out our party's radical heritage just as regularly." [13]

The ideologues at both ends of the spectrum misjudged the man. Tommy Douglas, who became in 1944 the first premier of the first social democratic government in North America, and who revolutionized his province, illustrated that his government was moved less by "doctrinaire socialism" than by pragmatic responses to reality. "In World War II, Saskatchewan farmers assumed, since horses were needed ... in World War I, they needed even more now. So they raised horses. But it was a war of machinery and by 1945 we had more horses than people and our treasury was empty. But we did not take away people's property to fill it. We built a plant, killed the horses and shipped the meat to Europe. We were neither ideologues nor sentimentalists." [14]

Most members of the Schreyer government, while perhaps a bit more sentimental—since they had fewer economic pressures, they could afford to be—were

---

[12] *The Winnipeg Tribune*, August 15, 1969.

[13] Toronto, June 4, 1974.

[14] During the 1958 federal election, I stopped for supper at a small restaurant on the Trans-Canada Highway east of Winnipeg and sat with a man who introduced himself as a long-distance trucker and pointed to a large rig parked outside. Her referred to the election and launched into a vigorous tirade against the Douglas government, how people were being cheated and how he had personally hauled horses out of Saskatchewan for which payments were made directly to Premier Douglas and his finance minister, Gordon Fines. I drew a pen and pad from my pocket and laid them in front of him:"I've been wanting to get those two sons-of-bitches for a long time," I told him, "and I'm so happy to have found someone who has the goods on them. If you will write down what you have just told me and sign it, I will fix them good." He disappeared as though beamed up by Startreck's Scotty and the next sound I heard was that of his big rig roaring out of the lot.

no less pragmatic. Ed Schreyer, despite his achievements in both academia and politics, was a small-town boy. He and his five siblings were raised in a family with no free riders. At ten, he worked in his father's bush camp; in his teens he worked in his brother's machine shop, and as a university student he earned tuition working in a morgue.[15] He knew, because his immigrant grandparents, his pioneer parents, and his industrious elder brothers had done it, what can be accomplished by individual action and freedom of enterprise. But he was not an ideologue on the subject.

Nor was he an ideologue on using government to achieve ends. But he had learned, from observation and reading, what can be done by collective effort —that indeed civilized society is the result of collective effort. So social policy would be changed; the wealth of society would be more equitably distributed; public corporations would be used as economic and social instruments.

His government would involve more people in decision making. Social and political elitism would be modified. The 'ordinary' people who did the work, paid the taxes and fought the wars—people like his callous-handed neighbours— would be empowered to reap more of the benefits of their labours and votes.

He saw nothing threatening in the NDP or its predecessor, the CCF; they were part of a non-revolutionary movement that had contributed to the health and humanization of the Canadian economy. But he knew others saw it differently. The corporate Titans, who used wealth to buy political power and political power to get more wealth, would not contemplate with equanimity anything that might modify their advantages, and others would support them in the hope of becoming Titans. Non-revolutionary change was glacier paced and attempts to operate without reference to context were doomed to failure.

But if he was no revolutionary, neither was he a reactionary. Change might come slowly, but it would come. To comfort those who held power and looked on his government with intense suspicion, he burnished his own image as a moderate.[16] He had a father and four brothers in business and would not apologize for the philosophy of his government, but he knew the fears of others and was willing to be conciliatory. He was not looking for a fight.

But he would fight. And the expected confrontation between his government and the business community was not long in coming. The transfer of Medicare premiums from poll tax to ability-to-pay tax was an election promise. A bill was prepared to reduce the Medicare premium by half, the resultant $14 million revenue loss to be made up by an increase of two per cent in personal and one per cent in corporate income taxes. A note came from a major Manitoba corporation: its board of directors was meeting and needed to know the government's intentions on the proposed tax increase, because it would influence their decisions on

---

[15] Colleague Russell Doern wrote: "The city had his mind, but the country held his heart." *Wednesdays are Cabinet Days*, p. 76.

[16] He was a fiscal conservative and, for a man who reached the age of majority at the beginning of the turbulent, iconoclastic Sixties, not that liberal in social policy either. But he understood that society was in flux and that there was no way back.

expansion and employment. The note was polite, but the shoe had been dropped.

The government enunciated what became its response to such approaches; the fiscal policy of Manitoba would be made not by private corporations, but by the democratically elected government.

The challenge was answered. The taxes were imposed.

The challenge came again when the minimum wage was raised from $1.25 to $1.50 per hour. The business community was hysterical. Higher wages would make workers lazy; business could not survive it; they would depart and leave Manitoba a vast wasteland.[17]

Schreyer was offended by such complaints when the economy was booming and a major concern was a shortage of labour, and appalled by the business community's blindness to its long-term interests. Members of the corporate elite were apparently too ideological to see wage earners as wage spenders; they spent millions on futile efforts to find foreign markets, while failing to appreciate that their best market was at home.

His Job-like patience snapped. He quoted Cromwell: "If some businessmen believe a wage of $1.50 hour for those who produce our wealth is too much, in God's name let them leave, for they have been here too long for the good they have done."

The new premier had drawn an inexorable line. It was a signal.

---

[17] Nothing has changed. Three decades later, when Manitoba's Conservative government raised the minimum wage to $6 an hour, mid-range among the provinces, Dan Kelly of the Canadian Federation of Independent Business protested: "I don't think we are prepared for a 60-cent increase ... It will definitely have a negative impact on job creation." *Winnipeg Free Press*, December 8, 1998.

V

Into the Breach

Glendower: "I can call the spirits from the vasty deep."
Hotspur: "So can I, but will they come when I call them?"
                    —Shakespeare, *Henry IV*

I n those glorious summers of 1969 and early 1970, it appeared the spirits would indeed come to the aid of the new government. We could do nothing wrong. We could triumph in the risks we took.

The New Democratic Party elected as the Government of Manitoba in 1969 had passed through several permutations since its tentative beginnings [1]. In the preceding half-century it had pulled together strains of progressive thinking, including British Trade Unionism, Utopianism, Christian Socialism, Fabianism, Gas-and-Water Socialism, Methodism, German Democratic-Socialism, Co-operativism, Marxism [2], and other movements rising in the wake of dislocations intiated by the Industrial Revolution and the desire to distribute its benefits more equitably. These had coalesced into the Independent Labour Party to send A.A. Heaps and J.S. Woodsworth to Parliament in 1921, and to elect a galaxy of men and women to legislatures, councils and school boards.

They had coalesced again in 1933, with Depression-sickened Eastern intellectuals and creators of the wheat pools and consumer cooperatives forming the Co-operative Commonwealth Federation (CCF). Its constitution, with its famous reference to the eradication of capitalism [3], still used by antisocialists to frighten

---

[1] For a study of the evolution of democratic socialism in Manitoba, and of the motivations of those who built the movement, see Nelson Wiseman's *Social Democracy in Manitoba*, University of Manitoba Press, Winnipeg, 1983. Also Lloyd Stinson's *Political Warriors*, Queenston House, Winnipeg, 1975.

[2] All except Marxism were non-revolutionary. The original core of the CCF leadership was not politically suspect Europeans, but rather Anglo-Saxons born in Canada or in Britain.

[3] "No CCF government will rest content until it has eradicated capitalism and put into operation (con't)

children—and voters—was written primarily by esteemed educator Frank Underhill, a mover in the League for Social Reconstruction. Woodsworth, first CCF Leader, T.C. Douglas, first CCF premier of Saskatchewan, and Stanley Knowles, longtime CCF/NDP member of Parliament, all came to politics through the Social Gospel Movement.[4]

Since the turn of the century, members of these movements had fought railroads, land barons, grain speculators, election fraud, gerrymandering and a philosophy English historian Thomas Carlyle described as "economic anarchy plus the policeman", which was producing obscene dualities of private wealth and public squalor. They fought for the vote for women—electing the first female MP; for social legislation (old age pensions, unemployment insurance, worker's compensation, public health care) and for unions to protect the interests of workers. They were willing to pay the price of their apostasy; some were charged with conspiracy and sedition, and threatened with deportation, after the 1919 Winnipeg General Strike. But while anathema to the authorities and the establishment, they were so popular with the people that several (John Queen, William Ivens, George Armstrong), had been elected to the Manitoba Legislature while in prison and the political ascendancy of others (S.J. Farmer, Fred Tipping, A.A. Heaps, W.S. Woodsworth) was permanently established by their leadership in the strike.

The strike was a watershed. It showed that the men with the guns had the power, that the populace valued law and order[5], that social change would be slow, and that it must be peaceful. Revolutionary proclivities gave way to reformism and the desire to create a political vehicle for a new philosophy. After 1945 when, instead of the expected post-war depression, prosperity resulted from the explosion of demand suppressed during the war, discretionary money to satisfy it, and burgeoning, technology propelled infrastucture, the CCF tailored itself to reality.

The party elbowed aside Cassandras and more radical elements, including the expulsion of several MLAs for taking independent positions on foreign policy.[6] In 1956, the Winnipeg Declaration, a constitutional concession to the majority of CCFers who did not believe in the efficacy of indiscriminate public ownership, exorcised the ghost of the Regina Manifesto. It pledged in future to work within, and with, the system, to civilize capitalism.

Despite this, in 1958 the national CCF was reduced to a corporal's guard by Progressive Conservative John Diefenbaker, a prairie populist who, at least in

---

[3] (con't) the full programme of socialized planning which will lead to the establishment in Canada of the Co-operative Commonwealth Federation."

[4] Knowles, who declined appointment to the Senate to continue his fight for pensions and was later accorded the unique honour of appointment as an officer of Parliament, came to politics through the church.

[5] As Lenin said of the Germans, there would be no revolution by Canadians, because they would not walk on the lawn grass.

[6] In 1949, the Manitoba CCF expelled two sitting MLAs, Berry Richards (The Pas) and Dr. D.L. Johnson (Brandon), and denied Wilbert Doneleyko (St. Clements) renomination, for "giving the impression that dissent from CCF policy was based on collusion with the Communist Party and its activities." Nelson Wiseman, *Social Democracy in Manitoba*, p. 59. This allowed the *Winnipeg Free Press* to claim that the CCF was sympathetic to the Soviet Union.

terms of rhetoric, appeared more radical than the elements of which the CCF was purging itself. In 1959, the same fate befell the CCF in Manitoba at the hands of Progressive Conservative Duff Roblin, who was progressive in more than name and implemented many policies with which the CCF could find little fault except in application.

In 1961, out of the ashes, rose the New Democratic Party, an organic union of CCF remnants and the Canadian Labour Congress. Organized labour would eschew its latent Gomperism and bring to the new political vehicle its organizational capacity, mass membership, and finances. The CCF would contribute its reputation as the social conscience of Canada, its hard-earned political experience and the government of Saskatchewan that Premier Douglas called "a beachhead of socialism on a continent of capitalism".

The architects of the NDP determined to broaden the party's base by attracting those who had a stake in the system rather than those who believed they did not. They appealed to both white- and blue-collar workers, the new upwardly mobile middle class, farmers, professionals and youth. In 1969, in Manitoba, the results were registered in the electoral statistics.

	ELECTORAL SEATS			PERCENTAGE OF POPULAR VOTE		
Year	1962	1966	1969	1962	1966	1969
NDP	7	11	28	15	23	38
PC	36	31	22	44	40	35
Liberal	13	14	5	36	33	24
Social Credit	1	1	1 (other)	4	4	2
Independent	0	0	1			

The almost 333,000 votes cast (sixty-three per cent of a total of 520,000 eligible voters) was virtually identical to that of 1966, but there had been a massive shift. The Liberals lost about 30,000 votes, the Progressive Conservatives 10,000, and the 11,000 first-time votes seemed to have gone almost entirely to the NDP.

The Tories had been severely damaged by levying a five per cent retail sales tax after Roblin's pledge, "as long as I am premier there will be no sales tax"[7]. And replacement of activist Roblin with opaque Weir robbed them of "progressive" pretensions. They were also damaged by persistent suspicions about hydro development, dark rumours about public money poured into the sinkhole of a forestry complex at The Pas, and anger at the election called after only a half-term in office. The Liberals committed political *hari-kiri* by replacing their retiring leader

---

[7]   Merchants quickly developed the habit of saying to angry customers: "This much for me and five per cent for Duffy." It was a killer.

with one even more conservative, and university students who traditionally gravitated to the Liberals resented the party establishment's selection of an aging rural reactionary. The generation of youth reaching adolescence in the iconoclastic Sixties was seeking a political figure to whom its members could relate.

The NDP had a moderate leader of proven ability and credibility who was both a product of, and had taught at, the University of Manitoba. He was rural-urban, multilingual, German Catholic[8] and friendly to the French fact precisely when non-English Manitobans had achieved a majority of the population and the Anglo-Orange hegemony that had governed Manitoba for a century was breaking down.[9] The party constituency organizations—Edmund Burke's "little platoons"—built a member at a time over a half-century, which had kept political fires stoked in difficult times and provided the shock troops to fight campaigns, turned their attention from election proselytizing to explaining the government's policies.

The Mennonite South had voted its faith, electing the lone Social Credit MLA—but ironically, one personally friendly to Schreyer. Redistribution had given Winnipeg twenty-seven of the total of fifty-seven seats which, with the two seats in Brandon and one in Thompson, gave the cities a majority for the first time, and the NDP had a strong urban policy. It won the seat in the mining city of Thompson, one of two in Brandon, and seventeen, including six of the eight new urban seats created, in Winnipeg, proving the Marxist contention that socialism grows among the urban proletariat. It also won eleven rural seats; Schreyer, son of a farmer and son-in-law of Jake Schulz, who had built the Manitoba Farmer's Union and politicized the rural areas, had a powerful rural image.[10]

On election night, while Bend lamented the decimation of his historic party and predicted it would make a comeback, and Weir asserted sourly that the people of Manitoba has made a mistake and predicted "they'll correct it next time", Schreyer had told a wildly cheering crowd at the Union Centre election headquarters: "The reason we have been able to win this kind of confidence is the excellent slate of candidates we were able to field and because the policies we have put forward to the people are enlightened and will take this province forward into the 1970s."

Later Desjardins announced he would sit as a "Liberal Democrat", loosely allied with the Schreyer government, and this was endorsed at a huge public meeting by his St. Boniface constituency. The government's crucial twenty-ninth seat seemed secure.

---

8. Before Schreyer, all CCF/NDP leaders in Manitoba had been urban, Anglo-Saxon and Protestant.

9. Nelson Wiseman has added a reason for the radical shift in voting patterns: "The first wave of settlers to Manitoba came from rural Ontario during the last quarter of the 19th century. They quickly occupied the best agricultural lands and secured homesteads along the new CPR. The Ontarians became Manitoba's charter group, and settled their greatest numbers in the rural southwest and in the fashionable areas of Winnipeg … [Their] continuing influence … in the 20th century was perhaps reflected in the fact that every Manitoba premier … until Schreyer in 1969, was either Ontario-born or of Ontario parentage." *Social Democracy in Manitoba*, p. 4.

10. The PCs won fourteen rural and eight urban seats; the Liberals won three rural and two urban seats, one of which defected to the NDP.

What was seen as a stunning victory for the NDP, could—and was— obversely translated into a stunning defeat for the political/business establishment. This mood was caught by the editor of the newspaper in Schreyer's home constituency, who quoted from a recent book by Peter Drucker that the new leaders need knowledge rather than an established pedigree or inherited status because: "The age of inherited power is over." [11]

But Schreyer, cool and quietly confident, did not see this as a win-lose situation of new versus old. He noted that most of the industrial and commercial base in Saskatchewan had been built under the CCF/NDP, and challenged those suspicious of his party's intentions: "I ask that the doom criers be written off as sour grapes until they have proof to the contrary ... Because of my upbringing as a member of a farm family, and with brothers with considerable investment in the Manitoba economy, I do not intend to lead a government which will go after businessmen in Manitoba, so they would lose by government infringing on their investment."

In appointing his cabinet he had sought to calm the business commmunity. Saul Cherniack, respected lawyer and political veteran at both the city and provincial levels, became Finance minister. Education went to another veteran of the legislature and former school board chairman and mayor of West Kildonan, Saul Miller. Labour was placed in the experienced hands of former Transcona mayor and fifteen-year veteran of the legislature, Russell Paulley. Schreyer himself—seen as a moderate—became minister of Industry and commerce. He saw it "psychologically important to allay business fears about investing in the Manitoba of the NDP." [12]

The media and the business community had predicted a short tenure for the NDP. *Winnipeg Tribune* associate editor Harry Mardon had written that the business community doubted the government would last and warned darkly the premier should listen to them. Insurance executives shrilled that any government touching their industry would be destroyed. The *Tribune* had proposed editorially that the premier "lean on his colleagues who may cling to a doctrinaire approach". The *Winnipeg Free Press* had editorialized that, if the government dared proceed with its agenda in the "House Divided", it would fall before winter.

Yet there they were, more than a year later, still in office. And it had been a productive and exhilarating year. Nineteen seventy was Manitoba's centennial year. Cabinet minister Phillip Petursson, the tall, patrician, impeccably dressed Unitarian minister, a Canadian Anthony Eden, guided the province through the festivities without a single gaucherie. The "postage-stamp" province with some 10,000 inhabitants brought into the Canadian Federation in 1870 was now larger than some European states, had a population of a million, and was bursting with activity.

---

[11] The *North Kildonan Herald*, June 27, 1969

[12] Throughout his tenure as premier, Schreyer ran well ahead of his party in the polls. No matter what the NDP did to improve the social and economic conditions of Manitoba, the public image remained: "Right man, wrong party."

Bobby Gimby, nationally famous for his rendition of "Ca-Na-Da" three years earlier, came to toot Manitoba's Hundred. Prime Minister Trudeau brought his entire cabinet for a meeting at Lower Fort Garry. Similarly, the annual premier's conference was held in Winnipeg and the other nine premiers came to pay tribute, to celebrate and to sense the energy pulsating through the province. Ebullient Social Credit Premier W.A.C. Bennett of British Columbia was so impressed he volunteered that, "Winnipeg should be the new capital for Canada's second century."

The royal family came, receiving tumultuous welcomes throughout Manitoba. NDP MLAs were treated like conquering heroes wherever they went. When the queen, regal and radiant, returned from the vibrant, developing north, accompanied by Manitoba's newly-minted hero, former hard-rock miner and anti-government demonstrator but now Highways minister, Joe Borowski, they were met in Winnipeg by a wildly enthusiastic crowd of more than 100,000 people. There was not a cloud in the NDP sky, not even the size of a man's hand.

Even the economy cooperated. Columnist Michael Best wrote:

> 'Boom' is the word Art Coulter, secretary-treasurer of the Manitoba Federation of Labour, used to describe conditions in his province … Unemployment averaged 2.7% compared with 3.4% in the previous year (4.7% for Canada). Builders and mining men complain of a shortage of help … Public and private investment [is up] … The North is booming with new mines and record exploration. Rod McIsaac, president of Midwest Drilling, the biggest mine-drilling company in the West, said he had more rigs working in Northern Manitoba than in the last dozen years. Retail sales were up a phenomenal 5.4%, and 1969 brought the province 63 new industries … Manitoba has halted its population drain [13] and gained 8,000 persons … A construction boom is changing Winnipeg's skyline … Winnipeg is where Bristol Aerospace is building the Black Brant rocket for space exploration [and] recently won a contract for components for the Lockheed jumbo … Boeing is putting in a parts plant for its jumbo. [14]

Not all businessmen were pleased. Michael Best reported:

> [The] president of a Winnipeg firm manufacturing grain handling equipment worries about the Schreyer government. 'The business climate is more difficult in Manitoba today than in the last 20 years,' but his major complaint was a shortage of labour. The president of a garment company

---

[13] Two years earlier, during a PC regime, sociologist Larry Shane stated: "Compared with other Canadian cities, Winnipeg ranked last in population growth." *Winnipeg Free Press*, October 12, 1967

[14] *The Winnipeg Tribune*, January 31, 1970.

(despite expecting a 20% growth in 1970) is worried that 'Tough new labor laws will likely damage Manitoba's garment industry.' "[15]

While the royals were being feted and the province launched into its second century, the legislature was in session. Commitments of the Throne Speech were being enacted and new initiatives undertaken: to guard against invasion of privacy; to establish fairer rules for the expropriation of private property; to advance self-rule in the North; to restore French as a language of instruction in schools; to launch an extensive home building program; to reduce crop insurance premiums. Construction of the giant hydro-electric project on the Nelson River was proceeding at full bore. And the budget was balanced.

It had been done by those who had been derided by detractors as "butchers, bakers and candlestick makers", "eggheads who have never had to meet a payroll", and "representatives of the unwashed masses who are prime examples of the people they represent". Manitoba, like Québec, was experiencing a 'Quiet Revolution'. Toynbee's thesis of historical evolution had come to fruition: the self-confident establishment at the centre was being displaced by those on the social, political and economic periphery who, by force of circumstances, worked harder, thought more, and represented a different set of interests.

By mid-1970 the NDP government had been sitting for seven of the thirteen months since being elected. It was coming to the end of a monumental session, the longest in the history of the province. It had passed 186 pieces of legislation. There was only one more little matter to take care of—passing Bill 56.

There were concerns expressed about Premier Schreyer being unable "to control his doctrinaire radicals", but he was winning people over. Columnist Douglas Marshall wrote:

> He is not a natural platform politician [but] communicates a
> steely-eyed integrity and seriousness of purpose that has captured popular
> imagination ... He is a New Dealer no more left than the quotation by FDR
> hanging behind his desk: 'The test of our progress is not in whether we
> add to the abundance of those with much, but in whether we provide for
> those with little.'[16]

Schreyer described his party's philosophy in anodyne terms: "The NDP and [and CCF] have been a coalition of groups and philosophies, only one of which is socialism. This coalition has become a traditional part of the Canadian political spectrum."

At the Liberal Party conference in Kingston in 1960, Maurice Lamontagne

---

[15] *Op. cit.* Socialist Schreyer could not satisfy the business community any more than plutocrat President John F. Kennedy who, exasperated after a fight with the steel industry, blurted: "My father always told me businessmen were sons-of-bitches."

[16.] *Maclean's*, December 1970.

had presented a paper which opened with the following words:

> The ultimate objective of economic activity is the maximum com-
> mon welfare. The majority of Canadians want to achieve that objective
> within a mixed economic system where the direction and the composition
> of the public and private sectors are determined by the democratic process
> and free markets.

That philosophy commended itself to moderate regimes such as Manitoba's NDP. But Schreyer explained: "The difference between social democracy and liberalism is the extent of its willingness to use the state to both create wealth and to distribute it."

No matter how non-confrontational those in the NDP government wished to be, they were part of a sixty-year continuum in social legislation propelled by men and women whose names had become more than footnotes in history books. They could not escape their convictions that there were public benefits in collective action, and that the public corporation was an instrument of democracy. They would not discard the state as an instrument through which a democratically elected government could act on behalf of its people. To them government was less an instrument for political control, than for social and economic development.

After a year in office it almost appeared the establishment had made its accommodation with the Schreyer government. Conversely, some in the party, particularly among the New Democratic Youth and the Waffle, which considered itself keeper of the socialist flame, had concluded the premier would conduct "business as usual": that he was too moderate to be a threat to the power structure and therefore of no value to themselves.

Both were wrong. In mid-July 1970, all appeared to be going well beyond expectation. It was an illusion. A month after the social democratic government of Manitoba had been given status by the royal tour, it was holding onto power by its fingernails. As Phoebus Apollo had forsaken beleaguered Hector at Troy, so in the hour of greatest need, the spirits would not heed our call.

The final item on the 1970 legislative agenda proposed to use the state to challenge the power and wealth of the entrenched insurance industry. All else the NDP had done or would do paled into insignificance compared to the momentous clash of the Government of Manitoba and the establishment over Autopac.

VI

Autopac I

If You Would See [Their] Monument, Look about You
          —On the tomb of Sir Christopher Wren,
          architect of St.Paul's Cathedral

"**C**all in the members.**"** The division bells shrilled. The Speaker of the Manitoba Legislature announced a standing vote on third reading of the Bill 56. It was the NDP government's revolutionary proposal to replace all private motor vehicle insurance companies in Manitoba with a publicly owned monopoly.

The government was risking its life. The combined opposition—twenty-two Conservatives, four Liberals and one Social Credit—totalled twenty-seven. That equalled the assured government votes. If the bill failed to pass, the first social democratic government in Manitoba and only the second in the history of North America, which had come to office thirteen months earlier, would die.

The visitor's gallery was filled far beyond allowed capacity. With less than standing room, people crowded against each other so tightly they almost had to breathe in unison and anyone suffering a heart attack would not have been able to fall down.

Among those in the crowd were representatives from sixteen American states, who had been sent to monitor the legislation, and witness either the birth of a publicly-owned corporate entity or the death of a government.

I stood with them that August 13, 1970, in the sweltering heat, fervently hoping the universe would unfold as it should. Below, in the cockpit of the chamber, the atmosphere was fighting tense, and the tension communicated itself to the gallery. Even those who knew nothing of the specifics of the issue knew that, this day, history would be made.

The official opposition, a year out of office and smelling blood, had tossed down its gauntlet. Conservative MLA Bud Sherman, with orotund vocabulary and evocative imagery, stated that his party heard in the 'socialist' government's bill, "the muffled cadence of marching jackboots", and warned this could be followed by nationalization of "trust companies, banks, trading exchanges, newspapers, radio and television stations and stores."[1]

All knew the buzzers summoning the members to their seats could be tolling the death-knell of the Government of Manitoba … "Never send to know for whom the bell tolls …"

Two wild cards in the legislative deck added to the tension. Gordon Beard, the gentle soul of Brobdingnagian proportions from Churchill for whom a special chair had been built in the chamber, was first elected as a Conservative, resigned his seat in 1968 because of his government's lack of attention to the North, and in 1969 was re-elected as an Independent. The previous day he had stated he would vote for the bill, but earlier he had repeatedly stated he could not vote for legislation that would result in nationalization of a private industry and loss of individual freedom. And he had consistently voted against the government on opposition amendments for delay. So how would Beard vote?

Laurent Desjardins, the stormy petrel from francophone St. Boniface had sat for years as a Liberal, representing a community that had voted primarily Liberal since Laurier. He had fought with his party shortly before the 1969 election because he felt it was not sufficiently aggressive in demanding more rights for francophones. Re-elected as a Liberal, he now sat as a Liberal Democrat and had not joined the NDP Caucus. He too had stated the previous day that he would support the bill but only two weeks earlier he had rocked the government by announcing he would vote against the "socialist" bill. On several occasions, he had expressed himself to be totally opposed to "nationalization" and for a year he had played Hamlet. So how would Desjardins vote?

In an atmosphere of palpable tension the clerk of the legislature, in sepulchral tones, began to call the roll. The issue that during the past year appeared to have brought Manitoba to the brink of revolution, was about to be decided …

THE TRAIN HAD BEEN SET IN MOTION years earlier when the CCF/NDP began arguing that the greater the vehicular traffic and the more frequent and expensive the accidents, the more selective the private insurers and the less satisfied the driving public became. Some drivers could not obtain insurance, meaning financial ruin for both perpetrator and victim in the event of an accident. In neighbouring Saskatchewan, the only social democratic government in North America had legislated no-fault, universal, compulsory motor vehicle insurance through a publicly owned monopoly in 1945 and it had proven an unqualified success.

---

1. *Winnipeg Free Press*, April 30, 1969.

Manitoba governments argued such things are best left to the private sector, but recognized such things could not be left to the 'Invisible Hand' and began intervening by regulation. In the 1950s, Premier Campbell's Liberals required the industry to accept high-risk drivers on 'assigned risk', which provided them with insurance but at a prohibitive cost. In the Sixties, Premier Roblin's Progressive Conservatives required all buyers of driver's licenses to pay an additional $25 into the Unsatisfied Judgement Fund, which was used to compensate victims for damages by uninsured drivers. Every regulatory move provided the private sector with a captive market—but without requiring accountability.

The Social Credit government of British Columbia appointed a Royal Commission to study complaints against the motor vehicle insurance industry. In 1968, Mr. Justice Wootten reported that the private industry was paying benefits of only sixty-three cents of the premium dollar, while the public monopoly in Saskatchewan was repaying eighty-three cents. In brief, private sector administration costs were double those of the public company. Wootten concluded:

> A major tenet of [Saskatchewan's] approach is application of liability
> of drivers to contribute to a fund that pays fairly for injuries to persons and
> damages to property, not attempting to shift losses on the basis of fault. A
> second characteristic is the savings inherent when all motorists work together
> ... providing the greatest return for the dollar paid."[2]

The Manitoba NDP seized on this report and the commitment to establish a universal, publicly owned insurance company became a major plank in its 1969 election platform. But once elected, the government found—as golfers have— there was "many a slip twixt the cup and the lip".

Initially, the insurance industry hardly took the new government seriously. Its members had learned from long experience that any party aspiring to the seats of the mighty must make obeisance to the unwashed masses, but quickly learned how the world really works after attaining office. Two days after the 1969 election, a *Winnipeg Tribune* survey showed all respondents doubting the NDP would proceed with a publicly owned insurance corporation.[3]

In the same issue, associate editor Harry Mardon quoted businessmen as stating that any government move smelling of socialism would drive away investment but saw Schreyer as "a man of moderation" and expected that he would stay that way.[4]

The *Winnipeg Free Press* editorialized that, with a minority government, any move to proceed with the promised insurance plan would mean, "Manitobans will

---

[2]   Government of British Columbia, Queen's Printer, 1968. Wootten wrote that the mess in the automobile insurance industry suggested that private companies should be nationalized, but, since that was not the "Canadian way", that they be given another chance.

[3]   "Insurance Men Ponder NDP", *The Winnipeg Tribune*, June 27, 1969.

[4]   "Business Circles Get Over Shock", *Ibid*.

be back to the ballot box before the snow flies."[5]

The hammer fell when the government tabled Bill 56. The raucous response, on April 29, 1970, was a giant rally of some 7,000 insurance agents and their supporters who paraded down Portage Avenue, filled every square inch of lawn at the Legislative Building, and shouted down Autopac Minister Howard Pawley when he came out to explain the bill. The call to arms had come two days earlier in a two-page *Winnipeg Free Press* advertisement with the huge headline YOUR FUTURE IS THREATENED. It concluded with the announcement of the mass rally, ostensibly sponsored by the Insurance Agents' Association of Manitoba.[6] Like the ancient tactic of troops advancing behind a screen of women and children, the industry was using the agents to front its attack.[7]

The advertisement was liberally sprinkled with the word "socialist" placed in juxtaposition to "free enterprise", free society", "unemployment", "bankruptcy" and "who will be next?". The rally was replete with posters reading: ED THE RED, and SEND SCHREYER TO SIBERIA. Those who saw a 'Communist Plot' in what they considered government intrusions into private preserves never understood they must deal with issues like Medicare and Autopac not on the basis of ideology but of economics.

The government treated the rally with jut-jawed resolve. Sidney Green dismissively commented: "If my boss gave me a day off with pay I would demonstrate too." But it alerted the government to the realization it would be a long, hot summer and that they must fight the entire insurance industry determined to stop the plan and kill the government. The industry and those at the commanding heights of the economy knew if Bill 56 passed the contagion could spread to other provinces—or states.[8] And the issue reached beyond the insurance industry. Like the war between God and Satan in Milton's *Paradise Lost,* this was trumpeted as the classical confrontation between free enterprise and socialism and politicized Manitobans as nothing had since the 1919 General Strike.

George Heffelfinger, president of National Grain Company, leader of the Liberal Party of Manitoba, well educated, an enlightened businessman, saw this confrontation in stark terms: "Because of Bill 56, my business friends display

---

[5] "A House Divided", *Winnipeg Free Press*, June 26, 1969.

[6] Reportedly, the Stop Bill 56 campaign was organized by the Insurance Bureau of Canada, and much of the thrust and material came from Allstate Insurance in the U.S. In June 1970, Consumers Report rated Allstate, in performance, at the bottom of a list of twenty-one insurance companies. Twenty-three years later, Allstate, sued by the Government of California, rebated $110 million to its California policy holders. *Los Angeles Times*, August 18, 1993.

[7] When it was clear that the government would proceed, it was quietly approached by a self-proclaimed insurance industry spokesman, proposing a tradeoff: the government should allow the private companies to continue providing insurance to Manitobans, but regulate them by having services delivered through government offices. If he was serious, the industry was proposing abandoning its agents who were fighting in the trenches for its benefit.

[8] Richard Cooper, manager of Insurance Central, an anti-Bill 56 lobby, stated: "If Autopac looked to be doing well [in Manitoba] other jurisdictions will obviously be interested." Quoted by Walter Stewart, *The Toronto Star*, January 28, 1972.

considerable apprehension. I feel pretty hard-pressed to recommend to my board of directors that we undertake expansion." [9]

The issue was being fought out not only in the public arena, but also inside the government caucus, which needed to resolve some fundamental questions: would this be a public company competing with the several score private companies already selling motor vehicle insurance in Manitoba, or a monopoly; would the services be delivered through government offices manned by civil servants, or by private agents paid earned commissions; would those now earning their livelihood selling insurance be absorbed into the apparatus of the public company, or bought out; if agents were compensated, would this also apply to companies?

And there was another fundamental question; an election promise had been made to establish a publicly owned auto insurance company, but did it make political—or common—sense to risk the life of the government on something so radical when it was in a minority position in the legislature? Some wanted to plunge ahead; they believed their government would be defeated by the combined opposition at some point in any case, so the government should choose the issue on which to be defeated. And they believed the concept of public insurance was so popular with the public that, if defeated in the legislature, the NDP would win a majority in the ensuing election. Others, including Schreyer, were more cautious. They did not want their government to be a passing meteor—no sooner seen than burned out, or be seen as recklessly throwing the dice with no chance of winning, or as political amateurs. They wanted time: time to prove they did not wear horns; time to mobilize the public; time to structure their position in more acceptable terms; time for the insurance lobby to overplay its hand; time to find the weak points in the opposition arguments; time for an opposition member to cross the floor, or to resign, or to become ill, or die.

The opposition argued fiercely that the government had a minority of seats and was elected with only thirty-nine per cent of the votes cast. Therefore, it had no mandate for the revolutionary course of establishing a public company that was socialistic, communistic, fascistic, unneeded, unwanted, would drive out business, reduce investment, create a massive bureaucracy, allow government to politically manipulate rates, be subsidized by the taxpayers, eliminate freedom of choice, destroy rights, and injure agents who rose at four o'clock in the morning to service client's needs.

Government members countered that the multiplicity of companies was overlapping and wasteful. They argued that administration cost more than one-third of the premium dollar; rate competition was artificial; many drivers were left uninsured; small claims were quickly settled but larger claims were taken to court, causing large backlogs; payments were delayed to force acceptance of inadequate settlements, and that the inadequacy of benefits paid was proven by the profits of the insurance industry which had, arguably, become the world's largest pool of investment capital.

---

[9] Quoted by Douglas Marshall, *Maclean's*, December 1970.

On June 24th, Premier Schreyer made a comprehensive statement to the legislature, methodically dealing with opposition arguments:

> The Opposition claims that, with a few minor adjustments, the current system of auto insurance is adequate! Yet the *Windsor Star*—not known as a socialist rag—has editorialized: 'The Government of Manitoba, in standing fast against criticism over the government's plan to introduce provincially legislated auto insurance, is performing a genuine service for the province and for Canadians. There can be little doubt about the inadequacies in the automobile insurance business. Anyone who has made a claim has fought through paper work, prolonged discussion and often insufficient settlements. The Manitoba Government deserves every encouragement for its efforts and good wishes for the success of its scheme. Detractors of the Manitoba plan are not the citizens who expect to save 15 or 20 per cent on their premiums.'
>
> The Opposition claims the government has no mandate for major initiatives! The Liberal government that established Manitoba Hydro was elected in 1953 with only 38.8% of the votes cast; the Conservative government elected in 1958 with only 40.22% of the votes, and with a minority of seats in the Legislature, undertook major initiatives; the Conservative government elected in 1966 with only 39.71% of the votes built the Winnipeg Floodway [larger than the Panama Canal]; the Diefenbaker government elected in 1957 had a minority of the seats in Parliament, and won with only 37% of the votes cast in the 1962 election; the Pearson government that legislated Medicare, the Canada Pension Plan and the Maple Leaf flag, was elected in 1966 with only 39% of the votes cast. So why are new rules being applied now?
>
> The Opposition claims a publicly-owned insurance company would reduce the freedom of Manitobans! Other jurisdictions in the British Commonwealth have government auto insurance, And I challenge them to say that liberty or freedom is any less to be seen in New South Wales, or New Zealand, or Saskatchewan, than it would be here after the implementation of this Bill.
>
> The Opposition claims a publicly-owned insurance company will develop a huge bureaucracy and be more expensive than the private system! Yet Saskatchewan has had public auto insurance since 1946 and has the lowest insurance premiums, lowest administration costs, and highest benefit payout as a percentage of the premium dollar, in North America. In 1964 Liberal Premier-elect Ross Thatcher was asked if he would abolish government auto insurance, and replied: 'No! I am not a socialist but neither am I crazy.'
>
> The Opposition claims Bill 56 will cause unemployment for many now in the insurance industry! They do not show the same concern when

private corporations lay off thousands. On the contrary, they argue layoffs
are needed for economic efficiency, so why do they not apply that argument
now? We know there will be dislocations, but every important change is
painful to somebody [and] we are obligated to ameliorate those dislocations. Those currently in the industry would have the right of first access
to employment with the public corporation, and those wishing to leave the
industry can apply to a Board of Adjudication to negotiate the buyout of
their agencies and scheduled transitional assistance.

The premier detailed how the opposition, in fighting the proposed
Insurance plan, had retreated from one position to another: (a) leave the
insurance industry alone; (b) regulate the industry; (c) reduce agent's commissions
to save money; (d) have the treasury subsidize the premiums of high-risk drivers
so the good drivers need not pay for them; (e) establish a review board to set
premiums; (f) legislate compulsory insurance for all drivers; (g) establish a publicly owned insurance company to compete with the private companies to keep
them honest.

> Each retreat demonstrated that the Opposition recognized the
> inadequacy and inefficiency of the industry, but was NOT willing to do
> anything to correct it! Indeed, every position they have taken means either
> taxpayer subsidization of the private companies, while being unable to
> exercise any control over them, or legislating compulsory insurance which
> would give the private companies a captive market of every driver in the
> province.
> And their worst position was their last one! The Opposition was
> saying 'all right already, perhaps something does need to be done and we
> will make some concession to the fact that you boxed yourselves into a
> corner by promising a public insurance company during the election cam-
> paign, so go ahead and establish one BUT UNDER NO CIRCUMSTANCES
> MUST THERE BE A MONOPOLY.'
> This would be a Godsend for the private insurance industry and a
> disaster for insurance purchasers. The private companies, already in pos-
> session of the record of every insured driver in Manitoba, would 'cream off'
> the best drivers and leave the high risks for the public company. The public
> company would be forced to increase premiums, giving the private sector
> the opportunity to raise its premiums ever higher, so long as they were just
> a little below those of the public company. This would guarantee the per-
> petual profitability of the private insurance Industry. And it would create
> a new and potent political issue by allowing the 'free enterprise' political
> parties to trumpet: 'we told you so—government cannot compete with
> the private sector'.

Schreyer concluded:

the 19th-century Luddites smashed the machinery in textile plants because
it was seen as a threat to jobs, so protecting themselves at the expense of
society by attempting to halt the Industrial Revolution. So too, the political
Opposition in Manitoba is willing to tax society with the costs of their
refusal to admit the essence of the modern technological revolution—that
there might be new and better ways of doing things which would redound
to the benefit of all.

Finally, establishment of a publicly-owned insurance company will
reduce premium rates a minimum of 15% through reduction of administration costs endemic in a competitive system. Equally important, investment capital currently leaving the province will be captured. Automobile
insurance companies currently harvest premiums of $37 million annually,
which are invested and the profits pocketed, and all that will remain in
Manitoba after the establishment of a publicly-owned insurance company.
The Saskatchewan Government Insurance office has, since its inception,
invested over $29 million in municipal debentures.

It was an epic performance. But it did nothing to ameliorate the debate —
or the death threats. Attorney General Al Mackling posted guards at the offices
and homes of the premier and the minister responsible for the bill, Howard Pawley.
The minister was skeptical and Schreyer philosophical: "They got Kennedy with
an army of Secret Service men around him. There is no way to guard effectively
against such eventualities. We must do what we must do and trust that
Manitobans will react in a civilized manner."

Bill 56 went to the Public Utilities Committee and hearings. In six weeks of
that hot and humid summer, some 140 presentations were made, most in opposition to the government plan. Those committed to the plan became a bit cynical
after hearing endless repetitions of the same points in brief after brief, seemingly
written by the same consulting agency. Yet one had to sympathize with the earnest
young salesmen with the clubby jackets and psychedelic ties who marched, one
by one, to the microphone to explain that both their personal future and that of
the country was at stake. They related the parable of the Little Red Hen, who had
worked hard and alone, only to see the economy of the corn patch ruined by
those wanting to reap where they had not sown.

Suddenly, help for the government came from a totally unexpected source.
Sylvan Leipsic was executive vice-president and general manager of Aronovitch
and Leipsic, the largest locally owned insurance agency in Winnipeg. He was a
leader in the fight to 'Stop Bill 56' and had been a speaker at the anti-government
rally in April. In his presentation to the committee, he made it clear he did not
welcome government intrusion into his business nor into the market economy
generally. However, he admitted that, rationally considered, the government plan,

while hard on the insurance industry, would be a boon for automobile drivers. The universal and compulsory features of the plan meant every driver would be insured. A monopoly meant elimination of the high costs of scores of companies, each with its own offices, executives, staffs, and salesmen, all competing against each other, and all being paid from the premium dollar. Ending this replication of administration would save drivers at least the "15 to 20%" of the current premium the premier had touted as a feature of the plan.

Leipsic had made himself a 'traitor to his class', and given the government hope. Perhaps things would go well after all and it might yet shepherd Bill 56 into law, despite its minority in the legislature. We now needed only to complete the committee hearings and report back to the legislature for the final vote.

The Public Utilities Committee was chaired by Desjardins. He had agreed to Schreyer's suggestion that, as a relative neutral, he was in the best position to moderate debate—and to assess the public mood. He was under enormous pressure. The industry knew the issue could be decided in the legislature by a single vote, and that they had to crack someone not totally committed to the government. Desjardins was their target. His exposure was emphasized manifold by his position at the head of the long table in historic Room 254. He sat like a large, brooding Buddha, alone and inscrutable, seeing all but saying nothing, day after torrid day, showing no anger or even perspiration, suffering abuse that would have driven lesser men to drink—or violence.

Not a whimper or word, except to call the next presenter—who would repeat the parable of the Little Red Hen. At the conclusion of the hearings, Desjardins summed up the proceedings and added: "I did not take issue with the deliberate insults—despite the fact that most of them were directed at me."

The pressure was not confined to the Legislative Chamber or the committee room. He was regularly accosted in corridors and on streets. His home phone number was, unfortunately, easily remembered and often dialed. His home became not a sanctuary but a cave, the sound of the ringing telephone bouncing off the walls through endless, sleepless nights. The industry knew they must break him to kill Bill 56. He accepted the abuse stoically, demonstrating no external signs of his inner turmoil; showing no sign of breaking.

On July 31st, he broke!

Just as the government was writing the final draft of the bill, with modifications for delivery of services by private agents and compensation for those leaving the field, Desjardins stood up in the chamber and announced he could not, in good conscience, support a bill implying "socialism for socialism's sake".

The effect on the NDP caucus was traumatic. It led to a furious fight between those who wanted to withdraw the bill, knowing that without Desjardins' vote—or that of a defector from the opposition, which seemed improbable—it could not pass, and those who, motivated by their election promise and/or the belief a snap election would result in an NDP majority, wanted to force the issue. The premier summarized the delicacy of the situation:

We are at a critical juncture. We are committed to Manitobans
to bring in a publicly-owned insurance company. We are also committed
to our party membership to remain in office the full four years if at all
possible. We are on the knife's edge and we must make a decision. There
is disagreement about whether to force the issue or abort the bill. Therefore
I am going to do the unusual. Normally we do not take votes here and the
caucus chair simply interprets the consensus. I am now going to ask for
a vote on whether we proceed, despite our circumstances. But let it be
understood that if we vote to proceed there will be no retreat by caucus
and no shirking by anyone. Also, let it be understood that we still have
some time and something might happen to give us the needed votes
provided we do not offend anyone. That will depend on how we, as
individuals and as a group, behave. As Alexander told his soldiers before
attacking Darius at the Issus: 'Remember, on the conduct of each depends
the fate of all.'

Caucus voted to proceed. The courting of opposition members and
particularly Desjardins and Beard, showed some progress.

On August 5th, everything blew up in the government's face. In the chamber,
Highways Minister Joe Borowski was asked what seemed an innocent question
about reported problems in his department. He responded gleefully, as it was a
scandal dating back to the previous Conservative government; he had fired several
departmental employees, laid charges against a contractor, and had a helicopter
looking for nineteen miles of road paid for but not found. The former minister of
Highways (Walter Weir, who was now leader of the opposition) must have known
of it, Borowski said, adding that his predecessor should be suspended from the
legislature until the investigation was completed.

The chamber exploded. Members shouted obscenities at each other. The
Speaker's attempt to restore order was ignored. Walter Weir, seeming to swell
even beyond his normally generous proportions, his handsome face dark with
fury, threw a copy of the thick house rules book onto the floor of the chamber in
front of the premier and demanded a retraction and an apology.

Borowski refused. He was appealed to by several members of the NDP
caucus: he had impugned the integrity of an honourable member of the legislature
and the house rules demanded he apologize. He refused. The Speaker threatened
to "name" him, withdrawing his right to sit in the legislature unless he apologized.
He refused: "If da opposition don't like it dey can go to hell."

It fell to Borowski's good friend Sid Green, as government house leader,
to do his duty. With tears in his eyes and voice breaking, he moved the requisite
motion that Joe Borowski be expelled from the chamber. He was. In the corridor
the ex-miner with a grade seven education, already a Manitoba legend, told the
media: "I told da trut and if I can't tell da trut in dat Goddam House I don't want
to sit in dat Goddam House."

Borowski was one of those who wanted an immediate election, firmly believing the electorate would return the NDP to office. It appeared he had broken faith with the premier and deliberately plotted the defeat of the government. He had not, but the consequences were the same: caucus was shaken; opposition members were furious and determined to get revenge; Borowski's vote could be lost on third reading of Bill 56, a week hence; gentle Gordon Beard, who might have been tempted to support the bill, was scandalized, and Larry Desjardins, without whose vote there would be no government insurance plan, challenged Borowski to a fistfight. It was a helluva mess, unexpected and irredeemable.

It fell to the premier to have a little chat with Borowski, who ultimately was persuaded of the consequences if he persisted. The next day he returned to the chamber and apologized. Under house rules, an honourable member's apology must be accepted. But the tensions in the chamber remained palpable, and doomsday was only a week away. And the government was still two votes short.

It also fell to the premier to speak with Desjardins and Beard: "You have both found favour with some aspects of this government and you have seen enough to know we are not ideological misfits cast into office by some quirk of the electoral process. Consider the consequences of our defeat. Do not abandon us now."

On August 12th, Desjardins, tearful and tortured, explained to the legislature that he would support Bill 56 because of "the cooperation shown" by the government in making the plan as painless as possible while honouring its pledge to the electorate. He had been impressed by Schreyer's sincerity, and his mind had pierced the veil of mythology hedging the private sector and he finally agreed, as he had with Medicare a year earlier, that "the old Order changeth and God fulfills Himself in many ways".

That left Beard. On May 15th, he had told the house: "I will not support compulsory insurance for Manitoba ... I wonder if people will accept this loss of freedoms ... creeping socialism will become running nationalization ... did those who voted (NDP) last spring know the impact of their vote? I ask the government to go to the people for their mandate as soon as possible." On May 24th, he had reiterated: "We are getting a snow job," and then voted with the opposition. Repeatedly, on divisions, he voted against the bill, forcing the speaker to break the tie in favour of the government "to leave the house opportunity to study the question".

Even if Desjardins supported the bill, Beard could cancel his vote. Theoretically, the Speaker could break the tie, but this was third reading. British Parliamentary tradition required that if the government could not get enough support for its own bill on third reading, it must be allowed to lapse. Conversely, if Ben Hanuschak ignored tradition and voted on final reading, he would be destroyed as Speaker. Bill 56 had reached the end of the road. It would die. And so would the government. It was show time.

On August 12th, Beard, the other tortured soul, MLA for the least-populated, largest, northernmost, most-ignored constituency in Manitoba, rose to state: "I do not feel that at this time it is necessary to have an election … Time wasted in fighting an election will bring the Manitoba economy to a halt for almost a year."

He gave a clue for his reversal of position: "I am against big government but I am, through my very location in this province, forced to turn to government for expanded northern programming … and no one can deny this government has dedicated itself to Northern development more than any predecessor." Then he added, "Two former Conservative cabinet members have indicated that deals for the North have been made to gain my vote on Bill 56. There have been no deals, but those who suggest this will do me a service if they go into the Churchill constituency and spread this tale of supersalesman to all my constituents."

He closed with the enigmatic, "I must thank members of the party opposite, and the insurance industry, for their detailed research, not only on my past, but on my past friends, from childhood right until now. They've done a good job; they've done a good job of making up my mind as to what stand I will take and who I must turn in trust to." [10]

Clearly, not only Desjardins was under severe pressure. Hearing Beard from the visitor's gallery, it was tempting to speculate whether, in the final analysis, the public insurance company would come into being because private industry had overplayed its hand—whether it had been too personal in its fight to stop Bill 56, even if that meant destroying two men whose philosophy they had always supported.

It was *der Tag*. The clerk tolled off the names of the members. All government members stood up to support the bill. Desjardins and Beard up stood with them. From the visitor's gallery, holding several score insurance industry personnel, boos, unprintable obscenities and calls of "goodbye Manitoba" rained down on them.

The negative vote of the total opposition was anticlimactical. The clerk announced: "Yeas—29; Nays—27." The Speaker intoned: "I declare the motion carried."

By two votes, neither belonging to members of the government, the Manitoba Public Insurance Corporation struggled into existence. The next day the province blossomed with bumper stickers: WILL THE LAST PERSON TO LEAVE MANITOBA PLEASE TURN OUT THE LIGHTS? But a new corporate entity had been legislated into being.

---

[10] Beard privately indicated that he believed the industry had investigated him and some friends to find some issue in their past that could be used to force him to oppose Bill 56.

VII

Autopac II

Long is the way, and hard;
That leads from hell up to the light.
 —John Milton, *Paradise Lost*

Autopac became operational on November 1, 1971. It provided a basic, compulsory package of $50,000 third-party liability and $200 deductible, with scheduled benefits for dismemberment, loss-of-income, or death. Extended insurance, providing lower deductibles and/or higher liability coverage, was available from Autopac—or from the private companies.[1] A driver merit system rewarded good drivers and required those who were accident-prone to pay extra charges, instead of loading the costs on the system. And the insurance package followed the driver, not the vehicle.

Passage of Bill 56 gave the Government of Manitoba authority to establish the Manitoba Public Insurance Corporation, and began dissipating the public tensions which, for a year, had brought Manitoba to the brink of civil disobedience. Conversely, it launched the government into a year of frenetic activity to give the new entity life. It was a complex operation: collecting data; feeding it into computers; creating the administrative apparatus; establishing the structure; appointing a board of directors experienced in the complexities of insurance and dedicated to making the new corporation a success, instead of sabotaging it; finding experienced and competent management; training staff; commissioning agents and establishing delivery of services and fees; computing premium schedules for more than 1,000 models of vehicle; negotiating rates with body shops and preparing materials to inform the public about the details of the program.

---

[1] One by one, the private companies found themselves unable to compete with Autopac and abandoned Manitoba.

Initial premiums ranged from ten to thirty per cent less than they would have been in the private sector. Sylvan Leipsic, an insurance expert appointed to the Autopac board of directors opined: "This is an excellent plan [and] could not have been instituted except as a government monopoly."[2]

In short, all was going superbly. Then it all blew up.

On February 18, 1972, ten days before the end of Autopac's first operational year, the minister that announced the system was on stream and all renewal forms had been sent to registered drivers. One week later, someone at the computer centre found a pile of 37,000 renewal forms that had not been sent out. Searches found more. They also revealed that some 12,000 renewal forms had been lost, and others were replicated. A friend received seven copies of his renewal form, and my next door neighbor received nine. The Autopac program was in a state of chaos. It was panic time.

The minister reported a series of very peculiar circumstances, adding that "Everything that could go wrong, did." A computer expert brought in from Toronto pronounced the system salvageable and spent the summer salvaging it. By autumn, Autopac seemed back on track. But I was still uneasy and called the minister.

Howard Pawley, whose low-key competence had guided Autopac into being, was a prince. His father, a tough man who had moved to Manitoba from the old Anglo-Saxon redoubt in southern Ontario, had proven to the chamber-of-commerce types that one could be both a socialist and a successful business-man. Howard was an only child who grew up in a book-filled home that was a stop-off point for itinerant socialist leaders. He spent many evenings listening to the men and women who were changing the social face of Canada.

He received his B.A. from United College and considered going into the ministry, but decided on law instead. Tall, slim, handsome, soft-spoken, infallibly courteous, he settled in Selkirk, set up a law practice, became the town's solicitor, joined the chamber of commerce, became known as a friendly, accommodating person, and married Ed Schreyer's cousin. At age twenty-three, he became president of the Manitoba CCF—its youngest president ever—and ran three times as a sacrifice candidate in unwinnable constituencies. On the philosophical left, he was disappointed when the new NDP included organized labour as an organic part of the party. He saw this as moving the party to the right, but he made his peace.

On June 25, 1969, his thirty-fifth birthday, while in hospital with a broken back resulting from a car accident, he was elected to the legislature for Selkirk. On July 15th, he was appointed minister of Municipal Affairs and became so popular that the Manitoba Union of Municipalities asked the premier to leave him in that portfolio after the 1973 election. In 1969-70, he was the minister charged with preparing Bill 56, shepherding it through the legislature, and making Autopac operational.

Pawley had a serious flaw, however. Largely because his education and

---

[2]   *The Winnipeg Tribune.* May 18, 1972.

training had been academic rather than practical, he simply could not believe ill of anyone. Even more than Schreyer, he was psychologically incapable of kicking stray dogs. He was no patsy, as those who thought him an easy mark during the Autopac debates discovered, and he ran his department with quiet confidence, but he had difficulty refusing any petitioner.

In June 1973, I received a telephone call from a resident of my old home community who refused to reveal his name: "Hello, who is speaking?"

"You know me."

"That's possible, but I need a name to confirm it."

"You do not know me favourably."

"That makes you one of many. So why are you calling?"

"I need a favour."

"What is the nature of this favour?"

"Get my brother out of jail into my custody."

"Why is he in jail?"

"He threatened to kill someone."

"Well, I can't get him out of jail unless I know his name."

"Bessaraba!"

Memories came flooding back. Fifteen years earlier, at a public meeting during the 1958 federal election campaign, his parents had thrown eggs at me, ruining my favourite tie, and made accusations that brought me to within an inch of arrest for inciting a riot. Now, as their son's almost tearful story unfolded, I realized with some chagrin that I was a public servant and had a responsibility beyond my personal feelings.

I phoned the acting attorney general. "Howard, I have received a plea and perhaps the boy is more volatile than malicious. I will quickly tell you the story and you decide if you should, or want to, intervene."

And Howard Pawley, who was in the middle of an election campaign, four days before E-Day, agreed to look at the file. Anyone in trouble, or with a problem, could count on him for help or consideration.

After the election I received another call from my former home town, this time from an old friend: "I understand your provincial employment program makes grants to municipalities for the purpose of creating jobs in the construction or renovation of publicly owned projects."

"You understand correctly."

"The Town of Grandview has received a PEP grant that was used to fund a privately owned project." He explained the details.

I phoned the deputy mayor: "I understand the PEP grant the town received was used for private purposes."

"No, it was used to dismantle and remove the old rink."

"But I am informed you had sold the rink to an individual and then he came to the town to get him a PEP grant to remove it."

"That's true."

"But in that case the grant went to a privately owned project. Regretfully, I must ask you to return the money."

"But we have already paid it to the man."

"I'm sorry, but them's the rules. If we allow you to get away with this, every municipality in Manitoba will do it and we will not be able to refuse. We would be ripped off from hell to breakfast and the objective of the program would be destroyed."

The Town of Grandview returned the funds. Weeks later another friend phoned, "There is a rumour the Town of Roblin used a PEP grant on private property." I phoned the mayor of Roblin and explained. He denied it. I phoned the PEP director: "Frank, send someone to Roblin to investigate."

PEP staff member Vivian Rosenberg went to Roblin, investigated, and sent me a written report detailing five projects paid for with the PEP grant. Again I phoned the mayor: "We have recovered from another municipality so the same rules must apply to you. I want your explanation or your cheque."

I received neither. A week later I received a call from the secretary to the minister responsible for PEP, Howard Pawley. The minister was meeting with some people from Roblin and he understood I was involved and was inviting me to the meeting.

The mayor of Roblin, the town secretary and their solicitor had come to tell the minister they had properly used the PEP grant and were entitled to keep it. I drew from my jacket pocket Rosenberg's report detailing the properties improved with the PEP money. They were embarrassed but defensive. Their solicitor said, "Roblin did not do anything wrong. Besides, we know of eight or nine other municipalities that did the same thing".

I whipped a pen and a piece of paper out of my shirt pocket: "Give me their names and I will recover the money from them."

He refused. The argument continued until I decided to end it: "Mr. Mayor, the Provincial Employment Program was established with certain guidelines and objectives. You claim you did not misspend the grant money. So I will make you a proposition. You put a letter in the *Roblin Review* explaining to the taxpayers of Roblin how you spent their money and I will forget the matter."

"I—I—I can't do that."

"Then I will expect your cheque." I returned to my office.

The minister had sat through the meeting, wordless but listening intently. A week later his secretary sent me a copy of the minister's letter to the Town of Roblin, advising the town that it could keep the money. I phoned the minister who explained that, while questions could be asked, he was satisfied the grant money was acceptably used, and in any case, it would cost more to recover it than it was worth.

"Howard," I said, "it's a good thing you are not a woman or you would be pregnant all the time. You just can't say 'No'."

He was a fine, decent man who put the best interpretation on everything.

But in November 1972, Autopac was preparing to send out the second year's renewal forms and I was worried about a repeat of the previous year's fiasco. We had discovered that the debacle had occurred because two control cards had been left out of the computer and the man responsible had suddenly left for England. I didn't know whether the problem had been carelessness or sabotage, but I wanted to be ready—just in case.

I phoned Pawley, the minister responsible, and told him that while the public might forgive us once for screwing up, they would not forgive us twice. I asked him to find out where the computer programmer had gone and prepare the necessary legal papers to extradite him and charge him with sabotage if the program was botched again. He agreed and phoned a week later.

"We found that man who left the computer centre last year," he said.

"Howard, great work. Are you preparing to extradite him?"

"Oh, that won't be necessary. He's here."

"Oh! Where?"

"He is working in the computer centre." Howard Pawley saw nothing incongruous about that; he was that kind of a guy. Despite the adversities of politics he never became cynical nor unwilling to give a person another chance.

And he never lost his zeal for social justice, both political and economic. Despite suffering the slings and arrows of an outraged industry and a sometimes vicious political opposition, he created a corporation owned by the people who use it, which has become as iconic provincially as Medicare has nationally.

MY FEARS WERE UNFOUNDED; during its second year Autopac worked like a charm. Part-time agents were dropped, reducing the total from 1,100 to about 400. Agencies were licensed to deliver Autopac services, or bought out.[3] Claims centres were established and operated with breathtaking efficiency: a damaged vehicle, if mobile, could be driven to a centre, the damages appraised in minutes, and the driver informed what Autopac would pay for repairs. The owner could then take the vehicle to his preferred privately-owned bodyshop, which would be paid directly by Autopac. Startup funds loaned by the government were repaid, and by mid-1973 Autopac had invested $6.1 million in hospital debentures. Administration costs, at seventeen cents of the premium dollar, were less than half that of the private sector. And we still made a profit.

By April 1973, Autopac had a profit of over $2 million. We were jubilant. We finally had a winner. The risk we took in 1970 was now paying off. Nothing could now spoil our success. Then we made a serious mistake; we reduced Autopac premiums!

---

[3] About $2.5 million in compensation was paid out to those wishing to discontinue their private agencies.

THIS IDEA DID NOT APPEAL TO EVERYONE. Sid Green was outraged. "Just before Autopac went into operation a car accident in southern Manitoba killed seven people. Two or three accidents like that will wipe out our surplus. Some people complain the premiums are too high, but some will complain no matter how low they are. With the possible exception of Saskatchewan we have the lowest rates in North America, but because of a small profit it's being proposed we reduce premiums and risk losses." He went on to remind us that we got thirty-nine per cent of the votes in the last election. "That means that sixty-one per cent of the people out there consider us sons-of-bitches and I prefer being a son-of-a-bitch for having a profit rather than a loss. Autopac has become a good thing and we can't stand it, so we want to screw it up."

Nevertheless, cutting costs was a tempting proposition. Autopac was supposed to operate at cost, so why not return the accumulated profit to the driving public through reduced premiums? That would be proper. And smart too; after all, 1973 was an election year.

So we reduced Autopac premiums by five per cent, making them twenty per cent rather than only fifteen per cent lower than the private sector. During the 1973 year Autopac had an operating loss of $8 million. In 1974, the loss was $9 million.[4] But it had been such a tempting proposition![5]

So we began the long, hard struggle to rebuild the financial integrity of Autopac. And it had to be done in a goldfish bowl.

Liberal leader Izzy Asper, who had been scathingly critical of Autopac in early 1973 because of its profit (a Crown corporation that shows a profit is clearly overcharging), was scathingly critical by early 1974 because it had a loss (clearly proving that government is a lousy businessman). It seemed we could do nothing right. But Autopac's financial position was recovering.

Then we made another mistake. In 1974, we reduced the gasoline tax by two cents a gallon.

THE ARAB-ISRAELI WAR had exploded in October 1973. OPEC—the Organization of Petroleum Exporting Countries—decided to punish Israel and its allies by shutting off the flow of oil. By mid-1974 world oil prices had quadrupled (in mid-1979 they were 1,000 per cent higher than they had been in 1973). Members of

---

[4]   Damage from one hailstorm cost Autopac more than $3 million. In 1973, the private insurance industry lost about $133 million and car insurance premiums in Ontario were increased by sixteen per cent. In 1974, the private sector lost a reported $250 million and premiums in Ontario were increased twice, by a total of nineteen per cent.

[5]   In 1986, the NDP government of Howard Pawley increased Autopac premiums before the election and increased them again the following year; this contributed to the government's defeat in 1988.

the petroleum industry in Canada—mostly foreign-owned—suddenly discovered their oil pool was considerably smaller than they had earlier estimated it to be. The "several hundred year" oil pool that they'd boasted of in 1972 when they sought export permits from the National Energy Board was, they confessed in 1974 as they sought higher prices, only a twenty-year supply."[6] And the Government of Alberta, with ninety per cent of Canada's oil, let it be known that it intended to become "blue-eyed Arabs", charging Canadians the world price or shutting off the supply.

With radically changing conditions came changes in government policy. In 1974, the government sought to reduce costs to gasoline users; in 1975, it sought to reduce gasoline use.

So in 1975 the Government of Manitoba increased the gasoline tax by two cents, moving it back up to seventeen cents a gallon—where it had been from 1964 to 1974—and dedicating the revenue from the increase to Autopac premiums. It was a rational response to the 'petroleum scare' that would serve the dual purpose of charging part of the insurance premium on the basis of miles driven—and thus exposure to accidents—and saving gasoline by discouraging needless driving and encouraging Manitobans to replace their gas-guzzling mastodons with more fuel-efficient vehicles.

But the political opposition, as well as the media, while both mouthing concerns about fuel wastage, the environment, fears of becoming hostage to OPEC, the 'greenhouse' effect, the possible melting of the polar ice caps and the hole in the ozone layer, nevertheless attacked us like sharks.

And their attack was effective. Seventeen municipalities from Conservative-held West-Central Manitoba wrote to the government—with copies to the media—demanding termination of "subsidization" of Autopac. The minister in charge, Billie Uruski, sent a reply that included numerous documents showing the various ways in which the municipalities themselves were being subsidized by government, ways to which they certainly had not objected. It was cathartic, but hardly politic. It was futile to argue with Conservative ideology that receiving subsidies from government is "free enterprise", but being asked to pay for services is "socialism".

The brush fires we had to fight seemed to increase in direct relation to the possibility of Autopac becoming a success. There were repeated stories of lineups at the claims centres, of bodyshops not being paid, of cars left in garages because their owners could not afford the Autopac premiums. Letters from car drivers and bodyshop owners, stating precisely the opposite and praising Autopac, had difficulty getting media attention.

There were demands by persons who, once Autopac became a success, wanted an agency. One agent, who handled both auto and property insurance, did

---

[6]   The federal Department of Energy Mines and Resources lost a zero. In mid-1973, they had reported Canada's petroleum reserves to be enough for eighty years. A year later, they reduced that estimate to eight years.

not wish to operate under Autopac and that portion of his business related to vehicle insurance was bought out. Then he sold his agency to a person who immediately applied for an Autopac license. Autopac refused. He persuaded his town council to write to the premier's office asking that he be licensed.

I responded that one reason for the substantial reduction in insurance premiums under Autopac was the phasing out of hundreds of agencies, which reduced duplication. The small town in question already had two agencies, which we considered to be sufficient. If we acceded to the request, we would open ourselves to similar applications from half the towns in Manitoba. Despite all this, we would license their protégé in question upon receipt of a letter acquiescing to the higher premiums that would result from the additional agency.[7] There was no reply.

We were also targeted by the fierce feminists of the new National Action Committee on the Status of Women who, desperately seeking issues, proclaimed themselves to be outraged because women were being charged $10 LESS than men for their driver's licenses. We pointed out that most of them were NDP members, who should appreciate what we were doing. Instead, they threatened to leave the party. We showed statistics proving that female drivers had fewer accidents and told them that charging women the same premium as male drivers would be ripping them off; they demanded "equality". We replied that equality of this kind would be a demotion because they had already proven themselves superior; they spurned this as the rankest form of anti-feminism. We argued that their position was ridiculous; they threatened to embarrass the government by going to the Manitoba Human Rights Commission. We surrendered; we made women "equal" with a $10 increase in their fees.

There were also those who saw nothing good coming from "government" and whose calls to Autopac agencies consisted of unrelenting bitching. Since Autopac was now the only automobile insurance corporation in Manitoba, all anger that had been previously dispersed among scores of companies about premium increases, loss of claims discounts, failure to have a hail-damaged car inspected within fifteen minutes of being reported, refusal to paint cars with a microscopic scratch, as well as compensation for a write-off that was deemed to be insufficient, was now focused on Autopac. No matter how low the premiums or fast the service, Autopac was suspect because it was 'government'.

The agency's best supporters were immigrants from other provinces, who made their own comparisons. The worst were the young, who had no previous experience and had been bombarded by editorials that convinced them government is "bad"[8]

---

[7] Autopac sought to limit the number of agencies to about 400.

[8] It was like the pig, Snowball, the agitator in George Orwell's *Animal Farm*, and his shorthand way to explain to the dumber animals how to tell the difference between friend and enemy: "Four legs good, two legs bad." (p. 21) Those present at the creation of Autopac must periodically remind ourselves that, since 1971, one and a half generations of Manitobans has been born and come to maturity with no knowledge of motor vehicle insurance rates or practices before Autopac.

Autopac also came under fire from insurance company personnel. C.C. Trites, president of Wawanesa Mutual Insurance Company, wrote to the premier, (with copies to the *Winnipeg Free Press*, *The Winnipeg Tribune*, and *The Financial Post*) noting that in its first five years total annual Autopac revenue had increased from $38 million to $68 million. "That looks like a 79% premium increase to me."

He neglected to mention that there were many more cars, that drivers were buying more coverage, and cars had become more expensive to repair. The premier replied that automobile insurance revenues to the private insurance companies in Manitoba had increased from $20,152,000 in 1965 to $35,646,000 in 1970. "That looks like 77% to me. Would you please explain what additional services you provided from 1965 to 1970 to warrant a 77% premium increase?"

And there was the *Winnipeg Free Press*. We had committed the unforgivable sin of challenging the establishment and the newspaper decided that we must pay. Autopac's unqualified success seemed to make our sacrilege more heinous. This visceral antagonism led them into an error. A scathing editorial entitled "Mr. Schreyer's Vision", about how he was soaking the rich to help the poor, made reference to Autopac: "which has, to use the government's own words, given residents the 'lowest cost' automobile insurance in Canada."

It was too good to be true. I wrote to editor Peter McLintock: "Your editorial, April 28, states Premier Schreyer's government 'to use the government's own words, has given residents the lowest cost automobile insurance rates in Canada.' I enclose a copy of the front page of your newspaper dated February 28, 1976, carrying across the entire page the flaming red headline proclaiming: CAR INSURANCE COSTLIEST IN MONTREAL, CHEAPEST IN MANITOBA. You must have forgotten." [9] There was no reply.

Conversely, Autopac received accolades from unexpected sources. Michael Leipsic, a third-generation insurance executive, son of Sylvan and president-elect of the Insurance Agent's Association of Manitoba, was quoted in a newspaper report headlined, "He Sees Autopac As Dead Issue Now". "Autopac is not a contentious issue now. It's here, we're living with it and we have good relations with the government insurance corporation and its people. They've got some pretty bright people." [10]

The headline meant, in essence, that if Autopac was a DEAD issue to the private sector, it was a LIVE issue for the NDP.

But the most satisfying accolade came after the Schreyer government's defeat. In the 1977 election, Conservative Leader Sterling Lyon promised to dismantle Autopac. As premier, he quickly appointed a commission to "study"

---

[9] Schulz to McLintock, May 7, 1976. On August 3, 2003, the *Free Press* published a news report entitled "Our Insurance the Envy of Many". The Fraser Institute published a study purportedly showing provinces with public auto insurance have more car accidents and fatalities (*Winnipeg Free Press*, September 5, 2003. This raises the question of why provinces with private insurance, and ostensibly fewer accidents, do not have lower insurance premiums.

[10] *The Winnipeg Tribune*, October 22, 1976.

it. The Burns Commission recommended it be abolished. Premier Lyon rejected the recommendation, saying, "The eggs cannot be unscrambled." Twenty years later Harry Enns, who had vehemently opposed Autopac as "communism", told the audience at a Schreyer roast that, "Autopac was the best thing he did."[11] The Manitoba Public Insurance Corporation, arguably the most radical undertaking of the Schreyer government, was finally assured of remaining as a monument to those who had risked their political future to put it in place, and to the men and women of the NDP who had sustained them. Autopac also stands as a monument to two tortured and courageous men, Laurent Desjardins and the late Gordon Beard, without whom it would not exist. They wrestled with the demons of their deepest convictions of the past—social, economic, political, and ideological —and voted for the future.

Not all our ventures were as successful—or as permanent.

---

[11] A note of comparison: in 2003, an eighteen-year-old driver with a perfect record, driving a 2002 Ford Taurus four-door, with $200 deductible and a $1 million third-party liability would pay $1,193 in Brandon (the lowest in the country); $1,248 in Winnipeg; $6,876 in Calgary and $8,267 in Toronto. *Winnipeg Sun*, July 11, 2003.

VIII

The Manitoba Hog Marketing Board

Nothing is more difficult to do, or doubtful of success, or dangerous to handle, than to initiate a new order of things. The reformer has enemies in all who profit by the old order, and only luke-warm defenders in those who will profit by the new order. The luke-warmness arises from fear of adversaries, who have the law in their favour; and from the incredulity of mankind, who do not believe in anything new until they have had the actual experience of it.
        —Niccolo Machiavelli, *The Prince*, 1513.

In **December 1971**, I approached the premier and told him I believed we were making a mistake by allowing the election of the directors of the new Hog Marketing Board.

He pointed out that, unlike the previous government, which appointed directors to its Hog Marketing Commission, he had promised that the new board would be elected by the hog producers themselves and would have real clout to make decisions.

I marshalled all my arguments. The situation, I told him, was unsettled and had become highly political. I was certain the opposition, which had asked about the dates for the board elections, was planning a coup. I asked him to consider that we could end up with a majority of directors who were actually opposed to board marketing. It would be equivalent to the Trojans dragging the Greek horse inside their city gates.

"But," he reminded me, "we made a promise."

"We made two promises: first, to establish a hog marketing board to give the producers an instrument to improve their prices, and second, to elect the members of that board. These two things need not be coincident. Let's go with the first," I argued, "and implement the second when the farmers have had some experience with the board." I was concerned that holding elections immediately might result in directors who would kill the board before it had a chance to prove itself.

"And how," the ever-practical Schreyer asked, "do you propose we do this without giving the opposition a stick with which to beat us?"

My arguments, that the opposition, being ideologically opposed to collective marketing, would invent something to beat us with, and that they were set upon sabotaging the idea, didn't wash with the premier.

"I must assume," he said, "that hog farmers are big boys. It is their product and presumably they will know what to do with it. We are giving them the opportunity to assert some control over the price of their product through collective bargaining. If they are unwilling to take advantage of this, it is they who will have to pay."

"But THEY will not pay," I sputtered, explaining that I was afraid the meat packers would keep prices low, encouraging the farmers to come to the government for another subsidy. And if we were to pay that subsidy, it would be the taxpayers that would pay. If, on the other hand, we refused the subsidy, the opposition would enlist the support of the hog producers, who would then be battling the government—rather than the packers—and WE could pay.

"Even if you have a point," the premier asked calmly, "how do we explain to the farmers that we are going to break our promise to them?"

"Shit!" I exploded. "Churchill promised Stalin a second front in 1941, but didn't deliver until 1944, when it had some hope of success. Tommy Douglas promised Medicare in 1944 but didn't institute it until 1962 when he had the means to honour the promise. Jesus, according to rumour, promised 2,000 years ago to return and might some day when the time is right. We promised an elected board and we will have one—when conditions favour getting supportive directors."

Perhaps my arguments were too persuasive. "If the majority of hog producers are opposed to the board system of marketing, perhaps we should reconsider our policy," he said.

I reminded him about the nature of the industry. Most of the 7,000 hog producers were small farmers and those small producers, which bred the majority of the hogs, supported board marketing. But the large producers, who delivered their hogs directly to the packers, were paid a premium and would fight to maintain that advantage.

Moreover, I was sure the packing companies would make every effort to kill the board; they would hire mouthpieces, coach others to join them and overrun meetings with those opposed to board marketing.

"There is an internal contradiction in your argument," the premier pointed out. "If, as you say, and with which I am inclined to agree, the majority of the hog farmers favour board marketing, they will elect the right people to the board because they have the votes."

I could see I wasn't getting anywhere with him. Could he not see that farmers in the Conservative ghetto of Southern Manitoba would be, at very least, reluctant to make themselves targets by standing up at public meetings to support a concept promoted by the NDP? Could he not understand that board marketing was alien to the political philosophy of that region? Could he not imagine how loath these producers would be to contend with the opposition shills?

"I don't follow your reasoning. If the hog producers support board marketing, they will attend the meetings, and if they have the majority they will not allow a hostile takeover."

"Dammit!" I was getting exasperated. "Don't tell me a meeting can't be taken over by a vocal minority. I have done it often. Some people are even better at it than I am."

He shook his head. "I find this strange. You have been fighting for a producer-elected hog marketing board for twenty years. It was you who informed me of this concept when I visited your farm a decade ago."

"Right! And because of that, now that we are on the verge of success, I don't want to see the whole damn thing jeopardized by those I have been fighting against for twenty years."

"So what do you propose?"

"That you tell Uskiw to cancel the board elections".

"No! We promised and we are not political prostitutes."[1]

The premier had spoken. The nature of his office gave his words a Delphic quality. The issue was settled. I could only hope for the best.

On January 1, 1972, pursuant to the commitment made during the 1969 election, the NDP government established the Manitoba Hog Producers Marketing Board, a central selling agency for all hogs, local or imported, shipped to meat processors in Manitoba. It was a revolutionary concept; hog prices would henceforth be set not by several purchasers negotiating with several thousand individual producers, but by several purchasers negotiating with a single selling agency that controlled the entire supply. It gave producers enormous market power by reversing the historic roles; the oligopoly formerly buying from competing suppliers must now compete against each other to purchase from a monopoly supplier. We had established a system of single-desk selling of hogs.

As individuals, hog producers had been disadvantaged in bargaining with processors, who could always go elsewhere if they felt the price was too high. In 1965, the Conservative government, inspired by Minister of Agriculture George Hutton, established a Hog Marketing Commission, aimed at giving producers some bargaining power. It was a beginning, but it was voluntary and because it had little authority, it failed. By 1971, farmers, desperate to market grain through livestock, had more than doubled hog production to over 1.2 million, but with no market protection the price went as low as nineteen cents per pound. Many hog farmers verged on bankruptcy.

Now Minister of Agriculture Sam Uskiw took the next logical step by converting the commission into a producers marketing board. Under the Natural Products Marketing Act, enacted in the 1930s, the board had monopoly power to market all hogs delivered in Manitoba.

---

[1] In 1963, as an NDP representative on a legislative committee, Schreyer had written a minority report supporting a hog marketing board—elected by the producers.

Processors argued that board control of imported hogs was tantamount to restraint on interprovincial trade, and therefore unconstitutional. Board chairman Maxwell Hofford assured them that Manitoba welcomed all hogs so long as they were marketed through the board. The processors challenged him by importing hogs from Saskatchewan, bypassing the board by bringing them directly to their plants in Winnipeg. When Hofford reached an agreement with Saskatchewan to ship its hogs to the board, the packers imported Alberta hogs. The issue was referred to the Manitoba Court of Queen's Bench.

Chief Justice George E. Tritschler ruled that the packers must buy from the board: "The plan is no threat to interprovincial trade. [It] does not restrict free flow [of hogs] between provinces ... It is essential to success that participation by producers and processors be compulsory. If Manitoba processors bypass the system, the plan would be destroyed with great damage to the industry."[2]

Warner Jorgenson, speaking for the Conservative opposition, protested that "Marketing boards encroach on the liberties of farmers."[3] He predicted that the board would not affect prices. Three days later the Manitoba Hog Producers Marketing Board [MHPMB] announced a seven-year agreement to sell ten per cent of Manitoba hogs, valued at $105 million, to the Itoh Company of Japan. Another $8 million would accrue to Manitoba because the hogs would be slaughtered locally.

Hofford explained: "This is the first time a Canadian marketing board has directly negotiated a long-term agreement for the sale of animal products on a continuing basis for an offshore market." MPHMB General Manager W.B. Munro added: "For the first time producers can systematically plan production of hogs, with a guaranteed market available for a good portion of their production." The board had achieved the fundamental objective of inducing increased production with longterm price stabilization. It was a coup!

But not to Jorgenson. On cue, he predicted the sale would not increase hog prices.[4] Believers in market competiton price setting should have argued that removing ten per cent of the product from the market would drive up the price of the remaining ninety per cent—but apparently Jorgenson didn't believe that would happen when it was done by a producer's marketing board.

While Jorgenson argued the board would not work at all, others argued it was working too well. When the MHPMB captured fifty-one per cent of live hog shipments to the United States, and hog prices in Manitoba increased from as low as nineteen cents per pound in mid-1971 to fifty-four cents in mid-1973, The Winnipeg Tribune editorialized: "Marketing boards have been pictured as ... essential to 'orderly marketing' [and] a form of consumer protection [by guaranteeing] supplies of foodstuffs ... [but they] are really a

---

[2] *Winnipeg Free Press*, December 15, 1972.
[3] *Ibid.*
[4] *Ibid*, December 20, 1972.

device for maintaining artificially high prices." [5]

To "free-enterprisers", it seemed the board could do nothing right. But it did. By the end of its first year of operations the traditional system of selling by processors bidding on the teletype had been augmented by two more: direct sales of pork to Japan, and direct sale of live hogs to the United States. During the 1973–74 market year, hog prices averaged about forty-six cents per pound. It was impossible to know how much the board contributed to price increases, but it had clearly established market power.

Now to attack another problem! Manitoba consumed a fraction of the pork it produced, so the balance was exported, mostly to Ontario. But the packers paid as much a seven cents per pound less in Winnipeg than in Toronto, claiming this was the cost of transporting hog carcasses from Manitoba to Ontario. The board calculated the differential should not be more than 1.9 cents. Discussions were held. The packers were adamant. The board acted.

The MHPMB notified the packers that after April 1, 1974 the Manitoba teletype system would no longer set prices, but only allocate purchases among packers, and the Toronto market would set prices. Then the Winnipeg price to be paid by the packers would be set at 1.9 cents per pound less than in Toronto.

The packers were furious. Board chairman Hofford phoned, "The presidents of the major packers have asked to meet with me on January 22nd. You may wish to attend so you will know the issues. Probably their next stop will be the premier's office."

"Surely that is a pigment of your imagination," I told him, but I attended. It was not a friendly meeting. The board was led by its soft-spoken but rock-hard chairman who had hacked a productive farm out of the wilderness after the war, had a substantial investment in hog production, and had learned the hard way that the monopsony structure of the touted 'free' market left the packers 'free' to offer what they wished and the producers 'free' to take what they were offered. He had long supported the concept of a single-desk selling agency, as had been done forty years earlier with wheat, to balance the uneven negotiations between a few buyers and many sellers. He now had market power and he knew how to use it.

Across the table sat the presidents of the four powerful meat processing companies—Canada Packers, Swifts, Burns, and Schneiders—led by William McLean, son of the founder of mighty Canada Packers of which he was now president. Tall, gaunt, intense, choleric, imperious and irascible, this was not a man who suffered fools—or anyone—gladly. He had been born into a command structure, was accustomed to having his way, and intended to have it now. He, too, had market power and he, too, knew how to use it.

The tension in the room signalled a meeting between an immovable object and an unstoppable force. The packers stated that they had served agriculture well for sixty years and considered the board an insulting intervention between

---

[5] August 27, 1973.

purchaser and producer. The board's function should be reduced to that of collector, bringing the hogs to assembly points, but leaving untouched the historical relationship between buyer and seller. In effect, the packers invited the board to abolish itself.

Hofford saw their position as understandable but unacceptable. His deep voice never rising, but hardening, he explained the reasons for the board and emphasized that it was here to stay. After seventy-five minutes, the meeting literally 'broke up', the spokesmen glaring at each other as they parted.

I left feeling depressed. The packers had not been expected to welcome the board, but surely, I felt, they would accept it as an evolution in marketing! Instead, they saw it as an impertinent challenge to their enterprise and authority. There would be no compromise.

Hofford had been prescient. Three months later later McLean phoned— I took the call. The four processor presidents wanted a meeting with Premier Schreyer. I advised the premier to decline. "This is a fight of packers against the farmers' marketing agency, not the government. They will demand we abolish the board and since we will not do that, why waste each other's time?"

I reminded him that the agency had hardly begun to operate and we did not yet know if it would survive without the full cooperation of the packers, but at least the board was showing some guts. We should wait, I told him, until the packers and the board have bloodied each other. We might then need to intervene as mediator. Not surprisingly, perhaps, the premier saw it differently: "Winnipeg once had the second-largest stockyards in the world, next only to Chicago, and the meat packing industry is still extremely important to the Manitoba economy. Your visceral anger may offer catharsis but it is not a good basis for public policy. It would be foolish to offend four major meat buyers if we can avoid it. We at least owe them the courtesy of a meeting."

We met in the Cabinet Room on May 31, 1974. On one side of the table sat the four presidents. On the other side sat the premier, Minister of Agriculture Sam Uskiw, his deputy minister, Willem Janssen, and marketing board chairman Maxwell Hofford. It was one of the few times I actually sat at the cabinet table.

With a minimum of formalities the brittle-voiced McLean, of arrogant poise and haughty mien who, but for the lack of duelling scars, looked like a pre-Weimar German count, quickly outlined the packers' position: (a) the board is an ideological intrusion into the marketplace, and unacceptable; (b) Hofford had made a good case for the Winnipeg-to-Toronto price differential of no more than 1.9 cents per pound, but it was unacceptable; (c) the marketing board's removal of sales from the teletype system was unacceptable, and (d) the board's direct off-shore sales were cutting into the packer's business, and was unacceptable.

The premier, as always polite and accommodating, recalled his own experiences as the son of a farmer, and briefly outlined the problems of farmers competing each other out of business. The board would not injure the processors; making the producers more secure would induce them to produce more hogs for the packers to process. In any case, the board was an autonomous instrument of the farmers, not of the government. He proposed that the concept be given time to be tested, and a new relationship be allowed to develop.

The four men across the table were not listening. To me the time had come to be as frank, and as difficult, as they were.

"Mr. McLean, back in 1954 your late father, then president of Canada Packers testified before a parliamentary committee and stated it was his practice to buy at the lowest possible cost and sell at the highest possible price. If buying low and selling high is good business for meat processors, it must also be good business for farmers. Through this board, hog producers can act collectively to sell their product at the highest possible price. You people must accustom yourselves to the fact this concept is going to be used by the people from whom you buy your supplies."

Arthur Childs, the soft-spoken president of Burns Foods, the second-largest meat packing company in Canada, responded courteously,[6] "Mr. Schulz, obviously you read only one paragraph in the *Hansard* report of the committee hearing in 1954. In the next paragraph the elder Mr. McLean stated that competition from the other buyers forced him to keep his prices up."

My mind filled with images. How many hundreds of hours I had spent crushing grain, carrying water, mixing feed, administering medicine, cleaning pens, standing ankle deep in stinking, sloppy manure, forking it out of the barn in clammy late June heat, the stench overpowering as I was buzzed by a billion flies? Or wrestling 240-pound squealing, recalcitrant porkers into a truck and taking them to loading pens in town and waiting for the cheque, the size of which was determined by a packer-buyer 250 miles away, who knew nothing of the producers who did the work?

I had never understood how farmers could be so indifferent to their own interests, surrendering control over the price of their product. I had spent twelve years and driven thousands of miles promoting the concept of a single-desk selling agency, and now we had the board that allowed the producers to assert their collective market power. I exploded: "Competition! Competition from whom? From the four of you who come here hand in hand and sit here shoulder to shoulder and repeat each other's words and have nothing to contribute to this debate but to demand abolition of the board so you can have a clear field in which there is nothing but cosmetic competition? Competition among you four, whose livelihood depends on keeping the farmers competing with each other instead of with you, so prices are forced down and their future is left in your hands?"

McLean abruptly stood up, his frame taut as a bowstring, glared at me, and without a word strode imperiously out of the room. His three associates, appearing somewhat embarrassed, followed him.

---

[6] Childs, the erudite mogul of the packing industry, died in 1997, reportedly leaving $1 million to the Reform Party of Canada.

As I returned to my office, I found Childs awaited me in the corridor. "You know, Schulz, you should remember we processors have a great deal of capital invested in Manitoba. You keep mistreating us like this and we might just close down our plants."[7]

"You do and we will expropriate them for a dollar as non-operating plants." He turned and left. I believe he almost believed me.

A MORE INSIDIOUS FIGHT was occurring between the supporters of the board, and the hog producers and their political mouthpieces, who had made destruction of the producer-controlled collective marketing agency a crusade. The fight was fierce.

In February 1974, I attended a meeting of hog producers at Carman, called by the board to report on its stewardship during the past year. Chairman Hofford stood at the front of the hall in a brown suit and green tie and, in his deep, quiet voice began his report, all the while writing figures and drawing diagrams on the large blackboard in a serious effort to demystify hog marketing. But the farmers, about 200 of them, were not there to hear a report on the board's activities—they were there to "get Hofford", to demolish what they saw as the representative of the NDP government. They were used to the Canadian Wheat Board system of grain marketing pioneered by their parents, but any extension of the collective marketing principle into other areas was heretical, a "socialistic" intrusion into the "sacred" market. So they snorted derisively, interrupted rudely, shouted profanely and urged one another into paroxysms of fury.

The meeting chairman, a local man clearly frightened by the display, did not even attempt to exercise control. Suddenly Hofford spun on his heel, eyes blazing, and faced the unruly mob. Like a lone gladiator in the Roman Colosseum, he stood defiantly, daring the infuriated spectators to turn down their thumbs: "Listen, you birds," he thundered. "It appears some people here think they know more about international pork marketing than I do. Why don't you come up here and show us how it's done. Here, *Weisenheimer*, you be the first one up." He threw his piece of chalk to a hog-buyer for the packers whom he recognized in the audience. No one moved. No one picked up the chalk—or the challenge.

But the most lethal challenge was within the board itself. When Uskiw lauched the MHPMB, he appointed the first board of directors, gave them terms of reference, and announced that directors would be elected as soon as the board developed the structure, defined the electoral base, organized the districts from which directors would be elected, and arranged for the elections.

Having predicted disaster, I waited in agony, carefully monitoring the progress of these elections. Then I phoned my old acquaintance and fellow

<hr>

[7] A decade later Canada Packers and Swifts abandoned their huge plants and went quietly away, leaving the city to clean up the debris. They sat derelict until they were demolished in 2000.

farm union organizer, Roy Atkinson, president of the National Farmer's Union in Saskatchewan: "Roy, the farmers need you. As I expect you know, we are currently proceeding with the election of the directors for the Manitoba Producer's Hog Marketing Board. Elections have already been held in several districts and some of those elected are anti-board.

"We can't afford any more of those. Attendance at meetings has been relatively small. A single vote could make the difference. Each district is crucial. You have farm union members here. Can you ask them to attend the meetings and support the pro-board candidate."

"No," he answered. "We don't want an elected board. We want a government-appointed board."

"Frankly," I responded, "under the circumstances, so do I. But that decision has been made and it is not about to be reargued at this point. The only thing left for us to do is to see that the right persons get elected to the board of directors. Can't you just send us some men?"

"Sorry, can't help you."

In one district, thirty-three votes were cast at the meeting. They split seventeen to sixteen—for an opponent of board marketing. By one vote we lost a board supporter. And by one director we lost control of the board. Twenty years of gruelling work was flushed into the pit. And the bloody, insidious fight began.

Don Cameron, in the Interlake, campaigned for election as director on the grounds he wanted to destroy the "Communistic" marketing board. He was elected. When the minister phoned him to inquire if the report about his antipathy to the board was true, he confirmed it. Then he refused the minister's request to resign. He made that announcement, flanked by Jorgenson and former Conservative Minister of Agriculture Harry Enns, at the annual meeting of the Conservative Party, to which he was a delegate. [8]

We Trojans had dragged the damned hollow wooden horse, filled with infiltrators, inside our city gates.

At the annual meeting of the Manitoba Pork Producers, an anti-board lobby group, Hofford was figuratively boiled in tallow. The major complaint was that Hofford had not provided a grant to subsidize their meeting; they demanded financing from the board they sought to kill. The demand was made by Felix Holtman, later a member of Parliament in the Mulroney government. [9]

Cameron became a fount of accusations of improper and "illegal" activities within the board: (a) Hofford did not report to producers how the board spent fees collected from them; (b) Hofford did not table the contract with Itoh; (c) the government had used producers' money to hide a loss on the Itoh contract; (d) at a board meeting "Hofford and the appointed majority rammed through an agreement for an interprovincial hog marketing agency"; (e) board meeting minutes are

---

[8] *The Winnipeg Tribune,* December 3, 1973
[9] *Ibid.*, November 29, 1973.

slanted, and (f) Hofford refused to reveal the pricing formula on the Itoh contract.

The minister quickly ordered an investigation by the Manitoba Natural Products Marketing Board, which policed all marketing boards. On December 28, 1973, the policing agency reported: (a) an audited financial statement for the year ending March 31, 1973, had been mailed to every hog producer in Manitoba; (b) a newsletter dated April 26, 1973, explaining the principles of the Itoh contract was mailed to all hog producers; (c) the government is not a party to the Itoh contract nor to setting or allocation of fees; (d) Cameron had supported the board motion endorsing the Itoh Agreement; (e) the motion to approve the board meeting minutes was seconded by Cameron at two of the four meetings he attended, and (f) the board, with one exception, voted to NOT reveal details of the pricing formula in the Itoh contract because "confidentiality is good business practice".[10]

A major complaint was that Hofford had not proceeded with elections of the board directors as promised by the government. The accusation was made at the anti-board pork producers meeting on November 29, 1973. An attendee had informed them that four of the seven directors had already been elected (plus one appointed by the Hutterite colonies) and elections in the remaining three districts, including Hofford's, were scheduled to be held within two weeks. These details did not deter those dedicated to killing the board. "The convention accepted the loud comment of George Vercaigne of Brandon: 'We want to show Hofford how unpopular he is.'"[11]

Then, as W.B. Yeats had discerned, when times get tough: "Things fall apart. The centre cannot hold. The best lack all conviction; the worst are filled with passionate intensity."[12]

The Supreme Court of Canada overturned the earlier Tritschler Decision, appealed by Canada Packers, Swifts and Burns. The court ruled that requiring hogs imported into Manitoba to be marketed through the board was "in restraint of interprovincial trade" and therefore illegal. The decision meant that the packers could again undermine the market by bringing in hogs from Saskatchewan and bypassing the board.[13]

But both Uskiw and the Government of Saskatchewan, which also had a hog marketing board, had anticipated this and taken steps to counter the effect. The two ministers of Agriculture agreed to establish a joint super-agency, Ex-Pork Canada West, with equal representation from each province, "to maximize the

---

[10] *The Winnipeg Tribune* editorialized that the investigating Natural Products Marketing Board was suspect, because its members were government appointed; presumably an ombudsman appointed by a newspaper to adjudicate on readers' complaints is suspect. The *Winnipeg Free Press* editorialized that while there was no formal denial of the Itoh pricing formula, hog producers were entitled to it; presumably then, newspapers should reveal their cost-price structure to readers—and competitors.

[11] *Ibid.*, November 29, 1973.

[12] "The Second Coming", 1921.

[13] It was a near thing. Brian Dickson, head of the Manitoba Appeal Court that upheld the Trichler Decision, had been appointed chief justice of the Supreme Court of Canada, but could not vote because of his previous involvement. The Supreme Court voted 4-3 against Manitoba.

value from the production and marketing of hogs in the two provinces from all markets, domestic or export". Therefore the court ruling would have no effect. Ex-Pork Canada West would simply designate the Manitoba board as its agent and declare all Saskatchewan hogs imported into Manitoba must be sold through the board. Market control, and upward price pressure, would be maintained.[14]

The preliminary structure of Ex-Pork Canada West had been worked out in general terms: the headquarters would be in Winnipeg where the major marketing facilites were; Hofford, who had already gained considerable expertise, would be chairman; Bill Munro, who had been general manager of the Manitoba Hog Commission and then the MHPMB for a total of nine years, would probably be general manager of the super-agency.

Then Saskatchewan collapsed. The death-knell of the super-agency came in early 1974 when Saskatchewan's minister of Agriculture wrote to Uskiw proposing Ex-Pork Canada West's activities be limited to offshore sales and its establishment proceed slowly, because the Saskatchewan board "is wary of becoming involved in the highly publicized controversy surrounding the Manitoba Hog Producer's Marketing Board."[15]

Instead of proceeding with orderly marketing, Saskatchewan decided to subsidize the difference between the market price and fifty-seven cents per pound. It allowed the packers to beat down the market price without producer protest.

Manitoba soldiered on. Following the meeting with the premier, at which the packers had agreed the board had made a good case for a price differential between Toronto and Winnipeg of no more than 1.9 cents per pound, they remained adamant at 3.5 cents. As he had warned, Hofford shut down the teletype and demanded reduction of the price differential. The packers reduced their daily purchases. The board asked hog producers to hold their hogs off the market, suffering some short-term pain for long-term gain. Some producers refused, claiming their hogs needed to be shipped at a weight calculated to the ounce. The packers were elated. The board hired trucks and pioneered shipping large quantities of live hogs to the United States. The packers threatened to stop buying. The board negotiated more contract sales to Japan, hired small local processors to custom-kill and store pork cuts for the board, and began arranging for a new inspection station at Grand Forks, North Dakota, for exported pork cuts.

During an eight-week period the accelerated shipments to the United States increased sales revenue by about $855,000, at a cost to the board of $420,000, for a net gain of $435,000 over what they would have earned had they accepted the packers' terms. The board was doing precisely what it was designed to do—represent the interests of hog producers. And it was winning.

Then it collapsed. Instead of fighting the packers, the anti-NDP, anti-board members of the board decided to fight the Government of Manitoba. They asked

---

[14] *Winnipeg Free Press*, December 22, 1973.
[15] Messer to Uskiw, January 17, 1974.

Uskiw for a subsidy to compensate for alleged "losses" while fighting the packers.

Uskiw refused. He argued that the board had made a profit on the sales to the United States, that their job was to get money from the packers, not from government, and that they had not exhausted all their options. The fight within the board became explosive.

Hofford made one more trip to Toronto to bargain with the packers about the 3.5 cent diferential. The board demanded he take along a director, Frank Lepp. After Hofford made his case, Lepp told the packers this was Hofford's opinion, not the board's.

Crusty Canada Packers president, William McLean, observed: "Max, you have been defeated, but not by us. You have been defeated by the farmers you are attempting to help."

As a test, board director Eugene Caldwell moved a motion stating that the board of directors supported single-desk hog marketing. Five of the eight members voted against the board they sat on. That led to the final casualty. In late 1974, Hofford resigned as both chairman and director. He told the annual meeting of the MHPMB: "Some board members seem more interested in getting me out of office than in selling Manitoba hogs. If they can do a better job than I have, they should be given the chance. As one who has worked for farm organizations for 25 years, I have come to the sad conclusion that the things I think farmers want and need [to get market power] are not accepted by many farmers."[16]

Agriculture Minister Sam Uskiw sympathized: "I completely understand why Max Hofford resigned ... There are board members whose purpose is to make the board not work."[17]

Confirming Uskiw's charge that the board had been made a political football by opposition politicians determined to kill it, Conservative Deputy Leader Harry Enns stated he was disappointed Hofford had resigned "because we'll miss him as our favourite target."[18]

The board of directors replaced Hofford as chairman with Lepp. But a metamorphosis had occurred. The sixty delegates elected from the districts to the meeting at which Hofford resigned, "gave a unanimous vote of confidence to their marketing board."[19] Having tasted its benefits[20], they would not surrender it voluntarily.

And the hog producing industry grew. By 1995, annual production in Manitoba was more than 2.3 million hogs, adding more than $500 million to the provincial economy. The end of the Crowsnest rates in 1995 tripled freight charges on grain shipped out of Manitoba, and it was estimated this would lead to over three million hogs, worth about a billion dollars, being produced by 1998.

[16] *Manitoba Cooperator*, December 12, 1974.
[17] *The Winnipeg Tribune*, December 6, 1974.
[18] *Ibid.*
[19] *Op. cit.*
[20] In 1973-74, the board reported net revenues of $718,000, working capital of $1 million and investment earnings of $200,000.

The meat packing industry adapted itself to the new reality. The board used its collective market power to get the best possible price. It worked so well that some virulent early detractors became ardent supporters. Now that hog producers had actual experience of it, they found it very positive.

The Manitoba Hog Producers Marketing Board became too successful for its own good. On July 1, 1996, Conservative Minister of Agriculture Harry Enns wounded it mortally. Despite loud protest from more than ninety per cent of Manitoba hog producers, he declared board marketing voluntary. This allowed large producers, who handled a substantial portion of Manitoba's hogs, to bypass the board and negotiate private deals directly with the packers. The board marketing system, designed to prevent the processors from playing farmers off against each other to drive down prices, was dead.

A newspaper announced the change with the headline: "End of Pork Monopoly Sets Hog Producers Free".[21] But most hog producers knew it was the processors who were being set free. At a meeting with Enns, 300 farmers carried signs: "THEY'RE OUR PIGS! DON'T TELL US HOW TO SELL THEM". A producer argued: "This government gives no consideration to hog producers, the major stakeholders."[22] Enns rejected their calls for a plebiscite; his decision was final and his government had four more years in office. He argued that the free market would bring processing plants to Manitoba.

They came, lured by subsidies and the power to suppress wages. The City of Winnipeg provided a reported $2.5 million in grants and tax concessions to subsidize Schneider's processing plant in Winnipeg. The Government of Manitoba and the City of Brandon contributed an estimated $13 million to induce Maple Leaf Foods to build a processing plant in Brandon. It then reduced wages at its Winnipeg plant by forty per cent. The Winnipeg Commodity Exchange, which profits on the difference between producer prices and consumer costs, rejoiced: 'WCE Ponders Hog Futures'[23]. Obviously, hog producers were made to make profits—for others.

In 2000, Maple Leaf Foods, Manitoba's major pork processor, bought out two major hog producers to secure supply. Then, to eliminate competition, Maple Leaf bought out J.M. Schneider's. Instead of single-desk *selling*, Manitoba hog producers now have single-desk *buying*. It had all been wasted effort.

---

[21] *Winnipeg Free Press*, July 2, 1996.
[22] *Ibid.*, February 14, 1996.
[23] *Ibid.*, October 9, 1996.

IX

Fun at The Ledge

Death is the end of life, so why, should life all labor be.
—Alfred Tennyson, *The Lotus Eaters*

"I want the premier to come to my home to inspect my breast."

The voice on the phone was middle-aged, urgent and female.

"What's the matter with your breast?"

"Nothing. Considering my age it is quite a nice breast. I don't think I have cancer, but since the premier is responsible for everything in the province, I want him to come and inspect it."

"I'm sorry. The premier is not a doctor so it is pointless for him to come and inspect your breast no matter how nice it is." I had an inspiration. City Hall had made a cottage industry of embarrassing the government. It was payback time: "This is a titillating invitation, but breast inspections are the responsibility of the city," I told the caller. "You should phone the mayor."

"I did phone Mayor Juba," she told me. "He told me to call the premier."

LIFE AT 'THE LEDGE' was not all work and worry. There were also delicious moments of diversion. Early in the NDP tenure, the main diversion was bomb threats. Wednesdays were for cabinet meetings and for phone calls informing the premier's office that the building would be blown up during the day. At first the building was evacuated, but after several scares with no explosive consequences except the tempers of those forced to vacate their offices, the ministers realized leaders must not show fear in front of the troops and notified the civil servants they could leave but they themselves remained, warily at first, at their meetings.

Later they concluded that they were either not important enough to be blown up, or the callers lacked the courage of their convictions. Assuming that serious bombers would not be giving warning of their intentions, they ignored the calls.

Most of us had not been victims of violence other than a punch on the nose, but the kooks had discovered the letter bomb and those responsible for our security, mostly war or police veterans, were mindful of the destructive proclivities of humans. A security guard phoned to ask me to meet him at the front door of The Ledge. I assumed it was another protester who had chained himself to a portico pillar, or a union delegation demanding to see the premier, or an inebriate unable to stagger up the grand staircase to my office, so I went down. The guard pointed to a small package and hesitantly asked if I would take delivery.

"But it's addressed to the premier, so why not take it to him?"

"Weeeellll," he said apologetically, "we don't know what's in it."

I suddenly felt like the food-taster at a royal court. It gave me a sensation of importance—the guards knew I had a function here other than as just a brother-in-law on the public payroll: "Oh, so you think it might be a bomb and I'm expendable?"

And naive! I set the parcel on my office desk and unwrapped it: a cardboard carton, a smaller carton—and then a small metal box with a copper wire across the top. With a panic-stricken movement I tossed the package out the open window of my second-floor office. Nothing happened, so I retrieved it from the shrubbery and gingerly opened it. It contained iron filings from some tool shop but nothing to indicate its source or congratulate whoever opened it on still being alive. My staff and colleagues laughed heartily when told about it and it was soon forgotten. After all, this was Manitoba and we did not receive bombs in the mail.

Two weeks later, at the Law Courts across the street, a senior civil servant opened a similar parcel that had arrived in the mail—and it blew off his hand.

THE TALL, THIN, STOOPED MAN, in black suit, white shirt and dark tie, looking like an undertaker, glided noiselessly into my office. Wordlessly, he laid his attache case on my desk, opened it, took out a sheaf of papers, laid them carefully in front of me, quietly closed his case, and, wraithlike, left. There were thirteen gold-stamped death certificates—one for Attorney General Al Mackling. I buzzed the guards, who nabbed my visitor at the exit door. He was angry, it seemed, about some land expropriation. He was later committed.

"I WANT WELFARE," shouted the rotund, middle-aged, fur-coated lady as she was ushered into my office. She had left her husband in Ontario, moved to Winnipeg, painted her apartment black, and spent her nights studying occultism. She had a job but wanted support from her husband, and welfare because, "My social worker said I would feel better on welfare than working."

Once a week, for two months, she went through the same drill. If I was not in when she arrived, she would take off her coat and shoes, curl up on my office chesterfield and wait. I did what I could but she was not an easy client and was testing my patience. One day I returned to my office to be greeted by screams that I was doing nothing for her and this damned socialist government was corrupt and there was no reason why I could not get her a larger apartment where she could better commune with the spirits. And just that morning, her social worker had again told her she "would feel better" if on welfare. It was too much already.

"Madam, I have done all I can. I arranged for you to meet the head of the welfare office and you refused to go. I set up a meeting for you with the minister of social services and you did not show up. At your request I made an appointment for you with a psychiatrist and you did not come. I wrote to the Ontario social services minister asking him to chase down your errant husband. I contacted the Ontario premier's office on your behalf. There is nothing more I can or will do for you. I suggest rather than demanding welfare that you be happy you have a job that gets you out of that black hole you made for yourself. And now, unless you are out of here in thirty seconds I will pick you up bodily, along with your fur coat, and throw you out of this window behind me."

"I am not leaving until you get me on welfare."

Defiantly I stood up, turned to the window, opened it, and turned back. In a single fluid motion she stood up, slipped into her shoes and coat and quietly padded out.

My receptionist came in: "You have a way with women. That lady was hysterical when she came in and when she left you had her completely calmed down."

I said nothing. Perspiration was forming in pools under my armpits. What if she had defied me? But there was no time to reflect. I phoned the minister of Health and Social Services: "René, find that God-damned social worker and fire her."

IT WAS LATE IN THE EVENING and The Ledge appeared deserted, except for me. The phone rang imperiously: "Your God-damn cobs toog my trug."

"Why would they do that?"

"Dey say I was drung."

"Were you drunk?"

"Yes, bud dey did not know dat".

"So how did they find out?"

"Dey stop me on da streed."

"Why would they do that when they did not know you were drunk?"

"My tail lide waz brog."

"So they stopped you just because you had a broken tail light?"

"I was driwin da wrong way on da one-way streed."

"For three little things like that they took your truck away?"

"I god no driwer licenz."

"You call to complain the police took your truck, but you admit you were driving the wrong way on a one-way street and your tail light was broken and you have no driver's license and you were drunk. I suggest they did you a favour by taking your truck."

The phone exploded: "Listen you fuckin' son-of-a-bitch, I gonna come ride up dere to you office and tear your fuckin' t'roat oud."

Suddenly I thought, from the darkness "something wicked this way comes."

SHE WAS TALL, statuesque, had long, dark hair no dye could keep from showing gray at the roots and she asked me to order Medicare to pay for what seemed an unnecessary facelift. I explained that in the early days of Medicare, wealthy women used cosmetic surgery to get facelifts, so it was delisted except for deformities or accidents.

"But if I could get a facelift I could get a better job than I have now, perhaps a modelling job, and I could get off welfare."

"You have a job but you are on welfare? That is not allowed."

"I know, but this is a good job and I don't want to give it up and if I can just get welfare for a few more years I could pay off my debts and make a new life. You know my circumstances."

I did. She had a son in prison I had helped her with, and a husband in an asylum, but there was nothing I could do about this.

"You have confided in me and I will not report you, but you must report this to your social worker. Government is not heartless and there may be some accommodation the department can make to help you, but if you are caught you are in big trouble."

She promised to speak with her social worker. Two months later, two uniformed city policemen came to my office at The Ledge and handed me a subpoena. She had been charged with welfare fraud and had named me as a witness at her trial in December 1975.

Her lawyer was aggressive: "Is it not true that you know this woman and you advised her to continue drawing welfare payments while working?" he thundered in the courtroom.

Did I know this woman! One sunny Sunday morning I was lying in my back yard, wearing nothing but shorts, listening to the grass grow, when a tenant came running from the apartment next door: "Come quick, come quick, the woman in Apartment One is being attacked."

Jerked from my reverie and still half-asleep I followed him, padding bare-footed across the gravel, down the carpeted corridor, and through the open door of the apartment.

A tall, dark-haired woman stood with arms extended as though to protect a boy, about six. The youngster was standing on the chair behind her and looking terrified, while the woman screamed hysterically, "Get him out of here. He wants to steal my boy." She was staring over my right shoulder and I turned slowly to follow her terrified gaze. A steroid mutant stood slightly to the right and behind me. He seemed the biggest man I had ever seen. He was in his mid-forties, over six feet tall, at least 240 pounds and dressed in a Harris tweed jacket that made him appear five feet across the shoulders and as powerful as Superman. I stood there, vulnerable, in my fig-leaf shorts and fearing my sphincter would give way as I raised my eyes to meet his a foot above mine and stammered apologetically: "I'm s-s-orry s-s-sir, you'll have to leave."

He glared down at me like the beanstalk giant at Jack, a slight sneer flitting acrosss his broad face, and growled in a voice that originated somewhere near his ankles: "And I suppose if I don't you're going to throw me out?"

He knew how to hurt a guy. From somewhere within my small, timid, fear-wracked body quavered a voice I did not recognize: "We-e-ellll, not unless I have to."

He glared at me a moment with a carnivorous glint in his eyes, then turned and walked out through the open doorway.

Did I know this woman! Waves of remembered terror still coursed through my body at the sight of her. Yes, I know this woman. No, I did not encourage her to continue drawing welfare. The judge believed me. The lady had to repay welfare benefits received while working. Had he believed her lawyer, it would have cost me my job. I had learned the difficulties, as a government functionary, of distinguishing between doing a favour and committing a crime.

SOMETIMES PROBLEMS WERE QUICKLY RESOLVED: "I'm callin' from _____ [a northern reserve]. I'm just lettin' you know we've had enough abuse by your government and we're goin' to blow up the hydro line from the Nelson River to Winnipeg."

The voice was clearly that of an Aboriginal Manitoban. "But Manitoba Hydro just built a transmission line to your reserve a few months ago and if you blow up the line you will have to go back to candles and wood stoves."

"Ohhh. Weeelll … yeeesss. Weeelll … we won't blow it up. But AIM [the American Indian Movement] might."

THE THICK DOOR VIRTUALLY EXPLODED as he burst into the Cabinet Room; big, parka-clad, fierce-eyed, red hair and a face to match, as Vikings must have appeared to the terrified ninth-century Anglo-Saxons. "You bastards better buy some of this native art," he shouted, waving a cloth sack.

As though electronically operated, the heads of seventeen cabinet ministers swivelled on their necks toward him, the arc of movement depending on where they sat around the table. The Cabinet Room was hallowed ground, entered only by those having risen to the rarified stratosphere of cabinet minister or, by lesser mortals, by special invitation only. No one was prepared for this wild-eyed stranger's propulsion into the Inner Sanctum. No minister rose to either invite him in or throw him out. Instead, seventeen heads swivelled back to look at me.

I slowly rose from my chair at the far side of the table and, as though watching a movie in slow motion, felt myself moving, trancelike, the dozen steps toward the apparition. My fear was palpable. As though in another dimension, I witnessed my disembodied self staring into the stranger's angry eyes and coldly ordering him to follow me to my office. There, he sat across the desk from me and took several carved trinkets out of the bag.

"I am selling these for the _____ Indian Reserve," he purred.

"The reserve should get a new salesman. If you want us to buy something you don't tell us, you ask us." To cover my fear I kept my face rock-hard and my voice two degrees below absolute zero.

"Well yes, but since I was in town ..."

"Get out."

THE ATTRACTIVE, if somewhat hard-faced, thirtyish woman stood behind her easel, painting the official portrait of the premier, which would be hung on the walls of stately Room 254, beside a long line of predecessors, after his departure from office.[1]

The premier sat at his desk working on a file as though oblivious to the presence of the artist with a multi-coloured palette in one hand and her brush in the other. I walked behind the easel and the artist (she wore a black blouse and skirt and had a good body and nice legs) to see the painting. It was an original.

Quite unlike the usual formal, brooding visages against dark, Rembrandtian backgrounds, this depicted a young man in a tan-coloured suit, standing with a large scroll like a rolled-up map in his hand, gazing across a river toward a rugged terrain. The effect was rather like Moses with his tablets gazing across the Jordan.

It was not what I had expected and I spoke just to make polite conversation:

---

[1] The portrait was hung on December 8, 1978, shortly after Schreyer, at forty-three, was named Governor General of Canada.

"Too formal," I said, immediately regretting my words, and smiling to show that I did not really mean them.

The portrait painter stopped in mid-stroke, took a step to the left, laid her brush on the miniscule bit of the polished oak of the premier's desk not covered by mounds of files, and turned to me with a look of pure, unadulterated disgust: "Oh. So you think it's too formal. Well, fuck you!!!"

I glanced at the artist, half-expecting a slap by the hand that had held the brush. Then I glanced at the premier and saw the shadow of a grin flit across his face. I fled.

TWO BLOND, MUSCULAR YOUNG MEN strode angrily into my office:" Unless we receive our unemployment insurance cheques by tomorrow noon we are going to blow up this building."

The Unemployment Insurance Comission was converting from manual to computer operations, which usually meant trouble. The premier's office received visits and phone calls from many who either did not know UIC was a federal agency, or felt that government problems should be handled by the nearest level of government. I would refer them to our Department of Labour, which would refer the information to the nearest UIC office. These two young men had apparently been referred once too often for their liking and were furious. Since they sought immediate satisfaction, I gave it to them: "Okay. It's your building, so go ahead and blow it up if you don't like it. What the hell's it to me?"

"What ... what do you mean it's our building?"

"It's owned by every person in Manitoba, and that includes you."

"Oh! We didn't know it was our building. That's different."

"ARE YOU AN MLA?"

"No. Just a worker in the political vineyard."

"You look like an MLA. Do you have anything to say to us?"

"Yes, as a matter of fact, I have."

The raging issue at the time was the government's announcement requiring motorcycle riders to wear helmets. Cyclists, because they saw this as an infringement of their inalienable democratic rights to damage their heads without hindrance, or because they believed the weight of a helmet invited a broken neck, or because they were enraptured by the caress of wind on face, or because ritual protesting was the norm in the Seventies, were furious.

Considering the dangers of motorcycling, I had little patience with them. Leaving my office about 7 o'clock on a beautiful June evening, wearing my tan -coloured, light-weight, parade-stopping Johnny Carson summer suit, which apparently caused me to be mistaken for an MLA, I walked unwittingly into a protest rally of several hundred bikers. I was introduced as a government official and handed a microphone. "I believe that in a democratic country each person should be free to choose to go the hell in his or her own way," I told them, "so if you people don't want to wear helmets you should not be forced to do so."

"Hooraaay," thundered 200 voices.

"I also believe if you are injured in a motorcycle accident and it can be shown that injury could have been avoided by wearing a helmet, then Medicare should not pay your bills."

"Booooooo."

They allowed me to escape with my life.

"WANT TO ACCOMPANY ME to do a bit of slumming?"

The caller was a friend, a doctor who substituted when the regular physician for the penal system was away. We drove to Headingley Gaol, built in 1932, which took its work seriously.

Here was the sturdy gallows with beam, trap, lever and twelve-foot drop, last used to hang Henry Malanik in 1952. The execution chamber was now used to store furniture and festive seasonal decorations. Here was the Potter's Field with the graves of fourteen men—most with non-Anglo-Saxon names—hanged here. I stood by while the doctor examined the parade of petty thieves, dope pedlars, purse-snatchers, etc.—mostly tall young men with no musculature—serving less than two years.

I noticed a lone man in a locked cell and asked the guard to let me in to speak with him. He pursed his lips hesitatingly but, knowing I was a 'big-shot' from the premier's office, he opened the cell door, and locked it behind me. I sat casually beside the prisoner on his cot in the small, barred cell within the larger secured area, I in my impressive light gray suit, white shirt and dark blue tie, and he in his prison garb. He was in his mid-twenties, a big, good-looking, fresh-faced, innocent-eyed young man: "So tell me, why are you here?"

"Killed my mother," he replied off-handedly.

Suddenly I felt like the mouse in Kafka's *Little Fable*, with the cell walls closing around me while the cat, in the form of the powerful young man, prepared to pounce. My throat went dry: "Oh. Oh, well, how … how, did you do that?"

"Drowned her in the bathtub."

Jesus Christ! "Guard! Get me out of here."

Later I was informed he was there on a lieutenant governor's warrant. Considered too dangerous and mentally unstable to be sentenced to a fixed term, he could be held for life.

MY RECEPTIONIST DIRECTED HIM to me. He came very quietly into my office and I asked him to sit down. He pulled the chair over to the side of my desk—the unusual nature of which did not register with me until later—so there was no obstruction between us. He was of medium height, slight, swarthy with curly black hair, and he slowly explained in bad, halting English that he was a recent immigrant from Portugal and a political refugee. Then: "I have message for Schreyer."

"Okay, I will take it."

"Message is for Schreyer."

"Yes. Okay. Give it to me."

"You Schreyer?"

Since he did not know the difference, I figured why not save some time. "Yes."

The switchblade appeared out of nowhere and the blade snicked into place. He leaned toward me, but hesitated. Oscar Wilde wrote that a man's mind can be wonderfully focused by the realization that he will be hanged in the morning; the threat of being stabbed had the same effect. His hesitation left me an opening. "If you use that knife on me, you will be shipped back to Portugal and the communists will get you."

He hesitated for what appeared an eternity while I sat, paralysed. Then in a single motion he closed the blade, stood up, slipped the knife into his pocket, and vanished. I was too petrified to call security guards until long after he was gone.

SHE WAS THIRTY-SOMETHING, five-foot-seven, dark-eyed, auburn-haired, and casually but carefully dressed in light brown slacks, a dark brown blouse and a tan coloured suede jacket. Obviously once attractive, but now somewhat shopworn, she appeared as though she should be pliant and soft-spoken, but she was now aggressive and voluble: "I demand that you take those cameras out of my bedroom."

She explained she had married in Germany and immigrated to Winnipeg with her husband, who had returned to Germany. She now lived with her fourth 'permanent' boyfriend, and her seventeen-year-old daughter looked at her accusingly in the mornings, as though she knew what those bumps in the night emanating from the master bedroom represented. So the government must have a camera hidden in the bedroom and was showing the photos to her daughter.

For perhaps thirty minutes, I repeatedly assured her that, while we government employees had a reputation for having little to do, we had more to do than to hide cameras in bedrooms. But her sense of guilt was deep and she was not dissuaded. Finally I asked: "Suppose we do have a camera hidden in your bedroom photographing your naked body while you frolic with your fourth permanent boyfriend, what would we do with the pictures?"

"Oh!" her brow and body arched. "Perhaps you are planning to make a movie of my body." I was nonplussed: "But … but … but … I don't think you are all that good."

For perhaps five seconds she sat stiffly as though she had not heard. Then she began to laugh, long and low and soft and pleasant and rippling and throaty and intimate and inviting until the sound and cadence permeated the space between us, while a great teasing smile illuminated her face, and her shoulder-length hair glistened and her body metamorphosed like a flower opening, becoming sinuous and curvaceous. Without a word she languidly uncoiled and sauntered, like a dancer, out of my office, leaving only her emanations and the sound of her laughter in her wake.

Later I related the incident to my colleague, Egon Frech. "So why did you not save yourself all that time by simply saying "Okay, we will remove the cameras."

I hadn't thought of that, but if I had, I'm glad I didn't do it; for the past thirty years, I have had, at random times, triggered by some vagrant unrelated incident, the exquisite memory of that undulating walk, seductive laugh and taunting smile.

Literally, life at the 'The Ledge' was more than labour. But the moments of diversion were few.

X

Anger on Olympus

He jests at scars who never felt a wound
      —Shakespeare, Romeo and Juliet

The premier had monumental self-control. He did not have inexhaustible patience, nor suffer fools gladly, but he revealed his periodic anger with little more than by abruptly changing the subject or with a slight tightening of his jawline. Therefore, it was all the more frightening when his anger did explode.

The first time I witnessed it, I was excited to note he was capable of such passion even though I thought it misdirected. The NDP government had been in office twenty months and had not yet done all the things some members of the young "ginger group" of college graduates thought should have been done. In brief, we had not yet created the New Jerusalem. They attributed this failure in part to being too timid—or too conservative—to clean out the Augean stable by firing civil servants we had inherited from the ancien regime. This charge led, at the party's annual convention in 1971, to an uncharacteristic outburst which left the premier's audience wide-eyed with surprise and the objects of his attack shaking with fear, when he strode to floor microphone and roared, "I am sick and tired of these carping criticisms of career civil servants being incompetent simply because they were hired by another administration or because they do not carry an NDP membership card. This government is dedicated to achieving certain stated objectives and as long as those in the public service work with us to those ends, their politics will not be an issue nor their loyalties questioned. To those here who are recent additions to the public service, largely because of their party member-ship card, who do not consider this the right way to run a government, I suggest they get off the public payroll and run for office and then THEY can make the political decisions."

His wrath had been aroused by two young men, Bruce Dryburgh and Myron Kuziak, the latter the son of a Saskatchewan NDP cabinet minister. They were civil servants who had signed on with the new Government of Manitoba to help create the new socialist revolution. And they were party members who believed the vaunted democracy and openness of NDP conventions gave delegates licence to speak freely. They would not make that mistake again.

The second time he did not raise his voice, but its savage intensity was even more frightening. "The next election will be won by whoever wins the soft Liberal votes," Premier-elect Schreyer told party insiders the day after the 1969 election that emasculated the Liberals. It was an astute observation, and for the next eight years he played to that audience, not objecting when the media—or NDP members—referred to him as a Liberal in disguise, or a Trojan horse in the NDP. With the by-election defeat of Paul Marion in February 1974, the resignation of Izzy Asper in March 1975, and defeat of the Liberal candidate in the Crescentwood by-election in June 1975, the Liberals were reduced to three members, one less than needed to maintain official party status with its perks of office and finances. Polls showed most Liberals who left their party had voted NDP, but Schreyer feared those remaining were of rightist persuasion and would vote Conservative in the next election, so he wanted to keep the Liberals in existence as a party. Also, he did not wish to humiliate the new, unelected, Liberal leader, the courtly gentleman and distinguished lawyer, Charles Huband.

Into these delicate manoeuvrings intruded Russ Doern. As minister of Public Works, he was responsible for assignment of offices in The Ledge. He saw the reduction of the Liberals as a politically exploitable coup for the NDP, and an opportunity to acquire their office for what he deemed more useful purposes. Followed by reporters and televison cameras, he marched down the long corridor and formally "expunged" the Liberal Party by removing the sign LIBERAL CAUCUS ROOM, from its office door.[1]

When the premier was informed, his face coloured, the muscles in his jaw pulsated, and his voice was barely controlled when he picked up the phone and snarled, "Russ! Get over here". On this occasion I completely agreed with him.[2]

But the third time his anger was directed at me.

"Mr. Speaker, I direct a question to the First Minister. I wonder if he could tell us if it is correct that the Manitoba Agricultural Credit Corporation denied a loan to an individual to purchase land and a loan was then made for the purchase of the same land—to the son of the chairman of the board of the MACC?"

Part of my self-assigned job was to sit in the visitor's gallery above the Legislative Chamber during Question Period, to get a sense of the direction of

---

[1] Doern later described this as "the worst mistake of my political career". *Wednesdays are Cabinet Days*, p. 94.

[2] In April 1979, Lloyd Axworthy resigned to run federally and expunged the Liberals in the Manitoba Legislature until the election of Sharon Carstairs in November 1981. As Schreyer had predicted, 'hard' Liberals voted PC in 1975, 1977 and 1981.

debates, note information needed, and assist government backbenchers in preparing questions. I was there during a late sitting that memorable evening in early 1973.

The questioner was Opposition Leader Sidney Spivak. My sphincter snapped shut!

Spivak had won a hard-fought battle for the leadership of the Progressive Conservative Party of Manitoba after the resignation of former Premier Weir in 1971. He was a fiscal conservative but a progressive in social policy, arguably to the left of a number of NDP members of the legislature, possibly influenced by his attractive, effervescent wife, Mira, who came of a relatively wealthy but socialistically-minded family. He was suspect in the eyes of the core base of Tory supporters, particularly its rural component, because of his "progressiveness". And he was not highly respected by some members of his own caucus because he was too "left" for some and too "right" for others, because some feared Manitoba was not ready for a Jewish premier, and because of his disconcerting habit of chewing energetically on a wad of gum while leaning far back in his chair and staring over the head of the person with whom he was speaking in private conversation.

He also had a chuckle-provoking habit of speaking rapidly and erratically and prefacing his questions in the chamber with; "I wonder if ..." This became so pronounced that, one day when he addressed a question to the minister of Northern Affairs, Ron McBryde failed to respond, was admonished by Spivak, and rose. "Mr. Speaker. I did not realize the Honourable Leader of the Opposition was asking a question. I thought he was just informing us he was wondering about something he was wondering about."

But Spivak, like Schreyer, had a quiet dignity that prohibited him from playing the fool. He won the prize for the highest standing during his four years at law school, and earned his Master of Law from Harvard. He, his father and his brother had, by hard work and intelligent investing, acquired a portfolio of revenue properties including a premier Winnipeg hotel. He was no political neophyte; he had entered the legislature in 1966, was appointed minister of Industry and Commerce and minister for the Manitoba Development Fund. He had travelled the world seeking investment capital and immigrants for Manitoba, and in politico/business circles was a power to be reckoned with.[3] More important, he had an intense desire to affirm himself, and perhaps his race, by becoming Premier of Manitoba. To do so he had to bring down the government and he worked at it diligently. No sniff of scandal swept up in the vacuum cleaner of political rumour was too minuscule for him to pursue and to ask devious questions about in an

---

[3] Sidney Joel Sprivak (1928 – 2002) was elected to the Manitoba Legislature in 1966, at age thirty-eight, was appointed minister of Industry and Commerce, served on Treasury Board and as minister for the Manitoba Development Fund, and succeeded Walter Weir as PC Party leader in 1971. While personally warm and friendly, his persona in The Ledge seemed cool and distant and he seemed never to be able to enjoy the camaraderie of his colleagues, nor focus his unquestioned intellect on issues while in opposition. He was defeated for the leadership by Sterling Lyon in 1975. He remained popular in the community and his funeral in July 2002 was attended by the Who's Who of Manitoba, as well as high-level representatives from Ottawa.

effort to embarrass the government. And I had inadvertently given him a golden opportunity to do so.

IN 1959, the Roblin government concluded farming had become a capital-intensive enterprise. Young men could not afford to buy farms, nor could their fathers afford to give them theirs. The Government of Manitoba devised a program to lend up to $35,000 to anyone under age thirty-five to buy land, and established the Manitoba Agricultural Credit Corporation to administer it. By 1968, it had loaned over $9,000,000 but annual loans were becoming less. Farmers needed MACC loans, but they had no collateral left against which loans could be made: that had been exhausted to guarantee advances from suppliers and other lenders. A 1971 survey of ten typical MACC loans made five years earlier showed they totalled $234,000 and were $53,000 in arrears making the debt to the MACC equal to the total value of the land. Such farmers must either declare bankruptcy, sell their farms, or borrow more money. But they had no security for another loan.

Sam Uskiw became minister of Agriculture in 1969 determined to make the farming sector a thriving industry. His answer to the above problem was the "consolidation loan". The Government of Manitoba, through the MACC, would lend farmers the money to clear up existing debts, and attach the land as collateral. The farmer would receive the maximum loan possible, would have one creditor instead of many, and could sleep at night knowing he would not be put into bankruptcy with a lien by a nervous creditor.

When the word went out that the Department of Agriculture was prepared to make "consolidation loans" allowing farmers to use government money to pay off existing debts to the Veteran's Land Act, the elevator agent, the fuel agent, the fertilizer agent, the crop insurance agent, the machinery agency, the feeder cattle supplier, the feed supplier, the lumber merchant, the dry-goods merchant, the well driller, the grocer, the Federal Credit Corporation, finance companies, credit unions and banks; the MACC was deluged with applications. Loan applications were for as much as $600,000. Some were of questionable merit and probably should not even have been given the courtesy of opening a file.

A farmer applied for a loan of $396,000, $105,000 to retire existing debt, $161,000 to guarantee operating loans at the bank, and the balance to buy the land. His net worth was minimal.

The loan was conditionally approved by the board. In late 1971, Maxwell Hofford was appointed chairman of the MACC. He scutinized the loan, did not like it, considered the ramifications of interfering with it, and proposed it be reviewed.

During the Schreyer government, the opposition frequently charged that the Premier's Office was "interfering" in matters that should have been left to "neutral" civil servants acting at arms length from government, and there were implied hints of political favours being granted—or bought—and of Schreyer being the King of Patronage. Actually, all too often these issues, and the troubles in their train, came to the Premier's Office uninvited; they were dumped on us. Some persons saw the affable Schreyer an easy mark; some, having been trained in another school, believed favours were always available from the head political honcho; some, having gone through the bureaucracy with no satisfaction, sought solace at the apex of power. Like Thomas Hobbes, they "fled from petty tyrants to the throne".

In January 1972, I was at my desk minding my own business. "Herb. We have been friends for many years but I have a feeling this morning our friendship comes to an end."

The visitor was an old friend, but since I had come to the Premier's Office he had become a pest, visiting me several times a week seeking favours for himself or his "clients". In my estimation he was becoming a professional leech. He must have sensed my disaffection, and his statement gave me an opening. "I don't think I can be that lucky but what do you want?"

"I am here to represent Mr. _____ The MACC has declined his loan application. He wants an appointment with the premier, or with you, and I am here to arrange it."

"Where is Mr._____?"

"He's at the St. Regis Hotel."

"Then go tell him if he wants to see the premier, or me, he should come here himself. We do not need an intermediary."

He stood up and glared at me for a long time:

"Okay! We don't need you anyway. I'm going over to the hog board meeting to see Sweetzer. I can get him to intervene." He grabbed his coat and stomped out of my office. [4]

I immediately phoned the hog board office. Chairman Max Hofford was also Chairman of the Manitoba Hog Marketing Board, and Leonard Sweetzer was also a member of both boards. The hog board was meeting that day. "Max. This guy is coming over there to put pressure on you and Leonard about the _____ loan application. He can only cause trouble and make things more complicated than they already are. When he gets there I suggest you throw him out." Hofford did.

I obtained a copy of the relevant file, scanned it, and concluded the board had acted responsibly by cancelling the loan.

---

[4] My old friend had developed a business offering to put people in touch with the "right" persons in government. He would sit in hotel lobbies, pick up bits of information from disgruntled persons, introduce himself, drop a few names, present his card, and offer to help—for a fee. He was a handsome man, of medium height, well built, always impeccably dressed, and both impressive and convincing in his approach to strangers. We were not aware of this "enterprise" until one day a stranger noticed the man had left his briefcase on the floor of a hotel lobby. Having heard him name-dropping and assuming this to be a government Mandarin and that perhaps the briefcase contained important papers, the stranger brought it to the Office of the Attorney-General. It contained, among other papers, receipts for fees collected for his consulting services.

On February 10th, a letter arrived from the farmer to the premier. "I believe in your sense of justice and fair play. I would beg you to have Rudy Usick as a first choice and Leo Fulliard as a second choice to be on [an arbitration] commission. The third member can be of your choice from anywhere in Manitoba BUT NOT FROM _____ [his home area]."

The premier replied in a letter, "You propose two gentlemen of your choosing to rule on your application. That would be tantamount to allowing any applicant for an MACC loan to select several friends to hear his case. That might be good for the applicant but not for the loan funds ... I am sure you are aware that approval or rejection of loan applications depend to some extent on the recommendations of those who know the applicant and have done business with him, and therefore your outright rejection of anyone from your vicinity [as an arbitrator] is hardly a recommendation."

Later Hofford casually informed me his son had applied to the MACC for a loan to buy land. It did not register with me it was the same land Mr. _____ had wanted to buy. Since I believed government employees and/or members of their family had the same right to government services as anyone else, provided no inside influence was used and their application was treated like any other, I mentally stored the information as insignificant. A year later, with Spivak's question, it exploded into significance.

Spivak was a political pro. His timing was impeccable; an election was pending. The case became a political cause célèbre. The opposition was certain they had an issue with which to taint the premier with political interference and patent favouritism.

My body turned suddenly warm as adrenalin shot through me, caused by fear of the implications of the question and embarrassment at having failed to detect them when Hofford had mentioned the matter. My usually politically sensitive antennae had been tuned out. I was about to pay the price.

My eyes were drawn, as to a magnet, to the premier. He rose, clearly embarrassed, mumbled that he would take the question as notice, and sat down. As soon as the opposition members were distracted by other questions, he glanced up at me in the gallery, caught my eye and almost imperceptibly jerked his head sideways—the signal for "Come to my office—NOW."

I slouched along the 300-foot-long corridor toward the Premier's Office, wishing I could disappear — that some great wind would blow me, like Dorothy, out of Kansas into Oz, or that, like the much older and more poignant plea, " this cup be taken from me". My mind worked furiously. There was no easy way out of this one. But a tactic emerged. I would take the aggressive approach.

I determinedly yanked open the door to the Premier's Office. "Now we have an issue," I said. "Now we can fight these Tory bastards!"

The premier's face darkened with suppressed fury. His jaw worked as he fought for self-control. His voice rasped, "I resent being forced into a fight we do not need. We have troubles enough without generating them. This is not just a case of the government in jeopardy but if what Spivak implies is true, we may owe someone an apology and compensation. If you knew of this you have been totally irresponsible in not informing me. And you are not being paid to deal cavalierly with citizens."

There followed a series of questions made famous by the Watergate investigation: "What did you know and when did you know it?". Suddenly I knew how it must have felt to be questioned by Torquemada. There was no escape; if I did not know I would be executed because I was not doing my job properly, and if I knew, I would be executed for neglecting to inform the premier, and for failing to take whatever action was needed to save a citizen from humiliation and the government from embarrassment.

"Go and do what is necessary to resolve this matter!"

The reaction of the public service to attack is to circle the wagons and "cover ass". It seemed like a good time to do so, but my instinct was to attack. Experience had taught me the opposition were usually more vulnerable than they appeared and that when they brought an issue of this nature to the chamber, it was usually embroidered to serve the interests of the politician rather than the citizen. There must be more to the story than implied in Spivak's question. I got the complete file.

Legally all was in order, but the political optics were daunting:

November 4/71—_____ loan approved by MACC Board of Directors;
November 19/71—Max Hofford appointed chair of MACC;
December 10/71— _____ loan withheld pending review;
January 14/72—_____ loan rescinded;
July 8/72—Trevor Hofford [chairman's son] applied for loan to buy same land;
July 28/72—Trevor Hofford interviewed by loans officer;
August 9/72—Trevor Hofford interviewed again;
September 21/72—Trevor Hofford loan approved.

But the files revealed something else: Mr. _____'s application was for almost $400,000 while Hofford's was for only $100,000; most of Mr. _____'s loan would go to paying off existing debt and guaranteeing future operating credit at the bank, while Hofford's would go entirely toward purchasing a farm; the loan to Mr. _____ would have been to someone farming over 1,100 acres of land while the loan to Hofford established a young farmer—precisely what MACC loans had originally been intended to do.[5]

The files also revealed that the two MACC directors who had moved and seconded the motion to approve Mr. _____'s loan, were the same persons who had moved and seconded its recession.

And I knew Max Hofford! We had become friends twenty years earlier

---

[5]   Trevor Hofford's loan was repaid within three years.

and had stood back to back during the decade of incessant turmoil caused by the fights between the Farmer's Union, the Manitoba Federation of Agriculture and Cooperation, the Canadian Federation of Agriculture, the United Grain Growers, the Dairy and Poultry Cooperative, the Manitoba Pool Elevator organization, and the political troglodytes, both Liberal and Conservative in both Winnipeg and Ottawa. We had participated in the birth pangs of the New Democratic Party. We had spent endless, sleepless hours, in the vilest conditions of weather and roads, driving through the night to meeting after meeting, planning our strategies and talking about life. I had sufficient confidence in his integrity to risk my future.

I went to the minister. "Sam. Here are the files on the _____/Hofford case. I suggest you table them in the chamber. No editorializing or commentary is necessary. Just table them and let the opposition and the media do what they wish with them. Let's see if Spivak and his people are prepared to take the political risk of defending Mr. _____'s application once the details are public."

Uskiw liked the idea, but as minister he had a responsibility. He made a quick phone call and informed me, "Our solicitor tells me MACC files are confidential and can't be made public without the consent of the principals." I raged, "This man has gone to the opposition and his criticism has been splattered all over the media and used to pillory the government. He long ago forfeited any claim to confidentiality."

Uskiw did something even better than I had proposed; he fired off telegrams to both principals requesting permission to table their files. A telegram came back from Trevor Hofford.

"I have no objections to having my MACC file tabled in the Legislature." The same day a telegram came from the other man, "Nothing in the tabling of my file would serve any useful purpose or shed any light. My file should remain confidential."

We were making progress but the water was up to our nostrils and we fearfully awaited another wave. Then Uskiw received an unsolicited letter from Erickson farmer, Rudolph Usick.

"When the MACC was formed [in 1959] I was appointed to the Board of Directors by George Hutton, the Conservative Minister of Agriculture ... I applied for the maximum loan available [which was] approved ... A loan to a director's son ... is more removed from the boardroom than my loan which was to an actual active director. You may use this letter as you see fit."

It was a valuable letter. But Usick was seen as friendly to the government and if indeed today's news wraps tomorrow's fish, the political wolves baying on our trail would not be dissuaded by what had happened a dozen years ago. The waves were receding, but the sea was rough. Then we received another unsolicited letter. "I am a person with no particular political leanings ... I say without equivocation the loan to Mr. Hofford's son was appraised and scrutinized without bias and when it was presented Mr. Hofford was excused from the board meeting. In his absence, the application was examined and found acceptable in all respects

... The fact that the land is the same property involved in a previous application, approval of which was subsequently rescinded, has no bearing on the matter. The two applications were completely dissimilar. I can only say anyone who questions this would agree after further examination."

The author of the letter phoned Uskiw offering to testify before legislative committees or anywhere else on the ethics of the loan. He was an MACC director who had first voted for the _____ loan and then to rescind it. He was also an ex-banker, appointed to the board by the previous Conservative government. He owed nothing to the NDP.

Uskiw brought the letter to the premier in his office. Several other cabinet ministers were present. There was a highly charged silence as the premier read the letter ... and then read it again.

The premier let out a long sigh and seemed to deflate with relief as he sat, staring into the distance, his elbow resting on the arm of his chair, the letter dangling loosely from his hand. "Gentlemen, this letter is a Godsend. It may have saved the government." He appeared on the verge of tears.

So was I. I left him there surrounded by his equally relieved cabinet colleagues, and quietly went back to my office. It was not one of my better days. I had come within a hair of being fired by my brother-in-law ... and of bringing down the government.

XI

Nineteen Seventy-Two

It was the best of times and the worst of times
—Charles Dickens, A Tale of Two Cities

Nineteen seventy-two promised to be a good year for the NDP. National leader David Lewis, with a blistering attack on the "corporate welfare bums", won thirty-one seats, the largest number ever. Pierre Trudeau, the philosopher-king of 1968, won a plurality of 109 seats and could be defeated at will by a combination of the NDP and/or Real Caouette's Creditistes plus Robert Stanfield's 107 Conservatives. So Trudeau made a deal with the NDP.

The NDP exacted a price: improved Old Age Pensions; Family Allowance and Unemployment Insurance; a Food Prices Review Board; changes to the Elections Act allowing income tax deductions for individual contributors to federal election campaigns; a Foreign Investment Review Act to analyze the value to Canada of the sale of local corporations to foreigners; an inquiry into the proposed McKenzie Valley Pipeline (later conducted by Mr. Justice Berger), and a new energy policy. And the *pièce-de-résistance*: creation of a publicly owned Petro-Canada, as a 'window' on the petroleum industry, which was about eighty per cent foreign-owned. This was to become a tool to mitigate the incipient blackmail of the petroleum industry when OPEC, in the months following the Arab-Israeli war in October 1973, embargoed oil deliveries and increased prices fourfold.

In the provinces also, the NDP was on the move. In British Columbia, ebullient former social worker David Barrett ended the nineteen-year reign of the Social Credit government and the buccaneer capitalists, in an upset almost as momentous as that of the Schreyer victory in 1969. A year earlier, self-disciplined Allan Blakeney had decisively retaken the sacred ground of Saskatchewan from Ross Thatcher's Liberals; passionate NDP leader Grant Notley had been elected to the Alberta Legislature—a different drummer in Peter Lougheed's orchestrated sweep and the young eagle, Stephen Lewis, had come within one seat of displacing the Liberals as the official opposition in Ontario. Within the NDP, the 'Waffle', the radical fringe that had organized within the party to guarantee its purity, but had become a band of intense ideological Nihilists creating tension with sterile philosophizing, was either absorbed (as in Manitoba) or expelled (as in Ontario).

In Manitoba, too, all was well. Cabinet ministers had found their footing in their departments and backbenchers consolation in their work. The Education Property Tax Credit had relieved low-income taxpayers. Senior's housing and nursing homes were being constructed to reduce health care costs; medicare premiums were reduced; a publicly-owned automobile insurance company had been established; programs to assist farmers had been devised; ex parte injunctions against striking employees had been ended; drug costs were reduced by requiring substitution of generic drugs for brand names; the thirteen municipalities of Greater Winnipeg had been reorganized into 'Unicity'; Lake Winnipeg was being regulated to ensure Manitoba Hydro power and the Conservative-proposed high-level diversion of South Indian Lake was being modified; the Churchill Forest Industries complex at The Pas had been seized from its foreign speculators to safeguard the taxpayers' investment and the veil of secrecy shrouding investments of public money by the Manitoba Development Fund had been removed. Premier Schreyer announced that his government had "fulfilled the commitments of the 1969 Throne Speech" and created "greater equality of the human condition".

Opposition efforts to create tensions between Schreyer and Sidney Green failed when the premier told a press conference, "Mr. Green is a hard-working, pragmatic, realistic person and our relationship is very good." When the *Winnipeg Tribune* failed to report the statement, Green publicized it in a paid advertisement.[1]

Best of all, for the first time the NDP government had a majority in the legislature! In April 1971, rancher "Pete" Adam was elected in the Ste. Rose seat vacated by Liberal leader Gildas Molgat's appointment to the Senate, and optician James Walding was elected in the St. Vital seat vacated when PC MLA Jack Hardy left Manitoba. In December, Laurent Desjardins was folded into cabinet as minister of Tourism and Recreation. Finally, the government had some breathing space.

Indeed, 1972 promised to be the best of times. The legislature was no longer "A House Divided" as described by the *Winnipeg Free Press* in June 1969. The Government of Manitoba had reason to feel pleased and proud and confident. Nothing could hurt us now. Then 1972 became our *Annus Horribilis*. By June, the NDP government was returned to sitting on a razor's edge, at the mercy of any disenchanted backbencher, just as in the first twenty-two months of its tenure.[2]

---

[1] *The Winnipeg Tribune*, December 2, 1971

[2] Standing: January 1, 1972: NDP—31; PC—21; Liberal—3; SC—1; Independent—1.
Standing: June 30, 1972: NDP—29; PC—20; Liberal—4; SC—1; Independent—3.

In June 1971, the election of Liberal leader "Izzy" Asper in the Wolseley seat, vacated by the death of PC MLA Leonard Clayton, resurrected the spectre of a Liberal alternative to the NDP. In March 1972, Sidney Green resigned from cabinet over a policy disagreement with his leader. In April, Jean Allard left the party due to "the influence of doctrinaire socialists". In May, Joe Borowski, who had caught the public's imagination, left the NDP.

Borowski, who became a living legend, burst upon the political scene like Prometheus bringing the gift of fire to benighted humanity, "A genuine, gold-plated folk-hero", as University of Manitoba historian Ed Rea described him. The fourth of ten children of Polish immigrants to a farm in Saskatchewan at the beginning of the Depression, he had worked at a paper mill in Ontario, a fishing camp on Vancouver Island, as a pipeline worker in Alberta, a farm labourer in Saskatchewan, a heavy equipment operator in British Columbia, and as a chef in an Army camp in the Yukon. In 1958, he became a hard-rock miner at the newly-opened nickel lode at Thompson, in Northern Manitoba, where he worked seven days a week to earn overtime.

His politicization began in 1960, when INCO took over the mine and reduced wages. He became active in the Steelworker's Union and by 1964 was local vice-president and chief negotiator. The union won its first contract, but the aggressive Borowski was fired, though not before he had been recognized as a spokesman for his fellow miners.

He and his wife established a small but lucrative gift shop, but when they sought to expand, permission was refused. Thompson was a company town, owned and controlled by INCO. In protest, Borowski took his sleeping bag and camped on the steps of the Legislative Building, where he held court for those, initially attracted by this "Polish joke", often came to scoff but left to ponder.

He demanded that Thompson be given its own municipal government, and won. INCO withdrew its jurisdiction and Thompson was created a town, with its own elected council. Borowski had his first victory: "And if I hadn't been fired," he said later, "I wouldn't have been able to picket the legislature." But his odyssey was just beginning.

Premier Roblin had stated there would be no retail sales tax "as long as I am premier", and declared the idea "as dead as a dodo-bird". In 1967, a year after Roblin was re-elected, the dodo-bird became a phoenix and Manitoba had a five per cent sales tax.

Borowski saw this as "election under false pretences" by a mendacious government and refused to collect the tax on sales at his shop. He paid the tax out of his own pocket but refused to act as a government agent to collect it from customers. For this he was jailed—three times. That brought him, with his sleeping bag, back to the steps of the legislature.

To shield himself from Winnipeg's bitter October winds, he moved into a trailer provided by a supporter. One evening, some university students who had adopted him as a symbol of 1960s rebellion, dragged the trailer up the steps so its

Joe Borowski, shown here with Premier Schreyer in the latter's office, represented his northern riding of Thompson with passion and ingenuity.

occupant could set up light housekeeping in the foyer of The Ledge. It was too much.

Stewart McLean, minister of Highways and responsible for the security of the building, ordered the trailer removed—and there was the news photo of a smiling Borowski sitting on the hitch of the trailer as it was hustled down the steps. But not before he had become recognized as a spokesman for his community and a cynosure for thousands of Manitobans.

Three years later, having assumed McLean's portfolio, Borowski became a phrasemaker with some rodomontade. "McLean made my life miserable. Today he is a circuit court judge in the sticks of Saskatchewan where I was born and I'm here with his car, his desk, his office and his secretary. And I'm enjoying them all."[3]

Borowski had been elected the NDP member for Thompson, the largest constituency in Canada, in a by-election in February 1969, after PC MLA Gordon Beard resigned to protest the way his government ignored the North. Borowski was re-elected in June and, at thirty-seven, appointed minister of Highways—the "dropout" in the best-educated cabinet in Canadian history. In short order, he became the stormy petrel of both caucus and chamber.

A vibrant six-footer weighing 220 pounds, powerfully built, with great hairy arms, he often seem like a MAC truck as he charged along the corridor of The Ledge. With only a grade seven education, but a high degree of native intelligence and political shrewdness, he never considered ignorance as an excuse for stupidity and no one ever doubted who was in charge of his department.

He struck terror into the hearts of gravel truckers he followed on the province's highways, ordering them to the nearest scales if they seemed overloaded. He seemed to have the same impact on the hearts of his staff. Once, when I attended his office, he asked his secretary to ask his assistant deputy minister to come to the office. We were still chatting when the ADM trotted in, shaking snow off his coat, wiping frost from his face, and puffing as though his lungs would burst: "You [puff, puff] called, Mr. Minister?" he gasped.

"Yes. But where were you?"

"I was at the Motor Vehicle Branch [puff,puff] at 1075 Portage."

"Oh. I thought you were in your office next door."

Petitioned by a delegation to pave a highway in southern Manitoba, Borowski replied: "You's guys voted Liberal and Conservative for a century and dey did not pave your highway, and neider will I. I was elected by the Nort where dey don't even have trails and dat's where I'm gonna build highways."

And he did so, brilliantly. The Government of Manitoba decided to build a 105-mile highway from Grand Rapids to Ponton, reducing travelling distance from Winnipeg to the burgeoning City of Thompson by more than 120 miles. Borowski, knowing non-native contractors hired Aboriginal Manitobans to do the bullwork,

---

[3] Article by Ted Allan, *The Winnipeg Tribune*, December 1969.

contracted instead with the Manitoba Indian Brotherhood to clear the right-of-way—and applauded when the MIB hired some white workers. He did it again to extend the highway 180 miles from Thompson to the mining towns of Leaf Rapids and Lynn Lake.

"You are seen as nuttin' but drunks," he told the native Manitobans, "but I'm gonna give you da chance to prove dat ain't true." The Aboriginal people accepted the challenge and set records for the speed with which the job was done.

But he was no patsy. Liberal leader Asper flew to the work site (he had a *Winnipeg Free Press* photo of himself in leather jacket and long white scarf like a 1920s barnstormer to prove it) and rose in the chamber to charge the government with abusing the workers by not providing trailers and forcing them to sleep in tents on spruce boughs. Borowski angrily replied that he had contracted with the MIB and it was up to them to provide their men with facilities, just like a non-native contractor would have to do. He was right, but it was not politic to be seen to be abusing Manitoba's Aboriginal people, and the incident embarrassed the government.

Borowski's philosophy was that "If you don't run with the lead dog the scenery never changes", and his aggressive nature and readiness to comment on issues quickly made him the darling of the media. On a slow day, they knew Borowski was good for a quotable comment that would sell papers, and his comments were not always politic. Asked his opinion about immigration policy, he created a furor with: "Well, da feds sent dese two guys here da udder day and one was an Eyetie and couldn't even speak English."

But he was also unusually forthright in a calling notorious for its equivocations. Visiting at his home at LaSalle one evening, I was surprised to find him playing softball with Gerry Haslam, the cerebral editor of *The Winnipeg Tribune*: "Gerry," I asked him, "you're considered an intellectual. Why are you associating with this barbarian?"

"Well, several years ago I was a reporter in Ontario and was informed the government was considering legislation related to intoxicated drivers. I interviewed the minister of Highways to inquire about the scope and purpose of the proposed law and he replied something like, 'Well, at times a couple may attend some social event and the man may imbibe too freely of alcoholic beverages and his wife may suggest she drive home, but his male ego is offended and he gets behind the wheel and there is an accident, so we are considering a law to control such situations by perhaps increasing penalties for over-consumption of intoxicants which, while inadvertent, can be damaging.'

"I transferred to Manitoba and learned the government was thinking of a similar legislation so I went to the new minister, Joe Borowski, and asked him his intentions and he replied, 'I'm gonna take da drunks off da road'. Now, THAT I understand."

Borowski's unapologetic partisanship made him a target in the chamber. He was often baited by the opposition and his responses did more to inflame than to inform, causing a colleague to write, "he believed in the mailed fist in the mailed glove."[4]

Discovering some chicanery in the letting of highway contracts under the previous government, he reported to the legislature that he had a helicopter searching for a road paid for by the Department of Highways that had disappeared, implying that the previous government was guilty of fraud.

Burly Walter Weir, former premier and minister of Highways and the new leader of the official opposition, roared a demand for an apology. Speaker 'Gentle' Ben Hanuschak rose and politely suggested the accusation should be withdrawn. But Borowski had developed a demonology about the "capitalist" parties, and he was tenacious to the point of folly. "If I can't tell da trut in dis house," he roared, "den I don't want to sit in dis God-damn house."

He was expelled from the chamber for the day's sitting. Persuaded to issue a partial retraction, which partially mollified the opposition, he returned the following day. But he had embarrassed the members of the legislature.

Ironically, Borowski's very rapport with the media led to his political descent. Flowing from his investigations, several employees of his department were charged with minor offences or fired. One sued the minister, personally, because his pay cheque was delayed. The minister was convicted and the government appealed on his behalf. When a reporter told Borowski, perhaps just to goad him into an intemperate remark, that the judge who convicted him might sit on the panel, he exploded: "If dat bastard hears da appeal he'll be defrocked and debarred."

The judge demanded an apology. Borowski refused and was charged with insulting a judge. The case was heard by Queen's Bench Justice Israel Nitikman and Borowski went to court carrying a small case with toothbrush, shaving kit, shorts and shirts, intending to make his point by going to jail if convicted. But the judge had anticipated him and would not allow him to martyr himself. He imposed a penalty of $1,000 and stated if it was not paid, Borowski's house would be sold and the proceeds used to pay the penalty. Borowski refused, so friends paid the fine. He made his point, but he had embarrassed his caucus colleagues.

Then he embarrassed his leader. Premier Schreyer, as was customary, sent a memo to all departments requesting that public employees be generous in donations to the United Way. Borowski had visited the shrine to Fatima in Portugal and become, in his words, "infested with religion". When told the United Way was contributing to the Mount Carmel Clinic, which was giving money to women having abortions, he sent a peremptory memo to his own department employees countermanding the premier's request. It was a direct challenge to the premier's authority. Twenty-six months after being appointed to cabinet, the unbending Borowski left it. He was a victim of self-righteousness and hubris, but also of inflexible principle for which he was prepared to pay a price. Like Herman Melville's anti-hero, "Ahab is forever Ahab, man."[5]

---

[4] Russel Doern, *Wednesdays are Cabinet Days,* p. 152

[5] Herman Melville, *Moby Dick.*

Nine months later he left the NDP over an issue that became a wrenching experience for the entire province, and Borowski blamed the premier for failing to do the impossible.

Premier Schreyer, to pursue his own philosophical inclinations and to satisfy a commitment to Desjardins, had chosen this time to promote a policy of public funding of private and parochial schools. This was to split the party, divide the caucus, humiliate the premier and almost destroy the government. And it all began so innocently.

When the Province of Manitoba was founded in 1870, education in Canada was in the hands of the church, as it had been since the collapse of the Roman Empire fourteen centuries earlier. The province, constitutionally responsible for education, left it there. In 1874, Ontario established a system of secular, state-funded schools, a policy adopted by Manitoba in 1890.[6] Grants to the churches to provide education were terminated, but private and parochial schools were allowed to continue on condition of voluntary attendance and private funding. For seventy-five years their appeals for money were resisted as Manitoba governments continued to fund only the public school system, which was open to all.

In 1965, the Roblin government agreed to provide bus service for children walking to parochial schools near public schools where the buses were depositing their charges. It seemed the decent thing to do. This led to the request that children from the poor, privately funded schools be allowed to use the library in the public school next door. Supporters of non-public schools, having breached the defences, pressed the attack: if public school buses could pick up children attending one private school, why not all? If public schools could "share services" of libraries, why not laboratories? Indeed, why not provide the same per-student grants to private schools as to public schools and let them run their own system? The government, sympathetic but fearful of public opinion, compromised by sharing public school services with the private schools and providing grants, primarily for textbooks, of about twenty per cent of the amount granted to the public system. But the government had acknowledged that the private school system was entitled to public funding—so if twenty per cent why not 100 per cent?

Premier Schreyer, a nominal but hardly devout Catholic, was viscerally offended by opposition to the funding of non-public schools based on most being "Catholic schools", seeing this as dangerously discriminatory. Religion provided a moral base without which no society can survive and private schools had classroom discipline that was being lost in the public school system. He sought freedom of the human intellect but, like philosopher Erich Fromm,[7] he questioned if "freedom" meant the absence of everything or the presence of something and, like G.K. Chesterton, he feared that those who no longer believed in God—by

---

[6] Supporters of parochial schools appealed to the Privy Council in England, then Canada's final court of appeal and lost, but "the issue of private and parochial schools was raised 80 years ago and has festered ever since." *The Winnipeg Tribune*, May 12, 1971.

[7] *Escape From Freedom*, 1941.

whatever name—would not believe in "nothing", but rather in "anything". He saw churches in secular societies as anchors in a world of shifting values, and alternate power centres in a world in which totalitarianism had a long history.

The classical philosophers had asserted that a totally homogenous state would be a tyranny, so would not a diversity of loyalties vitiate an easy acceptance of dictatorship? If, as English scientific historian and philosopher John E.E. Dahlberg Acton had warned, "absolute power corrupts absolutely", why not have societal structures that prevent concentration of absolute power?

Indeed, Schreyer did not regard this as an issue of religion, but of fairness. He lamented that it was impossible to have a pragmatic debate: "This issue of public funding of private and parochial schools is always clouded by reference to Catholicism, but how can [the bill he had introduced in the legislature] bear on religion when it makes no distinction between denominations?"

Schreyer also believed it was an issue of upbringing. "Many parents feel there is something desirable in the *esprit* and training of the private schools, so why penalize them?"

Economics was also involved in the debate. The non-public system comprised fifty-seven Manitoba schools with 564 teachers, which provided education for some 9,000 students who would otherwise be attending public schools. Since public schools are funded 100 per cent by the public purse, this would cost an additional $5.5 million, so why not reduce the "double taxation" of those financially supporting the private system?

Those opposing Schreyer's position were equally rational. Most also did not regard this an issue of religion but of social unity. Public funding of parochial schools would lead to fragmentation of a society still in its formative stages. The public school system took nothing from anyone and offered publicly funded education to all, while leaving private and parochial schools for those who wanted them. Those donating to the non-public schools were "double taxed" because they chose to be. Per student grants to "poor, religious schools" meant equal funding to rich elitist schools. Fully funded private schools would lure the best and brightest from the public system and promote elitism, and a class society, neither of which was supported by NDP philosophy. And if public funds were given to mainstream religious schools, how could government deny demands from peripheral cults without accusations of "religious discrimination"?

No! They believed the government should maintain the principle, arrived at after two centuries of bloody wars in European history, of separation of church and state. Let the publicly funded education system remain totally secular, allowing children in their formative years to learn the principles of physics and mathematics, while left free to disagree on philosophy and metaphysics.[8] Let logic reign in

---

[8] In 1609, contrary to Catholic church dogma, Galileo concluded that Earth revolved around the sun, not the reverse. Ordered to recant or burn, Galileo, not being the stuff of martyrs, recanted. But Earth continued to move around the sun and four centuries later the pope apologized to the long-dead Italian astronomer.

the school and faith, which many believe satisfies man's need to reach beyond himself, remain in churches. And if the private and parochial schools were able to maintain discipline, let that be adopted by the public school system.

At first the battle was waged at a subterranean level, within the government caucus. Initially only five of its thirty-one members (Schreyer, Desjardins, Borowski, Rev. Donald Malinowski and Jean Allard) supported Schreyer's proposal. However, a premier is not just 'primus inter pares', but also head honcho, numero uno, occupying the position of an autocrat who ultimately controls the direction of the government and the future of those he has appointed to positions of power. That makes his arm long and his whip, no matter how gently applied, felt. One by one his colleagues fell into line.

Sidney Green, minister of Natural Resources and government house leader, emerged as the spokesman for those in opposition. Some saw this as a continuation of the fight for the party leadership that he had lost to Schreyer in 1969, but this was belied when his position was supported by two cabinet titans and normally solid Schreyer supporters, Saul Cherniack and Saul Miller. Devastated by the premier's obduracy, they approached me at the NDP convention in Brandon in late 1971 and asked me to dissuade him from taking the irrevocable step of announcing his position to the convention the following day, when the vast majority of party members were opposed to legislating the funding. They argued that legislation, if defeated, would leave the premier in an untenable position. They were concerned that the outcome might be to hand the party over to Green, who was a fine man, but who thought in Manichean terms of absolute right and wrong and who would deliberately drive down a path because he had the right to do so, even though there was an immovable post in the way.

But I was not the right person to talk to. I could not condone the premier taking a position he knew to be anathema to the party, and believed he must either retreat or pay the price. "Who is running into the post now, Green or Schreyer?" I asked.[9]

But the premier's persuasiveness and rationality, along with the enormous moral authority he had won among his fellows in cabinet, caucus and party, were prevailing. Gradually, by some peculiar metamorphosis, it began to appear that the apostasy was being committed not by the person ignoring party policy to serve a principle, but by the person opposing the apostasy. Green, finding most caucus members agreed with him privately, but would not challenge the premier publicly, felt the sands slipping from beneath him. For both intellectual and political reasons he would not fight the premier from within cabinet, as Borowski had a year earlier. On March 2, 1972, he resigned his portfolio.[10]

---

[9] Convention delegates resolved to leave the premier the freedom to do as he thought best and fervently hoped he would use his power wisely.

[10] Green's note to the premier concluded: "My presence on Executive Council prevents me from properly representing my constituency [on the issue of public aid to private schools]. I accordingly hereby resign from the Executive Council."

The fight then went public. Schreyer and Green debated each other from the same platform at constituency meetings. They dealt with the issue on a high intellectual level and they treated each other with the immense respect born of their regard for each other's intellect and integrity, and of their realization the slightest venture into emotionalism could explode the party. The lines of battle swayed back and forth; party members were torn between supporting their long-held policy as articulated by Green, and their reluctance to humiliate their premier.

My office was inundated with phone calls and letters. Party members either supported Schreyer, or expressed disgust with his defiance of the party's philosophy, or attempted—sometimes poignantly—to understand his position and why he had taken it. Some argued that Schreyer was correcting an injustice against the private and parochial schools that went back to 1890, while others argued the "real injustice" lay in allowing such schools to continue when the public school system was established, and believed they should be abolished.

Many communications from non-party members argued that Canada needed a "state religion", believing two major religions could not coexist within a state, and saw in Catholic Schreyer's position evidence of a popish plot. They cited Ireland as an example of how two religions had spawned endless warring in the bosom of a single state. My response to such letters was that, in Britain, the concept of dual loyalties had been accepted some three centuries earlier, that Catholicism and Protestantism—plus a number of other religions—had coexisted in Canada since its founding, and that the conflict in Ireland had begun in 1164, 350 years before Martin Luther established Protestantism, when England's Henry II accepted the invitation of an Irish chieftain to come and help him fight another Irish chieftain —and had stayed.

But I was facing a personal dilemma. To me the issue was a cluster of ironies and contradictions. Because of government decency in not abolishing the non-public schools, they now claimed funding; those most vociferous in demanding separation of church and state were now also most demanding of public financing of religious schools. They wanted the state to carry their costs of religious education while their churches became bingo parlours. They wanted to control their educational system, but have others pay for it. As a final irony, they were allowed to teach religion only because they were privately funded, so what would be gained by obtaining public funding but losing their *raison d'etre*?

It seemed a replay of the fights for Medicare and Autopac; the private schools, not forced to take the physically handicapped, the slow learners and the social misfits, could operate more economically than the public schools. Soon the surreptitious, insidious and seductive campaign would begin to abandon the public school system and divert funding to a myriad of private schools as a cost-saving measure, thus recreating the conditions of intra-community conflict my parents had left Europe to escape. Finally, the concept of 'dual loyalties', spiritual or political, which led to men being free to worship as they pleased and to join political parties other than the 'Government Party', had been achieved through separation of church and state, which had taken two centuries of warfare to achieve.

Moreover, I was unhappy with the public school system and wanted it improved. It concentrated on elaborate buildings rather than improved minds, becoming a laboratory for experimentation by hippie products of the Sixties and academic theorists of the Seventies, eroding intellectual and pedagogic discipline,[11] and serving the interests of its bureaucracy rather than the students. When Leo Duguay, president of the Manitoba Teacher's Society, came to inform me that, unless the government agreed to a demand concerning what I saw as a peripheral issue,[12] there would be a teachers' strike, I replied, "Please strike so my son can stay home and learn something."

I feared that public funding of non-public schools would draw off not only the best students, but those parents most concerned about education, condemning the public school system to permanent mediocrity.

But most of all, to me public schools were primary socializing agencies in a new society, gradually knitting together disparate elements of race and nationality that had come from the ends of the Earth, to build a new culture and a new national identity through associations in which we bloodied each other's noses but chewed each other's gum, cursed each other's ancestors but married each other's sisters, and built evolving relationships:

> First across the gulf we cast
> Kite-born strings, til lines are passed
> And habit builds the bridge, at last.

And now, just as we were about to secure the bridge to the future, we were wantonly destroying it in deference to the past—to correct another 'historical injustice'. So I went to my boss,

"Mr. Premier. I have a problem. I answer your mail on aid to private schools, but I do not agree with your position and cannot promote it. Perhaps you should appoint someone else to do this."

"How have you been responding to date?"

"I state your position and the opposing position." I handed him a letter I had written. He scanned it, and handed it back.

"Carry on."

---

[11] Twenty years later, when theorists, parents and politicians had introduced into the curriculum AIDs programs, sex education, multi-cultural sensitivity training, drug, alchohol, suicide, anti-racism and anti-sexism counselling, trips to ski resorts, alternative programs for pupils not attending class because their parents were too drunk to waken them or "because I don't like my teacher", and teacher development days, there was little time or money left for what the children had presumably come to school to learn. A scathing U.S. Department of Education report declared the system was graduating children with "no values, no discipline, no goals". *Children at Risk*, 1988.

[12] Teachers who had left the classroom for military service in World War II had been included in the teachers' pension plan, but seven people who enlisted directly from teacher's college were not included. The MTS threatened to strike unless these seven were included.

The premier was losing his fight in the party and with the public, but winning it in the government caucus, whose members would vote in the legislature. They were forced into the agonizing grinder of choosing between publicly punishing their premier or quietly compromising their principles. He was winning by being flexible.

When some argued this was a matter of conscience, he agreed to allow a free vote. When some objected to this being a government bill, he agreed to introduce it as a private member's resolution. When some objected that a resolution to provide funding for non-public schools was too strong a remedy for the ailment and could create a backlash, he scaled it down to a request for a study. With every concession he gained more caucus support.

On June 1st, he tabled his private resolution. It proposed a special committee of the legislature "to study the matter of public financial aid to private and parochial schools". His proposal was so mild that we wiped our sweating brows with relief.

Except Green! He saw Schreyer's apparent retreat as subterfuge. The proposed resolution implicitly accepted the principle of public funding of non-public schools; the legislative committee to be established would be restricted to studying not IF but HOW MUCH funding was to be given to schools based on race or religion. Instead, he argued: "We should be seeking means of enhancing the public schools system in exciting ways that do not encourage division on the basis of race and religion and do not involve financing of particular religions and ideologies."

But the premier had made his last concession. Having extended the carrot, he applied the stick. Like Cortez after his invasion of Mexico, he figuratively burned his ships to end any hope of retreat; his troops now knew they must win or die.

The next day, at a routine Friday morning press conference the premier explained he could accept any proposal to provide a modicum of assured public funding to the non-public schools. The only course NOT acceptable was continuation of the status quo.

Then he dropped his bomb! To a question by Bob Beaton, chairman of the press gallery, about the possibility of resigning if his resolution were to be defeated in the legislature, he replied, "Yes, something must be done and if not, I would regard myself as having failed to do something that is necessary to bring some integrity into the operations of our Schools Act ... My resignation will be effective the day the matter is finally negatived."

The threat swept like wildfire through The Ledge. Those who had come here with the NDP government and would leave with it, were stunned. Suddenly a great black hole seemed to appear where the government had been. Would our political world end thus, not with a bang but with a whimper? Did this mean:

> There would be doubt, hesitation and pain
> Forced praise on our part—the glimmer of twilight
> Never glad, confident morning again?[13]

---

[13] Robert Browning, "Lost Leader", p. 11.

On Saturday afternoon, Sid Green visited my home. We were having lunch, pondering on the premier's statement and on what could have been done differently. We heard a car screech to a halt in the driveway and quick, heavy steps approaching the door. Harry Shafransky, the normally jolly, generous, bear-like, 250-pound NDP member for Radisson and NDP caucus chairman, burst in. Shafransky was a long-time party stalwart, who was often called upon when there was work to do, but seldom when larger decisions were being made. "Why are you two sitting here when Ed might be resigning?" he challenged us.

Green was silent and I was not sympathetic: "He walked into this with his eyes wide open and with plenty of warning about the consequences, so let him find his own way out."

Shafransky, who seldom used profanity in private and never in public, exploded: "You stupid, irresponsible bastard! This is our premier we are talking about. The only one we have ever had. He is also your brother-in-law. He is in trouble because of a responsibility he assumed, rightly or wrongly, and you owe him your sympathy and help. We worked too hard to become the government to lose it by default. Do something before its too late, for Christ's sake."

He dashed out to continue his campaign with "The Two Sauls". Cherniack and Miller had a long talk with their premier, who was also their friend, telling him he had a responsibility to the thousands who had given him their loyalty and their votes. This responsibility superceded whatever private obligations he might believe he had to other individuals or to himself, they told him; he had done all he could to fulfill those obligations and no one could ask more, but his resignation would spell the end of the first social democratic government in Manitoba. Finally, they said, he had no right to quit over what most would see as no more than a bruised ego.

On Monday, at a raucous noon meeting, the caucus members told their premier they did not appreciate him using a threat of resignation to whip them into line. Later that day he attended a press conference. Even his legendary self-control could not hide his agony as he explained in a tortured monotone, in response to questions, that, yes, he was withdrawing his threat to resign:

"I was reacting viscerally. I should not express my personal feelings in this way and I apologize to those who regarded that statement as intending to threaten their right to exercise independent judgement on the vote on the resolution."

He had come to terms with the issue, but there was a price to pay, not to the caucus whose members were emotionally exhausted, nor to party members who were relieved to have the paroxysm over, nor to the media personnel who were strangely sympathetic to this young man who had come so far so fast but had been prepared to sacrifice his future on the altar of a principle, but to himself.

His hands, which he attempted to keep hidden during the press conference, were black with blisters. He'd spent an agonizing weekend allowing his frustration to flow out of him through the handle of a spade. Like Voltaire's Candide, he had sought solace by digging in his garden. The pain of the blisters incurred in this self-flagellation must have been fierce. But he had made his peace with himself. The Angel of Death had passed over us. And we had our premier back.[14]

It was the last bill voted on before prorogation. The legislature sat past the witching hour. The tension was palpable. About 3 A.M. I climbed stiffly down the steep stairs from the visitor's gallery and entered the washroom in the members' lounge—just as Industry and Commerce Minister Len Evans was coming out. He was ghost white and visibly shaking. "Len. Are you ill?"

"No-o-o." He staggered against the wall and stammered, "I just had the most terrifying experience. I was at the urinal ... when the premier came in and stood beside me. I made the mistake of asking how things were going ... and he said, "All ministers except that bastard, Doern, will support me."[15]

"So I had to inform him ... I'm also vot-t-t-ing against him."

So did three other ministers and eight NDP backbenchers. Borowski, sitting as an Independent, who desperately wanted public aid to religious schools, voted against Schreyer's bill because it called only for a study, not for funding. But the decisive votes lay elsewhere. Liberals, Independents Beard and Allard, and Social Crediter Jake Froese, all supported Schreyer's resolution. But the PCs abandoned a long-held position to make a political kill; having found the premier's Achilles heel, they decided to destroy him.[16] All the PCs except Gabe Girard, MLA for Emerson, voted against the resolution. Their votes, added to those of the NDP defectors, formed a majority.

At 5:10 on the morning of Thursday, July 20, 1972, after the legislature had sat for fifteen hours, the longest sitting in twenty-two years and the last act in the longest legislative session in Manitoba's history, Schreyer's resolution was defeated, 30 to 22.[17] Then the lieutenant governor prorogued the legislature.

Four hours later, after the long and traumatic night, we were back at work, too physically and emotionally exhausted to concentrate. But the premier had two more jobs to do. At his post-session press conference he summarized the work done during the long and arduous session. On the issue that had exercised the

---

[14] Green, told of the withdrawal of the resignation threat, said, "I am very happy." Opposition leader Sid Spivak said, "The premier is the author of his own distress." The *Winnipeg Free Press* editorialized that in dredging up what had bedevilled Manitobans for ninety years, Schreyer "has done the province no service."

[15] Doern was the only cabinet minister to speak against Schreyer's resolution in the legislature. *Hansard*, July 15, 1972.

[16] After the defeat of the Schreyer government in October 1977, the Conservative governments of Sterling Lyon (1977-81) and Gary Filmon (1988-99) steadily increased funding to non-public schools. By 1995, the per pupil grants were sixty-eight per cent of public school grants, while grants to public schools were reduced to 1992 levels and frozen. (*Winnipeg Free Press*, September 7, 1995). Non public schools thrived while the public school system became "child centred"—a euphemism for letting kids do as they pleased as long as they did not disturb the teachers, or the parents. In some provinces, desperate parents turned to "back-to-basics" publicly funded, parent administered charter schools.

[17] Yeas: Jean Allard, Israel Asper, Leonard Barkman, Gordon Beard, Bud Boyce, Peter Burtniak, Saul Miller, Saul Cherniack, Laurent Desjardins, Jake Froese, Gabe Girard, John Gottfried, Ben Hasuschak, Ron McBryde, Al Mackling, Rev. Donald Malinowski, Steve Patrick, Russ Paulley, René Toupin, Ian Turnbull, Edward Schreyer, Harry Shafransky.

caucus, the party and the legislature, engaged the emotions of Manitobans for the past eight months, and almost toppled him from the apex of government, he spoke more in sorrow than anger and with the clear recognition that some social problems do not easily lend themselves to political solutions: "I feel that I have done all I can. Perhaps at some future date some other leader will be able to resolve this issue."

Then, despite some caucus opposition, in an act that showed the measure of the man, he reappointed Green to cabinet as minister of Mines, Resources and Environmental Management, minister of Urban Affairs, minister for the Manitoba Development Corporation, chairman of the cabinet subcommittee on resources and economic development, and Government House Leader.

And then we all went back to operating a government.

---

[17] (Con't.) Nays: (the names of NDP members voting negative are in italics) *Pete Adam, Tom Barrow,* David Blake, James Bilton, *Joe Borowski,* Donald Craik, *Russell Doern,* Henry Einarson, Harry Enns, *Leonard Evans,* James Ferguson, *Cy Gonick,* Harry Graham, *Sid Green, Bill Jenkins,* George Henderson, *Wally Johannson,* Frank Johnston, Wally Jorgenson, Morris McGregor, Earl McKellar, Wally McKenzie, Arthur Moug, *Howard Pawley,* Bud Sherman, Sidney Spivak, Inez Trueman, *Sam Uskiw, Billie Uruski, James Walding.* Toupin reversed his initial opposition because Schreyer's resolution called for a study, not for funding; Borowski reversed his initial support because the resolution did not call for funding. Absent were one NDP member (Phillip Petursson), two PCs (Ed McGill and Doug Watt) and one Liberal, Gordon Johnson.

Premier Schreyer, at left, along with Saskatchewan Premier Allan Blakeney, long-time federal MP Stanley Knowles, and British Columbia Premier Dave Barrett, attended the NDP Convention in July 1975.

XII

The Quick and the Dead

Taken all for all, he was a man.
　　　　　　　　—Shakespeare, *Hamlet*

"**T**he mayor is dead," the commentator intoned sepulchrally. No name was needed. For Winnipeggers, fifteen years after leaving office, there was still only one "once and future" mayor—Stephen Juba.

Thirty-seven years earlier he, a North End Catholic and son of Ukrainian immigrants, had shocked the Anglo-Saxon establishment by becoming Winnipeg's first non-Anglo-Saxon mayor. For the next twenty-one years, in the words of Ted Byfield, then a *Winnipeg Free Press* reporter who had helped plan that campaign, Juba was "an endless source of fascinating, outrageous, preposterous news stories [and] he made such delightful copy."[1] It ended on May 2, 1993, when at seventy-eight, he died peacefully among his beloved birds at his cottage at Petersfield, a tiny village thirty miles north of Winnipeg.

But from 1956 to 1977 he had given Winnipeg colour and identity. He had "made such delightful copy", which was his not-so-secret weapon, and made his a household name and, in 1986, the first name on Manitoba's Citizens Hall of Fame.

Newspaper headlines were adulatory: "Winnipeg Loses a Legend",[2] "A Winnipeg Original."[3] Juba was a man of vision, action, native intelligence and political adroitness. Former *Winnipeg Tribune* editor Eric Wells, who ran against him in 1968, commended his opponent: "Juba revitalized this bloody town: he

---

[1]　*Winnipeg Free Press*, May 5, 1993.
[2]　*Ibid.*, May 3, 1993.
[3]　*Ibid.*, May 4, 1993.

gave backbone to civic affairs."⁴ Ted Byfield wrote: "He made Winnipeg live as no one had before nor probably will again. He incarnated the sense of brawling adventure and raw fun that this great old city holds, both in the hearts of those who live here, or who have left it behind."⁵

His best epitaph may have been his own humorous reference, at an international mayors' conference, to the way mayors are addressed in various cities: "In Los Angeles they Honor the mayor; in Winnipeg they Worship him." He was also a ruthless gutter-fighter, his other not-so-secret weapon, which made his personna the source of fascination for two generations.

Steve Juba's reputation may be modified in the long perspective of history —one observer noted he had an insatiable wish to see his name on cornerstones and television, yet much of what he did cost the taxpayers. But he was a populist attuned to the temper of the times and had the courage to do things, which made him an icon. He also had an instinct for the unusual which made him, and his city, known throughout North America.

"Mayor Steve" first appeared in the political firmament as a member of the Manitoba Legislature in 1953 and remained until 1959. He knew the value of being 'different', sitting as an Independent, and he remained a maverick as mayor by identifying with neither the councillors nominated by the business-dominated Winnipeg Election Committee (later Independent Citizens Election Committee), which had governed Winnipeg since the General Strike in 1919, nor with the left-leaning representatives of labour and the CCF who aspired to do so. And he knew how to attract attention by using the media—a news photo on election night showed defeated Mayor George Edward Sharpe looking at Juba, and Juba looking into the camera.

More than a decade later, the inimitable Joseph Borowski displayed the same talents and briefly played a similar meteoric role in the political life of Manitoba, but Juba sustained it for three decades because he was something Borowski was not—an actor.

He found his true role in 1956 when, while still an MLA, he was elected mayor. This sent a shock wave of Richter scale magnitude through 'upper crust' and 'old money' Winnipeg—similar to the fear of the 'socialist hordes' elected to government in 1969—and a thrill of ecstasy through the 'marginalized' North End, but Juba was soon generally accepted. A decade after the end of World War II Winnipeggers were ready for a new—and naughty—idea, and Juba had won with virtually a one-plank platform—liberalized drinking.

In both his public and private lives, what he touched seemed to turn to gold. His campaign to legalize alcoholic beverages in restaurants shocked social conservatives, religious fundamentalists and old ladies in tennis shoes. But it led to the development of a mature attitude to "demon rum"; to restaurants of every size,

⁴ Paul Grescoe, *The Winnipeg Tribune*, August 13, 1977.
⁵ *Winnipeg Free Press*, August 5, 1993.

decor and appeal, and to some of the best dining in Canada.

He did not come to office as a philosopher; he was quite unlike the arms-maker's dilettante son in G.B. Shaw's *Major Barbara*, who knew nothing but the difference between right and wrong and was therefore suited to be a politician. He quit school at age fifteen to work when his father's business failed in the 1929 market crash. In 1945, he established a hardware business and hard work and the post-war boom made him a millionaire. North Enders never forgot that, when Juba became mayor, he disposed of the city-issue car and chauffeur and drove himself around in a plum-coloured Cadillac—his own.

His election as mayor electorally and socially enfranchised a sector of the population of the city and he never forgot his roots nor lost the common touch. At his death, Premier Gary Filmon, a former city councillor, remarked: "He had that magic quality that made people feel they had the ear of council. You could phone Steve and know he would call back." Former Governor General Schreyer who, as Premier of Manitoba, had felt the lash of Juba's publicity-seeking tongue, referred to his contribution: "He encouraged people to identify with civic democracy."

His business ventures had honed his natural instincts for salesmanship. The trunk of his car was filled with baubles and trinkets—always with the city crest and his name on them—which promoted him while identifying with the city. In 1974, Winnipeg's centenary, he gave away thousands of simulated leather diaries bearing the city's crest. Midway down were the words: Mid-Canada's Convention City, and in between, in eye-catching script: Stephen Juba—Mayor. Like presidential candidate Wendell Wilkie, he knew "a good catchword obscures analysis for years" and that a planted rumour was good twice—when initiated and again when denied. During his race for the mayor's chair, he recklessly tossed out the accusation that aldermen were junketing out to Pointe du Bois at the expense of city hydro. Since the city owned the plant that supplied it with electricity, that could hardly be classed as venal, but the uninitiated were scandalized and it got him reams of free publicity—and votes. He harvested more of both by contemptuously dismissing Mayor Sharpe as a "trained seal".[6]

His gift for the dramatic helped him get things done and his identification with the city and its populace was so complete he came to personify the city's Motto: *Unum cum virtute multorum* (One with the strength of many). An early triumph was to get a new city hall in 1962 by turning the old one into a joke. Calling it the "Gingerbread House", he made a sport of conducting guided tours through the vintage structure. Pan Am Pool on Grant Avenue is a permanent monument to his skill and flair in bringing the Pan-American Games to Winnipeg for the first time in 1967.[7]

---

[6] His talent for quotable quotes never faded. A decade after vacating the mayor's chair, when Québec was awarded the billion-dollar CF-18 contract after Manitoba had tendered a superior bid on both cost and technical merit, Juba quipped: "The only way for Manitoba to win a contract is to declare independence and call a referendum."

[7] They returned in 1999, thanks in part to the talents of another mayor with a talent for publicity, Susan Thompson.

He brought giant developer, Trizec, to Winnipeg to metamorphose an entire city block at Portage and Main, Western Canada's most famous intersection. He initiated construction of the Convention Centre, which lured Holiday Inn to Winnipeg. He left a city with office and residential towers reaching for the sky like medieval church spires in Europe.

He knew how to play the fool without being one, and was always completely in charge. He drove out to Wolseley Avenue to stop a city works crew from cutting down an old elm that was an obstruction to street development after local women were featured in the newspapers with their arms linked around the landmark tree. He donned a Mexican sombrero, mounted a horse, and rode around strumming a guitar to promote the St. Boniface Fiesta in 1972. His proposed "bubble-top" plastic dome, which would protect a huge area of the city from the savagery of the elements, seemed a bit space age, as was his obsession with building a monorail— an ambition he did not fulfill—but time may prove him wiser than we knew.

In 1973, while in Germany, I attended a demonstration at Wuppertahl, site of the world's first operating monorail. I recommended to the Government of Manitoba that, despite Juba's urging, we not consider building one because of the construction cost of $4 million per mile. Today it would cost that just to do a feasibility study of such a project, and I curse myself for that recommendation whenever I'm seeking a downtown parking spot.

Juba's political modus operandi was to identify an enemy—or create one— attack that enemy in the interests of some real or feigned threat to "My City", appeal to the public, proclaim victory, and then let the media make him a hero—yet again. He seemed to have swallowed 'Peter's Placebo': "An ounce of image is worth a pound of performance", and his self-induced, highly publicized fights sometimes resembled Jonathan Swift's wars between the "Big and Little Endians".

At times his choice of enemy was his own council and once, informed by a reporter that his policy committee—of which he was chairman—had voiced some criticism of him, he retorted "they can just go to hell". He did not always attend council meetings, but he was always in the chair when the finance committee presented the proposed budget. Invariably, the committee had sweated and strained for months to get it just right, and it would be read while Steve sat silently—it was rumoured he turned on his hearing aid only when HE was speaking. When the reading was completed, he would explode: "How can you do this?. You can't tax my people this way. Take it back and do it right."

And the chastised committee would slink back to the drawing board while "Mayor Steve" accepted the consequent accolades. When the Government of Manitoba created the Metropolitan Corporation of Greater Winnipeg (Metro Winnipeg), it automatically presented Juba with a new 'enemy' and his attacks upon it made the Welkin ring.

A phenomenon of post-war Canada was urban growth. Farmers, adopting new technology with a speed that suggested they were avenging themselves upon Nature for the millennia of drudgery their forebears had endured, revolutionized rural Canada in a generation. They became so productive that it required fewer to produce more than could have been imagined by dour Reverend Malthus 150 years earlier. Those made surplus in the rural community relocated to urban areas. This stream of humanity was enlarged to a deluge by rural families seeking a university education for their children—an aspiration long reserved for the children of doctors and lawyers. These young men and women, seeking escape from darkest Manitoba, much of which did not have electricity until the 1950s, for the bright lights of the city, were joined by underemployed persons in rural villages seeking work in burgeoning urban industries and thousands of veterans who were not about to return "to the farm after they've seen Paree", as Irving Berlin put it.

The population of Winnipeg and its environs doubled in the two decades after 1945. The city expanded like an octopus as towns with distinct identities and administrations became satellites. Magnified by local jealousies, this uncoordinated growth was heading toward a condition of incipient chaos. Streets and bridges were built leading to nowhere, taxes and services varied with each municipality, urban expansion had no defined limits and municipalities spread indiscriminately, leaving huge gaps of undeveloped land between them. The stage was set for that bane of developing population concentrations—urban sprawl.

In 1960, the Progressive Conservative government of Premier Duff Roblin sought to impose order upon, and give direction to, the metropolitan area that comprised thirteen municipalities with separate administrations and tax lists. Metro Winnipeg, their creation to consider the Big Picture, established a two-tiered system of urban government, with local affairs in local hands and overall planning of shared services —regional sewer and water trunks, parks, transit corridors, bridges among them —under the central authority. This was to be the essential instrument for directing future development and providing greater equity of taxation and services throughout member municipalities.

Juba saw all this as an attack on his city—and himself—by reducing his power. His fights with the urbane R.B. Bonnycastle, first chairman of 'Metro', became the stuff of legend. Metro successes were gained only by following Juba's prescription. At one point, the usually polite Bonnycastle, with Juba on the platform, publicly despaired: "Militating against a good Metro public image is the mayor of our city who has ... lost no opportunity to condemn it."[8]

In 1971, Juba scored his greatest triumph. By 1969, his attacks had reduced the Metro council to virtual paralysis, and the election of Ed Schreyer's NDP government introduced a new philosophy of urban development and decision making. Things had changed rapidly; the new middle class was moving from central Winnipeg to the quieter suburbs; satellite municipalities were offering cheap land and low taxes to businesses relocating. People and industry were sucked out of central Winnipeg, threatening to make it a slum, and taxation levels in contiguous jurisdictions were becoming increasingly unequal. Juba saw the evolving pattern

[8] *Winnipeg Free Press*, October 1, 1963.

and agitated for a single unified city. The Schreyer government agreed and enacted the City of Winnipeg Act.

The provincial government wanted a city council to replace the individuals loosely packaged as the Independent Citizen's Election Committee that governed Winnipeg with no program or platform, with a structure that forced an identifiable group to take responsibility for its decisions. It envisioned a parliamentary form with the fifty councillors elected in wards and the mayor chosen by them, ensuring that the mayor would speak for the council. Juba's relations with some councillors, whom he held in contempt, precluded his election as mayor by them. Besides, moved by ego and perception of the type of administration needed, he wanted to speak for the city, not just the council. He lobbied hard for a presidential-style mayor, who would be elected on a citywide basis.

The province, concluding that a new council elected from the old municipalities would be too ward-oriented, accepted the need for the unifying influence of a popularly elected mayor. Juba displayed his talent for publicity by choosing the sod-turning ceremony for the new Convention Centre to announce his candidacy for mayor of the new "unicity". And Steve Juba was elected Canada's first "super-mayor".

The Government of Manitoba had put enormous power into the hands of a politician who had never read Machiavelli, but knew his precepts intuitively. Juba ranked his 'territorial imperative' high, much like a wolf who marks his boundaries with his urine and then defends the territory within, and he attacked anyone who represented a real or manufactured threat to his power or domain. After 1969, he should have seen, and attacked, his natural enemy—Premier Schreyer. However, he was constrained by a problem he instinctively understood: Juba represented the breaking down of social barriers —but so did Schreyer. Juba's natural constituency was Winnipeg's ethnically diverse North End, but so was Schreyer's. Juba spoke several languages, but so did Schreyer. Juba drove his own car, but so did Schreyer. Juba was recognized as a populist, but so was Schreyer; Juba was an anti-establishment figure, but so was Schreyer; Juba had the image of being 'different', but so did Schreyer. In short, Schreyer represented a potent threat, but he was no easy target, for by attacking him Juba risked offending his own primary constituency. So he kept probing; there must be an Achilles heel. He demanded more money from the province and threatened to run against the NDP in the next election if he did not get it. When the province offered to reduce city costs by taking over its parks and health and welfare services, Juba charged it with stealing his property. When the government offered to let the city collect a share of growth (income, gasoline, tobacco) taxes, he demanded the province collect the taxes and give the proceeds to the city.

He briefly found an 'enemy' in the City of Winnipeg Act. At a meeting with the provincial government's urban affairs committee, he threw a copy of the act, which had attained epic proportions, on the table and stated loudly: "This is a terrible act. It should be reduced to four pages." Acting Urban Affairs Minister

Sidney Green immediately responded, "We agree. Just say which four pages you want." There was a thunderous silence from the mayor.

Then the 'enemy' became a paragraph in the act. Part of Winnipeg was served by its own city hydro and the balance, as well as the adjacent municipalities, by Manitoba Hydro. Winnipeg Hydro, which brought power from plants built many years earlier on the Winnipeg River, had lower rates than Manitoba Hydro. On amalgamation these were synchronized, requiring the city hydro to increase its rates to match those of the provincial utility. Juba had won publicity for supporting the amalgamation, but soon sought more by demanding independent rate setting for Winnipeg Hydro.

It was a typical "Juba-tactic": rate synchronization had given the City of Winnipeg windfall revenue of more than $15 million a year without raising taxes, but Juba needed an enemy. I suggested to the premier that we let him reduce his rates to get him off our backs, then wait for the city hydro's plants, one of which was sixty years old, to become obsolescent, and then tell Juba to go to hell when he came to us for money to rebuild them. The premier responded that we could not be that irresponsible, so I lost that argument to Juba.[9]

I lost to Juba again in September 1974, when agrochemical producer Ciba-Geigy opened its new plant in Transcona. Invited to represent the government, I planted a tree and told them warmly, "The Government of Manitoba knows how to welcome new industry." I was enjoying the plaudits of the crowd when Juba, who had also been invited, shouted, "And you know how to tax them too."

Juba's obsessive quest for dragons to slay ultimately paid off. He found in Russell Doern the 'enemy' he needed to maintain his 'hero' status. He was able to claim victory, and approving newspaper headlines across Canada, following his encounters with Doern not because he was right but because he made such delightful copy. The confrontations left Doern reduced in the eyes of the public and diminished in his own.

Among its initiatives, the Roblin government had rerouted Osborne Street and built a broad esplanade from the corner of Portage Avenue directly to the front of the Legislative Building, creating Memorial Park. Rather like the Champs Elysees as it approaches the Arc de Triomphe, the new boulevard had a broad expanse of manicured grass, benches where weary civil servants could revel in the Manitoba summers, and fountains with lights that emblazoned patterns on the blue-black northern sky at night.

By 1972, the esplanade had also become a hangout for hippies, homosexuals, hookers, drug pushers and anyone needing relief, bladder, bowel or sexual. Memorial Park was owned by the province and the government was deluged with

---

9 For twenty-five years, Juba and his successors boasted that Winnipeg Hydro was more efficient than Manitoba Hydro, and spent the $15-million plus annual windfall on tax reductions rather than plant maintenance. That ended in 2002, when Mayor Glen Murray announced that Winnipeg Hydro needed $232 million in new money to restore its aging power plants and then sold the facility to Manitoba Hydro.

complaints from those who frequented the park, or resided nearby or operated a business in the area. They all demanded that if we could not stop people from urinating, defecating or fornicating in the park, we should build a structure where they would be less exposed while doing so.

Russell Doern, minister of Public Works, was instructed to build "The Biffy" in Memorial Park. His department chose the location, drew up the architectural plans, applied to the City of Winnipeg for a building permit, hired a contractor and built a structure moulded so well into its environment that some Winnipeggers still do not seem to know it exists.[10] Technically the province did not need a building permit from one of its municipalities, but applied as a courtesy and, assuming it merely a formality, commenced construction. It proved to be a fateful miscalculation that was to rob Doern of the respect he craved, for it provided Juba with the 'enemy' he sought in the Schreyer government.

Juba struck like a shark. Former Manitoba CCF leader and alderman Lloyd Stinson wrote of him: "He pursues political opponents with the dedication of a bereaved relative in a Corsican vendetta,"[11] and that characteristic now surfaced. The city commissioner for the environment found no fault with the application, but three[12] of the five members of the environment committee opposed it, which Juba gleefully publicized. The dutiful media, eager for material to help peddle papers, were called into his service. Doern was charged with sacrilege. He was building a piss-house in a park dedicated to veterans and—*lese majesté*—he had insulted the sovereign City of Winnipeg. There was no need to check whether Doern needed the city's permission; it was enough that Juba said so.

Doern was a convenient target and was savaged. Juba spent $50 to rent a two-hole portable biffy (with building permit attached) and, followed by the fawning paparazzi, had it trucked to the front entrance of the Legislative Building. It was labelled:

THE DESERVING OFFICE OF HON. RUSS DOERN
PROPOSED BY MAYOR STEPHEN JUBA

A photo of the biffy flashed across Canada and within hours Doern became the object of national ridicule in print and on the electronic media.[13]

Not long after, the shark struck again. Having identified an enemy and hanged him, Juba proceeded, figuratively, to draw and quarter him and mount his severed head on a pike. In mid-December, a man drove his car onto a dormant flower bed on the legislative grounds. He was admonished by a commissionaire

---

[10] Twenty-six years later, columnist Bruce Cherney wrote that Juba halted construction on the structure. *The Real Estate News*, Winnipeg, October 9, 1999.

[11] Political Warriors, *Recollections of a Social Democrat*, p. 286.

[12] Phil Rizzuto, June Westbury and Robert Wilson. All ran against the NDP in the 1973 election and all were defeated.

[13] In 1999, the photo was still being published in newspapers.

and, perhaps wishing to protest, walked into the building, brushed past the secretary and entered the premier's private office. Finding the premier absent, the man entered cabinet clerk Derek Bedson's office, pulled a knife from his pocket, and slashed the prized Van Dyke portrait of an idealized King Charles I. He then walked down the corridor into the NDP caucus room, picked up a decorated Christmas tree and hurled it across the huge caucus table. Then he sauntered nonchalantly down the grand staircase, picked up a giant pot of poinsettias and dropped it to smash on the floor. Crossing to the other side of the staircase, he smashed the matching pot of poinsettias, and then casually walked past the astounded commissionaires and out the front door.

One commissionaire gave chase, caught the angry culprit on the Midtown Bridge and grappled with him, but the man escaped and disappeared. Another commissionaire phoned the city police. They arrived forty-five minutes later. A subsequent check showed that the constables had received the call in their patrol car, but had decided to have lunch before responding to it.

The following day Doern, the minister responsible for security in the building, explained details of the incident to enquiring reporters and casually remarked that it appeared the police took a long time to arrive at the scene. When this was reported, Juba went into orbit. In the newspapers and on the television screen "Mayor Steve" furiously attacked Doern for having insulted Winnipeg's finest. No one would be allowed to attack "his" police force with impunity.

Once again Doern was humiliated and again Juba, by deliberately creating an incident out of airy nothing, had destroyed an 'enemy' and emerged a hero.

It was bit much. I borrowed some stationery with the Department of Public Works letterhead, and typed a letter:

Dear Mayor Juba,

Several days ago an interloper did damage in the Legislative Building. City of Winnipeg police were called but took some 45 minutes to respond because they decided to have lunch first.

Several years ago, while feeding the birds at your cottage at Petersfield, you suffered a heart attack. Your wife phoned the city and an ambulance, escorted by police cars with sirens screaming, rushed to take you to the hospital.

Please check the record to see if your police, after receiving the distress call, decided to have lunch before picking you up.

Yours very truly,
Russell Doern
Minister of Public Works

I took the letter to Doern and laid it on his desk: "Russ, it's time to toast your tormentor (Doern always appreciated alliteration). This bastard has been getting away with political murder for years and you have now been given the opportunity to skewer him and simultaneously avenge yourself. I have prepared a letter for you. Read it and sign it."

He read the letter, paused, read it again with no flicker of expression on his face. He slowly picked up his pen—the one with the large fibre point that wrote in angry black ink—lowered it toward the paper, hesitated a moment, and looked away, through the door and down the long corridor past the office doors of the political colleagues with whom he must work and out into the world in which he must live, and laid down his pen.

The 'Battle of the Biffy' had taken its toll. He feared this was a fight he would lose, followed by more public ridicule. Challenging Juba to a public duel was like Pier Gynt fighting the formless Boig, who was everywhere and nowhere. And Doern had a character trait not always of advantage to one engaged in the cut and thrust of the political arena; whatever else he was or saw himself to be, he was essentially a decent man with no sense of malice and no desire to seek trouble when he could avoid it.

Russell Doern had no taste for the jugular.

JUBA COULD BE CONNIVING and vindictive. How it affected his judgement as chief magistrate must be left to history—and personal opinion—but what he wanted he got, no matter what the means. He reportedly kept secret files on fellow councillors and used the threat of making these public, in order to keep them "moral", particularly with respect to what he considered their obligations to the public … and to him. In 1977, when he had already privately determined to not run again, he decided to perform one more civic duty, to ensure that he would not be succeeded by Deputy Mayor Bernie Wolfe, who had announced he would not run if Juba did. With the media in tow, Juba placed his name in nomination. Then, quietly and alone, he sneaked back and withdrew his name, just minutes before the deadline and too late for Wolfe to register himself for nomination. It was a typical 'Juba-antic' but applauded by the media. He was 'Mayor Steve" and "he made such delightful copy".

I knew Steve Juba as a shadowy figure: his gaunt physiognomy with the large protruding ears and bulbous nose pictured in newspapers or on television as he made another attack on the government, or his lean six-foot frame haunting the Legislative Building like Banquo's ghost, seeking concessions. Whenever I noticed in the premier's diary that he had an appointment with Juba, or saw him flitting in or out of the premier's office, I ground my teeth involuntarily, for I knew it was no social visit. He always wanted something—a bridge, building code changes, provincial cost-sharing of some project, larger grants from the province, a share of growth taxes—and that he always had logical arguments for what he wanted, which invariably would cost the government money.

I always sensed he would milch us and discard us—but he fooled me. In a book about Schreyer, he wrote a laudatory foreword: "Edward Schreyer has made an outstanding contribution to Winnipeg, Manitoba and Canada ... During my political career ... as MLA and as Mayor of Winnipeg, I can think of no other political figure who has left such a lasting impression." [14]

Then he created a state of euphoria in the NDP. During the 1977 provincial election campaign, Juba appeared with Schreyer at a photo session, signed his nomination papers, mainstreeted with him locally, and fulsomely praised him: "I think the world of him. I've always found him liberal-headed and understanding." [15]

In the end, however, he confirmed my intuition by reverting to type. The day after the Schreyer government was defeated, there was Steve Juba in his Tory blue suit, telling the television audience: "It was time these guys were defeated. They were spending money like drunken sailors." And I bitterly recalled how we could have spent less money, and charged less taxes, and got more votes, by giving less to the city. But Juba knew how to play to the winners.

He also knew how to play to the gallery. I would see him at community or ethnic social functions, sipping a glass of milk, the recipient of hearty hand-shakes, whispered confidences, and the cynosure of admiring eyes, leaving as soon as it was polite to do so ... unless he had something specific in mind.

Such was the case one velvet-soft summer evening at the local yacht club. The premier had agreed to attend some function there but had been detained in Ottawa, so my wife and I were drafted to substitute. We spent an enjoyable several hours with cocktails and canapés, wandering through grounds to die for along the Red River, being introduced to persons of substance, being taken on guided tours of yachts with diesel engines large enough to propel destroyers.

I noticed Juba energetically pumping a group of a dozen persons in a corner of a room. Finally one detached himself, came over, and introduced himself: "I am a lawyer and represent a group of investors who want to build a shopping mall at the west end of the city (it became Unicity Mall). We have the money and are ready to go but we cannot get our project approved by your RAG (Resident Advisory Group). They are impossible people and unless we see some movement soon we may just take our money and go to Alberta. Why don't you just abolish your RAGs?"

Resident advisory groups were an outgrowth of the 1971 city amalgamation. [16] Each of the thirteen former municipalities, now a part of Unicity, was left with a community committee made up of the elected councillors from that

---

[14] Ed Schreyer: *A Social Democrat in Power*, Paul Beaulieu (ed.)

[15] *East Kildonan Examiner*, October 5, 1977.

[16] Twenty-five years later, the RAGs were considered ineffective, as few were taking the time to serve on them and the 1997 city-commissioned study, *Winnipeg: A Corporate Review* (also called the Cuff Report) proposed they be abolished. At the same time, Unicity Mall was being closed and demolished. Perhaps the RAG had reasoned better than anyone knew.

municipality and a resident advisory group, in place of its former council. The RAGs were concessions to the principle of citizen participation and were intended to provide advice to the regional councillors. With no formal structure, operating guidelines or money, they had little power to propose but, by arousing the public, they did have considerable power to oppose, and exercised it frequently.

With no mature system of election, members of the RAGs were largely self-selected and some had personal agendas less concerned with building a city economy than with conducting social experiments they had read about in the books which, during the 1960s and 1970s, tumbled off the printing presses like water off the Niagara precipice. They represented power without responsibility and a hurdle to be surmounted by those claiming to be imbued with the larger perspective. Understandably, their desire to protect the character of their communities was seen as a time wasting obstruction by prospective developers of shopping malls and the like, and sometimes by the city and the provincial government.

"A group of us were speaking with Mayor Juba and he says if he had the authority to abolish the RAGs he would do so but he does not have that authority and you do," the lawyer added.

An interesting proposition! The RAGs might be a pain in the posterior to developers and higher levels of government; in fact, I was not impressed with them either and considered them dilettantish, but Juba knew better than most that, politically, they could not be abolished and any government doing so would be eaten alive.

Communities would most certainly circle their wagons to protect local representation; RAG members would fight to the death to maintain their status; the media would crucify the government for "destroying the last vestiges of democracy"; Bud Sherman, Conservative MLA for Fort Garry, would dredge up superlatives from his extensive vocabulary to make another speech in the legislature about this action presaging "the muffled cadence of jackboots". And "Mayor Steve" would suddenly be on the side of the angels, defending the RAGs against the provincial bully.

The ploy was clear. The Machiavellian manipulator was at it again. Juba was practising his adroit intrigue: ingratiating himself with another interest group; setting up another simulated enemy that he could then kick to death in the arena to the roar of the approving crowd. The clever bastard! I had an inspiration: "Okay," I told the lawyer. "Let's do it. Tell Steve if he will propose publicly that the RAGs be abolished, we will legislate them out of existence."

The lawyer smiled broadly, thanked me profusely, turned on his heel, went back to the group, pulled Juba aside, had a brief, animated discussion. Then he returned, dejected: "Steve won't do it!"

Of course not! Juba was too smart to fall for such a sucker punch. I had outfoxed him. But I knew by the way he glared at me across the room that I had made a mortal enemy. So had Doern.

Russell Doern was a man out of his time and place. Raised in Winnipeg's

North End, in a modest home (his father did not own a car until age sixty and rode to work on a bicycle), he did not present the image of the archetypal North End working man. He was tall, athletic, handsome, blond, debonair, suave, impeccably dressed, immaculately coifed, and on social or ceremonial occasions always accompanied by some slim, long-legged, beautiful young woman. The term 'cherchez-la-femme' appeared to have been coined for him and when he and his consort entered a room, heads turned, or when they sauntered down the corridor of the Legislative Building, office doors opened and they were followed by envious, lascivious male eyes and convulsions of penis envy.

He was invariably quiet spoken, never displayed anger, seldom used vulgarity—except an overused four-letter word. He was always courteous to and respectful of his colleagues, had a Chestertonian sense of humour, and could be a master of understatement. Meticulously preparing for his death in 1987, he left his former wife a handwritten note beginning laconically: "Well, I guess this is it …"

He had a talent for droll wit. Told of a near-tragedy in which a farmer had his Mary Maxim sweater caught in a tractor power takeoff shaft and would have strangled had not the collar torn, he quipped, "Saved by a thread." During a report to cabinet that the price of baling twine had increased because some manufacturers had cornered the market, he remarked, "They have the twine all tied up." Noting some graffiti on the wall of a toilet cubicle at the Convention Centre: "My mother made me a homosexual," he wrote under it: "If I buy her the wool will she make me one too?" When City Councillor Ken Wong, a Chinese Canadian, left the Conservative party, Doern quipped, "This shows the chink in the Tory armour." During a cabinet discussion on the advisability of committing the entire production of the proposed Long Spruce hydro-electric plant on the Nelson River to an American utility for fifteen years, Doern, with tongue in cheek, asked, "Why give away our hydro for a mess of wattage?" At a caucus meeting, a furious Joe Borowski passed him a note on which some existentialist cynic had written: "God is dead." (signed) Neitzsche, and Doern appeased him by printing across the message: "Neitzsche is dead." GOD.

His ability to exploit humour allowed him to defuse potentially explosive situations. During a particularly tense caucus debate, Harry Shafransky interjected, "Russ is creating problems."

Mercurial, trigger-tempered Russ Paulley jumped to his feet, scooped up his papers, and strode toward the exit door. Red-faced and embarrassed, Shafransky shouted, "No, no, I meant the other Russ." Russ Paulley stopped. Russ Doern jumped up, dramatically scooped up his papers, strode toward the exit door, then turned and smiled. After a second's hesitation, the room exploded in uproarious laughter. Russ Paulley, embarrassed but mollified, returned to his chair. The tension was broken.

As a young man, Doern worked as an assistant accountant at Christie Biscuits, as sales trainee and clerk-typist with Ash Temple Ltd., and as advertising salesman for the *Free Press Prairie Farmer*. He indulged in the normal fantasies of youth and, as recounted in the moving eulogy at his funeral by his good friend in his high school and college years, Arthur Gillman: "We sought to conquer the world, not by war or politics, but by entertaining people with feats of magic." He graduated with a B.A. from United College (now the University of Winnipeg) in 1959 and worked toward an M.A. in economics and philosophy at the University of Manitoba. He taught history and english at several schools, both rural and urban. He was artistic and fancied himself both an artist and an actor. He worked in amateur theatre, became part-owner of a disco, and aspired toward a career in advertising.

He travelled extensively in the United States and Europe, and attended the Olympics in Rome (1960), Munich (1972) and Montreal (1976). He won an athletic scholarship to the University of Oregon (which he declined) and scored high in shot put competition in the Olympic trials. This became a cause for merriment in the political fraternity: other politicians were bull-shitters, but Doern was something much worse—a shot-putter.

He was involved in student politics and, in 1962, following his family's political traditions, became an early and ardent supporter of the newly-founded NDP. He was director of political education and in the 1962 election became a one-man advertising committee for the party, designing and writing the commercials, preparing the display posters, arranging the television material, and doing the voice spots for radio. Despite all his efforts, the NDP contingent in the legislature dropped from eleven to seven.

In 1966, Doern ran in the blue-collar NDP-held constituency of Elmwood when incumbent Steve Peters retired, and won against a member of a well-known local family. In February 1969, with Joe Borowski's victory in a by-election in Thompson, the NDP representation was increased to a round dozen, only one less than the Liberals. On June 25, 1969, the NDP was elected and Doern, who had laboured long and loyally in the political vineyard and had strongly supported Schreyer for the leadership, was confident of receiving a major portfolio.

But building a cabinet is a delicate operation, based on political considerations, not friendship or length of service to the party. Considerations are personality, geography, history, sociology, demography, psychology, ethnicity, the status of the individual among his/her peers, ethnic group and community, how well the person works with others, what an individual can contribute to the service of the public and to the success of the government at the polls. So, many call but few are chosen.[17]

---

[17] John Crosbie, a cabinet minister in Brian Mulroney's federal Conservative cabinet, wrote that cabinet-making is not just naming the best-qualified members of caucus. "The PM must construct a delicately balanced edifice, considering language, region, interests, ideology, age, stature in the party, sex, religion, length of service and whether an MP is rural or urban. There are [also] intangibles. A PM will like some MPs better than others. He will want to reward his supporters for the leadership and punish those without foresight, but he will administer retribution with caution. Prudence dictates that he invite a few erstwhile enemies into cabinet to keep them under surveillance, rather than leave them to stir up trouble." *No Holds Barred: My Life In Politics*, p. 245.

And Doern could appear arrogant and sardonic, more interested in style than substance, and he sometimes seemed to be cultivating an image of himself that damaged his relations with political colleagues. Other cabinet ministers lunched at the Shanghai; Doern dined at the Factor's Table. Other ministers bought their suits at Tip Top Tailors; Doern selected his at Handford-Drewitt. It was an unwritten rule that ministers drive cars one class lower than that driven by the premier: when the premier, anxious to reduce government costs and ostentation, indicated he intended replacing his government-issue Buick with a Chevrolet, Doern lobbied me strenuously to urge the premier to buy a more upscale car so he could order an Oldsmobile for himself.

In July 1969, Doern was appointed Deputy Speaker, later served as an acting minister and, in April 1972, was appointed minister of Public Works. He was given responsibility for the maintenance of government vehicles, leasing space, and for the renovation, construction and security of government buildings.

On the occasion of the opening of the legislature several hundred raucous university student protesters, demanding more money, invaded the huge foyer of the Legislative Building shortly before Lieutenant Governor Jack McKeag was to arrive to formally open the session. Having noted the huge increases in grants to universities, plus the student loan and bursary programs we had established, I concluded they should receive nothing more.

Devising a stratagem, I went to Doern's office: "Russ, a bunch of noisy students who think there is not enough slop in the trough for them have occupied the foyer and are psyching themselves up and daring each other to do something rash and exhibitionist. When the lieutenant governor arrives in a few minutes there is a possibility they might physically block his procession up the grand staircase. McKeag has a habit of wearing that cocked hat and coloured cape and if we get really lucky the students might even attempt to tear that plume out of his hat. If they do, and are caught by the all-seeing eye of the TV news cameras, the taxpayers of Manitoba will be so angry that we will receive a million phone calls and letters demanding that we don't give the universities another damned nickel and that we pack the students off to a leper colony or even worse, to Churchill. So let's just not take any precautions. Don't alert the guards. Just stay cool and let happen whatever happens."

It was the only time in twenty-five years that I saw him angry: "You may be getting some perverse pleasure out of what could become an ugly incident but I am the chief security officer for this building and I have a responsibility."

He immediately summoned the guards who formed a flying wedge just as the lieutenant governor, in all his traditional—and tempting—regalia, entered. He proceeded up the grand staircase unmolested, while the guards fended off the students. Russ Doern took his responsibilities seriously, but he felt diminished by having been given so few so late.

Over time, it seemed that Doern became the Rodney Dangerfield of the NDP. Being given a minor portfolio, he determined to lever it up, but all seemed to turn to ashes in his hands. When the Woodsworth Building, which was being built by his department, was nearing completion, he reserved half of the top floor for his ministerial suite. When this was discovered by the premier, these plans plummeted. Doern was instructed to construct a new dining room in the Legislative Building, but when the premier accidentally discovered the minister intended to import expensive carpeting from Atlanta, expensive crystal chandeliers from New York, to stock the shelves with expensive liquors, and to have piped-in music, these plans were abruptly vetoed.

In the 1973 election, the Liberals were reduced to three seats, one less than the four required to maintain official party status with its attendant perks of office and financing. At the same time that the NDP was courting Liberal votes for the next election, Doern deprived the Liberals of their caucus room, a humiliation that was witnessed by the television news cameras. His move was legal, but impolitic and the premier was furious. Once again, Doern felt humiliated. He tried so hard, but somehow respect eluded him.

He also had his triumphs. He had married a beautiful woman, and he doted on their young daughter, proudly introducing her to luminaries coming through Winnipeg, such as Pope John XXIII and Mother Teresa. The Woodsworth Building, named after the spiritual father of Canadian social democracy,[18] constructed while he was minister of Public Works, came in so far under budget that he was able to add two floors. After leaving cabinet he became a TV host and wrote two books.[19] In 1986, he ran against popular Mayor William Norrie and garnered over 50,000 votes—more than several previous 'personality' contenders: newspaper editor and radio commentator Eric Wells; former Metro chairman Jack Willis; lawyer, MLA and later judge, Brian Corrin; and esteemed lawyer, community activist and city coucillor, Joseph Zuken.

But by then his life had assumed a roller-coaster character. Upon Schreyer's precipitate departure to become governor general of Canada in December 1978, a substantial portion of the party was unsatisfied with the two contenders for the vacated leadership, Howard Pawley and Muriel Smith, but no one wanted to take the political risk of standing against them. So Doern did, but received only seven per cent of the convention delegate votes. In 1983, when the government of Howard Pawley, which had defeated Sterling Lyon's Conservatives in late 1981, attempted to legislate official bilingualism in Manitoba, Russ Doern rewrote what would have been the history of the province. He probably wanted appointment to Pawley's cabinet more than he had ever wanted anything in his life, but he took a stand and consciously nullified that ambition. He opposed the premier and

---

[18] The building honoured NDP icon James S. Woodsworth, a Methodist minster and parliamentarian dedicated to the causes of the underdog. First elected an MP in 1921, he became a prime mover and first leader of the CCF and its MP for Winnipeg North Centre from 1935 to his death in 1942. He fought for social reforms that were bitterly denounced at the time, but are now taken for granted: old age pensions, publicly administered health care, family allowances, unemployment insurance, collective bargaining for workers and more.

[19] *Wednesdays are Cabinet Days* (1981) and *The Battle over Bilingualism* (1985).

Attorney General Roland Penner, and though almost all his colleagues agreed with him, in the end they were too timid to oppose the proposal and left him to twist slowly in the wind. Not a single government MLA joined him. But later, during the elections of 1986 and 1988, when the electorate had reduced the NDP to twelve seats from thirty-one, perhaps many of them wished they had.

In 1976, Georges Forrest, a francophone insurance broker from St. Boniface, found a parking ticket on the windshield of his car printed in English only. It became a *cause célèbre*. Objecting to the ticket because it was not also printed in French, Forrest took the issue all the way to the Supreme Court—and won. In 1979, the court decided that, on the basis of the Manitoba Constitution, which had been written by Louis Riel in 1870, both English and French could be spoken in the legislature, all legislation must be passed in both languages, the journals of the legislature must be published in both languages, and all laws enacted since 1890 and published in English only, must be translated into French.

The Progressive Conservative government of Sterling Lyon, which had defeated the NDP in 1977, immediately established a French translation service and began complying with the court decision. But some wanted more. In 1981, Roger Bilodeau, another francophone from St. Boniface, was handed a speeding ticket printed in French only. Urged by the Franco-Manitoban Society, and financially supported by the Office of the Secretary of State, he, too, took his case through the courts to the Supreme Court of Canada.

In the spring of 1983, Roland Penner, attorney general in the new NDP government, announced he was "making a deal" with the francophone community of the province and would amend the Manitoba constitution to make the province officially bilingual.

Doern began to question the nature of the impending legislation in caucus, but his questions were evaded. Fearing the legislation would be approved without a public debate, he publicly declared his opposition to it. Immediately, he became a pariah among his colleagues and in the party he had vigorously served for twenty-one years, fourteen of those as an MLA. His opposition cost him his membership in the caucus, and he was unceremoniously removed from his spacious office into a tiny cubicle. But he proved to be a superb organizer, marshalling public opinion to his aid, and forcing the government into abject surrender.

Manitoba's francophone community was determined to regain the language rights it had had when the province was created and had lost, without any consultation in 1890. It also wanted the separate French schools and school boards, it had had until 1916. Francophones in Manitoba argued that these were their constitutional rights, and returning them would help to keep Canada united.

But Doern saw things differently. He feared equal rights for francophones would cause massive resentment in other racial communities, like the Ukrainian and German populations, each twice as large as the French, who considered themselves equally good citizens. He argued that Canada was not the property of the English and French, but of the several score racial and linguistic groups who also had done the nation's work and paid the nation's taxes and fought the nation's wars. He saw it as politically foolish, economically costly and socially disruptive to attempt to return to some mythologized Arcadia that never was, and that any society with respect for its children would look to the future instead of deliberately resurrecting hurts of a hundred years ago. He believed this proposal would recreate the animosities of linguistic communities within linguistic communities, which millions had come to Canada to escape from, that it would ignite the latent demands of Aboriginal Canadians and Métis for "sovereignty", and that Canada would ultimately be reduced to a collection of surly Bantustans based on race.

He foresaw francophone activists, prodded by politicians in Ottawa buying votes in Québec, demanding that every government department, agency, board, crown corporation, commission, and public office have its quota of francophones based not on their percentage of total population, but on being an "equal nation" entitled to half of everything. He believed francophone activists were less concerned with language than with power, and less with "righting a wrong" than with job creation for francophone Manitobans.[20]

Hundreds of thousands of Manitobans agreed with him. In a referendum conducted by the City of Winnipeg and sixteen rural municipalities in October, 1983, the government's proposal was opposed by seventy-eight per cent of voters. In February 1984, the government allowed its proposed legislation to lapse. One year later, Doern received almost unanimous approval at his constituency meeting when he announced he would run as an Independent in the next provincial election.

In June 1985, Bilodeau lost his case when the Supreme Court ruled the province had the right to decide in what language services would be provided. In May 1986, the Grand Ballroom of the elegant Hotel Fort Garry was filled to capacity at a dinner held in Doern's honour. The speakers included former premiers Sterling Lyon and Douglas Campbell and Doern's former caucus colleague Sidney Green. One of them, referring to the lonely role Doern had played to make it possible for the people of Manitoba to be heard on the issue of their constitution, quoted matador Domingo Ortega:

> Bullfight critics, ranked in rows,
> Fill the enormous plaza full;
> But only one is there who knows,
> And he's the man who fights the bull.

To crown his triumph, they presented him with a fine rosewood plaque bearing the eulogistic inscription from Arthur Clough:

He Set the Cause above Renoun

---

[20] At a social at the author's residence in August 1983, seven of the eight government MLAs in attendance stated categorically that they would NOT support Penner's proposal in the chamber. But they did.

It seemed that Russell Doern had been vindicated. But he had already lost the Elmwood electoral seat he had held since 1969 and was no longer an MLA. He had been hailed a hero by the public of Manitoba and in his own constituency for his position on the language issue, but this did not translate into votes. He had been ignominiously turfed out by his constituents, demonstrating political constituencies are usually the property of the party, not of the individual representative. His first marriage had ended in divorce and his second was dissolving. He had received surprising support in the mayoral contest, but nothing could assuage his self-perceived diminution by battles lost a decade earlier. He began to see himself as a failure: middle-aged with no job, no status and no prospects. His ensemble was as splendid and his wit as pungent as ever, but there was a shadow behind his eyes, haunted by humiliations of long ago.

I visited him briefly while delivering his automobile insurance policy to his high-rent, high-rise apartment on February 18, 1987. His appearance surprised me: it was already 11 A.M., but he was still in his bathrobe, unshaven, had not had breakfast. A shirt was thrown over the back of a chair, and unwashed dishes were on the kitchen table, all unusual for one so fastidious.

I asked, more as a formality than out of interest, "How are things going?" and he replied, "Not so good."

Someone more sensitive might have recognized the signals, but I did not.

Two days later he blew out his heart with a high-powered rifle.

Like Sophocles' Antigone:

> [He] is dead and we will never know,
> The nature of the fever that killed [him].

How different it had been fifteen years earlier when he stood, lithe and proud, in his trademark beautifully tailored light tan suit that matched his hair, and his button-down white shirt and clubby striped tie, as a newly minted cabinet minister. As an MLA from Winnipeg, he was a member of the government Urban Affairs Committee. The Urwick-Currie Study, commissioned by the city, had recommended dissolving Winnipeg's Works Department and farming out services to the private sector. Doern passionately believed these could more efficiently be provided collectively and saw this as an attack on one of the principles of the NDP. He publicly opposed the plan; an aroused public forced Mayor Juba to abandon it, and Doern was sustained.

But Russell Doern had created his own vindictive, clever and ruthless Nemesis—and Steve Juba had found his 'enemy'.

In 1973, responding to entreaties of Winnipeggers, the Government of Manitoba sprayed the city and it cost the taxpayers $1 million for the sledgehammer to kill a few mosquitoes. Also, the government was besieged by those damning the effects of methoxychlor on their children's respiratory system until we began to see ourselves as potential child murderers. The Manitoba Environmental

Council, and a group of pharmacologists and environmentalists calling themselves Citizens Against Slow Poisoning (CASP), argued spraying was ineffectual and little more than a political placebo. The government came to the same conclusion and, the following year, decided against spraying unless the mosquitoes were carrying avian encephalitis, which could cause 'sleeping sickness'. Vigilant monitoring showed no imminent danger, but Winnipeggers were suffering discomfort from mosquito bites.

It was ironic. Those of us raised on farms had worked in the fields when, at times, it appeared the sun was almost blotted out by clouds of mosquitoes, and we survived, but now on summer evenings we sat shirtless in our urban back yards, sipping cocktails, and the sound of a single mosquito roused the temptation to phone City Hall and demand they send a B-52 to nuke the pesky, man-eating beast. For those raised in the city it was worse. So Mayor Steve was getting it in the ear.

He kept making public noises that the Government of Manitoba should spray, and citizens kept phoning the Premier's Office demanding we spray, while others phoned to say their children's lives would be endangered if we sprayed, and we were caught in the middle attempting to pacify both sides and explaining we saw no need to spray, while every mosquito-bitten voter demanded that we do. It was a classic example of the public schizophrenia politicians must contend with ad infinitum: taxpayers, generally, demanding we save their tax money—so long as it did not inconvenience them individually. And all the while Mayor Steve was gleefully indulging in another feeding frenzy.

In the middle of the fray the premier proceeded with his usual Friday morning news conference. A few minutes before it was to begin, I walked across the corridor from my office to the cabinet room, the conference site. Most of the members of the media were already in the room, and just outside it stood Mayor Juba and two members of his executive committee, Gerald Mercier and John Gee. I assumed they had a later appointment with the premier and invited them to attend the news conference while waiting. Juba replied curtly, "No, we're waiting for Bernie (Deputy Mayor Bernie Wolfe)."

"Okay, well, feel free to come in when he arrives."

I entered the room just as the premier entered from the other end so I closed the door, and the news conference commenced. In a few minutes, I began feeling discourteous for leaving the mayor and his councillors standing in the corridor, so I went out. "Gentlemen, why don't you come in and attend the conference and I will wait for Bernie and bring him in when he arrives."

"No!" Juba spoke peremptorily.

I went back into the room. About five minutes later Juba, flanked by his Praetorian Guard (Wolfe, Mercier and Gee), walked in and sat in the row of chairs behind the reporters who surrounded the large table. The premier was being questioned on numerous topics which the reporters considered newsworthy when I heard a peculiar sound like that of a very large internal combustion engine, and rumbling, and grinding. I went to the window facing onto the grounds in front of the Ledge. A score of trucks, carrying tanks and spray booms, were being driven onto the driveway at the front entrance. What the hell?

At precisely that instant Juba stood up. "Mr. Premier and members of the press. If someone doesn't know, my name is Steve Juba and I am mayor of the City of Winnipeg."

There was total silence. Everyone sensed imminent drama.

Juba leaned forward, made circles in the air with a folded paper in his hand, and raised his voice: "Mr. Schreyer, I want you to know that if one of my 616,000 citizens dies of mosquito bites it will be your fault." The roar of the machinery outside was growing louder. "If you look out the window you will see some spraying equipment. We are delivering our city machinery to you in case you do not have enough of your own. You now have no excuse to not carry out a complete spraying program."

The premier was visibly embarrassed, which was unusual, because he seldom displayed emotion. I walked over to him and whispered: "That bastard is making fools of us again. Let's play his game. Let's accept his damned machinery and pretend we understood it is a gift, or we could seize it on the grounds that it is blocking our driveway, or some other pretext ..."

The premier shrugged me off. The die was cast. We sprayed. Juba's quest for an enemy, and a cause with which to beat him, cost the taxpayers in excess of $1.5 million to kill a handful of mosquitoes that offered nothing but momentary discomfort.[21]

Juba's attack "made such delightful copy." The following day a Winnipeg newspaper reported: "The premier's assistant, Herb Schulz, attempted to prevent the mayor and his colleagues from entering the room to attend the news conference."

I phoned the reporter. "I just read your report that I attempted to stop Juba and his cohorts from attending the news conference yesterday."

"Yeeees," he replied cautiously.

"Where did you get that information?"

"From Mayor Juba."

"Okay. I have a message for you. In the interests of accuracy, and also to give you a story to help you peddle your papers, I want you to report in tomorrow's paper that you interviewed me on this matter and I said Steve Juba is a lying son-of-a-bitch."

There was the sound of sucked-in breath. A pause. Then ... "I ... I ... I can't do that."

---

[21] The following year, the government rid itself of the pesky problem by transferring activities such as mosquito control to the city and municipalities, but they were required to obtain permission to spray from the Manitoba Clean Environment Commission. Councillor [later Mayor] William Norrie told the commission the city should be sprayed if a majority wanted it, even if it was injurious to health. "People in the real world are very unhappy [and] really not in the mood to discuss science ... Place your faith and confidence in City Council." *Winnipeg Free Press*, July 31, 1975.

"Then will you at least phone Juba and tell him—and I want you to quote me directly—that I said he is a fucking liar?"

"Weeellll, no-o-o-o."

So much for reportorial accuracy. Smart media people did not risk offending Mayor Steve. And "he made such delightful copy".

STEVE JUBA was fast with his mouth. But he was also fast with his mind. On the occasion of completion of the dazzling, op-art, bronze-glazed, twenty-storey Imperial Tower on Broadway, Manitoba Minister of Industry and Commerce Leonard Evans was invited to officiate and to formally name the building. I accompanied him. Mayor Juba was also invited.

The affable Evans, visibly proud to have another office building signifying economic development in the province, spoke briefly and was then handed a large bottle of champagne. In the traditional manner he announced the name of the building and drew back his arm to 'christen' it by smashing the bottle against the bucket of concrete hanging suspended four feet above the sidewalk as it was about to be hoisted up to the roof and the waiting finishing crew. Suddenly Steve Juba reached behind Evans' back, snatched the bottle out of his outstretched hand, and laid it on top of the wet concrete in the bucket.

"There is no point in wasting good champagne. The hard-working guys on the roof will enjoy it."

The cable whirred and the bucket, topped by the rescued bottle of champagne, rose to the roof and the coverall-clad, open-mouthed workers leaning over the parapet, waiting to consume it.

It was a gesture as gracious as it was unexpected. Aside from whatever concern it may or may not have demonstrated for the champagne tastes of the crew on the roof, it was arguably the most spontaneously astute political act I have ever witnessed.

And that is the way I will always remember him.

XIII

So What Did You Do in the War, Daddy?

It's not work unless you'd rather be doing something else.
— Anonymous

You will do case work, answer mail, whatever else is needed, and write speeches," the premier had told me on my first day at work. I was thrilled. I would write the words the premier would say to Manitobans and the world. My exalted thoughts would be echoed twenty years later by President Ronald Reagan's speech writer, Peggy Noonan, who wrote: "Speech writing is where the political, ideological and philosophical tensions of the administration get worked out. Speech writing is where the government gets re-invented every day."[1]

My ambition was soon realized. I wrote a speech to the annual convention of the National Farmer's Union. It distilled years of experience in farming and farm organizations, explained that Canadian farmers were in trouble because they sold their products on an open market, but bought supplies in protected markets,[2] and proposed collective action through marketing organizations. The speech was given to the premier just in time to deliver it, leaving him no time to delete the savage indictments and biting phrases he would consider too emotional—not because he did not feel deeply but because, like the hero in John Bunyan's *Pilgrim's Progress*, "he disliked emotion because he felt deeply". The speech was so good that the NFU gave 900 copies to its delegates.

It was to be almost the only full-dress speech I would write for the premier. He was not comfortable reading speeches. After a few attempts, I prepared notes and let him fill in the blanks. If the speech was on some technical subject, like

---

[1] *What I Saw at the Revolution*, Random House, N.Y., 1990.
[2] Twenty years later, little had changed.

hydro, or finance, notes were prepared by the relevant department and perhaps crossed my desk for vetting. But it became clear that, except on select issues, he was best speaking extemporaneously. His mind soaked up information like a sponge, and he had the rare ability to "think on his feet"—to sort out facts in logical sequence while presenting them, unrehearsed and seemingly unprepared.

One day, he remarked that he had been invited to address a service club and drawled quixotically: "Write me a speech entitled 'The Efficacy of Hypocrisy'." I wrote of how hypocrisy can be the balm that soothes, that eases human relationships. Is it hypocrisy, or kindness, to kiss a child's injury to ease the hurt, or tell a dying person he looks good, or to understate battle losses?

When a political leader states the economy is in a minor slump, when he knows it is collapsing, is it hypocrisy or common sense to avoid triggering panic, while natural and human forces are given time to correct it? The speech was sprinkled with references to Kirouac, Hegel, Pascal, Santayana and Churchill (who is reputed not to have warned the citizens of Coventry that they would be bombed because the Germans might learn their code had been cracked); St. Augustine ("Lord, give me continence and chastity—but not yet.") and Thomas Aquinas, who saw hypocrisy as intellectual prostitution, but noted that "prostitution in a society is like a cess-pool in a castle; it stinks but keeps the castle clean."

It was a great speech … but the meeting was cancelled.

Not ready to give up being the premier's amanuensis—if not his Svengali—I wrote a speech for him to present to the Chamber of Commerce. The chamber saw the NDP as its *bête noir,* and I saw the chamber members as nicely-dressed, self-centred persons drinking each other's bathwater. They were too ideological to understand that if not for induced circulation of money through wage laws and social programs, including Medicare,[3] their economy would collapse.

So I quoted eighteenth-century essayist and biographer Dr. Samuel Johnson, that "A merchant should rarely be consulted on designs of wide extent and distant result." And I liberally quoted Johnson's famous contemporary:

> The interests of traders and manufacturers is always … to widen the market and narrow competition … A proposed new law from them should be listened to with caution [for] it comes from men whose interest is never the same as that of the public, who want to deceive and oppress the public. Businessmen seldom meet, even for merriment, but the conversation ends in some conspiracy against the public or … to raise prices.[4]

---

[3] A decade earlier, the Canadian Chamber of Commerce had asked the Hall Commission on Health Care "to oppose 'socialized medicine' because Canadians can get health care through voluntary insurance. Those unable to pay should be subsidized by government … Those with catastrophic bills [should get] relief under the Income Tax Act." "Chamber of Commerce Denies Need for State Medicine", *Winnipeg Free Press,* March 20, 1962.

[4] *An Inquiry into the Nature and Causes of the Wealth of Nations: 1776, by Adam Smith,* William Benton, Toronto, 1952, pp. 51-57.

I had a fiendish thought: presumably few of the denizens of the chamber had read this author they so avidly claimed to quote. I suggested the premier read the passage and ask them who had written it. After hearing the chorus of "Karl Marx", he could reveal the true author—their icon, Adam Smith.

I handed it to him with obvious satisfaction. He scanned it: "I am not using this."

"But ... but ... why not? It's a barn-burner."

"And it will burn any bridges we might be able to build with the chamber and the business community."

"But I have even quoted their Saint Adam to them."

"The devil quoting scripture."

"But dammit, what I have written is true."

"True to you perhaps. It may have some substance, but I do not believe in this approach. The businessman has a role in our society." He went on to say that in an industrial economy the entrepreneur's talent for organization and risk-taking is essential to growth. Unless government is prepared to assume mobilization of the entire economy, we need the businessman. If government has made too many concessions to business, that can be rectified, but business is not the only special pleader.

"Suffice to say the interests of our government and the business community are not mutually exclusive," he concluded. "They may not know that but they will not be persuaded of it by your approach. You must learn that 'the soft answer turneth away wrath'."

So he spoke largely off the cuff, glancing at scribbled notes. He quoted John F. Kennedy, that "government and business are necessary allies". He stated that, contrary to their belief that "government should be run like a business" government is more, and has wider interests, than a business. He defined a political economy as the "allocation of limited resources to satisfy unlimited demands in a socially acceptable way", and explained that in a market economy it is the obligation of government to ensure the market allocates goods equitably. He stated that his government would not accede to the chamber's request to abolish estate taxes[5]—that it was an instrument of equity and the chamber was fooling itself by believing only high-income groups should benefit from tax policy.

He questioned the inconsistency of their belief in Galbraith's witticism: "too much money makes the poor lazy, but too little makes the rich quit." Then, having gently scourged them, he drew their attention to the fact that two equally tall, equally handsome men, Chamber President Graeme Haig and Highways Minister Peter Burtniak, were wearing identical dark-blue pin-striped suits. He considered it a metaphor for the symbiotic relationship between business and government and for the fact that, while the perspective of his government was not quite the

---

[5] In 1971, Ottawa vacated the field of estate taxes and invited the provinces to adopt them. All except Alberta did so.

same as that of the chamber, the NDP was not their mortal enemy.

He may as well have used my speech. The *Financial Times* report on the meeting was headed: "Business and Schreyer Declare War".

His speeches were usually long on fact and short on humour. His jokes were involved, stale, and elicited groans. His wife, speaking at a party dinner, related he had written a joke book of two pages, one for pictures of her and the kids. But he had a Chestertonian wit and his understated one-liners were hilarious.

When North Dakota announced it would build the Garrison Dam on the loop of the Souris River south of the Canadian border, there was concern biota from the Missouri River System would enter Manitoba's system and damage local species. At a Friday morning press conference, CBC reporter Bob Preston addressed the issue: "Mr. Premier, there is fear alien fish like the gizzard shad may get into Lake Winnipeg, but I believe he would freeze to death during the winter anyway." The premier, fatigued after having returned from Ottawa overnight, looked up, half-opened his eyes, and grunted: "Well, that would serve him right, wouldn't it?"

He had a habit, at press conferences, of seemingly seeking precision by circumlocution. He would say something, qualify it, then qualify the qualification, as though fearing his own words.

I found this disconcerting: "Why don't you take the hot potato out of your mouth and say what you want to say without apologizing?"

Then I learned why he was so careful. At a press conference he used the word "damn". We were deluged by phone calls and letters protesting such vile language by the premier. Deciding to turn the perceived *faux pas* into a public relations exercise, I wrote a brief form letter to send to all protesters. It stated that he had used improper language, there was no excuse for it, "you were right to draw it to my attention" and "I promise it will not happen again."

I sent it in for the premier's signature. He sent it back for a rewrite. He had deleted: "I promise it will not happen again."

There may have been another reason why the speeches I wrote for the premier did not appeal to him. Again, as Peggy Noonan wrote of the first speech she was assigned to write for Reagan, "I was looking for the grammar of the presidency—the sound and tone and sense of it. I wanted the triumphant cadence." I never found "the sound and tone of it", not because it was not there, but because our experience and thought patterns differed. We marched to a different drummer. But it did not matter. I had other things to do.

Three women came into my office one day. They lived in a public housing project in the premier's constituency. The Manitoba Housing and Renewal Corporation had given them thirty days to vacate and they demanded to see their MLA. I informed them that he was in Ottawa and asked why they had been asked to vacate.

The story unfolded. One couple had a boa constrictor in their apartment. The couple next door had a dog. One night the snake woke up the dog. The dog barked. The man with the snake fired a rifle through the wall to silence the dog.

The man with the dog kicked in the door of the man with the snake. A fist fight erupted. A third couple entered the fray. Garbage was thrown. A man was stabbed with a kitchen knife. Damage was done. Other tenants woke up. There was screaming and cursing. Residents threatened to move out. So the MHRC gave all three culprits notice to vacate.

"Well," I said, "you people have not behaved well. In public housing just like in private housing, if you don't behave you're kicked out."

"If you kick us out we are going to do whatever we can to defeat the Schreyer government in the election next week. Unless the notice to vacate is withdrawn immediately we'll set up a tent on the sidewalk outside the project and call Peter Warren."[6]

I reached for the phone and called the director of MHRC: "Frank, I have three ladies here who received notice from your office to vacate their apartments within thirty days. I want you to cancel those and give them notice to move out in FOUR days. I will suggest they come over right now and pick up the notices. If they don't, send them by courier." The women were furious:

"We'll go over to MHRC and pick up the notices and take them straight to the rentalsman". I dialed the phone: "Frank, these ladies are coming right over. Call the rentalsman and have him there when you hand them their four-day notices."

They left. They got their notices. They moved out. They did not set up a tent on the sidewalk, nor did they call Peter Warren.[6]

Fate moves in mysterious ways. A man walked in on two canes. He was from my old home town, but had been working in the mines in Northern Manitoba and had injured his back. He was on partial worker's compensation, but wanted more. I phoned the Worker's Compensation Board and suggested they review the case.

That was Wednesday. On Friday evening, my wife and I drove to our old home town to visit friends. I went with them to the pub for a beer, sat down and looked around. At the next table, his back to me, sat the man with the injured back. There were no canes in sight. Later, returning from the bathroom, he spotted me. After a long hesitation, and very red in the face, he came to my table, gulped several times and asked, "Well, so what are you thinking?"

"I'm thinking your compensation payments just ended."

People came to solicit jobs. Naomi Levine, who was working in a government department, came to ask if she must join the NDP to keep her job. Oddly, we thought little about that question. Appointments to commissions and boards went to political sympathizers because they required people who were attuned to party policy and they rewarded party supporters. Otherwise, hirings were based on merit. The premier did not allow a political test for prospective employees.

---

[6] Peter Warren was a well-known radio talk show host, who enjoyed situations that made the government squirm. His hit show now comes out of Vancouver.

On one regrettable occasion I broke that rule. When Sterling Lyon replaced Sidney Spivak as leader of the Conservative Party, Spivak's executive assistant quietly inquired if we had a place for him. I opposed his employment as being politically tainted. The assistant was William Neville, Rhodes Scholar, later city councillor, and then chair of the Department of Political Studies at the University of Manitoba. His entry into the public service would have been a coup for our government— and for Manitobans.

Even opposition MLAs came for help. When Robert Wilson was elected Conservative MLA for the Wolseley constituency, members of his own party were reluctant to have him in their caucus room. And he was *persona non grata* with me because he had defeated my friend, NDP candidate Murdoch MacKay. But one day Wilson came with a request: "It seems Wolseley has become a dumping ground for halfway houses. I would like to know how many there are and where they are, but the department refuses to tell me anything. I am the MLA and I have a right to know what is happening in my constituency."

I agreed, phoned the Department of Health, got the list, and gave it to him. He was grateful. But "politics is politics". He repaid me by mailing a questionnaire asking: "Are there any 'halfway houses' or other NDP government experiments on your street?"

Two days after my appointment as special assistant to the premier, the local representative of Canadian General Electric phoned for an appointment with the premier. "He is the minister responsible for Manitoba Hydro and we want to sell them some turbines for the Nelson River plant."

"You must make your presentation to Manitoba Hydro's executive board. They will evaluate all tenders and refer them to their minister."

"But I have been to Hydro. They say our bid is too high."

"Then you probably will not get the contract."

I refused his request to see the premier. He called again and I refused again. In the late afternoon Harry Shafransky, MLA and government appointee to the board of Manitoba Hydro, came bursting in. "Herb, we are going to supper with a guy from General Electric."

"Harry, this guy phoned twice today for an appointment with the premier. He wants to do an end run around Hydro. I don't want to feel obligated to him. If I go, he will phone again tomorrow. I'm not sure either of us should accept this man's invitation. If we buy turbines from CGE, the opposition may make a connection and claim we were bribed. Or we might be influenced to recommend against CGE to avoid that accusation."

Harry was not sympathetic. "Herb. This is your second day at a very important job. The longer you are here the more you will be approached by people who want something. Some will invite you to lunch. Acceptance does not mean you owe them anything but to listen."

He went on to say, contrary to the advice given to John F. Kennedy by his father, that if I was to guide my actions by what my political enemies might say,

I would be paralysed.[7] Whether or not I took advantage of some invitations for personal gain would depend on character, not on the law.

"Anyway," he told me, "The taxpayers will find anyone who is inclined to cheat. And if your character is so weak that you fear being bought with a supper, you should not be working in the Premier's Office."

We dined at the Charterhouse. Harry had two Harvey Wallbangers and a large steak, followed by two glasses of Cointreau.[8] I was uneasy. I had one rye, a small steak and no liqueur. The CGE representative, a cultured man and a good conversationalist, did not once mention turbines or appointments. My fears seemed groundless. The next day the cordial and generous CGE representative phoned three times for an appointment with the premier.[9]

Actually, there were few attempts at bribery. Free tickets to artistic performances were merely courtesies, as were most invitations to lunch by those seeking access to government or needing someone to listen to them. But once it was serious. "We are building a large office tower in the city," I was told by a developer. "There is $100,000 for you if you get the government to rent four floors for civil servants." His offer was regretfully declined, but we parted amicably. Later, when I was in the hospital he sent me a gift, a copy of Peter C. Newman's *The Canadian Establishment*.

If a clean desk connotes a sick mind, the litter of files on my desk suggested my mind was superbly healthy. My office was like Grand Central Station, assisting those passing through to other offices, those refusing to go anywhere but "the top", and those who had been passed from office to office with no satisfaction. The traffic and phone calls from ministers, deputy ministers, ministerial assistants, secretaries of cabinet committees, heads of publicly-owned companies, representatives of the NDP party office and of labour unions, and taxpayers, kept the joint jumping. Meanwhile the mail piled up and was taken home to be answered in my almost illegible longhand which, the following day, my staff, with furrowed brow but unruffled temper, rendered into legible type.

Attending cabinet meetings used up Wednesdays. Management committee meetings consumed Tuesday mornings. Caucus met for an hour at noon while the legislature sat. Spare time was used to write speeches for backbenchers. And there

---

[7] Patriarch Joseph P. Kennedy told his sons: "You are what others think you are."

[8] Shafransky, as a politician, was handicapped by an inability to be mean. In the 1968 federal election, he ran against PC candidate Vaughan Baird, who argued that he should not be forced to accept Medicare. I wrote a speech for Harry for a joint candidate debate. "Mr. Baird resents being forced to accept anything he does not want. Who is forcing him to accept anything? He pays taxes for the police, but need not accept their help if his office is robbed. He pays taxes for the fire department, but need not accept their help if his house burns ... He pays fees to the MMS, but need not accept help from doctors if he is ill. He can die if he wants to—and the sooner the better." When Harry arrived at that phrase, he turned red and began to laugh and would not read the punchline.

[9] In 1975, despite pressure from Ottawa and hints that CGE might build a plant at Brandon, we rejected a $102 million CGE bid for hydro-electric equipment in favour of Brown-Boveri, at $16 million less. Don Craik, PC deputy leader in the legislature, argued that a deal with CGE would bring jobs and new technology to Manitoba. Had we ignored the $16 million cost differential, however, we would have been accused of wasting taxpayers' money.

was attendance in the visitor's gallery during Question Period. It was the most exciting time of the day, as members shouted insults at each other across the legislative chamber from their seats, arranged, in the way of the British House of Commons, two sword's lengths apart.

The panoply and ceremony at the opening of daily sittings may seem arcane and unctuous, and the symbols devoid of meaning, but they represent centuries of human striving toward actualization of the proposition that men can govern themselves. But the best part was seeing the visitor's gallery fill with ordinary citizens witnessing what they had thought was foreclosed to them. Especially during the Autopac debates, the babas in babushkas sat listening to the debate, signalling support for their government with loud chuckles, occasionally being rebuked by the Speaker—and knitting. Few had heard of Madame Defarge, but figuratively at least, they saw the heads of the nobility rolling from the blade of the guillotine as a New Order was ushered in by those they could relate to.

Question Period provides the daily pyrotechnics in which the tensions and tactics of government and opposition are played out and, to aficionados, it is "the best show in town". But it is "opposition time". Opposition parties, taking full advantage of this being the only time of day when the press gallery is full, have an hour to hurl at the ministers questions designed more to embarrass than elicit information. They ask cleverly phrased 'Socratic' questions that make any answer appear wrong and do not allow for factual explanations.

It was always good theatre, but often left government members frustrated, the opposition jubilant, visitors confused, and me exasperated at apparent government impotence.

I had learned at high school and university, in farm organization wars and the construction industry, the Christian injunction to "turn the other cheek" should be taken only metaphorically. So as a counter ploy, I prepared questions for NDP backbenchers to ask their own ministers, providing opportunities to explain policies in detail and add laudatory remarks about the government. For example, during a fight with the Manitoba Medical Association, opposition members kept jumping up to assert rather than ask if it was not true that many Manitoba doctors were threatening to "opt out" of Medicare. When the opposition had worked itself into a frenzy, an NDP backbencher stood up: "Mr. Speaker, my question is to the Minister of Health. Is it correct that, despite threats of opting out, only 189 doctors of a total of more than 1,400, are not operating under Medicare and nine of the thirteen members of MMA executive have not opted out?"

"That is correct," nodded the minister, alerted in advance.

"Mr. Speaker, a supplementary question. Would the Minister explain how many Manitoba doctors were opted out in June 1969?"

The minister smilingly explained that after Progressive Conservative Premier Walter Weir threatened to sue the Government of Canada rather than accept Medicare in Manitoba, most Manitoba doctors remained "opted out". Opposition members howled with fury as my ploy proved effective. Later, however, as government, the Conservatives adopted it with devastating effect.

I was circumspect, but at The Ledge nothing remains secret—especially secrets. One day, when I sent a scribbled question, via a page, to Tom Barrow and he was having difficulty reading my writing, Harry Enns looked up into the gallery and called, "Where are you, Herb?"

Much of my work was done on the phone. A week after my arrival René Chartier, my shrewd and worldly-wise colleague in the Premiers' Office, saw the pile of files on my desk and advised: "Never do by letter what can be done by phone and always talk on the phone as though you believe it is bugged."

But letters were needed. On my third day, I was given a letter to the premier from a farmer who had been my neighbour. He was angry about rejection of a claim for crop insurance compensation. I wrote a reply delicately explaining the field representative's report, which indicated that his farming methods were so bad that it would be a travesty to pay him with premiums paid by other farmers. It was sent in to the premier for signature, with no indication of the author.

Leaving late that evening, I stopped to see if the premier was still in his office. He looked up from what he was reading: "This is a helluva good letter," he said. "I wonder who wrote it." It was my letter, but it would have been gauche to tell him. It was enough that I knew. [10]

My euphoria was brief. The next day a letter was awaiting my own signature when Sid Green walked in. Seeking more kudos, I handed it to him and asked, rather smugly, if he thought it was good. He read it: "No! You are using the premier's letterhead and anything you write might one day be on the front page of the *Free Press*." [11]

It was arguably the best advice I received in my six years there. After that I wrote letters I *wanted* on the front page, but they never were, even when sent directly to the editor. One such was to those writing about the "hypocrisy" of a "socialist" premier driving "a big, black, Buick Electra". I replied it was inherited from Premier Weir, changed only by removal of the expensive phone. Since writers sent copies of their letters to the papers, so did I. It was not published. The letters ceased when the black Buick was traded for a proletarian brown Chevrolet. [12]

The premier, asked at a press conference why he had hired his brother-in-law, replied: "Who did you expect me to appoint, a Conservative?" [13] The unapologetic response inspired a letter. Talk show host Peter Warren suggested his listeners ask if Schreyer's brother-in-law was working in the premier's office. So I wrote to

---

[10] Ministerial assistants need to decide whether to sign a letter, or prepare it for one's minister's signature, when to carry out an instruction, modify it or ignore it, and when to neglect to pass on information so that the minister can truthfully deny it.

[11] George Stephanopoulos, aide to President Bill Clinton, wrote, "I forgot the first rule of White House work; never say, or do or write anything that you would not want on the front page of the *Washington Post*." *All Too Human*, Little Brown and Co. 1997, p. 263.

[12] The unwritten rule was that ministers' cars be one grade below the premier's. Two ministers wanted him to get another top-of-the-line car so that they could maintain their status, car-wise.

[13] I might have added that my sister married Ed Schreyer, but my wife's first cousin was the wife of PC Leader Sterling Lyon

Warren, with copies to other members of the media, that this proved Schreyer did not discriminate against relatives and they should also ask if (Conservative MLA and former minister of Agriculture) Harry Enns' brother works for both (NDP ministers) Toupin and Green? If (Conservative MLA) Bud Sherman's daughter works for Toupin? If (Conservative MLA) Douglas Watt's brother works for Green? If (Conservative MLA) Warren Steen's brother is working for Toupin? If (Conservative leader) Sidney Spivak's cousin is working for Premier Schreyer?" As usual, there was no reply.

The Schreyer government was very sensitive to accusations of nepotism.[14] One very wet autumn, waterfowl were destroying much of the province's swathed grain. The relevant minister proposed to cabinet that, since the birds were protected by government it should compensate farmers for crops they destroyed. Cabinet agreed. The minister, aware of the sensitivities of his colleagues, then stated: "Now that we have agreed, I want to inform you the greatest single beneficiary of this program will be the premier's brother."

Several ministers, sensing the political fallout, visibly blanched. Had they been told this earlier, it is possible the farmers with damaged crops would not have received compensation—just because among them was George Schreyer.

Writing on the letterhead of the Office of the Premier gave me cachet, but held dangers. In the first Unicity elections the NDP ran twenty-one candidates, but elected only seven. It broke the party's hearts, but sharpened its tactics. In 1974, a group decided to run NDP candidates disguised as representatives of the Civic Reform Coalition. At a meeting, a proposal was made to run only CRC candidates, but Harry Lazarenko, a railway worker and NDP member, objected: "We have a government to protect and we must maintain the NDP presence at the municipal level. This is the North End. If we can't elect an NDPer here, where can we? I propose we have another meeting and discuss this further." Everyone agreed, but no meeting was called. So Lazarenko called a meeting, at which he was the sole attendee. He nominated himself the NDP candidate.

A letter arrived for the premier. It contained two membership cards, from people who stated that they could not remain in a party that allowed such undemocratic behaviour. By then the elections were over, with a peculiar result.

I wrote to the former members expressing my disappointment that they had left the party over frustrations that seemed rather minor compared with those experienced by elected members. Then, I added, "Re: the 'undemocratic activities' in the party, you will note that, in addition to the obscene act of having nominated himself as a candidate, the man in question has now committed the even more obscene act of electing himself to city council.[15]

Since it was highly political, I cleared the letter with the premier, signed it

---

[14] This sensitivity extended to the civil service. Spouses were not allowed to work in the same department.

[15] With a brief interruption, Lazarenko was still on council in 2005, though he had been expelled from the NDP. Only Evelyn Reese was elected as a member of the CRC. She later ran for the legislature—as a Liberal.

and sent it. Since the disillusioned former party members had sent a copy of their letter to their MLA, Saul Cherniack, I did likewise. The next day I was in the premier's office when Cherniack stormed in.

Saul Cherniack was an ornament to the legislature and a power in the government. He had grown up in Winnipeg's polyglot North End, served in military intelligence during the war, established a successful law practice and served on a school board and on the Metro council. In 1966, he was elected to the legislature, assumed star status, and in 1969 was appointed minister of Finance. A party grandee and a government 'heavyweight', who was listened to when he spoke, he moved between the social democratic cabinet and the conservative business community with confident semi-insouciance, exuding integrity and leaving the impression with friend and foe that his portfolio was in capable, careful, hands. I was reminded of Horace Walpole's statement about Charles Townsend, that, "no man can be as wise as he looked". But Cherniack was.

He was of medium height, well-built, urbane, quietly handsome and always impeccably dressed. In the early days of the Schreyer regime it made one proud to look down from the gallery and see Cherniack, in a stylish gray suit, modish mauve shirt and matching tie, answering opposition questions with courtesy and precision.

In both the chamber and the cabinet room, he was invariably articulate and spoke in a pleasant, resonant voice that he never raised. He did not need to; when he laid down his papers, raised his head, transfixed someone with half-hooded eyes and asked quietly, but with a chilling edge to his voice, "I trust you jest?" the object of his question invariably agreed that, yes, it was just a joke.

But now, in the Premier's Office, his face was red with fury. He nodded curtly to me. "I'm glad you're here. I want the premier to see how you're abusing his letterhead." He threw my letter on the premier's desk and almost snarled, "Read this."

The premier recognized the letter. Colour suffused his neck. It was an embarrassing moment. Would he reveal his complicity and risk the opprobrium of a senior minister or remain silent and risk losing my confidence in him? In the scheme of things, I was expendable. Would he rely on my silence and cause me to say, as the Earl of Strafford had said when his friend, King Charles I, signed his death warrant: "Put not your trust in princes"?

The premier feigned a quizzical expression. "But Solly, what do you find so wrong with this letter?"

"What is wrong with it is that your assistant is using your stationery to tell these people to go fuck themselves."

I was enormously relieved. The premier was temporizing. I would not need to fall on my sword. I smiled cheerfully at Cherniack: "Saul, I didn't know you were that perceptive."

✪   ✪   ✪

USUALLY THE PREMIER and I agreed over the things that I did. Larry Desjardins had been defeated in 1973, but the election was controverted and re-contested in December 1974. At the time, the union at Flyer Industries, a publicly owned company, was on strike. Union members sent Schreyer and Spivak a letter, which was also distributed to every household in St.Boniface, stating that its members would vote for the party that supported its demands.

Spivak replied cautiously but affirmatively. Determined that we must not surrender to this blatant blackmail, I wrote a response for the premier's signature and took it to his office. Thirty seconds later Green came in with a similar response. It remained for the premier to decide which letter, if either, would be sent.

He scanned them, deleted part of my letter, deleted part of Green's letter, put them together, and called his secretary: "Rita, would you type this for my signature?"

The letter outlined the government's position, stated that this was as far as we would go, and added that if union members wanted the key to the treasury they should vote for Spivak. A copy of the letter was distributed to every household in St. Boniface. We won the by-election.

At other times we disagreed. An associate deputy minister came to us highly recommended, but seemed to spend much of his time at home carousing. Work piled up on his desk and he was fired. For the next three weeks, he prowled the corridors of The Ledge, displaying his bulging briefcase and buttonholing anyone who would listen. I approached him in the cafeteria: "You no longer work here. You are demoralizing staff. I want you out of here. And take your damned briefcase with you."

"You must not be so abrasive with me. I have enough information in this briefcase to blow the minister out of his chair."

"Then take the minister with you, but get out."

He did. Two weeks later, I heard he had taken his government car with him. The next morning, on open line radio, he complained that he just wanted to help the people of Manitoba but this socialist government would not let him. I thought he could best serve the people of Manitoba by giving back their car. I went to the premier: "I want your authorization to personally collect that car."

"How do you propose to do it?"

"I will get CBC to set up a TV news camera in front of his house and then bang on his door and demand the keys."

The premier passed his hand across his face in exasperation: "Oh Christ, Herb, you just can't do things like that."

I stomped back to my office and called the relevant minister, the awesome authority of the Premier's Office in my voice: "Russ, it is now 10:25. If your department has not recovered that car by noon today I am personally going to get it. Fifty-seven minutes later the minister phoned. "It's okay, Herb. We've liberated the car."

Some things the premier and I did not disagree about because he did not know about them. When I was angry, which was often, I relieved frustrations by scribbling letters to the editor. I knew my boss would not be amused to see them published over my name, so I met with several members of the NDP executive: "I am on the inside and have more information than most of you," I told them. "I write letter to editors, especially in response to editorials, but cannot sign them because I am a government employee. If you people set up a committee to find signatories, I will write the letters and pass them to a contact who will pass them to you."

It worked quite well. During some weeks, several of my letters appeared in newspapers. Party members, unaware of who the author was, phoned to ask if I had read those great letters. I was jubilant. Information was getting out. One day one of my letters was in a paper. It was signed by a man from Brandon. I knew that man; he was a mortal enemy. I phoned my contact, a young man in the Department of Agriculture, to whom I had been passing my letters: "That committee of yours has some persuasive people on it."

"What committee?"

"That committee you pass my letters to after I write them."

"I don't know anything about any committee."

"Well, a while ago we arranged for me to write letters to editors, which I would pass to you, which you would pass to the committee, who would find signatories. One of my letters is in today's paper. It is signed by a farmer I know and someone on that committee is either very persuasive or threatened to dunk this guy's head in a bucket of pig-shit to get him to sign it."

"I don't know what you're talking about."

"Listen, for Christ's sake. I've sent letters to you and they have been getting into the papers after someone signs them …"

"I sign them."

"You sign them! Where in hell do you get the names?"

"I get them out of the telephone directory." [16]

MANY PERSONS approached the Premier's Office as though it was a candy store and had to be disabused, but it was impolitic to send them to the premier. Every chief executive officer needs a son-of-a-bitch and since I, in my several previous incarnations, had learned to say "No", I fell easily into that role. It made me the "bad cop" in the office, in contrast to René Chartier, who could continue presenting the smiling "good cop" image of the Premier's Office to the public. One day he told me, "Someone must take bad news to the premier. You are his brother-in-law

---

[16] Two years later, the assistant to the Premier of British Columbia was fired after being exposed doing the same thing.

and he probably would accept it better from you than anyone else, since you have nothing to gain by giving him bad news unless it's true."

Nevertheless, it proved an onerous role. One day, in the car on the way to a meeting, after I had burdened the premier with news he would have preferred to not hear, he said irritably, "Why is it that when I'm with René he makes me laugh and I enjoy myself but when I'm with you, you just make me angry?"

Nor did my 'son-of-a-bitch' role improve relations with others. The premier was always late. He was incorrigably late. His unhurried, unharried attitude bred confidence, but also annoyance. He was invariably late for the regular, bilingual [17] press conferences scheduled for Friday mornings at 10 A.M. At the last moment, someone would rush in with information he or she believed the premier must have for the scrum, while the media sat in the cabinet room fuming and waiting with nail-biting impatience, wondering if the premier was deliberately letting them cool their heels, and concerned about deadlines. [18]

René Chartier handled this with Gallic charm, entertaining the reporters with the latest round of ribald jokes and laughingly listening to their hints of government scandals about to burst. Then Chartier went on vacation, and for a brief time I became the press officer. Knowing the premier would be late, I entered the press room at 10:25. Sixteen reporters were sitting around the table chewing pencils and looking sour. CJOB reporter and press gallery chairman Bob Beaton, trying hard to conceal his irritation, said, "Well, Herb, since the premier is late as usual and we don't know how late he is going to be, why don't we just go back to our offices and you can call us back when he decides to come."

I was angry, not with the reporters, with whom I sympathized, but with the premier. But he was not there and they were. "Listen you bastards," I told them, "you know damn well the premier is late because he is busy and not because he is sitting with his feet on his desk trying to make life difficult for reporters. If any of you want to leave, go ahead, but I will not be calling you back."

No one left. After the news conference I followed the premier back into his office. "This is becoming embarrassing. We call the press conference for 10:00 and you arrive at 10:30, so why not call it for 10:30?"

He agreed. We changed to 10:30. After that he arrived at 11:00. I was very happy when Chartier returned.

Another problem with the premier was that he insisted on remaining true to his roots. It was impossible to control access to his office, because he wanted to speak with anyone who wanted to see him. [19]

---

[17] Long before Georges Forrest took his English-only parking ticket to court, and Franco-Manitobans began agitating to be served in French, Premier Schreyer was answering questions, in the chamber and in media scrums, in either English or French, depending on the language in which the question was asked.

[18] My relationship with the media, strained because I knew their interests and ours did not converge, was straightforward; they had the right to attack and I had the right to respond.

[19] Twenty years later, I was jealous when I read how carefully Premier Filmon's *apparatchniks* polished his image and guarded access to him. It was what I wanted to do, but failed miserably. "The Good Ship Filmon is Steered by a Small Band of Power Brokers", *Winnipeg Free Press,* March 21, 1997.

Worse, he left his home telephone number listed in the provincial directory[20]
It was used liberally. He often went home late, read a Hydro file or a Russian or
French dictionary until he fell asleep, to be awakened by the bedside phone being
rung incessantly by someone with another problem that simply could not wait
until morning. Then, occasionally, he would phone me. After all, what are assistants for?

One night, I dreamed there was a persistent ringing in my head. It woke
me up. It was not a dream. The phone was ringing. The clock showed 2:35 A.M.
I fumbled with the receiver and mumbled: "Hu-u-llo."

At the other end a very tired voice grunted: "Yes, this is Ed. A local man
died several days ago and his family has gathered here from as far away as Miami.
Now the doctor has decided he wants an autopsy, but the family wants a funeral
while they are all here. The son of the deceased just phoned. His number is XXX-
XXXX. Find them a body to bury."

Then he hung up and left me dangling at the end of the line.

---

[20] "Schreyer's ... telephone number remains in the Winnipeg directory and anyone who calls usually finds
himself talking to the premier." Douglas Marshall, *Maclean's,* December 1970.

XIV

Versatile

Historical events repeat themselves, first as tragedy and the second time as farce.
—Karl Marx

A **bane of government** is the lineup of businesses requesting help, often including those who publicly oppose 'government intervention' in business. Among the first petitioners seeking the newly-elected Premier Schreyer's 'intervention' was Versatile Manufacturing.

Versatile was a good company that made good farm machinery. It had been established in 1949 by two Toronto brothers-in-law, one a super inventor/mechanic and the other a super salesman. In 1952, they moved to Winnipeg to be nearer the grain-producing region. They built light farm equipment and by 1966 they were experimenting with new technology tractors and developing a large market.

In the late 1960s they over-expanded. Shortly after the election of the NDP government the two principals came to Premier Schreyer's office, explained they owed $6.5 million, the value of their shares had tumbled from $8 to less than $2, and their banks were threatening to foreclose. Versatile could end up as a heap of used machinery. Would the Government of Manitoba, through the Manitoba Development Corporation, take over their loan and get the banks off their backs so they could continue with their forte—manufacturing technologically-advanced farm machinery?

It was the first major loan application under the NDP and tested the mettle and methods of the new government. The machinery was good and there were over 800 jobs at stake, but was it the function of the MDC, using taxpayers' money, to bail out a failing privately owned enterprise? If the entrepreneurs were entitled to the profits of their endeavours, should they not also take the attendant risks, including bankruptcy? Also, perhaps allowing the company to go into bankruptcy would result in a new entrepreneur purchasing it for much less than the amount of the current loans and the capital write-down could result in a more financially viable operation and lower farm machinery prices.

Versatile's books showed the company was sound but was caught in a periodic squeeze: a temporary turndown in the farm economy resulting in supplier inventory buildup and reduced sales. It was decided it was indeed the function of the MDC to assist small business after the Big Banks turned their backs on them.

But there were problems. First, the major part of Versatile's production was being sold into the United States and it was already assembling machinery there, so what was to stop the company from taking our money, bailing itself out, and moving its plant south of the border? Second, what was to stop Versatile's shareholders from taking our money and paying it to themselves as dividends?

To forestall this, the loan was approved with two conditions: (a) the MDC would place three directors on the board of Versatile and (b) the MDC would purchase twenty-five per cent of the shares of Versatile.

This would give the MDC some influence over strategic decisions of the company and over the way the taxpayer's money was used. The principals of Versatile accepted the conditions and an agreement was drawn up.

Versatile's banks then decided if it was good enough for the government, it was good enough for them, so there was no need for the MDC loan. The government argued that the offer of Manitoba taxpayers money had kept the bank's money in the company, so the taxpayers were entitled to the conditions that had been accepted. But the contract was not explicit, so we saved the company from bankruptcy, but got nothing, except the survival of Versatile and 800 jobs.

Almost three years after the bailout, I received a phone call from the short, scrappy mechanical genius of Versatile. "We want to bring used machinery from our plant in Grand Forks to Winnipeg during the winter to repair it."

"Please do."

"Your tax system makes that very difficult. If we would bring machinery up here for repairing we could create off-season jobs."

"That would be most welcome. Tell me how our tax regime is interfering with such a process and we will see what we can do."

"We want the tax system changed. But if you socialists don't want jobs created by the private sector, it doesn't matter to us. You would probably rather take over our company."

"Listen, three years ago you people came to the Premier's Office virtually on your knees to plead with us to bail you out. We did and now we see your gratitude. Next time we will let your company go bankrupt and buy it for a dollar. Then we need not argue with you about what the government wants to do."

He hung up in my ear. Two hours later his partner, the tall, urbane salesman, called. It was not quite an apology. "I understand you had a fight with my partner. Perhaps he is a bit brusque, but he means well." His voice rose. "But listen, you have to do something about your tax system. Do you know the level of income taxes in this province is so high that I am forced to spend half my year living in a trailer in Mexico, where I have to carry my shit out in a pail."

"Well, that's what happens in a country that does not collect enough taxes to provide proper sewage disposal services. Tell me something. Is the tax system really so bad here that you feel compelled to spend the rest of your life living in a trailer in Mexico and carrying your shit out in a pail?"

There was a long silence. Then: "Well, maybe I should not object to paying some income taxes."

We exchanged correspondence in which he took the position that the lower the income tax and the higher the untaxed profits, the greater the capital investment and the lower the unemployment.

The farm economy exploded into growth and Versatile went into orbit. Wheat sold for the highest price in Canadian history. Farmers bought machinery as though it was going out of style—which, because of the massive technological changes, it was—and traded up their tractors to create a whole new mass market. Versatile developed into a world-class company. Living up to its name, it built a versatile and powerful articulated four-wheel drive tractor that caught the imagination of the agricultural community and found markets as far away as Australia.

Half a decade after the MDC intervention, Versatile was a roaring success with more than 1,300 employees, making it one of the largest private employers in Manitoba, and with sales of over $100 million making it one of the largest industrial firms headquartered in Winnipeg. Its machinery was on the leading edge of technology and a high percentage of its production was being sold outside Canada. Versatile was doing precisely what the government had hoped it would do when it offered help: making desired products, creating local jobs, earning foreign currency and contributing taxes to the provincial treasury.

Versatile was an outstanding MDC success. And the intervention of the government to rescue the company during its dog days was long forgotten. Harry Mardon, associate editor of the *The Winnipeg Tribune,* wrote that, while Versatile had received some $467,000 in grants from Ottawa, an official of the company had told him "the firm had received no grants from the Manitoba government."[1]

Such a bad memory could not go unchallenged. I wrote to Mardon. "For your information, in 1969 Versatile received a loan guarantee for $6,500,000 from the Government of Manitoba. Apparently Versatile, like the newspaper industry, has difficulty surviving without taxpayers' subsidies."[2]

Harry Mardon was not alone. In 1974, while in Misericordia Hospital enduring a skin-graft on an old burn, I was accosted by an aggressive nurse who, knowing I was "from the government" added to my pain by proudly informing me that her husband worked at Versatile which "has never asked for any help from government."

---

[1] *The Winnipeg Tribune*, December 26, 1975.

[2] At the time, subsidies to the newspaper industry by the Canadian government paid about eighty per cent of their mailing costs.

In 1977, the two principals sold their shares to Vancouver-based Cornat Corporation for a reported $28 million. By 1979, the plant size had been doubled, sales had reached $150 million, and the work force was about 1,800. But the agricultural economy can be as unpredictable and devastating for suppliers as for farmers. The subsequent combination of economic downturn and the high cost of carrying the capital load proved too much. By late 1986, Versatile's work force was down to about 650 and the possibility of plant closure was hanging over it like a dark cloud. The MDC had been wound down so was no longer there to help. Versatile was desperately seeking a buyer to save itself from bankruptcy.

This led to one of those bizarre situations showing how circumstances drive politicians to pragmatism—and hypocrisy. For more than a century one of the major issues of Canadian politics and of the Canadian economy has been the question of foreign ownership. This was particularly an issue, always good for tub-thumping "I love Canada" speeches, for the coalition of pseudo-intellectual leftists wanting to get their hands on the 'big levers' of government, the tunnel-visioned trade unionists whose advancement of the 'sheltered workshop' philosophy knew no limits, and the professional women's libbers who believed the government owed them a living because they were women.

The moment Prime Minister Brian Mulroney announced his intention to negotiate a free trade agreement with the United States in March 1987, it was met by a chorus, led by Manitoba Premier Howard Pawley and the political schemers at the provincial office of the NDP and backed by the Greek chorus at the head-quarters of the Manitoba Federation of Labour. Listening to them could force one to conclude trade agreements should be designed not to eliminate cross border tariffs, promote industrial efficiency, encourage mutual trade, and reduce costs to consumers, but rather to increase the ability of Canadian governments to main-tain an artificial economy, create artificial jobs, and pay for them with borrowed money.

They would not admit the logical end of the pursuit of their economic philosophy would result in Canada becoming an economic island with fewer and fewer goods being sold in a smaller and smaller market at higher and higher prices. Nothing must be done, they argued, that would jeopardize Canadian control of the Canadian economy and allow further penetration by foreign—read American—corporations. American corporations were BAD.

Except with regard to Versatile! Their fear of plant closure and loss of unionized jobs was greater than their economic xenophobia. The Deere Company of the United States offered to buy Versatile. The offer was accepted but the take-over was prohibited by the American Justice Department, which feared this would give Deere a monopoly in four-wheel drive tractor technology.

But did the trade unionists and the philosophical 'leftists' and the profes-sional anti-Americans heave a sigh of relief because one Canadian company had been rescued from the greedy grasp of an American corporation? Did Premier Pawley call a press conference and do a fandango on his desk-top and boast he had saved one for Canada? No! Premier Pawley fired off a telex to Prime Minister Mulroney telling him, in effect, to contact his Irish expatriate buddy in the Oval Office in Washington, President Ronald Reagan, and demand he call off his dogs and allow the takeover of Versatile by BAD Deere.

In early 1987, Versatile was sold to Ford New Holland, an American farm machinery corporation, for a reported $180 million.[3] Well, perhaps "sold" is not the correct terminology. In fact, the Government of Canada loaned Ford New Holland, a foreign corporation, $45 million of Canadian taxpayer's money, to be repaid over twenty years, to sweeten the purchase of Versatile.

The joy in Winnipeg knew no bounds! Principle was fine so long as it did not interfere with the opportunities of the pseudo-intellectual leftists to pretend they were doing something useful with the 'big levers' of government, or with the ability of the trade union panjundrums to maintain their myriad of job classifications, or demand government create artificial jobs with borrowed money.

All was wine and roses as newspaper headlines announced triumph after triumph for Versatile. In 1991, Fiat bought eighty per cent of Ford New Holland and moved the production of its two-wheel drive tractor from Belgium to Winnipeg. In 1996, Versatile celebrated the sale of its 10,000th product. In 1997, it was employing more than 700 persons and negotiating for a $40 million sale of tractors to the Ukraine. And it signed a three-year contract with its union.

In June 1999, this impressive business edifice began to collapse. Ford New Holland purchased the Case Corporation, one of the world's largest farm implement makers. American anti-combines regulators, alert to potential monopolies, allowed the purchase on condition that Ford New Holland divest itself of Versatile.

Suddenly Versatile was up for sale and the danse macabre of a decade earlier was repeated. Versatile was orphaned and desperately seeking a buyer— any buyer. On November 20, 1999, the union at Versatile placed a full-page advertisement in the *Winnipeg Free Press* appealing to the public to urge politicians to save the "critical research and development, engineering, design and manufacturing capabilities at the only farm tractor assembly plant left in Canada."

Ford New Holland reportedly moved twenty-five per cent of its work force, and its TV-140 bidirectional product line designed and developed in Winnipeg, out of Manitoba. The workforce fell to about 350 and annual sales of about $700 million were dwindling rapidly.

The company was also facing a severe downturn in the farm economy, the little matter of a debt of $32 million outstanding of the earlier $45 million loan from Ottawa, and a $100 million contract with the Case Corporation was at risk unless work on it began before February 1, 2001.

Winnipeg's Buhler Industries emerged as the only company prepared to accept the risk. Its owner, John Buhler, was a local businessman who had shown some talent for resuscitating companies in distress. In July 2000, he bought

---

[3] *Winnipeg Free Press,* February 18, 1987.

Versatile for a reported $15 million and assumption of the remaining debt of $32 million. Versatile escaped obliteration by the skin of its teeth. Three months later, the union struck and the labour-management dispute evolved into one of the most acrimonious in Manitoba history.

It became a test of wills between a hard-nosed entrepreneur who had achieved $100 million in sales from his stable of companies by doing things his way, and the Canadian Auto Workers Union, which had honed its negotiating skills and take-no-prisoners attitude by extracting lucrative agreements from the multi-billion dollar Big Three auto makers by doing things their way.

The disagreement was nominally over job security, seniority and outsourcing, but in fact it ran much deeper. The union considered Buhler anti-union and a scavenger, and had not been thrilled by his purchase of Versatile. [4] Buhler saw the union as an obstacle to reorganization of the plant into a viable operation in a declining market and saw no logic in being asked to guarantee job security to his employees with no security of sales for his products.

Negotiations proceeded as though one side was holding and the other side would not let go. Buhler threatened to operate with scab labour; the CAW implied such persons would be targeted. Buhler offered to go to compulsory arbitration; the CAW wanted negotiations. When the CAW agreed to compulsory arbitration, Buhler accepted, with conditions. With the CAW showing no sign of surrender, Buhler threatened to close the plant and move it to North Dakota.

On March 2, 2001, CAW President Buzz Hargrove came to Winnipeg to demand that the Government of Manitoba nationalize Versatile. When a spokesman for the Premier's Office responded that was "not in the cards", Hargrove replied that the government spokesman "should be fired".

Several private-sector Versatile owners had received financial assistance; now it was the turn of the union and the workers it represented. And they should have been able to have their way with an NDP government—a party of which the unions were an organic part. But the NDP government of Premier Gary Doer had learned the lessons of his predecessors, Premiers Schreyer and Pawley, and would not rush in just to save jobs by rescuing an industrial dog. Also, this was the perfect case for the acquisition and operation of a plant by the workers themselves. They conceivably could have acquired it for one dollar, and been granted millions in "research and development" funds. But Hargrove would not go there. The workers were employees, not businessmen. Taking risks was the responsibility of others. Socialism was for theorists.

So CAW sought its revenge elsewhere. They charged Buhler with "unfair labour practices". On June 7, 2001, The Manitoba Labour Board found Buhler Versatile guilty of "bargaining in bad faith" and assessed a penalty of $6 million.

The one-time pride of the Manitoba industrial scene was dying the death of a thousand cuts.

---

[4] John Buhler claimed that a CAW official told him that "out of a choice of 15 companies [they hoped would bid for Versatile], you would be number 20." *Winnipeg Free Press*, February 28, 2001.

But Buhler was not finished. He bought out the union contract for some $17 million and reorganized the plant on a non-union basis. He developed the unique B56 four-wheel drive articulated tractor to operate in tight spaces, and as this goes to print, Versatile appears to have achieved stability.

Reportedly, by the end of 2001, no former CAW members were working at the plant. And Buhler's tractor plant was reportedly "producing at prestrike levels with less than half the staff".[5]

In 1980, the chairman of the Cornat Corporation of Vancouver, which had purchased Versatile in 1976, was reported opposing federal help to refinance troubled Massey-Ferguson Ltd. because: "It is wrong for governments to bail out organizations that got themselves into trouble."[6]

That statement should be framed and placed on the desk of every premier —especially every social democratic—premier. On reflection, perhaps we should have let Versatile collapse in 1969 and be picked up by some entrepreneur at a fraction of its value. But it is not that easy to say "No" to mendicant businessmen.

---

[5] *Ibid.*, February 5, 2002.
[6] *Ibid.*, October 25, 1980.

XV

The Winnipeg Jets

Against arrant stupidity, even the gods contend in vain.
—Wilhelm Schiller

"**If you want to keep the Jets in Winnipeg,** buy some damn tickets," I told the belligerent caller to the Premier's Office. He, like many others, was obsessed with keeping the hockey team in Winnipeg by spending the last dollar of other people's money.

Ironically, some of the most vicious criticism of the 'socialists' resulted not from getting into business, but from attempting to stay out of one while the 'free-enterprisers' attempted to skate the government into a corner without a puck.

The government's trauma began on March 15, 1974, when Jets owner Ben Hatskin told the media he had lost about $250,000 the previous year, that there would be similar losses this year, that "that's no way for a private enterprise to operate very long", and that public ownership was the only way to keep the Jets in Winnipeg.[1] It ended in October 1995, when the Jets were sold for a reported $68 million (U.S.), and became the Phoenix Coyotes. The team's owners administered the final humiliation to Manitobans, and saved themselves a bundle in taxes, by shuffling the sale through Québec.

The departure was assured on August 15, 1995 when the Spirit of Manitoba, incorporated to buy the Jets with private money and keep them in Manitoba, announced that it had failed to raise the funds. David Whitson, a student of the relationship between sports and business, wrote, "The long-standing interests of Canadian fans, and of Canada itself, were becoming increasingly marginal to the commercial future of a game that Canadians had popularized and

---

[1] *Winnipeg Free Press*, March 15, 1974.

164

still occupies an important place in our popular culture."[2]

Carl Ridd, University of Winnipeg professor, former Olympic basketball champion, member of both the Manitoba and Canadian Sports Hall of Fame, activist in Thin Ice, a citizen's group opposing the ritual raid on the treasury to build a larger playpen for the Jets, analytically and graphically predicted, "Hockey franchises are going upscale, up-cost, up-market and down South."

David Whitson added, "From the perspective of NHL headquarters in New York City, these events were consistent with the league's strategy of building its presence in the prosperous and growing cities of the U.S. Sunbelt."[3]

I like to think that we saw it coming in 1974. That was when I told the angry caller the best way to keep the Jets in Winnipeg was to buy some tickets.[4] His unprintable retort was followed by the loud click of the telephone in my ear.

He was demanding that the Government of Manitoba levy taxes on the public to hand over to the private owners of the Winnipeg Jets, so that he could, from the other side of his mouth, or on alternate days of the week, attack the government for wasting his money. It was the classical example of people allowing themselves to be psyched into believing if government bought something it was free. Usually the understanding that this was their money came later—when the investment government had been urged to make went sour.

But then, this was an unusual case. Almost two years earlier, the incubus of the Jets had fastened its grip on the emotions of Manitobans and the treasury of the province. Few incidents better illustrated the hypocrisy of the elites or the cynical observation that we practice "socialism for the rich and private enterprise for the poor" than that initiated by the descent of the Jets upon Winnipeg like a secular Second Coming.

Benny Hatskin, larger-than-life, imaginative, former Blue Bombers football star who helped win two Grey Cups, was a major promoter on the Winnipeg sporting scene. Now he did what, even for him, seemed impossible, something that earned him many kudos and the title 'Man of the Year'. He brought to Winnipeg the World Hockey Association franchise and with it famed Chicago Black Hawks left winger and National Hockey League star, Bobby Hull.

On June 27, 1972, a crowd of 5,000 Manitobans gathered at Portage and Main to triumphantly witness the 'Golden Jet' sign a $3 million contract to play with the newly-minted Jets. The contract made him the highest-paid professional athlete in North America, and launched an upward spiral of athletic salaries that may never be brought under control.

---

[2] David Whitson in Jim Silver's *This Ice: Money, Politics and the Demise of an NHL Franchise,* Fern Publications, Halifax, 1996, p. 6.

[3] Whitson, *Ibid.*, p. 6.

[4] A generation later, the Ottawa Senators' owner threatened to sell his hockey team to Americans. On January 18, 2000, the federal government offered a $20 million annual subsidy plan for hockey teams. But politicians had not learned that all the people needed to do to keep hockey teams at home was to buy tickets, but the taxpayers had—and the resultant public uproar forced the government to retreat ... fast.

Less than two years later, Hatskin was announcing his sports losses and claiming that "a private businessman should not be asked to lose money". If Winnipeg wanted the Jets, he inferred, we must buy them.

There was no reason to believe that a public owner, or a new private owner subsidized with public funds, could operate the team any more profitably than the 'old pro'. But apparently it was acceptable for the public to be asked to lose money.

Winnipeg's newspapers bulged with horror stories of the city disappearing in a puff of smoke if the Jets folded or moved away. Any amount of subsidization was justified to keep them here. The literati waxed poetic in praise of the team, and predictions were dire; if by some arrant mischance, some stupendous lack of foresight, some regrettable absence of civic courage, some misconstrued sense of stewardship of public money, some fatal flaw in our thinking, some tragic defficiency of imagination, some genetic failure to adapt to conditions, some capitalistic impulse to love our money more than we love our children, if for any reason at all we failed to accept Hatskin's offer, we would condemn ourselves forever to descend into the Stygian darkness of our Northern winter night without the scintillating incandescence of the Jets to guide us.

Winnipeg, we were told, had developed a love affair with the Jets, and they must be kept here at any cost. Curiously, this love had not registered itself in ticket purchases at the box office during the previous two seasons, but we were vociferously assured, particularly by those whose tickets were often purchased by their corporate employers with tax writeoff money, that it was so. Therefore, so this love could be requited, the Jets must be kept alive, and here, no matter the cost.

Immediately, a citizens' committee was established to find money to buy the Jets. Their early fundraising foray was to City Hall, where they got a $300,000 interest free loan.[5] Then they came to the Government of Manitoba for an equal loan, also interest free. The government recognized the contribution of the Jets made in taking the edge off the Winnipeg's long, cold winters, that Bobby Hull had contributed to a gleam in the eyes of the province's younger population, and that the WHA franchise itself had a market value. There were also some ardent sportsmen in the NDP caucus who would have felt bereft if the Jets had forsaken the city, and there were other MLAs and party supporters who aged visibly at the thought of having to inform their children that the Jets might be leaving.

In ordinary circumstances we might have provided the loan. But the circumstances were not ordinary. After five years in office we were floating, submerged to our nostrils, in the jetsam and flotsam of wreckage of projects that had gone into bankruptcy after receiving government loans, and the waves were rising. Ironically, the turbulence was created by some of the same people now asking us for money.

It seemed everything we touched was turning to ashes; what would be

---

[5] The loan was never repaid. The purchasers of the team disclaimed all responsibility.

different about this project? Also, the Blue Bombers, the community-owned football team, was having financial difficulties—again. And could we buy or bail out the Jets without inviting the demand we do likewise for the privately-owned Assiniboia Downs race track, which seemed to be on its death bed?

Granted, these projects might be for the public good, but were not all the failures in which we had invested for the good of the public? Granted, these projects would create jobs, but was that not the seductive argument that stuck us to the tar-baby of Churchill Forest Industries, Saunders Aircraft and Flyer Bus? Could we afford, politically or financially, to invest in another questionable venture?

Granted also, $300,000 was not a large slice of a half-billion dollar budget to risk, but could we be sure this would be the only dip into the till on behalf of the Jets? It was feared that, as soon as the loan was made, the team's promoters would hint to the media that the 'Golden Jet' could not play his optimum game without a couple of star wingers, and there were a couple in Sweden who would do him justice, which we really must have, if only to show our kids—and those in the box seats—what a great game hockey is. If only the government can be tapped for money to buy the Jets, it would be almost forced to buy the Swedes to protect the original loan.

We could purchase the Jets as a community-owned operation, like the Blue Bombers, but would this be a legitimate business proposal? The franchise originally acquired for a reported $250,000 now had a price tag of $2,300,000 (and *Winnipeg Tribune* sports columnist Jack Matheson was claiming it was worth $4 million), with $500,000 to be paid in cash and the balance amortized over seven years at nine per cent interest.

Nor were the prospects inspiring. Attendance increased in the second season, but so did the losses. And the back-of-the-envelope projections for the team's future viability were suspect, to say the least. Average attendance per game had been 5,761 in 1972–73, perhaps 6,317 for 1973–74, but was projected at 7,500 for 1974–75. Similarly, losses had been $251,056 in 1972–73 and $314,531 in 1973-74, but were projected at only $74,763 for 1974–75. But in preparing these projections, they had neglected to add arena rental ($148,256 in 1973–74) or interest charges on the proposed $300,000 interest-free loan, plus the $500,000 cash payment, plus the $1,800,000 to be paid over seven years at nine per cent interest.

And there was one more little wrinkle: the government was being asked to pick up a share of any future operating deficits. [6]

Nonetheless, it was not an easy decision: "These pressures [to create a new 'post-industrial' civic image] create very real dilemmas for political leaders because, even when self-serving claims about the contributions of pro sports to the civic

---

[6] Harry Mardon, *Winnipeg Tribune* business editor, considered the deal so bad he took issue with his colleague Jack Matheson by pointing out these deficits (*Tribune*, April 27, 1974. Matheson snarled back that defending Schreyer was most unusual for Mardon).

economy are revealed as inflated, the symbolic effects cannot be discounted."[7]

But we said NO!

Winnipeg went wild. Sports commentators were frantic. The guys in the box seats were not amused. The public was aroused. The government received more than 1,000 phone calls, letters and telegrams demanding that we make the loan. Many stated that our negative response was proof positive that we were indeed just "a bunch of God-damned socialists", determined to destroy the country, as the authors of these missives had suspected since we took office. Larry Desjardins, a well-known and highly-esteemed hockey player and ardent sports fan, and now minister of sports and recreation, was hung in effigy at Western Canada's most famous intersection—the corner of Portage and Main.

Bumper stickers that had first appeared during the gut-wrenching fight over public auto insurance in 1970, reappeared: WILL THE LAST PERSON TO LEAVE MANITOBA TURN OUT THE LIGHTS?

And a joke began making the rounds on the cocktail circuit. Question: What is the difference between a politician and a catfish? Answer: One is a big-mouthed, slime-sucking, bottom-feeder. The other is some kind of fish.

Sports columnist Jack Matheson vented his spleen:

> The people of Manitoba [now] know Mr. Schreyer's ... reputation as a sports fan is a fraud ... [He] doesn't give damn about sport ... If you want to catch a glimpse of him, try the Union Centre or a Labour temple, where his bread is buttered for him ... I guess the Jets weren't as unsuccessful as they should have been last year. If they had floundered and gone into receivership, Premier Schreyer would have the money to pump them up [as] he keeps pouring your money ... into an aircraft factory nobody wants ... If Premier Schreyer doesn't want the Jets here ... perhaps he could tell us where he'll find the million dollars in revenue the hockey team generated last season [including] provincial income tax from players and staff.
>
> So what do good corporate citizens do now? I'd like to think they could tell Mr. Schreyer where to put his 300 grand, a bill at a time ... I wonder what would happen if they called Eaton's and The Bay and BACM and Great West Life and Greater Winnipeg Gas and Inter-City Gas and Sears and Canada Packers ... and the breweries ... I wouldn't be surprised if they came up with quite a bundle ... The future of the Jets is up to people like Bob Graham [president of Inter-City Gas], Bill Shields [of Clarkson, Gordon and Company] and Jim Burns [president of Great West Life], who are big in business here, and that may be a tip-off, too, when you consider how our socialist friends under the dome feel about anybody making an honest buck through hard work and enterprise."[8]

---

[7] Whitson, in Silver, *Thin Ice*, p.7.
[8] Matheson, *The Winnipeg Tribune*, April 25, 1974.

Jack Matheson forgot—or ignored—that, a week earlier, William Shields and James Burns had approached the City of Winnipeg and the Government of Manitoba for the $300,000 interest-free loan for the Jets. And he either was not aware—or chose to ignore—the statement, made the same day, by one of his corporate heroes: "James W. Burns, president of Great West Life Assurance Company said Wednesday reduced government spending would be the strongest step possible toward reducing inflation rates."[9]

But perhaps Jack Matheson did not even notice it. After all, it was so normal; demand that government finance your pet projects; criticize it if it doesn't; criticize it even more if it does.

And then there was the article by columnist Phillip Anwyl:

> A sum of $300,000 represents peanuts by today's standards of excessive government spending ... So what's all the fuss about a $300,000 loan from the taxpayers? To the government the sum represents a drop in the bucket. What changed the mind of Premier Schreyer, who earlier reportedly aired a receptive view to the idea? Possibly pressure from some members of the NDP caucus who have never been particularly sympathetic to anyone who is reasonably well-off.
>
> Mr. Hatskin, owner of the Jets, is reported to be a millionaire, not the best credentials when your name crops up in the caucus room of the NDP ... Mr. Hatskin paid $250,000 when he bought the WHA franchise. Although the Jets have been a financially losing proposition in its two years of operations here, Mr. Hatskin's losses will be more than made up if he sells the Jets. The franchise is worth anything up to $4 million—and that, in the eyes of many a good socialist, is an unconscionable profit."[10]

Lenin had described the phenomenon. "In the last analysis we are all special pleaders." Overuse of a few dollars of welfare by some city-core indigent drove the elites and their media handmaidens into fits protesting government negligence and waste of public money, but refusal to bail out the Jets, owned by a reputed millionaire, was seen as treason, or at best, *lèse majesté*.

Actually, Anwyl had a point; Schreyer was quite receptive to contributing to the Jets—until he read the contract. It gave the $250,000 team, which had never filled the arena and had lost more than $500,000, a value of $2.3 million and required the government to pick up part of future losses. Giving money to the Jets would have been tantamount to throwing it down a rat-hole.

We were constantly being damned for wasting public money, when we were not being damned for NOT wasting it.

---

[9] "Govt Spending Cut urged by Businessmen", *Winnipeg Free Press*, April 25, 1974 Twenty years later, Burns urged Premier Gary Filmon to buy the Jets, for $32 million. *Ibid.*, June 19, 1994.

[10] Anwyl, *Ibid.*, April 27, 1974.

And the main promotion appeared to emanate from the corporate community. But when the corporate boxes were purchased with pretax money they contributed little, merely allowing the REAL taxpayers to purchase the seats for them. We were aware of the speciousness of the propaganda that the Jets were bringing "millions" into the provincial economy. And we feared that the infusion of public subsidies would result in higher salaries and higher ticket fees; subject to the law of normal bureaucratic corruption, more money would mean more waste, not reduced prices.

But the fix was in. When those demanding we bail out the Jets were told to show their support for the team by buying tickets rather than demanding subsidies, they would reply that the symphony and the art gallery were subsidized so why not the Jets? They saw no difference between such services in which the community had chosen to invest and a privately owned, for-profit enterprise that had failed in the marketplace and now sought a bailout.

In any case, by 1974 the government already had a bellyfull of the Jets. Their owners did not allow the early adulation lavished upon them as patrons of the sports to interfere with their acumen as hard-headed businessmen. They would do much for Winnipeg—if government gave them enough tax concessions to make the team profitable.

When the Jets arrived, their owners immediately asked the Government of Manitoba to legislate cancellation of amusement taxes on Jets games. And that bunch of socialists encamped—temporarily it was devoutly hoped—in the Graeco-Roman mausoleum on Broadway, were apparently expected to pine for just such an opportunity to ingratiate themselves with the business community.

No, we could not cancel the tax for the Jets without opening a can of worms, but we would support the Jets in true free enterprise fashion—through the box office. The government would buy Jets tickets for $100,000 annually (21,000 of them in 1973). This was equal to the amusement tax, but would be of much more value to the team, because it would not be just a subsidy. The tickets would be distributed to Manitobans who did not normally attend games. This would both add new money to, and new interest in, the Jets.

And then we set about selecting the lucky recipients of the free tickets to the games of the vaunted Jets! Among the first names drawn was that of an inmate of Headingley jail. We needed to hire a car and a driver, as well as a commissionaire to guard the prisoner, pick him up, drive him to the arena and return him to his snug billet.

It marked the beginning of the melancholy relationship between the Government of Manitoba and the Jets. And it turned out to be not the best way to win friends and influence voters.

XVI

The Stamp

Before we came here we thought of ourselves as good people.
—Vincent Foster, White House Counsel
to U.S. President Bill Clinton

It was another routine Monday. The plaque on my desk read: "I came here to contemplate the futility of it all but alas, it's no use." And I was facing the endless minutiae of administration, reflecting aspirations or anger of Manitobans. In the potpourri of correspondence was a letter to the premier. The chairman of a northern school division demanded more teachers, social workers, and funding. If there was no affirmative reply by 2 P.M. Wednesday, he would call a press conference to denounce the government to the people of Northern Manitoba who had strongly supported it in the last election. I vizualized board members psyching each other into writing that letter—and knew if they received no money, they would have a political issue. This needed special treatment.

We received frequent ultimatums. The question was, if they came from an area on which the government depended for its political life, should it accede, or would an affirmative response make the recipient hungrier for power? Concessions invariably invoked Zymurgy's First Law of Evolving Dynamics, which postulates that if one opens a can of worms the only way to get them back in is to get a larger can. An affirmative response would circulate through the province at the speed of light—or at least at the speed with which telephones could be dialed—and lead to demands from other divisions.

Mail of this nature should be referred to the premier or to the relevant minister. But was it good politics for the premier to respond to ultimatums? And the minister was out of town. I could not leave this to his bureaucracy; they would either not respond in forty-eight hours, or worse, they might give the division what it demanded and open the floodgates. Besides, this was too good to leave to others.

I sent a night letter informing the chairman that his division had already received three more teachers, four more social workers, and several hundred thousand dollars more in grants than it was entitled to. My letter concluded with: "Please advise when you wish me to give your file to the media."

The next morning, about 11 o'clock, my secretary came in to discuss several matters. Apropos of nothing in particular, I remarked: "About now I should be receiving an apologetic phone call from the chairman of a ..." I was interrupted by the urgently ringing phone.

"Mr. Schulz, this is _____ from the _____ School Division. I just received your letter. I am very sorry about offending you." He assured me, due to the information in my letter, that there would be no news conference. The conversation ended on a friendly note.

As usual, a copy of the correspondence was sent to the relevant minister, in this case Education Minister Ben Hanuschak. And then I began to feel uneasy. I had interfered in the affairs of a department and the minister might not appreciate it. So what to do? I could phone the minister and, like Macbeth, boldly admit, "I have done the deed." But the minister already knew that and aggressiveness would not spare me a reprimand—or even dismissal—if the minister reported my indiscretion to the premier. The more guilty I felt the more uneasy I became and the more uneasy I became the more guilty I felt. I had made a serious error.

At the next cabinet meeting I sat, as usual, behind the premier's large, ornate chair, listening to the discussions and taking notes so I could explain to callers the reasons for policy decisions. Hanuschak came in late and sat, facing me, in his chair at the far end of the huge table. I attempted to make eye contact, but he appeared to be avoiding my gaze. I was in trouble!

Time passed—very slowly. I frequently glanced toward Hanuschak, but he did not acknowledge my presence. Guilt played havoc with my taut synapses. The tension was creating body heat. Half an hour later, Hanuschak pushed back his chair and rose. My frayed nerve ends informed me that my hour had come. But not yet—he slowly reached into his pocket and pulled out his eight-inch pipe. Even more slowly he pulled out his pouch and tamped the tobacco into his pipe. Slowly he lit it and took several deep, satisfying puffs. The tension was unbearable. He never looked in my direction, but I knew he was thinking about me. I was in greater trouble than I had thought. In what appeared slow motion, like an apparition partially obscured by the huge cloud of smoke from his omnipresent pipe, he took the dozen steps to where I sat, still not making eye contact, and took another puff. "Herb!" His voice sounded sepulchral. "I suspect you spend a great deal of time writing letters."

I had transgressed the unwritten rule of inter-departmental relations once too often and I was about to pay the price.

"Weeeeelll, yeeeessss," I responded.

"Would you like to hear a suggestion about how you could save yourself a considerable amount of time?"

He finally looked into my eyes. The challenge was clear. Sweat formed on my forehead and under my armpits. My body shrank but my mind, as though in another dimension, admired his approach: his next words, dripping with sarcasm, would undoubtedly be, "by keeping your fucking nose out of my business."

"Weeeeelll, Mr. Minister, as always, I would be pleased to hear any advice you have for me."

I groped in a fog. He took another draw on his pipe. It was a bad dream but frighteningly real. He was torturing me. He withdrew the pipe and his mouth formed words: "You should get a stamp with a rude message on it that would instantly be recognized as your personal imprimatur." Then he chuckled and returned to his chair. Two weeks later Anna Gordon, his executive assistant, came with a small gift-wrapped parcel: "From the minister," she said. "To save you time answering mail in future."

I opened the box. In it was a large rubber stamp. It read: FUCK YOU! STRONG LETTER FOLLOWS.

NEWS OF 'THE STAMP' marched in quick-step through The Ledge. Government employees came to inquire if this rumoured instrument really existed and if they could see it? Ministerial assistants, bedevilled by demands they could not possibly satisfy, and required to run interference for their minister, would pick it up caressingly, relating occasions when they might have used it had they had it, and borrow a piece of paper on which to stamp the inscription as a souvenir. I never used it of course; the premier would not have been amused. But at times I was tempted.

Demands on government are constant and, contrary to conventional wisdom, emanate less from 'welfare bums' living their lives of quiet desperation in the rotting core of the city, than from powerful persons, organizations and corporations. The more powerful they were and the more they boasted at their clubs of their fervent devotion to 'free enterprise", the more they sought access to the public pocket. When these demands were not acceded to, the cacophony of criticism about how we were destroying free enterprise by refusing them government assistance was such that it would have caused Socrates to voluntarily reach for the hemlock. It caused ME to reach for The Stamp—figuratively, of course.

THE WINNIPEG TRIBUNE editorially criticized farm subsidies, stating many industries do not receive subsidies, do not ask for subsidies, were doing very nicely, thank you, without subsidies, and perhaps this was a lesson for farmers. The editor was sent a letter reminding him that his industry had its mailing charges heavily subsidized by the taxpayers, and including a rough estimate of how many dollars this would annually drop into the pockets of the owners of the paper.

The long-delayed reply stated that government payment of newspaper's mailing costs is not a subsidy because (a) it is government policy and (b) it had been in effect for so long it can no longer be called a subsidy.[1] Stripped of its rationalizing cant, it meant "our subsidy is not a subsidy because a subsidy is a subsidy only when received by others." I visualized the mark of The Stamp on the editor's forehead.

THE PREMIER'S OFFICE was both a Court of Last Resort and a one-stop problem-solving centre. People with problems would be either directed to the appropriate department or we would phone the relevant department, obtain the information, and resolve the issue. If someone came with a complaint that a department was not providing service or that the issue involved several departments and was lost in the maze, we would pull together all the relevant information and attempt to solve the problem. We often worked into the night and devoted our time to satisfying citizens. For those who looked helpless, or politely requested assistance, we virtually stood on our heads to help.

But there were others. "Listen, if you bastards don't give me that MDC loan pretty damn soon I'm moving my shoe factory to Hawaii." The call was from a very angry man. He perhaps spent much time complaining about too-high taxes and too much government involvement in business, but now his concern was that his $1 million loan application had not been answered with a cheque by return mail. He was advising the Office of the Head Honcho of the government to prod the MDC board with a sharp stick or Manitobans would be walking in their stockinged feet. The answer was easy. "Well, I hear the weather is beautiful in Hawaii. Goodbye."

MOST IRRITATING WERE THOSE who came with a problem already dragged through several departments and hopelessly tangled, and would then phone several times a day to inquire if we had yet cut the Gordian Knot on their behalf. We would listen carefully, make copies of material, undertake to do our best with the issue, but caution that this would take time to unwind. The citizen invariably assured us that he/she had spent so much time on the matter that a few more days did not matter. Invariably, when I arrived at the office next morning, a call would already have been received from that person, inquiring whether we had solved the problem yet.

A man arrived and deposited an armload of papers on my desk. His problem

---

[1] Second-class mail (newspapers and periodicals) are subsidized through Canada Post. In 1972–73, the subsidy listed in federal accounts was $36,569,000. In 1974-75, the subsidy was estimated at $45,548,000, or about seventy-six per cent of Canada's newspaper mailing costs.

involved three separate departments plus Manitoba Hydro. He had been working on it for four months, he needed help, and we could have all the time we needed. Predictably, in the next three days my staff gave me several phone messages a day asking about the status of his problem. On the fourth day, his letter peremptorily demanded results. I replied briefly, stating he had said there was no rush, that I am working on it, and will call when it is done. The letter almost bore the imprint of The Stamp and I was pleased with myself. But I was dealing with a superior intellect: he replied with a letter, addressed to me, blank except for the signature, "Marcel Marceau"—the mime artist. He was implying that my letter had said nothing. The mark of The Stamp was on my forehead.

THERE WAS A VAST DISCREPANCY between what people publicly pronounced should be the relationship between the government and its agencies, and what they wanted that relationship to be when they sought service. This applied particularly to applicants for Manitoba Development Corporation loans. Publicly, they demanded that the agency be at "arms length" from government and zealously ferreted out "government interference", but privately, if they were refused a loan, or response to a delayed application, they immediately contacted the government.

They appeared oblivious to the fact that it took time to decide to loan money—even if it was only taxpayers' money—and an affirmative response took longer to process than a simple negative might.

One letter from a company executive was straightforward and peremptory; his company had applied to the MDC for a substantial loan several weeks ago and had not yet received a response, either accepting or declining, and he was a businessman with no time to waste waiting for government bureaucrats to get off their inertia, and he was entitled to an answer, either "Yes" or "No".

I called in my secretary and dictated a one-word reply: "Sir: NO. Sincerely, (signed) Assistant to the Premier."

THE MESSAGE OF THE STAMP was sometimes applied to matters political. Civil servants came and went. Having left the public service, they were free to live their private lives, including freedom to attack the government members at whose table they had dined. We would hear about these disaffected persons on the radio, or read about them in the papers, and grimace, and forget about them. But occasionally that attack was too blatant to be ignored.

A senior civil servant took early retirement and went public. Newspapers carried explosive headlines: "Government Accused of Filling Jobs With Friends"; "Tourism Department Probe Urged". One morning he was on an open-line radio program informing the world that he had quit the public service because of "patronage", "nepotism", "pork-barrelling" and "NDP infiltration" that had been rampant since the election of the "socialist" Schreyer government. Now he was eschewing a lifetime of non-partisanship to help elect a Lyon government.

We were within a year of our quadrennial rendezvous with the electorate of Manitoba. Sterling Lyon, new leader of the Conservative party, was attacking with a vengeance. Our hold on government appeared daily more tenuous. We did not need this.

A quick phone call to the Civil Service Commission placed the culprit's personnel file was on my desk. A quick perusal showed he had been elevated, in stages, over time, to the senior position of director in the Department of Tourism.

This was commendable—but there was a peculiarity. In the competition for the position of director, he had placed fourth. So how did he get the job? The minister had ignored the competition ranking, chosen the man who was at that moment on the radio, and written a letter to the Civil Service Commission instructing them to "signify your approval on the attached Order-in-Council so it can be presented to Cabinet as soon as possible." In short, the man who was complaining so publicly about patronage in the Schreyer government had attained his senior position through patronage. I dialed the station: "Is it not true you did not win the competition for the position of director and you were not selected by the politically neutral Civil Service Commission, but by order of the minister?" I asked on-air.

There was the sound of indrawn breath.

"Oh, so that's how you got your job too?" the radio-show host asked, and clearly annoyed, abruptly terminated the interview. The former civil servant had lost a bruising contest with The Stamp.

A DIFFICULT AND DELICATE ACTIVITY of government is in dealing with unhappy party members. Election of a political party to office does not automatically guarantee its members entree to the perks of government; in fact, sometimes it is the opposite. Nor does it guarantee implementation of long-held party policies. By mid-1973, we had some 20,000 party members and it seemed at least half were disaffected. We had annual conventions, attended by 700 to 1,000 party members, giving the government an opportunity to report on the past year's activities and the members an opportunity to report on how the people in their constituencies were reacting to what the government was doing, and to lay down policy for the government to pursue in the coming year. We also had tri-monthly provincial council meetings at which the party elite, two from each constituency, provided advice to the government.

But the party, elected, is the government, and 'government' is a serious business, not a Boy Scout picnic. It could not govern, much as the elected members might wish, in the interests of the 120 provincial council members, or the 1,000 annual convention delegates, or the 20,000 party members, or even in the interests of the several hundred thousand supportive voters. Faced with the responsibility of governing, and privy to information available only to those who are governing, policy goals so clear while in opposition become blurred, the path to them previously arrow-straight becomes serpentine, and time parameters for their implementation that were assumed to be immediate, recede into the distance.

Psychological rationalizations involved in governing are never more apparent than when elected members attempt to maintain a very difficult balancing act. They must maintain to party members that convention resolutions are policy directives to the government and will be zealously pursued, but on the other hand reassure the world at large, frightened by the sound and fury emanating from the convention, that these are merely guidelines.

In the early 1960s, at the national convention of the Liberal Party, a group of young Turks forced a number of resolutions through that the government found embarrassing. Prime Minister Lester B. Pearson assured the electorate that these were merely expressions of opinion by a wing of the party and no solid citizen need worry they would become policy.

For the New Democratic Party it is not that easy. Policy making at NDP Conventions was democratic almost to a fault. Members of the media commented cynically when the premier was seen standing in a long line of delegates waiting to speak on a resolution, and heard, on arriving at the microphone, identifying himself as "Schreyer, from Rossmere". But we believed that party members, like the Italian immigrant reputed to have described the essence of American democracy by marvelling "the President is Mister and I am Mister, too", prided themselves on standing in the same line as their premier, arguing with a position he was taking, and sometimes defeating a resolution he was supporting. Unlike the world-weary journalists, they did not see this as a denigration of the premier but as an elevation of themselves. These were the people who walked the city streets or drove the rutted country roads, proselytizing for the party, signing up new members, and distributing election literature because we did not have the corporate donations to buy time on radio and that new, powerful but enormously expensive media, television. Now, having elected their party to office, they demanded their due: that policy resolutions passed at conventions be precisely that—policy.

But, through the process of the "swearing in" ceremony on July 15, 1969, a metamorphosis had occurred, subtly, but permanently. Like a volcano heaving itself out of the level cornfields of southern Mexico, a hierarchy had developed. Sloping from its apex, the premier, down through its various strata were the cabinet ministers, the caucus members, and the gatekeepers in the form of secretaries and ministerial assistants, who saw as their role the responsibility to guard access. In future, whether in or out of office, like those very ordinary mortals who have entered the priesthood, those who had entered this inner sanctum would never again be looked upon the same way by party members.

Dissolute young Henry V had warned his former drinking companions,

"Presume not I am the thing I was," and rigorous Cromwell executed his former most ardent supporters because, on achieving power, they wanted too much change too fast. Similarly, those forming 'government' quickly found it imposed upon them certain strictures and responsibilities that often abruptly ended old friendships.

The government became an entity distinct from the party. The chemistry between those in office and those not, changed. While the great majority of party members saw their reward in seeing their party in office and left the hydra-headed problems of governing to those elected, some believed the elevation to office was a form of reverse alchemy, which transmogrified their former friends into enemies to be suspected. Still others began looking upon "their" government as a candy store to be plundered. To elected members and political assistants was left the Sisyphusian task of explaining what government could and could not do for them. Sometimes that was easy—apply The Stamp.

A university professor took umbrage with some minor action of government. Instead of asking for an explanation, or explaining why he objected and how this could have been done differently, he simply sent the premier a terse note stating that, unless this action was reversed, he would return his party membership card. I sent an equally terse reply: "Sir: Kindly return membership card."

A PARTY MEMBER WROTE to the premier explaining that her daughter had recently graduated from the university with a B.A. (Hons), and had been diligently seeking a job but the only offers to date were menial ones, such as bill collecting and telephone solicitation, so, "I am sending this letter to the leaders of all our political parties. We have five votes in the house and they will go to whoever offers my daughter the best job."

It called for The Stamp, and an insight into the real world. "Madam," I wrote back, "Thank you for your letter to the premier. The taxpayers of Manitoba, through government, have spent considerable money paying 85% of the tuition required to get your daughter a university degree. We would be most pleased to have her get a good job so she can earn a high salary and pay enough income tax to repay the taxpayers the money they invested in her. But sometimes one must begin with jobs available and improve one's position over time. For example, Sam Uskiw started his working career as a school janitor and is now minister of Agriculture. Sidney Green delivered coal and is now minister of Natural Resources. Ed Schreyer earned university tuition fees working in a morgue and is now Premier of Manitoba. So you see, there is no predicting how far your daughter might go so long as she is not too proud to take a job that is available, instead of waiting for government to create one for her."

A CIRCULAR LETTER appeared on my desk, purportedly sent by the management committee. Entitled "New Sick Leave Policy—Effective Immediately", it outlined the new conditions of employment:

SICKNESS (NO EXCUSES). Doctor's certificate as proof no longer acceptable. If you can go to the doctor you can come to work.

DEATH (OTHER THAN YOUR OWN). No excuse. There is nothing you can do for them and someone else can see to the arrangements.

DEATH (YOUR OWN). This will be accepted as an excuse. However we will require two weeks notice to train a replacement.

It was good for a laugh, probably penned by one of the Mao-jacketed, long-haired young hot-shots who infested the Planning and Priorities Committee of cabinet. I had a fiendish idea. I sent a memo to the secretary of the Management Committee: "I want whoever wasted precious taxpayers' money preparing and distributing the enclosed to be found and summarily fired. (Signed) Assistant to the Premier."

Three days later Shirley Bradshaw, an acknowledged mandarin of the Manitoba public service, walked hesitantly into my office clutching a piece of paper in her white-knuckled hand:

"Mr. Schulz," she stammered, "We have turned the civil service upside down seeking the culprit who wrote this memo but no one will admit to having been involved with it and I do not know what more to do." She appeared to be holding her breath.

Embarrassed, I explained it was intended as a joke. She was too relieved to complain as she began to breathe again. The incident gave me a sudden sense of the power of the office I occupied and the terror created by its irresponsible use. And it gave me a sense of the power of The Stamp, even if used figuratively.

"UNCLE BEN" GINTER was raised in Manitoba's Swan River Valley and went elsewhere to make a fortune. Energetic, ebullient, engaging, he had a fateful tendency to allow his entrepreneurial enthusiasm to outrun his negotiating capacity. He returned to Manitoba, purchased a building in Transcona, and announced he would establish "Uncle Ben's Brewery" to brew up local beer and sell it in brown bottles featuring on the label a likeness of "Uncle Ben" himself, exuding the macho image of his sturdy body in checkered woodsman's mackinaw shirt and sporting a beard.

Then, in what appeared to be becoming the primary characteristic of Manitoba entrepreneurs, he applied for an MDC loan.

The Schreyer government, early in its tenure and uncertain of the ventures in which it wanted to invest public money, was hesitant. The MDC directors, unsure of the direction of the new government, were cautious. Ginter may have received the loan but, in an effort to force the government's hand by appealing to the public directly, he told the media that, unless the government gave him the loan poste haste, he would build the brewery with his own money. I took the press clipping to the premier who quickly announced, somewhat ingenuously, that "Uncle Ben" was precisely the kind of businessman we needed in Manitoba— one who would use his own money instead of asking the government to take the risk while he pocketed the profit.

Ben Ginter's impatience was to cost him a bundle—and save the taxpayers the equivalent amount.

Ginter built his plant but his beer was not selling, so he complained to the government that hotels, too attached to the established breweries, were not stocking his product. The word was passed to the Liquor Control Commission, which issued an order; all beer outlets must carry all brands brewed in Canada. To ensure compliance, several of us ordered Uncle Ben's at every opportunity. We would go to the two hotels owned by PC Party Leader Sidney Spivak, order lunch and an Uncle Ben's, and report them to the Liquor Control Commission if they did not have it. We forced several hotels to stock the product no matter how much they resented it, and we gradually enlarged Ben's market.

But I eventually concluded I really did not like 'Uncle Ben's'. It tasted too malty. After two years of making life difficult for hotel owners, my taste buds rebelled against being abused to peddle Uncle Ben brew. And perhaps other Manitobans also were not drinking it not because it was not stocked by hotels but because—like me—they did not like it. I so advised the government.

Ginter's market remained minuscule and he continued to complain that the hotels were shunning his product and to lobby the government for legislation to redress the balance. The government was anxious to preserve a local enterprise, particularly one giving vigorous price competition to the long-time oligopoly of the established brewing industry. Attorney General Al Mackling was instructed to draft legislation allowing the sale of beer in grocery stores. The decision was made reluctantly, but this would test if, indeed, Uncle Ben's was being discriminated against.

Leaving my office late one evening, I went into the Premier's Office to check his itinerary. He was not there but his diary listed "Meeting Ben Ginter, International Inn, 9 P.M.". The next morning, on my way to work, Uncle Ben's voice boomed on my car radio as he announced on a open-line program that the previous evening, he'd had a "secret meeting" with the premier and had been promised legislation advancing the sale of his brew.

I parked my car and went raging into my office just in time to pick up the ringing phone. It was my sister: "Oh, Herb, I just received the most beautiful vase of flowers."

"They are from Uncle Ben!"

"How did you know?"

"Is the delivery truck still there?"

"Yes. He is having trouble turning around."

"Catch him and tell him to take the flowers back to where he picked them up. Where are they from?" I phoned the florist: "Listen to me carefully. We are returning some flowers you sent out this morning. Do not, under any circumstances, ever again send flowers to the Schreyer residence from Ben Ginter."

Early that morning the premier had departed on a long-scheduled trip to the Soviet Union. I went to Mackling. Public perception would now be that we were enacting legislation to favour sale of Uncle Ben's beer not because of a policy carefully thought out by the government caucus and cabinet to crack the hold of the big breweries and support a home-grown industry, but because of a "secret meeting" at the International Inn between Ginter and the premier, and an expensive bouquet of flowers to the premier's wife. The legislation was scrapped. The Stamp had spoken.

THE GOVERNMENT WAS DAILY BUFFETED between the Scylla of those complaining we were spending too much taxpayers' money on others and the Charybdis of those complaining we were not spending enough on them. One group could become as demanding and vicious as the other. Many days there were calls or letters, often with copies to the media, by those knowing of some instance of government waste. These were interspersed with calls or letters, often with copies to the media, complaining about some request for a service or a loan which had been denied or delayed.

The spring of 1975 was unusually dry. Particularly from southeastern Manitoba, we were inundated by complaints about a lack of water (a year earlier, from the same region, we had been inundated by complaints about a surfeit of water) and requests for help. When a problem overwhelms individuals they turn to government. We helped where we could, but sometimes we couldn't. A farmer called: "There is no water or grass out here. My cattle are going to die of hunger and thirst. I need help."

I patiently explained that the drought was what is called an "Act of God" rather than of government, that as mere mortals our power to control nature was limited, and that we were doing all we could to assist, including hauling hay from other areas to the affected regions. But he had not called for a sermon. He wanted help, like yesterday, and in his rage he made a mistake: "You bastards are not helping me because I voted Conservative."

"I didn't know that until you told me. However, it is written that we must all pay for our transgressions. Pity that it is your livestock, not you, that is paying."

He became more irate: "What's this God-damned Schreyer going to do for me?"

"Nothing."

"What should I do with my cattle?" he screamed into the phone.

"If you, as a farmer, don't know how to procure feed and water for your livestock, I suggest you kill them and eat them."

He probably did not appreciate the message of The Stamp.

A PROPOS OF THE MANITOBA GOVERNMENT'S establishment of the French Education Branch in our Department of Education in 1975,[2] we received a hand-scribbled letter from Saskatchewan:

> Dear Mr. Schreyer,
>
> You Damn premier will stoop to anything to get votes, you wouldn't think twice about selling English Manitoba out to the Godamn french in Quebec. Where in hell is your brain? Have the French bought them from you? So you should really and truly be completely ashamed of yourself, trying to sell English Manitoba to the Godamn Quebec. The next time we fight the Godamn French we will beat the damn shit right out of them for fair, so they will never but never mention their Godamn culture again. Keep Manitoba and all western Canada English, and piss on Quebec, let them separate, or let them go plumb to hell for ever. They are nothing but trouble anyway.

I noticed a peculiarity. It was just too good to ignore.

> Dear Sir,
>
> This is to acknowledge receipt of your letter to Premier Schreyer politely and sensitively analyzing the problems of the Canadian Federation. I note you have a German name and therefore remind you that a generation ago much of the world's population felt exactly the same way about you as you now feel about those 'Godamn French' in Quebec.
>
> Sincerely, Herb Schulz ,
> Assistant to the Premier [3]

---

[2] This was long before Georges Forrest's English-only parking ticket and the subsequent multi-million translation of musty statutes that few read in English, let alone in French.

[3] Also having a German name, I felt I could get away with that.

The writer had sent a copy of his letter to Saskatchewan Premier Allan Blakeney, so I sent him a copy of my reply. Blakeney's office responded: "We received a letter from Mr. _____ very similar to the one to Premier Schreyer. Your response was much appreciated here."

The Stamp was acquiring a national reputation.

BUT ONCE THE STAMP WAS VIGOUROUSLY APPLIED—and regretted. A man had established, in a rural town, a small but active plant that manufactured light farm equipment and employed up to 200 persons. In 1970, the company borrowed money from the Manitoba Development Corporation, expanded the plant, brought in shareholders, and repaid the loan. Then the farm economy declined, the market dried up, and the company applied for a $500,000 MDC loan.

I had requested MDC chairman Sid Parsons to keep me apprised of bad outstanding loans and of loans under consideration for projects of arguable viability. This was not to interfere in decisions of the MDC but to provide the premier with basic information in case a reporter, at weekly press conference, asked about the MDC. After 1973, as it became clear that many loans (most made by previous governments but for which responsibility was fixed on the NDP) were insecure, it became a sport among media persons to ask how much taxpayer's money we had "wasted" lately.

A function of the MDC was to provide support for firms which, by failing, would damage the economy. Parsons informed me this one was delicate, but it met government criteria; it was rural, involved secondary industry, manufactured locally purchased products, earned foreign currency through exports, produced off-farm income, and created new jobs. Therefore the board would probably approve the loan at the next meeting. I intuitively expected that if this loan was made it would soon hit the front pages of papers as another example of "socialist incompetence", but I could only prepare the premier for the deluge.

Libraries are filled with tomes analyzing the fortuitousness of accident— the *deus ex machina* unexpectedly and irrationally intervening—and this now occurred. The following day I noticed an article in the business section of *The Winnipeg Tribune*.

Business editor Harry Mardon, had virtually made a career of attacking the "socialist" government of Manitoba. He focused on our hapless floundering among the flotsam and jetsam of wrecked MDC loans, and on what he deemed the fundamental dangers of government intervention in the economy ... if only to rescue businesses for which he considered himself guardian. In this column, Mardon described a meeting of very angry shareholders of this particular firm, asking why it was in trouble and what was being done about it. And then the fateful sentence: "All agreed they wanted no interference from government."

Mardon's article was like manna; if the firm's shareholders did not want "government interference", we certainly should not force it on them. I quickly wrote a letter, copy to the MDC, and sent it to the president of the firm.

> This is to advise that the article by Harry Mardon in *The Winnipeg Tribune* (copy enclosed) stating that the shareholders of [your firm] do not want government interference in the form of a loan, is being forwarded to the Board of Directors of the MDC for information.

> (Signed) Assistant to the Premier.

It was disingenuous but it got results. Two days later I received a phone call from a very angry president of the firm. "What right has the Premier's Office to interfere with the MDC, when it is supposed to be at arm's length from government?" he demanded.

"We were not interfering in the loan decision, which is made by the MDC board. However, I am sure you are aware that the government is usually smeared with responsibility for loans that go sour. Therefore I considered it my responsibility to refer to the MDC any information which could be relevant to an application and I believe you will agree the fact that your shareholders do not want government interference is relevant."

"But you are interfering in my business. And what right do you have to listen to Harry Mardon on this matter anyway?"

"Since Harry Mardon was reporting on a shareholders' meeting I must assume he is a shareholder and in a position to express the wishes of the shareholders."

After a prodigious effort on both sides to control tensions, the dialogue became less heated and ended when he asked, "I would like to meet with you to explain this situation. Could we have lunch?"

The following day he came to my office to pick me up. He was tall, lean, well-built, balding and had a look of defeat in his eyes. We lunched at the Sherbrooke Hotel and the story unfolded. He had worked hard all his life, developed a business which was now in financial trouble, was sixty-three years of age, and was about to lose everything including the home he had mortgaged. He desperately needed the MDC loan. As for Harry Mardon's report: "That son-of-a-bitch bought one lousy share just so he could attend the meeting. He had no right to say we don't want government interference. We want money from wherever we can get it."

How easy to wound from a distance, but not when one is looking into another's eyes. A man's life's work was going down the drain because of on unfortunate business decision four years earlier. But was it even that? How was he to know the world price of wheat would drop, that cash flow to farmers would suddenly plummet, that the market for farm equipment would virtually disappear, that because of a business decision made in the halcyon days of $5-a-bushel wheat, he was now threatened with bankruptcy? I was losing my resolve to apply the lesson of The Stamp.

But I had invited myself into this situation, and I was responsible for the taxpayer's money. Yet, perhaps there was a way. "We are not insensitive to your situation," I told him, "and certainly we have an obligation to promote rural industry, but we also have an obligation to invest public funds wisely. Clearly you need the loan, but there is a problem. You owe a considerable amount to a chartered bank and what guarantee do we have that your firm will not just become a conduit to funnel our $500,000 to your bank? That would be of no value to you or the government or the economy of Manitoba. The bank would be happy, but you would still be out of business, the taxpayers of Manitoba would be out $500,000, and the MDC would be stuck with a bankrupt plant."

He reluctantly agreed with my analysis. I made a proposal: "If you can provide us with written assurance from your bank that they will leave their money in your plant, the MDC might find your application more attractive."

A look close to ecstacy passed across his face. He saw no reason why they would not do that if the MDC agreed to invest. After all, the bank's money was already invested in the business and there was little chance of getting back much —if any—of it if it went into bankruptcy.

We parted amicably. Several days later he phoned. He did not plead, nor bargain, nor ask for a review. He simply thanked me for my time and for what he described as my "generous proposal", delivered his message and hung up the phone: "The bank will not do it."

So the MDC declined the loan. Shortly after, the plant was placed in receivership. The bank had applied The Stamp.

"The Stamp": coveted by all, but employed by none.

XVII

Rendezvous

The test of our progress as a society is not in whether we add to the abundance of those who already have much, but in whether we provide more for those who have little.
—F. D. Roosevelt

Four busy years had flashed by. Three hundred pieces of legislation were enacted. The face of Manitoba was changed, primarily by tax shifts and construction projects, based on the belief we get the society we make and on the desire to make the society we want.

In striking contrast to the preceding government's philosophy, the NDP government had decided that, rather than reduce the number of farmers to fit the income, they would increase total income to fit the number of farmers. They advanced the concept of the "stay option", which included mortgages for farm homes, family housing, schools, development of rural infrastructure, municipal grid roads, schools, hospitals, senior citizen's housing, nursing homes, recreational facilities, grants to events such as the stampedes in Morris and Swan River, and economic opportunities in small towns. To break the 'perimeter psychology' that nothing of worth happens outside Winnipeg, government departments were partially decentralized to locations outside Winnipeg, moving to Portage la Prairie, Thompson, Brandon, Beausejour, Arborg and Dauphin, among others.

The 'stay option' was not a Luddite desire to recreate a past "where the village smithy stood". Rather, the NDP saw agriculture as a crucial industry and the family farm a social as well as an economic unit. To assist it in remaining that way, the department of agriculture had made loans for land acquisition through the Manitoba Agricultural Credit Corporation, and provided grants to improve dairy and beef herds, install farm and rural town sewer and water services, and provide for acreage payments when Ottawa refused to help. The department had recovered $6 million in federal milk supports lost to eastern dairy farmers by the Weir government, included hail damage in the crop insurance plan, and established veterinary clinics, a feed grain commission to protect farmers when the bottom dropped out of the market, a marketing branch to seek foreign markets and encourage farm diversification, and marketing boards for hogs, eggs and turkeys to give farmers the advantage of collective marketing.

The government was committed to providing affordable health services to all in the most economical way. To serve this objective, it abolished health care premiums, reduced drug costs through bulk buying and substitution of generic for brand names,[1] enacted Pharmacare for seniors, began training dental nurses to substitute in rural areas and began moving the mentally ill from institutions into communities and sheltered workshops. The government attempted to control escalation of health care costs in two ways: (a) allowing shifts from expensive acute care to cheaper longterm care by developing a hierarchy of health care facilities (acute care, extended care, nursing homes, personal care homes and home care) that were better suited to the care needed and in descending order of costs and (b) establishing community clinics supervised by locally elected community health boards that were given a budget and the authority to decide how to use it.

The government was also determined to provide affordable housing for middle-income Manitobans. A 1969 survey showed 10,000 units were overcrowded, thirty-seven per cent of the housing stock needed repairs, housing starts were at only about 5,000 per year, the vacancy rate was at 1.6 per cent, and the average price of a single-family home was moving beyond the reach of many families.[2] The government responded by constructing 7,900 units of public rental housing; establishing the Manitoba Housing and Renewal Corporation, which compensated for the reluctance of the Canadian Mortgage and Housing Corporation by providing long term, low-interest mortgages to modest income families, and providing rental subsidies of up to $300 for low-income families. Between 1970 and 1973, housing starts increased to more than 9,000 annually and the vacancy rate rose to 4.5 per cent, forcing market competition in rents.

"The young are forgetful and the old are forgotten" was an adage the NDP government was determined would not be applied to it. This led to programs, including the pensioner home repair program, which granted up to $1,000, depending on income, to repair bathrooms, roofs and windows, etc. These improved the existing housing stock and kept many elderly people in their homes instead of personal care and nursing homes. The government also provided housing (both public and rent-subsidized) in rural areas, which gave substance to the "stay option" by allowing the elderly to retire in the communities where their

---

[1] "Alphonse Poirier, external relations manager for Hoffman-Laroche, a Montreal drug manufacturer and pharmaceutical supply company, criticized Manitoba for allowing substitution of drugs," stating that this would block research. *Winnipeg Free Press*, February 27, 1970. More than thirty years later, the refrain of pharmaceutical companies remains the same.

[2] From 1961 to 1968, home prices had increased by almost forty per cent, to $21,000, and then virtually doubled between 1971 and 1977.

friends were; offered property tax credits of between $100 and $200 (eighty-one per cent received the $200 maximum) that relieved most pensioners of school taxes; constructed nursing and personal care homes and assisted with improvement of their services.[3]

Like the golden boy atop the Grecian-columned Legislative Building, many NDP policies pointed to the north, and produced a cluster of programs. These included the creation of a Department of Northern Affairs; allowing election of local community councils in unorganized territories and giving them reponsibility for local housing, services, economic development; the construction and partial paving of Highway 391 from Thompson to Lynn Lake, via Leaf Rapids, which opened access to the mining communities; construction of the town of Leaf Rapids (awarded a prize for the best-planned town in Canada), which deviated from the traditional 'company town' and put the Sherritt-Gordon Mining Corporation on the municipal tax roll. The NDP government also created the Community Economic Development Fund to encourage optimum economic development in isolated communities and assist local enterprises; constructed a network of winter roads to remote communities and built thirty-four airstrips in communities that had no road access.

The Northern Manpower Training Corps was created to develop new employment opportunities and ensure northerners access to them; standard or radio phone telephone service was extended to remote communities (by 1973 every community of more than fifty inhabitants was served) and live television was extended to larger areas. The Patient Air Transport (PAT) service was also created to provide improved access to health care for northerners.

The huge Churchill Forest Industries complex at The Pas was developed, as was the massive hydro-electric project on the Nelson and Churchill Rivers. A radical new tax regime for the mining industry was established, doubling royalties, encouraging development, and dedicating resource revenue to supporting individuals and towns when mining was suspended. It was an attempt to ensure that Manitobans, particularly in the north, would reap the benefits of nature's bounty.

The basic philosophy of the government's industrial strategy was to abstain from incentive wars with other jurisdictions and to create a plethora of grants and tax incentives to private firms to do what they should be doing in the normal course of a 'free enterprise' economy. The government also assisted industry through a variety of other programs, including loans by the Manitoba Development Corporation and managerial assistance (through the Manitoba Institute of Management) to assist local firms to become competitive. The Manitoba Trading Corporation was established to seek markets outside Manitoba; provide short-term credit to assist off-shore trade; help local firms with international shipping arrangements, insurance, import regulations and

---

[3] One grateful lady wrote to the Department of Health: "I am 88. I thank you for the hair dryer Care Services gave me. The lady in the next bed is 86 ... she had a hair dryer for years. She never let me use it. Yesterday, her hair dryer fell and got smashed. She asked me if she could use mine. I said 'fuck you'."

licencing, and assist in services such as checking credit of foreign corporations and collecting accounts receivable. Finally, if the private sector would not take the risks attendant upon developing the economy, the government would use crown corporations.

The hallmark of social democratic governments—social legislation—sought to advance and protect the rights of all citizens. This included: an ombudsman to guard against administrative injustice against citizens by government; a rentalsman to police the Landlord and Tenant Act by arbitrating on rents, damage deposits, lockouts, privacy, noise, etc; a consumer's bureau to protect consumers against shoddy goods or unscrupulous dealers (Manitoba had the most advanced legislation in Canada and the first to prohibit pyramid selling, which caused 3,448 complaints in 1972 alone); Legal Aid to ensure "equality before the law" by providing full legal services in both civil and criminal cases to those unable to pay, understand English or the court processes, and the small claims court to expedite minor cases without overloading the courts.

The government legislated: the Criminal Injuries Compensation Act, based on the principle that the government owes individuals protection, and should compensate innocent victims of criminal activities; protection from abuse by personal reporting agencies by allowing individuals to demand disclosure by private agencies and demand changes if the information was inaccurate; the Human Rights Commission to show the law is not just a Sunday instrument by giving citizens protection against discrimination in housing, employment, gender, colour, race, ethnicity, national origin, the courts and the marketplace; labour legislation that established a Women's Bureau, increased the minimum wage to $1.75; made it easier for workers to organize, and improved the enforcement of labour laws.

The government remained true to its philosophy of redistributing the costs of society. Manitoba had the highest income taxes in Canada, reflecting the NDP's deeply-held determination to shift costs from poll taxes to the 'ability to pay' taxes and to use the taxation system as a vehicle for economic redistribution. This was based on the belief that no one becomes wealthy except in a social context and therefore the greater one's wealth, the more one owes society. Moreover, without an adequate income, people cannot contribute to the health of the economy. Thus, while a family of four with an income of $8,000 paid $43 more in income tax in 1973 than 1969, the elimination of the Medicare premium of $204, plus a Property Tax Credit of $159 (which, as stated above, relieved most pensioners of school taxes) meant a total saving of $320.

When Ottawa abandoned the tax on estates of the deceased, Manitoba assumed it (with a $200,000 exemption) on the principle it was unfair and inequitable for some to pay income tax as they worked to acquire an estate, while those who inherited an estate paid nothing.

After four years, the statistics were revealing. Manitoba's total farm cash receipts were up thirty-eight per cent (to $485 million). The value of manufactured goods shipped was up nineteen per cent (to $1,465 million) and retail trade was up thirty-one per cent (to $1,470 million).

Capital investment was up twenty-eight per cent (to $1,051 million), and in 1972 alone eighty-three companies had been established or expanded. Construction was up twenty-two per cent (to 804 million) and residential construction was up eighty-six per cent (12,068 units). Primary resource production was up forty-two per cent (to $990 million). Unemployment, at 4.1 per cent, was 2.3 per cent below the national average—lowest of any province—and 2,287 new jobs had been created, including twenty-four per cent in rural areas.

Average weekly earnings were up fifteen per cent ($124), personal per capita income by thirty-six per cent ($3,558) and personal disposable per capita income by thirty-two per cent ($2,936), while the inflation rate was among the lowest in Canada.

Manitoba's gross provincial product was up thirty-five per cent ($4,447 million) and in 1972, Manitoba grew 10.8 per cent compared with 10.6 per cent for Canada. The population, which had decreased in the two years prior to 1969, was up by 21,000 (to 992,000).

Comments about Manitoba during 1972 told the same story. *The Winnipeg Tribune* admonished Liberal Leader Izzy Asper for predicting doom and editorialized: "Manitoba's economy is doing well [and] at last report had the lowest unemployment rate in Canada." [4] A report in the *Ottawa Citizen* showed that, despite higher income taxes in Manitoba, a comparison of taxes and fees meant 'Manitobans Paying Less Than Ontarians'.[5] *The Manitoba Cooperator* carried a banner headline, 'Manitoba Leads Nation in Economic Progress'.[6] Daniel Sprague, president of the Canadian Manufacturers Association, which had predicted a rapid exodus of business from Manitoba after the 1969 election, now stated: "Reluctance for private industry to move to Manitoba is more talk than fact," and advised his members in British Columbia that "it would be wise to cooperate with the [new] NDP government."[7]

The budget of 1973 brought commendations. The *Montreal Star* editorialized: "The feast of ideas pouring forth from the parliament buildings in Winnipeg is in impressive contrast to the dearth of imagination which marks most Canadian administrations at both federal and provincial levels." [8] Winnipeg's Mayor Juba lauded: "If I could assume a budget like this every year I would be the happiest man in Manitoba."[9] Socialism's nemesis, associate editor Harry Mardon, admitted: "Manitobans earning up to $50,000 a year are better off under the new

---

[4] May 26, 1972.
[5] April 8, 1972.
[6] September 27, 1972.
[7] *The Winnipeg Tribune*, November 18, 1972.
[8] April 5, 1973.
[9] March 29, 1973.

budget than they were under the former government."[10] Both opposition parties voted to support the budget, and Liberal Leader Asper expressed "relief and gratitude and applause for the government".

The public also seemed pleased with their government. A survey asking: (a) Do you agree with the government's efforts to shift school property taxes? (b) Would you support government programs to stop rural depopulation? (c) Should the government continue to provide work and training projects? and (d) Do you support the government's Winter Works Program? received affirmative responses from eighty-two to eighty-nine per cent. The same survey showed 71.5 per cent of Manitobans rated the government's four-year performance as 'Good' or 'Excellent'.

And the *pièce de résistance*: Autopac had proved to be a stunning success (tables showed the premium in Calgary, a similarly sized city, for an under-25 driver, was double that in Winnipeg). In its first year of operations, it had kept its rates about fifteen per cent below the estimated private rates, reduced administration costs as a percentage of the premium dollar to half that of the private sector, made a profit, and invested $6.2 million in hospital and municipal bonds— money that would have had to be borrowed outside Manitoba. Sylvan Leipsic, president of the largest locally-owned insurance agency in Winnipeg, who had fought hard against the establishment of public insurance was quoted in a banner headline: "Autopac Is Working: Autopac Is a Money Saver"[11].

It was time for our rendezvous with the sovereign electorate.

---

[10] *The Winnipeg Tribune*, March 29, 1973
[11] *Ibid.*, May 18, 1972.

XVIII

Vignettes of a Campaign: Election 1973

Another such victory and we are undone.
> —Greek General Pyrrhus after defeating the Romans
> in 280 BC, but suffering great losses

The premier sounded the tocsin and we rushed into the campaign. We were reasonably sure of victory. We saw ourselves as a good government and expected that to be recognized by the electorate. And we were aided by a crack team of office staff, professional organizers, advance men, media relations advisors, and relays of cars, planes and helicopters for the premier and his retinue.

Recollections of the campaign flash by as series of vignettes.

We flew, aboard the Saunders aircraft manufactured at Gimli and leased for the campaign, to a nominating convention/rally at Thompson. Surrounded by lake and forest, the urban jewel of the North had, in twenty years, sprung from the discovery of minerals into Manitoba's third-largest city. The party nominated Ken Dillen, a darkly handsome, well-built, well-dressed, soft-spoken Métis ex-paratrooper-cum-miner. The rally, organized by Len Stevens, a tough talking, hard-edged, ex-steelworker who was president of the Manitoba Federation of Labour, was boisterous. Buoyed by the crowd and the atmosphere, the premier spoke well, and then retired to the hotel with a handful of friends to nurse a double rum and coke while talking—though mostly listening—about politics and policies and economic development and—his favorite subject—The North.

The next morning we toured the mine and the plant in which we observed the magic of great masses of gray rock being crushed and fed into the electric furnaces (Thompson used more electric power than the old City of Winnipeg) to come out as gleaming ingots of nickel. Then we flew north and east, following the Churchill River, while writer Farley Mowat, one of our troupe, gazed out the window and spoke softly into his tape recorder, describing the tundra, the high, alkaline striated banks and the rippling river as it wended its serpentine way to the sea.

My mind leaped: I would see Churchill for the first time and "I marshalled the battalions of my fancy to my aid". This was where Captain Monck had wintered a century before LaVeredrye saw Lake of the Woods. For two centuries, this was the entry point into North America for the world's greatest fur trading, and now the world's oldest, company. This was where the old world met the new —the emporium of The Company of Gentleman Adventurers, the gift of King Charles II to his cavalier nephew, dashing Prince Rupert, who skewered the Roundheads and received a grant of two million square miles of uncharted territory and riches beyond the dreams of Croesus.

This was the post that launched Henry Kelsey across the plains, dark with buffalo, to the "Shining Mountains", Alexander Mackenzie to the frozen Arctic and David Thompson on his decade-long journey to the Pacific Northwest. Here, too, was Hudson Bay, which had witnessed the travails of the seekers of the fabled North-West Passage and held the secrets of luckless Henry Hudson. Here was the water that bore the ships that carried the Selkirk Settlers to plant their colony at the historic confluence of the Red and Assiniboine Rivers a century and a half before, and, fifty years later, another group to establish the autonomous Republic of New Iceland on the shore of Lake Winnipeg.

Here, today, was the terminus of the Hudson's Bay Railway and the anchorage for the ships that carried their golden cargo of wheat to exotic lands. Here lay Canada's largest airfield and the anchor of the DEW Line, built to alert Strategic Air Command of the approach of Soviet bombers.

I felt like a Muslim awaiting his first glimpse of Mecca ...

The plane slipped down through the cloud cover. My eager eyes beheld a vast crescent of blue-gray water edged in white. Ah-h-h-h! White sand beaches just like the Gulf of Mexico—oh no—that was ICE! Jesus Christ! It was mid-June, the days would soon shorten ... did this damnable place never unfreeze? The plane landed. The icy winds swept off the bay. A clutter of shopworn buildings along a single street lay to the right, and to the left, a collection of small houses, windows broken and doors hanging askew, the village built for a band of Dene relocated from farther north (later moved to Tadoule Lake). In the distance the grain terminal clung to the rocks, much less impressive than I had imagined as an ardent member of the Bay Route Association. This was not the city of my romantic imagination. This was where a magnificent fortress, rivalled only by Louisburg on the Atlantic, had been surrendered without a shot; this was a community that had the largest *abandoned* airfield in Canada; a city that had shrunk from a population of 5,000 to 1,500 when the military establishment left; a town that had persuaded the Government of Manitoba to build it a $10 million city centre, and then shamed us into subsidizing the $300,000 annual heating costs; in short, this was a frontier settlement hanging on by its fingernails, surviving on its public payroll, awaiting rediscovery.

The premier and Farley Mowat and several local residents spent the night in a shack on an ice flow. I sought sleep in a ramshackle hotel listening to the night sounds, mostly of inebriated men shouting at each other. I recalled, fifteen years earlier, at a social, approaching a young woman and gushing: "I hear you spent two years at Churchill and I have read about its role in our history and I wondered what you thought of it."

She surveyed me with what I later sensed was pity, gazed into space, and spoke with the cool voice of a cultured young lady: "Well, if the world should ever need an enema, that would be the logical place to administer it."

We flew south, along the Nelson River, and I suddenly clutched at the ceiling, terrified, as the plane hit an air pocket, and then landed at Gillam, the roaring town built by Manitoba Hydro, filled with several thousand men and women completing the giant 1100-megawatt facility and preparing the site for the similar Long Spruce project a dozen miles down river. After midnight and a long evening of consuming a variety of alcoholic beverages and sandwiches in the huge mess hall, and politicking by attempting to meet every resident while avoiding Conservative leader Sidney Spivak who, embarrassingly for both parties, had arrived at the same time, we boarded our plane. The turbo-prop groaned through the night and the awe-inspiring pyrotechnics of a violent storm.

Just after 4 A.M., we glided into Winnipeg International Airport. Among the party of politicians and reporters was a young man sent by the Canadian Labour Congress as a media relations person. Too little sleep and too much liquor had laid him out. *Free Press* columnist Egon Frech and I carried him into the terminal. I went back to the plane to fetch our luggage and found a bottle of rye.

The premier and the out-of-town journalists roared away in all the available taxis, leaving Frech, Mowat, the CLC man and me, in front of the terminal, fatigued and shivering in the cool dawn, waiting for another taxi. I produced the stray bottle of rye and offered Mowat the first drink. He began raising it to his mouth, "Oh, this is Premier Piss!"

I was tired and dog-dirty and cold and in no mood for practical jokes, even by Farley Mowat, who was notorious for them.

"I've heard of Liebfraumilch and Teacher's Highland Cream, but I have never heard of Premier Piss. Who in hell makes that?"

"No, this is the genuine article." The designers of the twenty-three-seat commuter with optimum range of 200 miles had not felt the need for a toilet so, during the three-hour flight, the premier had relieved his overflowing bladder into an empty rye bottle.

I re-corked the bottle, held it up to let the first rays of "rosy-fingered dawn", creeping across the river and over the roofs, shine through the clear light amber fluid, and set it behind a pillar in the airport terminal. I have always wondered what lucky fellow found the free swig of that potent brew.

THE ELECTION PLANNING COMMITTEE instructed me to find a candidate for a rock hard Conservative, southwestern Manitoba constituency where we had less hope of winning than of catching a ride on a space commuter. I made some calls and then phoned an acquaintance, Boissevain schoolteacher John Bucklaschuk: "John, you are going to be our candidate in Souris-Killarney."

"No! I ran in the federal election last year and it cost me a lot of time and money and I just can't do it again."

"John, the party demands that every man do his duty and we have tried but have been unable to find anyone else so you are 'it'."

John Bucklaschuk was a good and decent man and totally committed. A membership meeting nominated him. The next morning, I picked up the urgently -ringing phone to hear the quavering but persistent voice of our Brandon-area political organizer.

John Vershagin had won his spurs as a constituency organizer in Saskatchewan, where he had been since Tommy Douglas won it in 1944. He lived for the party, and knew electoral victory required both an acceptable platform and a good candidate. His plaintive voice was urgent: "Herb, I don't know how you're going to do this but I just found a great candidate for Souris-Killarney and if we could get him nominated we could win that constituency ..."

"John, in the event you haven't heard, we had a meeting last night and we nominated a candidate for Souris-Killarney ..."

"Oh I know, Herb, and I don't know how you're going to do it, but this is a super candidate who is very well known and if we could get him nominated we could win that constituency."

"John, you haven't listened. We nominated a candidate ..."

"Yes, Herb, I know." The voice was becoming less pleading and more urgent. "I don't know how you're going to do it. But this is a prince of a candidate of old Anglo-Saxon pioneer stock and extremely well respected and the municipal reeve and the chairman of the hospital board and the chairman of the school board and if we could just get him nominated we could win that constituency."

"Who is this superman?" I could not disguise my exasperation.

"Howard Nixon. From Margaret."

I phoned John Bucklaschuk: "John, I'm just calling to inform you that you are ill."

"But ... but ... I am feeling fine."

"When I explain what is about to happen to you, you will become ill. We found a better candidate and we will arrange to have him nominated. We will explain your sudden and regrettable illness."

"You son-of-a-bitch! You pleaded with me to run and I agreed against my better judgment and I informed my school board that I will be taking leave, and now you dare to call me with this."

"John, the party expects every man to do his duty, so you will contribute by suddenly becoming ill."

John Bucklaschuk knew he was being used, but he was a good and decent man and totally committed. We arranged for a new nominating meeting.

On the morning of day of the meeting I received an urgent phone call from Howard Nixon's wife: "My husband has been rushed to the hospital with a blood clot in his leg. He will not be a candidate."

I dialed the phone: "John, you are well again." [1]

THE SEARCH FOR A CANDIDATE for Souris-Killarney had a sequel. Assuming Nixon would be running, the managers of his campaign suggested his chances would be enhanced if the government were to commit to rehabilitating the old sanitarium at Ninette. The institution, largest of its kind west of Ontario, had been built in 1910 and housed up to 200 patients when tuberculosis was a threat to the public and it appeared the only option was to contain the victims in a controlled environment. By 1973, the disease was no longer a threat and the facility had been closed.

But many communities, particularly those claiming to have never met a government they liked, spent half their time complaining about government spending, and the other half seeking a government payroll to sustain them. Ninette was no different. And restoring the building for some function would serve the government's 'stay option' policy, bring money into the community via the public payroll, and—crucial to the government in June 1973—might get the NDP some votes in a constituency where we historically had not enough supporters to fill a telephone, let alone a polling, booth.

So the decision was made to restore the building, but for what purpose? Marvin Blauer, secretary of cabinet's Health, Education and Social Policy Sub-committee, was assigned the task of finding some practical use for it. And the Department of Health was directed to assess the costs of renovating it.

A fast appraisal showed some rotting wood and some rusted pipes, meaning that it would cost perhaps $250,000 to restore the building. In practical terms, this really meant it would cost double that. But Blauer had also found a use for the building; we could relocate some mentally handicapped Manitobans from the Portage la Prairie institution to Ninette.

The assessment left us in a discomfiting proposition. Should we commit money we did not really have to something that did not really need to be done? How did this affect our morality as politicians and our integrity as individuals? What was the right thing to do and what was the politic thing to do, and could they be made to coincide?

In the end, we decided a case could be made for the renovation, no matter

---

[1] John Bucklaschuk was elected to the legislature in 1981 and served as a minister in Premier Howard Pawley's cabinet.

how tenuous. And our candidate would be given some hope, no matter how minuscule. After all, that was the whole point of the exercise in the first place. So Blauer was given his instructions: "Let's do it."

Shortly afterward, Howard Nixon became a non-candidate and any hope of winning in Souris-Killarney was expunged. I phoned Blauer and, in his absence, left word at his office to cancel the project because its *raison d'être* had disappeared, and then left to accompany the premier on an extended electoral tour.

Nixon's precipitate illness had solved our moral dilemma—I thought—but I had failed to realize that once the ponderous machinery of government begins to move, it is difficult to stop.

Several days later I phoned from out of town to ensure that the project was off. Blauer was out again, but his office informed me they were proceeding full speed ahead. Again, I instructed them to halt. Two days later I caught up with a despairing Blauer; renovation of the old sanitarium had begun and would be difficult—and embarrassing—to stop; the people of Ninette had already been informed of their good fortune; the people operating the facility at Portage had been informed that it would become less crowded, and he was receiving pleas from the NDP office from those who felt we were obliged to assist our candidate in Souris-Killarney no matter who it was. Moreover, Blauer himself had become convinced this restoration, and this transfer of patients, should be made on their own merits, entirely aside from any political considerations.

"Marvin, this project was based entirely on the political consideration inspired by the hope of Nixon's candidacy. Since that is no longer the case it is pointless to continue. If it has any merit other than the political we will reconsider it after the election, but meanwhile, for Christ's sake stop already."

One of the maddening frustrations of working with government is in discovering the speed with which it can move, when doing the wrong thing. The project did finally, slowly, grind to a halt. After the election the bills came in—in excess of $500,000—and all for nothing, either political or economic, I thought.

Serendipidously, there was to be a benign consequence. A spark had been generated. Two years later the project was reassessed on a non-political basis and found to be viable. The buildings were restored to become the Pelican Lake Training Centre for the Mentally Handicapped. A number of people were transferred from the Portage la Prairie facility and in the next twenty years more than 100 clients were helped to start independent lives in their respective home communities.

By the mid-1990s, the centre had seventy live-in clients and a staff of about sixty. Ninette got its government payroll of some $2 million annually until 1998, when it was closed.

"SILENT" JOHN GOTTFRIED was the NDP member for the Gimli constituency. A former school principal, he was the premier's cousin and as soft-spoken as all that extended clan. Indeed, he hardly spoke at all and I wondered how anyone had heard enough from him to elect him, but here he was in the legislature.

In a pre-election coup, a quasi-political meeting disguised as a development conference was arranged in Gimli by the Department of Industry and Commerce. I accompanied the troupe of members and departmental staff to assess how our programs and our MLA for Gimli were faring. During the hour-long car ride, I studied our 'silent' member, who would introduce the minister and chair the meeting, and wondered what damage-control would be needed to cover his verbal gaffes ... or his inability to verbalize at all.

We arrived at Gimli. The department staff set up displays. Some forty people gathered around the coffee urn, half-whispered ribald jokes, and settled into chairs. The dreaded moment had come ...

Gottfried strode to the podium, his chiseled features topped by a shock of dark, wavy hair, his tall, lean form elegantly dressed in a nicely-tailored, pencil-striped suit. Impressive but ...?

Then 'it' spoke, in a clear and resonant voice: "Ladies and gentlemen. This is Gimli, the home of the gods and the Gottfrieds."

He launched easily into an eloquent description of the pioneers who arrived more than a century ago. Immigrants from Iceland, represented by the heroic, horn-helmeted statue of a Viking in the park at the edge of the town, they had braved the rigours of this somewhat inhospitable place to found a new republic that was later absorbed into the burgeoning Province of Manitoba. They had established their homes and their families, created a robust economy and a distinct society and how their descendants now looked to the future with quiet confidence in their own strength of character, ready to meet any challenge.

And the words of Pontius Pilate, who came to scoff but was strangely moved, flashed into my mind: *"Ecce homo."* Behold the man.

CAMPAIGN STORIES ARE LEGION. There is the one about the serious candidate who knocked on a door and asked the man who anwered: "Sir, do you agree our real issues are ignorance and apathy?"

"I don't know and I don't care," he said.

Or the Conservative candidate, a rather severe middle-aged lady, who was progressing down a street, preceded by her scouts. In response to a knock, a door was opened by a pretty young woman—completely nude. The scout, trained to repeat his spiel no matter what, asked: "Would you like to come out and meet the candidate?"

"No thanks, I don't live here."

Then there's the tale of Doreen Dodick, a stunning blonde with a perpetual smile, always immaculately dressed, who was campaigning in the Wolseley constituency. She knocked on a door through which strange sounds emanated. It was opened by a naked man, who looked her over carefully before inviting: "Hi doll, come on in and join the orgy."

But not all campaign trail experiences are humorous.

We were on the way to a political rally in Brandon, Manitoba's second-largest city and the site of a large commercial fertilizer plant built in 1967 by world-class, Idaho-based Simplot Corporation. It had received a $5 million grant from Ottawa and a $23 million loan from Manitoba's Conservative government via the Manitoba Development Corporation. At the opening, Simplot's president had stated that his company seldom uses its own money in such ventures.[2]

While driving, I informed the premier that Simplot was using our money and our resouces to make fertilizer in our province but selling it in the U.S. for less than it sold in Brandon. Fighting foreign corporations is good for votes so why not tell the rally that, unless this stopped, our loan would be called. And if Simplot threatened to close its plant? We would get more votes by stating the Manitoba government would reopen it within a day. The premier demurred: "This is a legitimate loan and cannot be abused that way."

In short, he was not ready to take my advice.[3] It would not be a good day.

The rally was huge. Floating balloons displayed the names of regional candidates. The hall was packed to the rafters. The only vacant chair was at the press table, beside *Winnipeg Free Press* columnist Egon Frech. Across from us sat the CBC's Henry Champ.

The premier, inspired by the enthusiastic audience and seeing this as a crucial meeting in a politically critical area, spoke at length. After thirty minutes Champ leaned across the table to Frech: "How long does this guy speak? In Ontario, Bill Davis would have said his piece and been out of here twenty minutes ago."

The premier continued. The audience was entranced, but Champ was visibly bored. He leaned across to Frech and said conspiratorially, "I hear this premier of yours is quite a stud." A moment later he added, "I hear his wife is rather loose too."

Frech, visibly embarrassed, looked directly at him. "Why don't you ask Herb here. She's his sister."

I leaned across the table. "Yes. Why don't you ask me. She's my sister."

The six-foot-plus Henry Champ appeared to shrink a bit. He mumbled an incoherent apology and muttered that in a civilized province no political person would be permitted to sit at the press table.

---

[2] Five days before the 1999 election, when Progressive Conservative Premier Gary Filmon was running for a fourth term, the ninety-year-old founder of Simplot opened a large addition to the Brandon plant.

[3] A 1974 study by Toronto's Topcon Group reported that Simplot had admitted "discriminatory pricing policies", which cost Manitoba farmers excessive prices for fertilizer, and lamented, "It is ironic that the benefits of a public investment accrue to ... Simplot of Idaho, and U.S. farmers who get low-priced fertilizers from Brandon." *The Winnipeg Tribune*, February 27, 1974.

✪ ✪ ✪

WE HAD A GOOD MEETING AT GRETNA, which nominated party faithful Jake Heinrichs to run against the lone but solidly entrenched Social Credit incumbent, and then we raced across country to another nominating meeting for sitting member René Toupin at St. Malo. I was driving the huge black Buick we had inherited from former Premier Weir and had the pedal to the metal on the beautiful June evening, the setting sun red behind us as we roared eastward into the darkening blue. The mastodon of the highway purred like a racing engine while the rises and dips in the road gave us the sensation of being airborne. The premier, in the rear seat with briefing notes, sensed the speed, "Herb, we do not need to be in a such great rush. We have time."

"Well, in fact we do need to rush. And besides, with all these horses under the hood this beast is difficult to control."

"Well, okay."

I crossed the Red River at Ste. Agathe, whipped along the narrow road to Highway 59, rocketed southward, turned sharply right into the town, sharply left onto Main Street, and skidded to a stop in front of the hall on the dot of 9 P.M., just as I had promised Toupin. The premier jumped out to enter the hall while I cruised the street seeking a parking spot. An RCMP patrol car pulled up. A young officer came over and asked almost apologetically, "How fast were you driving back there on the highway?"

"Well, officer, I was so preoccupied with watching the road that I didn't notice my speedometer."

"We couldn't clock you but you sure as hell were moving."

"Well yes, I was in a bit of a hurry."

"We realize you're driving the premier, but we just can't let you get away with this. We have to do something."

"I understand, officer. You have to do what you have to do."

With a suggestion of reluctance, he wrote a speeding ticket and handed it to me and I, making the best of an unhappy situation, commended him for doing his duty. I said nothing to the premier.

That was Wednesday evening. On returning home my wife asked what exciting things had happened to me during the day and I told her about the speeding ticket. She was not amused:

"You should know better than drive like that with the premier in the car. It would be tragic to have an accident at this time. Perhaps having to pay for that ticket will smarten you up."

"Oh well, I will just turn in the ticket with my expense account. After all, I was chauffering the premier of the province and there is no reason why incidentals such as traffic tickets should not be a government expense."

"You should be careful doing things like that. We are in an election campaign and you must realize you are working in a goldfish bowl. If the media ever finds out you let the taxpayers pay that ticket it might be used to embarrass the premier, which is not exactly what he needs at this time."

So on Thursday afternoon, I walked across Broadway to the Law Courts Building and paid the ticket out of my own pocket.

The following day, at the regular Friday morning press conference, Bob Beaton of CJOB Radio pointedly asked the premier if the government had paid my speeding ticket.

ON THE DRIVE TO GIMLI, the premier and I argued about fishing. Shortly after the election of the NDP government in 1969, it was discovered that fish in Lake Winnipeg were contaminated with mercury. Legal action was taken against a Saskatchewan fertilizer plant that was dumping its effluent into the river of the same name, which flowed through Lake Winnipeg on its way to Hudson Bay, and the lake was closed to fishing. Two years later, when the lake was reopened, it was discovered the fish had proliferated enormously during the hiatus. Immediately thousands of potential fishermen became anxious to harvest this bonanza. The government, fearing the fish would not long survive this onslaught, and seeking to preserve a permanent harvest of fish, immediately began establishing regulations to govern commercial fishing.

The announcement that regulations would be established was greeted by a stampede of applicants, some of whom had sold their boats years ago and/or left the province. A furious debate resulted at two levels: first, between those who considered it their God-given right to fish out every fingerling, and the government determined to regulate in the interests of maintaining a sustainable industry; and second, between those in the government caucus charged with the responsibility of establishing the regulations, and those whose constituencies bordered on the lake and who, for both economic and political reasons, wanted liberal regulations.

The arguments focused on (a) licensing criteria that would determine who would be allowed to fish commercially, (b) quotas determining total fish catch allowed, and (c) mesh size, which would determine the maturity of the fish allowed to be caught.

Eventually, it was established that those who had fished commercially in the three years prior to the closing of the lake and could verify that they had sold enough fish to constitute a significant part of their income would be eligible for licenses. Quotas were based on anticipated rates of reproduction and the mesh size of the nets was set at four-and-a-half inches. Some modifications were made, but the pressure continued; prospective fishermen wanted lower entry qualifications, larger quotas and smaller meshes. Some would have used cheese cloth as the mesh, had it been allowed.

This is what we were discussing on the drive to Gimli. I had been through the blood bath of Canadian Wheat Board regulations and took the hard line. The premier, always ready to accommodate and impelled by both his nature and the practical political considerations of an election campaign, was prepared to make any modifications possible without damaging the principle.

"Could we not at least modify the eligibility qualifications so more persons could obtain licenses?" he asked me.

"We have been wrestling with this issue for a year now and the pressures for further accommodations continue. A system of regulation must have some integrity. The softer the regulations, the more complaints we will have and the more difficult policing will be. We must become accustomed to the realization that, no matter what we do, not everyone will love us. Furthermore, the major complainants are probably also the major violators."

That evening, following the premier's speech, he was approached by a number of individuals while I stood at a discreet distance just within earshot. I recognized one as a man who had come to my office to seek a $1 million MDC loan to construct a building in which he could mount some cables and pulleys to demonstrate that he had solved man's quest for perpetual motion. Now he wanted an MDC loan to demonstrate that he had perfected fireproof plastic.

Another man spoke to the premier, who then called to me, "Herb, come over here. This man has a request to make of you."

The premier introduced us to each other and the man explained, "I want you to tighten the licensing regulations. I know two guys with good incomes other than from fishing and they should have their licenses pulled."

It was time to illustrate a point. "So _____ drives a school bus and _____ is a barber and you want us to take them off the lake?"

"Well, I didn't mention any names."

"But I did."

"Okay. Yes. Those two should not be fishing."

"All right. As soon as we get back to Winnipeg I will check out those two and if they are receiving more than half their income from sources other than fishing, we will revoke their licenses."

The man, obviously impressed that the problem he had complained of should be rectified so expeditiously, smiled and reached to shake my hand. The premier looked somewhat quizzical.

"And then, Sir, I'm going to check you out."

The man took a step back, and raised his hands in surrender, "It's okay. Forget I ever mentioned the subject."

The premier did something unusual for him in public—he began to laugh. It was our last debate on the licensing of fishermen.

IT WAS MY FAULT. For the premier, the campaign was a triumphal march through the province. The press reported 250 at his meeting in the little town of Pine Falls (June 10th), 600 at his own nominating meeting in Rossmere (June 12th), 800 at Dauphin (June 13th), 400 at Thompson (June 14th), 600 at Swan River (June 19th), and a capacity crowd of more than 900 at Brandon (June 20th).

This was climaxed with a massive open air rally of 3,500 noisy, cheering, banner-waving celebrants on a lovely Sunday afternoon (June 24th) at Kildonan Park's Rainbow Stage. The rally was addressed by author and environmentalist Farley Mowat, who allayed some concerns with his approval to the government's northern hydro-electric program. The crowd cheered itself hoarse as the premier, with thirty candidates on the stage with him, regaled them with stories of the opposition leaders who "could profitably run a peanut stand only if they inherited it", could operate an industrial complex "only if they found someone with brains in Switzerland" and who were unable to put together a coalition in constituencies where they were both weak "despite three years of coaching by the *Winnipeg Free Press*".

Even in southwest Manitoba, where NDP votes were historically as sparse as Russian thistles growing out of the dust dunes along the fence lines in the Dirty Thirties, we found friends. In small towns, people requested the premier's photo and autograph. In the constituency of Arthur, our candidate was soft-spoken Lorne Watt—who was running against his brother, Douglas Watt, former minister of Agriculture in the Weir regime.

In Virden, Manitoba's Oil Capital, the premier was met by sitting Conservative MLA Morris McGregor, who was anxious to introduce him to one and all and offered to vote with the NDP if they were returned with a minority. "I thought I should be here to greet him," McGregor said. "He is the premier and whatever his politics, I think I should defend him. I always got along well with Ed and I could work with him easily. He comes across better than either of the other two leaders." [4]

All was well. It was not the time to be careless. But I was. I did not appreciate the load the premier was bearing, or the need to buoy him up with pleasant thoughts between speeches and interviews. I had never appreciated the role of the court jester in keeping the king happy with humour—until this incident.

It is axiomatic; the larger the crowd the lonelier the person. City dwellers seldom know their neighbours, which is anti-social, but there is safety in anonymity. Conversely, in less populated rural areas, most people know their neighbours within a large radius, But KNOWING them means knowing ABOUT them. This, combined with a peculiarly Calvinistic tendency among rural people, particularly farmers, to regard those not making their own way in the world as not only lazy, but morally flawed, makes 'welfare' payments a potent issue, waiting to be politically exploited.

---

[4] Frances Russell, "Premier In Toyland", *Winnipeg Free Press*, June 20, 1973

Among the most frequent, and virulent, tormentors of the NDP government on this subject were two rural MLAs. Wally McKenzie and James Bilton, Conservative MLAs from Roblin and Swan River respectively, (sometimes joined by Conservative MLA Harry Graham from adjacent Birtle-Russell) were politicians who made the term 'Progressive Conservative' an oxymoron. They were ideologues of the first magnitude who made a fetish of never seeing anything good in any action of a "socialist" government, even when it favoured people in their own constituencies. McKenzie never missed an opportunity to wax cynically critical of any government expenditure he could pitch as an intervention in the "free enterprise" economy, and his twin was always alert for some excuse to bludgeon the "profligate socialists", sometimes verging on the bizarre.

The Manitoba government, appalled at the wide disparities among municipalities, decided to regulate welfare payments. The two rural Tories saw this as a political bonanza, for two reasons: to get votes by quietly obtaining welfare for constituents and to get more votes by fiercely attacking the "welfare" government.

McKenzie was an affable country grocer whose rumpled appearance disguised his political acuity. He saw his chance and attacked. "The municipalities thought they had control of the welfare system [but] ... they have no power, because the Welfare Advisory Committee can overrule them on any issue ... I've got farmers in my constituency that make $15,000 bucks but are on welfare."[5]

Then he gave Health and Welfare Minister René Toupin some advice:

> For gosh sakes let's have no dreamers in your department. I want some hard-nosed businessmen that know a buck's a buck. The minister has in his department some of the most red-eyed socialists Manitoba has ever seen ... He's got these dreamers, philosophers, politicians there's hundreds of them ... And this is what the people of my constituency are concerned about.[6]

Bilton was a hard-bitten veteran of both World War II and many political battles, an insurance broker and a former speaker. He was quick to anger, sharp of tongue, and a vocal guardian of pubic funds:

> I have old age pensioners coming to me and saying what am I going to do with all this money? The supplementary cheque, the old age pension ... those old timers, they're not asking this government for anything, and don't know what to do with the money they're getting ... You are doing them a disservice ... I hear it on every hand ... where is this money coming from?

---

[5]   *Winnipeg Free Press*, June 20, 1972.

[6]   *Hansard*, June 16, 1972

> Never in the history of the valley, Mr. Speaker, did we need the charity this government is handing out. The people are not asking for it, it is being forced on them, and they don't want it ... For Heaven's sake, don't be pouring out your charity in the Swan River Valley ... you're not going to win that seat.[7]

It was all so patently political, as though pension programs have no utility but to buy votes. But their real *bête noir* was welfare—the government was forcing welfare payments on people who did not need it and did not want it, and particularly on those who did not deserve it, and this was the 'socialist' way of destroying the economy, the work ethic, and community values.

On impulse, I phoned the Department of Social Services: "I want to know if Wally McKenzie and James Bilton have been referring constituents to the welfare offices. Send me whatever reports you have from your district offices. For the sake of comparison also give me reports on the Burtniak and Adam, the two government MLAs from the Parklands area."[8]

The reports were revealing and the hypocrisy appalling. During the period from April 1st to August 2nd in 1972, staff reported a total of fifteen written referrals from Mr. McKenzie. Moreover, they reported that "Mr. Bilton is in the office constantly referring many, many cases to us and putting as much pressure as he possibly can on us to have his own referrals enrolled even when we explain to him these people are clearly ineligible."

The summary went on to say:

> Of the four MLAs involved with the Dauphin Region (McKenzie, Bilton, Burtniak and Adam) Mr. McKenzie leads in the number of written referrals made to us ... Mr. Bilton often tries to exert pressure in getting staff to make enrollments, even when ineligibility is explained ... *We cannot recall a written referral from Mr. Burtniak or Mr. Adam.*[9]

One of McKenzie's letters complained a recipient's welfare was reduced by $5 and "he had difficulty providing for himself." A second letter stated a welfare recipient was having difficulties and "No doubt the cost of his car insurance and license have much bearing on the problem." (This was six months after the advent of Autopac, which all but one Conservative MLA had voted against). A third letter requested increased welfare for a recipient "to buy a decent car". These referrals were NOT to obtain welfare, but to obtain more welfare than the department thought adequate.

---

[7] *Hansard*, May 25, 1972.

[8] Peter Burtniak, MLA for Dauphin and the minister of Highways, and Peter Adam, MLA for Ste. Rose, were both members of the NDP.

[9] Author's italics. Departmental memos, August 2, 3 and 9, 1972.

I gave the material to the premier who referred to "people who say one thing and practice another" in the chamber the next time 'the troglodyte twins' reared a head. The reaction was peculiar; the ministers in question attacked him for attacking them for doing their job,[10] the opposition attacked him for attacking elected members; the media attacked him for revealing 'confidential' records.

We lost that round. We now had another opportunity. It was three days before E-Day. We were flying into the belly of the beast, the three constituencies along the Saskatchewan border that we had lost by less than 200 votes to the Conservatives in 1969.

Had my colleague, René Chartier, taken this trip he probably would have told jokes and funny stories about the campaign and kept the conversation light and the premier amused, but I was different, and besides, the premier and I seldom indulged in small talk. In the plane on the way to the evening meeting at Russell, I briefed him on recent developments in general and then bore in on what I deemed the primary purpose of this evening's exercise—to destroy three Conservative MLAs. "We have been wasting time visiting constituencies in which Jesus Christ would be crucified if he ran as an NDP candidate," I told him, "and I have always objected to dispersing our limited resources on barren ground. Tonight we are in the heart of northwest Manitoba and the town of Russell is the nodal point of the constituencies held by Bilton, McKenzie and Graham."

I reminded him that the NDP and the CCF before it always had a strong core of support here and that we lost these constituencies by a hair in 1969. "Tonight we have a chance to give our people cause to fight harder by undermining our opponents. These buggers have been getting support by calling us the 'welfare government' and on that issue we now have them by the short hairs."

Any perusal of records would show that we have been uncommonly generous in constituencies held by the opposition, I said, particularly through the Departments of Agriculture, Health, Municipal Affairs and Housing."But all we get from that off-key Greek chorus across the way is the constant harping that we are spending too much money. It is time we told the people of Manitoba where most of the money is being spent and tonight you have a unique opportunity to do that. We have been good to their constituencies in spite of them and tonight you can skewer these malicious, hypocritical vote whores with their own words."

I had scored some tactical successes with my *modus operandi* of 'attack faster and harder'. Success had bred a hubris, which had made me careless. Most of my advice to the premier was modified or ignored. This time, to my profound regret, it was accepted.

---

[10] The exposé had a salutary effect on Bilton. A year later, the district office reported: "Within the last year, Mr. Bilton's referrals have become quite reasonable and have decreased in number. Most have been conveyed to us verbally in the office or on the phone and we have generally agreed with the referrals." Not so with McKenzie: "McKenzie's referrals are on the increase." They included "requesting additional benefits for a single 52-year-old man, a long-term social assistance recipient on full budget. Mr. McKenzie advised the man should be on B and R with his mother. Four visits to this man's home were all futile, since [he] was out riding about the country on his truck and a neighbour advised that [his] mother was visiting this winter with her daughter in B.C." Departmental memo, April 27, 1973.

The hall was full to bursting and the audience was partisan and enthusiastic and clearly expected this time they would be voting with the majority. The premier spoke well and persuasively and related the initiatives undertaken in Manitoba generally and in their constituencies particularly during his administration. Then he eased into an area he had been persuaded should be broached, but which his political instincts informed him was delicate.

He explained that his government had treated fairly constituencies represented by opposition MLAs and indeed there were complaints from his own people that they were being treated too well. His government had not rewarded those who supported it and punished those who voted against it, but had responded to need. However, there are MLAs who use public money to the maximum extent and then maliciously criticize the government for spending too much money. If this continued, the time would come when it would be difficult to justify expenditures in their constituencies.

He referred to lone Social Credit MLA Jake Froese, who had taken out an election advertisement stating his constituency of Rhineland had been "virtually ignored under the old Conservative administration, [but[Ed Schreyer respects the opinion of our MLA". The ad went on to list a number of projects, including drainage works, highways and schools that had been brought there by the NDP government. Then:

> You know, when the Conservatives were in office they did have a
> habit of freezing out constituencies that didn't vote the right way.[11] We
> have tried to be fair, but I want to make it very clear that we will not
> bend over backwards and try and treat fairly equally a constituency the
> MLA of which—and some of them are worse than others—is vicious and
> malicious and vindictive.
>
> A man can be of the opposition, as Mr. Froese is, but if he is not
> vicious and malicious, we try to be fair.

He merely meant to explain that while his government had been fair to a fault, NDP politicians were not stupid, and would be reluctant to support efforts that appeared to be 'leaning over backwards' just to prove they were being fair, particularly in the constituencies of patently unfair opposition MLAs.

But his convoluted syntax was wrong. It didn't come our right and he knew it. He intuitively felt himself slipping down the slope to an election threat. His effort to modify it made it worse: "But I'm serving notice now, if we're the government, any maliciousness on the part of an opposition MLA really is some-

---

[11] A confidential Manitoba Treasury Board paper entitled 'Financial Management and Planned Program Budgeting', prepared by the PC government in June 1968, proposed "a weighting of constituencies according to the threat to the overall security of their government." It classified the fifty-seven constituencies as a) Solid Opposition, b) Solid Government, c) Volatile Opposition, d) Volatile Government, e) Marginal Opposition and f) Marginal Government and concluded "The implications for Cabinet are obvious." p. 22.

thing which the government would be foolish to reward with kindness."

My political antenna jerked up. For one usually so sensitive to both the tone and content of what he said, qualifying his words and qualifying the qualifications, always cognizant of Orwell's dictum to "let the meaning choose the word", this seemed a gaffe. Was I being paranoid? Were the heightened sensitivities inherent in election campaigning making me overly cautious about nuances?

The crowd was applauding wildly—they were figuratively drinking Conservative blood as I had hoped they would. Clearly this would put our people in a fighting mood and mobilize their energies for the final push. No sweat, I thought, no one had even noticed. I turned my head just in time to see *Winnipeg Tribune* columnist Richard Purser, a press corps luminary who had once occupied the Washington desk. In a single motion he closed his tape recorder, picked up his notebook, stood up and fairly ran out of the hall.

The shit was about to hit the fan. In politics perception is reality and the reality would be what Purser would say it was and it was clear he had already decided what spin he would give it.

Worse, he did not need to give it a spin at all. The words, no matter what the intention, would be construed as a threat.[12]

Late that evening, I mentioned to the premier that we had a problem. But he, knowing only what was in his mind rather than what he had said, did not appreciate the danger. I explained how his comment would be interpreted, but he was confident he knew what he had said, and what he had meant, and it was no threat.

The next morning, when we landed at the Dauphin airfield, the switchboard was red with phone calls for us—from my secretary, from several ministers, from the chairman of the election planning committee, from the provincial secretary of the NDP, from the provincial election organizer, from the local MLA, and from several other organizers and candidates throughout the province. Some were just inquiring about what had been said. But the party's election officers recognized the danger and were adamant; the premier must deny that he had said what was being said he had said. Clearly Purser's report had hit like an unspent meteor and the shock waves were being felt throughout the province.

Radio reports showed the opposition leaders having a field day at our expense. Sidney Spivak told a large crowd at Dauphin—a seat we had to win— "This is the sign of a frightened government. [Schreyer] said if he didn't like the MLA the people chose, his government would ignore the needs of that area."

---

[12] I had planned a clever strategem. Ed McGill, a Conservative MLA and candidate in Brandon West, had made a statement about the premier, which a newspaper had reported under the banner headline: 'Schreyer is a Liar'. I arranged to have a copy of that headline dropped into every mailbox in the Brandon West constituency the evening before the election. Since the premier was known as "Honest Ed" and his integrity was respected by friend and foe alike, I believed many recipients would vent their disgust with McGill's attack by voting NDP. After the incident at Russell, I quickly cancelled the distribution. I recalled this incident when Conservative aparatchniks Taras Sokolyk and Jules Benson confessed to a judicial inquiry about some vote-rigging during the 1995 Manitoba election. We political warriors consider 'dirty tricks' an election device, not an indictable offence.

And Izzy Asper added: "The premier has made a cynical, ruthless statement. He said vote NDP or get punished ... It's political blackmail."

After a brief meeting with local party people, we sat in morose silence in the cramped cabin while the tiny plane hiccupped its uncertain way to Cross Lake and then Jenpeg, to be again besieged by telephonic demands to deny, deny, deny. After a brief meeting with the chief and council, and the Manitoba Hydro crew, we prepared to leave for an evening meeting at Wabowden.

I said to the premier, "I'm staying here. I want to call Winnipeg and resolve this matter. My instinct is our organizers are so wrapped up in their work that they are ignoring some political nuances. This issue is too political to be ignored and too sensitive to be left to the party bureaucracy. I'll see you when you return from Wabowden."

I called several people in Winnipeg and explained that while the premier had not intended to say what was being said that he said, what he had said could be sufficiently misinterpreted for the media and our political opponents to be able to say the premier had said what they were saying he had said. I left instructions to do nothing and say nothing until we returned to Winnipeg.

I met the premier when he returned to Jenpeg: "We've got to get back to Winnipeg. We have a problem."

"Oh, that's all been resolved." He explained while at Wabowden he had been phoned by our election organizer, who told him all was under control; party spokesmen would deny he had said anything that could be construed as a threat, and a friendly reporter would explain it all on the CBC television news at 10 P.M.

It was now 9:25. I ran to the nearest phone and dialed: "Allan. You bunch of idiots. Shut up and listen to me closely. We are coming back. Don't say anything more to anyone about this.

"And for Christ's sake, don't let that reporter anywhere near that TV station. Call a press conference for tomorrow morning."

"But Herb, you are being irrational. Everyone knows Schreyer does not make threats even when he should. There were hundreds of people in the hall and no two will remember the same words. Why can't we say the premier did not say what is being said he said?"

"Because, you asshole, Purser has it on his frigging tape."

The next morning we flew to Winnipeg, without conversation. The emotions at the press conference in the huge room were palpable. What would the premier say? He was having trouble with his voice: "Ladies and gentlemen of the media ..."

The tension was unbearable. I had the sensation of teetering on the edge of an abyss.

"I have difficulty believing I said what I am accused of having said. It was unintentional and not intended as a threat."

Goddamn it! The party bureaucracy had won. He would deny it.

"But it was close enough to be so interpreted," he went on. "Therefore, for saying what I said I am deeply sorry."

He knew too well the Gresham's Law of politics: that bad news expunges good news. He knew what this would cost him, but he would not evade the issue. There was moment's pause as he struggled for self-control. Was he formulating an excuse? Would he indulge in bathos?

"Nor can I excuse myself on the grounds of fatigue." I began to feel warm inside as my sympathy flowed out to him. He would not seek refuge in an excuse certainly available to him under the circumstances. It was almost embarrassing, as though watching through a keyhole while a man wrestled with his deepest emotions.

"I am the leader of the party and the premier of the province. That imposes obligations. People look to me for leadership. I dishonoured my supporters and insulted the people of Manitoba. For that I must take the responsibility."

He was drinking the hemlock. A refrain ran through my head:

> Tears were in [my] eyes, and in [my] ears,
> The music of a thousand years.

We never spoke of this again. He never knew that it was here at the moment of his greatest humiliation, that I most honoured him. We lost some votes but regained the initiative. More critically, we would no longer be pursued by innuendo. The matter was out of the way and, for the rest of the campaign, we could concentrate on real issues. No one knew that better than Richard Purser. That evening the premier spoke at Winkler. I dropped him at the hall and sought a parking spot. When I entered the hall, Purser stood in the doorway. As I walked by, he glared at me with what I could only interpret as hate. Into my face he hissed, "We almost got him. He almost denied it. We almost got him."

Alone in the crowd, Premier Schreyer takes part in an NDP convention.

XIX

The Morning After

Today is the first day of the rest of our troubles.
        —Old Russian proverb

It was 'the morning after' and we had a sour taste in our mouths. It was a glorious day, not only because it was June in Manitoba and we had won a majority, but because we had proven our election in 1969 was not an aberration. We were part of the political culture and we occupied "the seats of the mighty". The re-elected premier described the election results as "a victory for social democracy and the average Manitoban". It was a good day to be alive and to be a member of the New Democratic Party, something close to Heaven.

So why were we not deliriously happy? *The Winnipeg Tribune* summarized our discomfiture in a huge, glaring red margin-to-margin headline: SCHREYER HAS CAKE, BUT NOT THE ICING.

"It's a very strange election when the winner should be disappointed while the loser is a kind of winner. The PCs won a moral victory by simply standing still. Why? Because they faced a government with as good a record as any in Canada, a government that had kept its promises and maintained a close human relationship with the electorate."[1]

We had thrown everything we had into what was arguably the most intense political campaign in the history of Manitoba. We had 18,000 party members and their enthusiasm was that of winners.

Every pre-election poll had predicted our victory, and commentators had given us up to forty-two seats, thirteen more than at dissolution. The premier, by far the most popular politician in Manitoba, who ran ahead of the opposition

---

[1] June 29, 1973.

leaders even among their party members, spoke in thirty-seven constituencies, twice in some. We had fifty-eight full-time campaign organizers, thirty-seven from other provinces, plus experienced persons provided by labour unions.[2]

More important, many of our programs were so popular with the public that our political opponents were forced to be circumspect in criticizing them. Autopac had become wildly popular; Medicare was already part of the social culture; senior citizen's homes, nursing homes, home care, the home repair program, PEP programs to build provincial infrastructure, student loans and employment programs, the property tax credits that had relieved most pensioners of the education tax, farm supports, northern development, were all popular programs.

Then it was E-Day. It was a frenetic day, answering a hundred phone calls, visiting polling booths to encourage volunteer workers, receiving minute-by-minute reports from the Party office; resolving a dozen last-minute disputes that were miniscule in the great scheme of things, but critically important to individuals or communities whose support we needed; there was mediating between candidates concerned with local sensitivities and their professional organizers looking at the overall picture; fending off media while not being difficult, assuring all we would win while not appearing arrogant.

Then came the wait. We felt certain of victory. The result seemed written in the stars. Recent surveys had us well in the lead. A public opinion poll rated Schreyer's popularity far above that of the other two leaders. And it had been a great campaign. It was just a question of how many seats we would win. Schreyer, the realist with a sensitive political nose, predicted thirty-three seats, but media commentators gave us up to forty-two of the province's fifty-seven seats.

But elections always bring the titillation of uncertainty. The public can confound the prognosticators and in elections *vox populi, vox dei*. Results can surprise—as they had in 1969 when we unexpectedly won. And just winning had created its own problems. Now the question was, would the electorate give us a large enough majority for room to manoeuvre? Or would the government again be condemned to the frustrations of working with a minority, unable to move without looking over its shoulder to note if a caucus member was ill, or a disgruntled back-bencher was making noises, just before a crucial vote, about either he or his constituency being neglected?

Minority governments, by definition, might be seen as good by the public, but not by those responsible for the day-to-day conducting of public affairs and the making of long-term policy decisions with no possibility of short-term benefits.

The polls closed. Results trickled in. Constituencies switched back and forth on the television screen like the high ground on battlefields. Figures slowly stabilized. It appeared we had won thirty-one seats. It was not what we had hoped or believed we had earned.

Members of the media, panels of commentators, analysts popping out of

---

[2]   CLC, CUPE, CFAW and the Steelworkers' Union.

the polished woodwork of political science departments, explained why the voters had done what they had, and assessed the consequences.

Disappointing! But at least we had a majority. The pressures would be somewhat eased. We would have some breathing space. But that was tomorrow. Tonight we would celebrate. Tonight, shortly after 10 P.M. when the electoral results were clear, the premier would appear like a conquering hero, wafted on waves of adulation and frenzied applause of party aficionados at the Union Centre …

THE UNION CENTRE! It was not quite all over. That afternoon, my secretary had received a phone call, in a deep male voice: "Tonight, at the Union Centre, your premier will be killed."

Killed? By whom? How? Why? Was this possible? Was this not a civilized country? The premier was informed but shrugged it off: "They got the Kennedy brothers and Martin Luther King, so it can happen to anyone."

He felt this came with the territory and there was no secure defence against a determined assassin. Nor was this the first threat during the past four years; we had almost become inured to them, yet none had materialized. But this was a special occasion. And political assassinations were not unknown. We had to take whatever precautions were possible.

The Winnipeg police and the RCMP were alerted and sent several plain-clothed officers. The premier's assistants and some close friends, amid the smoke and satisfying smell of sweat and stale beer, maintained a loose cordon around him, discretely diverting anxious petitioners or over-exuberant supporters. Others watched from strategic positions, attempting to remain alert amid the tumult and the shouting, the distracting Cyclopean lights of television cameras and the hundreds of beer bottles and banners waved overhead like trophies.

"At the time of victory no one is tired," some Roman scribe had written, but we were. The rigours of the campaign, and the less-than-expected results, had taken their toll. Our adrenalin was no longer pumping. And we tried to not look too foolish playing Walter Mitty imitations of James Bond pretending to protect the Captain of our Ship of State.

As it turned out, no assassination attempt was made, no shots were fired, no bombs burst, no blood flowed. It was all so anti-climactic.

In the end, the NDP popular vote had increased four points, from thirty-eight to forty-two per cent, the third-highest popular vote since 1920, but it netted us only thirty-one legislative seats, two more than at dissolution and the same number we had a year earlier, before being deserted by Borowski and Allard.

Meanwhile, the PC popular vote had, rather than decreasing as we had expected, increased one point, from thirty-five to thirty-six per cent, and netted them an additional seat, increasing their representation from twenty to twenty-one. Liberal popular support had decreased five points, from twenty-four to nineteen per cent, but their representation had increased by one seat, from four to five. We had swept the north, as expected, but the PCs had unexpectedly swept the

south, including the seat of lone Social Creditor Jake Froese, who had been ideologically opposed to the government but personally friendly to Schreyer. And we
had lost two cabinet ministers, Desjardins and Mackling. With everything going
for us, including the abolition of Medicare premiums and the reduction of Autopac
premiums shortly before the election, and with most of the Liberal defectors
coming to us, it had still been, like Waterloo, "a damn close-fought thing".

Our popular vote was four percent less than our own pre-election polls had
predicted. With a four-year registered voter increase of 66,000 (523,000 to 599,000),
and an election day turnout of a record of 78.3 per cent (compared to 64.3 per
cent in 1969), we had barely held our own. Humiliatingly, we again lost the
three western border farm seats we believed we would win; the Tory MLAs who
criticized us as a "welfare government" while ladling out welfare to their constituents were re-elected by increased majorities (111 to 131, 161 to 236, and 576
to 702 respectively).[4]

We had taken one seat from the Tories, but largely because their popular
MLA, Gabriel Girard, had retired. We had won the remaining three of the five
northern seats, but from Independents, and two of those we had held before
their incumbents, Allard and Borowski, left us. We had struggled mightily and
barely gained while the Tories had triumphed simply by not being decimated.
Something had gone terribly wrong.

But what? It was time for self-evaluation. Did we lose what we thought we
had won because 'socialism' was still a four-letter word among Manitobans generally? Was it because of the 'One Candidate' strategy of the other two parties,
which resulted in only a Liberal or a PC running in nine seats, one being St.
Boniface, where we lost Desjardins? Had our Land Lease Option, which both
parties had used so effectively against us, roused fears of "nationalization" of farm
land? Was it because of the premier's "gaffe" at Russell? Had it been a mistake to
base the campaign largely on the personal popularity of the premier instead of the
party? Was it the primal passions, exploited by our opponents, roused by our uni-
ficaton of thirteen municipalites into Unicity? Did businessmen still regard us as
'Barbarians at the Gates'? Had we allowed hubris to blind us to reality? Had we
misread the signs; were we not as good—or as popular—as we had thought? Was
columnist Frances Russell right in stating that the publication of our *Guidelines
for the Seventies*, which proposed future directions, demonstrated a "Death Wish"?
Was Tory MLA James Bilton correct in stating that "people don't want all that
money you are handing out?"

The questions were titillating—but unanswerable. And we were gripped by
fatigue and post-election ennui. First things first.

Harry Shafransky and I rented a truck with a camper and took our families
on a trip. We drove the 750 kilometres through the little towns and rocky terrain

---

[4] Sidney Green attributes the disappointing results, at least in part, to the publicity about Schreyer's
"gaffe" in Russell, and to his own display of anger at "some of [Izzy] Asper's outrageous statements" in
a TV debate. *Rise and Fall of a Political Animal*, p. 89.

between Lakes Winnipeg and Manitoba, past Grand Rapids where the great Saskatchewan River flows from the "Shining Mountains" through Cedar Lake into Lake Winnipeg and then north along the Nelson River to the mining centre at Thompson. Then we bounced over the rain-slippery, axle-deep ruts the 120 miles to Leaf Rapids. In that inviting model town snuggled in the thick forest against the Churchill River, we spent a wondrous and restful several days.

In a large motorboat belonging to Shafransky's brother Anton, who lived there, we cruised among the scenic, rocked-ledged, tree-crowned islets in the great spreading river. From one, we cast our hooks into the water, reeled in the tasty trout, tossed them into the pans on the open fire, and langorously feasted like ancient royalty.

One day we commandeered a Manitoba Hydro helicopter and flew the eighty-five kilometres to the Cree village of South Indian Lake, which Manitobans had been led to believe would be destroyed by the planned diversion of the Churchill River into the Nelson. There we saw construction activity to almost rival that of Winnipeg, with fine frame houses and a huge school being built. And it was a beautiful place. Perhaps Izzy Asper's proposal for a monorail from the city made more sense than we had thought.

It was a therapeutic week. We witnessed the beauty and expanse of a part of the province most Manitobans would never see, and enjoyed what we experienced. And then we went back to work.

The election was not quite over. Liberal Leader Israel. H. (Izzy) Asper had held his seat in Wolseley by defeating NDP candidate Murdoch MacKay [5] by two votes. [6] Laurent Desjardins, who had won as a Liberal by 1,325 votes in 1969, was now running as an NDP candidate and was crucial to us as both a seat and a symbol. [7] He had been defeated in St. Boniface by Liberal Paul Marion by eighteen votes. John Gottfried, who had won Gimli for us in 1969 had his majority reduced from 223 votes to thirty by Conservative candidate Ted Reval. Cy Gonick had retired and Crescentwood had been held for us by Harvey Patterson, [8] but our majority had been reduced from 273 votes to fifty-seven by Conservative Laurie Pollard.

And Schreyer had his majority reduced from 2,343 votes in 1969 to 568. All five seats could be challenged, either by us or by our opponents. If they were,

---

[5] MacKay, a Winnipeg lawyer and former Liberal, was elected president of the NDP for a two-year term. The government had appointed him to the Manitoba Development Corporation board and as chairman of the Manitoba Labour Board. In the latter capacity, he so offended the Winnipeg Chamber of Commerce that they requested that the premier remove him on the grounds that he was 'too fair'.

[6] We even knew who the two votes were. A couple, both good friends of the Schreyers and strong NDP supporters, came home from work and decided to have a short nap before going out to vote. They awoke at 8:10 P.M. and realized the polls had closed.

[7] As outlined in earlier chapters, Desjardins had crossed the floor from the Liberals to the NDP after the 1969 election, giving the government the working majority it needed to enact Autopac, Unicity and abolish Medicare fees.

[8] Patterson was a railroader, a long-time union activist, and a prominent member of the Winnipeg Labour Council.

depending on the final outcomes, we could have thirty-two seats —or twenty-seven. We could end up with neither the icing nor the cake.

To challenge or not to challenge, that was the question. Desjardins had received 49.9 per cent of the votes cast, so could we leave him hanging out to dry? And MacKay, slated for the attorney general's portfolio, had come too achingly close to ignore; when Asper's assistant came in to explain how good we looked because we had not challenged, we knew Asper was nervous. But would a challenge, no matter how legitimate, be perceived by the public as a refusal to accept the will of the sovereign electorate. After all, was not *vox populi, vox dei*?

As in some eighteenth-century European battles, each side sought the moral high ground by waiting for the other to fire first. In late July, Conservative candidate in Rossmere, Alfred Penner, broke the impasse by challenging Schreyer.

Penner, a high school civics teacher and City of Winnipeg councillor, had conducted an execrable campaign. Rossmere had the largest concentration of Mennonites of any constituency in Canada, many of them first- or second-generation emigrés from the Soviet Union, and he played to the prejudices of his constituents. He billed his candidacy as offering 'A Choice Between Freedom of Opportunity, or Socialism'. A striking red, white and blue leaflet bore his photo and the words "I Believe", as though about to confess the Apostles Creed, followed by: "We now have a government that stifles initiative, restricts freedom of choice, downgrades standards of decency and morality and compensates lawbreakers." Additionally, he wanted "studies of Socialist, Communist and Marxist doctrines" in schools replaced with "the Bible and Christian principles". He lost by almost 600 votes, but he found novel grounds for a challenge.

As in all elections, the government appointed the returning officers, one for each constituency. For Rossmere it was George Epp. He was non-partisan, had never held a party membership card, appointed more PCs than NDPers as deputy returning officers, and had run what even Penner admitted was a flawless election day organization, without a single complaint despite having the highest percentage of voter turnout of any constituency in Manitoba. He was at that time completing his Ph.D. in history and was a teacher by profession. He was also a part-time lay preacher in a Mennonite Church. And the Elections Act prohibited "ministers, priests or ecclesiatics under any form or profession of religious faith or worship" from being a returning officer.

On this ground, Penner wanted the election invalidated and the courts to give him what the electorate had denied. He had known Epp was a preacher long before and had indeed discussed it with him five days before E-Day, but had said nothing publicly, impelling the conclusion that, had he won, Epp's status would not have been an issue.

In February 1974, the case went to the Court of Queen's Bench. The question was when is a preacher a minister. A host of witnesses were called and long legal arguments made. In March the case was thrown out of court. Schreyer was safe.

In Gimli, after recounts by the returning officer, the county court and the

Court of Appeal, on August 17, 1973, NDP candidate Gottfried was declared winner, his majority increased to fifty-six votes. In St. Boniface, a county court recount tied the two candidates at 4,293 votes each. In the Court of Appeal two judges disagreed, one giving Marion a majority of three (4,301 to 4,298) and the other a majority of one (4,301 to 4,300). The counting was over and Desjardins had lost. But a voter had left us a gift. He had been a patient in St. Boniface Hospital on election day and had voted on a hospital ballot. On these, instead of marking an X, the voter writes the name of the candidate he is voting for. Paul Laville had inadvertently written his own name on the ballot, then stroked out "Laville" and written Marion over it. But "Laville" was still visible. All those who had counted and recounted the ballots had accepted this one. We did not. We challenged it on the grounds it identified the voter, a No-No in any election. Paul Laville had died on October 18, 1973, and we had to identify his headstone in the cemetery. The election was controverted. In the consequent by-election, on December 20, 1974, Desjardins won decisively with 3,711 votes to 3,092.

The recounts in St. Boniface and Wolseley, which kept the crucial St. Boniface seat for the NDP, had a second consequence; they demonstrated that ballot counting is not an exact science. In St. Boniface, a ballot for Marion was marked / X, with a small slanted stroke about an inch from the X. It was accepted. In Wolseley a ballot for MacKay, almost identical—as though made by the same person but with the stroke slanted in the opposite direction—was rejected by a different judge. A third judge counted both. In Wolseley, a ballot on which the voter had marked an X and then written "Murdoch MacKay" over it, presumably to ensure there was no misunderstanding, was rejected as possibly identifying the voter. In St. Boniface, the ballot for Marion, showing the name of the voter, had been accepted.

In the contested Wolseley and Crescentwood constituencies, the counters also danced on the heads of pins. Ballots were clinically examined, counted and recounted. In Wolseley, on election night, the returning officer had broken the tie in favour of MacKay, a subsequent recount had given Asper a majority of two votes and a county court judge increased this to three votes. In the Court of Appeal, two judges increased that to four votes but a third reduced it to two votes (3,124 to 3,122).

In Crescentwood, a returning officer's recount reduced Patterson's fifty-seven -vote majority to two. A second recount gave Pollard a two-vote majority and a third gave Patterson a single-vote majority (3,730 to 3,729). An entire poll of 196 ballots was thrown out because the deputy returning officer had neglected to initial them. A county court recount tied the vote. The returning officer opted for Patterson, and he was sworn in as an MLA in January 1974. A year later, the election was controverted and the NDP majority reduced.

This necessitated a by-election in Crescentwood. The long, arduous and costly recount process had taken its toll. Pollard withdrew as candidate. The process had also taken its toll elsewhere. Asper had seen his majority slip from

1,259 to two in two years. And he had found other pursuits more suited to his talents. In March 1975, he resigned from his legislative seat and as leader of the Liberal Party of Manitoba.

The premier called the two by-elections for June 25, 1975. We lost both to two former city councillors and PC candidates, Warren Steen in Crescentwood and Robert Wilson in Wolseley.

When the dust of battles re-fought settled, Schreyer, Gottfried and Desjardins were saved but MacKay and Patterson were lost. And so, after two years almost to the day after the 1973 general election, after five electoral challenges, four judicial recounts, three by-elections and one court case, and after all the agonizing and the expenditure of time and staggering court costs which had drained some private pockets as well as that of the party, our representation in the legislature was exactly what it had been after the 1973 election, and what it had been in June 1972, before the departure of Allard and Borowski.

Furthermore, the Independents, from whom we had sometimes drawn support, were wiped out, the Liberal Party was eliminated as a serious contender, and we had reaped all the Liberal defectors we could reasonably expect. The Tories were basking in their new-found confidence, which derived from having increased their seats from twenty-one to twenty-three in the by-elections. Worse, the electorate was polarized. And it was only two years to the next election.

XX

The NDP and The MMA

Troubles do not come as single spies but in battalions.
—Shakespeare, *Hamlet*

**want to congratulate you** on your speech." He stood before me, fiftyish, wafer-thin, 5' 7" of bone and gristle, his narrow shoulders almost protruding through the jacket of his dark suit, with graying hair, an ascetic face, a small neatly clipped moustache and unassuming wire-rimmed spectacles. I happily accepted his extended hand. I had defied the party establishment and only Saul Miller appeared willing to forgive me.

In 1966, the NDP elected eleven MLAs to the legislature, the most ever. Seven years earlier, party leader Russell Paulley had inherited a battered four-member caucus following the slaughter of the party at the polls by Duff Roblin. Over time, Manitobans had come to terms with the image of the NDP as "the conscience of the legislature", but it seems we were never thought of as government material.

Not so, however, the phalanx of ambitious young men who were elected for the first time in 1966. These newcomers were unwilling to accept the 'token' role political commentators—and the electorate—had assigned to the party. Increasingly influential among them was the articulate thirty-six-year-old lawyer with a forensic mind, Sidney Green. And it was inevitable, perhaps, that tensions would develop between the pallid Paulley and the young Icarus. Green was a team player; experience in sports and city politics had taught him that collegial support is needed to achieve large ends. But he could not deny his nature, which demanded that he reach for the brass ring no matter what the field of endeavour.

In mid-1968, Green announced he would challenge Paulley at the annual convention in October. The party caucus was traumatized. Privately they were

critical of Paulley's unspectacular persona and his non-confrontational performance and Green had interpreted that as an endorsation of his own emerging desire
to change the party's image from 'conscience' to 'contender'. But party veterans
found the prospect of him being leader almost as alarming as they found that of
Paulley pedestrian. Russ might be slow but he was safe, while Green's mind was
too swift and agile for comfort. And some feared conservative Manitoba was not
ready for a Jewish premier.

Ben Hanuschak, the only caucus member who supported Green, dealt
with this issue wittily. When asked why he was supporting a Jew, Hanuschak
replied smilingly: "Oh, I'm not supporting Green just because he is a Jew." Some
were not amused.

But Paulley had found a prospective successor more acceptable to caucus.
In 1958, the soft-spoken, cerebral Edward Schreyer, barely old enough to vote,
had been elected to the Manitoba Legislature and become popular with political
friend and foe alike. In 1965, and again in June 1968, he had been elected to the
federal Parliament. Five months later Paulley, to thwart Green's lunge for the leadership and to choose his own time of departure, tapped Schreyer on the shoulder.

There were also strategic considerations. To the west, the CCF had become
a political force, and had conducted its social experiments after its election in
Saskatchewan in 1944. Euphoria reigned when the party elected twenty-five MPs
to Ottawa in June 1957, but just a year later they were reduced to eight, and the
leadership decapitated, with the defeat of such luminaries as Tommy Douglas,
Major James William Coldwell, David Orlikow and Stanley Knowles. In 1961, the
CCF was reorganized as the New Democratic Party, which sought a broader base
and included organized labour as an organic component. But the hoped-for rush
to its ranks did not come and after the federal elections in 1962, 1963, 1965 and
1968, it had not regained the 1957 strength of its predecessor.

The party hierarchy concluded that, to win nationally, they must begin
provincially. Manitoba, where the energetic Duff Roblin had been replaced by
lacklustre Walter Weir, became a target. The national executive's decision to "go
provincial" coincided with the Manitoba NDP's realization that it was time for a
new leader. But Schreyer, just re-elected to Ottawa, considered it a breach of faith
with his constituency to resign so soon.

Despite considerable opposition from members of the party and the caucus,
both provincially and federally—but never from Schreyer—I agreed to nominate
Green:

> I am here today to talk about the best thing that has happened to
> the New Democratic Party in a long time—Sidney Green ... [H]e is a
> product of the times with whom young people can identify, and in whom
> those who have devoted much to the party can see their own hopes and
> aspirations ... We are told that Green must not challenge Mr. Paulley but
> Mr. Paulley got into the legislature by defeating incumbent CCF MLA
> George Olive at a nominating convention.

Green's speech was calm, detailed and powerful. The image of the ogre frothing at the mouth that had been created by those in the party terrified by the fear he might become leader was not at all evident. He explained that the party had long played the role of providing ideas for others, that we had done our work and won our political spurs, and that we were now "ready to govern". He concluded, presciently, with Brutus's celebrated call to action:

> There is a tide in the affairs of men, which,
> Taken at the flood, leads on to fortune
> On such a full sea are we now afloat ...[1]

It brought the audience to its feet. Paulley saw himself defeated. He stood at the podium, trembling visibly, and began reading a prepared speech. After the first paragraph he paused. stood facing the audience as though communing with himself. Then he tore up his speaking notes and launched into an oration.

It was reminiscent of a younger Paulley who had often moved audiences, though small, in basements and legion halls throughout Manitoba. It was a Russ Paulley who had learned his politics at the feet of party icons: legendary party founder W.S. Woodsworth, long-time M.P. Stanley Knowles, savant 'M.J.' Coldwell, Winnipeg Mayor John Queen and other leaders of the 1919 General Strike. It was a Paulley who had fumed with helpless rage when friends with families to feed, working for the rival CPR, were dismissed just before retirement, with minimal pensions, while the corporation abandoned railbeds built with public funds and shifted profits to airlines and foreign luxury hotels. He spoke of the NDP as a political vehicle for the dispossessed. Then he acknowledged that "the Old Order changeth" and perhaps it was time for a new leader and he had one in mind and wanted the honour of keeping the seat warm until that man, like a modern Lochinvar, could ride back to the West and assume the leader's mantle—"young Eddie Schreyer".

The speech was bellicose, rambling, passionate—and successful. Russ Paulley was re-elected party leader. His supporters were delirious. We were weary and defeated. Then Saul Miller, a passionate supporter of Paulley as the surrogate for the unavailable Schreyer, and a fierce opponent of Green, defied his associates and crossed the hall to shake my hand.

Miller was a Mensch.

The party hierarchy had planned well. Eight months later, Schreyer became premier of Manitoba and Saul Miller, at fifty-two, was appointed minister of Youth and Education and in the next eight years held so many portfolios—Colleges and Universities, Urban Affairs, Public housing, Health and Social Development—that he became known as "Minister of Everything". In 1971, a "Super Committee" was established to coordinate the activities of the Departments of Health, Education

---

[1] Shakespeare, *Julius Caesar.*

and Social Policy, and Miller, as its chairman, became the first "Super Minister".

He was a product of Winnipeg's North End and had received his education there and at the University of Manitoba. A war veteran, he had built up a successful metal fabricating business, belying the image that the NDP was comprised of academics and ideologues who "never had to meet a payroll". He was a respected member of the Jewish community, and had served as Director of Rainbow Stage, the Canadian Legion and the Manitoba Urban Association. Like many CCF and NDP members, he had experience at lower levels of government, as board member and then chairman of the Seven Oaks School Board, and as councillor for and then mayor of the City of West Kildonan. First elected in 1966, he was already a veteran and, oxymoronic considering his frail physique, immediately became seen as a "heavyweight".

He proved to be a highly competent, compassionate and dedicated minister. Often the only ministerial office light on in the dead of night was Miller's, as he sat at his desk until three in the morning reading briefs or studying budgets line by line. His opinions on any subject, in cabinet and in caucus, were sought and prized. He was known as a "detail" man who "knew his stuff".

He would be often tested. In 1975, the Manitoba Government Employees Association demanded wage increases up to fifty-three per cent. During negotiations Labour Minister Paulley was rushed to the hospital and Acting Labour Minister Miller stepped into the breach. At a supper meeting of a small cabinet committee at the Shanghai Restaurant in the city's Chinatown, Miller took a serviette and sketched a proposal that became government policy and broke the normal mould of flat increases that annually increased the gap between low and high earners. Instead, he proposed a flat base increase of $2,400 to every employee plus an escalating increase of between four and eight per cent, in inverse ratio to salaries: the higher the salary the lower the percentage of increase.[2]

The MGEA leaped into the perceived gap in ministerial control, by calling about 2,000 civil servants to a demonstration in front of the Legislative Building during the lunch break. Miller went out and asked for the leaders. Four men stepped forward. He asked them to accompany him to his office. They did, followed by a troop of reporters. Miller stopped at his office door: "I want negotiators only. Everybody else OUT. EVERYBODY." That included me. The last words I heard through the closing door were: "Okay, gentlemen, you have had a lot of fun at our expense. That is now over. I am going to ask you a question and I am only going to ask it once. I want to know; do you want to talk or fight? The choice is yours." They talked. And they accepted his formula.

Miller was tough.

The conflict of the NDP government and the Manitoba Medical Association was endemic. "Medicare" had been legislated by the NDP in Saskatchewan in 1962. The doctors struck. The contest left emotional and political scars. Most

---

[2] Miller was a realist. Two years later, the policy was modified when Miller reported, "Unless we do so, we will have the highest-paid floor sweepers and lowest-paid deputy ministers in Canada."

welcomed the government's universal health care plan. Others feared bureaucratic interference in the relationship with their patients, and loss of cost control.[3] Some members of the medical profession agreed that health care is best provided on a collective basis, but others feared government intervention would reduce both the quality of health care and their status and income. Basically, it became a vicious fight between individuals who believed health care was a public good and that a one-payer concept was the most effective and efficient way of providing it, and those who believed health care must remain a private relationship between doctor and patient.

Against all pressures, the Government of Saskatchewan prevailed. In 1966, Pearson's minority Liberal government wanting "no enemies to the left", legislated the National Health Insurance Act. It set general principles but, since the 1867 BNA Act left health as a provincial responsibility, administration of the plan was left to the provinces. Alberta Social Credit Premier Ernest Manning raged against the compulsory features of Medicare. Manitoba PC Premier Weir threatened to take the Government of Canada to court.

Sidney Green, the newly-elected NDP member of the Manitoba Legislature, dealt with the issue in a monumental speech: "Certain political groups say this plan is compulsory because everyone must contribute to it. That is the only compulsory feature ... [You] can go to a doctor and say: 'I want my medical care outside the program,' and any doctor can say: 'I won't accept you if you pay me through Medicare.' The only compulsory feature is that we must all pay for the program."

He went on to explain:

> Not everyone goes to [a public school], but we must all pay for it, but I have heard no one speak of a 'compulsory' school system ... [People] can let their homes burn. They need not use the [fire department], but they must pay for it; yet no one speaks of a 'compulsory' fire protection system. Why not refer to a 'compulsory' police protection program ... Nobody has to use [police] services, but they [must pay] for the system. What of the compulsory nuclear protection program? Every citizen pays for it whether they want it or not, but they don't refer to it as a 'compulsory' program. What of mosquito control? Whether these programs are used is an individual option, but nobody escapes the social responsibility of paying for them. What is the difference between such programs and medical care program?

---

[3] A quarter-century after its advent, Medicare's single-payer administration costs was three cents per health care dollar, versus the eleven-cent cost of some 1,500 private insurance company payers in the U.S. The Paris-based OECD reported in 1989 that the U.S. spent $2,683 per capita on health care versus $1,918 in Canada. Oregon's Health Policy Office reported in 1990 that Canada's health care system works better, provides more and costs less that health care in the U.S. The apolitical comptroller general of the U.S. reported in 1991 to the House of Representatives that adoption of the Canadian Medicare system would save enough to cover the thirty-four million Americans then uninsured.

There is no such thing as voluntary taxation, so unless we
refer to every program financed by taxation as 'compulsory', let's stop
talking about the 'compulsory' medicare program. If you want to make
[Medicare] a completely voluntary program, wipe out the premiums.
Have this paid out of general revenues. Then nobody has to pay premiums, but everyone can use medical care.

[Someone] said this [will lead] to freeloaders. He is saying in this
system people will use the service when they don't need it. Perhaps 70%
of the population are members of MMS [doctor-sponsored Manitoba
Medical Services insurance]. I am a member of MMS and most members
of this legislature are members of MMS—but he says we 70% don't use
more medical services than we need because we are good people. He
says the other 30%—the low-income [citizens] are bad people and will
overuse it. I suggest the availability of adequate and affordable health
services will no more [make hypochondriacs] of them than it has of us.[4]

The Government of Canada sweetened the pot by offering to pay fifty per
cent of the cost of Medicare in the provinces that adopted it. By April 1969, one
by one, the provinces had acceded.

In Manitoba, fees for medical services were established by negotiation,
but doctors were left free to opt out and levy fees higher than those specified by
the schedule. Normally a patient attended the office of a doctor, who sent the bill
to the Manitoba Health Services Commission, which sent the cheque to the doctor. But if a doctor opted out, the bill was sent to the patient, who sent it to
the MHSC, which sent the cheque to the patient, who would—or would not—
relay it to the physician. Prompted by a citizens' committee spearheaded by the
Manitoba Federation of Labour, many stopped relaying their cheques to their
doctors. It worked. By 1973, more than ninety per cent of Manitoba physicians
were working under Medicare.

Medicare is a system of public funding for private providers. However,
some physicians never forgave the NDP for being the main protagonist of the plan
and sought revenge during the annual fee negotiations. Usually these began early
in the year, went public by mid-year, reached their crescendo of threats and counter
threats late in the year, and were quietly resolved by year end.

In 1973 it was different.

On August 8[th.] the MMA submitted to the minister of health a sixteen-page
proposal for an "Agreement". It demanded: (a) an agreed-to fee schedule; (b) two
members of the Manitoba Health Services Commission to be appointed by the
MMA; (c) binding third-party arbitration for any "grievance" by a physician; (d)
any changes to the health care delivery system to be subject to the approval of
the MMA; (e) "the [Manitoba Health Services] Commission shall deduct at source

---

[4] *Manitoba Hansard*, March 31, 1967, pp. 2141–2146.

from every medical Practitioner, whether or not a member of the MMA, the amount of the dues payable (to the) MMA."

And then: "The Government and the MHSC shall recognize the MMA as the sole and exclusive bargaining agent for the purpose of negotiating and concluding an Agreement … *[but] a Physician shall not be bound by the conditions of this Agreement.*"[5]

The MMA had demanded an agreement to bind government, but not doctors. They wanted to be treated like a trade union without, like a trade union, committing its members to conditions it negotiated.[6] But the primary question was whether future health policy would be made by a craft union, i.e.: the Manitoba Medical Association, or by the elected Government of Manitoba.

The MMA wanted an iron-clad agreement with the government relating to working conditions, fee schedules and health care policy, none to be changed without their approval. Doctors feared an anti-professional bias on the part of a "doctrinaire socialist"[7] government, which could enact policies to limit the doctor's freedom to practice in or out of Medicare, the location in which they could practice,[8] and freedom of patients to choose their doctors.

They feared the loss of their treasured fee-for-service mode of payment and status as independent practitioners. They feared this would lead to bad medicine, bad economics and bad doctor-patient relationships. And they feared the zeal of government planners—particularly "Wild Man" Ted Tulchinsky.

Conversely, the government feared loss of control of health care policy if they gave the MMA inflated status by agreeing to negotiate policy with them, and feared escalating health care costs if they agreed to third-party arbitration of fees. A study in mid-1972 suggested some doctors were made scalpel-happy by the fact their income depended on procedures performed—the providers of health services were creating their own demand. The government feared that failure to modify the fee-for-service form of payment could tempt too many doctors to see too many patients, order too many diagnostic tests, prescribe too many drugs, perform too many surgeries and keep too many patients in hospital beds for too many days. Doctoring might become more financial than medical.

The government knew that costly acute-care hospitals were overfilled, because they were the only fully insured facilities with no financial barriers to access; a 1972 study suggested that thirty per cent of hospital patients could be in other, less expensive, facilities. The study envisioned a range of long term alternatives to hospitals, in descending order of cost: nursing homes; senior citizen's

---

[5] Author's italics.

[6] "Doctors are attempting to combine the best of two worlds. They want to remain self-employed professionals charging fees and not being paid salaries. But they want all the protection and guarantees of a trade union contract with an employer." Frances Russell, *Winnipeg Free Press*, June 12, 1975.

[7] In the industrialized world, only South Africa and the U.S., where health costs were becoming the primary cause of bankruptcy—have no publicly-administered health care system.

[8] While approximately half the people in Manitoba lived in rural areas in 1973, seventy-four per cent of the doctors practiced in Winnipeg.

housing; outpatient services and home care. They wanted to experiment with community clinics, which combined health care and social services and emphasized preventive care. These would be administered by lay boards, financed by government grants, and would receive primary care by nurses and salaried doctors. To implement these ideas, the government imported Dr. Tulchinsky, medical director of the St. Catherines District Community Health Foundation. He was a respected practicing physician, but to the MMA he had a fatal flaw—he was the son-in-law of national NDP Leader Tommy Douglas—which made everything he did or thought suspect.

The atmosphere of suspicion and distrust became palpable, but the government wanted no destructive confrontations. The minister of Health was conciliatory. He replied to the MMA, agreeing to enter into an agreement because: "the Government of Manitoba recognizes that any health policy requires participation of [those] engaged in delivery of services," but adding, "The government cannot abdicate its responsibility to the public by [agreeing] ... to not make changes in the health care delivery system without previously negotiating such changes with your Association."[9]

The government would concede much to the MMA—except that government policy be made by a non-elected interest group.

Attacks on the government by members of the MMA, supported by the opposition in the legislature, became increasingly fierce. On September 25th, the MMA released its version of the negotiations to the media, and the 'war' entered the public arena. Doctors placed petitions in their offices asking patients to support their demands.[10] Most Manitobans supported Medicare, disliked the MMA's demands and tactics, and knew doctors were not being reduced to taking in washing or selling tickets on street corner to put their children through university.[11] But doctors held the power of life and death and nobody wanted to die, so many signed.

The Premier's Office was deluged with letters, telegrams and petitions. It was time to challenge this incipient blackmail.

In 1934, my mother became ill. My father placed her on a wagon and began driving to town, seven miles away. Part way to town, they realized a call at the doctor's office would cost a dollar, and they did not have a dollar. Perhaps the doctor would have ignored that as doctors did in those days, but they were proud people; if they did not have the money they would not request the service. They turned and drove back home. From that experience my father concluded, "A

---

[9] R. Toupin to Dr. K.O. Wylie, October 22, 1973.

[10] Manitoba Medical Association Information Sheet #2
"Manitobans Need a Government-Doctor Contract: Current troubles between your doctor and our government can be solved by the government signing a contract which ensures consolidations with your doctor's association concerning proposed changes in health services; ensures medical services for you and your family. If you agree with your doctor's stand, please sign and leave with the receptionist."

[11] 'Half of Manitoba's MDs earned $50,000 in 1973', Manfred Jager, *Winnipeg Free Press*, January 9, 1975

person who is ill has problems enough without having to worry about how to pay with money not being earned during that illness." It was his introduction to the embryonic concept of collective, pre-paid health insurance.

It also gave him cause for introspection. He was thirty-three, stood 5'10', weighed 200 pounds, was strong as an ox, had a college education and normal intelligence, and was ready and willing to work. And yet, in a country rich beyond the dreams of Croesus, he could not earn a dollar. He was impelled to self-examination and concluded it was not his fault. Next year he joined the fledgling CCF. In 1957, he was elected to Parliament and dedicated himself to promoting national health insurance. Now it was my turn.

To make health care more assured and payment more certain, doctors established their own Manitoba Medical Services Plan. I enrolled and it was helpful but selective, and because the client base was low, the premium was high. Also, after we had two children, I purchased a health and accident policy. After making three annual premium payments I suffered an injury. The insurance company paid me, but refused to renew my policy because I was "accident-prone". I found the primary function of private health insurance plans is to earn dividends for shareholders, not to provide care for the ill, and not available when needed most.

Medicare was conceived by the Government of Canada as a group plan to include every citizen. Since actuaries agree the larger the client base the smaller the per-capita administration costs, a single payer concept was deemed more economical than myriad private plans. It was designed to be universal (entitlement to services by virtue of citizenship), comprehensive (entitlement to all services listed), portable (services in every province to be accessed by premiums paid in any one), accessible (health care facilities to be sufficient to provide basic services), with a public, non-profit, administration of the Plan. In brief, it provided equity of access; the best health care modern medical science could provide would be available as a condition of citizenship, not income, of health, not wealth.

The government could not have proceeded without the support of at least a substantial portion of the medical profession and most, under the leadership of the aging but legendary Dr. Paul Thorlakson, founder of the Winnipeg Clinic, supported the plan. Nor was that support necessarily all philanthropic: aside from the ill, the greatest single group of beneficiaries were the doctors; they were spared the odious task of collecting bills.[12]

In the spring of 1962, during the most incendiary days of the doctors' strike in Saskatchewan, I visited my home town (population 800) dentist. With his hands in my mouth, he began cursing like a sailor about the "God-damned socialists" who were "nationalizing the doctors" and "I suppose when you have them under control you will nationalize dentists."

---

[12] "While (Laureen Fingas) runs Care4U in the Russell-Roblin area from her Inglis home, she's hesitant to ask people to pay for her services," *Ibid.*, October 26, 1997.

When I was finally able to speak, with my mouth full of blood and nostrils full of the burning smell of a high-speed drill, I responded, "Yes, and high time too."

He walked to his desk and opened a large ledger. "Come here, I want to show you something."

I scanned the list of names. Many in the community owed him money. "I wish to Christ you would nationalize me," he barked, "and collect my bills."

By 1973, most Manitobans, while initially skeptical, had discovered the benefits of pre-paid universal health insurance, and most members of the medical community, while initially suspicious, had discovered the benefits of the one-payer concept. Doctors found they were still licensed and policed by the College of Physicians and Surgeons; as before, they were still represented by the Manitoba Medical Association; as before, the doctor-patient relationship was still private; as before, the monitoring of services provided by the paymaster, the Manitoba Health Services Commission, was no more onerous than when the paymaster was their doctor controlled Manitoba Medical Services, and now their remuneration for work done was totally secure. Indeed, by 1973, the fight between doctors and government seemed less over principle than pay—the schedule of fees for each medical procedure. It was this schedule, subject to the number and nature of the services provided, that determined the physician's income.

But the fight was savage. Those physicians who saw Medicare as a milch cow were determined to get at the cream immediately. Conversely, the government suspected the long-term health of the plan would depend on its cost. This proved prescient; during the 1993 national election campaign, despite reports showing that the costs of Medicare were much less than American private plans, and despite the cost of Medicare as a percentage of GDP being little more than it was twenty years earlier, Reform Party leader Preston Manning, a proponent of private health insurance, argued those costs were exceeding predictions "by a magnitude of ten." [13]

Fee negotiations were to be conducted between the Manitoba Medical Association for the physicians and the Manitoba Health Services Commission as paymaster, and they normally began that way. However, invariably the government was compelled to intervene because it set the financial parameters for the MHSC and established health care policy, and because the MMA insisted on government participation in the negotiations. It appeared at times they wanted this participation simply to embarrass the government. Accordingly, at their request, on October 16th, representatives of the MMA met with the minister of Health and Social Development.

René Toupin was educated at St. Boniface College and Laval University. Before election to the Manitoba Legislature in 1969, he had worked for three aircraft companies and as manager of the Centrale de Caisse Populaire in St. Boniface for seven years. From 1969 to 1977, he served as minister of Consumer and

---

[13] In twenty years, between 1982 and 2002, despite the addition of multiple services, Manitoba Health Department spending increased only 1.5 per cent of GPP.

Corporate Affairs; minister of Tourism, Recreation and Culture; and chairman of the cabinet sub-committee on Health, Education and Social Policy (HESP). From December 1969 to February 1974, he was minister of Health and Social Development.

The meeting provided a study in contrasting approaches. Toupin, under his Peter Pan facade, was much tougher than he appeared but he did not comprehend then, nor accept later, that the MMA representatives[14] had apparently come less to negotiate than to humiliate him. Attending as an observer, I reported to the premier that the MMA representatives had been smug, aggressive and contemptuous while the minister had been correct, polite and overwhelmed. The premier responded by appointing a committee to work with the minister, including Saul Cherniack, Saul Miller and Sidney Green.

The two committees met in late November. The government representatives, seeking to avoid a public confrontation with the members of this powerful profession who were the gatekeepers in terms of provision of health services, and on whose willing cooperation rested the future of their beloved Medicare, were courteous and forthcoming. The men of the MMA, perhaps sensing vulnerability, were cold and unequivocal. The president of the MMA was Dr. Kenneth Wylie, but the main spokesman was Dr. Garth Mosher. His Ben Casey jacket with the stand-up collar, matched by his stand-up crew cut hair, made him look more like a soldier of fortune than a practitioner of the profession of Hippocrates, and he attacked with a vengeance. Conversely Sid Green, usually aggressive as a junkyard dog in debate, was on his best behaviour. Several times, attempting to placate his adversaries by stroking egos and placing the discussion on a friendly rather than formal basis, he addressed Dr. Mosher as "Garth".

Suddenly the latter exploded, "Listen Green, to you I am not Garth. I am Doctor Mosher."

Green was briefly nonplussed. Then he leaned across the table. "Fine. Then to you I am not Green. I am Mister Minister."

There was a momentary, ominous silence, as each side realized it had overstepped the bounds of civility, and then a shuffling of feet as the combatants departed in mutual discomfiture. There was nothing left to say. Several mornings later, while driving to my office at The Ledge, I turned on the car radio. There was the usually calm Dr. Wylie, now audibly agitated, explaining to the world that the Manitoba medical profession was being victimized, that the premier had taken negotiations away from the minister of Health and turned it over to the tender mercies of a committee, that the committee was impossible to negotiate with, and "Next time we meet with that committee we want the media there so Manitobans can see how we are being abused."

I thought, "The Lord hath delivered mine enemy into mine hands." I parked my car, went to Toupin's office, and dictated a letter for his signature. "Dear Dr.

---

[14] 'Ninety-two per cent of Manitoba's physicians practiced under Medicare, but the majority of the MMA negotiating committee had 'opted out'.

Wylie, I propose that the next meeting of our negotiating committees be on December 20, 1973, at 2.30 P.M., in Room 254 at the Legislative Building. The media will be invited as per your request."[15]

I was certain the MMA did not want the media at the committee meeting and, on receipt of Toupin's letter, they would contact Toupin and suggest, "Mr. Minister, if you do not really want the media at the meeting that is fine with us." Affable Toupin would agree and the media would not be invited. But I desperately wanted the media at the meeting. I instructed Toupin's secretary to divert to me any calls for the minister from the MMA.

We could not allow Medicare to be destroyed, either by frontal assault or by milching it. We could not tolerate development of a health care system that produced miraculous medical technology, but which many citizens could not afford.[16] I recalled my mother being unable to attend a doctor's office for want of a dollar. I recalled driving my wife's brother, who was helping me with the harvest, from his field to Dauphin, forty miles away, because there was no doctor at Grandview ten miles away or at Gilbert Plains twenty miles away. I recalled carrying him into the hospital, in agony, because his appendix had ruptured, being stopped at the door and required to pay a deposit and being fortunate in having my wallet in my coveralls or there would have been some broken glass.

And what did the physicians have to complain about? They continued to practice their craft as always, the only government "intervention" being in raising the money to pay them. Payments were more secure—indeed the physicians had agreed at the commencement of Medicare to accept payment of only eighty-five per cent of their regular fees because of that security—and the fee schedule was renegotiated annually. Doctors were free to "opt out" and bill patients directly for any amount desired, yet ninety-two per cent of Manitoba physicians were practicing under Medicare. If Medicare violated the doctor-patient relationships, or if the fee schedule was reducing them to penury, why not "opt out"?

But they wanted it both ways! Doctors, by the nature of their profession, carried in their satchels the gift of life and help for pain, and were therefore able to establish an association (a euphemism for a craft union) too powerful for even government to defy. And some blatantly displayed that power. At the meeting with the minister in October, one doctor stated that his profession had historically enjoyed the highest average income in Canada and they intended to continue doing so, and the statement was made with a self-assurance that suggested it was a Kantian Imperative.[17]

---

[15] Richard Sprague, executive vice-president of the MMA reportedly told the press that the MMA would "not oppose a government proposal to open the session to newsmen". *Ibid.*, December 19, 1973.

[16] A study by a major health insurance company showed that fees varied up to 52% between Minneapolis and Winnipeg hospitals. Average costs of a day in a Minneapolis hospital was $167, compared to $96 in Manitoba. In Minneapolis, a gall bladder operation is $450 and an appendectomy $280, while Manitoba costs for the same surgery are $280 and $126. *Winnipeg Free Press*, June 5, 1975.

[17] "Doctors have done very well under Medicare, rising to top income brackets in most of Canada." Editorial, *Winnipeg Tribune*, October 1972.

I remembered the phone call from a doctor, for whom I arranged a luncheon appointment with the premier, who explained how our public health care purse was being pilfered. A colleague had left a patient, requiring only a minor procedure, in a hospital bed for nine days, "And there is nothing wrong with her, but he gets paid a capitation rate per patient-day so he left her there. Yesterday I told him it he did not have that woman out of there by this morning I am going to see the premier, and this morning she was gone, but I decided to see the premier anyway."

Yet clearly, the doctors were the gatekeepers and could easily sabotage the system. We needed their cooperation, and to get it we needed to be nice. And there was another dimension. At age nine, I was thrown by a bucking horse and broke my arm and the gruff, elderly doctor with the hamlike hands left his Sunday dinner to knead, with unbelievable gentleness, the jagged bone under the purpled skin and repair my arm. At age fourteen, I was caught in a gasoline fire and suffered second- and third-degree burns and spent fifteen months in three separate hospitals while a series of doctors experimented with assorted remedies (egg white, butter, beeswax, cod liver oil, gentian violet—all these before sulfa drugs were available), cursing because nothing was effective and they finally restored both my life and the use of my severely burned arm. In 1962, I was awakened by the strident ring of the phone to be told by the cheerful—at 4.30 A.M.—voice of the doctor that (after two daughters) we had a son. And in 1971, I was told I had cancer of the throat and the gentle doctor had made a professional (and perhaps personal) decision and saved both my life and my larynx.

But there was no *deus ex machina* to intervene to both please the MMA and save the health care system, our crowning achievement that had become synonymous with our party. Neither government nor market action could evade the confrontation between those who had decided the manner of paying for health services and those on whom the system depended to deliver those services. Later, with another confrontation looming, pending a health ministers' meeting in Montréal, I approached our minister, Laurent Desjardins. "Larry, our MMA-types who are giving us most trouble seem to want to return to the halcyon days of free enterprise, so let's give them some. In the marketplace prices are set by the amount of competition available. Suggest to the other ministers at the meeting that we send a plane to Europe and import a load of the best doctors they have and let them give our domestic doctors some real competition.[18] That should knock the bottom out of the damn fee schedule and the starch out of the MMA."[19]

---

[18] In 1974, the Canadian Medical Association (with 25,000 doctors in its membership) asked Ottawa to reduce immigration of foreign doctors and stop granting landed immigrant status to medical students already here because their own countries needed them. "Reducing the drain of talented people from underdeveloped countries will provide more aid than any other program." *Ibid.*, February 26, 1974.

[19] One reason the MMA demanded recognition as the sole bargaining agent for doctors is revealed in a letter by their lawyer. "[If there is no recognition] physicians could be brought to Manitoba ... to render services for less than those established ... by the proposed agreement." Walter Ritchie to MHSC, November 28, 1973.

Several days later, the media reported that, with one exception, the ministers had voted against importing foreign doctors. I angrily awaited Desjardins' return: "Larry, what in hell did you guys do with my proposal?"

"Hold it! I was the one exception. I presented your proposal, but it isn't worth a shit. The discussion on it went something like this: if we have more doctors we must build more hospitals so they will have a place to practice, then we must equip those hospitals so they have tools to work with, then we must hire nurses to work with them, then we must hire technicians to operate the equipment, then we must hire service staff to maintain the buildings, and then comes the real cost—we must fill the hospitals with sick people so the doctors and the nurses and the technicians and the maintenance staff will have some reason to do what they do. The doctors' unions are too powerful to be influenced by the marketplace. The only way we can reduce costs is to have fewer doctors[20] rather than more."[21]

It appeared we were helpless. But perhaps there was still a way short of public confrontation. I made a proposal to caucus: "This is becoming a vicious fight and we need to get the public on our side. There is a way. It is time our doctors justified their incomes to the public that pays them. Let's publish the name of every doctor paid by MHSC, and the amount each was paid, in Public Accounts."[22] The response was not favourable. "It would be read as implied criticism of their income levels."

"No, we simply publish the physicians' names in alphabetical order, along with their incomes, with no editorial comment."

"There is a matter of trust and confidentiality involved here."

"My salary is published in Public Accounts for the taxpayers to read and I note no solicitude for my tender sensibilities," I responded.

"You are a direct employee of government and are paid directly by government and the doctors are neither."

"But the government collects the taxes to pay them and simply funnels it through the MHSC that pays them."

"It would be a distortion because payments to doctors shows gross income, out of which they pay their expenses, not net."

---

[20] Earlier: "Health ministers agreed to restrict immigration of foreign doctors ... Ontario Health minister Frank Miller said [it] could knock $500 million off Canada's health costs ... a glut of doctors means the medical care fund is billed to the limit [and] expensive medical facilities were required in proportion to the number of doctors." *Winnipeg Tribune*, January 16, 1975.

[21] Twenty-two years later, Conservative Manitoba Health Minister Darren Praznick announced that he would import foreign doctors, not to control fees, but to fill rural doctor shortages. *Winnipeg Free Press*, September 10, 1997. At the time, foreign-trained doctors were being stonewalled by the College of Physicians and Surgeons despite adequate training and knowledge of language.

[22] Three years later, doctors were furious when a similar report was leaked to media by an NDP member of the Ontario legislature. It showed that in 1974-75, OHIP had paid 812 doctors (of a total of 3,000) more than $100,000 and eleven more than $1 million, with average gross payments of more than $70,000. *Ibid.*, December 17, 1976.

"When Tony Schreyer, the premier's brother, builds a highway for the province, public accounts simply lists his name and the gross amount paid to him, without a footnote indicating that he must pay his employees and operating costs out of that and that in fact he might have lost money on the contract."[23]

The premier ended the debate:

> Gentlemen, the discussion is futile. Tough annual negotiations with the physicians and their organizations were anticipated when Medicare was legislated. After all, the Saskatchewan experience of 1962 is within easy memory for all of us. Harsh words and confrontation are endemic in such negotiations, but if we believe in the principle we must have patience with the process. We decided we would not take the route of forcing physicians on salary,[24] because that would have meant a total confrontation with the entire profession, and also because we believe there is no substitute for the principle of people being paid on the basis of the amount of work they do.[25] So long as we operate, and I am not being punny, on a fee-for-service basis, despite the inherent dangers of this type of remuneration leading to a form of Parkinson's Law in which the medical services expand to fill the income needs of the physicians providing the services, no health plan such as ours can long endure without the willing cooperation of those who deliver those services. The people of Manitoba do not want a revolution; they want more assured, better and less costly medical services than they have had.
>
> Our government simply cannot afford to antagonize a group of professionals who may refuse to work effectively if their power and prestige is threatened.[26] We cannot be seen, either by the medical profession or by the public, to be doing anything which may escalate the current conflict or add to the bitterness that will follow in the wake of a settlement, no matter

---

[23] Twenty-four years later, Premier Filmon's Conservative government passed the Public Sector Compensation Disclosure Act, requiring publication of the name of anyone paid more than $50,000 a year by the government. A newspaper reported, "Highest Billing MD Made $710,781; Seven Topped $500,000". Dr. Ian White, MMA president said ... "the figures don't tell the whole story because they don't include the doctors' overhead or taxes." *Ibid.*, September 22, 1997.

[24] A salary system was tempting. From 1969 to 1973, there was no increase in fees, but total payments to physicians increased by $8 million or seventeen per cent. With no equivalent increase in physicians or population, this was from performing more procedures. Vera Chernecki, Manitoba Nurses Union president, said a "fee-for-service system encourages over-treatment and over-billing." *Ibid.*

[25] The MMA feared a salaried doctors policy would give government total control of health policy and argued that salaried doctors would work "union hours" and not properly service patients. Twenty-four years later, despite a considerable increase in the number of physicians and little increase in population, doctors in rural Manitoba complained of "low fee-for-service fees and long hours" and refused to service emergency wards unless they were placed on hourly salaries. The government complied. The minister said in Portage la Prairie, doctors "can now work 40-hour weeks and earn more than $140,000." *Ibid.*, September 25, 1997.

[26] S.M. Lipsett wrote of Saskatchewan's introduction of Medicare, "To threaten the power, privileges or beliefs of any socially necessary group may lead that group to refuse to continue its work. Such 'sabotage' could temporarily deprive the public of services previously received." *Agrarian Socialism*, p. 295.

what its terms. In brief, the program must prevail, but we cannot make a desert and call it peace. We owe it to Manitobans, and to our colleagues who fought for a publicly-administered, prepaid, universal health insurance plan for a generation before we got it, to bargain as effectively, but as inoffensively, as possible.

The premier was one of those rare members of the political species who spoke in complete sentences, with implied punctuation marks. Now, as so often, he had spoken the 'last word' on the subject. He had summarized the current situation, placed it in historical context, made obeisance to both sides of the argument, injected a touch of wry humour, and set the course.

But there was no easy way out. So I prepared my letter. It was not a nice letter. It gave notice to both the professionals and the public that the Government of Manitoba intended to fight. The preparation of this letter created the only occasion for an argument between myself and one of my secretaries. She came with the letter I had written in longhand, and threw it on my desk: "I refuse to type this."

"What's the problem?"

"Look at this sentence. I will not type this."

I had written: "To listen to the MMA's list of complaints about government interference, [27] one would think the government had nothing to do but stand and look over the doctor's shoulders while they take down the patient's pants in triplicate." [28]

"What do you find inappropriate about that?"

"You might be referring to a woman."

I reluctantly admitted defeat. It was such a graphic sentence, which would certainly catch the attention of the media and guarantee its publication, which was precisely what I wanted.

However, I deferred to female wisdom and changed the sentence to "take the patient's pulse in triplicate.

The staff rebellion was resolved. And the letters went out at the faintest excuse.

---

[27] Conversely, California doctors struck to demand government intervention—to force private insurance companies to reduce malpractice fees. *Winnipeg Free Press*, January 10, 1976. Also: "Obstetricians in Canada will stop delivering babies as of January 1 rather than pay the 'absolutely crazy' increase in malpractice fees, the head of the Society of Obstetricians and Gynocologists of Canada warns." Ibid, November 1, 1997.

[28] In 1990, a doctor who left Manitoba for Texas fifteen years earlier because he objected to government control of health care, returned to report: "Government control of health insurance is so much better than insurance company control. I spent more time on paperwork than I did looking after patients." [32] (*Ibid.*, December 15, 1990) Another Winnipegger who left to practice in Los Angeles reported, "Initially, I practiced optimal medicine [but] ... a major change caused medicine to be business driven so costs would not increase and business would reap large profits at the expense of hospitals and health providers. The result was a micro-managed system that limited access and care." *Ibid.*, September 27, 1997. Clearly, in the U.S., the ideological captive of the NRA ad the AMA, where gun control and socialized medicine are seen as "Communist plots", it is the insurance companies that "look over the doctors' shoulders while they take down the patients' pants in triplicate."

The MMA saturated physician's offices with leaflets stating that all the doctors wanted was that government agree to "the standards of medical practice established by the College of Physicians and Surgeons ... the Code of Ethics of the Canadian Medical Association ... the hospital standards established by the Canadian Council on Hospital Accreditation", as well as "freedom from intimidation and coercion".[29] It was sheer sophistry, to make it appear the issue between government and the MMA was *medicine*.

My letter made it clear the issue was *money*.[30] It summarized the situation and the government's position in unequivocal terms. Thousands of copies were sent. Anyone who phoned or wrote was sent a copy of the letter. All those who had signed the petitions conveniently placed in the offices by the MMA and remitted to us by diligent receptionists, were sent copies. Those who phoned to express the hope all my family become infected with an incurable and agonizing illness, or that someone nail my scrotum to the top of a fencepost and push me off backward to hang there while the crows picked my eyes out, were read excerpts from the letter ... if they stayed on the line long enough.

Toupin sent a letter, with attached copies of correspondence between the government and the MMA, to every Manitoba physician. It made a weighty package. It was so effective it elicited a reply (with copies to the media) from Dr. P.M.F. McGarry, complaining: "The missive consisted of 32 pages of photostatic copies. I feel the total bill to the taxpayer was $3,000 ... equivalent to the maintenance of a hospital bed for 50 days."[31]

Toupin replied: "Since the taxpayers of Manitoba will be paying over $55 million to doctors like you in the coming year, you should not object to spending $3,000 to inform you of the status of current discussions between the government and the MMA."[32]

A new tone crept into the minister's correspondence. The MMA was informed that henceforth the government would follow the association's practice of releasing correspondence to the media.[33] A letter from the MMA demanding "all differences be settled by January 15, 1974," was sent the startling reply: "I acknowledge receipt of your ultimatum, [but] to [accede to your demands] would make the MMA the Government of Manitoba on health policy."[34]

---

[29] This was the reddest of herrings. Three decades after the advent of Medicare, doctors continued to be policed by the College of Physicians and Surgeons, not the government.

[30] "Despite all protests to the contrary, both the level of fees and the method of payment remain the main concern of doctors." Manfred Jager, *Winnipeg Free Press*, January 12, 1974.

[31] *Ibid.*, December 29, 1973.

[32] cc. Dr. K.O. Wylie; Mr. W. Ritchie.

[33] An MMA tactic was to write to, or meet with, the government, release correspondence to the media and immediately complain that it had not received a response. After the election of Sterling Lyon's Conservative government in late 1977, this practice was continued, but when the media asked the new Health minister why he had not responded to the MMA, Bud Sherman—whom I had once considered a lightweight, replied, "I did. I told them 'No'."

[34] Toupin to Wylie, December 11, 1973.

A letter from the MMA to the minister threatened to call off the scheduled December 20th meeting unless (a) you withdraw your precondition and (b) the [Manitoba Health Services] Commission is authorized to negotiate fees ..." [35]

Toupin replied curtly: (a) "We have always been prepared to continue our discussions without establishing preconditions and (b) as has been explained to you many times by many persons, including the premier, you should negotiate fees with the MHS Commission."[36]

The newspapers told the story. "The Manitoba government has thrown down an iron-clad, spiked and studded gauntlet in a new get tough policy toward organized medicine." [37]

"The Manitoba government has again toughened its stand toward the province's doctors, advising the MMA that it does not intend to negotiate any agreement on public health policy that would subject such policy to third-party arbitration by a non-elected tribunal." [38]

And then, suddenly, it was December 20th. *Der Tag*. So far so good. Just before 2:30 P.M. I walked down the long granite-floored corridor, past the grand staircase flanked by the two large, well-endowed statues of buffalo; past the Tyndall stone walls with their fossilized skeletons of ancient sea creatures; past the magnificent marble-floored rotunda, which opened to the vast dome topped by the long-striding, torch-bearing Golden Boy soaring 255 feet above ground level; past the doors of party caucus rooms to the far end of the building, and into Room 254, the elegant, high-ceilinged, elaborately decorated room hung with portraits of former premiers.

Behind a table sat the four government ministers, all appearing slightly apprehensive. Behind them, in a wide arc, sat or stood a score of reporters, with pencils poised. And over all, like eagles hoisted over the ancient Roman legions, hovered the ubiquitous, allseeing and unforgiving eyes of the television cameras.

I sat down behind Toupin. He turned to me: "It's after 2.30. I wonder if the doctors are not coming?"

"They're coming. I saw them in the corridor when I came in."

Toupin seemed satisfied. But about a minute later he rose and walked out of the room. The significance did not register with me for a moment ... and then I broke into a sweat. "Jesus Christ, the whole damn thing is going to be ruined at the last minute." I rushed out the doorway and down the corridor to where Toupin was surrounded by the four MMA committee members and their lawyer, Walter Ritchie, just in time to hear Dr. Wylie say: "Mr. Minister, we are not going into that room to negotiate until you order the media to get out."

---

[35] Wylie to Toupin, December 19, 1973.

[36] Toupin to Wylie, December 19, 1973.

[37] Manfred Jager, *Winnipeg Free Press*, December 12, 1973

[38] Egon Frech, *Winnipeg Free Press*, December 19, 1973

And the minister, affable, accomodating René Toupin, replied: "Okay, I'll tell them to leave." And he turned to go.

The Sisyphusian rock had just rolled back down to the bottom of the hill. I grabbed Toupin's arm and addressed the others: "Doctor Wylie, my name is Schulz and I am special assistant to the premier. I am the person who heard you on the radio, after our last meeting, stating you want the media present at this one and I advised the minister to invite the media, as you requested.

"Now you people can do one of three things. You can go back home and the negotiations will end and the government will impose a fee schedule and begin hiring doctors on salary and you can learn to like it or opt out and return to collecting your own fees. Or, you can go into that room and negotiate in front of the media as you told the people of Manitoba you wanted to do. Or … YOU go in there and tell the media to get out." [39]

Toupin looked at me with uncharacteristic anger and stalked back into Room 254, leaving me with the MMA representatives. After what seemed an interminable silence, Dr. Wylie said, "Give us a moment to discuss this among ourselves."

I returned to Room 254. Toupin glared at me. I avoided his eyes and sat down. Chronos counted off the seconds and the only sounds in the room were guarded whispers. No one told the media about the confrontation in the corridor, but they all sensed something significant was occurring. Then the door opened. The five representatives of the MMA walked in and stopped in the middle of the room. Manitoba Medical Association president Dr. Kenneth Wylie, [40] visibly perturbed, said quietly but firmly: "Ladies and gentlemen of the media, we would ask you to leave." [40]

They did. So did I. This was for principals, not functionaries. There remained only the four ministers and the four doctors with their lawyer. In that cavernous room, in the next two hours, they sought to lay the basis for conditions the doctors would accept, and fees Manitobans would pay for medical services, for the next year.

But the truce did not hold. The MMA immediately began setting the stage for a new confrontation. They cancelled a meeting scheduled for December 31st, and another for January 7th, 1974. They continued their attack on the government through the media and some doctors continued to attack through their patients. News headlines announced: "Possibility of Strike by Doctors". [41]

But the media had isolated the MMA's reason for the threatened strike. It was not health care, but money: "Doctors' Fees At Issue; Strike Deadline Near". [42]

---

[39] My wife was not amused about all this. She informed me, "Dr. Wylie is our son's pediatrician, and an excellent one."

[40] The Winnipeg Tribune, December 21, 1973.

[41] Winnipeg Free Press, January 14, 1974.

[42] Ibid., January 12, 1974.

And we had won an advantage: no matter how much they respected physicians as individuals and believed they were needed to effect our social revolution in health care or how much they feared the MMA as a political force, all members of the government caucus now agreed there would be no "peaceful solution" and that we must do what we must do.

Cabinet put in motion the ponderous wheels of the government which, like the mills of the gods, grind slowly—but they grind. Desjardins, the rugged former hockey player, was chairman of the MHSC. A committee of non-government persons was appointed to liaise between the government and the MMA.

The premier, because he needed the rest and because we wanted to get him out of the direct line of fire, in the event he would be needed as a "neutral" final arbiter, was packed off to the Caribbean for a brief vacation. Saul Cherniack became acting premier. Saul Miller—reliable, unflappable and tough—took over the role of organizing the forces of government.

Every MMA attack was countered. The MMA pushed; the government pushed back. The MMA threatened a "withdrawal of services" (a euphemism for a doctors' strike);[43] government responses made it clear that this strike would be against patients, not the government.

The MMA threatened to abandon entire hospitals; the government arranged with airlines and buslines to move patients from abandoned hospitals into functioning facilities or, if needed, to hospitals in the United States or Ontario. The MMA spoke of abandoning Manitoba; the government negotiated with the Manitoba College of Physicians and Surgeons to bring in out-of-province doctors.[44]

Copies of my letter flooded the province. Answering the mail and phone calls became full time work. The letters had the intended effect: people were beginning to ask what this fight was about. I was pleased to explain. People, sensitive to the powers of the ancient cult of the healer, were loath to offend the physicians, but they had tasted the fruits of Medicare. Our campaign was gaining momentum, and public opinion was swinging to our support. We were challenging the most powerful interest group in Western society, and winning. The government had sent the signal; this was one fight we did not intend to lose.

On January 14, 1974, Acting Premier Saul Cherniack called a full dress press conference to explain to the people of Manitoba that the Government of Manitoba had agreed to:

- recognition of the MMA as the bargaining agent for doctors
- a permanent consultative process on all health services

---

[43] On December 5, 1973, offices and clinics closed and hospitals were manned by skeleton staffs while a meeting of 820 doctors agreed that if their demands were not met by January 12, 1974, the MMA executive would be authorized to recommend whatever action, including a strike, it deemed necessary to get an agreement.

[44] The oft-threatened exocus did not materialize. "The registrar (of the College of Physicians and Surgeons) says Manitoba is gaining more practicing MDs than it is losing," said the *Winnipeg Free Press* on November 19, 1976. During the Schreyer years, the number of physicians increased by about twenty-seven per cent and Manitoba's doctor/population ratio remained above the national average.

- the right of doctors to 'opt out' and bill patients directly
- no change in health policy without consultation with the MMA
- the Canadian Council on Hospital Accreditation to remain the provider of guidelines for the operation of hospital facilities
- The College of Physicians and Surgeons to remain the sole supervisor and enforcer of medical standards and ethics.

Conversely:
- there would be no third-party arbitration of government policy
- the government was prepared to submit itself to public opinion
- the government was flexible on the proposed fee schedule but made it clear that "this country is faced with a serious problem in health care. All provinces are on notice from the federal government that it will reduce its participation in sharing of health costs. The escalation of costs is such that expenditures may double every five or six years —*this simply can not be allowed to happen.*

Finally, the government emphasized that "any doctor's strike will not be over substantive issues *but over a simple disagreement over the fee schedule.*"[45]

Then, on a cold January afternoon, we met in the cabinet room to analyze the situation and make plans for instant response if doctors proceeded with the threatened strike on January 15th.

There was Cherniack, the acting premier, and Toupin, ready to do cabinet's bidding, and Miller—steady, steel-tough Saul Miller—the government's point man in the campaign. And there were the three members of the 'civilian' liaison committee between the government and the MMA. The committee's report was concise and precise; the doctors wanted to quit the fight and go back to their work. The MMA saw itself outclassed in the political arena and wanted to strike its tents and retire with what dignity they could salvage. Indeed, the MMA was no longer a factor and the doctors would take whatever was offered.

It was finished!

Victory was sweet. The enemy had surrendered unconditionally. Now we could fix Medicare as a permanent feature of our society and set the terms for participating physicians. Now our health care system would be safe from the twin dangers of incessant frontal attack, political and professional, or of being clawed to death by those determined to destroy, from the inside, what they saw as 'socialized medicine'. Now we could end the debilitating feud between government and health care professionals which, since its inception, had followed Medicare like a black dog. Satisfied looks and congratulatory comments pervaded the

---

[45] In 1985, the Government of Manitoba agreed to arbitrate the fee schedule, but then refused to honour the arbitrator's award of a 6.5 per cent increase and cancelled future arbitrations. In Alberta, an arbitrator's award cause Premier Peter Lougheed to assert that arbitrators seem to live on a small distant planet and henceforth would be given strict limits on what they could award.

room. The fight was over. We were fatigued. But we had won.

I was elated. For half a year I had been at the core of the battle, taking the fight to the enemy, exposed to criticism—some from my colleagues because of my adamant position—and offending a profession some of whose members I deeply respected, to whom I owed my life, and who my family might some day desperately need. Now I was anxious to know what penalty we would levy on the MMA to ensure there would be no repetition of this confrontation. I wanted to hear that a stake would be driven through the heart of organized opposition to Medicare.

All eyes shifted to Miller. He sat gazing into the distance, the gauntness of his features emphasized by his concentration, a thin wisp of smoke curling up from the omnipresent cigarette in his nicotine-stained fingers. For a month he had carried on his frail shoulders the weight of history and reality. He must be pleased. As chairman of HESP he was entitled to the last word. "Gentlemen, now that we have beaten them, perhaps we should give them what they want." [46]

---

[46] "War between Doctors, Government Never Ends" ran the headline on an article by Arlene Billinkoff, *Winnipeg Free Press*, December 12, 1989. "MDs Tighten Grip on Health Policy: Doctors Control Advisory Panel on Medicare Reform" ran the headline on an article by Doug Nairn, *Ibid.*, May 19, 1994.

Life was not all lengthy skirmishes. Here, with Lily, left, at his side, Premier Schreyer tries his hand at the bagpipes.

XXI

Job Creation

The best-laid schemes of mice and men
Gang aft agley.

—Robert Burns, "To a Mouse"

"I feel obliged to tell you that if you give us more money, we will just hire more damn fools to waste it."

The attractive, agitated American woman from the United Nations Food and Agricultural Organization was addressing the Annual Convention of the Manitoba Farmer's Union. "I have been sent here to ask for money. But before I do so, I want to explain how we have been spending the money we have."

She had recently returned from southern Egypt where she was sent to develop projects to create new jobs and improve the economy. To aid this enter prise, the Food and Agricultural Organization had sent millions of dollars worth of heavy farm machinery—tractors, seed drills and combines—which was of absolutely no benefit to anyone except the employees and owners of the corporations from which they were purchased.

"No one there knows how to operate these machines and even if they did, the fields are much too small to operate them on. There would need to be an agricultural revolution before we could get any value out of this equipment."

She explained that on the tiny plots, a farm operation consisted of a man hitching his wife to a forked stick—twice as efficient as a single-pronged stick—who pulled it with a string while he guided it to make two shallow furrows. Seed was dropped into the furrows, the children dragged tree branches over the ground to cover the seed, and then the family gathered to pray … and wait.

"My colleagues and I concluded these people needed a garden hoe, but they had never seen a hoe and could not visualize one. Before we could get them to make some locally, we needed a prototype."

But FAO, with its hundreds of millions of dollars allocated, could not find four dollars to buy a hoe and send it there. "Finally an American Boy Scout troop held a dance and collected the money to buy a garden hoe and send it to us. Now we have 200 people employed in southern Egypt making hoes and production on the farms has been improved by a magnitude. But the huge machines sent by those knowing nothing of local conditions, and concerned more with jobs and status for themselves than with the needs of the local economy, sit there to rust, as useless as the pyramids."

It was ever thus. An allegory can be imagined. Once upon a time, in ancient Egypt, the pharaoh's advisors advised him that there was unemployment in his realm. Presumably the pharaoh ordered them shortened by a head, but bad news forces itself even upon a pharaoh and he eventually acknowledged the problem. Well, since the advisors had advised there was a problem, what did the advisors advise be done about it? But advisors are not as quick with solutions as with problems; it is problems, after all, not solutions, that create the need for advisors. And there was the consideration of the price advisors must pay if they advise badly.

But as Lenin was to say, revolutionaries are always revolting and advisors are always advising. Eventually one advisor, as yet uninitiated in the art of keeping his light under a bushel to keep his head on his shoulders, suggested jobs could be created by building dams on the Nile to control the river's flow. This drew cries of horror from those arguing that the dams would produce larger crops, and since the rich could not eat more and the poor could not afford more, there would be huge surpluses requiring either destruction of the food (which would be impolitic) or paying farmers to not grow food (which would be uneconomic).

But the neophyte had forced discussion. Another advised dredging the Nile so boats could carry greater loads. This was scuttled by those who argued that boats would then be able to ply the river from source to mouth, instead of unloading and reloading at every sandbar, and thus destroy legitimate jobs.[1] So an advisor made a third proposal; if sandbars in the Nile created jobs, rather than dredging them out, more should be added to create more jobs. But this was frantically opposed on the grounds that would be useful work and the prime prerequisite of make work projects was that it not be useful or it would create unemployment among those actually employed at useful work.

A fourth boldly suggested an extension of the empire. This would make jobs in the military services, create a new tier of bureaucracy, busy giddy minds with foreign broils, provide new territories for the Favored Few to exploit, and provide ordinary Egyptians with people to look down upon. This roused the ire

---

[1] In the 1840s, the French government began building a railway from Paris to Madrid. The council of a city on the route proposed a gap in the track, so that jobs could be created for local carters, bargemen and hoteliers to move the goods through the town to reload on the train on the other side. The French economist, Frederic Bastiat, wrote satirically that more jobs could be created if all towns along the route adopted that initiative ... and even more by building a *negative* railway.

of small 'l' liberals who preferred trade to aid, imperialists who feared placing arms in the hands of so many men, young men who preferred making love to war, anti-imperialists who considered the empire large enough, elitists who did not want the sun god's realm mongrelized by "the lesser breeds without the law", and the "lunatic fringe" who wanted to give the empire back. At this the pharaoh growled menacingly that he had not been anointed son of Osiris to preside over the dissolution of the empire.

Ultimately, despite the advisors, a solution was found. It was decided to collect stones from all over the empire and make a huge pile of them. The decision having been made, justification needed to be manufactured. And since any form of economic imbecility can be justified in the interests of national defence, it was proposed this work be undertaken as a defence project.

So the pharaoh demanded that his advisors be creative, and one who had waited with his advice until he knew what advice the pharaoh wanted, advised that the pile of stones be given the exotic name of 'pyramid', a word he had read in ancient scrolls. He also advised that, despite the plentiful polished panegyrics to slave societies, more work was derived from the led than the driven and it would be most productive if Egyptians were induced to believe some urgent need dictated construction of the pyramid. And so the word went forth that the 'enemy'—those Babylonians plying their nefarious trade on the red sands of the Euphrates—were building a pile of stones they had given the barbaric name of 'ziggurat' and if the ziggurat was completed before the pyramid, the locusts would come, the Hebrews would leave, the social parasites would stay, and the empire would suffer a fate worse than death.

And so it came to pass that the great pharaoh commanded his people to gather stones from the farthest reaches of the realm and that they be brought to the appointed place, and a great pile of stones rose from the face of the plain and the people of Egypt united as one man and laboured mightily and begat the pyramid. And there they are today, great gray piles of stones in a ravaged land, permanent monuments to bureaucratic boondoggle.

Later the NDP government would be accused of make work projects like those of antiquity—conceptually magnificent but essentially non-utilitarian. And indeed the pyramid could be a metaphor for the difficulties of coping with special interest groups inimical to job creation projects.

But, of course, it is easy to be clever after the fact. What we saw at the time was rising unemployment which was NOT, as held by classical economics, paralleled by decreasing prices. The unique phenomenon, which Swedish economist Gunnar Myrdal named "stagflation", was not understood. Unemployment loomed large and we, as products of Depression-inspired Keynesian economics, responded with a plethora of public spending programs to make jobs, to train persons for jobs, to retrain persons for other jobs, to teach persons to teach others to do jobs, to educate persons to provide services, and to experiment with new initiatives.

The Provincial Capital Works Acceleration Program (PCWAP) speeded up public works projects like construction of the thirteen-storey Woodsworth Building and conversion of the old Winnipeg Auditorium into the Provincial Library and Archives Building. It also built many public housing units for elderly persons and low-income families, and developed wilderness campsites for tourists.

The Provincial Employment Program (PEP) provided funds for the labour portion of a variety of projects. Municipalities received grants to build or repair municipal offices, equipment shelters, fire halls, bridges, sidewalks, streets, recreation centres, schools, hospitals; by 1975 it was difficult to find a community without a PEP project. Small cooperatives were established or improved, particularly in the North where economic development was limited. Native reserves and remote communities received labour cost funds to develop garbage dumps, workshops, drop-in centres. Farm PEP provided labour grants to farmers for jobs building hog and cattle barns, pole sheds, dairy facilities. Arguably the most popular program, in terms of job creation and value gained by the community, was the Pensioners Housing PEP. It provided off-season work for tradesmen and enormously improved the province's housing stock. Grants ranged from $150 to $500, depending on the amount of Old Age Pension and Social Allowance received, and about fifty per cent of the all pensioner-owned homes received new bathrooms, attic repairs, insulation and water and sewer pipe replacement. In older areas, entire streets of houses proudly displayed new roofs, concrete basements, triple-paned windows and vinyl siding.

Government determination to provide equality of education to the greatest possible extent led to programs to improve education and create jobs in the teaching sector. The Schools For Urban Neighborhoods (SUN) gave education and training to the socioeconomically disadvantaged in Winnipeg's inner city. The Community Assessment Program (CAP) promoted community access to schools in Winnipeg and Brandon. The Immigrant Program for Access to Education (IMPACTE) provided job-related education for new immigrants so they could find jobs and keep them. Brandon University's Northern Teacher's Employment Program (BUNTEP), provided education and teacher-training for northern First Nations.

New Careers was a two-year rehabilitation and training program for those sidelined by some technological development or personal disaster to deadend jobs or welfare. Many hundreds of welfare recipients, and the disadvantaged seeking to reenter the job market, were provided with jobs, largely in areas of health care, recreation, and mid-level civil service positions. New Careers provided education, training and opportunities for second-generation Aboriginal leaders, including George Hicks, elected to the legislature in 1990 and later appointed speaker.

The ACCESS program provided financial aid to students who would not otherwise have received a university education. It was intended primarily for Aboriginal Manitobans and graduated a number of professionals, including Ovide Mercredi, a lawyer, former grand chief of the Assembly of First Nations, and professor at Lakehead University.

The Student Temporary Employment Program (STEP) provided employment for university and high school students during vacations. It led to performance of work of social value and provided students with experience in managing projects and with money for tuition.

SOME LEARNED TO MILK THE PROGRAMS. At least one municipality hired a person just to read Government Information Bulletins and immediately apply for any programs announced. Others took the funds intended for public use and reportedly used them to improve private property. While investigating one municipality that I suspected had misused a PEP grant, I concluded it had also misused a federal Local Initiatives Program (LIP) grant. I phoned the local LIP director to suggest the taxpayers were being fleeced and that we coordinate efforts to recover our respective grants. He said he would check and call back. He did not. I phoned him seven times and left messages to call me. He did not.

Others learned to milk the government. A southern Manitoba town applied for a $15,000 PEP grant to improve a community building. When notified that the application had been approved, they requested that the cheque be sent in time to be announced at a large community dinner being planned. But since Southern Manitoba was comprised primarily of displaced Anglo-Saxon progeny of United Empire Loyalists from Ontario, who preferred stability to unpredictable change and considered themselves the bedrock of Manitoba, along with displaced Russian Mennonites who considered "socialists" as Godless communists and voted Conservative unless they could find something more right wing, we saw an opportunity to reap some political credit. We would show these people that the NDP was not a vampire seeking their life-blood. So one of our more affable, low-key ministers, who did not believe in the iron fist even in a velvet glove, was delegated to deliver the cheque in person, and the community was so notified.

The morning after the event the minister came to my office.

> My wife and I drove out to _____ last night to deliver that PEP cheque at their dinner. When we entered the hall, no one came to greet us. We sat down on a bench along the wall and finally someone came over to say "Hello", but appeared rather embarrassed and did not offer to introduce us to anyone. We noticed some whispered conferencing and furtive glances in our direction. Finally, two more chairs were set and we were invited to sit at the head table. The chairman introduced everyone at the head table but when he got to us, he seemed embarrassed and stumbled over our names. After dinner he called on the chairman of the local Tory constituency association, who made a tub-thumping partisan political speech. Then he called on the Tory MLA from the neighbouring constituency, who made a rip-snorting partisan political speech. Then he called

on the local Tory MLA, who made a red-hot partisan political speech. Then he called on the local Tory MP, who made an impassioned partisan political speech. They all congratulated the people of the community on their private initiative, and community works, which did not require help from 'that NDP government'.

The chairman did not call on me. So while they were busy hand-pumping and back-slapping, I put the $15,000 cheque back in my wallet, and my wife and I drove home.

Then, early this morning, while we were still asleep, the phone rang. It was the man who had been chairman at the dinner. He expressed regret for having forgotten to ask me for the cheque.

The people of Southern Manitoba had lived long, seen much and knew that after the temporary socialist interregnum, there would be a return to a government they wanted and programs specifically tailored to their needs. Meanwhile, they would take our money, refuse us credit and evict us from office when the time came. The genial minister, having received the message, responded in kind:

So I said, well, my wife and I drove out there just to deliver that cheque but you people did not appear in any hurry to receive it so I assume you do not really need it. So here is what I am going to do. I am going to put your cheque back into the pile at the bottom of the applications we have received. At the end of the year, when all the other applications have been satisfied, if there is any money left, we will send it to you.

SOME, HAVING RECEIVED SOMETHING, wanted more. A lady phoned me. "I received $500 from your government through the Pensioner's Home Repair program to rebuild my bathroom."

"Well, I am glad you were able to take advantage of one of our programs to improve your home and also create some jobs."

"Yes, but it cost me $800 to repair my bathroom."

"Well, no, it only cost you $300. We paid the other $500."

"That's my point. It cost me $800, but you only gave me $500."

"Madame, let me ask you a question. Why did you phone me?"

"Because I need another $300 to pay for my bathroom."

"No. Without our $500 you would not have repaired your home and you would not be $300 out of pocket and would have no reason to call me. You are calling because we gave you $500 free money." [2]

---

[2] Sometimes I felt like the Vietnam veteran who quipped, "We were the unwilling working for the unqualified doing the unnecessary for the ungrateful."

OTHERS WERE MORE FORCEFUL. While lunching in the basement cafeteria at The Ledge, I was approached by a tall, intense, hawk-faced man in his mid-thirties who leaned over me menacingly, "I want to get back on New Careers."

"So you have already been on the New Careers Program?"

"Yes. And I got a job. And I got fired. And I want back on."

"Well, since you have already been on the program once, you will probably have to stand at the end of a long line."

"I don't stand at the end of nobody's line."

"I suppose there could be some exceptions if there is real need. Tell me, why did you get fired after being on the program?"

"I smashed my God-damned brother's fucking head in with a baseball bat and they sent me to jail and I'll fucking well do the same for you if you don't stop asking stupid questions and get me back on that program."

OBVIOUSLY, WE HAD SOME PROBLEMS out there. But we also had some problems inside. Sometimes it appeared we were making more jobs for the job-makers than for job-seekers. The City of Thompson was a one-industry town where jobs came or vanished with the periodic pendulum swings that are endemic to mining. This created problems for Aboriginal Manitobans who were moving from reserves into town and needed help to locate, get an education and some training, and find work.

A Northern Manpower Office was established in Thompson to assist with these complex economic and social adjustments. When I stopped in one day to see how they were doing, I found they had twelve employees ... and four clients.

The Minimum Income Program (Mincome) was intended to resolve a conundrum: how to build work incentives into the social welfare program. The regulations discouraged job seeking by ending all welfare payments as soon as a job was found, but there was a fear that liberalization of the rules would encourage wholesale abuse. The problem was not with 'the lame and the halt and the blind', but with able-bodied unemployed but employable people who had lost their work ethic—or had never had it—or whose quantum of dependents was such that the income from welfare was higher than the earnings from working in a low-wage industry.

This presented two problems: economic, in that it drained money from the treasury with no reciprocal production added to the economy; and political, since low-income workers were developing a fury with governments supporting their "lazy" neighbours. Threats to cut people off welfare were futile because they knew society would not leave them without food and shelter. And ignoring the issue was not an option because the 'disease' would eventually infect those working at low-wage jobs. The only rational alternative was to supplement the incomes of welfare recipients willing to work at low wages. But how should it be structured? What should be the parameters? How could it be made most effective? The concept needed systematic testing.

We found an ally in federal Health Minister Marc Lalonde. An energetic, rawhide-tough visionary, he had the same concerns and was determined to find a solution. He wanted to experiment with some variation of a guaranteed annual income and measure its effects on the working poor. Moreover, he was prepared to commit seventy-five per cent of the $17 million deemed needed for that purpose. Manitoba agreed to conduct the three-year pilot project. Cabinet approved the program allowing for the gradual reduction of welfare, instead of having payments immediately stopped when a person found a job. Three test areas (rural, urban and the North) would be mapped out. Individuals within these regions would be selected for the test. Rigorous records would be kept and all data collated from which valid conclusions could be drawn at the termination of the experiment.

A year later, I met friend a who told me his daughter had resigned from the Mincome program, where she had been a computer operator, because "she and others spent most of their time sitting around with their finger up their ass." I was surprised. "I don't believe you. You're exaggerating."

"So how many people do you think are working there?

"At a guess I would say between thirty and forty."

His daughter had brought home a computer printout of a list of employees. We counted them. There were 208.

The next day some quick checking showed it was costing, at that time, about $2 in salaries for every $1 we were delivering to poor people. While setting up such an innovative program was no easy matter—there were high front-end costs and the payoff, if any, was in the dim future—I was appalled. I went to Saul Miller, the chairman of the Health, Education and Social Policies (HESP) committee, who was ultimately responsible for the program. "Saul, we started this program to create jobs and get money into the hands of the working poor, but it seems the only jobs we have created are for government employees." He smiled wistfully. "Well, I guess those are jobs too."[3]

The For Open Campus University Services (FOCUS) program was a service to improve knowledge, lifestyle and job opportunities. In northern communities—Thompson, Churchill, The Pas—there were many young, energetic people seeking to improve their education and become more employment versatile, but could

---

[3] "Seven years and $17 million later, the federal and Manitoba governments have yet to draw any conclusions from Mincome, their massive research experiment with guaranteed annual incomes ... [The] project director conceded that Mincome still has not answered the main question it was designed to deal with, namely, what effect a minimum annual wage has on a person's incentive to work ... It is estimated that analysing the data could cost as much as $5 million and take several years to complete ... [The] assistant deputy minister in the federal Health Department wasn't sure whether the project was originally intended to analyse the result and publish the conclusions." "Mincome Analysis Delay May Waste $17 Million", *Winnipeg Free Press*, March 14, 1980.

not afford to leave their jobs to attend university. Brandon University developed a program to provide a variety of courses (politics, economics, trade unionism, labour law and women's issues, among others) on closed-circuit television to counter such circumstances. The Government of Manitoba acquired the program, appointed a director, and allocated a budget of $300,000.

I assumed a staff of six could deliver the program. Three months later the director called me. "Would you tell your brother-in-law I need another $100,000?"

"Listen, he may be a brother-in-law to me, but to you he is the premier. In any case, we gave you $300,000 for the year. You have nine months left in that year and you already need more money?"

"Well, I had to hire staff …"

"That was assumed when you were appointed and it was included in the $300,000 you were given. I want to know how in hell you spent your entire annual budget in three months. Send me a list of all the people you hired and the salaries you're paying them."

She did. She had hired nineteen people. Her secretary was being paid more than mine. She had dedicated $292,507.83 to staff salaries. That left $7,492.17 to give the program effect. I phoned her. "You are not getting another nickel."

"Then you are going to have a mass resignation on your hands."

"That's the best news I've had for a long time. Please resign and take your whole baggage with you."

'EDUCATIONAL LEAVE' became an ersatz 'job creator'. Perhaps after World War II, when government was expanding rapidly and there were few university graduates, there was a rationale for sending deserving and experienced civil servants to learn the theory of why they were doing what they did, and to familiarize themselves with the latest techniques and technology. But by the 1970s, if we needed university graduates, they were a dime a dozen. And if civil servants wanted to be *au courant* in the latest academic thinking, could they not attend summer school or night school?

Occupying the office that received the complaints—from those who did not receive the grants they wanted, or did not receive as much as they wanted, or knew of others who received too much—I developed a jaundiced view of artificial job creation. While spending a weekend in the country, I was approached by farmers who complained that they and their wives were working themselves into early graves because they could not hire help; many young people were working on government-funded make-work projects. Surely the desire by government to be socially soft-hearted did not obviate the need to be fiscally hard-headed.

When a letter came from a man in Thompson complaining that his two sons, twenty-one and eighteen, were on welfare (which paid their parents for their board and room) and wanted to work but "there seems to be no effort made by City Hall to find them jobs". His sons had sought jobs with the city but failed because "they had no experience". And his sons could not get jobs elsewhere either because "Employees from INCO take jobs at Manitoba Hydro during their vacation." Finally: "I have always been critical of City Hall because of the way they waste money."

I was not sympathetic. "If the city is not creating jobs for your sons it might be because they fear the criticism that they are wasting money … If INCO employees are spending their holidays working on Hydro projects we must conclude they are enterprising men who go where the jobs are. You may wish to inquire where those INCO men go on their working vacations and follow them."

Indeed, the concept of 'job creation' among the bureaucracy, and the emerging expectations among the public that there were no jobs available unless the government created them, began to take on a life of its own. Gradually, the unidimensional intention to create new jobs seemed to obliterate the need to examine the value of the jobs to society. In older times, someone wanting a job produced something others wanted and the market created the job. Now the noble idea that everyone who wanted to work should be able to do so threatened to reverse that process; we created the job first and hoped it would produce something society would want. We were courting the danger that our good intentions were turning into little more than organized time-wasting.[4]

And there was a danger that we would begin to measure the value of the jobs by what they cost rather than by what they produced. Natural Resources Minister Sidney Green put it all in perspective at a job-creation committee meeting. "What is our purpose here? I keep hearing that we are going to create jobs. What will be the social utility of these jobs? I want to know what these jobs will produce and of what value they are to our society. If our only criterion is to create jobs for people, whether or not they are doing anything that needs to be done, I have a proposal. Why not move Winnipeg six inches north?"

And indeed sometimes it appeared we were obsessed with the concept of job creation to the point of farce. One man was sent to an American college for two years to learn how to operate a furnace. Another was offered funds for a two-year course at an American college to learn the art of shoeing horses. The memo approving the grant was intercepted by an opposition MLA, who read it in the chamber. The man had to get a less exotic job.

A *Winnipeg Tribune* columnist wrote a tongue-in-cheek piece describing a job creation project: "A $13,000 grant to 11 university students to study the social impact of people opening revolving doors with their left hand." Joe Borowski, waiting for a caucus meeting to begin, read the article and exploded: "Hey, youse guys, look at da kinda junk we're blowin' money on."

Russ Doern, having read the article earlier, pointed out it was a fiction and,

---

[4] James Grey wrote of Depression-era work programs, "We kidded about make-work jobs such as adding up columns in the telephone directory, or keeping ledgers in invisible ink … The fatuous nature of the projects quickly brought the entire make-work concept into disrepect." *The Winter Years*, 1966, pp. 38-47.

as the caucus Puck, added playfully, "The real projects are worse."

And some were. I was on the phone when my secretary came in to ask if someone could measure my office. I nodded in the affirmative and continued with my phone call while two eager young men came in with tape and clipboard and proceeded with their task. I finished the call just as they were leaving and casually asked, "By the way gentlemen, why are you doing this?"

"Oh, the Department of Public Works instructed us to measure all the offices in the Legislative Building."

I thought no more of it then. It was a large office and perhaps the department was subdividing some offices rather than building or leasing more space. But that night, as though by premonition, I woke up wondering. The next morning I phoned the minister, "Russ, why are your people measuring my office?"

"We are having them measure all the offices in The Ledge."

"For what purpose?"

"We are planning to go metric."

"Why? We own the building. We are not paying rent. What the hell difference does it make to us what size it is?"

"Well, that's true, but we decided to go metric anyway."

"So why not just get the blueprints and give someone a pocket calculator for half an hour and he'll tell you the size."

"Well, yes, we could do that. But you see, we hired four university students for the summer and we have nothing for them to do so we told them to go measure the offices." [5]

---

[5] We did not descend to the rage of the '80s (in both the U.S., and Canada) in paying for programs such as $215,000 to study latrines in Guatemala; $14,000 to study the attitudes of Nova Scotians to animals; $88,000 to "study the detectability of tracks in snow"; $13,500 "to study the social value of lawn ornaments"; $10,300 to translate a book entitled "*If It Weren't for Sex I'd Have to Get a Job*"; $36,000 "to study the flatus-inducing factors in dry beans," $200,000 to teach civil servants how to shake hands and how to be civil (apparently firing them if they were uncivil was not considered an option). The spirit was contagious. Washington reportedly gave a $168,000 grant to someone to study whether a child likes its own mother best (he concluded it did). In his mid-Sixties book *The Lonely Crowd*, American sociologist David Reisman postulated that North American society was within reach of producing enough for our needs and that we should now turn our attention to the constructive use of leisure time. Perhaps it is from that study that some American universities drew the inspiration for such exotic credit courses as Sand Castle Building, Frisbee Throwing and Doing Nothing.

XXII

"Doctor NO"

Go tell the Spartans that here, according to their laws, I lie dead.
  —Message to his king by Leonides, leader of the Spartan troops,
  before being killed by Persians at Thermopylae, 480 BC

"**I'm appointing you to Management Committee.**"

The Management Committee of cabinet (Treasury Board) was a vital element in the control function of government. It comprised several ministers who monitored government expenditures and assessed proposals for programs not included in the annual departmental budgets so required special warrants.

I attended a committee meeting to observe a proposal being shepherded through by a deputy minister and reported to the premier. "This is not a particularly effective control mechanism. The ministers are too polite to each other and reluctant to deny funding to colleagues. There is a tendency to approve requests and let them go to cabinet. Some tension should be built into this process to make it more discriminating. It needs a shit-disturber to ask embarrassing questions."

The premier's cryptic response required me, for five years, to attend Management Committee meetings where I became 'Dr. NO'[1].

My initiation was rapid. The Department of Health requested approval of a special warrant for $100,000 for a program to provide milk for children in inner-city schools. They reported that city core poverty breeds frustration so some parents over-imbibe and suffer from hangovers in the morning and so their kids come to school hungry. Therefore, "we should provide them breakfast and lunch, which may come later, but we want to begin with milk."

---

[1] My staff gave me a small, snarling statuette with the caption on the base:"The answer is NO! Now what did you want?"

Peter St. John

Nobody ever called him a 'Yes Man', but just in case ...

I saw this as another 'pilot' program, which would soon mushroom into an entire department if we let it get out of hand. "If we are concerned about the kids we should hire some men with sledge hammers to smash the pop vending machines in the schools, because if the kids have a choice of milk and Coke they will drink Coke.[2] Then let's throw out the machines dispensing potato chips, because they are so greasy they will give the kids acne that makes medical history. But there is something more basic at issue here."

I explained that this was not a problem for schools, but for parents. When I went to school all families were poor but if kids had come to school with no food their parents would have been visited by the school trustees. If, with our army of social workers and our galaxy of social programs kids come to school hungry, there is more wrong than is being described. Instead of relieving parents of their responsibilities, let's instruct our social workers to knock on the doors of drunken parents and tell them to feed their kids before school or the next knock on the door will be by a policeman.

Without parental responsibility there is no parental control, and eventually their children end up on the doorstep of the government as hungry children to be fed or arrested offenders to be jailed. "What makes us believe that we have *carte blanche* to use unlimited amounts of taxpayer's money to assume obligations of irresponsible parents?"

But what truly troubled me was the second part of the proposal; of the $100,000 requested, $20,000 was to be used to pay a doctor to determine the effectiveness of the program by measuring the size of the children's heads, before and after the program.

"What the hell is this? First, at the end of the program the kids will be a year older so presumably the size of their heads will be larger whether they drink milk or not. Second, I suspect the basic size of the human head has not changed much in the last thousand years, yet we are asked to believe the consumption of a few quarts of milk will cause the kids' heads to swell in months. It seems to me the only swelling emanating from this program would be the heads of the bureaucrats administering this imbecility, and the wallets of the doctors hired to supervise it. "I'm inclined to suspect this must have been proposed by some medical student seeking a summer job to earn tuition."

But two ministers at the Management Committee table were ex-school teachers from the city's core. They had deep concerns born of experience, and did not consider $100,000 outrageous for a pilot program that might lead to alleviating deep and abiding problems. And children could not be held responsible for irresponsible parents. The program was approved, subject to approval by cabinet. I had lost.

Well, not quite. I would appeal to the premier. But he too believed the sins of the parents should not be visited upon the children, and that whatever could

---

[2] Thirty years later, soft drink vending machines were removed from schools.

be done to improve the health and morale of the children of the inner city should be done. Also, he was unlikely to countermand the recommendation of five ministers. One reason he wielded such enormous moral authority over his colleagues was because he used it sparingly; he never challenged his colleagues on minor matters and he knew when to accept defeat gracefully, even though skeptical about the outcome. No, I could not expect the premier to challenge the decision.

Then I remembered! The premier would be in Ottawa and cabinet would be presided over by Deputy Premier Russ Paulley.

Andrew Russell Paulley was a treasure. With the face of an aging leprechaun, he could be choleric and irrascible, but he had substance. A product of the Great Depression, he had worked simultaneously as a CNR upholsterer (becoming foreman) and at several other jobs to feed his family. He had been a union leader, a school trustee, a two-term mayor of Transcona and was elected to the Manitoba Legislature in 1953 to become its dean in years of service.

He had become leader of the CCF (later NDP) in 1959 when former leader Lloyd Stinson was defeated and the party reduced to a corporal's guard in the Roblin sweep. In 1969, he had happily surrendered the leadership to Ed Schreyer, and after the election he was appointed minister of Labour and deputy premier.

He was the oldest person in the Schreyer cabinet and, with the exception of Borowski, the least educated. This caused some unkind, if muted, comments among his colleagues, such as Doern's cruel nifty about a man he considered unlettered and uncultured: "If Russ heard someone yell, 'out, out damned spot', he would think it was someone kicking the dog out of the living room."

Awareness of such an attitude made Russ somewhat ill at ease among his university-educated colleagues, which occasionally caused him to overreach in an attempt to be funny, or clever, and his malapropisms became legendary. Such was the case one day when the premier had slipped out of a tight spot and Russ looked across the cabinet table admiringly and chuckled: "Again Schreyer falls into a pit of shit and comes out smiling like a rose." [3]

He was also inclined to histrionics and, when he lost his self-control in the chamber, shouting and windmilling his arms, the opposition would sit back and smile indulgently, knowing he was doing more harm to himself than to them. He would occasionally lose his train of thought and harangue to fill the void with sound. Or he would miss the point of an issue, if made subtly, and dig himself into deep doo-doo by pretending he had understood. Despite this, he was generally admired. On one occasion, he announced in tears that he was resigning and left the chamber, followed by friend and foe pleading with him to reconsider and regretting whatever they may have said that had infuriated him to the point of resignation. The next day it was discovered, with some chagrin, that he had merely resigned from some minor subcommittee, not from his portfolio.

But Russ loved the legislature and all it stood for, including allowing him to

---

[3] Other "Russisms" were: "I received a standing ovulation"; "It's a fact accompli" and "'Til the crows come back from Capistrano".

speak for the blue-collar, railway worker town of Transcona, which sent him there in six successive elections. He was a shrewd, pretelevision politician who cared little for the niceties of clothes or of political correctness, and was seen as "genuine".

He could hold his own in debate. Severely afflicted with emphysema, his tenure as minister was repeatedly interrupted by sojourns in a hospital under an oxygen tent, and on one such occasion he was given a psychiatric examination. Later, when he was speaking in the chamber and stammering under the influence of the copious quantities of medication taken to relieve his illness and an opposition member muttered something about "Russ needs his head examined again", he turned to the speaker in mid-sentence: "Sir. It amuses the alleged Honourable Member across the way to make sport at my expense, but I want him to know I am the only person in this chamber who has been medically certified as sane."

And Russ Paulley was a man of blunt honesty and deep compassion, who understood human foibles. One afternoon I received a call from the premier's private secretary: "Herb, there is a man here. I think this is for you to handle."

I crossed the hall to the premier's reception room. A very angry truck driver was demanding to see the premier. I advised him he was in the chamber, which was in session, and asked him to come to my office. Instead, he brushed by me and, with me following, marched in determined strides down the long corridor, burst through the door of the chamber where "strangers" are not allowed, and shouted that he wanted to see the premier.

The commissionaires hustled him out. The premier, followed by a furious Russ Paulley, came out of the chamber and, accompanied by the culprit and his escorts, we went to the Premier's Office.

The man explained he had been given an undeserved speeding ticket and had come to see the head of the government who, he assumed, controlled everything including the traffic police.

I had little sympathy. "Mr. Premier, anyone with the intelligence to drive a cross-country transport truck must know you do not come to the premier with a traffic ticket. I suggest this man is seeking marytrdom and we should accomodate him by having him arrested."

Russ Paulley's voice cut through the air like a knife: "Listen, my truck driver friend, you have done a bad thing. There are certain rules in our society. One is that if you get a speeding ticket you either pay it or go to court. You do not ask the premier to interfere with the law. We also have certain rules in this legislature. One is that no one comes into the chamber when it is in session without an invitation. You have placed yourself in serious jeopardy. By the way, where do you work?"

The man named a major national trucking company. Russ picked up the phone and called the manager. "You'll be reading about one of your drivers bursting into the legislature and causing some commotion. He didn't do any damage and I hope you will ensure this doesn't affect his job with you."

Then he turned to the now-chastened truck driver. "Get the hell out of here before I change my mind."

While the truck driver was fleeing, Russ turned to me, standing there making fists in my pockets and fuming at what I saw as another prime example of government pusillanimity. "Aw hell, Herb, why make a waterfall out of a spit in the lake. So the guy invaded the Holy of Holies of the Old Boy's Club. So what? Sometimes we need to be shook up and see things through the eyes of those out in the real world. We tend to forget what it was like when we were ordinary little people. Besides, maybe that poor bugger really believed the premier would fix his ticket."

On another occasion, Russ was visited by a delegation of barbers and invited me to attend. The barbers had a problem. The younger ones, with big bills to pay, wanted to work evenings and weekends. The older ones, with mortgages paid and cottages at the lake, wanted time out, but were afraid if they left their places vacant their business would soon migrate to those working. They had come to ask the minister of Labour to pass a law limiting the working hours of barbers.

Russ Paulley patiently and politely heard them out. Then he reached across his desk for a sheet of paper. "Gentlemen, when I was appointed a minister of the crown, I made a list of things I want to do while in office. I don't see on my list anything to suggest that I want to tell barbers how long they can work. I suggest you settle this among yourselves."

To this no-nonsense man I explained my concerns about the school milk proposal. He listened intently, a large grin passed across his laugh-lined, pug-nosed, Puckish face. "Okay, Herb, I'll fix it up."

The next day I entered the cabinet room in a self-congratulatory mood. I felt even more so when cabinet reached the final item on the agenda and Russ entered the debate with fine fury. "This is a ridiculous proposal. Where in hell do we find the people who make such proposals? This is the sort of thing that should not be countenanced. This should have been killed at MCC. Just look at this. They want to use $20,000 of the milk money to pay a doctor to measure the kids' heads. There is no way I will stand by while doctors are being paid with the kids' milk money."

Russ Paulley, power in the cabinet, was in full oratorical flight, making his points repeatedly, his voice rising and hands gesticulating. I felt good. The proposal was dead. Then: "I move that we add $20,000 to the program to pay the doctor so the kids will have the full benefit of the $100,000 for milk."

He had missed my point. By attempting to save the taxpayers $100,000, I had cost them an additional $20,000. I had struck out. That was to largely symbolize my tenure on MCC.

The School Milk Program proceeded, followed by the School Breakfast Program and the School Lunch Program.[4] In the 1995 Manitoba election Liberal

---

[4] Three years later "Principals involved in the controversial free meals program say attendance has improved [and] the meals offer an enticement to children to come to school [but] attendance is lower in the afternoon than in the morning, when it appears the meals are being offered." *The Winnipeg Tribune*, December 9, 1977. It seemed that children were being sent to school to eat, not to learn.

Leader Paul Edwards "vowed to ensure that every child in Manitoba has breakfast before school begins in the morning."[5]

The syndrome of relieving parents of responsibility for the welfare and actions of their children continued to fester.[6] Meanwhile Troy Rupert, director of Native Alliance stated: "The problem is not in the streets or in the school [but] in the homes."[7] And, "The province's chief medical examiner is calling for new legislation to crack down on parents whose children die as a result of parental intoxication."[8]

Sometimes proposals were rejected because they were outrageous. The premier was once in flight—economy class—to Ottawa, studying a topographical map of Manitoba. He turned to his seat mate, Manitoba Hydro chairman Len Bateman. "Len, we have some two dozen remote reserves with no road approaches. All supplies are taken in by plane, or tractor train in the winter, or by water." He went on to say that he could see a number of places where, with the construction of short canals, rivers and lakes could be linked into an almost continuous system. Supplies could then be hauled in by barge, which was much more economical. Anything storable could be transported in summer. In fact, barges could be built and given to the residents of the reserves and allow them haul the supplies and create jobs for themselves. And since these canals would be an integral part of an interprovincial waterway system, Ottawa might cost share. "All we would need to do is build some barges," he concluded.

Several minutes later Bateman replied: "Mr. Premier, I just remembered that when the Roblin government built the Grand Rapids Dam we built a barge to haul supplies. It is out on Lake Winnipeg somewhere and we have no more use for it. You can have it for a nominal fee." Suddenly Bateman spoke again, "Mr. Premier, if I recall correctly, we built two barges. They are of no value to us. We will find them and you can have them."

On his return the premier sent a brief note to the Department of Northern Affairs suggesting it consider the feasibility of using barges to haul supplies to the affected remote reserves.

Several weeks later MCC received a proposal for funding a new, unbudgeted program. The department had taken the premier's suggestion seriously and had worked at it diligently. They proposed construction of nineteen barges and hiring seventy employees to operate them. Something had been lost in translation. A suggestion intended to save money in haulage charges had grown, like Topsy, into a proposal for an expensive new program. It was declined.

---

[5] *Winnipeg Free Press*, April 11, 1995.

[6] By 1993, several Winnipeg school boards were discussing hiring security guards to patrol school hallways because of violence. In a survey asking "what are the biggest problems facing Winnipeg schools?" twenty-five per cent reported "lack of discipline", higher than funding problems at twenty-one per cent. *Ibid.*, November 20, 1993. It appeared our peaceful society would soon be hiring half the population to police the other half.

[7] CBC Interview, March 21, 1997.

[8] *Winnipeg Free Press.*, March 18, 1996.

There was another program that grew like Topsy. One Tuesday morning Harry Taylor, coordinator of the government fleet of motor vehicles, brought a message to MCC. "We are going to have to buy about 750 new vehicles this year."

Ministers, deputy ministers, associate and assistant deputy ministers, agency directors, and a myriad of other government employees had access to government-owned vehicles. Those using their own cars were reimbursed for mileage driven for public purposes, but a government car made them a two-car family with no capital cost. And who would check if it was used only for public purposes? The fleet administration had lost control. Who were they to deny a minister a car for an assistant? Driving a government vehicle became another perk that was used liberally. Now Taylor explained that he operated on a three- to four-year replacement cycle that required the purchase of between 700 and 800 vehicles this fiscal year.

My hair stood on end; how do we justify that to the public? And I was annoyed parking spaces at The Ledge were full of government cars, leaving no room for taxpayers calling on government. "Harry, next Tuesday morning, I want a complete list of how many vehicles we have, who has them, and where they are."

He brought the list. We had in excess of 3,000 vehicles. Four of them, three cars and a truck, were at Berens River. I had been to Berens River a year earlier. It was a tiny Aboriginal village. There were about four miles of road in the village. There was no road in or out. The vehicles had to be transported there by ferry or on the ice. And when they arrived they had nowhere to go.

We never got that situation under control. It took a recession and change of government to do it. By 1995, the Filmon government had reduced the vehicles to about 2,400 by requiring the fleet to operate on a self-sustaining basis. They charged mileage, plus per diem, ending the practice of a car sitting at a civil servant's office for weeks at a time, travelling no further than from home to office, but tying up capital. It brought responsibility into the system. Many found they did not need a car if they were required to pay for it.[9]

Sometimes I won an argument simply because someone feared I had more authority than I actually had. A primary pillar of NDP policy was to make education, like health care, available to all. Most NDP members, aware of how much their own North End or rural circumstances had been changed by their schools and teachers, saw education not just as the rote learning of reading and writing, but as the passport to a better life. It raised youthful visions above their immediate horizons and inspired them to look upon the world with eyes of wonder. Therefore education should be based on a student's intellectual capacity rather than on his or her parents' bank account.

This led to an extensive program of student loans. Every year applications for loans increased. So did complaints received by my office. Many were not about

---

[9] "Filmon announces government now meeting needs with 729 fewer vehicles than in 1987, saving $3 million." *Winnipeg Free Press*, March 29, 1995.

applications being declined, but about the length of time it took to inform them. The complaints were something like: "I applied for a loan in March and it is now August and university begins next week and I still don't know."

I referred complaints to the Student Loans Office in the Department of Education. Finally I asked the auditor at MCC to inquire. He reported that they could not keep up with processing applications manually and the director of the Student Loans Office recommended going to computers.

"Then go to computers. The Government of Manitoba has just purchased a whole computer company. Use it."[10]

The complaints continued. Several months later, I inquired again. The program auditor reported that computer processing was not proving effective and they may be forced to go back to manual processing.

"Then tell them to go back to manual, but get the damn thing cleared up. And pass the word along to the director that unless this is cleared up soon, someone is going to get fired."

Then I was told that the director of the Student Loan Program was hinting that he was not concerned about threats from me. He had been Premier Schreyer's classmate at university and knew he would never be fired. I phoned the executive secretary of MCC.. "Hans, on Tuesday I want student loans on the agenda and I want the director at the meeting. And tell him to be prepared."

When I walked through the reception office to the MCC boardroom, I noticed the director sitting, half-hidden behind a newspaper, pretending he was not there. When we arrived at the student loans item on the agenda, I asked: "Hans, I asked you to have the director at this meeting. Why is he not here?"

"He is available but I did not invite him in here because I was afraid you would just get into a big fight with him."

There were five cabinet ministers present. Without having to say so, they clearly agreed with the secretary. And they seemed to be suggesting I was going a bit too far in using my authority. But it was not they who were receiving the calls and letters from angry student applicants, it was I. But I knew the director was just beyond the door where he could hear me if I shouted. "Listen, dammit! I want him here because I WANT a fight. We are spending $7.5 million a year on student aid and all we get is complaints. I'm fed up with this shit. I don't give a damn if they go to computer or to manual, but next time I get a complaint from a student about an application not processed expeditiously, the director is fired. And I don't give a shit if he WAS the premier's classmate at university, he's fired."

When I left, the director was gone. I asked the receptionist, "When I was shouting in there, do you think Mr. _____ heard me?"

Chalk-white, with eyes round with fright, she stammered, "Oh-h-h, Mr. Schulz. Yes-s-s-s. He he-he-hea-ard you."

---

[10] The Government of Manitoba had acquired a computer company when an MDC loan to its former owners went sour.

I never learned how they accomplished the miracle, but I never received another complaint about student loan applications. Later I heard a rumour that they hired about forty university students during the summer to process the applications manually. So sometimes I won, but only by accident. [11]

The Department of Northern Affairs, always alert for new ways to improve incomes of the people of northern Manitoba, concluded that native fishermen were not making enough money because they were not catching enough fish. This could be rectified by providing them with two-man fishing canoes, powered by outboard motors. Income would mushroom, and prosperity come to native fishermen. And there would be spin-off benefits; two-man canoes would double the number of fishermen and the greater catch would make more jobs at fish processing plants. The aluminium used in making the canoes could lead to construction of a smelter. Jobs would be created in building both plant and canoes. And the plant could be in a rural town, building up the rural economy.

The proposal was brought to Management Committee. Flowing from the simple axiom that more fish could be caught from two-man rather than one-man canoes, a new multifaceted and integrated industry was being spun into being right before our eyes. The possibilities were limitless. They wanted to hire experts to do planning and workers to build canoes and find motors and erect the plant and move in equipment. They came to MCC for money.

The ministers on MCC saw the proposal of dubious feasibility, but the relevant minister himself had brought the proposal to MCC and unless it was patently absurd, ministers were reluctant to shoot down a proposal from a colleague. After all, the minister responsible for the department presumably knew best what the department wanted to do, and why, and each minister knew he might one day need the others. So again, we were slipping into supporting what appeared a minor expenditure, but which could blossom into another monstrosity.

I objected. The proposal was to build bigger boats to catch more fish and improve fishermen's income, but we already had fourteen million pounds of fish in storage at the freshwater fish marketing plant in Transcona. To help fishermen we should first sell the fish already caught and give the market a chance to increase the price, rather than provide the means to catch more fish to depress the market further. Fishermen, like farmers, were being seduced into believing that if they cannot get a sufficient return on what they are producing, they should produce more, which would increase costs and depress incomes and result in them producing themselves out of business.

Second, since the fishing canoes were mostly for Aboriginal Manitobans, who had no money, the plan necessitated long-term credit. But once they have the canoes, there is the possibility that some will plead inability to pay and if we attempted to repossess them there will be an outcry about yet another example of

---

[11] "The average student loan upon graduation is expected to be $25,000 ... A record number of students are walking away from their loans." *Ibid.*, October 23, 1997.

"systemic racism". The media will kick the snot out of the government.

Then, I explained, when we realize the program is another loser, we will be unable to close down the plant without paying a huge political price. There will be an outcry from organized labour that we are destroying jobs, from the town council that we are ruining their economy, from the media that we are pre-judiced against our native people, and from our own lunatic fringe that we lack the courage to carry the program through to its logical conclusions.

"Worst of all," I said, "we will have created expectations from which there will be no escape if all turns to rat-shit. We will have created another vehicle for welfare, we will have made the current situation worse, and we will have given our political opponents another stick to beat us with."

I lost that argument. A prototype canoe was built, an outboard motor was mounted, and two men took it for a test spin. They cracked the hull. It knocked the heart out of the program. Except for the accrued bills, I never heard of the two-man, outboard-driven, super-dooper, aluminum fishing canoe again.

The logging operation was worse. When the Jenpeg power plant was built at the north end of Lake Winnipeg, it raised the question of what to do with the trees along the channel. They could be left to rot, but it was decided they should be removed: to harvest the trees; reduce the potential of later blockages, and pro-vide jobs for Aboriginal workers. Soon after, the Department of Northern Affairs came to MCC with a request in excess of $400,000 to purchase heavy machinery. I asked, "What are these tractors and tree-cutters for?"

"To give to men to cut the trees along the channel."

"Why do we not give them chainsaws instead?"

"The native people won't work with chain saws. They want tractors."

"We decided to harvest the trees to make jobs for native Manitobans. If we give them heavy equipment the work will soon be completed. If we buy this equipment for people with no experience it will soon break down. We will have to fly in mechanics by helicopter. Soon everyone will get tired of the whole thing and revert to cutting the trees in the normal manner. Our equipment will be abandoned and we will be left with expensive, rusted junk."

But the machinery was purchased. The next government sold it.

Sometimes I won because of the fickle finger of fate. Civil servants were allowed 1.5 days per month sick leave. Some took their leave whether they needed it or not, while others treated it like any other benefit (unemployment, car or home insurance), to be used when needed and be glad when it was not needed, and prudently banked unused time in the event of a lengthy illness.

Then the union began agitating that employees leaving the public service should be paid for unused sick leave. It was like being paid for the portion of unemployment insurance that had not been used, or demanding the return of an insurance premium because one's house did not burn down. We kept saying "No", but pressure mounted. Committee members were pitched with the rationale that if we did not pay for accumulated sick time, employees would regularly take time off, sick or not. Requiring a doctor's certificate for every day taken would be impractical. The government was losing again.

Then it happened! Just when it appeared that MCC might give in, a request came in to extend sick leave for a civil servant who had been ill for several months and had used up all his banked sick time. [12]

I called the MGEA representative. "There is no way we are going to extend this guy's sick leave."

"But if he leaves the hospital he might die."

"Death comes to us all. In four days his sick leave ends and he is fired, sick or not. And he will be informed that you, not I, killed him."

We compromised. The man's sick leave would be extended, but there would be no more demands for pay for unused sick leave. [13]

Another item repeatedly returning to MCC was the demand to make "merit pay" (an annual non-negotiated salary increase) automatic. A previous government had instituted this to be selectively used to keep "meritorious" people with the public service instead of risking losing them to the private sector. Now the civil service was demanding this become part of the pay package for every civil servant. I did not believe every civil servant was "meritorious".

But it had become expected, and what minister would bell the cat by refusing it? Finally, one took the risk. He denied the "merit" increase to three of his employees. The uproar was ear-shattering. They complained to the Civil Service Commission, and to the opposition, and to the media. The minister suffered enormous abuse. The civil service was furious and the public indifferent. We won no political kudos. It would have been so much easier to just pay.

Sometimes a program just spun out of control. We needed a quick study on how northern transportation (roads, winter roads, airstrips, water transport) could be integrated. I was instructed to find someone to do the job. I phoned someone I knew. "Dave, do you know the North well enough to do a fast study for us on the best utilization of transportation facilities?"

"I know it like the back of my hand. I spent twenty years up there buying fish and freighting supplies."

"What would you charge us?"

He thought a moment:"$15,000."

I reported back to MCC. The proposal was accepted and so was the man. Then a minister had an inspiration. "Ottawa will cost-share a study on Northern transportation. But I must ask if this consultant is acceptable to them."

He was not. But they knew someone who was acceptable. We hired him. The study was done. The bill was more than $80,000. [14]

---

[12] A morbid but relevant joke at the time went: "I ran out of sick time, so I called in dead."

[13] Two decades later, City of Winnipeg employees won this clause in their collective agreement. When Manitoba Hydro was sold in 2002, the union demanded some $10 million for "accumulated, unused sick time" (an average of $15,000 for each of 580 employees). *Winnipeg Free Press*, February 22, 2002.

[14] How often we were beguiled into programs by cost-sharing!

Sometimes I won an argument I should have lost. Bud Boyce, the cerebral, concerned MLA for Winnipeg Centre (he read Buckminster Fuller, Northrop Frye, and Frank Lloyd Wright in his spare time) was appalled at the many abandoned motor vehicles along highways and littering junk yards and back yards in residential areas. He saw this as unsightly and an inexcusable waste of resources. A local car-crushing firm had overextended itself and needed money. He proposed that the government buy the plant and operate it as a public enterprise. Junked vehicles would be collected, dismantled and salvaged material sold as spare parts or recycled. The plant would be self-sustaining; costs would be recovered from the sale of salvage and from a fee of $1 added to each driver's licence issued by the province.

The proposal was intended to clean up the environment, salvage a resource, and create new jobs ... at no cost to the treasury. MCC agreed that it sounded good and should be brought back in four weeks for further consideration and possible recommendation to cabinet.

Then some suspicious citizen did some arithmetic. One dollar per driver's licence was not much, but multiplied by the number of driver's licenses issued it put more than $500,000 a year into the greedy hands of government. The mathematical genius must have had a large network of friends, for letters and phone calls, poured in. They came to the Premier's Office. I panicked. I questioned MCC; did we really need another political problem? The proposal was abandoned. The firm recovered, became a singular success, and was sold two decades later for millions of dollars. Had we pursued Boyce's proposal, it might have become one of our few successes.

Sometimes I misunderstood and saw trouble where there was none. It had been a long, frustrating morning. Several projects approved earlier had asked for more funding. Several departments had requested unbudgeted money for new programs to do things I did not consider necessary, except to give the department headlines. We reached the last item on the agenda.

The young program auditor for the Department of Industry and Commerce explained that the department needed a special warrant for $19,000 to study the sewage treatment plant at Brandon.

I exploded: "For Christ's sake, can't we even build a stinking sewage plant that works? Get the damned contractor who built it to repair it. What in hell is the matter with the damned sewage treatment plant at Brandon anyway?" He blanched at my angry tone, half-rose as though preparing for a fast escape, and stammered: "Oh, oh ... nothing ... nothing, sir. In fact, it's ... it's working v-v-very well. We just w-w-want to know why."

XXIII

The Civil Service: The Ogre Triumphs

Government ought never to underestimate the power of our complicated systems to pervert their good intentions into unintentional results.

—Allan Greenspan

"**Herb, would you like to go to Washington?**" The question need not have been asked.

"The American State Department has issued an invitation for four Canadian non-elected political persons to visit for a week at their expense. I managed to reserve a spot for Manitoba. You are owed vacation time so you might wish to go. My office will make the arrangements. You will meet the others in Washington."

It was Derek Bedson's first trip to my office from his dark-panelled, history-haunted retreat next to the premier's office. He was clerk to the cabinet and I resented him as a residue of the *'ancien regime'* I hoped to extirpate.

❂   ❂   ❂

SHORTLY AFTER ED SCHREYER assumed the premier's chair, he was given some advice by the national leader of the NDP, Tommy Douglas. "When the people change government fundamentally, they expect fundamental change in government. That will not occur unless you change your senior administrators."[1]

---

[1] S.M. Lipsett, in his epochal study of the CCF in Saskatchewan wrote, "Administrative functions cannot be separated from policy-making power. Members of the civil service [have] power to amend, initiate and veto actions proposed ... The political problem of the power and influence of the permanent civil service with its own goals and traditions was not important so long as the social and economic values of the bureaucracy and governing politicians did not conflict. The problem becomes crucial when a new political movement takes office and proposes to enact reforms that go beyond traditional frames of reference ... and upsets existing regulations within the bureaucracy. It is especially important when the explicit ... goals of many democratic states are changing from the laissez-faire ... regulation of society to those of a social welfare state." *Agrarian Socialism: The Co-operative Commonweath Federation in Saskatchewan*, p. 309.

The advice was based on the experience of the legendary former premier of Saskatchewan who changed his province fundamentally, but experienced sabotage of programs by inherited bureaucrats. He informed Schreyer:

> I am aware there are different theories of how a civil service should be treated by a new government. These include leaving all at their post and hoping for the best, which is unrealistic, to quietly replacing as many as possible, which is both difficult and unfair, to bringing in a new tier of super-bureaucrats, which is a good idea for new programs designed to serve the ideological needs of the government but is both expensive and confusing if applied generally. We learned in Saskatchewan there is a tendency, human but unfortunate in this case, for public servants to become so identified with, and so protective of, the programs they have been administering that they become obstacles to changes determined upon by a newly-elected government.[2]

The new premier too, was a student of political science and responded, "But some historians theorize that the easy success of the Nazi coup was in part due to Germany's civil service having been so well trained to 'follow orders' that they unquestioningly obeyed their new political masters even when they were morally wrong."

Douglas agreed, but argued that other historians have written that the same bureaucracy that did the will of the imperial regime and later of the Nazis, resisted the Weimar administration after 1918. Ironically, it seemed those who obey their political masters are primarily in authoritarian regimes where the bureaucracy should resist, while those who resist are products of democratic regimes where people choose their government and should have commitments honoured.

"So from the perspective of government, which is preferable?" Premier Schreyer wanted to know.

"Neither," responded Douglas, and explained that as opposed to politicians, who are transitory, the civil service provides continuity in administration of public affairs. Consequently it is their duty to prepare the government for all consequences that might flow from a policy decision. But they should be neither Horatius at the bridge, holding back change, nor sycophants eager to respond to a passing political fancy. A new government should expect the civil service to give its best advice based on experience, but accept change when representatives of the public will require it. "The politician," he said, "and not the civil servant, must face the electorate and should have the last word."

"So, Tommy, does the new, in your phrase, 'fundamentally different'

---

[2] Perhaps the most significant examples, during the Schreyer years, of public servants over-identifying with a program of the previous government were that of Rex Grose, CEO of the Manitoba Development Corporation and lawyer Walter Newman, in the case of CFI. See also James McAllister, *The Government of Edward Schreyer*, p. 157.

government's desire to implement new programs require a wholesale massacre of civil servants?"

No, said Douglas, for each department is a hierarchy with the deputy minister at its apex. The minister is the political head of the department who reports to cabinet on the initiatives of his department and brings back government policy decisions for departmental action. But the deputy is the administrative head and is virtually sovereign in his sphere of responsibility. The wise minister will not become involved in the minutiae of departmental activities, but that leaves him totally dependent on his deputy for the information he takes to cabinet.

Worse, directives to the departmental machinery flow down from the deputy. Therefore ministers, and by extension, the government, are totally dependent on the deputies for both the information on which they base policy decisions and for the manner in which policy directives are administered. A determined deputy can both manipulate information resulting in undesirable policy decisions, or implement a policy in name but not in substance.

"So how does a government best ensure adequacy of information to itself and compliance with its directives?" asked Schreyer.

"Find deputy ministers on whom you can depend explicitly. Competence is of the essence but you are undertaking a small revolution and ideology will prove of importance. And a person is not necessarily incompetent just because he supports the NDP," advised Douglas.

Douglas' advice was not taken. It was not part of Schreyer's nature or purpose to initiate his regime with a basketful of severed heads of deputy ministers. In eight years, one deputy minister was fired, and he was an NDP supporter. [3]

Mostly, the giant machine of the bureaucracy continued at its own pace. Civil servants knew they were permanent, while politicians were temporary and by the time they learned their role they were already on the way out. Deputies had perhaps served a dozen ministers in a half-dozen administrations, knew how their departments functioned, and how to have things done or stopped. And within a short time, they knew where the bodies were buried by their new masters. Sometimes, within days of his assumption of office, a new minister was taken captive by his bureaucrats, either because he was unsure of himself and overdependent on them, or because they were privy to damaging information. By the second term, when the bureaucracy would accept the NDP government as a fact rather than an aberration, some ministers had lost both their resolve and their energy.

Ironically, a minister's control over his department appeared to be in inverse ratio to the amount of his involvement in it. It seemed the less paper on a minister's desk, the more efficient the operations of the department. Some considered themselves responsible for every sparrow that fell; their desk was piled high with

---

[3] "Almost two-thirds of those employed as deputy ministers or assistant deputy ministers or at similarly high levels in 1975-76 had been employed by the Manitoba government prior to the 1969 election." McAllister, *Ibid.*, p. 159.

files, their desire to check program progress caused them to reach into the bowels of their department, and consequent problems with senior administrators at times became debilitative. Conversely, there were those with desks that were maddeningly clean; these took a cold and analytical approach to the department, but gave senior administrators precise directives and expected precise reports on what had been done to effect them. Some wag has quipped that "a clean desk is evidence of a sick mind". Perhaps, but it may also be evidence of clear objectives and iron control, and of a minister thinking of policy rather than administration.

The ways that civil servants were kept on the payroll regardless of competence sometimes seemed almost scandalous. Administrators were transferred from department to department to agency to commission to committee, to find a niche to fit them. In cases of perceived *non compos mentis en extremis*, names were "red-circled", which froze salaries, but never reduced them. That created the demoralizing situation in which a senior administrator, transferred to an agency, would have a salary perhaps double that of the other, often eager young employees, doing identical work.

It also led to a perceptible loss of "edge" on the part of those required to work at the same level as those they had been accustomed to command, and who knew that everyone else knew they were here because they had not "cut it" at a higher level. At meetings of Management Committee, our *modus operandi* on Tuesday mornings was to have departmental program auditors hand each of us a paper with relevant documents attached, and provide a fast verbal summary. The depleted level of energy and interest became painfully clear one morning when a former deputy minister, now reduced to program auditor, handed us copies of his report, which I quickly scanned, and then began to mumble his summary.

I interrupted, "What you are saying is the opposite of what is in your paper."

"Oh! We-l-l-l, I really did not write that paper."

"But your signature is on it."

"Oh! We-l-l-l, I guess my secretary must have signed it."

Sometimes it was worse. When one assistant deputy minister was transferred to an agency to get him out of harm's way, and then fired by the board of directors of that agency, an appeal by the man's wife kept him on the payroll. This was to be for a three-month period to ease his transition into the private sector, but then he was appointed assistant deputy by the minister to whom he had been transferred for reasons of compassion, not competence.

There was the egregious practice of "rug-ranking", by which senior employees maintained a sumptuous style and established their comparative status. That meant changing everything—rugs, desks, paint, paintings—whenever a bureaucrat became part of the expensive game of musical offices. At one point the Department of Public Works, responsible for the management of the building, felt impelled to get into the act, both to play the game and to control its costs, by issuing a booklet meticulously detailing entitlements—and limitations—of rank.[4]

The effect was insidious and galvanized some into action for the first time since passing their probation, changing offices or decorating theirs. The effect was also disturbing. When the Woodsworth Building was nearing completion the Attorney General's Department was given the honour of being first to leave cubicles in The Ledge basement and move to the steel-and-glass structure across Broadway. Two assistant deputy ministers from that department appeared before Management Committee to complain that their new offices were too small. Would MCC order the minister of Public Works to have them enlarged?

The taxpayers had spent some $10 million in improving quarters for bureaucrats and they were complaining! MCC delined to intervene. The following week the ADMs, and their deputy, returned with the same request. Again MCC declined. A week later the ADMs and the deputy minister came again, like Abou Ben Adhem's angel, with their minister. He said nothing, but his presence was intended to pressure MCC.

I was furious. They had wanted new offices, which we built, and now they wanted larger offices! Why in hell didn't they go to the private sector and get a taste of the cost of rent? But mostly I was angry with their minister; he had sat through several cabinet meetings while the minister of Public Works laid his blue-prints on the table and explained in detail what was being done, and he had said nothing. Now that the walls were up he was supporting his bureaucrats' demand for the expenditure of moving them.

Probing for some functional utility of larger offices, I asked why they were needed. One ADM said loud and clear, "Because our status is judged by the size of our offices." Even his minister lowered his head in embarrassment.

Competence, ideology and status-seeking were not the only problems; there was productivity. It is not true that the civil servant winks by opening one eye, but to the beleaguered taxpayer or businessman needing information and not familiar with the routine of public administration, it appears that way. I had operated a farm and a construction company, and when there was something to be done a way was found to do it. A machine was repaired or a hole dug or a ramp built or a lifting device rigged, but the job was done. If the hours of the day were not sufficient, we used the night. In the world of the small business operator the last— the absolute last—option was hiring additional help.

It seemed to me that in the civil service it was the first option. And one thing became evident; hire one civil servant and he works for the public; hire two and they work for each other.

---

[4] A lowly program director rated an office of ten by twelve feet (space and salaries approximate), one modern, metal desk of a certain size, and three chairs—one for the bureaucrat and two for visitors—and one ashtray. An assistant deputy minister could claim an office of twelve by eighteen feet, three chairs (including one that swivelled), one wall painting and one ashtray. Someone having reached the exalted status of deputy minister was entitled to an office of twenty by thirty feet, a private washroom, three wall paintings, a large oak desk, a leather upholstered swivel chair for himself, plus three padded wooden chairs for visitors, a glass-topped coffee table and TWO ashtrays.

No modern industrial/welfare state can operate without a permanent civil service. No review can ignore the invaluable contribution of deputy ministers with long experience and no civil service protection, the secretaries with computer memories who are first in line for abuse by their bosses and by the public, or of the thousands of faceless dogs-bodies who labour in quiet anonymity, dedicated to the public service, not knowing when their political masters might abandon them to "downsizing" or sacrifice them to political ends. In an operation in which billions of dollars pass through their hands and temptation is real, be it as trivial as abusing a government credit card or a free parking pass,[5] the few times such scandals erupt demonstrates the high moral responsibility of the civil service.

But the civil service adage: "Politicians come and go, but we go on forever," tends to make some less industrious than they might be. And the self-aggrandizing upper echelons who see themselves entrenched in command/control positions know, if all else fails, they can bury their new ministers in paper. This leads to a Gresham's Law, by which the truly dedicated are driven out of public service by the devaluation they see around them.[6]

When I questioned an ADM about why a certain action had not been taken, I was told "I have been here long enough to know I will never be fired for what I do not do." A $30,000-a-year civil servant came to complain that his department would not assign him work because they considered him incompetent, I raged to the premier, "The only damned reason this man is here is because he was a good Conservative when the previous government hired him. He is contributing nothing and probably never will. We are not doing either him or the taxpayers any favours by keeping him on the payroll. I appreciate your fabled aversion to confrontation but as a student of political history you must surely be aware of Machiavelli's injunction that, "A prince, to maintain his power, is forced to govern in ways contrary to charity and humanity."

The premier was not amused."And surely you," he responded, "as a student of historical literature, must be aware of Le Maistre's injunction that, 'The true warrior remains human in the midst of the blood he sheds.' I am surprised that you like many others have fallen prey to the belief those in the public service do not produce simply because their productivity cannot be mathematically measured." He proceeded to give examples:

> Firemen and city services crews may spend time sliding down
> greasy poles or playing cards, but when the alarm sounds or the snow falls
> the public wants more of them, not fewer. How do we presume to measure
> productivity in areas of intangibles like education and health care? What

---

[5] I was always irked when the parking lot at The Ledge seemed to have room for everyone except taxpayers. Also, a standing joke was that at times there was no parking space downtown, because of government cars with free parking decals.

[6] In 1981, Auditor-General J.J. Macdonell reported that the federal government was not getting a day's work for a day's pay and that civil service staff was working at only sixty-one per cent of potential.

can be measured is comparisons and, per capita, we have fewer civil servants than most other provinces, including free enterprise Alberta. I suspect much of the antipathy toward the civil service results from jealously, which is ironic because if public servants are such parasites, why do their detractors covet their places? Also, our civil service complement is growing largely because government has entered services such as Medicare and Autopac and employees have been transferred from the private to the public payroll. That, incidentally, is a case in point. By what process do these people, previously considered hard-working and productive members of society, suddenly become seen as drones simply by virtue of moving from the private to the public sector?

The premier's question deserved an answer.

Because even to the casual observer it is clear there is an ineluctable dynamic that tends to make them so. Any program director with a modicum of intelligence knows by the time he has served his six-month probation period that, if he has ten staff and is paid $16,000 and can increase his payroll to twenty employees, he can apply for promotion to senior officer I at $20,000. If he hires forty persons, he can go to SO II at $26,000 and if he hires eighty, he could be an assistant deputy minister at $32,000. If he is clever and determined, and doubles his payroll again, he could get his own department and be a deputy minister at $38,000.

And that's the good news. Small pyramids form inside the larger one. Those in on the ground floor find reasons to develop subunits for administrative purposes, with themselves as director, and needing their own complement of employees and secretarial staff and offices. This does not result from maliciousness or venality, but from each person's belief that their work is important to humanity, and that they can get more work done with more personnel doing it. The result is empire-building, irresistible to ambitious persons, which bloats our payroll and makes the civil servant both envied and despised.

The premier was not persuaded. He pointed out that the ministers, who must sooner or later go back to the electorate if they wish to remain in office, would be on guard against such accretions. Second, overstaffing is not a disease of government but of gargantuanism. He offered the suspicion that the staff of General Motors was likely much more bloated than ours and predicted that this would manifest itself in the next economic crunch.[7] He added that overstaffing in the private sector is excused on the grounds it is a "private' cost", but said that the

---

[7] Shortly after our conversation, during the 1981 recession, General Motors laid off about 17,000 and Chrysler about 8,000 middle management, white-collar employees.

only difference is that it filches the consumer's rather than the taxpayer's pocket.

Third, he said, civil servants are condemned to be both envied and despised by the very nature of their position, which is perceived as providing secure jobs, good salaries and benefits, with no credit given for the expertise they provide.

"Then perhaps we could clean up their image by reducing their salaries and benefits," I argued, "such as pensions."

That is a fallacy, he told me, reminding me that once upon a time, the public service, like armies, foraged. They lived on what they could steal. Even today in much of the world, public servants, including the gendarmerie, receive such low pay that they live on bribes and citizens get nothing done without greasing palms with lucre. "I daresay the amount of corruption increases in inverse proportion to the salaries," he said.

Our public servants, on the other hand, receive decent pay and retirement pensions because they are in positions of public trust and we do not want them to be tempted to pilfer or accept bribes. "Surely you have sensed, Herb, that considering the quantities of money passing across the desks of our public servants, some could easily stick to their hands if they were so inclined, no matter how stringent the controls."

While I agreed with his final remark, I was not completely persuaded. "That's understood, but the public objection appears primarily to the permanency of their positions, which is interpreted as paying them forever no matter how little they do or how badly they do it. Taxpayers and voters are both subject to economic and political changes, and they resent the fact that, no matter how often they change government, the civil service seems immune to the ills ordinary flesh falls heir to."

The premier reminded me of a time when public workers were considered employees of the government, not the state, and every change of government resulted in their wholesale replacement. About a century ago, the British government realized that the complexities of modern industrial states required administrative continuity. They also realized that government employees sent to administer the colonies had only the limited time between elections to enrich themselves and were plundering the colonies and alienating them from the empire.

The result was a system of exams that allowed people to enter the public service because of WHAT rather than WHO they knew. And this led to the concept of civil servants as employees of the state, with a degree of permanency conditional only on good behaviour.

"Cynics may argue this gives them more time to debauch the economy," the premier said, "but an honest appraisal would favour our current system. Even then it is not all that firmly rooted and only a generation ago, particularly at the municipal level, lusting for the blood of public employees was still endemic. I suggest that sentiment is latent and it would be both irresponsible and atavistic to act in a way that could loose that beast again."

While I appreciated the lecture, the information was not new. And I still believed that a few publicized firings could have a salutary effect, like the British Navy executing an admiral on his own quarter-deck "to encourage the others".

The premier did not consider that a good idea. "Civil servants are employed for their technical qualifications and if we wish to encourage them to advise us, they must be protected against arbitrary dismissal."

Moreover, he reminded me that if we had too many employees doing too little, it was our fault, not theirs. "It is a demonstrated fact of industrial and bureaucratic life," he said, "that inefficiencies result primarily not from the way employees do their work, but from the way their work is organized for them. In your position you are expected to be more far-sighted than those who have never experienced seeing government from the inside."

"But it is precisely because of that experience that I state, to abuse a famous phrase, that never in the history of organized society have so many paid so much for so little."

The premier was irked. "If you perceive such problems, do something about it. But I say this with all the emphasis I can muster, THERE WILL BE NO POLITICAL FIRINGS. We came here to govern in the interests of a great enterprise, not to feast on bodies of defeated opponents. Remember, to perhaps misquote Burke slightly, 'Magnanimity in politics is often the truest wisdom and a great enterprise and little minds go ill together."

And then I knew why he was premier, and I was not.

We brought in new personnel by the hundreds, but there appeared to be little increase in the quality of competence. The problem seemed to be that the knowledge the bright, well-educated newcomers brought to their positions came primarily from university text books rather than from life. They were long on learning but short on experience.

One example of the triumph of theory over political sensibility was the major study produced for the Policies and Priorities Committee of Cabinet, 'Guidelines for the Seventies'. This proud production was a commendable summary of current situations, lucidly pointing to future directions and complete with analyses of their implications. However, parts of it read like a left-wing political manifesto; its authors seemed unaware that if one wants support for policy changes from a society already suspicious of the government, one should not begin by frightening its members, and it had to be carefully rewritten.[8]

The eager young people at PPCC were doing precisely what they were supposed to be doing, but I was of a different generation with whom measurable outcomes were required to exceed inputs, and with whom a superb academic education did not necessarily equate to practical intelligence. I was not alone.

One evening Frank Syms, Liquor Control Commission chairman (and formerly NDP president), rushed into the premier's home. "Ed, you've just got to hire

---

[8] The government determined to keep the document confidential until it was rewritten and ordered all copies locked up, but a week later excerpts were published in *The Winnipeg Tribune*.

this guy, perhaps for one of your cabinet committees." There followed a list of the person's awards and accomplishments, "and the best part is that he has a Ph.D."

The premier's hand crossed his face in frustration. "Oh, God save me from another Ph.D.". As a farm boy with several university degrees, he appreciated intellect, education and imagination, but in operating an activist government he also needed 'can do' men and women who dealt in tangibles.

Nor did these new people bring with them any perceptible increase in loyalty. Entree into PPCC, as the government's think tank, depended as much on having a party card as a Ph.D., but when the party organized a dinner to honour long-time Labour leader "Jimmy" James and raise funds for the party, very few tickets were purchased by committee personnel.[9]

Among those we inherited, we found there is such a thing as a professional civil service, and that lapses were on an individual rather than a collective basis, even among the "relics".

The most notable "relic" was Derek Bedson, whose presence many considered an insult to the new era ostensibly ushered in by the election of the NDP, and a lip-curling reminder of the premier's essentially conservative approach to management of government.

Bedson was a true Manitoban, descendant of a Hudson's Bay Company factor, grandson of a member of the Wolseley Expedition sent to expel Riel, and son of a World War I regimental commander. He served in World War II and then studied at Oxford, where he became a history aficionado, which allowed him, in conversation, to sweep across the centuries like a television montage. He was so well known as a mind at large that Professor George Grant dedicated his epochal *Lament for a Nation*[10] to him. He worked in External Affairs, serving a term in New York with the Canadian mission to the United Nations. He served as executive assistant to national Conservative opposition leader George Drew and to Prime Minister John Diefenbaker.

When Duff Roblin became premier in 1958, Bedson was recalled to Manitoba and appointed clerk (which he pronounced "clark", in the English way) of the Executive Council. For twenty-two years, through four governments, he was an authentic Manitoba mandarin at the apex of the provincial bureaucracy, providing historical perspective and practical experience to premiers, and being their contact with the bureaucracy. Unknown to most, he had an acute mind, a lively wit and a droll sense of humour, but his austere, arrogant, forbidding appearance and impatient, terse, dismissive manner caused him to be known to the bureaucracy as "The Ogre".

His sudden apparition-like appearance in the office of a junior civil servant, and the sound of his voice, half sigh and half whine, as though attempting to

---

[9] It did not commend them to the next government. Premier Sterling Lyon declared the committee, which had mushroomed to about ninety, redundant and all staff was dismissed.

[10] George Grant, *Lament For a Nation: The Defeat of Canadian Nationalism*, Toronto, McClelland and Stewart, 1965.

control his contempt, caused palpitations that rattled the walls.

The function in government of this once-powerful super bureaucrat and confidante of heads of state seemed to have been reduced to little more than protocol officer. It was somewhat pathetic to see the tall, lean, slightly stooping, clearly balding, visibly aging, obviously cerebral, Micawber-like figure, scurrying around in dark jacket and striped gray trousers during swearing-in ceremonies, carrying the Bible from NDP minister to NDP minister against whose appointment his very being, as a Conservative and monarchist, must have cried out.

I considered his retention a classic sinecure, but the premier made his position clear when I broached the matter. "Derek is here because I want him here. You, as a student of history, should be among the first to appreciate that neither our public image nor our policy objectives will be damaged by maintaining some semblance of continuity and stability."

So he continued to occupy his dark, forbidding lair, papered with the huge portrait of his putative ancestor, the luckless King Charles I whom Cromwell's regicides had shortened by a head, while recording and processing minutes of cabinet meetings.

I, too, attended cabinet meetings, every Wednesday morning, sitting at the small table directly behind the premier's chair, assiduously answering mail while carefully listening for nuances in the discussions. This was less to note the decisions, which were recorded, than the reasons for them. Across the table from me sat Derek, doodling, reading French novels, and periodically sighing audibly as though pained by the thought of the "socialist hordes" having stormed through the gates of the citadel, certain that investors would leave and welfare bums would stay, fearful the province would disappear in a puff of opium smoke, and feeling betrayed by the fate the electorate had perversely visited upon him. When the thump of the premier's gavel announced the ministers at the great oak table had reached a decision, he would make a brief notation.

One day Cherniack called me to his chair and asked me to fetch a document from his office. When I returned, the matter under discussion when I left had been resolved and the ministers were on to another subject. I walked around the table and whispered, "Derek, what was the disposition of the previous item?" He turned slightly, glared at me and grunted sharply, "I don't know. And I don't care. And I am not going to tell you. Go and sit down."

I was too stunned to respond, so returned to my chair. But when the meeting ended about twenty minutes later, the bile had worked its way through my corpus. The ministers departed quickly while Derek collected papers. I walked over to him. "Derek. I could wait until my ire is under control but I won't. I attend cabinet meetings at the invitation of the premier and the ministers, not by your sufferance. I am here because I answer the letters and phone calls to the Premier's Office and I need to hear the ministers' discussions so that I can more adequately explain the reasons for policy decisions. Today I was absent briefly to do an errand for Cherniack. The matter under discussion was of particular importance, so I asked you about its disposition."

Before he had time to answer, I continued, "I resent your response. From now on when I ask you a question I will expect a proper answer. If sitting here a few hours a week, doodling and reading porngraphy, is so stressful that you cannot act civilly, I suggest you ask the premier to be relieved of your position and find something to do which you can handle."

Bedson flinched as though physically struck. Two months later, he brought the invitation from the American State Department. I saw it as a peace offering. I had my revenge.

ON MARCH 31, 1973, I arrived in Washington, the nexus of the political universe, a symphony of colourful shubbery and white marble. For five days, I inhaled the fragrance of Japanese cherry blossoms, revelled in the grandeur of the city, toured the Oval Office and visited the memorial to Jefferson, surrounded by his declaration,[11] which had launched a new nation and changed the history of the world. I stood serenely gazing across the tidal basin, and I marvelled at the seated, brooding, lifelike Lincoln in his columned replica of a Greek temple, his inspired words at Gettysburg chiselled into the Carrara marble walls of his shrine. I observed the long reflecting pool stretching to the dark, austere 500-foot obelisk that dominates the Washington skyline and commemorates the first president of the United States of America.

I walked reverently across General Robert E. Lee's old plantation, now the Arlington National Cemetery and the final resting place of some 360,000 of America's heroic dead, and felt an involuntary constriction in my throat while standing by the eternal flame over the grave of President John F. Kennedy, "The pillar of a people's hope; The centre of a world's desire."

I gazed with wonder across the historic Potomac River at the edifice of Watergate, which a "fourth-rate burglary" was elevating into a generic term that generated a constitutional crisis and humbled a president. I listened, enraptured, while my taxi driver lived up to the reputation of his profession by explaining in fine detail that Nixon was "finito". The only question, he emphasized, was whether he would be expunged by his nemesis, the Democrats, who despised him but were mindful of the political consequences of regicide, or by his friends, the Republicans he had led to the greatest electoral triumph in the country's history, winning every state but one, but to whom he had become an unbearable liability.[12]

We toured the halls of Congress and attended a session of the Senate, where

---

[11] "We hold these truths to be self-evident: that all men are created equal; that they are endowed by their Creator with certain inalienable rights; that among these are life, liberty and the pursuit of happiness; that to secure these rights governments are instituted among men."

[12] Four months later, Nixon resigned under threat of impeachment, proving the vaunted omniscience of taxi drivers.

Senator Mark Hatfield told us their tax system was so riddled with loopholes that $87 million annually remained unpaid. A Finance Department bureaucrat explained that nineteenth-century Britain had no deficits because they had no statisticians. And Washington's black mayor informed us the flight of whites to suburbia had left some of the city's schools ninety per cent black.

I experienced the snub of a black girl (Washington's population was then more than thirty per cent black) at a drug store counter. When I asked for a film for my camera she stared through me, unblinkingly, chin in hand and elbow on counter, ignoring me until I took the subtle hint and left. And I endured the scorn of another, my seat mate on a bus, stunningly attractive in red shift and ferocious "Mrs. Eldridge Cleaver" Afro hairdo. When I attempted a conversation by remarking on the unseasonably hot weather, she glared at me and gave me a lesson in the "new" race relations by snarling, "Don't you dare patronize me with small talk." For the rest of the ride she stared straight ahead, defiantly masticating a great wad of gum while, on her lap, a copy of *The Negro American* lay unopened. Clearly, blacks intent on revenge for centuries of abuse did not differentiate between white tormentors and liberal whites.

I spent long, pleasant sessions with my fellow travellers, one each from Québec, Ontario and British Columbia, touring the city, asking endless questions of congressmen and members of the diplomatic corps, feasting on street vendor hot dogs. And I almost ignited an international incident with an impromptu but fierce nose-to-nose tiff with a member of the State Department.

They laid on a fine dinner for us at the Brookings Institute. There were twenty men around the table and we were enjoying each other's company. I had just picked up my knife and fork when the man across the table addressed me in a peremptory tone, "We don't like the way you people are continuing trade and diplomatic relations with Cuba. We consider it an insult to us."

The adrenalin surged. I laid down my utensils. My voice rose. "Listen! When I left Canada it was a sovereign country and I suspect it still is. We live on the same continent, we speak the same language, we cross each other's border more than any other people, and usually we end up on the same side of international issues. One would think then, that if you want us to go along with you on this one, you would ask us instead of telling us."

There was silence around the table. Slowly we continued our meal, but the conversation had lost its flavour.

Then we departed. On the way home we would visit the capital of Michigan. Flying from Chicago to Lansing, we were caught in a cyclone that killed nineteen persons in the Windsor-Detroit area and swept south to demolish several small towns. Our plane was tossed about like a piece of paper caught in an up draft, buffeted so violently that luggage kept falling from the overhead racks, while outside it was made day-bright by non-stop lightning and torrents of rain seemed about to drown the plane. The flight attendants, ghost white with fright, one frantically fingering her rosary and audibly mumbling a prayer, buckled themselves into seats. It was terrifying testimony to the vulnerability of man in this sophisticated, technological age. It was not reassuring ...

As the oldest of our little group, and having been instructed by my father that leaders must not show fear in front of their troops, I attempted to maintain a silly, somewhat incoherent banter, while realizing it was less to comfort my companions than to cover my own terror.

Life had been good ... could it really end like this? Was it really possible that I should die in such a prosaic and wasted way? Just a grease spot splashed on the rain-soaked earth, without the opportunity to face the Red Slayer, without my spear broken on the dragon's armour, without family to wish me well on my journey to that bourne from which no traveller returns.

Ah, but we were not dead yet, the plane seemed to be weathering the storm, and the pilot was a pro. Then he voice of the pilot, dripping with shattered confidence, came over the intercom: "We-e-e-e-l-l, if no-o-thing goes wro-o-ong, we should be la-a-nding in about ... ten ... minutes. His tone made it clear he could just about guarantee something would, indeed, go terribly wrong.

And oddly, the voice sounded peculiarly like the half-sigh, half-whine of Derek Bedson. He was having his revenge.

XXIV

De Profundis

Damned in the midst of Paradise.
> —Herman Melville, *Moby Dick*

Life was good. I felt a bit guilty for not being at the office, despite the fact it was a Saturday, but having decided I would not go, the rationalizations came easily. It was January 4, 1975 and the work would be piled up and I recalled the sign my secretary had hung on my wall: *If it was not for the last minute panic, nothing would ever get done here.*

But I knew my capacity for work, and it would still be there on Monday. Like the work of the proverbial housewife, my work at the office would never be completed in any case. At times I felt like Sisyphus perpetually pushing that damned rock up the hill only to have it roll down again as another batch of files was deposited on my desk. It was a twenty-five-hour-a-day job, and not always fun. But it was feverishly exciting, and it was probably as near to Heaven as I would get.

Besides it was too nice a day to go to work, as attested to by the sun's rays streaming through the living room window, playing with the suspended dust particles in the room, and reflecting off the expanse of virginal snow spread in delicate patterns across our large back yard in a desirable part of the city. The sun was bright but the day was very cold so I put on my parka, the indestructible old Army-green one, heavy as a dead priest, but warm. I warmed up our 1968 Chrysler New Yorker, two-toned green with the black vinyl roof and all the bells and whistles and 383 horses under the hood, a mastodon of the highway, which had taken my family so many interesting and enjoyable miles across the vast expanses of North America, often off the main highways, because both my wife and I believed "a bend in the road is as good as a rest". I eased the car into reverse through the crunchy snow out onto the street. No. 1 Highway past our back yard was clear and the snow shading into the shadows under the trees made it appear, "The woods are lovely, dark and deep." [1]

But I had "promises to keep". My wife had asked me to get some groceries at Safeway, just a couple of blocks away. I would also get some supplies at the Canadian Tire store next to it. All was well. The huge engine purred as though preparing for a race, my hand rested lightly on the steering wheel, the diamond brilliance of sun on snow inspired thoughts of how far I had come since ...

ROMANIA ... well, it was Romania when I was born there, but it had been part of the giant Russian Empire when my parents were born there and part of the Ottoman Empire until 1812. This was a decade before my ancestors had followed the stream of Germans who had accepted the invitation of Catherine the Great to bring their Teutonic energies and advanced farming practices to the outreaches of her vast and growing domain. These adventurous and adaptable people, drawn by the ancient call of free land for the peasant, had sunk their roots into communities with German names that stretched like a giant string of beads—"Islands in the Steppe", in Al Reimer's graphic phrase [2]—over a thousand miles from the eastern limits of the ramshackle Austrian Empire to the Volga, Ukraine, and the productive northern slope of the Black Sea to become the legendary Schwartzmerdeutche.

My own forebears, Prussian Lutherans, had come to the province of Bessarabia from which the Russian Army had expelled the Turks, and their tiny settlement later became incorporated as the nillage of Friedenstal. It was seventy-five miles north of Odessa and partway between the Pruth River to the west, which formed the border with Romania, and the Dneister to the east which formed the border with the Ukraine. Local place names evoked images of Arabian Nights and fables of Byzantium, and it was adjacent to Transylvania, the home of the legendary Vlad the Impaler, the prototype for Dracula, a name long invoked to frighten nubile young maidens into remaining at home on inviting summer evenings.

The German farmers mixed their labour with the rich black alluvial soil of the area and prospered. This was prairie with few trees, so they erected buildings of stone and painted them with gleaming whitewash. They erected low stone walls on both sides of the long street that led through the village and built schools, hospitals, sanatoria, municipal buildings, and an elegant church that became the pride of the village and a tourist attraction. They established a credit union, an insurance cooperative, a cooperative store, and a cooperative creamery to make butter and cheese to sell to neighbouring towns as a cash crop. They developed herds of

---

[1]   Robert Frost, "Walking in the Woods on a Snowy Evening".
[2]   *My Harp is Turned to Mourning.*

cows, sheep, goats, hogs, flocks of poultry, and bred heavy draught horses to pull their plows and light Arabian horses for riding or pulling their spring-mounted carriages. They grew cereal crops and their gardens produced all the vegetables hungry, hardworking people needed.

The seasons were long so they produced fruits including grapes, from which they made wine which they drank like water. Over a period of five generations they had created a secular paradise.

But my father was uneasy. In 1917, at the collapse of the Russian Army, Romania had seized Bessarabia, so my father had done his compulsory military service as a sergeant in the Romanian cavalry, where he observed recruits reduced to eating their breakfast of corn kernels they picked out of their horse's manure and he concluded in the event of war these soldiers would shoot their officers and go home. He was one of the very few who had graduated from high school and had learned to read widely and knew of the Soviet Union's purge of the Kulaks who were killed on the spot or transported to Siberia. And he believed the U.S.S.R. would come to recover Bessarabia as soon as it had rebuilt its military strength and the German farmers would be seen as kulaks.

He was frustrated with the form of land holding that required spending many hours on wagons driving from one small field to another, and he wanted a large farm where modern machinery could be used efficiently and with his homestead in the middle so he could look around and survey his crops and herds.

He was an only son who would have inherited a substantial estate, but his thoughts were elsewhere. At twenty-three he acquired his own farm, at twenty-five he built a straw-cutting machine and hired men to do custom work, so he had only to drive around in his car (one of the few) and collect the fees. At twenty-six he was the youngest person ever elected to the village council, and a gentleman farmer. In the spring of 1930, when he was twenty-eight and I was three, he decided to go "Away from Europe, from her blasted hopes, Her fields of carnage and polluted air."[3]

My parents settled in west central Manitoba and made a payment on a quarter-section farm with a fine house set in a grove of trees, bought six cows for $60 each, and a Fordson tractor for $200. By the following spring, the Depression had reduced the value of the cows to $6 each and the tractor was traded for $25 worth of seed wheat. They could not make further payments on the farm since the Romanian government had prohibited the export of investments, and the $1,000 they had brought with them was spent. They were strangers in a strange land, and they were broke. The bright images of Canada as "a land of milk and honey" had turned to black. The man who had been financially independent and a political power in the community a year earlier, was reduced to farming with four wind-blown horses and a two-bottom plow, earning grocery money by doing casual labour for neighbors. They rented a half-section, four miles away, which had been

---

[3] J.M. Keynes, *The Carthaginian Peace*, 1919.

abandoned by another bankrupt farmer. It had a two-storey clapboard house that had not been painted in twenty years, sat on the bald prairie without a tree near it, and was so cold that we feared the only inhabitants that would survive the winter were the bed bugs. But it had a large barn which we slowly filled with cows, hogs and horses. During the Depression currency virtually went out of existence, so my father traded custom work for wild range broncos a neighbour had imported from Alberta. My father believed anyone over six years of age should contribute to the family income and by age eight, I was driving a six-horse outfit hitched to a cultivator and saddle breaking the broncos that threw me in great arcs, breaking my arm and nearly breaking my back.

When I was ten, we acquired a half-section of treed land that had to be grubbed out one tree at a time. The work was almost beyond endurance, but it was the only way to clear the land and when it was cleared, it was productive and a farm enterprise was slowly built. Then, at age thirteen, a few days after graduating from Grade 8, I was caught in a fire, spent fourteen months in a series of hospitals and was twice given up for dead. But I had survived.

It might not have been so had we remained in Europe. My father had warned anyone prepared to listen, "I smell gunpowder, we live in an incendiary part of the world, one day the Russians will come to take back Bessarabia," and the difficulties he had predicted had come to pass. In July 1940, just as I was lying in the hospital passing in and out of delirium from the pain of the burns, the Soviet Union repossessed Bessarabia. Pursuant to the Hitler-Stalin Pact of August 1939, the ethnic Germans in Bessarabia were allowed to leave, but they lost their property. Five generations of striving was reduced to the seventy-pound packs they carried aboard the ships that took them westward to be resettled in Poland. There, near the end of the war, they were caught between Polish partisans and the Red Army and were killed on the spot or transported to the Gulags.

The years 1930 to 1946 had been difficult as we grubbed a living out of the wilderness, but we were the lucky ones. My parents had not wanted to go to Canada alone and had pleaded with relatives, particularly my mother's three sisters and their husbands, who were excellent farmers and esteemed persons, to accompany them. But they did not see the same dangers and stayed where they were, and they were there ten years later when the Red Army came. By the end of 1946, four were dead as a result of the war and the other two remained in Soviet labour camps until 1955. Among the 2,130 persons who vacated Friedenstal in 1940, the toll in lives during the war and its immediate aftermath was twenty-five per cent. As my parents prepared Care packages to send to the relatives that were left, the tears that glistened in their eyes testified to the fact that they were profoundly grateful to whatever Fates had moved them to leave their ancestral home and come to Canada.

Here they had slowly rebuilt the paradise they had lost. And fifty years after we came to Canada I said to my father, half in jest: "Life is wonderful. Here you are, one of those legendary sheepskin-clad peasants from Eastern Europe who came with nothing but what you could carry on your back, but your daughter is the first lady of Canada and living at Rideau Hall as the wife of the governor general, a man who is also the offspring of German transplants from Eastern Europe. Now isn't life wonderful?"

He gazed into the distance and his eyes misted slightly and he shook his head slowly and said: "No, it is not life that did this. It's this wonderful country. This could not have happened anywhere else."

Meanwhile, the fire that left me with third-degree burns and a crippled arm had a salutary effect. Most farm boys did not get beyond Grade 8, but since my body was damaged, I attended high school and then studied Agriculture at the University of Manitoba. In 1949, at twenty-three, I married a local school teacher and we took over the family farm while my parents moved into town. Within a year we were deeply involved in farm organization activities through the Manitoba Farmer's Union, founded by my father, and in politics through the Cooperative Commonwealth Federation. In the next twelve years we operated a productive farm and I became a recognized spokesman for the farm community.

In 1962, we sold our farm and moved to Winnipeg. For eight years I worked in partnership with my father in a company established to build apartment blocks, while simultaneously earning a B.A., an M.A., and doing course work toward a Ph.D. I had been sitting at the kitchen table thinking about that work when Premier Schreyer phoned to request my assistance.

IF LOCKE WAS RIGHT that "no man's knowledge can go beyond his experience", I came to my government position knowledgeable. As a friend had said to me two decades earlier when we were fighting the Manitoba Federation of Agriculture, the Canadian Federation of Agriculture, the Manitoba Dairy and Poultry Cooperative, Manitoba Pool Elevators, United Grain Growers, the provincial and national Liberal parties, the provincial and national Conservative parties, and the Social Credit Party, "after this, whatever you may do will be easy". He was right. And my position as special assistant to the premier gave me opportunities to see the world from a different perspective and to do some of the things I believed needed doing. I soon developed my own niche and base of influence within both the government and the party and, while not in position to make government policies, I could influence them, and observe their development and results.

I had reached the zenith of my ambition. I was now the arbiter of disputes rather than a petitioner. I was in a position where I need not lose many arguments. People came and laid their problems at my door and it was good to know they had confidence in my ability and authority to help solve them. And sometimes I was able to do so and that induced an even better feeling. My position was relatively secure. I had come a long way from that powder keg of the Balkans to this country where I had achieved influence and where nothing could hurt me.

❂   ❂   ❂

I PURCHASED THE GROCERIES on the list my wife had given me, deposited them in the car, and then went into the Canadian Tire store. Only two blocks from my home, it was a familiar place because I regularly had my car serviced there. But I did not go shopping often. My wife forbade it. I had a tendency to browse when I got into a store, and a habit of buying things because of their appearance. My wife was not amused: "Why did you buy this? Its nothing we need now or in the foreseeable future. And if we should need it we know where to get it. You have a fatal attraction for things just because they are wrapped in attractive packages."

I was always apologetic and admitted the validity of her criticism. Then I found a way to mollify her: "Okay, that's true. But then, that's the way I got you."

So I was browsing, aimlessly, knowing there were several items I wanted but there was no rush. My trips to stores were so seldom that when they occurred I was always intrigued and wandered about looking at new products on the shelves, wondering what genius, or what happenstance, had caused them to be made.

I picked up a package of bicycle spokes for my twelve-year-old son who had ordered me to buy them on pain of being scalped (he was in his cowboys and Indians stage) so he could ready his bike to do wheelies in the spring. I picked up a roll of electrician's tape because it attracted my attention and was always handy to have. While examining some shelving that might fit into our daughter's room I laid down the package of bicycle spokes, and the tape, and had to return to retrieve them. I spotted some cross-country skis and remembered my wife had spoken of getting a pair and stopped to feel their varnished surfaces, but decided to leave them for another time and walked away and again laid down the spokes, and the tape, and had to return for them.

I picked up a gallon container of antifreeze for the car, but returned it to the shelf because I wanted to browse some more and did not want to carry it so would get it before leaving. I passed a shelf of variable sized bolts and nuts and suddenly remembered the nut holding the centre leg on our expandable dining-room table had been lost and the leg fell off whenever the table was moved. It needed a half-inch nut but with an unusual thread.

Idea! The attached vehicle centre where I often had my car serviced had all shapes and sizes and thread types lying around. They might have an old used one that fit. I would go there before leaving to see what they had.

Suddenly I saw them! For a year I had sought a set of cables with which to attach the stereo in the living room to speakers in the basement rec room. Now, here they were. I picked up the package. But the cables were only thirty-five feet long. I needed sixty. I would take two and splice them. I checked the price tag —$5.95 each—I would have paid four times that. There were four packages on the shelf. What if I should decide to install another speaker in the garage, or the workshop? What the hell, I would take them all.

But I wanted to go to the service shop for a nut and did not want to risk putting the precious cables back on the shelf and having someone else buy them, or worse, absent-mindedly laying them down and forgetting them.

"When you get Alzheimer's I won't know the difference," my wife had commented several times, triggered by the fact that she had asked me to get something —a bottle of milk on the way home, or taking some baking out of the oven when she went to shop for groceries—and I would forget.

"You remember when Caesar crossed the Rubicon and when Varus lost his Legions to Germanicus in the Teutoberg Forest and when the Vandals sacked Rome and when the Rosetta Stone was found and when Carter exhumed poor little dessicated King Tutankhamen and verbatim who said what during a particular political debate and poems you heard once on the radio and a dozen reasons the Manitoba government decided to do or not to do some particular thing and the detailed history of Manitoba's Crown Corporations since their inception, but you can't remember what you are to do today."

Indeed, my absent mindedness had become almost a scandal. "What's that red yarn around your face for?" a friend had asked me when we met on the main street of our home town.

I was driving into town from our farm and my wife had asked me to get something for her and I had said I would forget so she had written it on a piece of paper and slipped it into my shirt pocket. I had said I would forget to look in my pocket, so she had playfully tied some red yarn over my forehead and behind by ears and knotted it under my chin. Bouncing along in my truck over rutted roads and thinking about other things, I had forgotten the red yarn. As I walked along the street, I noticed glances in my direction and checked to see if my fly was open, but otherwise paid no attention until a friend asked why I the red yarn was tied around my face. I could not remember and had to phone home to ask my wife.

I could not risk mislaying the precious cables. So I put them, the spokes and the tape, in my parka pocket. I would pay when I came back from the service shop to get the antifreeze.

I walked to the far end of the store and through the door into the eight-by-eight foot cubicle and turned to go through another door that led into the vehicle service shop. A man stood there. "I want to talk to you!" he said.

I thought it was some petitioner who recognized me and wanted something from government or wanted to give me hell about something the government had done—or had not done—and it was a Saturday and I had decided long ago that despite working for government I was occasionally entitled to some personal think-time. And I had learned that when approached by someone who had a problem that had appeared spontaneously upon catching sight of me, if I made some excuse about being busy for a moment and returned later the petitioner had often already solved his problem. "Would you excuse me for a moment," I said. "I want to go into the service shop briefly and we can discuss it when I return."

"No! I want to talk to you now."

"All right. What's the problem?"

"Do you have some merchandise in your pocket?"

"As a matter of fact I have, but what's that to you?"

"I'm the store manager. You are walking out with unpaid goods."

The adrenalin pumped. My body became suddenly warm. The neurons of my brain furiously shot impulses back and forth. Of course! I had passed many times through this door when I came from the service shop to pay my bill. To me it was the same store.[4] But from the cubicle there was one door into the service shop and another out to the parking lot. Yes! It could be suspected that I was attempting to walk out.

"Well, let me explain ...

"No! Follow us."

I suddenly noticed a second man stood at the door leading outside, and a third man stood behind me. The three men escorted me through the length of the store and up the stairs to the manager's office on the mezzanine.

"What do you have in your pockets?" The store manager snarled.

I took the cables, the tape and the spokes out of my parka pocket and placed them on his desk.

"Got anything else?"

"Here's my damn parka. Look and see for yourself."

The store manager phoned the police. The three men stood and glared at me and I glared back, wordlessly, for about ten minutes until the police arrived. Two burly parka-clad officers took the manager's written statement. They examined my wallet, with $143 dollars in cash. "Come with us."

The two officers, one in front and the other behind, escorted me through the store. Everyone seemed to be staring accusingly at me. I got into the rear seat of the police cruiser. They drove across the highway, down a side road, and parked. "You have the right to call a lawyer. You do not need to give a statement now, but you can if you want to."

"I don't need a lawyer and I want to make a statement."

I explained my meanderings through the store, why I was going through the door to the car service shop, and concluded, "I guess it was stupid of me putting those goods in my pocket."

They wrote down what I said and their polite questions showed sympathy. They drove me back to the Canadian Tire parking lot and I stepped out of their car. They handed me a piece of paper, smiled and waved a friendly goodbye as they drove away. They were real gentlemen. I read the document. They had charged me with shop lifting!

The police charge had raised questions. Should I resign? But that would imply admission of guilt. Should I get a lawyer? But our political tormentors

---

[4] After this incident, Canadian Tire put up a large sign: NO UNPAID GOODS PAST THIS POINT, separating the hardware store from the vehicle service shop.

would whisper that the premier or Attorney General Howard Pawley were pulling strings. Should I tell my family? But the court date was only ten days away and there would be nothing in the media unless I was convicted, so until then it was enough that I knew.

As commanded by the police document, on the appointed day I went to the Public Safety Building and attended the police lab where they took my mug shot, full-face and profile, and moved my fingers and thumb, one by one, from ink-blot to paper. Then I entered the courtroom and sat, like Sampson, "eyeless in Gaza, at the mill with slaves", among a night's sweep of drug pushers, pick-pockets, petty thieves, hookers, pimps, and a would-be murderer. The last of these was a slender, handsome, blond boy in his late teens who confessed in a clear voice that he had stabbed another man, and while his tearful mother screamed repeatedly, "No! No! He didn't do it," the boy muttered to his companion, "I should have killed the son-of-a-bitch."

Three hours later, I walked my melancholy Via Dolorossa to where the bailiff stood. The judge asked how I would plead: "Not Guilty." My voice cracked into falsetto and I had to repeat myself twice before being understood.

The judge was sympathetic: "You are in the wrong court."

The trial was booked for Queen's Bench on June 13th. It meant five months of mental agony, reading my guilt in every passing eye. Hope of avoiding publicity until the trial date was ended a month later by the bold headline: "Premier's Assistant Arrested".[5]

When the dread day came, I left my resignation, "To be opened if I am convicted" on the premier's desk and crossed the street. This time I lacked the courage to go alone. My lawyer questioned my accusers and then asked for my statement. "I went to the store to get bicycle spokes. I also got some electrician's tape. I found some television extension cables I had wanted for some time. I did not want to lose them, so I put them in my pocket. I was going to the auto service centre to see if I could get a nut for a bolt and then come back to get some antifreeze. Had I not been interrupted I would have ended up at the check-out counter with the roll of tape, the bicycle spokes, the electrical cables, a gallon of antifreeze and a used nut."

Judge John Enns was kind. "Technically, moving articles from one shelf to another can be construed as theft. I give the accused the benefit of doubt."[6]

---

[5]   *Winnipeg Free Press*, February 8, 1975.

[6]   Criticism came quickly from several quarters, including Gerald A.V. Hart, the bane of governments for refusing to pay income taxes. He wrote (with copies to the media) "How will [you] squirm out of this typical n.d.pee debacle? I suggest Schreyer create the Dept. of Ali Baba & 30 thugs. Schultz could be Chief Thief, which would be most fitting with his peculiar propensities."

XXV

Never Judge a Book by its Movie

What has happened to the crusading spirit of the Schreyer administration that took Manitoba by storm in 1969?
—Egon Frech[1]

Being government imposes responsibilities. The crusading was succeeded by the need for administration, exuberance by reality, the careless rapture of 1969 by the realization of the limits of power. Yet those fearing that the fire-in-the-belly of those who had stormed the Shining City on the Hill was reduced to embers would have been surprised at the hectic activities inside government.

A post-election cabinet shuffle rested on experience—and caution. Saul "The Fixer" Miller was appointed to Urban Affairs. Ben Hanuschak went to Colleges and University Affairs and kept Education. Howard Pawley replaced defeated Al Mackling as Attorney General and retained Municipal Affairs. Ever-smiling, thirty-one-year-old turkey farmer and ex-RCMP officer Billie Uruski, seasoned as legislative assistant to the premier, became minister for MPIC. Steady Ian Turnbull, after four years as legislative assistant to the minister of Industry, government representative on the MTS board, and chairman of the Standing Committee on Public Utilities, became minister of Consumer Affairs.

The 1973 election brought the government caucus new faces. They were ex-paratrooper-cum-miner Ken Dillen (replacing Borowski), ex-union official Harvey Patterson (replacing Gonick), Les Osland, ex-naval officer from Churchill, and soft-spoken Harvey Bostrom (replacing Allard). Bostrom, raised in a remote northern community, winner of prizes and scholarships while earning his M.A. in Economics, at eighteen the youngest high school teacher in Manitoba, became, at twenty-eight, minister of Cooperative Development.

---

[1] Columnist Egon Frech, *Winnipeg Free Press*, September 29, 1973

But outward appearances that nothing dramatic was happening inside government did not mean nothing was happening inside government—at least not for those inside government.

Adequate salaries for legislators, who hold the destiny of the nation in their hands, was a tenet of social democratic parties. It was more than money; they believed laws reflect the values of those who make them. England, the source of Canada's political system, did not pay its members of Parliament from 1649 to 1901. It was argued that salaries would corrupt them. The result was the ascendancy of the neo-feudal landed aristocracy, who could afford a job with no pay, and the corruption of the laws to serve their interests. This changed when Labour members appeared and argued that if the public wanted laws to benefit all, legislators must be paid by all. But how much? British Columbia Premier David Barrett doubled member's salaries to $24,000 by calling two sessions of the legislature annually.[2] He explained, "Politics is too important to be left to part-time politicians," and added that low salaries keep out middle-income workers and businessmen who do not want to leave their jobs in their best earning years, which leaves law-making to the very rich or the very poor. It was a logical argument, but in only three and a half years Barrett was swept out of office.

In Manitoba, the eager beavers of 1969, regardless of party, found the aphorism that politicians are "oversexed, under-worked and overpaid" was not true—at least not the last two items. In 1972, the salary of MLAs was $9,600 ($15,000 more for ministers) leaving them the lowest paid in Canada, apart from P.E.I. Some needed two homes; inflation was grinding them down and costs were rising but income was fixed. Some had left professions and both income and careers were passing them by.[3]

But it is difficult to increase one's own salary when the taxpayers are watching and MLAs held their breath whenever the subject was raised. Opposition MLAs also wanted increases and would vote for them, but the government must enact them. Nevertheless, the practical consideration of low pay robbing the legislature of good people had to be faced. In 1975, a delicately balanced formula was created; salaries were set at $14,000 and future increases tied to the cost-of-living index. The principle of better pay was served, and future salaries held to that of the populace.[4]

Day care had become a timely idea. A social revolution had occurred. Most Canadians no longer lived in rural areas amid extended families and

---

[2] Premier Schreyer was such a penny pincher that when he did call a second session, he paid only a half-indemnity.

[3] Only three of the eight teachers in caucus were able to re-enter their profession. As someone has stated, those who go into politics as a business have no business in politics.

[4] In the mid-1990s, the Filmon government rid itself of this responsibility by appointing an independent commission to set salaries. As of April 2005, the basic salary of MLAs was $67,173, third-lowest in Canada. Nova Scotia and P.E.I paid less.

women graduating en masse from universities were seeking jobs worthy of their talents and education. But who would take care of the children? And it was more than a personal issue. Did it make sense for a society to provide eighty per cent of the tuition costs of young women and then deprive the economy of their knowledge by sending them back to *"Küche, Kirche und Kinder"*? And since the fecundity of women appeared to decrease inversely to the increase in their education and income, if a wealthy society wants to maintain its population must it not give women incentives to bear children?

The government was caught between those who argued that day care was an instrument to force one-earner families to pay the child rearing costs of two-earner families, and the women's movement, armed with the 1970 *Report of the Royal Commission on the Status of Women,* which showed that women were going to work outside the home in droves and therefore day care was a legitimate social expense. But there were questions. Should day care centres be public or private? If day care was subsidized, what of those who pay taxes but forego a second income to raise their own children? If women rented out their children, were they really better off after paying for child care?[5] Where formerly neighbours took care of each other's children, now both the working mother and child-care worker would appear on the employment roll and would demand that the government create new jobs for them if one, or both, lost theirs, so would day care merely distort the economy? And how would day care effect children[6] and the family?[7]

Despite these concerns, the government proceeded apace. In 1974, our day-care budget was $500,000 for 375 spaces in twelve centres. Three years later, it was $4.5 million for 5,000 spaces in 165 centres[8] and cost became an issue. Day care could be visualized as blossoming into a parallel education system with its own free standing facilities, professional staff, government department, claim to independent funding, and status as a job creator.

During the 1977 election campaign, the Election Planning Committee discussed how to manage the costs of day care. EPC member Sidney Green, mentally wrestling with how to proceed with this multi-faceted program without creating another expensive black hole, and speaking tentatively, posed a question. "When I was young, whether at home or school or camp, the older children took care of the younger ones. Instead of costly free-standing facilities, could we not establish day care in schools, which already exist and are being paid for. Instead of hiring a new tier of day care workers, could we not have professional supervision but have

---

[5] Years later, *The Globe and Mail* editorialized, "Couples need two incomes to pay for child care, so that one spouse is free to work to earn enough to pay for child care." April 3, 1995.

[6] In 1986, an American was paid almost $200,000 to research whether children like their own mothers best. He concluded that they do.

[7] "Women were 27% of the work force in 1961 and 45% in 1991; the divorce rate went from 55 per 100,000 population in 1961 to 278 in 1992; the birth rate dropped from 116 per 1,000 women in 1959 to 55 in 1994; the average age of women having a first child rose from 23 in 1961 to 27 in 1990." *The Globe and Mail*, August 11, 1995

[8] In 2003-04, the day care budget was more than $65 million.

older school children trained to look after those dropped off by their mothers on the way to work?"

The question was answered, quickly and firmly, by the labour member of the EPC, a senior official with CUPE, "No! We don't want that. Our people want those jobs."

THE PROPOSAL FOR TREASURY BRANCHES, provincially registered quasi-banks, flowed from the government's desire to establish a publicly owned financial institution to enlarge the measure of democracy through increased public participation in investment. They also wanted to bring investment decisions closer to home, to stop the haemorrhage of an estimated $300 million annually from Manitoba (as Autopac had shown could be done), to give the chartered banks real competition, and to curtail the tendency of banks to take the easy money and run. *The Winnipeg Tribune* agreed. "Premier Schreyer is correct in stating that private lending institutions have engaged in 'creaming' the profits from accounts that involve little work … The West has long been aware that the Eastern-based banks have little appetite for dealing in high-risk capital for Western-based business." [9]

Alberta, Ontario and North Dakota had publicly owned financial institutions, so our proposal should not have been seen as radical. But it was, and the primary objections came from credit unions. In 1971, the NDP government had enacted legislation to greatly expand the ambit of credit unions by permitting them, for the first time, to deal with municipalities, towns, cities and governments. But now it was a question of "what have you done for us lately?" as they rushed to protect their turf—and that of the banks.

The manager of the Morden Credit Union wrote to oppose treasury branches because the credit unions and the "existing financial institutions" were serving the people of Manitoba very well and "when you mention you will be offering loans, the first thought that comes to mind is the Manitoba Development Corporation and how efficient it has been."

It was the unkindest cut of all, and deserved a reply, "Your bank will be pleased that it has found a champion in you and that you and the bank do not feel the need for Treasury Branches. I remind you that forty years ago, banks saw no need for credit unions. You are correct in stating the MDC, started by the Roblin government in 1960, has not been a success. One of its disastrous accounts is with Morden Fine Foods. Please advise if you want the MDC to stop losing money in Morden."

But the treasury branch proposal was aborted. Most NDP members had an almost religious attachment to credit unions.

---

[9] March 11, 1975.

A PROGRAM WE DID PROCEED WITH was public property insurance. Unlike Autopac, this was voluntary. It was established because some schools and home owners could not get insurance from private companies because of fear of vandalism. I feared it would be another loser and advised the minister, Billie Uruski, to set the premiums so high that we could not sell any policies so we would not lose any money. I was wrong. It became so successful that it was one of the first programs terminated by the Lyon government.

New programs got two kinds of complaints: from those who saw them as too niggardly—to themselves, and from those who saw them too generous— to others. The Provincial Employment Program, giving grants for local improvements, induced a letter from a man who sarcastically observed that his town had not received a grant for an enclosed, heated hockey rink but others had, so it must have been a "political" decision. He was informed, "When I lived in a rural community and we needed a rink, we built one. I now live in Winnipeg and our son plays hockey at an open air rink while his mother and I stand on snowbanks to watch."

The Crime Victim's Compensation Act, based on the principle that government is obliged to keep its people safe or compensate them if it fails to do so, generated a spate of complaints. It was judged the most generous in Canada, but some beneficiaries wanted more, while taxpayers argued individuals should take private legal action against those who had injured them. [10]

Welfare, while not new, was an endless source of fierce and virulent complaints. It seemed everyone knew someone who knew someone who was cheating on welfare. One erudite protester quoted Tolstoi: "The more that is given the less people will work for themselves and the less they work the more their poverty increases." The NDP government agreed with that sentiment but knew the history of welfare from the Elizabethan Poor Laws to its application in a modern industrial economy, so our time was divided between explaining the concept of social assistance and devising carrots and a sticks to put welfare recipients to work.

The establishment of the Clean Environment Commission invited problems. People did not object in theory but it interfered with their way of doing things. Two commission employees went to check on reports of a water problem in a creek running through a small town in eastern Manitoba. They found that a farmer had built a corral from his stable to the creek so his cattle could drink at will. In winter they defecated on the ice and dead animals were dragged there. In spring, like Hercules cleansing the Augean stables, the water swept away the winter's accumulation of feces and carcasses. People downriver got the taste in their water.

---

[10] Some programs had strange results. The NDP government proudly enacted legal aid to give low-income people equal access to the protection of the law. Thirty years later, a group of Hell's Angels, charged with a menu of crimes, demanded to be released without trial because legal aid would not pay the high fees of the lawyers they claimed they were entitled to under the law.

The two eager young men explained to the elderly farmer that "The Law" no longer allowed this form of disposal. The farmer, a burly, overall clad, mackinaw -shirted product of the 1930s, who had worked very hard to achieve his estate, was proud of his labour-saving innovation and was not amused with city folk telling him how to run his business. He went into his house and returned with a shotgun: "I god it a bigger law. Ged oudda here!"

The Town of Churchill, shrinking into a ghost town, desperately wanted better services and the stability of a government payroll. So we built them an enclosed town centre large enough to house all its major services. The town council was properly grateful, at least briefly. Then it informed us it could not keep the complex open unless the government contributed $300,000 a year toward the heating costs. We protested, but we paid.

There was the perennial fight with the Canadian Pacific Railway over the Crowsnest Pass Rates. In 1896, the federal government had subsidized the cost of a line into coal-rich southern British Columbia on condition that the CPR haul grain from Western Canada at a fixed rate in perpetuity. "Perpetuity" ended when the CPR complained it was losing money on grain haulage. In 1976, a federal commission reported that despite subsidies of $55 million from Ottawa, the two railways (CPR and CNR) lost $87 million. The railway companies demanded permission to tear up the Crow Rates and many miles of branch rail lines. Elevator companies saw profits in closing elevators ten miles apart and building large inland terminals 100 miles apart. Some farmers and rural businessmen agreed; they believed if farmers were required to pay the full cost of exporting grain from the West, they would utilize it locally. That would re-create the failing hog, livestock and milling industries, diversifying and improving the farm economy.

The Schreyer government was anxious to diversify agriculture but saw farmers as losers in the above scenario. They believed farm diversification and maintenance of rural communities lay in keeping more young people on the farm, which would not be done by raising farm costs. They argued that the CPR had built the largest conglomerate in Canada—a huge, diversified empire including telecommunications, hotels, airlines, flour mills, real estate and petroleum, not to mention the railroad [11]—with profits taken out of the railway paid for by the taxpayers of Canada, and they resented the CPR escaping its obligations. Paying the full freight would quadruple costs and damage grain farmers in favour of a hog/livestock industry owned not by farmers but by processor controlled agribusiness.[12] Also, longer distances between elevators meant longer transport by truck on roads paid for by the provincial taxpayers instead of by rail, maintained by the railways. The NDP government saw the transfer of bulk freight from rail to

---

[11] By 2000, the CPR owned CP Ships, its eighty vessels making it the largest container carrier in the world; PanCanadian Petroleum, one of the largest producers and marketers of crude oil and natural gas; Fording Coal, which produced sixty per cent of Canada's coal, and Canadian Pacific Hotels, the largest luxury hotel operator in North America. *Winnipeg Free Press*, February 14, 2001.

[12] It happened precisely that way. See the chapter on The Hog Board.

road as economic insanity. The fight involved labour, railways, elevator companies, livestock feeders, millers, farmers, truckers and businessmen. We lost the fight.[13]

Agricultural Minister Sam Uskiw's messianic determination to diversify farming led us into a cul-de-sac. He encouraged two-score farmers in southern Manitoba to undertake a two-year experiment growing black beans. They grew well. As an incentive, he promised them eighteen cents per pound if they could not get more on the market. They could not. So Uskiw sold the beans to Cuba— analogous to selling ice to the Inuit—for 16.5 cents per pound.

"Professional" anti-communist Harry Enns attacked Uskiw in the Legislative Chamber, mockingly commending his "compassion" in providing food to the "hungry people of Cuba where many are in jail and there are no elections". Uskiw replied that, for twenty years, the survival of Canadian farmers had depended on selling millions of bushels of wheat to the Soviet Union and China "where people are hungry, many are in jail, and there are no elections". It was a brilliant retort, but the experiment cost Manitoba $153,000 and the taxpayers—and voters—were not amused.

In 1972, the bottom fell out of the feed grain market. Hog and beef feeders were delighted with the low price of feed. Feed producers attempted to compensate for low prices with more sales. When this threatened to bankrupt them, they appealed to Uskiw. He saw no benefits in feeding cheap grain to cheap cattle but did not want to establish another subsidy program, so he established the Feed Grain Marketing Commission, which set a floor price for feed grains. That infuriated hog producers and feedlot owners.

The following year, the private American grain companies oversold to the Soviet Union and grain prices shot up to the highest on record. About 150 hog producers and feedlot owners filled the visitor's gallery, shouting at Uskiw to bail them out or they would go home and get their guns. That led to the cow-calf loans, the beef stocker program, and the Beef Assurance Income Plan.

Defending the Canadian Wheat Board was a recurring task. It was established in 1935 when the Government of Canada concluded that the Western grain industry was too important to be left to the Winnipeg Grain Exchange. Hence, all commercially sold wheat, and later barley and oats, was sold through the board. It stabilized the market to the benefit of the rural community, but it seems that nothing of benefit to the general community can be allowed if it limits profit for a few. The board always had ideological enemies, but by 1970 a new generation of farmers seemed to believe their pocket calculator gave them more information than the board with its forty years of marketing experience, banks of computers, storehouses of information, established world market connections, history of capacity to deliver the world's best wheat when and where it was wanted, and

---

[13] Twenty years later, the railways won their long fight. They were relieved of the Crow Rates; grain freight rates quadrupled, a hog industry blossomed, largely controlled by agri-business, and many of the province's magnificent bodies of water, including Lake Winnipeg, rapidly became polluted by the waste of such concentrated livestock operations..

information on future market trends. So there was pressure to abolish the Canadian Wheat Board in favour of the "free market". But the NDP government believed the "free" market was controlled by a handful of multinational grain companies, and the Canadian farmer's only protection was collective marketing through the CWB. We attended many public meetings and made repeated representations to Ottawa to prevent what we saw as a disaster resulting in more demands for subsidies.

Dead animals encroached upon our time. Legislation required carcasses to be buried at least three feet deep, or disposed of at registered rendering plants. The minister for the Environment issued directives to that effect. That brought a letter from the owner of a rendering plant providing us with the names and addresses of a number of farmers "who chose not to take advantage of my dead stock removal service when informed of the $10 fee for farm pick up." Obviously dumping the carcasses into the nearest creek was cheaper. So those on the list needed to be hunted down.

Another massive encroachment on the government's time was the Garrison Diversion. Conceived by North Dakota as a combined flood control and irrigation project, it threatened to introduce foreign biota from the Missouri River System into Lake Winnipeg. Also, the return flow from the Souris River, which rises in Saskatchewan, loops through North Dakota, and returns into Manitoba, would bring salts, chemicals, pesticide residues, animal waste, plant nutrients and eroded soils to degrade the quality of the water used by thousands of Manitobans. I proposed a ditch, just north of the American border, to drain the south flow of the Souris into the return flow in Manitoba and deny the U.S. the Souris water, but that was considered too radical by half—and a violation of international law. We repeatedly petitioned the Government of Canada to persuade the Government of the United States to demand that the Government of North Dakota submit the issue to the International Joint Commission created by the Canada-U.S. Boundary Waters Treaty of 1909. Finally, in 1974, Washington informed Ottawa it "would comply with its obligation to Canada to not pollute water crossing the boundary to the injury of health of property in Canada." [14]

In February 1973, the Government of Manitoba received *The Report on Natural Resources in Manitoba*, [15] which stated:

> The ownership of land and resources belongs to the people collectively ... In 1968–70 the people of Manitoba received only 2.3 cents as pay for every dollar of resources produced [and] 14% of the net profit, while the operators received 85%. By turning over management of resources to the private sector, the Government of Manitoba has received only $15

---

[14]   In 2005, North Dakota's Devil's Lake project caused similar fears, but the George W. Bush administration was less cooperative.

[15]   Government of Manitoba, Queen's Printer, 1973.

million of the $192 million [earned by the private sector] in the last three
years ... I recommend that mining income above the normal profit be
taxed 100% ... that the property tax be high enough to force return of all
mineral reserves to the Crown within 10 years."

This heresy was not spewed by the ghost of Che Guevara, but by self-made
millionaire, former president of the Montreal Stock Exchange, former minister in
the Liberal government of Québec and former minister in the Trudeau government,
Eric Kierans.

Before 1969, the resource companies were the darlings of the Manitoba
Treasury. Mineral leases could be obtained for up to sixty-three years at less than
twenty cents per acre per year, development was not required, cheap electricity was
provided, and much infrastructure (roads, etc) was provided by the taxpayers.
In 1968, the people of Manitoba, the owners of the resources, received less from
royalties than they spent servicing the industry.

The NDP government doubled the royalties, required exploration spending
of at least four dollars per acre per year on leased land, and imposed a two-tier
tax regime—fifteen per cent on normal net profits and thirty-five per cent on windfall profits. Because mining companies are mobile and could threaten to leave
whenever changes were made in the high-subsidy, low-tax regime, the government
created a backup position by establishing the publicly owned Manitoba Mineral
Exploration Corporation. It would explore and develop on its own, and take a
minority position in new private development, sharing risks and profits or losses
based on equity.[16] Now, if mining companies did leave because of tax changes, or
were lured away by other jurisdictions,[17] we would know where the minerals are,
and we had the capacity and expertise to exploit them.

But there was one place the government would not go. Kierans had recommended confiscatory taxes and this found favour with elements in the party but
not with the government. Mines Minister Green explained that mining in Manitoba
was a $300-million-a-year industry, that steps had been taken to make the prov-
ince less dependent on the private sector, but that private operators had the right
to a fair return on their investment. Then the minister that the business community and the opposition parties feared as a fanatical Marxist itching to take over the
"means of production" told the NDP convention, "I will not expropriate private
property without compensation." However, the image of the NDP was fixed in the

---

[16] The MMEC became a qualified success, with interests in gold, nickel, copper and oil. In 1978, the Lyon
government "fulfilled an election promise" by abandoning joint ventures, returning to subsidizing the
private mining industry. In 1994, the Filmon government sold its share of "the jewel of the MMEC" at
Trout Lake to HBM&S. This gutted the MMEC, which had paid the province $16 million in dividends the
previous year.

[17] In 1974, G.A. Jewett, executive director of the mines division of the Government of Ontario, told the
annual convention of the Prospectors and Developers Association, "Mineral development will decline
rapidly unless governments provide financial assistance to mining companies." *Winnipeg Free Press*,
March 16, 1974.

mind of the business community and Green's statement succeeded only in alienating the left wing of the NDP.

Much time was spent just putting out brush fires. After Watergate every political story to which "gate" could be attached became an instantaneous scandal. So with "Wabodengate". The manager of a business at Waboden, in northern Manitoba, went to Opposition Leader Sidney Spivak with a charge of vote-buying, by means of loans by the Community Economic Development Fund to the business he was managing. Government denials were condemned as "deceit, lies, arrogance, cover-up and obstruction of justice"—all politically-loaded terms flowing from Watergate.

The incident was to involve a local radio station, the premier, the MDC, the management of the CEDF, a court receiver, the RCMP, Autopac, the License Suspension Appeal Board, the Canadian Radio and Televison Commission, the Canadian Pension Plan, the federal Department of Regional Economic Expansion, the Department of Revenue, the Unemployment Insurance Commission, the Provincial Employment Program, the Winter Warmth Home Program, several legal firms, the attorney general, and a threat on the life of Sidney Green. Five men from a radio station, with an armload of papers, visited the premier to demand investigation, but stated repeatedly "there is absolutely no evidence of vote-buying", leaving us wondering what we were supposed to investigate. Two CEDF directors demanded investigation of an expense account they had approved earlier, of a third member. Spivak demanded a "judicial inquiry" and an RCMP investigation. Green replied Manitoba would degenerate into a police state if the RCMP investigated every accusation made by the opposition. For a year charges reverberated and we expended much physical and psychic energy chasing shadows. The agony ended when the man who had ignited the fire by complaining to Spivak about vote-buying came to my office, broke into tears, apologized for causing us so much trouble, and explained his target had not been the government, but his boss.

PEOPLE CAME TO US with problems and we would virtually stand on our heads to assist them. A second group was the chronic bitchers who had got up on the wrong side of the floor in the morning, or had a bad hair day, or noticed the moon was full, so they called the Premier's Office, and they too were accepted as part of our job. And there was a third category. It was surprising how many people believe any demand for assistance or policy change must be preceded by insults, with "socialist" being the ultimate. They believe government must give them whatever they demand, and that an affirmative response is ensured by letters or phone calls rich with expletives and allegations about the intellect, integrity, morality and ancestry of politicians.

My replies were in kind. A letter from a marina owner invited such a reply:

Thank you for your letter, copies to the media, implying you are the only person who has ever worked for a living, that taxation, welfare and intervention in business began with election of the NDP and that members of this government are lazy, stupid parasites and lousy businessmen ... You write 'You have never worked, or mortgaged your homes, for your take-home pay because it has always been provided from public funds.'

In fact, those in the NDP caucus have worked as packing-house workers, coal miners, sailors, engineers, clergymen, undertakers, lawyers, school teachers, janitors, taxi drivers, residential builders, restaurant operators, policemen, farmers, loggers, railwaymen, social workers, storekeepers, electricians, merchants, miners, recreation camp directors, and high-riggers. The premier has worked on a farm, in a logging camp, in a machine shop, as a university teacher, and in a morgue. Twelve of the seventeen members of cabinet are university graduates, with up to four degrees.

All members of caucus managed to make a living before they came here, although I do not know if any ever sold a boat. Also, twelve of the thirty-one members of the government caucus are veterans of World War II. Do you really believe it fair to sneer at them?

A letter from southern Manitoba complained bitterly that the NDP government was killing "free enterprise", and then added "you have been in office five years and have done nothing to help the small farmer stop rip-offs in farm input costs". It was answered, "The system that permits such rip-offs is called 'free enterprise' ... We have introduced many programs to strengthen the buying and/or selling power of farmers and to reduce the market power of those ripping him off, but most of them have been denounced in your part of the province as interference with the free-enterprise system."

The proposal to require motorcyclists to wear helmets became a political flashpoint. A fierce letter from the Faculty of Science at the University of Manitoba, elicited the following reply:

You write that this legislation has probably been proposed 'by some self-righteous minister who knows nothing of the mechanics of a motorcycle nor the joy of operating it'. In fact, the minister has been a soldier, a farmer, a musician, a salesman, a hockey player, a machine repairman, a heavy machine operator, a union organizer, a director of the Manitoba Farmer's Union, minister of Tourism and Recreation, and is currently minister of Highways. He has driven cars, trucks, jeeps, construction equipment, tractors, bicycles—and motorcycles. While his other activities have left him little time for escapism on a motorbike—with or without a helmet —he is familiar with what you describe as 'the euphoria of driving with the glow of the sun and the flow of the wind on his face'.

Those who wrote to harangue about "NDP socialists" being "soft on crime", as evinced by light sentences, needed an education.

> Two centuries ago the English jurist, Blackstone, listed 160 capital crimes. Despite the savagery of the sentences, criminal activities, mostly against property, continued and the rulers responded by increasing the list so that by 1819 there were 220 actions, including stealing from a clothes-line, for which one could be executed. Marx wrote a famous essay about property having more rights than people, and juries refused to convict. The system had to change if it was to retain integrity … Today, in England, there is only one capital crime—the murder of a policeman on duty—and are there more or fewer crimes today?

Reduction of the voting age from twenty-one to eighteen drew a surprising flow of protests. I felt one, from a lady, needed a response. "When inducted into the Army at age 18, no one asked if I was mature enough to do what was expected of me … Incidentally, in Britain, before 1929, women were not considered intelligent enough to vote until they were 30."

Those accusing the "NDP socialists" of pawning off our wealth and resources to foreign racketeers, were sent a standard reply, "Since there is some disagreement over which government is responsible for the CFI [Churchill Forest Industries] Agreement, I enclose a copy of the Orders-In-Council of February 25, 1966, showing who signed it. Present were Roblin, Evans, Weir, McLean, Johnson, Carroll, Whitney, Hutton, Baizley, Smellie, Steinkopf, and Lyon. You will not find the name of an NDP minister on that list."

Those demanding, invariably with sarcastic references to "tax-and-spend NDP socialists", that we reduce taxes and leave them more freedom to spend their own money, were informed:

> This year [1976] we could reduce taxes $300 million by freeing families to educate their own children, $150 million by freeing Manitobans to pay the same Medicare premiums as Ontario, $50 million by ending Nursing Home subsidies, $80 million by ending Property Tax Credits which resulted in most seniors paying no school taxes, $18 million by refusing to rescue livestock producers when the 'free market' failed them, $6 million by abolishing the Department of Industry which assists the business community, and $89 million by abolishing our Department of Highways so you can put your car up on blocks.

Writers of vituperative missives, mostly businessmen, about the NDP support for the loathed "social welfare state" needed a lesson in history and economics:

> In 1975, federal Post-Master General Bryce Mackasey told the

Canadian Newspaper Association 'defenders of the faith forget the welfare state grew on the corporate refusal to pay the social costs of its growth'. The chief economist for the Ford Motor Company [whose opinion you surely value] recognized the realities of the modern industrial economy by referring to rising unemployment and stating 'Unemployment insurance and welfare are two reasons why there is no blood in the streets.'

Complaints about lack of spending on health care, almost invariably juxtaposed with a paragraph complaining about high taxes, were a staple. A lady from the premier's constituency wrote she would never again vote NDP because of the government's lack of concern for her cancer-stricken aunt and its obvious lack of familiarity with the consequences. She was sent a letter expressing the premier's sympathy for her aunt, and, "I have not given the premier your letter stating if he ever has anyone near and dear to him afflicted with cancer 'may you not have the money to take them where they can get help'. Bill Jenkins, our Deputy Speaker, has been taking cobalt treatments for cancer for many months. Francis Eady, my predecessor in this office, died of cancer two years ago. Just before I came here I had surgery for cancer which necessitated the removal of my thyroid. You are not alone in your familiarity with cancer."

A letter (with copies to opposition leaders) from a local business executive demanding withdrawal of a bill to strengthen labour bargaining power evoked a reply (with copies to opposition leaders), "Your assumption that a decent income will destroy the 'pride and initiative' of the working people of Manitoba is an insult to anyone who had ever worked for a living. Even worse is your assumption that a good wage for labourers will destroy our business community. If your assumptions were correct we should have had a superfluity of 'pride and initiative', and business should have been booming, in the Thirties."

Another socialist hater, who believed the NDP government was much too lenient with misfits and too generous with the property of others, quoted from Will Durand's *Roman History*. "Plato says that from the exaggerated 'license men call liberty' tyrants spring up," he wrote. "From out of such an ungoverned populace one is chosen leader ... who curries favor with people by giving them other men's property ... surrounds himself with armed guards and emerges as a tyrant over the very people who raised him to power."

The opportunity was irresistible. "What Plato referred to as 'the license men call liberty" is now called 'democracy' ... The huge demonstration of insurance personnel that stormed the legislature several years ago did not find the socialist premier surrounded by armed guards."

Changing the Censor Board, which could ban "pornographic" movies or books from Manitoba, to the Classification Board which could only classify them and leave people free to choose what to see or read, ignited the fury of those who claimed this would make Manitoba the "Porno Capital" of Canada. We government *apparatchniks* were kept busy answering letters and calls to explain the government caucus did not like pornography any more than they did, but sincerely believed censorship gave pornography an unnaturally high value, that people left to their intelligence would do the right thing, and that abolishing censorship did not make government members professional purveyors of pornography.

Some communications were as scatalogical as the works they abhorred. A lady's vulgar letter stating that the end of censorship would destroy the morality of her children, was answered, "You consider yourself a moral person despite the pornography available when you were young, and I expect your children will do as well. Society has survived worse imbicilities than the garbage in books and films disguised as art, which has become popular largely because we have drawn so much attention to it."

A priest demanding "tougher" censorship needed a reminder. "How shall we define 'pornographic'? I did not know of 'fornication' and 'sodomy' until I read about these activities by the patriarchs of the Old Testament."

After heavy rains in early 1974, the government hired university students to help the aged and infirm clean up flood damage. A peremptory telex arrived stating that, while the sender was able-bodied, he was a victim of "irresponsible escalation of property taxes" and entitled to assistance cleaning up his basement. He was telexed some advice: "Refer complaints about 'escalation of property taxes' to City of Winnipeg, which imposed them. If able-bodied, clean up your own dirty basement just like I did."

The issues we needed to contend with were rich in variety. The Freshwater Fish Marketing Board, established in 1969 by Ottawa, was a crown corporation with exclusive authority to buy and sell most freshwater fish caught in Manitoba, Saskatchewan and the Northwest Territories. A plant built in Winnipeg processed the fish, sold what it could, and freeze-stored the balance until markets were found. This brought order to a chaotic market, evened out prices to fishers, and maintained a sustainable industry. It gave fishers in a $50 million industry spread over five million square kilometres access to the world market, and offered buyers diversity of product and security of supply.

The provinces were responsible for setting and administering quotas, mesh sizes and criteria for licensing fishermen. We were nearer than Ottawa, so we got the full force of complaints. No matter what we did to modify the program, some people were simply not satisfied, and determined to protest until the government gave them what they wanted. One found a unique way to do so.

A man came to the legislature and gave a wrapped package to a page to deliver to Environment Minister Sidney Green in the chamber, then sat in the visitor's gallery to watch. The page delivered it to Green's desk. He regarded it with suspicion and other members held their breath. Then, slowly, he unwrapped it. It was a large, freshly-caught whitefish.[18]

---

[18] Thirty years later, the plant was processing about 2.2 million pounds of freshwater fish a week and selling up to fifty million pounds a year for some 4,000 fishers, [Continued on p. 303]

The next day the man came to my office. "I sent a fish to Green in the chamber yesterday to emphasize my anger with his regulations. I wonder what he did with it?"

"He invited my wife and me for supper and we ate it."

Karen Schulz

Her father's vivid stories inspired the artist in Karen Schulz. The result, completed just as the book went to press, shows the nightmarish side of life at The Ledge.

---

[18] (Con't.) including 2,400 in Manitoba. Most were satisfied, but as with farmers relative to the Canadian Wheat Board, some claimed the fisheries board was playing favourites, or that transport costs were too high, or that there should be a string of processing plants in the North, or that it did not make proper obeisance to treaty rights, or there were opportunity markets in Poland and Indonesia that individuals should be free to access, or that any fisher should be free to circumvent the board by selling his catch off the dock, or that single-desk selling was uncompetitive and probably unconstitutional. Some people appeared to be motivated by the philosophy that "nothing good should be left untouched". Differing opinions are expected, but one wonders why any sane government would become involved in such operations. Why not let them eat cake!

XXVI

Agriculture

Beyond this place there be dragons.
—Inscription on ancient maps
on areas beyond the known world

In 1975, I accompanied the Agricultural Committee of the legislature on a series of public hearings to hear the reaction of Manitoba farmers to government proposals for acquiring, holding and disposing of land. In brief, what could the government do to maintain family farms as viable economic and social units and stabilize the economy of rural Manitoba, so that young people would stay there?

That question had long perplexed both farmers and governments. Years earlier the Conservative government of Premier Duff Roblin had wrestled with the problem of agricultural viability in a fast-changing, capital intensive economy, and with the question of the intergenerational transfer of family farms. How do children acquire the family farm without reducing their parents, or themselves, to penury. Farming had changed by a magnitude since a generation earlier when a young couple could buy a team of horses and basic equipment for several hundred dollars, CPR land for a dollar an acre, and create an enterprise. Thirty years later the farm was productive, the machinery modern, the buildings painted—house white and barn red—but there was no money in the bank.

Now the parents wanted to retire and the sons, who had worked on the farm since childhood with no remuneration but free board and room, use of the family car to court the neighbours' daughters and a bit of money for beer and movies, wanted to acquire it. But the sons had no cash to buy the farm and the parents could not afford to give it to them. There were no options but to subdivide the farm, which generally made it uneconomic, or to allow the work of a lifetime to pass to strangers. That meant the old folks moved into the local town and their children to the city, robbing the rural community of their energy and its future.

The search for a solution resulted in the establishment, in 1959, of the Manitoba Agricultural Credit Corporation, "a credit fund to assist establishment of new farm units and reorganization of exisiting ones". Directors were appointed to administer it and the terms of reference were modest and limited: loans were restricted to $35,000 and applicants to those under thirty-five years of age. The loans were intended to buy the family farm or to add a small parcel to make it more viable. The MACC provided a vehicle for retirees to transfer their farms to their children for cash, while the children assumed a long-term, low-interest debt with the Government of Manitoba—and the family estate.

And it worked! Briefly. The Sixties were good to farmers and and prices increased. In the Red River Valley $100-an-acre land became $200-an-acre land and political pressure forced the MACC to increase its limits. The same political pressures, and jealousy because the provinces were reaping political capital from their farm loans, induced the Government of Canada to increase loans through its Federal Farm Credit Corporation; these new sources of capital caused land prices to go to $300 an acre.

Suddenly the banks, which had largely abandoned farm loans after taking a terrible beating in the 1930s, could not resist what they saw as a lucrative investment. They established special agricultural loans sections and trumpeted the availability of their money … and the price of land went to $400 an acre. During 1973 and 1974, a combination of petroleum-fueled inflation and heavy grain buying by the Soviet Union and China increased wheat prices to over $5 per bushel,[1] the highest in Canadian history. All this, plus a series of good crops, created in farmers a hunger for land, and for loans to buy it at prices that had risen to $500 an acre.

Then came the foreigners! The Americans had taken an unprecedented beating in Vietnam. Soviet space vehicles were filling the stratosphere. China was testing nuclear bombs. Strategic Air Command B-52s, each plane an arsenal of dreaded weapons, were leaving vapour contrails flying twenty-four-hour "alerts". The Old World was again smelling of cordite and burning flesh, and as a haven, Canada seemed the world's last best hope.

So Europeans came to Canada. They came from France where encroaching towns were paying huge prices for land, from Belgium where it was too crowded for ambitious farmers, from England where settling in the "colonies" sounded romantic, from West Germany where 300,000 Soviet troops, armed to the teeth, were glaring across the trip-wire at Check Point Charlie. They came from Italy where governments were changing on an average of every eleven months, where the political situation appeared no more stable than in 1945, where the Communists appeared only one coalition away from forming the government[2] and where parents preferred that their military-age sons be lovers, not fighters.

---

[1] In 1973-74, farmers received the wheat board price of $5.07 per bushel for No. 2 spring wheat.

[2] On October 9, 1997, the Communist Party left the coalition and brought down the fifty-fifth post war government in Italy. In May 2001, Italy elected its sixty-first government in fifty-six years.

They did not come in multitudes, but they came with cash. The price of land, compared with that of Europe, made it appear, literally, dirt cheap. So they bought, and the price of land went as high as $600 an acre. Farmers began to see themselves as potential millionaires; the joke went around that for a farmer to become a millionaire, he needed to work late and early, live frugally ... and sell his over-priced farm to a foreigner. Then he needed to persuade the government to abolish the estates tax so that the family could keep the capital gains. Meanwhile he needed MACC loans to buy land to sell to foreigners at inflated prices.

The election of Liberal Leader Izzy Asper in 1971 brought new excitement to the legislature. Intellectually agile and swift of tongue, he delighted in keeping the government off balance with oblique assertions disguised as questions: a niggling point here, an implied accusation there; a scholastic argumentation on an obscure issue, sometimes farcical but enough to embarrass the government. One day he revealed, with appropriate fanfare, that Americans were buying up Canada. Actually, they had been buying Canada at a prodigious rate since 1947. Journalist and author Peter C. Newman, had written:

> By [1968] nearly two-thirds of the country's manufacturing capacity was owned outside the country, while the percentage of foreign ownership in such key industries as automobiles, petroleum, mining, chemicals and rubber ranged up to the high nineties. Nine out of ten factories in Canada with at least five thousand names on the payroll were controlled by parent corporations in the United States.[3]

Asper claimed the NDP government was letting foreigners deprive Manitobans of recreational land. When the issue did not catch fire, he discovered foreigners were also buying agricultural land. This time it worked. Government departments began receiving communications warning of dire consequences if this continued. Economists feared our farmers would be reduced to tenants paying rent to foreign owners; environmentalists feared foreigners would not treat the land with the same respect as Canadians; professional nationalists saw Canada disappearing acre by acre; young farmers reported parcels of coveted land purchased by foreigners at a higher price than they themselves could pay.

A subsequent study by the Department of Agriculture showed only about three per cent of Manitoba farm land was owned by non-Manitobans, including Canadians. But Asper had created a political problem; the NDP government could not allow itself to be perceived as not moving to prevent alienation of land. As Will Rogers had quipped, "Buy land, they ain't making no more of it." It must be preserved. So the government limited non-resident purchase of farm land.[4]

---

[3]   *The Distemper of Our Times*, M & S, Toronto, p. 221.

[4]   Ironically, five years later, when the policy began to be vigorously pursued, some foreigners were dumping their land and returning to Europe, while local farmers, caught in the squeeze of a recession and twenty per cent interest rates, were praying for foreigners to buy their land before it was seized by creditors.

While doing so, it discovered the real problem in agriculture was much deeper, more basic and more complex.

Following the NDP victory in 1969, Sam Uskiw, whose parents had immigrated from Ukraine, became minister of Agriculture. He was raised on a small farm across the river from the town of Selkirk, which was situated in Red River Valley gumbo. As a youth, he had travelled in a boxcar to work as a machinist in a Toronto railroad shop to augment family income and later returned to work as a meat cutter. At the death of his father in 1957, he took over the family farm and converted it to potato growing just when that was becoming lucrative.

A keen observer of politico/economic developments, he became active in public life as school board trustee, as director of the Manitoba Farmers Union, and, in 1966, at age thirty-three, as member of the Manitoba Legislature for Brokenhead. As minister, he determined to restore the importance agriculture had lost in the mindless rush to industrialization, and to make farm life more rewarding for those without whose toil and risk-taking there would be no towering buildings, paved streets, art, music or anything else representing the technological genius and psychic aspirations of humankind. Unlike the previous government's plan for reducing the number of farmers to fit available income, he sought to increase income to fit the number of farmers. He was a powerful spokesman for agriculture and his department became notorious for spending money, sometimes to the distraction of cabinet. One MLA wrote:

> As Agricultural Minister Sam Uskiw brought in a never-ending series of new programs and subsidies for farmers—so many in fact, that one day he would simply grind to a halt. No words would come from his lips. No new proposals. No sounds. Because he would have introduced and implemented every single, solitary agricultural proposal the human mind could conceive.[5]

But Uskiw was difficult to say "No" to. Serenely rational, he would show that his proposal for farmers was good for all. Despite criticism, programs sprang from his department like mythical Minerva from the head of Jove.[6] He promoted rural drainage, cooperatives, a hog marketing board, a beef marketing board, and farm produce diversification. One of his early programs was the provision of grants to install sewer and water in rural homes; the irreverent press immediately dubbed it the "Sam-Can program".

The equal of Schreyer in hiding emotion—and he did it with a smile— Uskiw never appeared angry or impatient but he always had something on the front burner. "Here comes Sam with another program," became the impatient

---

[5]   Doern, *Wednesdays are Cabinet Days,* p. 76.

[6]   When Uskiw introduced legislation requiring three-year warranties on tractors and combines sold in Manitoba, Harry Mardon, associate editor of *The Winnipeg Tribune,* worried that this could increase prices and induce some farmers to become careless with their machinery. *The Winnipeg Tribune,* June 8, 1973.

refrain of cabinet members, when he walked in, always neatly dressed in suit or jacket a size too large, appearing bulkier than his 5'5" and 165 pounds, with white shirt and colour-coded, Windsor-knotted tie, and every jet black hair in place, his extensive and precise vocabulary belying his limited formal education, and a sheaf of papers under his arm. But "Smiling Sam" was determined that, while in the grand scheme of things, Ceres could never be returned to her ancient estate, at least on his watch she would receive her share of the loot.

Once I complained to the premier about the cost of our farm programs, all of which had to be wrestled through the legislature and squared with the taxpayers. He looked pensive a moment, then remarked ruefully, "Well, Sammy always was a big spender." But the premier too was a farm boy, and painfully familiar with the heartbreak of having a life's work destroyed in hours by a hailstorm or an early frost.[7] He was aware of the billions of taxpayers' dollars spent annually on industrial subsidies to make a few rich richer, and he was not about to apologize for spending a small percentage of that to keep 30,000 families on the land.

Uskiw's chosen instrument for restoring and maintaining farm prosperity was the Manitoba Agricultural Credit Corporation. "Go spend some money," he told his board of directors, and the directive was taken literally. But there were some concerns. In mid-1971, an old friend who was a member of the MACC board, came to my house one evening with an armload of files: "Look at these. See if you think we are doing the right thing."

I was appalled. Both age limit and loan limit had been removed. Anyone could apply for a loan and applications were for up to $650,000. One application, already tentatively approved, was for some $400,000, mostly to be used to pay off debts. Another, for about $350,000, also tentatively approved, was to purchase a dairy farm including a number of cows at $1,100 each. I phoned my friend, who was himself a dairy farmer. "Emil, what is the market price of a good dairy cow?"

"About $500."

"Then why is your board lending $1,100 to buy a cow?"

"The other $600 is for the milk quota."

Milk quotas—the permit to sell an agreed amount of milk at a guaranteed price—was established in 1937. The competitive nature of farming made farmers easy prey to the vortex of downward spiralling prices of the Depression. As they competed each other out of business, the government feared a shortage of milk for the children. Today they would perhaps be told to "drink Coke"—or beer—but at that time milk appeared virtuous ... and nutritious. So the government enacted the legislation and appointed the Milk Control Board to allocate production quotas. The board calculated the amount of milk required, divided that by the number of cows needed to produce it, gave each milk producer a permit to deliver a quota of milk based on the number of cows owned, and the government guaranteed the

---

7   In 1999, hundreds of farmers in southwestern Manitoba and parts of Saskatchewan were bankrupted when heavy spring rains delayed seeding and early frosts killed what was seeded. In 2002, many more were bankrupted by drought.

price. Surplus milk was destroyed and its producer fined. Competition was traded for price guarantees; it made milk producers the princes of the agricultural industry.

But by intervening to limit the number of producers while guaranteeing the market and the price per unit of production, the government created a marketable product—the delivery quota. Without it there was no access to the market. The first generation of milk producers, having received their quota gratis from the government, envisioned the proceeds from its sale as a retirement pension. But monetizing the quota raised prices for dairy farms, and demands for higher milk prices by their purchasers. As the price of milk to the dairy farmer increased, so did the value of the quota, and the price of the milk to pay for it, just as a liquor license enhances the value of a hotel and increases the price of liquor to pay for it. MACC loans to purchase milk quotas added to costs for Manitobans twice, as taxpayers subsidizing low-interest loans, and as consumers paying more for milk.

In 1975, Uskiw ended this by offering free delivery quotas to anyone wanting to start a dairy farm. The fury among producers who saw their unearned pensions wiped out was palpable; had Uskiw visited them he might have been fed to the pigs. Meanwhile, the MACC was being used, in part, not to transfer farms from parents to children, or to add land to make a family farm more viable, but to allow some farmers to retire rich while leaving purchasers with an impossible debt to the taxpayers of Manitoba.

I met with the MACC board of directors. "Look at the size of these damned loans you are approving. What in hell are you people doing?"

"The minister told us to spend some money."

"But surely he did not tell you to spend it all on half a dozen applicants at the cost of more debt for the taxpayers."

I went to the minister. "Sam. The MACC is becoming a farce. You may want to put someone in charge who knows what he is doing." And he did.

MAXWELL HOFFORD was of that rare breed who does anything and does it well. Raised in Calgary (he boasted of being strapped by then school principal and later Alberta premier, "Bible" Bill Aberhardt, "and he was a powerful bugger"), his school teacher father moved the family to a farm near Roblin, Manitoba, in the Thirties. At the beginning of the war, Maxwell joined the Air Force. He became a pilot-navigator, parachuted out of a crashing plane, flew thirty-eight missions over enemy territory including such *verboten* targets as submarine pens off the French coast and V-2 rocket site at Peenemunde, as well as the abortive attempt to sink the German warships *Scharnhorst* and *Gneisnau* escaping through the fog-shrouded English Channel.

He was transferred to Transport Command and ferried officers and VIPs around the world, including a trip to Dumbarton Oaks in September 1944, where the basis was laid for the United Nations.

After the war he and his wife settled on a farm at Bowsman, in north-western Manitoba, and each did the work of at least two ordinary mortals. Their motto appeared to be "They who think they can't, can't." By the mid-Fifties they had a large farm, a good set of buildings, and fields of waving grain; the primal sounds of cows and hogs paid lyrical tribute to their industry and husbandry.

Slim of build at 5'8" but with a whipcord body, huge pectorals and biceps, and the elastic walk of a boxer, he was not a man frightened by things that go bump in the night, yet his deep voice and quiet mien made him appear deceptively placid. While Hofford was chairman of the Manitoba Agricultural Credit Corporation, an acquaintance reported to me, "I was very late with my MACC loan payment and got a letter requesting payment or action would be taken. I met the board and there was a gray-haired, hunched-over farmer in a plaid shirt in the chair, and I knew I could scare him, so I read them the riot act and said if they pressed me I would go to the media and make their name stink from coast to coast. The little man looked up and said in a very deep voice, 'You are free to do that, Sir, but in the meantime we will take your farm.' So I paid—quickly."

Hofford was practical, resolute and literate, able to discourse on any subject. Hard work and minute attention to the science of agriculture had not robbed him of the magic of wonder and he read avidly—huge, heavy, hard-cover tomes. (I would borrow them, read in bed, fall asleep and let them crash to the floor, panicking my wife into bolting upright.) And his success had not made him a Mammon worshipper; he had an integrity and a moral gyroscope that often left him standing alone, but never compromised.

We had met twenty years earlier when I advertised a meeting at my farm at Grandview to discuss organizing the Manitoba Farmer's Union. That day a man got out of his car and said, "I'm Max Hofford from Bowsman and I want to help." After that we travelled many hot, cold, dark, icy, tired miles together. We were on some boards requiring driving into Winnipeg twenty or more times a year. Hofford would rise at 2 A.M. and arrive at my farm 150 miles away at 4 A.M. We would have toast and coffee and then roar through the night at warp speed, traversing the 250 miles between my farm and the city, discussing farming and farm organization and the general economy and the state of the universe and our place in time and space and the joy of living and the evanescence of life: "The bird of youth has but a little way to flutter, And lo, the bird is on the wing."[8]

We would arrive in Winnipeg at 8 A.M., have breakfast, be at the board meeting at 9 A.M., usually sit until 7 P.M., have supper, drive back to my farm, have toast and coffee, and then he would drive home, arriving about 3 A.M. For any sensible person, spending ten hours at a board meeting would be a day's work, but Hofford did that plus drive 800 miles. It was a helluva way to live, but we were young and had a world to save.

Hofford's words to me, "I want to help", were to define our relationship.

---

[8] The *Rubiyat* of Omar Khayam.

When I, or those I worked with, needed help, we called on Hofford. He helped organize the Manitoba Farmers Union and fight Manitoba Pool Elevators. He became a director of the Manitoba Federation of Agriculture and president of the Manitoba Dairy and Poultry Coop. As president of the new Manitoba Hog Marketing Board, he broke the monopoly of the meat packers by selling hogs directly to Japan. The only role he had trouble with was that of politician. As NDP candidate in the 1966 provincial election, he visited a constituent's farm. The barn roof had collapsed, the machinery was decrepit, the little unpainted house had a manure berm around the base to keep out winter winds and weeds had grown out of it to block the windows. Approaching the owner, who was repairing an old seven-foot binder when most farmers had combines, he introduced himself. The farmer retorted angrily: "You're from that communist NDP that wants to take away all I have."

And the aspiring politician responded impolitically, "Well, if we took everything you have we wouldn't get much, would we?" He was not elected to the legislature.

In 1972, as the new president and CEO of the MACC, he quickly analysed the situation. While Asper was fearing that farm prices were being driven up by foreigners, Hofford was finding that much of the upward pressure came less from non-residents than from local farmers expanding their holdings, some in anticipation of selling to a foreigner and borrowing money from the MACC to do it! Instead of a public policy instrument with a precise objective, the MACC had become just another bank. Worse, it had become a bank to the commercial banks.

Agriculture Minister Uskiw had accepted the concept of the "consolidation loan". The MACC had been declining loans because applicants already owed debts to a multiplicity of lenders. When a farmer had exhausted all sources of credit and was pursued by a creditor, he came to the MACC. By then he had no collateral left.

An applicant for an MACC loan was informed, "The purpose of the MACC is to improve a farm operation, not merely to bail out existing creditors. You request a $292,000 loan, of which $266,000 is for debt consolidation. Of this, $167,000 is owed to the Royal Bank and $33,250 to Manitoba Pool Elevators. You already owe the MACC $31,950, including $2,000 in interest arrears. Approval of your application would merely add $26,000 to your total debt and increase your MACC debt by $260,000. The taxpayers will merely rescue your creditors."

Alternately, a farmer obtains a loan to buy land. The loan is a percentage of the market value of the land. Produce prices drop, reducing the land's market value. The lender (bank, credit union, etc.) is overexposed and demands the farmer pay down the loan, but he has no money. The lender moves to attach the land. The farmer, desperate, applies to the MACC for a loan to pay down his debt. But the lender has the land as collateral, so there is nothing left.

The consolidation loan concept allowed the MACC to rescue the desperate farmer, using his land as collateral, by loaning him public money to retire his debts to the private creditors. Often the first in line were the banks. In the four-year period from 1970-74, from the commencement of the debt consolidation concept until the government turned to other measures, the MACC committed about $13.2 million to paying off existing farm debts. Of this, about $7.8 million went to banks and credit unions—more than $2.7 million to the Royal Bank alone—and $730,000 to the federal government. Manitoba taxpayers were bailing out the federal government and the commercial lenders.

Demands upon the MACC became bizarre. A decade earlier, to assist farm diversification and accommodate farmers, who preferred borrowing money to fighting for better prices for their products, Manitoba Pool Elevators began lending money to livestock feeders. In 1972, MPE president H.B. Sneath wrote to the MACC requesting that it guarantee some of the "more problematical loans" because "the possibility of catastrophe to some herds is always on the minds of our bankers." [9]

Hofford replied, "You wish the MACC to relieve the anxieties of your bankers with public funds to repay losses they might suffer by lending your organization money to loan to cattle feeders … We are not in the business of underwriting bank loans."

Collecting outstanding accounts could prove equally bizarre. A farmer died and the MACC attached the estate against a $10,000 debt. A lawyer wrote a poignant letter informing the MACC the deceased "also owed the Royal Bank $6,500 and … approximately $4,000 in other debts." The widow was attempting to carry on the operation but "all her milk money is going directly to the Royal Bank," so she was unable to repay the MACC, and hopefully the MACC would forgive the debt so the widow would not be worse off "than prior to [her husband's] death."

Hofford reponded with equal compassion: "The MACC appreciates your concern [for your client] … You write that you 'do not know how my client is going to pay the [MACC] claim against the estate'. Could you please advise if such a statement [requesting forgiveness of debts] has been sent to the other creditors, including your law firm?"

I had long aspired to attend a meeting of the Winnipeg Chamber of Commerce. As a farmer, it seemed an exotic place to go and now, as a government functionary, I went. The meeting was addressed by Charles Hunt, a government representative who spoke informatively of government programs designed to reduce market (as opposed to natural) risks for farmers. As soon as the presentation was completed a tall, well-built man about forty jumped up. "My name is Doug McRorie," he said. "I am the agricultural representative with the Royal Bank, I am a free enterpriser and a believer in competition, and I am proud of it." After thunderous applause, he went on to say that farmers' greatest problem was

---

[9] Sneath to Hofford, Sept.15, 1972.

government interference and all would be well if farmers were just left alone to take market risks, the way the banks do.

It was not going to be a good day for me. I leapt to my feet. "Mr. Chairman, My name is Herb Schulz and I work in the Office of the Premier of Manitoba. I am very pleased to hear the Royal Bank thrives on competition and risk. I want to ask Mr. McRorie if tomorrow he will join me in writing a letter to his president asking him to write a letter to the premier stating he no longer wants Royal Bank farm loans guaranteed by the Manitoba Agricultural Credit Corporation."

Dropping the proverbial pin would have sounded like a bomb.McRorie came over, sat down, contritely apologized and suggested such a letter would not endear him to his president. He had suddenly become risk-averse.

The episode was good catharsis but did nothing to solve the long-term problems of agriculture. The conclusions flowing from Hofford's analysis were that: MACC consolidation loans were of less value to farmers than to their creditors; the payment of bank loans by the MACC encouraged banks to get other farmers into trouble; a loan used to buy land often left the farmer with inadequate machinery to farm it without incurring more debt; a loan used by an urban land company to buy land to lease back to its former owners reduced the yeoman farmer to a tenant, and a loan used to buy land to sell to a foreigner served no social or economic purpose. All this resulted in increasing land prices, and ultimately increased food prices. In other words, Manitobans as taxpayers were having their money used to increase their costs as consumers.

Hofford's analysis raised at least two dilemmas; should the government leave agriculture to the mercies of the market and risk land ownership by a handful of rural oligarchs while the middle-class farmer who maintained the rural economic and social infrastructure was destroyed? And, using public funds, how does the government assist in maintaining the family farm as both an economic and a social unit without contributing to the inflation of land prices, requiring ever larger loans to establish young farmers?

At a farmers' meeting at Brunkild in 1972, I outlined the problems. The number of Manitoba farmers had dropped by half to about 30,000 since 1941 and was continuing to drop at about 1,000 per year. Half the farmers in Manitoba were over fifty-five and, unlike the situation in industry, sons were prohibited from replacing their fathers by the need for capital. Though farm productivity had increased at twice the rate of industry since 1945, the only solution proposed by universities and governments[10] was to increase efficiency with larger farms and fewer farmers. To this end, many millions had been loaned to farmers by govern-

---

[10] In March 1969, a $500,000 study proposed to the Conservative government of Walter Weir that the number of Manitoba farmers be reduced to 20,000 by 1980 and that "The decline should be faster than the natural attrition rate and people will have to seek new employment." 'Targets for Economic Development' report, Queen's Printer, p.59. The figure of 20,000 was arrived at by dividing projected total income by forecasted individual farm need. By contrast, the NDP government was determined to increase total farm income to sustain those on the land.

ments. That had enlarged farms—and debts—until sixty-five per cent of farm investment was in land. Increasing loans burdened young farmers with impossible debts and many would soon sell to a foreigner, or a neighbour, who borrowed the money from government and the loans would again drive up the price of land.[11]

We were going around in ever larger concentric circles, getting nowhere. This must end. Governments must devise programs to provide young farmers with opportunities to obtain land without impossible outlays of capital, more risk for taxpayers, and inflating land prices. I would recommend ending MACC loans. The farmers in the audience responded with looks of panic. How would they survive? The dilemma demanded solutions and crystallized into a policy—the Land Lease Option.

The concept was developed by Uskiw's cerebral, articulate, kinetic Dutch-born chief program analyst (later deputy minister), Willem Janssen, dubbed "Red Bill" by Tory MLA Warner Jorgenson. It was simple and straightforward; instead of lending the farmer the money to pay his debts, the government would pay them but keep the title and lease the land back to the former owner. The farmer would receive market price and the rental fees would be based on that price. The lease would be for a "lifetime" and could be passed on to heirs for as long as they wanted it. This solved a number of problems: the farmer could not lose the land except for failure to pay rent, as would be the case if he failed to pay loan interest; the money previously needed to buy land could then be invested in machinery and equipment to make the enterprise more efficient, or in buildings to make life more pleasant; the heirs could inherit the farm without having capital debts; the farm could not be sold to foreigners; the land, removed from the market, would no longer be subject to price inflation; the taxpayers who provided the money to buy the land would, as consumers, get lower long-term food prices, and finally, Manitoba farm products would become more competitive on the world market.

The proposal was similar to having developers, to reduce capital costs, building on land leased for ninety-nine years from banks, except there was no termination date. No farmer would be forced to sell to the government or encouraged to sell if he approached the MACC. The farm community would simply be informed that the program was available to those who wished to use it, in which case their land would be purchased at market price. It was simply an option.

The NDP government had concluded that no economic or social advantage was gained by enlarging cities at the expense of rural Manitoba. But this required development of roads, municipal recreational facilities, housing, improvement of educational and economic opportunities and industrial initiatives that allowed people—particularly young people—to stay in the rural areas. The Land Lease

---

[11] The Faculty of Agriculture at the University of Manitoba showed that after 1959, despite cash receipts per acre remaining stable, farmland prices had increased dramatically, in direct proportion to the amount of farm loans by government. *Spotlight*, Winter 1975.

Option fitted uniquely into what, in 1972, became known as the concept of "The Stay Option".

It looked so rational—on paper. But it went terribly wrong. The minister of Agriculture proposed the program to the government in April 1973. It was accepted, reluctantly, but as a necessity. Ministers were prepared to support it intellectually but were viscerally uneasy. Sidney Green commented presciently, "This may be the most radical program our government will ever introduce. Before we proceed let us be certain that we know what we are doing. And let us determine that if we proceed, there will be no compromising later to cause its death by a thousand cuts."

After the cabinet meeting, I approached the minister. "Sam. This is an excellent program but must be very carefully explained, which will take time. We will be into an election in two months. If you introduce this now it will become part of the campaign. We will be accused of being communists wanting to seize farmers' land. We will not have the opportunity to explain it properly and we will pay a political price. I suggest you keep this under wraps until after the election. Then we can conduct public meetings to explain the program and get public input."

I thought we had agreement on that approach, but something happened. Four weeks before election day the proposed legislation was reported in the media. I was terrified. My political antenna was gyrating. But nothing happened. The election campaign was on. We were in the belly of the beast and had other concerns. I relaxed.

Then, a week before E-Day they hit us! The PCs struck with a powerful commercial showing a multi-armed octopus reaching from the Legislative Building and seizing farm land. It was devastating. It tainted the opportunity for rational debate and/or explanation. Media analysts later claimed the introduction of the program at that time, and the opposition's response to it, cost the NDP several rural seats in the 1973 election. Nevertheless, we won and for the first time in four years we had a secure majority. We would now have the opportunity to explain.

Uskiw, determined to end the raids on the treasury, enacted the legislation and announced public meetings to discuss it. The MACC began purchasing parcels of farm land when approached by farmers needing to retire debts or simply wishing to retire. The land was leased back, mostly to the former owner, and the lease was for life, making it much more secure than a private lease.[12] The volume of mail and phone calls to the Premier's Office, attacking the program, was enormous … and fierce. The opposition parties were killing us and it made me wonder, like King Arthur in Camelot, "How did we get into this agonizing absurdity?"

---

[12] The program died "the death of a thousand cuts". Political survival soon required that we promise to sell the land after five years, destroying the essence of the program. The succeeding Conservative government sold off all the land and by 1979, the innovative program was dead. Twenty years later, the newspapers were filled with reports of farmers losing their land. The provincial government pledged $50 million to guarantee a quarter of any bank loans to farmers (*Winnipeg Free Press*, March 29, 2001) and a farm spokesman asked the government to "buy out" distressed farmers (*Winnipeg Free Press*, March 23, 2001).

Then one day an old friend brought some information, a rumour, actually. I phoned the director of the Department of Agriculture's Lands Branch. "By 5 o'clock today," I told him, "I want a complete list of all Manitobans who have land leased from the government. I want the name, the address, the lease number, and the number of acres in each lease. And I want the names listed in alphabetical order."

Just after 5 P.M. an exhausted director came puffing into my office and placed a thick folder on my desk. I was aghast. More than 3,000 leases comprising about two million acres, had accumulated under previous "free enterprise" governments. I had asked that the names be in alphabetical order so, while the director stood at what in retrospect appeared uneasy attention, I flipped to the "Es" and ran my eyes down the list. Without looking up, and not certain of my information, I said, "I'm looking for a name beginning with "E". I do not see it."

Silence. I looked up. The director was ghost white.

"Is that who you are after?"

"I have been given certain information and I want to know if it is correct, but I do not see the name here."

"Give me back that file. I'll put it in and bring it back."[13]

He did. And there, like Abu ben Adhem's[14] name written by an angel in a book of gold, was the name of Harry Enns, former PC minister of Agriculture, whose party was damning the Land Lease Option as "communism". He had 1,735 acres of land leased from the Manitoba government. The list also showed that James Ferguson, PC MLA for Gladstone, had 160 acres of leased land.

After that it was a piece of cake. Anyone giving me the faintest excuse was sent a letter explaining the genesis, nature and purpose of the Land Lease Option. Thousands were sent. And in each was the bold statement that the program cannot be as bad as some, particularly in the Progressive Conservative party, were saying because, after all, Harry Enns, Progressive Conservative MLA, former minister of Agriculture and bitter critic of anything communistic, has 1,735 acres of land leased from the government.

Harry Enns was a consummate thespian. He had spent time on the stage and could create a circus atmosphere with his performances in the chamber. He would stand in his place and make a speech. Whether or not it made sense was of no consequence, as long as he had an opportunity to orate, and he could work himself into a simulated state of fury while he was doing it. Then he would walk outside the chamber, slap his thigh in glee and laugh uproariously. He had done it to us again. Some government members had even taken him seriously.

But he was not as vacuous as some thought. He was a member of a highly esteemed Manitoba family. His father was a bishop of the Mennonite Brethren and Harry's four brothers included a member of Parliament, a hospital administrator, a

---

[13] The director had worked for Harry Enns when he was minister of Agriculture in the Roblin government.

[14] Leigh Hunt, *Abou den Adhem.*

judge of the Court of Queen's Bench, and a school principal. Harry was a rancher by vocation but a politician by avocation, a minister of the crown in three governments, and would become the dean of the Manitoba Legislature before announcing his retirement in 2002. He was eloquent, affable and friendly, aggressive in attacks on his political opponents but never malicious. His blind spot derived from the folk memory of the Mennonites in Russia having their farms seized by the Communists and his analysis of any legislation was circumscribed by that experience. One night, when the legislature sat beyond the witching hour, he invited me into the Conservative caucus room, poured us each a copious shot of rye, and proceeded, in a beautiful tenor voice and in flawless German, to sing the breath-catching *Horst Wessel Lied*. Afterwards, whenever he referred to me as a communist, I reminded him he was the only person I had ever heard sing the theme song of the Nazi Party.

One day Harry Enns walked into my office. "Herb. You have a problem."

"So what is the nature of this problem you say I have?"

"I have read some of your letters to some of my constituents about your Land Lease Program, and I note they all state that I have 1,735 acres of land leased from the Government of Manitoba."

"But you are our favourite lessee so why not boast about it?"

"I understand that, but this morning I received a letter from your minister of Agriculture stating he is revoking my lease."

"So how does that create a problem for me?"

"If my lease is revoked, you will no longer be able to defend your Land Lease Program by informing people that 'Harry Enns has 1,735 acres of land leased from the government.'"

I admired at how neatly he had trapped me with his imaginative deviousness. Of elected persons I worked with, he remains one of my favourites. I made an appointment for him with the minister, who had received letters from Enns' neighbours complaining he was leasing land from the government at nominal rates and, with no livestock, was subletting it to neighbours at a profit. A compromise was reached and Enns kept his lease. And he responded gracefully. During the debate on the Lease Option, challenged by Uskiw, Enns replied, "Nowhere in this chamber nor in the public arena have I indicated any opposition to leasing of land or that it was an undesirable feature of farming." [15]

The Manitoba Department of Agriculture prepared a 120-page White Paper, which with inexcusable political insensitivity it wrapped in a red cover, causing endless suggestive comments, that listed the facts and figures that had led the government to its conclusions about land ownership, and distributed copies. On May 30, 1974, the legislature appointed a special committee "to enquire into matters relating to property rights in lands within the province, and to hold such public hearings as may be deemed advisable."

---

[15] *Hansard*, March 13, 1975, p. 238.

In early 1975, I attended a farmer's meeting at Fisher Branch, in the Interlake. The hall was filled with farmers and Bill Janssen was explaining the lease option. It took only a few moments to realize it was an exercise in futility. These men and women largely of Ukrainian stock, whose parents or grandparents —or even they themselves—had come to Canada to satisfy an ancient hunger of the peasant for land. They had settled amid the spruce, swamp and stone of the Interlake and made it into productive land that nourished them and sent their children to university. No one should even hallucinate about selling them on a program that implied that they might turn their land over to the government.

Things were bad, but they had seen worse. They might lose their farm to creditors, but they would find another. Young farmers were having difficulty getting started, but what else was new?[16] They liked the NDP and Premier Schreyer and their MLA, Billie Uruski, but they did not like this program. For them, owning a farm was not just a matter of economics; it was an affair of the heart. The Land Lease Option might look good, on paper, but they were having none of it.

In our zeal to stabilize the agricultural industry we had crossed the pale of what even our best political supporters were willing to accept. The policy may have been good, but the optics were bad. It was a classical example of a policy making good economic sense but proving a massive political blunder. We had made the politically unforgivable, and unredeemable, error of attempting to sell the solution before selling the problem.

Opposition propaganda had done its work. Fear of the program was burned into the farmer's psyche. The government was taking their land; all else was inconsequential. We had ventured onto *terra incognita* inhabited by dragons. And we were about to be consumed.

In the public hearings throughout Manitoba, the special committee heard from bankers arguing it was good for government to support their loans to farmers; realtors claiming it was sacrilege to take property off the market; lawyers representing foreign buyers claiming these improved agriculture by burning the houses of those whose farms they bought; opposition politicians claiming it was much better to lease land from foreign landlords than from government; farmers claiming to be "free enterprisers", who considered the market sacred but wanting more subsidized interest government loans; a farm business association claiming "government subsidies cost us our rights" but wanting more subsidized interest loans to farmers while being relieved of the estates tax, gift tax, capital gains tax, school tax, sales tax and income tax; a farm organization stating it might be necessary to prohibit foreign purchases of land, but convinced that farmers must be left free to sell to anyone of their choosing—except to the government.

---

[16] Twenty years later, a report based on the 1991 census showed "the average age of Canadian farmers is 49, fewer Canadians under 35 are entering farming, and more farmers make incomes at other jobs." Farm families had declined by almost a quarter since 1971 and those under thirty-five had declined by fifty per cent between 1986 and 1991. "The costs of owning a farm are beyond many people ... it is difficult for parents to even transfer farms to their children ... To start, a potential farmer would need about $500,000 to purchase land and equipment for a 200-hectare commercial farm." StatsCan, *op.cit.*, October 25, 1994.

The hearings assumed an air of unreality and futility. Committee members were saying one thing, but farmers were hearing something else. At Brandon, after a masterful explanation of the genesis and objectives of the program by Sidney Green, a man spoke, "Mr. Green. I don't believe you."

Patiently, Green went through his repertoire again.

The same man stood up. "Mr. Green, I still don't believe you."

We took a helluva beating. But there were moments …!

At Steinbach, the farmers did not want to discuss the option; they wanted to discuss property taxes. Reduction of taxes would vitiate the need for MACC loans or land lease programs. When the meeting ended, I walked to where a man the NDP had been wooing to be a candidate was haranguing some farmers about the astronomical property taxes fixed on them by government. I asked, "By the way, how much property taxes are you paying this year?"

"Sixteen hundred dollars."

"On how many acres?"

"Nine hundred."

"Shit! In the city I pay that much on an acre."

Then there was the meeting when Bill Janssen was invited to discuss the Land Lease Option with the Winnipeg Chamber of Commerce. Janssen was a short, slim, fiftyish dynamo with prematurely gray hair, who had come from The Netherlands with an excellent education in agricultural economics and in the political economy of the world at large. He also had a mind that could absorb a multitude of disparate facts and convert them into sequential statements of irrefutable logic. He had come to the department as a program planner and analyst and was now deputy minister of Agriculture. Irreverent and passionate, he never skirted an issue just to be polite and always made his case in perfect English with a noticeable accent and awesome erudition.

On March 18, 1975, he made his usual detailed presentation, explaining the history and contributions of agriculture and farm problems in Manitoba. He explained that the option would not rob the farmer of his land, but rather ensure he kept it safe from creditors so he could continue farming. He explained that the series of public hearings had been hijacked and subverted into a campaign of "ideological warfare" by those with a political agenda, who were using this option as a stick with which to beat the government, and by special interest groups who knew little and cared less about agriculture, except as a milch cow for themselves. And he explained that since 1971, every province in Canada except Alberta, regardless of political persuasion, had begun land-banking programs, including Tory Ontario, where it was funded with $200 million.[17]

But this audience of self-important sophisticates, most of whom seemed to know squat about agriculture, were not there to listen and learn; they were there

---

[17] In October 1975, Senators George McGovern, Walter Mondale and Hubert Humphrey, all U.S. presidential candidates, sponsored the U.S. Senate's Young Farmers Homestead Act, based on Saskatchewan's Land-Lease Program, which had 500,000 acres leased to farmers at the time.

to "get Janssen". Several stated they could not take Janssen seriously and were highly suspicious of the government's intentions. Finally a former Liberal candidate from Southern Manitoba rose. "Mr. Janssen, it really doesn't matter what you say. We know exactly what your government wants to do with this program. You want to take away the farmers' land."

I stood up, "Mr. Chairman, with the exception of the last speaker, who has such deep insight into government policy, there appears to be some question here about the nature of the government's intentions in having proposed the Land Lease Option. As some of you are aware, I attend cabinet meetings and am privy to the secrets of the government. Since you people appear so interested, I am going to tell you precisely the intentions of the government. You must appreciate this secret has never before been revealed outside the door of the cabinet room."

I paused for dramatic effect while all eyes swung expectantly in my direction, including that of the minister of Agriculture, aware of the rule that cabinet secrets must not be divulged. "Mr. Chairman. The government's intention is this ..." There was rapt attention. *"We don't want your God-damned land."* My anger and frustration vented itself as I shouted, "The only reason we started this program is because too many people are borrowing too much money from the government because you can't get it from the banks. If you want to kill this program so you need not worry about the government stealing your land, stop coming to us for loans to buy land or to pay off your debts. Go to your God-damned banker instead."

It did not get us any votes, but it got their attention.

Columnist Richard Purser, scathingly critical of the program, reported after the meeting: "Is then [the land lease program's] opponents' assumption that the government is crazy for land nationalization a horrible misunderstanding of the government's intentions? If Mr. Janssen and Mr. Schulz were as sincere as they appeared to be, it would appear so."[18]

So I sent a letter to *Winnipeg Tribune* editor Tom Green:

> The attached article by Mr. Purser indicates that at a recent meeting of the Winnipeg C of C (which was always solicitous of the welfare of agriculture), "the Premier's brother-in-law", livid with rage, shouted, 'We don't want your damned land.' Now that 'the Premier's brother-in-law' has revealed government policy on this matter and laid to rest suspicions of farmers and your columnist, would you with your usual fairness, give this revelation the same publicity your publication gave to the government's purported mania for land nationalization?

There was no reply.

---

[18] *The Winnipeg Tribune*, March 21, 1975.

IN FEBRUARY 1975, sixteen years after the Roblin government's massive intervention into the agricultural economy with the MACC and a year after the Schreyer government's intervention with the Land Lease Option, the special committee held its last hearing. We were in Morden, a well-kept town in southern Manitoba, a productive and prosperous area of the province, on a cold but sunny winter day. The area had been settled more than a century earlier by Anglo-Saxons who had planted their seed and culture and were pleased with their work. They were joined in 1875 by German-speaking Mennonites from Ukraine who came to get land, and two generations later, by relatives whose defining historical experience had been the violent expropriation and subsequent destruction of the Wirtschafts they had lovingly built there since the 1770s. Their relocation to Canada had not robbed them of their mystic union with the soil and its fruit:

> Pile the bodies high at Austerlitz and Waterloo
> Shovel them under and let me work. I am the grass.[19]

These were two proud peoples who did not want to be seen taking money from government, but who knew their large place in the provincial economy, and their tendency to block-vote in elections, made it easy for them to get money if they wanted it. They knew that governments salivated for an opportunity to serve them; all they needed do was ask … and they were about to do so.

All day we listened to briefs, mostly sarcastic or vacuous. There was the usual obeisance to "saving the family farm" and "keeping young farmers on the land", but few proposals on how to achieve either. The Land Lease Option was largely dismissed as an insult and referred to with derision. Instead, the central theme of most presentations, perhaps written by the same consultants, was that "all would be well on the farm if the government just abolished the estates tax" (taxes on estates inherited after the death of their owner). "Abolish the estates tax," we were exhorted repeatedly, "and farmers will get along just fine."

To me this seemed sheer hypocrisy; they were playing games with the detested socialists. Hardly a week passed without the government being besieged by farmers and farm organizations pleading for government assistance to rescue them from markets or banks. They were helpless, caught in the unpredictability of turbulent world markets and in the giant scissors of rising costs and falling prices, and without the intervention of government as regulator or lender they were lost and their farms forfeit. Now, we were here to listen to what ailed the industry generally and discuss a radical solution in particular, and we were told the farmers' primary problem was that they had more wealth than they could spend while living and did not want it taxed when they died.

---

[19] Carl Sandberg, "Grass"

Granted, average farm net income had increased substantially from 1969 to 1975. However, this was largely due to a unique—and brief—sharp upward spike in wheat prices because of unusually heavy purchases by the Soviet Union [20] and China, and because of price inflation in the wake of the sudden quadrupling of world oil prices after 1973. All looked good on paper. But not all was well. In the three years between 1971 and 1973 (after which the land purchase program commenced) MACC loans had increased by more than $23 million, [21] for a total of more than $85 million since 1960, most of it to south-central Manitoba. And repayment of capital and interest was in arrears by over sixteen per cent.

Nor were farmers in Conservative southern Manitoba reticent about taking advantage of the new Land Lease Option, no matter how "communistic" they deemed it. In the program's first year, on a purely voluntary basis with no solicitation, the MACC was offered 303 properties, purchased 154, and leased out fifty-nine, mostly to the farmers they were purchased from; fifty-eight per cent of those were in southern Manitoba.

And while Conservative MLAs in the legislature were accusing the government of paying too much for land, out-bidding local buyers, farmers in the Conservative south were hiring lawyers to demand they be paid more. One couple offered their land to the MACC, but were unhappy with the price offered. Their solicitor wrote, "Our clients are most anxious to dispose of their land ... subject to the property being leased to their son ... but your offer is for considerably less than [their] evaluation. I would suggest you re-evaluate your position."

The MACC replied, "The value placed on [your client's] farm constitutes what we consider market value ... [they] are at liberty to dispose of their farm to anyone offering more."

As for the hated estates tax, three days earlier a Bank of Montreal agent had come to demand abolition of this tax but admitted only one-third of one per-cent of estates processed the previous year—a total of twenty-four farms—were taxable. According to the 1971 census, only 708 farms had a value above the taxable bracket. Minus debts, there were almost none. But the general prosperity of the 1970s, unexpected income from a market blip, and Uskiw's taxpayer-financed programs, had put real money into farmers' pockets, and prospects of selling their land to foreigners made them millionaires in their own minds.

Psychologically they had gone from country cousin to country club. They envisioned the establishment of dynasties, and they resented the general community requiring repayment, through estates taxes, of unearned profits from the funds it had invested in them.

---

[20] The Soviet Union bought so much wheat from American grain brokers that the U.S. government was forced to stop sales and buy back some grain already sold.

[21] In 1979, the Federal Farm Credit Corporation reported that during the last half of the decade Manitoba farmers were above the national average in borrowing money to buy land. "In 1976-77 Manitoba farm loans ... [went] 72% for land purchase and 14% for debt consolidation." *Winnipeg Free Press*, February 10, 1979.

At supper I sat with MLA and committee member Tom Barrow. I attended caucus meetings for six weeks before knowing Barrow was capable of speech. He had been a coal miner in Nova Scotia where, in 1958 in the murderous Springhill mine, seventy-five miners were sucked into eternity. He had relocated to Flin Flon, become a hard-rock miner, and in 1969 was elected to the legislature for that arid, uninviting community in northern Manitoba. He had also been a boxer, shown by the elasticity in his step when he walked, but when sitting he sometimes exhibited the classic symptoms of having taken too many punches to the head. He would sit at the long, mirror-polished caucus room table, the personification of the broken soldier on the battlefield of life, staring down, skin stretched tightly over craggy features, hair white at age fifty-one, "bowed by the weight of centuries", visage brooding, tortured, inscrutable. Then, one day, he erupted like a smoldering volcano.

The outburst was occasioned by a visit to caucus of the sign painters union, seeking permission for billboard advertising of liquor, which was illegal at the time. It was self-serving job creation and caucus was opposed, almost to a man. Still, the discussion demonstrated the openness of the NDP caucus to any group or individual with an issue or a problem. And it demonstrated that Barrow was vocal, for suddenly he spoke, with a surprising torrent of words.

> B-b-but, Mr. Chairman. What's wrong with billboards? For centuries
> billboards have been used by people to carry messages and they were
> mostly our kind of people who could not afford other forms of media and
> we should be proud that in this world of expensive and esoteric communi-
> cations technology billboards are still available and we should do what is
> necessary to promote their use and preserve them and they should not be
> considered from the purely economic perspective because billboards also
> have intrinsic value if you can imagine the utter tedium of driving from
> here to Calgary across 700 miles of featureless prairie topography without
> being able to observe the occasional billboard and at times the only expres-
> sion of civilization in the midst of arid monotony and the only joy in life is
> a billboard and I have been caught in situations when my only shelter from
> the stormy blast and prying eyes when I needed to relieve my bladder was
> a billboard and billboards have multiple uses and I had my first piece of
> tail behind a billboard and …

Caucus exploded in raucous guffaws. Tom had made his case—with all except Caucus Chairman James Walding, whose laconic, cultured English voice caused another explosion of laughter with, "Granted, Tom, but as great as you appear to believe billboards are, would you want your daughter to marry one?"

In private conversation, Barrow was loquacious, displaying a lust for life reserved primarily to those familiar with the ease of losing it. When in pensive mood, he reflected on life in the coal mines, black and eerie, with every sound potentially presaging sudden death, or worse, slow death by entombment. He recalled the terror of his younger days, when entering the ominous shafts required an effort of will, and every day might be their last:

> Life, to be sure, is nothing much to lose,
> But young men think it is, and we were young. [22]

He spoke of the vicious fights with the mining companies for wages sufficient to validate themselves as sentient humans and to compensate their families for wrestling with the ever-present shadow of the nearness of the death of their breadwinner. "But we sometimes got our revenge. We knew they had delivery quotas and we would work as slowly as possible all week. And suddenly they would realize they didn't have the supply. And then they would have to pay us double-time-and-a-half all weekend."

Barrow never felt apologetic. This was part of the bargaining process and of economic survival, and he considered any extra income miners could make by such means as deserved because he had often witnessed the unforgiving nature of their work. He stood in his place one day, tears in his eyes, his low voice holding the rapt attention of his colleagues in the chamber as he graphically and poignantly described how the skin and flesh were stripped off the body of a Manitoba miner who had fallen to his death down a narrow mine-shaft that morning. He would become impassioned in pleas to the legislature for better working conditions for miners and supervision by government inspectors, instead of entrusting that to company foremen. One day, describing relationships between owners and workers, his voice suddenly rose. "Mr. Speaker. Mr. Speaker. I tell you Mr. Speaker, that foreman is a bastard. That foreman is a real bastard."

Martinet Speaker Peter Fox's darkening visage and immediate motion to rise from his thronelike chair was warning he was about to declare such language "unparliamentary" and demand retraction on pain of expulsion, but Barrow anticipated him, "Mr. Speaker. Mr. Speaker. Please. Before you say my language is unparliamentary, Mr. Speaker, I just want to say, Mr. Speaker, that in a mining community, 'bastard' is a term of endearment."

And Barrow was tough as nails. One day he reported to caucus, hesitatingly, more in sorrow than in anger, on a recent trip to Thompson, accompanied by Rupertsland MLA Jean Allard. He had overheard Allard telling a Liberal party organizer that, under certain circumstances, he would consider abandoning the NDP to run as a Liberal candidate in the 1972 federal election.

The tension rose as Barrow haltingly described what he considered an act of betrayal by a caucus colleague. He sat, bowed over the caucus table, and Allard was sitting directly behind him on a chesterfield. A sound came from Allard as though he intended to say something in contradiction. Like a tiger Barrow spun in his chair, leaned toward Allard three feet away, his wiry, six-foot body slightly

---

[22] Alfred E. Houseman, *Poems.*

bent like a tautened bow. "Jean, you son-of-a-bitch. Say a word and I'll kill you."

Allard slowly uncoiled his long, lithe body and stood up, tall as a tree. An intelligent, educated, articulate Métis, descendant of Jean-Baptiste Lagimodière, who walked from Winnipeg to Montreal to tell Lord Selkirk of the massacre of his settlers at Seven Oaks in 1816, and nephew of a Rhodes Scholar who had been ambassador to Cuba and Denmark, Allard was proud, confident, vital. His finely-chiselled classical features topped by a shock of wavy, graying hair; he was an aristocrat. He stood briefly while the air crackled with tension. Then, without a word the man who helped the NDP government legislate Autopac and Unicity, and abolish Medicare premiums, turned and walked out of the caucus room—and out of the caucus—to sit as an Independent.

Back at the land lease committee meeting, Barrow's reckless toughness was now needed: "Tom," I said, "What we have been fed this afternoon is pure, number one, unadulterated, grade A, triple-distilled bullshit. Those presenting briefs consider us a joke because we represent the NDP government. They are entertaining each other by making sport of us. We are being led to believe the farmers' only problem is that this socialist—read "communist"—government will not allow them to die without paying a tax on their unearned gains." I reminded him that the estates tax applies only to the portion of net worth exceeding $200,000 per estate and added that they all want to leave the impression they are worth more than $200,000 and that they all accrued that wealth all by themselves, without any help from government or from society in general, and intended to keep it.

"A large amount of public money is going into southern Manitoba in one form or another," I continued, "and it has become almost an industry here to ask for tax concessions or assistance from government. For some of these people to live without applying for a grant or loan—especially from an NDP government—would be as cataclysmic as for a good Catholic to die unshriven."

I had an idea. "Tom. We are going to put an end to their merriment. When we go back there after supper and another brief is presented demanding abolition of the estates tax, I want you to stand up and demand a show of hands by those with a net worth of more than $200,000."

Barrow laid down his knife and fork and looked at me, unsure. "B-b-but Herb. There are a lot of rich farmers down here."

"Tom. There will be two kinds of farmers in the hall. There will be those who, when you ask that question, will want to impress us, as strangers, by having us believe they are worth more than $200,000, but they know their neighbours know they are not so they will not raise their hands. Then there is another kind of farmer, especially here in the south, who are worth more than $200,000, but they don't want the Income Tax Department to know, so they will not raise their hands. Tom, I believe if you ask that question, not a single hand will be raised. We can cut these hypocrites off at the knees and you're the man to do it."

Barrow looked skeptical, but said nothing.

We returned to the hall and the hearing reconvened. The first presenter informed us, with emphasis and with smug, sidelong glances at his associates, that the greatest single problem facing the farmer was the estates tax ...

Tom Barrow leaped to his feet, visibly perturbed, "Mr. Chairman. Mr. Chairman. I want a show of hands to see how many here are worth more than two hundred thousand dollars net."

The chairman, somewhat startled, put the question. Not a single hand went up. The balloon was punctured. The farce was ended. After a moment the farmers, singly or in groups, began to leave.

THREE YEARS LATER, after the NDP government had been defeated, I had found a new vocation and was attending a meeting of Pioneer Life Insurance agents. All morning the big, middle-aged man from southern Manitoba had been glaring at me. The meeting recessed for coffee. He walked around the table and leaned menacingly over me. "You were at that meeting of that land committee in Morden a couple of years ago?" It was both a question and an assertion.

"Ye-e-es-s."

"You're the guy who was taking all the notes?" This time it was both a question and an accusation, and his voice was hardening. "Ye-e-e-ess." I felt exposed, as though naked in the streets. "You're the guy who put Tom Barrow up to asking that question about how many of us were worth more than two hundred thousand dollars." His voice was laden with accusation.

"Yes." My initial apprehension was giving way to defiance.

"You knew damn well there were people in that hall that day, like me, who were worth more than $200,000."

"So why in hell didn't you raise your hand?"

"You know damn well why. I didn't want the income tax people to know. You son-of-a-bitch. I could have killed you that day."

XXVII

The Government and the 'Indians'[1]

Men and nations will do the right thing only after all other avenues
of recourse have been exhausted.
> —Katz's Law

Dear **Mr. Premier,** I refer to the Cross Lake Band's need for a rock
crusher and your election promise. Enclosed is a copy of a letter received
from the chief of the Cross Lake band … He points out that there were
witnesses at the time when you made your election promise … I urge you
to honour your word. The time has gone when our people will accept
promises not backed by action … We will no longer put up with words
from forked tongues.

> Yours in Brotherhood
> (signed) Chief Dave Courchene
> President

The missive came on the letterhead of the Manitoba Indian Brotherhoood.
The time had come to put an end to this farce:

> Dear Chief Courchene, I enclose a letter received under MIB letter-
> head and purportedly signed by you. Since you have had constant access
> to Premier Schreyer's office, and are aware of his efforts on behalf of the
> native people of this province, and since you are aware the decision to pro-
> ceed at Cross Lake has been made but that the work must await heavy

---

[1] In the past thirty years, the terminology has metamorphosed from the term "Indian", which resulted
from the erroneous belief of early Spanish adventurers that they had stumbled onto the shores of
India, to 'native' to 'Aboriginal' and finally to 'First Nations'. In the period about which this chapter is
written, the term "Indian" was widely used and in fact is still used by some Aboriginal Manitobans
today. While most of this section uses modern terminology, "Indian" is used here without prejudice.

frost, and that criticism for lack of action should be directed at the Federal Department of Indian Affairs, I am certain you would never insult Premier Schreyer by accusing him of 'promises not backed by action' or using 'words from forked tongues'. Consequently, I conclude that someone less knowledgeable than you are is misusing your name and I attach the letter for your perusal.

Sincerely
(signed) Herb Schulz, Assistant to the Premier

It had begun in April when the premier, on a flight to Thompson, and curious about what was happening in Manitoba, landed at Cross Lake. Rain had made the grass landing strip muddy, clogging the wheels of the small plane which tipped and bent the propeller. He left the plane muttering that the runway should be gravelled. He was picked up by another plane and continued his tour. Before he returned to Winnipeg, a phone call from Cross Lake informed me the premier had made an "election promise" to gravel their airstrip. Thereafter, every few weeks, by letter or phone, the "promise" escalated to include gravelling the airstrip and community roads, providing a water truck, a fire truck and a rock crusher, and building a bridge over a river, with no road on the other side.

No matter how often we explained some things would not be done and others would take time, the demands continued and became more imperious. They ended with my letter to Courchene. He never spoke to me again. He never looked at me directly again, even through the dark "cheaters" he affected. But Courchene was an aggressive leader who fought hard for his people and did not allow the loss of a few battles to deflect his firm resolve to win the war. And he was astute at snatching opportunities to promote his objectives.

The letters from Courchene and the chief of Cross Lake exemplified the nature of much of their correspondence—brief, direct, leaving no doubt about what they wanted and usually in very good English. Similarly, in meetings with Aboriginal leaders, I marvelled at their verbal facility. And many bureaucrats, ignorantly believing them to be inarticulate, were surprised on meeting them.[2]

The correspondence with Courchene and the chief also marked the metamorphosis of my relationship with Aboriginal people. As a member of a minority before that became exotic, I needed no instructions on the raging frustrations it generates. And since I had never believed myself to be bigoted or racist, I saw no need for pseudo-liberal self-flagellations or contorted apologia. Furthermore, having grown up in a pioneer family that hacked its living out of the bush, I viewed the conditions on reserves differently than did some others. While they saw "third world conditions", I saw millions of dollars dedicated to improving the lives of Aboriginal Canadians, with no noticeable improvement.

---

[2]   U.S. President George W. Bush has defined this attitude as "the soft racism of low expectations".

As a child I was taught all humans are equal, that "race" was a fictitious division imposed by demagogues and power seekers. By my late teens, it had become clear to me this was not a universal attitude. On Saturday evenings, when the people of the community gathered in town to shop and socialize, there was often a fight at the "hotel corner", and usually one of the combatants was from the reserve west of town. I noticed that he would often be goaded into the fight and then arrested and deposited in the lockup by the town policeman, who often arrived just after the Aboriginal combatant had been beaten to a pulp.

Determined to try to change this scenario, I waited until the fight commenced, reported it to the police, and demanded that he arrest the non-native pugilists who had started it. I never got anyone arrested, but the attacks on the young men from the reserve became more circumspect.

I also became acquainted with the residents of a local reserve and watched in anger as the Indian agent allowed their herds to dwindle and leased their land to white farmers, while their machinery was left in the fields to rust and they became dependent on welfare. The result was despair, which resulted in many of them poisoning themselves with home-made liquor brewed in zinc-plated tubs.

I visited at the home of Tommy Prince, a gentle man who was one of Canada's genuine war heroes. Dust blew by the blanket that was used as a door to his stifling hot one-room shack, and flies feasted on the face of his feverish year-old child. And I questioned what manner of society would permit this to happen to someone who had risked his life so valiantly on our behalf.

During those years, offended white Canadians often regarded me with contempt for speaking of "equality" for our native people. Later, the Aboriginal people themselves regarded me with contempt for suggesting "equality" implied supporting themselves, while the new "liberal" whites, unable to distinguish between liberalism and lunacy, saw me as a bigot and a racist.

NOW THAT I WAS PART OF a government seeking to help Aboriginal Manitobans to become self-sustaining, through the funding of economic development programs, I met mostly those who came to the Premier's Office to borrow money (which came out of my pocket) for bus fare back to a reserve, or to stay at a hotel overnight. And there were their leaders, who came to complain to the premier that "our people" (they always used the possessive) were being mistreated and to demand that Canada be returned to them because "we were here first".[3] I concluded they were prepared to do anything except contribute usefully to the objectives

---

[3] This often reminded me of Central European history, which for the past three millennia has been crossed by invading Celts, Gauls, Romans, Goths, Lombards, Franks, Saxons, Huns, Thuringians, Friesens, Danes, Magyars, Vikings, Slavs, Mongols, Swedes and Turks. Unless driven back, each group established itself by either absorbing or killing those who "were here first". No tribe even hallucinated about giving land they had occupied back to its former owners—unless they were strong enough to take it.

they ostensibly desired, and to discuss anything except reality. I attended a meeting at which a dozen native leaders sat at the cabinet table telling the premier what they wanted, which involved everything except work. After they left, I said, "Mr. Premier, I listened patiently while your guests demanded roads, houses, hydro, phones, sewer and water, tourist lodges, shopping centres, and a "land base" to put all this on. Normally people earn these things by working. What do these people do?"

"I don't know. Why do you ask?"

"While you were listening to them I was looking at their hands. None has as many callouses as I have and I do very little."[4]

ONE AUTUMN DAY I accompanied the relief doctor to Headingley Gaol. Prisoners were sitting, mostly on corridor floors, playing musical instruments, reading, playing cards. They seemed relaxed. Most were Aboriginal. Later the doctor explained: "It happens every autumn. They come to the city with no marketable skills and no homes. They live on the streets or in rabbit-warren rooming houses with friends. Headingley offers food and shelter. When it gets cold they do something that gets them a six-month sentence. That's what you saw today."

I recall that incident when treated to heart-rending stories of "racism" causing the over-representation of Aboriginals in our prisons.

THE CEO of the then publicly-owned Manitoba Telephone System phoned. The utility had been instructed to extend phone services onto the _____ Reserve. The chief wanted $300 for every pole emplacement.

"So what's the problem?"

"We pay only $50 per pole emplacement in white communities."

"So pay them $50 like you do elsewhere."

"They won't take only $50. They demand $300. What shall I do?"

"The answer is simple. You just don't build the line."

I recall that incident when I hear the heart-rending stories of how First Nations people are being systemically discriminated against.

---

[4] My sentiments were echoed by the late John Rogers, the long-time, streetwise—and sympathetic—director of the Main Street Project, Winnipeg's major detoxification shelter. He said that native leaders should put their energy into solving their problems instead of blaming whites. "I don't see any here getting their hands dirty." "Mister Rogers' Neighbourhood", *Winnipeg Free Press*, March 19, 1989.

IT OFTEN SEEMED TO ME that the galaxy of programs for native Manitobans had taught them everything except how to get their hands dirty. Clem Blakeslee, a Cherokee with a Ph.D. in Sociology, came to our public service via a professorship at the University of Calgary. He feared that the government was not committing enough manpower to help natives in the North, while I argued we had too many programs for the good they were doing. We talked frequently.

He was sight-impaired and one morning I heard his cane tapping along the marble corridor toward my office and anticipated another verbal joust. Instead, he said, "I just returned from two weeks in the North and I found out what our problem is there. We have too damn many civil servants there simply because they are not happy at home. Instead of our development officers concentrating on economic programs, they are social animators, persuading the people to be even more unhappy than they already are. They are teaching them everything except how to do something useful. They do little but get into mischief. I call them The Great Ass Patrol."

In October 1973, the government caucus took a weekend tour on the *MS Lord Selkirk* and stopped at Berens River Reserve. The premier met with the council. They wanted village roads gravelled, a school bus, a phone in each house instead of booths in the village and television. Back aboard I approached the premier. "The village is only a couple of miles long," I said, "so it is a short walk to school and there are no roads to the outside, so there are few vehicles. Instead of school buses, gravelled roads, private phones and television, what these people need is something to do. Ken Dillen [our MLA for Thompson] and I walked the length of the village. There is substantial poplar growth which usually means soil suited to growing grain or legumes. Probably all the bread and meat is freighted in here. Why not give the community a caterpillar tractor, a brush-cutter and a good plow, so they can break up land and grow feed? We can give them livestock and they can produce milk and fresh meat for themselves."

"That's an interesting idea. Check out some cost figures."

I phoned an acquaintance who was in the land clearing business and knew machinery, explained my intentions, and asked, "Wally, can you get us the necessary equipment?"

"Sure. But it's of no use. We did that at [he named a reserve] a number of years ago. We broke up about 1,100 acres. Half of it has now been leased out to whites and the rest has gone back to bush. It won't work. Save the taxpayers the money."

I recall that incident when treated to heart-rending stories about there being no economic opportunities on reserves.[5]

---

[5] John Rodgers told the commission of inquiry into the shooting death of native leader J J Harper by a policeman, "Natives are over-represented in the prison system because they are over-represented in the commission of crime ... If you break the law, it's not racism if the cops bust you ... the natives will stop being hassled by [police] when the stereotype changes. [But] the leaders of some native organizations have an interest in promoting the idea that racism exists in the system."

IN THE SPRING OF 1974, waters from melting snows, augmented by a four-inch deluge on the Victoria Day weekend, burst the banks of the Red and Assiniboine Rivers and spread across the flatlands of southern Manitoba. The situation was critical and the government went on twenty-four-hour alert. Departments mounted relief programs; ministers did helicopter reconnaissance of affected areas; the Emergency Measures Organization was activated; several hundred troops with trucks, amphibious vehicles and helicopters were brought from Alberta; people and livestock were moved out just ahead of the enveloping water and sometimes in it. We enlisted municipalities, set up regional offices, notified hospitals to prepare for emergencies, and prepared lists of facilities for evacuees.

We moved like Satan's minions in Milton's *Paradise Lost*, "in perfect phalanx to the Dorian mood". Each noon the premier and members of relevant committees of cabinet met with the director of the EMO and his regional lieutenants to hear reports, assess developments, plan evacuations, and issue orders. One day, the reports were being given by responsible officials in the usual concise, precise, almost military manner: "Mr. Premier, at Portage la Prairie the water has risen three inches in the past twenty-four hours. The Portage Diversion is full. If the water rises four more inches we must begin evacuations of the towns along the Assiniboine between Winnipeg and Portage."

"Mr. Premier. The Americans are predicting a four-inch rise at Emerson, barring more rain. If the rise is more than five inches we may need to evacuate everyone within ten miles of the Red."

"Mr. Premier. The Army is evacuating persons and farm animals by helicopter and amphibious vehicles. People are being cooperative, but we may need more health care facilities for the ill and elderly."

We sat in the sombre cabinet room, tense and tired, nervous and threatened, the premier forming the calm centre of the storm, knowing we may be facing a catastrophe, and knowing "the buck stops here". It was a helluva mess, but so far so good. No one had died, no one had gone berserk, no one had threatened to shoot government officials for letting their grain rot, no one had asked for favours, no one had refused to evacuate.

Then, "Mr. Premier, the chief of Roseau River has sent an ultimatum. No one will move until the government promises a private house for each family to move into, with at least one coloured television set in each house, and the government promises to provide catering service three times a day for the able-bodied men who remain on the reserve."

The room became a vacuum as breaths were sucked in. I rose: "Mr. Premier. Should we not just let them drown?" His frown showed he was not amused. But they were treated just like every other Manitoban.

I recall that incident when treated to heart-rending stories of people on reserves being mistreated.

JULY 29, 1973, the day after the provincial election, was a glorious day. Not as many seats as we wanted but enough to prove our election in 1969 was no aberration. It was a good day to be alive, and to be a member of the New Democratic Party and a senior political functionary of the Government of Manitoba, was close to Heaven.

I walked across the wide, marble-floored corridor, through the dark-panelled Cabinet Room exuding majesty, and into the Premier's Office. It was only mid-morning on the first day of the new mandate, but already a pile of files lay in front of him. The premier's secretary, the keeper of the gate through whom all seeking an audience with the premier must pass, entered.

"Mr. Premier, Mr. Courchene and his men are here to see you."

In another age, Dave Courchene might have been a warrior leader holding the eastern Marches for Charlemagne, or a merchant prince accompanying Marco Polo to the myth-shrouded Orient, or a scout for Captain Hawkins collecting African blacks to be transported aboard the good ship *Jesus* to some Carribean sugar island. In 1973, he was the powerful, articulate, irreverent "Super Chief", president of the Manitoba Indian Brotherhood. And he knew his power. Accused of being arrogant, he responded publicly, "You should get used to it because there is going to be more of it."

Informed that Courchene often sat in the first class section of the same plane to Ottawa in which the premier flew economy, I had approached Jean Allard, an articulate NDP member of the legislature, and a Métis who knew Courchene well. "Jean, our policy is that government personnel fly economy and if its good enough for the premier, it should be good enough for Courchene. Manitoba taxpayers pay part of the cost of his tickets and if they find out he is flying first class it will cause political problems and make it harder for us to help him."

Several days later Allard said he had spoken with Courchene. "Davie said, 'We've been fucked by the white man long enough and it's our turn to fuck the white man.'" Obviously Dave Courchene was going first class all the way … and with no apologies.

Now I rose to leave, but the premier invited me to remain: "They want to talk about farming, with which you are familiar."

Courchene, a powerfully-built 5'8", 200-pound bundle of swarthy self confidence, wearing his trademark fringed buckskin jacket and dark sunglasses, strode rapidly into the room and sat down at the desk, facing the premier. The two six-foot Anderson brothers, native farmers from the Interlake, neat in work shirts and jeans, followed him in and sat down, one at each end of the premier's desk. From my position on a chesterfield out of harm's way, the premier appeared surrounded; he didn't have a chance.

Without preliminaries, Courchene slapped his hand on the desk: "Listen Eddie. Right now. We need $20,000 from you. The Feds are giving us $19 million for Indian farmers. We need $20,000 from Manitoba to hire a consultant to show us how to use it."

"Well Davie, why not take that $20,000 out of the $19 million?"

"The Feds won't allow it. The $19 million is strictly for investment in agriculture. We need the extra money to hire a consultant. Only then will we get the $19 million."[6]

The discussion continued. The premier was sympathetic and cooperative but appeared skeptical. I had an idea. "Mr. Premier, why not loan Mr. Courchene and his people an expert from our Department of Agriculture. We will pay his salary as we are doing now, and he can provide the consulting services."

Courchene smashed his fist on the premier's desk top: "No! We want someone we can tell what to do."

I was incensed. "If you already know so much about agriculture that you can tell your consultant what to do, you don't need a consultant."

The atmosphere became tense. The premier played peacemaker. "Well Davie, do you have anyone in particular in mind?"

"Yes." He mentioned a name I recognized. "Listen," I told him, "I believe the primary interest of this consultant will be to get you funding, but Ottawa is already giving more money than you know what to do with. What your people need now is not a consultant, but a practical farmer who can show you how to plow a furrow and nurse a sick cow and distinguish between soil types and repair a tractor and mend a fence and build a shed. We can provide you with such persons if you are serious about farming."

The air suddenly smelled of cordite. Courchene was livid. The discussion came to an embarrassing halt and he and his men departed. They were not pleased. Neither was the premier.

"It is not good enough to simply say 'No' to these people because their proposals appear impractical. Dave may be fantasizing a bit and they are feeling their way along a path new and strange to them, but we should be happy they are attempting something. They need help and if Ottawa is financing this venture, that should be sufficient to enlist our assistance.

"Instead of dismissing them cavalierly, why don't you inquire if our Department of Agriculture is aware of this federal initiative and discuss with them if there is something practical we can do?"

I approached the long-time deputy minister, a respected figure in agricultural circles (later general manager of Manitoba Pool Elevators) and related the discussion in the Premier's Office. "Assuming the Feds are serious about this venture and the Indians are serious about farming, do you have any suggestions for how we

---

[6] I was skeptical about this explanation, but later had cause to wonder when we had an application from a reserve applying to the Manitoba Agricultural Credit Corporation for a loan to purchase a snowmobile "for fishing". The application had been declined because he already had a snowmobile from the Department of Indian Affairs. He claimed Indian Affairs only allowed him to use it for trapping, not fishing, and a call to Ottawa confirmed this.

might help make this work?" I asked him.

"Oh yes, we're away ahead of you. Several months ago we learned of Ottawa's initiative and we established a committee to plan how to proceed in the most rational way. There are six men on the committee, including Chief Courchene. In fact, we have a report to show how we envision this program proceeding."

I read the report. It proposed establishing 300 native families on farms, each with a minimum of 500 acres of land and 100 head of livestock. On the committee that produced the report was the consultant Courchene had mentioned. I went back to the deputy. "What in hell are you people doing?" I asked him. "Farming is not a sentimental exercise for people with nothing else to do. It is learned by experience, not by borrowing a bunch of money and waving a magic wand. You start small, learn the business, and if you survive you acquire a larger operation.

I asked him whether his committee was really serious. "You are proposing entrusting 100 head of cattle to people with no experience with domesticated animals except dogs. By the end of the first year several animals will have been eaten and most of the others will be dead of pneumonia, hoof rot, milk fever, bloat or starvation."

I told him not to set them up for another expensive failure. "The only possible consequence of this preposterous proposal will be to leave the natives more cynical and the taxpayers more angry. Let's develop a program that is within their competence.[7]

"And incidentally, what in hell is this consultant doing on this committee? I assume this outrageous report is his creation."

Two days later, a man in his early forties, well built and well-dressed, walked unannounced into my office. He stared down at me through dark sunglasses and said, quietly but emphatically, "I hear you have something against me."

"Who are you?" I asked impatiently.

"I'm _____, the consultant from _____"

My sphincter snapped shut. A pall descended over the day as though a curtain had been suddenly drawn. The "seats of the mighty" had my buttocks in a vice-grip. I groped for words, "O-o-hhh, I have nothing against you personally. I don't even know you". My breath was returning and my heart palpitations were slowing. "However, I do have something against the philosophy emanating from your area that all would be well on the farm if farmers just borrow more money, preferably from government."

I was surprised to be so suddenly confronted. Obviously this was not a man to be trifled with, and he was much bigger than I. So I invited him to the downstairs cafeteria for coffee. He was, fortunately for me, a civilized man. We related well to each other. The fact that I had been a farmer was helpful. I learned

---

[7] "Tribal Wi Chi Way Win Capital Corporation has some 11 delinquent loans left from the approximately 300 acquired when it took over the portfolio of bankrupt Manitoba Indian Agricultural Program of 1994 ... Some [loans] date back 20 years." "Tribal trying to collect loans", *Winnipeg Free Press*, January 22, 1998.

that he and his brothers had established a farm corporation, and were experimenting with special crops and developing warehouse facilities and markets. In brief, they were master farmers, on excellent land, with a wealth of accumulated family experience, and were conducting a highly capitalized agri-business operation.

There was much about which we agreed and we developed an almost friendly relationship while dancing around the salient issue which had brought him here. It appeared the beauty of the day was returning and that the "seats of the mighty" had been contoured to fit my posterior, and then he asked the fateful question, "Have you read my report on native agricultural development?"

"Yes."

"What did you think of it?"

"Frankly, when I completed reading your report I had a mental picture of six men sitting around a table and saying to each other, 'The Feds are giving us $19 million; how do we blow it?'"

He sat there, in his fine-textured dark brown suit, white shirt and colour-coded tie, fine-featured and sun-browned, the picture of an educated, competent, confident gentlemen farmer. I expected a violent reaction, though he didn't look like a violent man.

He looked down and stared at the table for what appeared a long time. Then he raised his head, looked directly at me, and said quietly, but with a hint of inner agitation, "That is a very astute observation. But look … I was not the worst … Dave Courchene was much worse than I."

Several months later, I accompanied a group of ministers to a local hotel to meet with Chief Courchene and several others. I was immediately accosted by the two Anderson brothers from Lake St. Martins, who had been at Courchene's meeting with the premier the day after the election. "You refused to give us that money because we are Indians," one of them growled.

I sought to disabuse him. "No. There are many unhappy white petitioners out there who also consider me a son-of-a-bitch."

"GEORGE MUNROE."

The name reverberated off the dark-panelled ceiling of the cabinet room and wafted down into a void of stunned silence.

The Government of Manitoba had decided to establish a Native Branch within the Department of Education and needed a director. Ideally, it should be someone with experience and ability, who had some competence in the area, and already had a constituency to sustain him when—as it would—all appeared to turn to ratshit. Also, it should be someone who took this seriously and appreciated the fact that education provided a way out of poverty and into social and economic mobility for the native people.

"We could ask the Manitoba Indian Brotherhood for names," suggested one of our ministers.

"No! We would incur their wrath if we reject their nominee," responded another.

"Are we confining ourselves to native people in this search?"

"No, but we named a francophone as head of our recently established French Education Branch. In any case we want to have role models for the natives and this is such an opportunity."

"There may be a paucity of material to draw from, but to not appoint a native as director of the Native Education Branch would be inexcusable and would conceivably endanger all we want to accomplish with this exercise. We need a native."

But who? This vexing question elicited the awesome name from a minister.

"But ... but ... he hates whites," stammered one of his colleagues.

"That's precisely why I suggested him. For that reason he will work very hard to provide service to the native people."

Munroe was not a "new age Indian" like the later prodigies of the galaxy of native organizations, who expected Canada to be handed back to them, gift-wrapped. Nor was he a romantic like the academics who had never seen a reserve and feared Aboriginals would feel deprived if Manitoba Hydro replaced their tar-paper shacks with frame houses. Asked "What does the Indian want?" he replied tartly, "The Indian wants what the white man wants."

A former school teacher, he was articulate, had a quick, humourless wit, and the will to use it. He developed a reputation as a white hater, but his talent for sarcastic one-liners was not confined to non-natives. Later, running as a Liberal in the provincial seat of Rupertsland and losing to another educated and articulate native, NDP candidate Eric Robinson, Munroe quipped, "The old guard got in. It's the well known and the well worn."

In 1971, he won a seat for the NDP in Winnipeg's first Unicity election, but did not run again and accepted the government's invitation to become director of the Native Education Branch. Within a week of his appointment, he sent a peremptory memo to Management Committee of Cabinet; he was appointing four native assistants at a specified salary, and he virtually demanded approval.

MCC checked departmental expenditures and assessed departmental requests for non-budgeted spending. We were incensed by the prospect of adding four civil servants and by Munroe's demand being made almost before he had time to warm his chair. However, we were committed to the project and could not allow diversion from our objective by the acerbic personality of the new director.

But our uneasiness found consensus in a desire to buy time. The auditor for the Department of Education was instructed to see if the salaries Munroe specified for his men conformed to the civil service scale. It was a legitimate concern and had the virtue of postponing the decision. The next Tuesday, the auditor reported the proper salary for this job description was $2,000 less than requested. Munroe was sent a memo agreeing to the hirings, but at the lower salary. The following week, his response awaited us.

"Indians will not work for only $_____ a year."

The memo showed admirable economy with words—and a concern with reducing the oft-quoted "90% unemployment" among natives. He felt it was better to leave them unemployed than working for the wage paid white civil servants.

He was sent an equally cryptic reply, "Hire whites."

Several weeks later the ministers were taking their places at the cabinet table when the door literally burst open. Education Minister Ben Hanuschak was the personification of the unexcitable man, with an always active mind but giving the impression of good natured insouciance, and was always surrounded by a cloud of smoke from an eight-inch pipe. This day the pipe was nowhere in sight as he slammed the huge, heavy oak door shut. "Gentlemen, I want to tell you something. And I am not asking you … I am telling you … I have just fired George Munroe."

He tossed a letter on the polished oak table. It explained in spirited language that the NDP government's expressed concern with the welfare of Aboriginal Manitobans was a sham, and the appointment of the signatory as director of the Native Education Branch was merely a political ploy to hire a "token Indian". The letter was signed by George Munroe, and copied to about twenty people. For whatever his sufferings, real or imagined, he had his revenge. He had also, as they say on the farm, shit in his nest. No one dared argue with the minister.

George Munroe gravitated to other endeavours. He purchased an older house, converted it to an Indian-Métis Friendship Centre, renovated it at a cost of $26,500 … and sent the bill to the premier. The mail office brought it to me. I read it and pushed it to the side of the desk with other matters to be handled when I had time for non-essentials.

One week later I received a phone call from Corrections Minister Bud Boyce. Bud was the pleasant, well-liked fifty-year-old MLA for the city core constituency of Winnipeg Centre. He had served in the Canadian Navy on the Murmansk run, earned a degree in Agriculture and another in Education, and had been a teacher with the Winnipeg School Division. A reformed alcoholic, he cared deeply about his unfortunate brethren and sometimes appeared, like a tired Atlas, to be carrying the weight of the world. He always had unlimited time to listen to the problems of his constituents, and a supreme sense of compassion, which left him prey to every supplicant and panhandler in Winnipeg.

"Herb, I need to see you. I'm bringing George Munroe with me."

I riffled through the papers on my desk for Munroe's letter. Bud and George came in, sat down, and Bud came right to the point.

"George tells me he sent a letter to the premier a week ago asking for money to pay for the renovations to his Friendship Centre and he has not yet received a reply."

"No, he hasn't. I have the letter." I turned to Munroe. "George, you have been with government and know you cannot send us a bill and expect a cheque by return mail. You know we want to help your people but we have no budgetary appropriation for this. In future, we would appreciate it if you ask before you spend our money. But it is spent and we will find a way to help you. Desjardins handles the lotteries funds. We have grants for cultural groups and we will break some of that loose for you. I'll explain to Desjardins and arrange for you to pick up the cheque ..."

Munroe had stood up. He was arrow-straight, of medium height, slim and lean and lithe and tough as whipcord, overall giving the impression of a coiled spring. His hard, dark eyes, fairly burning in their sockets, transfixed me and his voice was quiet and even, but filled with suppressed intensity. "WE are not a cultural group. We are a nation."

I picked up his letter with the demand for $26,500 on something about which we had not been consulted, and extended it to him, "George, nations pay their own way. You can begin by paying this."

He hesitated momentarily, then took the letter, turned on his heel, and quickly walked out. I never saw him again.

XXVIII

The Greening of the NDP

What is right in practice will prove right in theory.
                    —Francis Bacon,
                         sixteenth-century English scientist and philosopher

Sidney Green considered politics a noble calling. He was an adornment to the legislature, a champion to his friends, a guide for the party caucus, a scourge for his political opponents, a flaming radical who would burn down the world to remake it in his own image for members of the Chamber of Commerce, and a conservative for the government he repeatedly saved, with his cautious approach, from potential embarrassment.

"If there is no need to legislate, let us not legislate," he would say, reminiscent of the British peer credited with the classic definition of Conservatism: "If it is not necessary to change, it is necessary to not change." But Green would not have defined this as 'Conservatism', but as social and political realism; changes must be made—that is why he and his colleagues were in politics—but for the purposes of expanding the sphere of freedom and equality, not for their own sake.

He did not see politics as war by other means, but as an arena in which men and women contended peacefully and respectfully, with weapons of ideas. And he believed the greatest "right" in a democracy is the right to be wrong. The contention of ideas, in a democratic forum, was the human path to self-actualization, but he was too much a student of history to expect this to happen quickly, if ever. As Milton's cerebral Satan had cautioned: "Long is the way, and hard, that out of darkness leads to light."

A logician par excellence, he often infuriated eager new cabinet colleagues after they had completed a presentation on a departmental initiative and its expected consequences, by beginning his rebuttal, "Let me explain how the opposite will happen." He cited 'The Law of Unanticipated Consequences' to illustrate that results desired were not always the results obtained.[1] He had seen too much havoc wrought by legislation designed more to embellish the image of a minister or a departmental bureaucracy than to correct a problem or move society forward, and too much money wasted on programs designed more to appease some noisy interest group than to serve the interests of the general public.

Colleague Russell Doern wrote of Green, "He could instantly read the politics of any situation."[2] The Land Lease Option to allow financially troubled farmers to sell land to the government and lease it back, which was proposed in 1973 and was to follow us like a black dog for the balance of our tenure, induced this warning from Green, "Be careful, this is the most radical thing we will ever do." Human rights promoters agitating for racial quotas impelled this observation, "That would mean there could not be three Jews in this cabinet." The Official Languages Act caused him to learn French because, "French Catholics in Québec as part of Canada means I can be a Jew and attend synagogue in Winnipeg." A major financial institution called to hint that any increase in corporate income tax, which offset a reduction of the Medicare premium, could influence its decision to remain in Manitoba. Learning that its board was meeting to await a reply, he was roused to declare, "There are two board rooms where meetings are now taking place. One board room is at the financial institution. The other board room is this Cabinet Room. The question we must decide is not whether or not medical premiums will be reduced and the income tax increased. The real question is 'In which room does the Government of Manitoba sit?'"[3]

Since, historically, laws reflect the interests of those who make them—i.e. the financially and politically powerful—he sometimes felt, like Tolstoi, that "Where there is law there is injustice." But he was a politician, not a poet, and knew laws were essential to any society, so he thought in terms of Oliver Wendell Holmes, who referred to "those wise restraints we call the law". However, he believed that laws should be understandable, and as few as possible, leaving freedom for citizens to do that not expressly forbidden. He was a lawyer who believed laws should be so clear that citizens would need no lawyers to interpret them, and so few that they did not impinge on the liberty of individuals.

He read prodigiously: political science, philosophy, economics, history, religion. His first stop when driving through a city was a bookstore, not for the latest 'top ten' novel, but for seminal books by such authors as Spinoza, Kant, Rousseau, Voltaire, Paine, Milton, Hegel, Tolstoy, Veblen, Dostoevsky, Henry George, Marx, Keynes, Adam Smith, Locke, Hobbes, Ricardo, Mill, Lincoln Steffens, Upton Sinclair, Galbraith, and the plethora of books by implementers of Franklin Delano Roosevelt 's New Deal. A product of the Enlightenment, he

---

[1] In 1982, Premier Pawley's NDP government enacted legislation permitting plebiscites, expecting it to be used by a movement to vote Manitoba 'nuclear free'. Instead, it was used the following year to vote against his bill to make Manitoba officially bilingual.

[2] In *Wednesdays Are Cabinet Days*, p. 134.

[3] Sidney Green, *Rise and Fall of a Political Animal*, p. 85.

believed that to improve humanity, one must improve its social environment. If people steal to pay for medical services, one must create a public health system that provides care as a condition of health, not wealth; if striking laborers become violent when picketing is prohibited, change the laws and let them legally advertise their grievances.

But he was not blinded by ideological assumptions of how the world works, nor bounded by rigidities in his determination to make it work better. Essentially a student of *Realpolitik*, he had no illusions about the moral superiority of those who had joined the NDP—making him unpopular with some—but he believed in the social superiority of the party's philosophy. He felt it was the embodiment of the Hegelian dialectic which saw history as teleological, moving in an upward spiral to progressive enlargement of the sphere of individual human freedom. A political party must have a clear goal which, like the Jewish concept of Heaven, could never be attained but must be striven toward. Too practical and too aware of the frailties of humans and of the institutions they developed, he was never a Utopian but, like Oscar Wilde, he believed "No map without a Utopia on it is worth a glance."

And he did not suffer fools ... at all. Shortly after we met, we went to the YMHA Recreational Centre for lunch and waited for some time while waitresses served several persons who had come in after us. Green complained to the manager who, embarrassed, explained the waitresses were more helpful to guests who tip.

"So how much do they tip?"

"Usually fifty cents."

"From now on I'll tip a dollar, but I want to be served first."

The day after the 1969 election we again went to the YMHA, showered and entered the sauna. Eight men sat on the benches, sweat streaming down their naked bodies. One immediately pulled the cigar from his mouth, waved it imperiously, and called: "Hey, Green, if you become minister of Welfare,[4] I want you to promise me you will take the bums off welfare."

It was an incongruous place for an argument but Green pounced, "Okay! If you promise me to stop cheating on your income tax."

Acting for a group in a rural school division that was challenging the proposed location of a new school, he called as a witness a supporter for the other side and pointed out that, at a public meeting held earlier, the residents of the division had voted against the location decided upon by the board. The witness allowed that, yes, there was such a meeting, and yes, the people there had voted the other way, but this was a meaningless vote because no attempt had been made to explain the situation or to advocate the position he was supporting.

Green looked quizzical,"But is it not true that the leader of your group got on the platform and made a speech on this issue?"

The witness appeared to be wondering what a big city lawyer could possibly

---

[4]   Three weeks later, Green became minister of Health and Welfare.

know about what occurs at country meetings, "Well, yes, but he wasn't really trying to persuade anyone."

"Oh, so that is why people out here get on platforms and make speeches, to not persuade anyone."

He was fiercely competitive. At 5'6" and of slight build, he was quarterback of the all star football team at the University of Manitoba. He was active in the YMHA from age ten, played on its junior basketball team and varsity volleyball team, participated in its dramatic presentations, was president of the YMHA House Council, program chairman of the Jewish Youth Council and of the YMHA, and director of the B'nai B'rith Camp. He became president of the New Democratic Party of Manitoba and vice-president of the national New Democratic Party. He served on the board of Red River Cooperative, on the Winnipeg Metro Council and as president of the Winnipeg Film Society. He became president of the U of M Alumni Association after graduating with two gold medals: one from the University of Manitoba, and one from the U of M Law School.

Son of a minor coal merchant and product of Winnipeg's polyglot North End, the crucible from which non-Anglo-Saxon immigrants emerged to shake the political and commercial establishment of Canada, he earned his degrees while simultaneously working at as many as three jobs. He articled with highly respected community activist, alderman and lawyer Joseph Zuken, "who taught me the law", and more notably, taught him that the thrust of laws depended on the social philosophy of the politicians who made them.

It was in his capacity as a lawyer that I met him. Infuriated by the procedural manipulations of the Manitoba Federation of Agriculture, I spontaneously threatened to obtain a court injunction to stop the annual convention in its tracks. When the only response was loud guffaws and hoots of "You just do that little thing," my wife and I left the hall and I turned to her, "Dear, what's an injunction?"

"I don't know, but I think you need a lawyer to get one."

We knew no lawyers. We walked hand in hand along north Main Street seeking one. On the door of an older office building we chanced to see a plaque announcing Mitchell and Green: Barristers and Solicitors. We had read Mitchell's name in a newspaper earlier, so we entered. Leon Mitchell, the noted labour lawyer, was busy, so we got his newly-graduated partner, Sidney Green. I briefly explained the situation and then added, "Mr. Green, we'll lose the case but I want to fight it anyway."

"Mr. Schulz, I do not fight cases to lose them."

"Furthermore," I said, "this is a political case, but the organization is incapable of dealing with it so it must be fought in the courts."

"I do not fight political cases in the courts."

Fifteen years later, Green came to my office and said: "You were right that time. I should have fought that as a political case." I called in my secretary to witness the statement. Admitting a mistake was virtually unique for him.

The brief he prepared was so impressive that I blurted, "If there is such a thing as justice, we will win."

"There is no such thing as justice. There is only the law."

We lost the case; one does not challenge the establishment with impunity, but we became friends and political colleagues. And he explained to me that 'justice' had to be sought in another place, not where the law was interpreted, but where it was made.

He announced his presence in the legislature after the 1966 election with several epic speeches, primarily on the issues of labour law, which he considered punitive, and Medicare, which was being legislated in Ottawa, and it became clear to his colleagues and to the media that a star had been born. His speeches, models of reason and lucidity designed to inform, never read as well as they sounded when one was present to sense the passion and burning intellect that went into them. Hearing him was an experience, and throughout his political career the visitor's gallery filled when word went out that Green would speak. He was a man who had never met a controversy he didn't like and soon developed a reputation for the fast and effective retort.

When Premier Roblin defended his government's investment in the forestry complex at The Pas (which became a major boondoggle) as a good deal for Manitoba, Green compared it to the "sale of Manhattan Island by the Indians", who undoubtedly then boasted, "Boy, did we put it over on those Dutchmen."

During the Medicare debates, the government, as a condition of paying physicians directly, offered them eighty-five per cent of the fees set by the MMA. A doctor asked, "How would your union membership like it if they were told they would receive only eighty-five per cent of their wages?" Green silenced him with: "They would be delighted provided they could set their own wages like you do."

At one point, "Super Chief" Dave Courchene demanded that the government market the wild rice harvested by natives, then complained that the government's efforts were insufficient. Banging his fist on the cabinet room table, he thundered, "Buy me an air ticket and I'll go to Europe and sell it myself." Green ended the discussion with a question, only half in jest: "Would you accept a one-way ticket, Dave?"

When Manitoba public automobile insurance was introduced, Harley Vannon of the Insurance Bureau of Canada implied that the Government of Manitoba was seeking a license to steal. Green responded: "Vannon knows all about that because he now has that licence and does not want to give it up."

In the early days of the Schreyer government, when there was much tension between right and left wings of the party, MLA Jean Allard confronted Green in the corridor of The Ledge. Hovering over him by nearly a foot, he pointed down and declared: "It's the radicals in the party we have to watch." Green, in no doubt to whom Allard was referring, looked up and replied: "Jean, I couldn't care less what you call me, as long as it's not a Conservative or a Liberal."

During the 1973 election campaign, when Conservative leader Sidney

Spivak stated Ed Schreyer was a nice fellow "but if you elect his party you have to take Green", Green terminated the "bogeyman" tactic by retorting "there are nice Conservatives, but if you elect that party you have to take Spivak".

On an open line radio program, when a sympathizer phoned in to encourage him with, "Mr. Green, you are a man of principle who would rather be right than be premier," he quipped, "No, I want to be both."

But twice I saw him stumped for a retort. Reverend Phillip Petursson, the tall, courtly, soft-spoken, Anthony Eden look-alike Unitarian Church minister and government MLA, notified Green, the caucus whip, that he would not be in the legislature that afternoon because he was to officiate at a funeral. The next day Green, striding along the corridor of The Ledge, deep in thought, passed Petursson and, wanting to acknowledge recognition, asked absent-mindedly, "Hello Phillip. How was the funeral?" Petursson stopped in mid-stride, looked at Green, smiled quizzically, and replied, "It was a success." Green was nonplussed.

On one occasion, members of Green's constituency executive arranged for a debate between their MLA and Joe Borowski on capital punishment. It was an emotional issue both within the party and among the public. Green, the fierce debater who never lost an argument, cogently reviewed the history of jurisprudence, that historically many crimes declared "capital" were against property, not persons, and that laws made by humans were not precise and could lead to the execution of innocent persons. He acknowledged that this was a matter of individual conscience, that debate on the issue would continue no matter how the law read, but that he, personally, could never agree to give the state power over human life. As always, his argument was virtually impossible to refute.

Borowski, a committed spokesman for the anti-abortion movement, did not attempt to refute it. He rose and stated: "All I am asking is that those opposed to capital punishment show the same consideration for the unborn child."

He sat down. Green sat open mouthed. He had been finessed.

He was, by nature, a "single combat warrior", who enjoyed pitting himself against apparently impossible odds and the more vicious the attacks the more he welcomed them. Unlike Hamlet, he never asked if it was noble "to suffer the slings and arrows of outrageous fortune", but rather, his entire being was programmed "To take up arms against a sea of troubles, And, by opposing, end them."[5]

During the tense and vicious debates on the government's policy to divert the Churchill River to help spin the hydro-electric turbines in the Nelson River, Green, the minister of Natural Resources and responsible for the regulation of Manitoba's water, was invited to speak at a public meeting at the University of Manitoba. The large hall in the Students Union Building was filled to capacity with students, professors, "professional" environmentalists wanting to save nature and "professional" sociologists wanting to save the Aboriginal people, whose lands and reserves would be affected. Green stood alone on the platform,

---

[5] Shakespeare, *Hamlet.*

before a hostile crowd, and delivered a superb presentation on the history of the project (initiated by the previous PC government) and the objectives of the government (to secure maximum power to develop Manitoba and the North). But the audience had not come to listen; it had come to demolish the government's position and anyone who dared defend it. Green did not allow himself to be distracted by boos, catcalls or critical comments, but continued his presentation, answered questions informatively, and cogently explained that if our society wanted to become more industrialized and comfortable, the energy needed to make this possible had to be obtained from some source.

Finally a man rose in the audience, criticized Green and the government for choosing this option, detailed problems it would cause, and concluded by stating that really, the best solution was for Manitobans to use less energy. It was precisely the direction in which Green had been discreetly tending. But he was neither about to permit diversion from the issue he had come to address nor to allow anyone to diminish his singularity. He agreed with the man, and then added, "But listen, I do not want friends where I do not have any. You people came here to argue that this is the wrong project at the wrong time in the wrong place and I am here to inform you that we have studied this as thoroughly as we know how, and have considered every conceivable option, and we are proceeding."

A man in the audience asked a colleague, "Have you noticed when Green leaves a room after a debate there is an odour of sulphur in the air?"

He had respect for the Conservatives, whom he believed had a rational political philosophy, and particularly for Sterling Lyon, a former law school classmate and Conservative Party leader after 1976. However, he despised what he perceived to be the political ambiguity and opportunism of the Liberals.

A mid-1972 by-election in the Wolseley constituency brought forty-year-old lawyer and businessman Israel (Izzy) Asper to the legislature as leader of the four-man Liberal caucus. A slim, 5'7", ambitious, peripatetic, nattily-dressed chain smoker, Asper had permanent dark bags under his hooded eyes from lack of sleep, a keen mind, and a coiled-spring body that appeared congenitally unable to relax. He had been raised in scenic Minnedosa and cut his business teeth managing his family's movie theatres. He had honoured his home town by building a distillery (with more than a million dollars borrowed from governments), which he sold to Melcher's Distilleries (which in turn closed it). He headed his own law firm and was to make his indelible mark in business by investing in several media outlets and becoming a billionaire.[6] Meanwhile he was making a gift of his talents

---

[6] Asper (1932-2003) was to become an international print and electronic media mogul. *Maclean's* magazine named him "Tycoon of the Tube" (November 27, 1995) and *Forbes Magazine* listed him as a billionaire. He became a philanthropist extraordinare and was inducted (1999) into Winnipeg's Citizen Hall of Fame for his public service. His name is found on the Asper School of Business at the U of M, the Asper Comunity Clinical Research Institute at St. Boniface Hospital and the Asper Community Campus, while the name of his company can be found at Winnipeg's Canwest Global Ball Park, the Canwest Performing Arts Centre and the Red River Canwest Global Multimedia Classroom and Studio. His funeral, in October 2003, was attended by 1,600 people, including Prime Minister Jean Chrétien.

to the people of Manitoba. He seemed out of his element in the cloying confines of the legislature. An unreconstructed capitalist, even his most liberal interpretations of problems seemed to lead to conservative solutions, and he would have agreed with Swiss historian Jacob Burkhardt that, "the only means of advancement are talent and calculation", but government loans could be helpful …

Asper was a one-man band. He had an instant answer to every question, no matter how complex, and, seemingly, solutions to problems not yet invented. The aggressive, quick-off-the-mark style which made him a tiger in the courtroom and a star in the corporate boardroom, proved his Achilles heel in politics. The public intuitively sensed if problems were that easy to solve they would already have been solved. His tendency to arrogate to himself all the attention that came to the Liberal Party, and to personally deal with every issue in the chamber without reference to his caucus colleagues, left them humiliated and disillusioned. Gordon Johnston, his deputy leader, and house leader during the party's dog days after the 1969 election,[7] became lax in attending sittings. Asper's political career was one of meteoric rise and equally fast fall, a record of prodigious talent circumscribed by perceived self-aggrandisement burning out his welcome in the legislature within two years.

In a speech that filled seventeen pages of *Hansard*,[8] Asper called the throne speech barren, lethargic, disappointing, disillusioning, innocuous, inadequate, frightening, frustrating, torturing, smug, evasive, platitudinous, propagandistic, ideological, complacent, unimaginative, astonishing, and a failure. Then he proposed the government should defer, reduce or abolish a whole range of taxes and charges (sales taxes, personal and corporate income taxes, estates taxes, capital gains taxes, property taxes, utility charges, long distance telephone charges between north and south) and warned the government should be wary of increasing mineral taxes or selling hydro-electric power outside Manitoba. Conversely the government should spend more to develop Denticare, expand Pharmacare, provide free eyeglasses, wheelchairs and prosthetics, supplement old age pensions, rebate child care expenses to single-parent families, increase home ownership assistance, build acute care hospitals, day care centres and senior citizen's homes, expand universities, and provide more grants and tax incentives for urban transport, rural industrialization, regional development, programs for the North, and to keep young people in Manitoba by creating new jobs.

In Asper, Green found a foil. At first glance they appeared evenly matched—of similar age and height, wiry of body, mercurial of temperament, equally driven, complex of intellect, fast with repartee, super-confident in debate, but in contests Green invariably won. Green knew, as H. L. Mencken did, that "to every problem there is a solution that is quick, easy, popular … and wrong", and was appalled by Asper's easy habit of producing rabbits without even a hat to pull them from.

---

[7] Between Liberal Leader Gildas Molgat's appointment to the Senate and the election of Asper to the legislature.

[8] *Hansard*, February 5, 1974, pp. 61-78.

If Asper's unpredictable forays kept the government off balance, Green's responses kept Asper off balance. When Green and Asper squared off, one could almost hear the mournful sound of trumpets playing the Duguello, the signal no quarter would be asked or given, and Green's periodic methodical evisceration of Asper made one wonder if he really believed in the humane slaughter of animals.

One day after entering the legislature, in an epic speech during a debate on a labour bill intended to loosen legislative control of organized labour, Asper vowed his undying support for organized labour, but added that government should beware of passing legislation giving labour too many rights. He also stated his belief that labour unions should be Canadian rather than international.[9]

Green responded by explaining the intent of the legislation and proceeded with a learned dissertation giving the history of working conditions leading to the formation of labour unions, how they functioned, the forces against which they had to contend, and that labour organizations were international because capital, and many industrial employers, are international. Referring to Asper's fear that the legislation might give organized labour too much freedom, Green spoke of the British Combinations Act of 1799, which prohibited unionization, and displayed his Classical liberal philosophy: "The Honourable Member for Wolseley thinks the only thing that is permitted by law is what we enact in the legislature. I say the reverse is true. The only thing that is prohibited by law is what we enact here."[10]

It was Green's usual superb performance and for any ordinary person it would have been sufficient, but not for Green. He not only had to counter the argument; he also had to slay the dragon. He stated that he was impressed by Asper's assertion that he supported the concept of labour unions, but, "The Honourable Member says there is something holy about a Canadian union ... That is the typical employer pitch. When he wants to weaken his union he says the Americans are taking your dues from you ... Well, if a Canadian union is better than an American union, I'm sure the Honourable Member ... would say a western Canadian union is better than a Canadian union."

Asper took the bait and smiled assent. Green continued, "And if a western Canadian union is better than a Canadian union then a Manitoba Union is better than a western union." Misreading the direction the debate was taking, Asper again nodded agreement and Green bore in relentlessly, "And if a Manitoba union is better than a western union, then a Winnipeg union is better than a Manitoba union, then a North End union is better than a Winnipeg union ... and if a plant union is better than an industry-wide union, then surely that ... [of] the machinists in the plant ... is better than a union that takes into account the whole plant ... and if a union within a plant is better than a total plant union the best thing to do ... is to fight for yourself, don't be involved with anyone."[11]

---

[9] *Ibid.*, July 4, 1972, pp. 3767-8.

[10] *Ibid.*, p. 3773.

[11] *Ibid.*, p. 3774.

In brief, Green sought to show Asper did not support unions at all.

Then there was the time Asper, in another barn-burner speech, wandered into a minefield and was trapped beyond hope of redemption. Waxing loquacious, he accused the government of politicizing the civil service, and Green of "leaning on people" who disagreed with him, and of causing the departure from the public service of good and dedicated mandarins. Green, his body taut as a bowstring, rose on a point of privilege: "Mr. Chairman, the Honourable Member has charged that I have intimidated people within my department so they cannot without fear or favour give me their professional advice based on their best information. I suggest ... the remarks be withdrawn."[12]

Asper, on a roll and feeling as combative as Green, strode farther into the minefield.

"... I expressed the opinion that he who disagrees with the minister mysteriously disappears ... A member of his staff, seeing the parade of dismissals, would not be intimidated ... in the last few months we have lost the deputy minister, Winston Mair."[13]

Green responded by bringing to the chamber an unusually laudatory letter in which the writer stated Green was the best minister for whom he had ever worked and thanked him sincerely for the opportunity to do so. The letter was signed by Green's former deputy minister, who had left Manitoba for a civil service position in Ontario—Winston Mair.

The chamber was stunned into silence. Of any of the some 14,000 government employees Asper might have chosen, he had, with unbelievably bad luck, named a man who had written Green the kind of letter for which a cabinet minister would kill.

Contrary to the perception among many that he was a subversive using the party for some Mephistophelian experiment, Green's principles were inflexible, his analysis rigorous, his positions based on practicality and his expositions models of logic and clarity. During a debate in the chamber when his explanation of the benefits of Medicare drew a shout of "Communism" from an opposition MLA, it was answered by the revered Douglas Campbell, a former Liberal premier but a philosophical conservative, who interjected, "If that is communism then I am a communist."

Hearing Green explain and defend government policy in the chamber reminded one of Lincoln. Informed that his most successful general, Ulysses Grant, was a drunk, he replied: "Find out what brand of whiskey he drinks and send it to my other generals."

That was his strength—and his weakness. Like Achilles, he was the hero with a fatal flaw; he was psychologically incapable of losing an argument. Going through the wrenching experience of questioning him reminded one of Hitler,

---

[12] *Ibid.*, March 13, 1973, p. 587.
[13] *Ibid.*, p. 588.

who when returning from meeting with Spain's General Franco, told his advisors, "I'd rather have four teeth pulled than debate with that man again."

Many who sought to dialogue with him went away less convinced than humiliated. Being such a formidable debater, he did not realize he was not converting people, but merely silencing them. My pleas to "lose an argument just to prove you are human," begot the reply, "But I am right." And much of the time he was, but in politics, as in personal relationships, being right is often not enough.

To most of his elected colleagues, particularly the backbenchers seeking excitement, he was a hero. Often he carried his cold, unrelenting logic to the outer limits where it threatened to become illogic, which invariably led to a delicate balance of emotional consternation and intellectual titillation among the backbenchers, and while the breathtaking scope of his thinking often left them vaguely uneasy, it was easier to go along than risk debating with him. Besides, he usually had a challenging idea—preposterous perhaps, at first glance, but challenging.

Not so with the NDP provincial council. This was the body, comprising two persons from each of the fifty-seven constituencies, which governed the party between annual conventions. It met four times a year, on weekends, when most ministers wanted to relax or had constituency functions. Green considered it an obligation to the party to attend, sometimes making him the only minister there, and thus the lightning rod for those who saw themselves keepers of the flame and sought an audience with government.

Councillors, in daily contact with grassroots opinion, usually just wanted to be heard and to vent their frustrations resulting from having to defend the government on the ground. But Green, his mind on strategic realities and intent on having it clearly understood why the government did what it did, and not coy about expressing himself, too often ignored the adage that "the soft answer turneth away wrath". He treated them as he did caucus colleagues, familiar with the reasons for specific policies and from whom he expected more than from non-party members. But they did not see his commitment to them and to the party by attending their meetings and answering their questions, only his impatience when questioned. Attempts at dialogue often ended in contention.

They did not recognize his intellect, only his anger. Council meetings became fractious. Defeated in debate, councillors sulked. Toward the end of the Schreyer regime, Green was a power in government and a hero in caucus, but he was looked upon with increasing disfavour by many members of the party, particularly the labour contingent of the party. Despite having been an aggressive labour lawyer, and largely responsible for liberating organized labour from legal strictures against picketing at strike sites, he fell afoul of his old friends.

He did not believe in separate laws for labour any more than for conglomerates of capital, or for professionals such as lawyers. When labour demanded anti-scab laws to prohibit anyone from working in a struck plant, Green infuriated them by asking if that would mean that, in the event of a doctor's strike, the government could not enlist other doctors to staff the struck hospitals.

He believed in freedom as a Kantian imperative and sought to enlarge its scope by democratic means. Therefore neither labour nor capital should be granted legal powers which would allow them to blackmail society, but should be left as free as possible to follow their own best interests. Speaking to the Canadian Institute of Managment about labour-business bargaining, he stated: "Freedom is not only desirable intrinsically, but because it works best." [14]

The same philosophy informed his view on income distribution; it was not just nice, but utilitarian. A candidate in the 1965 federal election, Green was asked why he, a gold-medal law student with clear prospects of prestige and wealth, was in a socialist party. He replied that if he were the richest man in Winnipeg and living in a palatial residence, but surrounded by poor people, he would be a very insecure person, needing the protection of moats and guards, and he preferred seeking security through the more equitable distribution of the nation's wealth. In 1976, columnist Steve Kerstetter wrote: "When the NDP was elected in 1969, Mr. Green was already well known as an advocate of a more equitable society and a defender of its underprivileged members." [15]

With the government's defeat in October 1977, and Schreyer's departure for Rideau Hall a year later, Green should have been the logical successor, but the party turned elsewhere. And he found himself with a different caucus. Among the more aggressive were those who had learned their conception of government from the textbooks, not by coming up through the ranks of school boards and municipal councils. They did not recognize the Baconian imperative; they believed if the theory seemed good, the practical application must be forced to follow. It drove him from the NDP, and to founding his own Progressive Party. Perhaps his concept of increasing political freedom by reducing the number of laws, and of extending economic freedom through publicly owned enterprises, was too esoteric for many to grasp.

His position, in both the party and the public, deteriorated while in office. In the 1973 election, Social Credit MLA Jake Froese promoted himself in his Mennonite constituency by arguing that his reelection would help Schreyer who was "a man I can work with", and warning that if Schreyer left, his successor as NDP leader would be Green "who is the most radical socialist in the NDP". Two years later, a profile of Green by columnist Joan Bowman was headlined: "He's The Most Feared NDPer In Manitoba." [16]

He lost his seat in the 1981 election, which swept Howard Pawley's NDP government into office with the largest majority the party ever had. He was defeated by an NDP candidate, and by the people of the constituency he had served so well for fifteen years, but who voted the party rather than the individual

---

[14] *Ibid.*, p. 588.

[15] *Winnipeg Free Press*, January 19, 1976.

[16] *Winnipeg Tribune*, December 20, 1975. Green commented, "It could have been worse. She might have called me the least feared."

who had broken with it. That defeat robbed the legislature of a protean talent and the people of Manitoba of a powerful advocate of democracy in economics and of rationality in politics.

But he had left his mark. He had coined the phrase "Ready To Govern" in 1969, and had done as much as any single person to transform the New Democratic Party from the "conscience of the legislature" into a powerful political force which has formed the Manitoba government in twenty of the thirty-five years from 1969 to 2004.[17]

Having helped elect the New Democratic government of Manitoba, he had served as minister of Health and Social Services, minister of Urban Affairs, commissioner of Northern Affairs, minister of Mines, Resources and Environmental Management, chair of the cabinet subcommittee on Economic and Resource Development and, after 1973, minister for the Manitoba Development Corporation.

The affairs of the corporation had been kept confidential by its creator, the Roblin government. The Schreyer government, believing Manitoba taxpayers should know where their money was going, opened the books. With that they unwittingly opened a Pandora's Box, releasing the evils that lurked therein.[18] Green was to preside over this hydra-headed monster, vainly attempting to explain that public enterprise is the economic equivalent of political democracy, but that public investments, just like private investments, are not always successful.

[17] The NDP was defeated in 1977, re-elected in 1981, defeated in 1988 and re-elected in 1999.

[18] This refers to Pandora's Box from which, according to myth, the evils had escaped leaving only HOPE. With the problems of the MDC, we lost even hope.

The Manitoba Development Corporation

We wanted economic development so much we would have given away our daughters to get it.

—Premier Joey Smallwood of Newfoundland.

Tꞁhe *Winnipeg Free Press* made a boo-boo!

The paper's lead editorial on February 25, 1972, intriguingly entitled "Midas in Reverse", listed a doleful litany of twelve failed privately owned but government financed businesses. While obliquely admitting some culpability by the preceding Progressive Conservative government, these failures were charged to the NDP government, for "keeping the Manitoba Development Corporation ... [as] a useful tool for government intrusion into business." Future PC Premier Sterling Lyon later asked what could be expected of "socialists", who "can't run a peanut stand" and "would run the Sahara desert out of sand".

There was just one problem; nine of the twelve failed firms listed, and another nine not listed, had been financed by, and failed under, the "good business" PC government,[1] in which Sterling Lyon had been a prominent minister and future PC Party leader, Sidney Spivak, had been the minister responsible for the government agency that had made the loans.

In 1973, MDC chairman Sydney Parsons reported to the legislature that of the 458 loans made, twenty-five had failed, including eighteen before June 25, 1969, when, by March 31, 1975, of the total of $335,404,000 approved, $238,845,000, or seventy-one per cent, was to projects conceived or committed to by the

---

[1] Public Cold Storage—Brandon; Midwest Expanded Ores Ltd.—Winnipeg; Fieldmaster Industries—Morris; Teulon Hosiery Mills Ltd.—Brandon; Brandon Poultry Products; Futronics Ltd.—Selkirk; Lake Winnipeg Navigation—Selkirk; Morton Timber Preservers Ltd.—Neepawa and Churchill Forest Industries at The Pas. The three actually initiated by the NDP were: King Choy Ready Foods—Winnipeg; Unicraft Enterprises—St. Boniface and Dents Foods Ltd.—Winnipeg.

Conservatives and $96,559,000 by the NDP. Of the total losses of $77,465,000 during the same period, $44,188,000, or fifty-seven per cent, was attributable to accounts initiated by the Conservatives and $33,277,000 to the NDP.[2]

When Conservative MLA George Minaker attempted to embarrass the government by asking for the names of MDC-financed companies in receivership or bankruptcy and a listing of how much they owed, Sidney Green, minister responsible for the MDC, responded by tabling a complete list of all MDC accounts since the corporation's inception in 1958.[3] It showed only ten per cent of the accounts in receivership, but of the total of some $212 million in loans outstanding, about $188 million was owed by two companies in bankruptcy; both had been established by the preceding Conservative government. The PC benches howled like banshees. It was not what they wanted; they were determined to promote the impression that the MDC was an NDP creation and that everything it touched turned to dross. They hated being reminded of their own imprudent past.

GOVERNMENT INTERVENTION in business in Canada has a long history. In the 1890s American journalist and "King of the muckrakers", Lincoln Steffens, travelled through America's mushrooming cities and drew conclusions: if public services were installed by several companies it caused high costs resulting from duplication; if done through franchised monopolies it caused high costs because of venal combinations of developers willing to buy the politicians who issued the franchises and politicians willing to be bought. At a meeting in Los Angeles, he spoke of the high cost and low quality of their public services and of the political corruption resulting from competition among developers—not to improve services, but to buy franchises to operate privately-owned monopolies which were, effectively, licenses to print money. An Episcopal bishop present agreed there was corruption at the municipal level, but said that this must be lived with since it was innate in man. Steffens responded:

> Many claim corruption began with Adam, but the men argue it was with Eve, and the women insist it was with the serpent. I am here to tell you the corruption around us is not the fault of Adam or Eve or the serpent. It is the fault of the apple. The apple is the opportunity of monopoly profit. If a businessman obtains a franchise to install city services or utilities, it guarantees him a perpetual profit. For this men will bribe and corrupt and kill. To end the corruption, remove the prize of that apple by taking the utilities into public ownership.[4]

---

[2] Report by MDC Minister Sidney Green, September 14, 1975.
[3] Return to Order of the House, #15 and #16, March 17, 1975.
[4] *The Autobiography of Lincoln Stephens*, Harcourt, Brace and Co., NY, 1931, pp. 570-74.

Simultaneously, during the rapid industrialization and urbanization in Britain, a group that became known as "gas and water socialists"[5] concluded vital services (water, gas for heating and lighting, sewage disposal, streetcar railways and so on) were most economically provided by monopolies to eliminate duplication of infrastructure, and that such monopolies should be publicly owned for maximum social control. This legacy was brought to Canada[6] by immigrants and implemented in vital areas such as city services, hydro-electric power, radio and telephone systems, air transportation, grain marketing, auto insurance, mail services, and in the mining and harnessing of dangerous substances such as uranium.

But the 'free enterprise' ethos was powerful, assiduously promoted by the captains of industry reaching for the golden apple, and accepted by the general populace who either aspired to wealth or were true believers in the virtue of private sector competition. It was generally agreed that development of a national economy required government intervention, particularly in areas of instruments of national policy, natural monopoly, the perceived need for regional development, and the failure of private enterprise, but that it should be minimal. Debates on the degree of government intervention in the economy often reduced normally articulate politicians to quivering masses of ectoplasm and roused chamber of commerce speakers to paroxysms of pained outrage—either against intervention in general or in support of intervention for a pet project. Intervention to provide funding for private ventures in the construction of infrastructure (canals and railways, among others), or to take them over when they failed, was so prevalent that Canadian historian Herschel Hardin concluded that, as opposed to the 'free enterprise' of the United States, the key to the Canadian identity is our "public-enterprise economic culture".[7]

It was usually the captains of industry who benefited. If a small business was failing, who cared? But, if major corporations could not pay their creditors (Canadian Pacific Railways) or threatened employee layoffs (such as Chrysler Corporation, Ford Motor Company and Massey Ferguson), they came running, often accompanied by the employee unions they normally sought to destroy, to governments[8] and governments came running with bags full of money. If these private firms were in such bad condition that government had to take them over

---

[5] Including cognoscenti like playwright G.B. Shaw, and Sidney and Beatrice Webb, who founded the London School of Economics.

[6] Americans continued to see the serpent as the cause of corruption and rejected public ownership in favour of regulation. But the dynamic of regulation required regulators to be more concerned with the solvency of the utility than with service to the public, making them captives of corporations they were appointed to regulate. Canada is now moving in the same direction. The Manitoba Telephone System, privatized in 1997, is a case in point. The regulator, the CRTC, agreed with the privatized MTS that income tax is an operating expense and can be charged to the consumers instead of being paid by the shareholders.

[7] *A Nation Unaware*, J.J. Douglas, Vancouver, 1974

[8] "In public deliberations, Labour's voice is little heard and less regarded, except on occasions, when his clamour is animated and supported by employers … for their own purposes." Adam Smith, *The Wealth of Nations.*

to save them (Canadian National Railways, Steel Company of Quebec, Sydney Steel in Nova Scotia, Sheehan Oil Refinery in Newfoundland, Ocean Falls Pulp and Paper Company in B.C., Canadair in Montreal, DeHaviland Aircraft in Toronto, among them)[9] taxpayers became the unhappy owners of firms that were bankrupt before government acquired them. If a publicly owned enterprise made the cardinal error of becoming profitable, such as Polymer Corporation, which was established to make synthetic rubber during World War II, it would be sold to maintain the fiction that government "can't run a peanut stand".

In 1976, for the first time in twenty years, the publicly owned CNR made a profit and Transport Minister Otto Lang announced it would be sold, though only the profitable parts. The lucky taxpayers would keep the losers.[10]

THE FRENETIC PUBLIC INTERVENTION in the economy in the 1960s and 1970s was not a symbol of socialism, but rather a symptom of the times. It was an ideologically based program for financing private entrepreneurship and ownership with public funds.

The process and psychology of this compulsion of two decades was insightfully captured in the title of the book: *Forced Growth: Government Involvement in Industrial Development.*[11] Author Phillip Mathias, assistant editor of *The Financial Post* defined this as "hastening growth of a plant by an artificial environment and application of growth promoting substances from external sources." Its intent was "to end poverty and redress social disorders created by sweeping changes in economic patterns and disparities of income and opportunity in the undeveloped regions and cement ethnic ties of the mosaic culture."

"Forced growth" was the product of an ebullient, optimistic, expansionist and socially liberal mindset. After fifteen years of relative prosperity and growth, much of it fuelled by wartime and post-war public spending, governments believed they had learned not only how to manage an economy, but how to regulate its tempo of growth. And they believed the future was inflationary, so funds expended to stimulate the economy would provide public benefits and private profits and be repaid from future growth.

The compulsion cut across provinces and politics. Newfoundland's Liberal Premier Joey Smallwood invested prodigiously in stimulative ventures with disastrous results[12] and one that suceeded, the Churchill Falls Hydro-Electric Project,

---

[9] When these firms failed under public ownership, they became known as examples of "Lemon Socialism", but they were lemons before being socialized and socialized because they were lemons.

[10] Manitoba Liberal Leader Izzy Asper argued that public enterprise should be confined to doing what the private section did not do because it was not profitable, but that the enterprise should be sold to the private sector as soon as it becomes profitable.

[11] James Lewis and Samuel Publishers, Toronto, 1971, p. 2.

[12] *No Holds Barred: My Life in Politics*, Toronto, M&S, 1998.

though it did so at enormous cost to the province. Nova Scotia's cautious PC premier, Robert Stanfield, invested in production of "heavy water" as a coolant for nuclear energy plants and was left with a $100 million pile of rusted junk.[13] New Brunswick's Conservative Premier Richard Hatfield fell prey to the job creation urge, and a persuasive promoter, and blew more than $20 million of taxpayer's money on the "sculptured beauty" of the fibre glass, gull-wing Bricklin car, which would not sell.

Saskatchewan's Liberal Premier Ross Thatcher committed his province to sixty per cent of costs, for thirty per cent ownership, of a pulp and paper plant and the succeeding NDP government paid the contractor $6 million, just to go away. Alberta's PC Premier Peter (the Red) Lougheed, invested public money in a forestry complex at Whitecourt ($28 million), Pacific Western Airlines ($38 million), Syncrude Oil and related projects ($485 million) and many others. When asked why he, the personification of private enterprise, did this, he replied, "Because it is good for Alberta."

Manitoba Premier Duff Roblin's PC government was committed to the very practical and highly complex goal of guiding conversion of Manitoba's economy from agriculture to industry, diversifying industry to guard against future shocks, and accelerating growth to produce a larger economic pie. In 1958, to serve this multi-faceted objective, the Roblin government established the Manitoba Development Fund (later Corporation) "to further economic development of the province by encouraging growth of business", appointed a board of directors to administer it, and provided funding.

The MDC was to operate at arms length from government "so matters are conducted in a businesslike way",[14] and lend only to private ventures "unable to obtain funds from other sources on reasonable terms". Commendable in theory, this became a recipe for disaster; political control was lost and loans were confined to projects conventional lenders had rejected as losers. There were some notable successes[15] and a number of small accounts prospered, creating new jobs, producing value-added goods and growing the economy, but what was remembered was a province littered with bones of failed MDC financed ventures. As President John. F. Kennedy had mused: "When I am right no one remembers; when I am wrong no one forgets." The MDC brought hair-tearing grief to every government after its establishment. Worse, if the venture succeeded the entrepreneur got the profits and plaudits but if it failed, government got the bills and the execration.

The recipe for disaster was complete when the Conservatives, who had promoted the MDC as a shiny development tool, branded it a "socialist slush

---

[13] In announcing the plant in 1967, Premier Stanfield saw it as "a symbol of hope for the future of the area." By 1972, when the tangle of salt-water corroded pipes and pumps was disassembled, it had produced not a drop of water—heavy or otherwise.

[14] Premier Roblin, *Hansard*, December 12, 1966, p. 109.

[15] Simplot Chemicals became the second-largest employer in Brandon and the Minnedosa Distillery, after several changes in ownership and purpose, became Mohawk's producer of ethanol.

fund" after it fell into the hands of the NDP, questioning every loan, and shamelessly politicizing it. After the 1969 election, Conservative leader Sidney Spivak, former MDC minister, demanded its abolition. However, in the 1973 election, speaking at Gimli, the site of Saunders Aircraft, which was an MDC account profusely bleeding red ink, he promised to keep it.

Despite the hundreds of new businesses and thousands of new jobs it created, the public image of the MDC became so bad that even when we had a success, like Versatile,[16] it was not believed and the mordant motto appeared: "To stop crime being profitable, let government run it." The business community, which benefited greatly from this largesse of the public purse,[17] but did not want to be seen supporting it, was reminiscent of J.M. Keynes pungent assessment: "The British Parliament [in 1919] was full of hard-faced men who had done well during the war."[18]

And they were determined to maintain their advantage. When the MDC was changed from a "lender of last resort" to a conventional lender seeking to make a profit and free itself of losers,[19] the business community was furious. In April 1975, the Manitoba Chamber of Commerce passed a resolution demanding the MDC "act solely as a guarantor of loans..in excess of those from the conventional market".[20] They wanted the MDC to guarantee that share of bank loans for which there was no security; they wanted the MDC to lose money.

Green responded, "I love the Chamber of Commerce. They make my job so much easier. [When they] make such stupid statements, and are known as great supporters of the Liberal and Conservative Parties, people say 'we've got to go to the NDP'."[21]

There was created, over tinkling cocktail glasses in the most affluent parts of the province, the twin myths that government intervention in business began with the "socialist" Schreyer government, and that government business is bad business and invariably fails. Both were wrong, but the NDP government, in its naivete, invited the mythology by making a tactical error; it opened the books of the MDC to public scrutiny.

Article 32 of the Development Fund Act stated: "The Fund shall not be required to produce to the Legislature or any Committee any application for a loan or other information [from] anyone ... who has applied for or obtained financial

---

[16] See chapter on Versatile.

[17] In 1968, the "free enterprise" PC government issued a laudatory statement showing two major plants in Minnedosa, Premier Weir's home town. Both were financed by the MDC. The Winnipeg Convention Centre, built and subsidized totally with public funds, has been a financial disaster for its funders, losing up to $4 million a year, but a bonanza for the business community.

[18] *The Economic Consequences of the Peace*; 1919: *The Carthaginian Peace*.

[19] MDC Minister Sid Green explained, "Our purpose in the future is to build crown corporations in the public sector, rather than using public funds to support so-called free enterprisers who relish ridiculing the public competence that has been feeding them." Speech to Finance Executive's Institute, January 17, 1977.

[20] 'Make MDC Guarantor, Chambers Recommend', *Winnipeg Free Press*, April 22, 1975.

[21] *Hansard*, May 16, 1975.

assistance from the corporation." When an incredulous NDP Leader Russ Paulley asked in the legislature: "Has not the government the authority to investigate the use of public funds in the province?" Premier Roblin replied, "Not unless we change the statute." [22]

The Schreyer government changed the statute; it required the MDC chairman to report annually to the Economic Development Committee of the legislature—and opened a Pandora's Box. [23] Since the evils therein were now released, it was easy for the public to assume, and for the political opposition to assiduously promote, these had been placed there by the "socialists". It was like John Locke's tree falling in the forest not really making a sound unless someone heard it, and now it was heard. The NDP struggled to explain that some major losers were initiated by the preceding government, and that it should not be expected that all public investments will be successful any more than all private investments [24] are. But the evils in the box had escaped, and finally even Hope had fled.

THE HYPERACTIVE ROBLIN GOVERNMENT, determined to force the growth of the economy but ideologically opposed to public enterprise, forged an instrument for intervention—the MDC—to select ventures in the private sector and fertilize them with public money. It was a noble goal, but by 1969 when the government changed, the MDC was little more than an instrument for bailing out private failures. [25] Many chosen "winners" had become losers and were to bedevil the Schreyer administration throughout its tenure. Instead of taxpayer-owned firms at the commanding heights of the economy, to be directed to desired goals, it inherited a stable of sick investments, many of which had to be written off.

But sometimes something worse occurred; the government made the mistake of assuming a venture could be made profitable. Such was the case with Lake Winnipeg Navigation, which owned a ship.

The MS Lord Selkirk was a beautiful ship. At 1,500 tons its displacement was fifteen times that of the Golden Hind that Sir Francis Drake used to circumnavigate the globe and bring back enough treasure to lay the base for the fortune which, four centuries later, made Queen Elizabeth II one of the richest women in

---

[22] *Hansard*, December 12, 1966, p. 110.

[23] When Premier Schreyer, responding to Liberal Leader Izzy Asper's persistent criticism of the MDC, revealed that the Minnedosa Distillery, of which Asper was president, and which had been sold and closed, had been funded by the MDC, Asper charged the premier with violating the act that governed the discussion of fund investments.

[24] A U.S. Senate committee reported that of sixteen million private businesses established between 1900 and 1939, eighty-five per cent went broke.

[25] Green explained, "No economist argues for pouring public money into private hands. Some say public money should be used as investment capital and they are called socialists, others say private people should be free to use their initiative and they are called capitalists, but only idiots say the public should finance private investments." *Hansard*, February 21, 1979, p. 90.

the world. It was of all-steel construction and had 128 berths, a seventy-five-seat dining room, a 130-seat cocktail lounge, two lifeboats and a 100-ton hold. It was equipped with state-of-the-art navigational equipment and cost more than $1.3 million to build.

In 1967 several Manitoba businessmen conceived the idea of using the ship to ply the waters of Lake Winnipeg with tourists aboard, interested some shareholders, and approached the MDC for money. The Conservative government thought it was a brilliant idea. The ship would ply the waters of Lake Winnipeg as an admirable adjunct to the tourist trade. This was the seventh-largest fresh-water lake in North America, its waters dotted with mysterious islands and its shores adorned with pine-dark forests, native villages and picturesque geological formations. A major hotel and golf course would be built on historic Hecla Island, once part of the Republic of New Iceland, which was being brought into the public domain.[26] It would create jobs and attract foreign currency. The MDC loaned the company about $650,000. In June 1969, a month before the NDP became government, the ship was launched—into a sea of red ink.

Tourists did not come, and no amount of advertising could bring them in sufficient numbers,[27] nor did the ship make a big splash among Manitobans. Two years later, the MDC placed the ship in receivership to protect the public investment, and sought to sell it. The best offer was about $225,000. Len Evans, then minister of Industry and Commerce and responsible for the MDC, considered it "sacrilege" to sell such a beautiful ship and potential attraction, for its scrap value. So it was kept, money was poured into it, and various schemes to make it profitable were proposed. But the tourists would not come.

In 1974, the Lord Selkirk almost broke even. The MDC proposed the ship be cut in two and 100 berths added, at a cost equal to the original cost of construction. I gave the premier a memo:

> The proposed extension of the MS Lord Selkirk shows this investment, which lost $306,000 in the last three years, is threatening to make a profit and the MDC bureaucrats can't stand it ... To believe it will attract hordes of tourists, foreign or domestic, is nonsense.[28] To argue the extension will produce a profit through economies of scale is the same sick economics the Tories applied to ruin agriculture and even General Motors is questioning ... In August 1973, I paid $10 for a 10-hour cruise on the Rhine River, past mythologized landscapes, hanging vineyards, Medieval castles, Roman ruins and history beyond belief. In October the same year, I paid $88 for a weekend on the Lord Selkirk and saw the Netley marshes.

---

[26] The Gull Harbour Hotel, intended as part of the attraction of the MS Lord Selkirk tours, was completed in 1977 at a cost of about $4 million and has been awash in red ink for most its existence.

[27] As Yogi Berra famously said,"If they won't come, you can't stop 'em."

[28] Actually, by 1980, tourism was Manitoba's third-largest industry, with revenues of $427 million, including $177 million from non-residents. They were just not boarding the MS Lord Selkirk.

I have had my cruise on the ship and will not be going again. Similarly,
I expect repeaters are few ... The ship is an attraction we acquired by
accident. It gives pleasure to 4,000 to 5,000 persons a year. If we write
off the capital cost, with good luck and good management it might pay
its operating costs. If not, it can be absorbed by the Department of Tourism
and its costs written off like other recreational services. Extending the
ship will solve nothing and invite unneeded problems.

The *MS Lord Selkirk* was not stretched. The following year the fond hopes
for crowded gangplanks evaporated. Later, so did the hopes for the reelection of
the NDP, killed in part by the swirl of bad publicity from media and opposition
claiming "the socialists cannot run a peanut stand—or a ship," which did nothing
to attract tourists and made the ship a floating joke.

In 1978, the Lyon government sold the *MS Lord Selkirk* to two Manitoba
businessmen for $250,000—the scrap value. One enthused, "It's a lovely ship and
a wonderful asset to own." [29]

The *Winnipeg Free Press* commended the new government: "It (is) better
business for the government to take half the profits of a well-managed company
through taxes than to prop up a poorly-managed public corporation with tax
dollars." [30]

The owners spent about another $100,000 upgrading the ship. It reportedly
lost $300,000 in 1979 and $200,000 in 1980 but the *Winnipeg Free Press* headlined, 'The MS Lord Selkirk May Soon Sail Into Sea Of Black'. [31] In June 1983, the
bank called its loan. The ship was purchased by two other Manitoba investors.
Its replacement cost was estimated at $7 million. Three years later, it was tied up
in a cove in the Red River at Selkirk. There it rests and rots. The government's
only consolation is that it was such a bad investment that even the much touted
private sector could not make it succeed. There were no editorials about "bad
management" by the private sector. Was this a naive extravagance or a botched
opportunity? It was such a lovely ship!

The NDP government wanted to kill off some chronic bleeders initiated
by the Conservatives, but could not. Among these was Columbia Forest Products.
In 1960, the Roblin government had turned its laser gaze on southeast Manitoba,
where scrub forest was a major resource, and the MDC envisioned a particle-board
plant at Sprague. By 1967, it had been abandoned twice by American firms invited
to take advantage of Manitoba's cheap labour and taxpayers' money. A study
reported there was nothing wrong with the project, except lack of supply, lack of
markets and lack of plant facilities. So the MDC raised the ante: seventy-five per
cent of the shares of the plant, having consumed $1.5 million of taxpayer's money,

---

[29] *Winnipeg Free Press*, February 3, 1978.

[30] *Ibid.*, November 23, 1977.

[31] *Ibid.*, August 3, 1981.

were sold to a Canadian corporation for $1, an additional $2 million was tossed in, and a sawmill added. Then the remaining twenty-five per cent of the $3.5 million public investment was sold to the same corporation for another $1.

And an interesting clause was written into the contract: "Subject to the provisions of this agreement the [MDC] shall lend to the Company ... *all necessary working capital.*" [32]

Manitoba taxpayers were stuck with providing a blank cheque. The MDC kept paying whatever the company requested. By June 1971, this totalled $4.3 million. In July, the corporation applied for another $313,000 they claimed was needed to keep the plant operating to the end of the year. The MDC, supported by the NDP government that saw this as a bottomless pit, refused to pay.

The corporation closed the plant. [33] The MDC demanded $500,000 in penalties for closing without permission. The corporation sent its shares to the MDC and said they were no longer the owners and thus had no responsibility. The MDC refused to accept the shares; it wanted its money back, not the worthless shares, and sued the corporation for the $500,000 penalty. The MDC argued the "all necessary working capital" clause was a "one-shot obligation", while the corporation argued that it was entitled to a perpetual subsidy and called in an officer of the MDC to testify in court that in 1967 (under a PC government) the corporation was told if they took over the plant "it would not cost them a nickel". The corporation argued that the MDC had therefore breached the agreement. The judge agreed and penalized the MDC for stopping payments.

So Manitoba taxpayers became the proud owners of a plant that had cost them $4.3 million but was evaluated at $800,000. Alas, that was not the end of the agony. While the corporation and the MDC were playing 'take it, it's yours', the community, which did not care who owned the plant so long as it was working, had a seventy-five-person work force that wanted its jobs. A receiver began operating the plant, with the government paying the bills. In October 1972, fire destroyed half the plant—the profitable half.

I sent the premier a memo entitled "Fire: Final Solution To Publicly-Owned Plants". The local Conservative MLA—suddenly appreciating public enterprise—demanded that the government spend $2 million to rebuild the plant. His leader, Sidney Spivak, argued that the government was the real owner and must act, when he was not arguing that the government should not be in business at all. In February 1974, with the plant losing $20,000 a month, the union struck for higher wages. Calculations showed it would cost much less to leave the workers on welfare than to employ them and the plant was sold for about $200,000.

Not all our disasters were inherited. The reasons for investing were varied and the desire to improve the economy insidious. The MDC, under the NDP government, made a loan to Dauphin Alfalfa Products because local entrepreneurs

---

[32] Author's italics.

[33] The corporation reportedly left Sprague with $56,000 in unpaid taxes.

believed the verdant local alfalfa could be pelleted and sold offshore; it seemed a good idea, but the business failed. We invested in Misawa Homes of Japan because the world's largest home builder offered to apply its unique structural methods at Gimli if we partnered with them on a 50/50 basis: it seemed like a Mikado-sent gift, but the pre-fab homes did not sell. Answering a cry for help, we bought Morden Fine Foods after thirty vegetable producing farmers were left stranded when a major canning company closed its doors. We lost money every year but one and the multi-million dollar plant was sold by the Lyon government for about the value of the canned goods on the shelf. Wanting to create native role models, management and income sources, we made a loan to Dave Courchene's fly-in Thunderbird Lodge, but the project was in bankruptcy almost before our cheque was cashed. We partnered with four good businessmen in the Evergreen Fertilizer Plant at Beausejour in order to exploit a local resource and earn foreign currency by exporting peat moss from the bogs. While government-financed, the management was left to the four apparently experienced businessmen. When the operation collapsed, one of them commented: "Nobody at the management level seemed to know what they were doing."

And then there was the aircraft plant, and the bus plant, and CFI …

The Crash of Saunders Aircraft

Nothing is true until it has been officially denied by the government.
—German Chancellor Otto von Bismarck

"We want to see the premier!"

My wife and I were babysitting the premier's children at his home at the 'Cabbage Patch' in the summer of 1970, while he and his wife attended some Sunday political function. The knock on the door separated me, with some relief, from Henry George's fascinating but difficult tome, *Progress and Poverty.* Two dark-suited, impressive looking men stood at the door.

"Why?"

"We understand the Government of Manitoba is seeking companies to move into your new industrial park at Gimli."

"Yes we are. And you are most welcome. But you do not see the premier for that. You see the minister of Industry and Commerce. Incidentally, what is the name of your company?"

"Saunders Aircraft."

How I was to be haunted by that name!

DURING WORLD WAR II, the Government of Canada had developed an air training base at Gimli, in the Interlake area of Manitoba.[1] In the next six years some 20,000 young men from the Allied countries won their wings there. The

---

[1] By war's end, the Commonwealth Air Training Plan, from its bases across Canada, had graduated more than 131,000 pilots and air crew from Allied countries, and Canada had won the title "aerodrome of democracy" from U.S. President Franklin D. Roosevelt.

subsequent Cold War kept the Gimli base alive for another twenty-five years, but in 1970 the federal government announced it would be closed.

Civic officials and businessmen in the Interlake knew that the removal of the government payroll would leave a $9-million-a-year hole in their economy, and sought help. They found it in the newly-elected NDP government, which was committed to rural economic diversification, and particularly in Minister of Industry and Commerce Leonard Evans, who saw every unemployed person a fallen sparrow for whom he was personally responsible. Ottawa was persuaded to transfer the base to Manitoba to convert into an industrial park.

The NDP government immediately invited individuals and companies to occupy the premises and establish industries. More than twenty businesses did so, and most were successful. But, subject to the Gresham's Law of the news industry, bad news supercedes good news and the only Gimli venture of which Manitobans seemed aware was that wretched failure, Saunders Aircraft.

Saunders had established a small plant in Montréal, collecting old Heron hulks and converting them into stretched, twenty-three-seat, turbo-prop, short hop, intercity commuters. He would move his plant to Gimli; all he needed— what else?—was a bit of money. The Manitoba Development Corporation responded to his application with a loan of $750,000, not a huge loan, we thought, as we fantasized about this new industry establishing in Manitoba and bringing new jobs. We would rescue the Interlake economy.

Our admiring public was duly, and repeatedly, informed of this auspicious event; of the advent of this new and vibrant industry that promised to make Gimli —"The Home of the Gods" in Icelandic—into the Seattle of the North. Our political opponents scowled into their cocktail glasses at our presumptive success.

Saunders Aircraft was soon back for more money. When we had committed about $4 million and it was clear Saunders could not repay the loan, it was converted to shares and Manitobans, via the MDC, became the owners of an aircraft manufacturing company.

When the loan reached $14 million, I drove out to see this bottomless pit. There was no need even to get out of the car: two planes were being rebuilt in the huge hangar, while most of the workforce lolled around, waiting for those working to take a break. An optimum workforce might have been twenty-five per cent of those on the payroll. It was a classic example of how easily—and inadvertently— an intended industrial production project can slip into being a make-work fiasco. Barring a miracle, Saunders Aircraft was doomed.

But hope springs eternal! Government statements about future prospects of Saunders were not as euphoric as earlier, but any suggestions by the opposition that the project was a disaster were emphatically denied. In retrospect, it is easy to know what should have been done, but the government wanted rural industrialization to sustain communities for which agriculture was of decreasing economic importance, and Saunders Aircraft seemed an excellent vehicle for that purpose.

The government also wanted job creation, and Saunders Aircraft was certainly doing that.

How many should be employed there? That was a decision for on-site management, which reported to Saunders' board of directors, which reported to the MDC board of directors, which reported to the minister, who reported to the government. Should the government become more directly involved in individual MDC projects? If it did, our political adversaries would attack like rabid hyenas. In any case, the MDC's charter required it to operate at "arm's length" from government. That way the MDC would not be induced to make "political" loans and the government, theoretically, could not be attacked for individual loans made by the corporation.

It's a pretty theory, but those to whom government intervention in business —except on their behalf—is abhorrent, have no concerns with theory. Ultimately, the executive branch must be responsible for the actions of its administrative apparatus including "arms length" agencies. The theory of crown corporation independence from its political masters leaves the government helpless in the administration of specific projects, but the theory of responsible government holds the government responsible for the actions of its appointees. Thus the government became ever more deeply enmeshed in justifying continued infusion of public funds into Saunders Aircraft, while explaining that not all investments—public or private—are successful, but hoping this one would be.

Anyone who has ever invested in an enterprise knows that the most difficult decision is when to stop, and that the greater the amount invested the more difficult it becomes to admit failure. That decision is even more difficult for government with its myriad considerations—economic, social and political. Will the income taxes paid by those employed recoup the losses on a public loan? What will be the cost to the public treasury if the plant closes and its employees go on Unemployment Insurance or social assistance? Are we losing our nerve too soon and will just a little more patience and money ensure success?

When in total darkness, a pinhead of light is seductive ... and sometimes disastrous. The news was not all bad. Three Saunders planes, built at Gimli, were sold to an airline in Colombia. In the 1973 Manitoba election campaign, the premier and those accompanying him, including national reporters and journalists, had flown on the Saunders plane and found it comfortable. But the news was not all good either. Further sales were slow or nonexistent. Of the three planes sold to the South American airline for minimal cash deposits, one disappeared, a second had crashed against a stone wall and the purchasers claimed they must make payments only when it was flying, the third was abandoned and a pilot, at great cost, was sent to retrieve it. By late April 1974, some $16 million had been invested in Saunders. Even the most sanguine among us admitted the government had been caught *en flagrante delicto* with the taxpayers. Like the Man of La Mancha, we must summon our last ounce of courage, and admit defeat. The government decided Saunders Aircraft must be shut down.

Then the miracle! The following day, the Government of Canada called an election. Two days later, Transport Minister Donald Jameison held a news conference in our cabinet room and announced to startled reporters, and to an equally startled Government of Manitoba, that Ottawa would inject $6 million into Saunders Aircraft, and would purchase two planes for use by Air Canada to fly the Winnipeg-Brandon-Regina-Saskatoon-Dauphin-Winnipeg route. A week later Prime Minister Pierre Elliot Trudeau, questioned about this by reporters at the Winnipeg Airport, shrugged and allowed that if his minister of Transport had stated this was so, it must be so.

Within the Government of Manitoba the joy was palpable. Now that the feds were in we could hardly get out. Granted, there were only a dozen old Heron hulks to convert but forward planning had been done; by the time the Herons had been bisected, stretched, retrofitted and new engines mounted, the workforce at Gimli would have developed the skills to build a brand new plane.

That novelty materialized as the ST-28. Modelled on the Saunders, it was a sleek, aerodynamic STOL (short take-off and landing) plane. Those who flew it, including test pilots, looked upon the work and found it good. When the opposition charged it was an expensive make-work project for a plane with no market, MDC Minister Sid Green stated, half-facetiously, the planes could be flown up and shot down, which seems to provide markets and prosperity for the business community during wartime.[2]

Government statements were again encouraging. Probing questions by the opposition were easily deflected. No, the government was not closing Saunders. Yes, the government was putting more money into Saunders. No, the government did not admit Saunders was a bad investment. Yes, Saunders Aircraft was ready for take-off.

"Are you free for lunch?"

Tom Bernes phoned in early 1975. We had been classmates at the University of Manitoba a decade earlier. We were both politically active, he in the Liberal Party and I in the NDP, so we became acquainted and I had always enjoyed our discussions because he was bright, articulate and committed. After the election of the Trudeau government in 1968, he had gone to Ottawa and was now assistant to Defence Minister James Richardson.

"Always happy to be dragged from my cloister for a free lunch."

During lunch we reminisced and congratulated each other for having climbed so high, even if, unlike Cyrano de Bergerac, we had not done it alone. Then Tom got down to business.

"We're not of the same political persuasion but we know each other and I want to deliver a message. Your government is hanging its political future on the weak peg of Saunders Aircraft. I want to inform you your new ST-28 will not be licensed."

---

[2] *Hansard*, March 26, 1974, p. 1891

"But … but … why not? Everyone who has flown it, or has flown in it, claims it is a great little plane."

"Perhaps, but we have a problem. We have an agreement with the United States. Any plane licensed by their government is allowed to fly in Canada. Reciprocally, any plane licensed by our Federal Aeronautics Board is allowed to fly in the United States. Boeing and Lockheed are both in trouble and have received substantial subsidies from Washington. They have built too many large argosies and now want to build small intercity commuters to fill a perceived niche in the market. And they don't want competition from Saunders Aircraft." Tom was always direct and clear.

The fate of the CF-105 Avro Arrow flashed through my mind.[3] "Tom, this is ludicrous. We build three or four planes a year at Gimli and you are saying mighty Boeing and Lockheed, the world's largest aircraft makers, fear competition from us?"

"It may be ludicrous, but that's the way it is."

For a brief moment we had seen the light at the end of the tunnel; now someone had lengthened the tunnel. I reported the conversation to the premier and we agreed it was ludicrous to think Ottawa would do that to us.

But Ottawa did. For whatever reasons, the federal authorities never licensed the ST-28. That meant it could not legally carry paying passengers. That made it unsaleable. And we received only about $300,000 of the promised $6 million from Ottawa. Meanwhile Ottawa had provided about $380 million to Eastern aircraft companies including Canadair, United Aircraft and DeHaviland.

In June 1975, cabinet ordered the Saunders Aircraft plant closed. Management was called in and informed the decision was irrevocable, that we had lost some $27 million, and that was enough. Management then informed us they had pre-ordered some Pratt and Whitney aircraft engines from Montreal at a cost of about $11 million and that these must be paid for.

A great pall appeared to envelope the room. Like Captain Ahab in *Moby Dick*, Saunders Aircraft had become "darkness leaping into light". Saunders Aircraft ended as a $40 million boondoggle.

That month, June 1975, two Manitoba by-elections were being hard fought. Crescentwood and Wolseley had been won by the NDP in 1969, the results taken to court after the 1973 general election, and were back at the polls. The by-elections were a week hence. Was it not the better part of political valour to keep our decision secret until after the by-elections? Did it make any sense to give aid and comfort to our enemies? Or did we owe it to Manitobans, who had entrusted us with government office, to be honest with them?

Ben Franklin had moralized that, "Honesty is the best policy, but he who lives by that principle is not an honest man." In brief, honesty is visceral, not

---

[3] In February 1959, Prime Minister John Diefenbaker cancelled construction of the Mach-2, delta-wing, CF-105 Avro Arrow, reputed to be the world's most advanced fighter-interceptor. Reportedly this was done in deference to the Americans who were developing a continental defence program based on the Bomarc missile and the Voodoo jet fighter.

cerebral; the need to think about whether or not to act honestly in itself implies dishonesty. But is it that simple? Does not an individual, or a government, have a right to defend its self-interest? What harm would be done?

The money was already lost and delaying the announcement a week would not hurt our taxpayers more than they already were. And if we revealed ourselves undone, the media, the business community and our political opposition would crucify us at an inconvenient time, considering the by-elections. Conversely, would not the people of Manitoba who claimed to want "honesty in government" applaud us? Would not our virtue be rewarded by the public and our opposition be thwarted by our forthrightness?

Like Shakespeare's Hotspur, we would "tell the truth and shame the devil". The next day we announced our decision to close Saunders. We lost both by-elections.

XXXI

Flyer Bus

Success is only delayed failure.
—Graham Greene, *A Sort of Life*

Flyer Industries became a classical example of McDiarmid's Law, that "Murphy was an optimist". Intermittently successful, it became a seductive teaser, like the mythical Lorelei, luring three successive governments to shipwreck. In retrospect the question was not that it finally failed, but that it lived so long.

Western Flyer Coach Ltd., a Manitoba bus manufacturer since 1930, applied to the MDC for a loan in 1964, 1965, 1968 and 1969. Finally, in 1970, the MDC provided a loan of $2 million. When repayments failed, the MDC took equity and ended up owning the company. Renamed Flyer Industries, it expanded with a new plant in Transcona, became a major competitor in the diesel bus market in Canada, made an agreement with General Motors to supply shells for buses sold in the United States, and became virtually the sole electric trolley bus supplier in North America.

In December 1972, Premier Schreyer told his party convention: "School bus manufacturing existed only in Ontario and the United States. Now we are making our own, jobs are being created in Morris and Winnipeg, and we just sold sixty buses to B.C. Hydro."

Then Flyer began showing its dark side. It seemed the more it threatened to succeed, the more savagely it was attacked by the political opposition and the media. By the end of 1974, ten managers and thirty skilled workmen had left, in part because the criticism convinced them the company had no future. By September 1974, the detractors had their way. Despite $17 million in investments and 500 people on the payroll, overall production was down and some was simply bad. Whether from sabotage, bad management or bad workmanship, brakes were failing and windows were falling out of buses that had been sold.

On October 1, 1974, the union struck, Flyer offered a twenty-four per cent wage increase over two years. The union demanded twenty-six per cent over eighteen months, and a profit-sharing plan.[1] Flyer workers paraded around the homes of Labour Minister Paulley, MDC Minister Green and Premier Schreyer (who invited them in for breakfast), carrying anti-NDP placards. The union blanketed the city, the media and the opposition with horror stories of Flyer as a bad company badly run and accusations of government as "the worst employer".

It threatened that "there will be no support from this local in the forthcoming by-election in St. Boniface (where about 200 Flyer employees were eligible to vote) or any other election."

The Conservatives reversed their traditional position; after ritually accusing the government of being in thrall to unions, they suddenly began accusing the government of "callousness" toward the Flyer employees. The *Winnipeg Free Press*, instead of editorially implying that unions struck at the drop of a monkey wrench, now claimed they struck only when they believe they are about to be exploited by management. "Workers at Flyer … fear such exploitation by their employer … the socialist-oriented provincial government."[2] There were "human interest" stories, complete with photos of wives and children, portraying the difficulties of striking workers.[3] Media and opposition argued that the strike was an issue between the workers and the government, not between workers and management. Flyer, by the way, lost about $14 million in 1974.

The arrangement with General Motors failed. The assumption that Canadian provinces would prefer to buy made-in-Canada buses was shattered when, despite Flyer's lowest bid, cities in Québec and Ontario bought from General Motors, due to instructions and/or subsidies from their governments. The City of Winnipeg became a problem. The government, to improve public transportation, reduce downtown congestion, encourage zero fares for seniors, and create new jobs, offered to pay half the capital cost if Winnipeg bought its buses from Flyer. The offer was accepted but Mayor Juba, as usual seeking an issue he could turn into political capital, soon began making noises the government was blackmailing the city.

One day during Question Period, I was in the visitor's gallery of the chamber. The opposition was damning the government for "forcing" Winnipeg to buy buses from Flyer without tendering. Behind me, synchronous with the accusations from the opposition benches, Mayor Juba and Deputy Mayor Olga Fuga were chorusing loudly that, indeed, the government should give the city the money and let them decide where to buy buses. I turned to them, "Listen you two. If you use your own money you can buy your damn buses wherever you wish, but if you

---

[1] See chapter on Labours Lost, p. 445
[2] *Winnipeg Free Press*, January 8, 1975.
[3] *Ibid.*, January 9, 1975.

want to use our money you will buy from our company."

The company had a brief recovery. The strike allowed the board of directors to hire a new general manager—at $300 a day—who cleaned out the flotsam, material and human, and soon had the plant producing twice as many buses— eight per week—with half the pre-strike workforce. In 1976, Flyer produced 480 buses and sold 343 to San Francisco, fifty to Boston and sixty-four to Dayton, Ohio. Sales totalled $34 million, with a profit of $4 million and the accumulated debt was reduced to $16 million. But the renaissance was brief. The strike had cost four months of production, public goodwill, and confidence among potential bus buyers. A $30 million bid to supply Seattle and Philadelphia was dropped when the United States required built-in lifts for handicapped passengers. The production delay, along with a sudden period of inflation caused buses to be sold at a loss. The constant public questioning of the viability of the company caused concern among both suppliers and buyers. And new markets failed to materialize.

Options were explored to combine other products with bus making. Among them were talks with Volvo as a potential buyer of Flyer. Skyrocketing gasoline prices (at least they seemed high at the time) heightened prospects because of Flyer's electrical trolley capability. And the sliding Canadian dollar made the American market more accessible. But ...

On February 21, 1977, MDC Minister Sidney Green made a concise statement to the legislature. It began optimistically, stating that in 1976, Flyer Industries had made and delivered 470 buses valued at $32 million, ranking the company fifth in total value of business sales for manufacturing concerns in Manitoba. It continued with a short history of the company, including its public funding, and outlined both the early challenges and more recent successes. "For the past seven months," said Green, "the company has produced between nine and ten buses a week." Yet, he continued, "The company's every move [has been] scrutinized by a hostile media [and] its difficulties were exaggerated by persons who would normally try to assist a Manitoba enterprise."

He stated that the government had authorized the MDC to keep Flyer operating and explore all options for improving its position. "Suppliers and customers are assured the government intends to honour all obligations made by the company regarding accounts."

In October 1977, the government changed, and so did the policy relative to Flyer Industries—almost. On September 16th, PC Leader Sterling Lyon had told Manitobans he would reduce their income tax with savings from selling Flyer. On November 25th, the newly-elected Premier Lyon stated "Government can't create orders [for buses] where none exist," while Industry Minister Robert Banman added that Flyer would be sold or closed.[4]

Three days later, Flyer received a forty-bus order from Hamilton and Mississauga, Ont. And the same day Banman announced Flyer would fill a seventy-

---

[4]   *The Winnipeg Tribune,* November 26, 1977.

bus contract with Winnipeg. In December, buses were delivered to Kitchener, Ontario, where the transit manager had rejected media criticism that they were costlier and less reliable than General Motors buses. Thus Flyer ended 1977 with a $1.2 million profit. In 1978, Flyer lost $1 million, but contracted to supply 144 buses to Seattle and in 1979, Flyer received orders for 100 buses from San Mateo, Cal., 118 from Seattle, and 175, valued at $33 million, from Oakland, California, where Flyer had under-bid General Motors by $11,000 a bus. By late 1979, Flyer had a backlog of 600 buses on order. MDC chairman Sydney Parsons told the government that this would be a good time to sell Flyer to the private sector.

But it was too late. The government was caught in the trap. Whether a failing enterprise is public or private, there comes a time when the question must be asked; should this dog be sold or can it be made to run, in short, is there a possibility of recovery? This is a much more delicate and agonizing issue in the public sector, for it is not simply an economic, but also a social and political question. The longer one stays in the harder it is to get out.

Flyer had 450 employees, was injecting $14 million annually into the Manitoba economy, and was projecting a profit for 1980. Should this be ignored? If the current investment was written off, how does a government explain that to its taxpayers? Industry Minister Banman equivocated, telling the media, "Selling Flyer hastily might lend credence to NDP claims that the Conservatives are unloading a government-owned enterprise at fire-sale prices for ideological reasons."[5] The Lyon government, elected to relieve the taxpayers of public investments, had been seduced. Flyer ended 1979 with a $4 million loss, but had won a reprieve.

In 1980, Flyer doubled its sales to $41 million and had a profit of $1 million. It won a $13 million, 107 diesel bus order from Toronto and a $45 million, 220 trolley bus, order from Vancouver. The workforce had expanded to 540, the highest on record. In 1981, Flyer won a $21 million order for 168 diesel buses from Boston and ended the year with a $2.5 million profit, the third in its twelve-year history.

In November 1981, the government changed again; the NDP was back. At the end of that year, Flyer received orders from Calgary and Anchorage, Alaska and in 1982, orders totalled $70 million. In October 1982, the company won a $31 million order for 200 diesel buses from Chicago, underbidding its American competitors by twelve per cent.

Zounds! The beast had more lives than the proverbial cat. It would not die. It kept producing buses and the workforce had grown to 600. Then everything turned to rat-shit!

Building buses and creating jobs did not necessarily mean financial viability. A bus sold in Peru was not paid for and could not be retrieved. A proposal to sell 300 buses, for $58 million, to the Peruvian Ministry of Transport proved to be a

---

[5] *Op. cit.,* August 4, 1979.

figment of a commission agent's imagination. Chicago imposed a late delivery penalty and 1983 ended with a loss of $1.4 million.

Nor did selling hundreds of buses mean Flyer was producing a credible product. Reports indicated that buses built since 1979 were defective. Seattle withheld $700,000 and Vancouver $6 million, pending correction of mechanical problems to their respective orders.

In January 1984, a newspaper reported, "Crippled Flyer buses littering Vancouver streets have been front-page news and a king-sized headache for the Winnipeg firm."[6] Salt used on city streets was short-circuiting insulators in the trolley buses. The electrical system was built by Westinghouse of Pittsburgh, but Flyer of Winnipeg got the blame. And the repair bills.

A month later Calgary, Los Angeles and San Mateo reported shifting fuel tanks, bulging floors, loose rivets, and defective exterior panels, frame members, chain drives, suspension bolts and wiper arms. Most buses were still on warranty. Flyer was required, at its expense, to replace the suspension bolts on Boston's 168 coaches and the front axle bolts on Seattle's entire 259-bus Flyer fleet. Chicago demanded the 163 buses delivered on the initial 200-bus contract be repaired, and a second order for 380 buses, valued at $63 million, was cancelled.

First we could not build buses, then we could not sell them, and finally we could not keep them sold. The *Winnipeg Free Press* editorialized acidly, and accurately, "Flyer Industries, Manitoba's own bus building company, has proven that, given sufficient tax money, it is possible to crack, at least once, the international markets for public transit buses. The company however, appears in real danger of proving also that a poor product can be sold only once."[7]

Flyer Bus, carrying the hopes of three successive governments, the taxpayers of Manitoba, numerous suppliers and hundreds of employees, had become nothing more than a vehicle for welfare.

Hope springs eternal in the breast of businessmen and governments, but the self-delusion could not continue. In January 1986, three days after returning from their Christmas break, 220 of the 335-member workforce were laid off, some for the fourth time in four years. Morale was shattered. Canadian Industrial Mechanical and Allied Workers Union (CAIMAW) regional vice-president Pat McEvoy charged: "The union is very suspicious that this [layoff] is being done to make the operation more appealing to new owners."[8] He was right, but not all were unhappy. One worker commented, "The best thing that could happen to Flyer is a change of management that would come if the company was sold."

In 1983, Flyer had lost $17,500 on each bus built. The following year ended with an operating loss of over $12 million, an accumulated deficit of over $32 million, and a loss of $10 million was anticipated for 1985. The government

---

[6] *Ibid.*, January 28, 1984.

[7] *Winnipeg Free Press*, February 13, 1984.

[8] *Ibid.*, January 12, 1986.

injected another $8 million just to keep the doors open, but the more buses were built, the more money was lost.[9] When Chicago cancelled a second order, Flyer chairman Hugh Jones commented with gallows humour that he was relieved, "Had they taken the order we would have lost $50,000 on every bus we sold." By early 1985, Flyer was seriously seeking an angel.

There were tentative offers, including one from a local firm and another from an Ontario company, accompanied by media speculation that the offers had been rejected because the government did not want to sell this flea-bitten dog. But the dog was not sold because the government was desperately attempting to salvage the jobs and to rid itself of the costs of refitting defective buses it had sold, conditions no prospective buyer would accept. But at last the bubble had burst; the rationalizations could not be sustained.

An offer came from Carrosierfabriek den Oudsten, a Dutch bus manufacturer. The nature of the offer signalled the government's desperation. On April 24, 1986 the *Winnipeg Free Press* announced the sale with the shocking headline, "Flyer carrying costs pegged at $116 million: defects, severance payments, bills fall to province".[9]

The Manitoba government would write off its $51 million equity investment, pay off the $30.5 million owed to the Bank of Montreal, pay an expected $27 million to repair defects on buses already sold, settle all outstanding bills, and cover severance to workers laid off. The balance of $8 million would go to the buyer to consolidate and expand the plant, to transfer its bus designs and technology to Winnipeg, and to retrain Flyer workers.

The cost of the sale of Flyer was $3 million more than it would have cost to close it down, and as the minister responsible explained, "The government decided to spend the extra money because it believes Flyer can be viable under new management."[10]

It had cost the government $3 million just to give Flyer away.

Hugh Jones said taxpayers would not recover $96 million pumped into Flyer since public support began fifteen years earlier and added that the company had lost $14.5 million in 1985, or about $59,000 on each of the 245 buses produced. He explained that the transfer could not be described as a sale because, "The company was worth nothing, absolutely nothing."

And Finance Minister Eugene Kostyra delivered the *coup de gras*, "Flyer, for all intents and purposes, is a bankrupt company." Gary Filmon, leader of the opposition Conservatives, was not sympathetic, "They drove the company into such disrepute over the past four years that they're having to pay someone just to take it."[11]

The government, however, was rid of a burden, the union got a guarantee

---

[9] The private sector also had white elephants. In 1981, Dupont wrote off a $70 million polyester plant that failed. In 1984, Bechtel, one of the world's largest engineering companies, lost $150 million in an effort to move coal by pipeline.

[10] *Winnipeg Free Press*, April 23, 1986

[11] *Ibid*

of a minimum of 250 jobs, Winnipeg got qualified assurance of a major transportation centre, and den Oudsten got a toehold in the North American market—for free. Asked what the people of Manitoba got out of the deal, den Oudsten replied, "They got a factory with a good future and a lot of employment."

The sixteen-year public ownership experiment ended July 15, 1986.

FIFTEEN MONTHS LATER, the renamed "New Flyer" announced its first major sale: fifty-six buses for $9.7 million to Oakland, California. It then won a sixty-bus contract with Toronto, and was retrofitting the 368 buses earlier delivered to Boston, for which the Manitoba government paid the company $7 million. New Flyer had 300 employees.

On September 15, 1987, New Flyer got its first major contract to supply the City of Winnipeg. At $173,000 per bus, the $5.1 million contract was $86,000 more than the tender from General Motors, but since it was now dealing with a private company, the city saw the value of buying a "Manitoba-made" product. Mayor Bill Norrie explained, "It's good for New Flyer and for Winnipeg."

In the next dozen years, New Flyer won repeated multi-million dollar contracts to deliver buses to Atlanta, New York, Las Vegas, San Francisco, Los Angeles, San Mateo, Minneapolis, Seattle, Toronto and British Columbia. It developed an articulated, double-length bus, a new suspension technology for easier passenger mounting, and engines designed to burn ethanol or propane for pollution control. It sold several hundred compressed natural gas buses to the American market, experimented with the Ballard fuel cell burning hydrogen and expelling water instead of carbon dioxide, and added (aided by Ottawa and "free enterprise" Manitoba PC Premier Filmon) a $10 million, 200-person, expansion in Winnipeg. It built two satellite plants in Minnesota to comply with U.S. content and subsidy requirements. On July 15, 1996, its 10th anniversary, New Flyer held a party for its 1,000 employees.

In October 1999, New Flyer unveiled a sleek new, forty-four-passenger low-floor bus. It had 1,450 employeees, orders for 3,300 buses with a value of $1.3 billion, and had captured thirty per cent of the North American market. By late 2000 it was producing some 2,000 buses a year, had orders to mid-2002, had 1,500 employees in Winnipeg and 1,200 in Minnesota, and was exporting eighty per cent of its production to the United States. New Flyer was creating jobs, earning foreign currency, and supporting the Manitoba economy ... precisely as it was intended to do when the government bailed it out in 1970.

New Flyer grew so fast that it outran its financing capacity. In late 2001, it announced it would shrink its work force by 500 and seek a partner. In March 2002, a New York private equity fund, KPS Special Situations, injected $44 million but took a majority stake in New Flyer. Company control was traded away to cover debts and obtain working capital and again government was called upon for financial help to prevent collapse.[12] It was sold again in 2004,[13] and a federal loan was written off, to help sell a Manitoba firm to a U.S. firm that could buy it at an enormous discount because of a Canadian dollar worth 65 cents US. However, New Flyer remains the leading bus maker in North America.

SO WHAT HAD BEEN THE PROBLEM with the 'Old Flyer?' It was plagued with problems; managers came and went; there was a lack of administrative, financial and quality control; management and labour were not communicating; there was rampant absenteeism, a crippling strike, and a general malaise among the work-force. Further, the employees were working in a goldfish bowl that was under daily attack by political opposition and media.

Were the attacks triggered by political and business ideology or by the poor performance of the company? Flyer's performance can hardly be defended, but the sale, promoted by business and the media, two decades later of the phenomenally successful, publicly owned, Manitoba Telephone System suggests the attacks on Flyer were motivated by more than red ink. Would a struggling private company be treated the same way? Of course not! The disparity is excused on the grounds that a private company loses only PRIVATE money, yet that is the reddest of red herrings, since private corporations charge their losses, and management mistakes, to their customers.

Eldon Gregory of CAIMAW feared the board inadvertently appointed managers who were not committed to public ownership; "Someone wants to get rid of the company. Maybe someone wants to buy it cheap."[14]

Ken Clark, appointed CEO in 1983, saw it differently. "It was laughable. There were people falling over each other. I fired 90 people in the first 90 days."[15]

President Hugh Jones blamed management for misleading the board of directors: "Boards received a comfort level from the people in [operations] that has been proven unjustifiable."[16]

MDC Minister Kostyra agreed. "Previous managers, supported by previous boards, were selling buses at less than cost. The last manager thought he could do that. He is no longer there."[17]

---

[12] New Flyer was not alone. Privately owned Motor Coach got a government bailout of about $20 million and then laid off 600 workers. In November 2003, its unions saved half the jobs by accepting a four-day work week with the fifth day paid by UIC.

[13] KPS sold New Flyer to Harvest Partners and Lightyear Capital in February, reportedly for about $300 million, after only paying $28 million in 2002. *Ibid.*, April 2, 2004.

[14] *Canadian Business*, November 1984.

[15] *Ibid.*

[16] *Ibid.*

[17] *Ibid.*

Conservative Leader Spivak (with commendable prescience) had much earlier blamed the concept of publicly operated enterprises. "Since the [bus] market is there, [success] may be achieved but only if [Flyer] is sold to private industry."[18]

The man who had owned Flyer before the government took it over agreed. He had been appointed to the board of Flyer to operate the company of which he had lost control. In 1974, he resigned, stating that government should not be involved in business because "Government does not have the same access to information and knowledge as the private sector has."[19]

But talk is cheap. He, as a private businessman, had not done so well either; the Government of Manitoba became involved in his firm because he borrowed money from the MDC and could not repay it.

IRONICALLY, the MDC and its stable of acquisitions was not run by "government", but by boards of directors comprising prominent businessmen, lawyers, accountants and engineers, so why did their private success not transfer to the public sector?

Provincial Auditor William Ziprick claimed the real problem was lack of cost accounting, and that Flyer survived as long as it did only because it had unlimited access to public money. "When you remove the bankruptcy discipline, it's pretty hard to create an artificial environment to take its place."

The PC approach to economic development was to have privately owned, privately managed but publicly funded companies. The NDP approach, based on the concept that those who supply the money should own the plant, was to use publicly owned, publicly funded, but privately managed companies. Ziprick theorized that only the incipient threat of losing their own money triggers the businessman's acumen. But are businessmen not also taxpayers?

Or was Flyer's problem more insidious and generic? Sixty years earlier German sociologist Robert Michels wrote that any organization not rigorously controlled has an ineluctable dynamic to bureaucratization. Everyone wants to be a chief; every minor manager aspires to a suit and every worker to a white collar.[20]

New Flyer president den Oudsten commented that the plant had a good work force and equipment but poor organization, inflexible work rules, stingent job classification and too many of the wrong kind of employees: "When we first came here, there were as many white-collar people as blue-collar. That's incredible."[21]

Since New Flyer's success was based on the nucleus of the old work force,

---

[18] Not only the public sector fails. The business acumen of the Eaton epigone of business aristocracy, was displayed in the demolished remnants of the Eaton Building on Portage Avenue in 2003.

[19] *Winnipeg Free Press*, October 28, 1974.

[20] *The Iron Law of Oligarchy*, Germany, 1915.

[21] *Winnipeg Free Press*, July 16, 1986.

which produced well under private management, was the real problem less with the workers than with how management organized the work for them? Or is there a tendency for workers in a publicly owned plant, with a "friendly" government in office, to believe the treasury is bottomless, and to milk it?

The union called a four-month strike when the firm was losing millions, and the resultant deficit dogged Flyer from that date. Union members behaved as if they believed if they destroyed that firm the government would buy them a new one. Perhaps the government should have listened better when the union described Flyer as a "headless monster", but perhaps the government would have been more inclined to listen had they come to us without first going to the media, without embroidering every miniscule plant problem into a "government" problem, without threats of political action, without assuming that if they created enough hysteria the government would surrender to them, and without claiming no reorganization can take place without their consent. Would they have behaved that way with a private employer?

An irony of Flyer was that the odious task of ridding the crown of "this turbulent beast" fell to Finance Minister Eugene Kostryra. He was the soft-spoken, hardworking former senior official of the Manitoba Federation of Labour, who had spent his adult life fighting for worker security and union empowerment, sometimes in defiance of a firm's bottom line. Now the bottom line became the deciding factor and he sold. It was a wise—and courageous—decision. He stated that he had not consulted the union.

Of course, it would have been an even wiser decision for government to have not acquired Flyer at all. But while it is easy to be wise in retrospect, why DID the Schreyer government become involved in a firm already showing signs of failing?

Three years after its acquisition by den Oudsten, New Flyer announced a $30 million, 151-bus order from Atlanta, its largest contract to that date. The next day, Minister of Industry and Commerce Leonard Evans, who was responsible for the MDC when the decision was made to take equity in Flyer, revisited the experience, "I recall a cabinet meeting where the MDC Board of Directors recommended putting money into Flyer. They thought it a wise decision ... to get into what they thought would be the lucrative bus and electric trolley building market." Evans explained that the MDC board of directors included proven businessman Robert Kipp, who founded a Winnipeg firm (Kipp-Kelly), and prominent lawyer Abe Simpkin, while the chairman and CEO of the MDC was a super promoter of business in Manitoba, Rex Grose. Then he added ruefully: "But Grose also recommended going into Churchill Forest Industries." [22]

And that was the greatest and most costly scandal of all.

---

[22] *Ibid*, September 15, 1989.

XXXII

Churchill Forest Industries

How could one man fool so many people?
> —Bob Preston, CBC reporter, following release of the
> Report of the Commission of Inquiry into The Pas Forestry
> and Industrial Complex, 1974

At precisely **7 p.m.**, January 8, 1971, the RCMP and a phalanx of accountants and lawyers, carrying court orders, fanned out in a quasi-military operation to seize the Churchill Forest Industries pulp and paper complex at The Pas, and about $8 million in bank accounts in Canada and the U.S. At the same moment, Premier Schreyer announced and explained the takeover.

In August 1974, the official Inquiry Commission Report was released. It stated, "Taking physical possession of the [CFI] plant was properly carried out under orders of the court and the behaviour of those who did so ... was proper."[1]

This should have been the end of the movie, with the heroes, to public acclaim, walking into the glowing sunset. Instead, it was merely a comma in the sad commentary on what had become, and remains, the most politically charged and financially costly episode in Manitoba's resource development saga. It included betrayal of trust, ambition, financial manipulation, naiveté, legal suits, and a trail of dashed hopes that would continue for another twenty years before fading into unrelieved black.

WHEN ED SCHREYER first sat in the leather upholstered chair as Premier of Manitoba, the first item he saw on his huge oak desk was a bulky document including "a lengthy statement on Forest Products Development in Manitoba, the

---

[1]   *ICR*, p. 1959

financial statements of the Manitoba Development Fund (later Corporation)[2] prepared by McDonald Currie, and a legal audit certifying the activities of the MDC had been conducted in accordance with the Act."[3] On top lay a memo assuring him that, rumours to the contrary, all was well at Churchill Forest Industries at The Pas.[4] The memo was signed by Rex Grose, chairman and general manager of the MDC.

Premier Schreyer was greatly relieved. There had been questions about the identity of those involved with the government in the project[5] and the amount of public money at risk.[6] There were rumours of problems—and perhaps skulduggery—at The Pas, and it had been an issue in the 1969 election. Schreyer had stated that this project was "the darkest moment in Manitoba's economic history" and "the only way to clear the air is with an inquiry". But the new premier was not inclined, by experience or nature, to begin his tenure by firing "Mr. Manitoba", the title Grose had been awarded as the province's most energetic promoter of enterprise and industrialization, and he accepted Grose's assurance.

It was a decision he would profoundly regret.

In this sentiment he was not alone. Thirty years later, former Premier Duff Roblin, during whose tenure the CFI project had begun, wrote that in 1967, the Liberals in the legislature asked questions about the project, to which Grose prepared answers that did not satisfy them and, "They should not have satisfied me."[7]

The commission of inquiry later reported, "Some statements in (the documents Grose gave Schreyer) were known by Grose to be untrue[8] at the time." It also found that Grose had deliberately misled the premier and misused the "universal confidence" placed in him.

Six days after taking office, Premier Schreyer met with Grose and was again assured that loans to CFI were monitored and had been certified by the noted firm of Arthur D. Little of Massachusetts. On July 31st, Schreyer, Finance Minister Saul Cherniack, and several MDC directors, met with CFI principals Oskar Reiser and Alexander Kasser and were satisfied the MDC funds were being properly used.

But it was already too late. They would not know until much later that a week earlier, control of the funds had been taken out of government hands. While

[2] The fund is popularly known as the Manitoba Development Corporation, so shall be referred to throughout as MDC.

[3] ICR, p. 1416.

[4] Churchill Forest Industries was one of four interrelated plants at The Pas (they included CFI, for woodlands operation; River Sawmills, for lumber; MP Industrial, the pulp and paper maker, and James Bertram and Sons, manufacturer of the paper-making machinery). All were controlled by one person, so the complex was referred to as CFI.

[5] "The public has a right to know who its partners are and their credentials for executing the agreement." Winnipeg Free Press, April 19, 1966.

[6] "Some public concessions to the developer are inevitable, but ... the Roblin government paid a king's ransom." Ibid., April 28, 1966.

[7] Speaking for Myself: Politics and Other Pursuits, p. 137.

[8] Grose had written, "The MDC is providing about 2/3 of the total capital for the project." (ICR, p. 1417) In fact, the MDC would pay 100 per cent.

they were meeting, millions in public money was being spirited from Manitoba into Swiss bank accounts.

Initially, MDC disbursements to CFI were made against invoices supported by detailed documentation. Later this was changed to loans made against purchase orders only. This made it easy to put the money into safe bank accounts rather than pay suppliers.

The inquiry reported,

> At a meeting on July 22, 1969, in Montclair, N.J., attended by David Rodgers, Assistant Manager [later GM] of the MDC, and others, it was decided to speed up the flow of money to Zurich ... because of fear the NDP government might cut off funds ... The MDC and [certifying agent] Arthur D. Little fully cooperated in this reprehensible action [p. 1935]
> ... The principals were aided in their deception by Rex Grose [p. 1444].

Rodgers testified to the inquiry, "There was consternation among the principals [of CFI] ... The new government indicated it would examine [the project]. The meeting restructured payout procedures [p. 1441] ... The flow of money [from the MDC to CFI] was speeded up by the July 22nd meeting ... \$30 million went out in the next three months [p. 1444]."

Rex Grose and ADL were not alone in leaving the government with a false sense of security. The inquiry commission wrote that from December 1958, to March 1970, the law firm of Newman, McLean was counsel for the MDC, but in October 1969, "Mr. Walter Newman [senior partner in Newman, McLean] was actually retained by [Kasser's son-in-law] on behalf of CFI [while his partner] Mel Neuman, was acting for the MDC [the lender], without knowledge that his senior partner was representing the borrower [pp. 1541-43]."

In short, Newman was meeting with the borrowers when the MDC and the government were in contention with them, and his partner, Mel Neuman, was advising the MDC side. "No one in the MDC or government knew Newman was advising CFI [9] [p. 1562]."

Despite assurances from Grose that MDC was contributing only its share of the funds, from ADL that the MDC funds were going where they were supposed to be going, and from Newman, McLean that all was proper and legal, Schreyer became concerned. In October 1969, he asked Alistair Stewart, an old friend and vice-chairman of the Manitoba Economic Advisory Board, to quietly investigate without causing a panic. Stewart, with his high forehead, clipped moustache and aggressive manner, resembled a British brigadier, but was in fact a chartered accountant. He went to work with a will.

---

[9] Testifying to the inquiry, Walter Newman argued that he was merely acting as a consultant, but the commission concluded that Kasser and Reiser sought "his advice as a lawyer" (p. 1581). In 1975, after a special investigation, Walter Newman was cleared of "conflict of interest" allegations by the Manitoba Law Society.

Schreyer later testified to the inquiry commission, "It wasn't to look for problems but to confirm statements that there was satisfactory backup for the government in the whole development ... I had no concern about payout procedures. I felt [the money] was adequately protected [by ADL] ... I expected confirmation that all was going on in an orderly way [p. 1444]."

But that is not what Stewart found. He addressed some questions to Grose and received answers [later proven wrong] with enough discrepancies to arouse his suspicions. And he came to the momentous conclusion that the MDC had given CFI a "blank cheque".

Stewart followed his suspicions to New Jersey. One afternoon, he phoned Premier Schreyer to say he had found something of extreme interest and would reveal it when he returned to Winnipeg next morning. That night in the airport in New York, Stewart died, apparently of a heart attack.

Grose's response also triggered suspicions elsewhere. Phillip Mathias, a journalist with *The Financial Times*, had followed the CFI project and developed certain concerns. In August 1969, Grose told him the project would cost $81.7 million. Six months later, Grose informed Stewart the capital cost would be $142.6 million.

In March 1970, Mathias came to The Ledge to see the premier. Schreyer would not see him; he had been warned by Grose that Mathias was linked to Abitibi Pulp and Paper, a competitor that opposed the CFI project, and therefore could not be trusted. Mathias took his memo to Green, who scanned it quickly and immediately took it to Schreyer. The game was over.

At a special cabinet meeting on Sunday, March 22, 1970, Grose tearfully confessed to lying. The commission reported:

> Premier Schreyer testified Grose stated to cabinet that the figures
> he had given ... were wrong ... When asked if they were intended to mis-
> lead, he admitted so ... and indicated that he had an impossible task over
> the previous four years because the [CFI agreement] was dumped into his
> lap [by Premier Roblin] and he had been instructed to accommodate its
> financing [pp. 1456-7].

Roblin later denied this: "At no time did cabinet as such negotiate with Kasser over the CFI arrangement. That was the function of the MDC."[10] But the inquiry commission concluded:

> An informal committee of cabinet composed of [Premier Duff]
> Roblin, [Industry Minister Gurney] Evans, [Mines and Resources Minister
> Sterling] Lyon and [Provincial Secretary] Maitland S. Steinkopf, conducted
> the negotiations with Oscar Reiser in September 1965, which led to

---

[10] *Speaking for Myself,* p. 141..

acceptance of Monoca's [the supposed parent company of CFI] proposal ...
The cabinet group made no adequate inquiries about Reiser ... [and] laid
the foundation of the fraudulent activities that later occurred [p. 1912].

Meaningful debate was made impossible by assurances given
Monoca and CFI that financial relationships were confidential. Moreover, the Roblin cabinet instructed Grose to take all documents with him
when he left the Department of Industry in 1966 to be fulltime general
manager of the MDC. The MDC closed off any possibility of searches of
the public record by interposing a trust company between borrower and
lender [p. 1963].

On March 31, 1970, the premier blew the whistle. He told the legislature
that the CFI owners' equity was not thirty-three per cent as believed, but zero. The
same day Grose resigned.[11] After Stewart's report, Mathias's revelations, and Grose's
confession, Schreyer directed the provincial auditor to check the MDC accounts,
and appointed Stothert Engineering of Vancouver to audit the CFI project.

Stothert soon found that "tens of millions of dollars went out of the
MDC improperly". In May, the government temporarily halted loans, pending
arrangements to monitor spending. But the lender could not catch up to the borrower. The inquiry commission wrote, "In [1966] MDC had committed itself to an
open-ended loan to CFI ... By March 1969, commitments to [CFI] had reached
$51 million [p. 1968]." By June 1970, MDC loan advances reached $73 million.

THE GOLDEN BOY atop the classical dome of the Legislative Building in Winnipeg
looks symbolically northward, and so did the Liberal government of Premier
Douglas Campbell. It tapped the Nelson River for hydro-electricity to power the
nickel smelters at the boom town of Thompson, and then turned to timber. In
1956, the Liberals commissioned the firm of Arthur D. Little to study possibilities
for northern development. ADL reported distance from markets, freight costs,
high costs of town site development, and extremely slow growth all created insur-
mountable obstacles to development—unless the government provided incentives.

Campbell's successor picked up the report and ran with it. Duff Roblin
described his first view of Manitoba's North this way:

> The town of The Pas, the centre of the Old North, was a stagnant
> community. It had a splendid history interwoven with the Hudson's Bay
> Company and the fur trade, but its future was doubtful—except for the
> possibilities of the forest around it. The difficulties were numerous ...
> but a forest industry could be visualized. It was worth pursuing [12]

[11] Grose became an economic development officer in P.E.I.
[12] *Ibid.*, p. 134.

The Roblin government, at its active best, was prepared to make the necessary concessions and take the concomitant risks. It was a courageous decision. And it cost the people of Manitoba their shirts.

In Rex Grose, deputy minister of the Department of Industry and Commerce and general manager and later chairman and CEO of the MDC, the government found a willing instrument for pursuing their interrelated objectives of spurring regional development, luring the private sector to develop northern resources, and making jobs for northerners, particularly Aboriginals, among whom unemployment was stratospheric and endemic. This grew into a determination to develop an integrated lumber, pulp and paper operation.

Grose contacted many companies. They were offered electrical transmission lines, power at extremely low rates, generous tax concessions, development allowances, no realty or business taxes, and the lowest stumpage fees in Canada. No one would touch it.

In retrospect, given this bonanza of concessions, one assumes if no experienced firm would do it, it was not worth doing. But former Wing Commander Duff Roblin, who had flown heroic missions over enemy territory, was no stranger to risk. His government had vision and will and would not be deterred by the faint of heart.

In July 1965, in what later seemed an act of desperation, the Conservatives gave wide circulation to Operation Industrial Breakthrough. "We believe key industries ... like pulp and paper ... should locate in this province ... The Government of Manitoba will provide $100 million to ensure that these projects take place." The advertisement was signed: Duff Roblin, Premier of Manitoba.

The inquiry commission wrote with commendable hindsight, "The government was unwise to advertise ... $100 million was available. That solicited the interest of profiteers and racketeers."

Out of nowhere came a Swiss company, Monoca AG[13] and its principals, the suave, dignified Dr. Otto Reiser and the charismatic, enigmatic Alexander Kasser, whom Walter Newman described as "a small, explosively energetic man with staring eyes who dominated any group."[14] If the government was willing to give away that money, they were willing to take it, and they did.

The commission commented, "When Monoca appeared, the government and the MDC accepted its proposal after minimum negotiation. The principals of Monoca demanded non-disclosure. Credit reports of Kasser's wealth gave no security, because he refused to give his personal guarantee. Yet the government granted much greater concessions than ever before and the loan was the largest ever made [pp. 173-6]."

Kasser, Hungarian-born but resident in the United States, who later emerged as the brains behind the Monoca/CFI scheme was, in Walter Newman's words, "an

---

[13] Monoca proved to be a shell company controlled by Kasser, and used, with its president, Oskar Reiser, as a front.

[14] Walter C. Newman, *What Happened when Kasser Came to Northern Manitoba*, p. 19.

unconventional genius [pursuing] his financial objective by methods as deceptive as ingenious."[15] He seemed to sit like a spider at the centre of his web, Technopulp Inc., of Montclair, New Jersey, which controlled a raft of companies established to extract money from the public purse.

Like the nineteenth-century railway magnates, who believed if government was subsidizing railroads by the mile, then a crooked line was the shortest distance between two points, so Kasser apparently concluded, if government was subsidizing companies then the more companies he owned the more free money he would receive.

Columnist Richard Purser wrote that "[Kasser's] financial objective was to build the project at The Pas entirely with public money, without the government knowing it was paying the entire bill."[16]

He did it by overcharging the MDC, putting part of the surplus back as his share of project costs and pocketing the balance, by getting kickbacks from hungry suppliers, and by controlling the entire operation through affiliates and shell companies in faraway places like Lichtenstein. He succeeded because he found a government so anxious to develop the North that it accepted his insistence upon confidentiality.

Monoca was given the host of concessions the MDC had earlier offered to others, plus exclusive cutting rights to 43,000 square miles of Manitoba, and unlimited access to money. Asked on December 15, 1965, if there were any financial commitments to Monoca, Premier Roblin told the legislature, "The government promised nothing. The MDC is available to this company as to any other. There was no special deal made."[17]

Three months later, Liberal MLA Elman Guttormson asked Industry Minister Gurney Evans, "Will the government lend Monoca money through the MDC?"

Evans replied, "The government has no financial commitment ... Monoca has financial resources."

Guttormson probed, "They have no commitment from the government that they can get money from the MDC?"

And Evans replied, "That is correct."[18]

Six years later Sterling Lyon, Mines minister in the Roblin government, testified to the inquiry commission. Asked if he knew in early 1966 that the government (via the MDC) would be providing CFI financing, he replied, "I think that was understood by everyone."

And the commission commented, "Mr. Roblin misled the Legislature on

---

[15] Newman's detection of Kasser's methods did not stop him from working for Kasser. The inquiry reported, "Mr Newman continued to take a direct interest ... and performed certain services for CFI ... for which he submitted bills to CFI."

[16] *Winnipeg Tribune*, November 6, 1976.

[17] *Hansard*, p. 249.

[18] *Ibid.*, p. 242.

December 15, 1965, by stating the government had promised Monoca nothing [p. 1962]" … "Gurney Evans misled the Legislature on March 8, 1966, by stating Monoca had no financial commitments from the government. This he knew to be untrue since he had signed the letter of October 8, 1965 accepting Monoca's proposals [p. 1962]. The financing memorandum, accepted in writing on October 8, 1965, was open ended with no ceiling on the amount of the loan to be made by the MDC to CFI [p. 1914]."

On March 4, 1966, four days before Evans made his statement to the legislature, Roblin had met with Reiser in Zurich for a ceremonial signing of the agreement with Monoca. *The Winnipeg Tribune* reported, "Premier Duff Roblin has landed a fully integrated forest industry for Manitoba's northland." [19] And the government trumpeted that this meant 4,000 new jobs.

Roblin called an election for June 23, 1967. The government touted its "northern vison" of hydro and forest development. His government was returned with a reduced majority. On June 25, 1969, the Conservatives, now led by Premier Weir, were defeated.

ON JULY 22nd, one week after the NDP government took office, at the meeting at Montclair, New Jersey, attended by representatives of the MDC, a gigantic swindle was plotted. The payout schedule was rejigged so MDC money would flow out to CFI much faster than needed. And it would flow to Switzerland instead of to suppliers of equipment and labour for the plant at The Pas.

During 1970, the MDC advanced money by the millions, CFI kept asking for more, and complaints were arriving that CFI was not paying bills for which MDC had advanced funding. Mechanics' liens for $8 million were submitted to the MDC and some trades verged on bankruptcy. In November, NDP Industry and Commerce Minister Leonard Evans visited The Pas and was appalled by what he heard. On December 4, 1970, Stothert sent a memo, "In view of … delayed construction, poor performance, lack of planning, lack of recruitment, lack of financial strength, inability to raise capital, lack of ownership equity, excessive mechanics liens, failure to pay contractors, failure to provide documentation to the government [on] expenditure, the MDC should take possession of the assets of CFI (*ICR* p. 1514)."

The legal team, usually cautious, drew the same conclusion. CFI was appearing as an operation not to make pulp and paper, but to extract money from the MDC. Court orders were obtained.

On January 8, 1971, without warning, the plant was seized. On the desk of general manager, the RCMP found a hand-written document showing how CFI could purchase the paper making plant for $1 and continue receiving funding

---

[19] Op. cit., March 8, 1966.

from the MDC. Had the seizure occurred a week later, Kasser et al. probably would have received $12 million in area development grants from Ottawa.[20]

Leifur Hallgrimson of the attorney general's Civil Litigations Division, became the court-appointed receiver to complete and operate the plant. By then the people of Manitoba were "out of pocket" $95.2 million for a plant evaluated at $71 million.

On January 27, 1971, the government appointed the commission of inquiry, composed of former Chief Justice C. Rhodes Smith (chair), Murray Donnelly, Political Science professor at the University of Manitoba, and Leon Mitchell, prominent lawyer and chairman of the Manitoba Municipal Board. Three and a half years, $2 million, eighty witnesses, and hearings in ten countries later, after following the elusive trail of evidence like Theseus hunting the Minotaur in the labyrinths of ancient Crete, they published a six-volume, 2,800-page report, which concluded that the CFI operation was: "a massive fraud, planned and executed by Dr. Kasser, of which the MDC and the people of Manitoba were the victims."

They also concluded that Kasser had taken away $33 million, $26 million of it in excess fees, virtually all tax free.

Twenty-six charges were laid against some companies and seven individuals, including Reiser and Kasser. Kasser abruptly fled to Switzerland with which Canada had no extradition treaty. He was declared a fugitive from justice and Interpol was alerted.

When a reporter wrote that Reiser claimed the inquiry commission had refused to hear him, Comission Counsel D'Arcy McCaffrey replied, "Vern Fowlie enjoyed a week of Dr. Reiser's hospitality in Switzerland and now reports his side of the story ... We were prepared go any place to hear their story ... They would not appear. Now, from behind their Swiss curtain, Reiser says he had no access to our Courts. He is lying."[21]

Kasser was charged with "conspiracy to defraud" and sued for recovery of $36.6 million. He countersued the government and Premier Schreyer for $405 million for "conspiracy" to take his plant. In 1973, the court threw out Kasser's claim as "vexatious" and awarded Manitoba $103.5 million from those named in the suit. By 1986, when ADL paid $3 million, Manitoba had recovered a total of about $5.5 million—considerably less than it cost to collect it.

THE INQUIRY COMMISSION also concluded: "The Schreyer Government's retaining of Stothert Engineering [in March 1970] to conduct an audit was a prudent action. The Commission believes it should have been done earlier [p.1957]."

---

[20] It was several years before Ottawa gave Manitoba the money it had committed to unknown foreign operators. During the 1972 federal election, Schreyer was informed it might be easier to get the money if he stayed out of the election campaign.

[21] *Winnipeg Free Press*, May 24, 1975

The *Winnipeg Free Press* editorialized: "The commission has painted a startling picture of how men in high places can be duped, how experts can be confused and misled, and how the ordinary taxpayer can be taken to the cleaners ... nobody comes out smelling like a rose ... Premier Schreyer's administration comes in for criticism for not halting the deal after the NDP came into office." [22]

After the commission's revelations, from the perspective of 1974, it was easy to conclude that the NDP government should have acted on its initial suspicions. and immediately seized the plant at The Pas, arrested those involved before they escaped to safe havens, and decapitated the MDC of its senior officers.

But Premier Schreyer defended his government for moving slowly, "The only basis we could have had for not accepting those assurances [by Grose, ADL, et al] is if we believed everyone involved in the agreement were ... crooks." [23]

Former Premier Roblin later hinted that Schreyer was at fault: "He had pledged to investigate CFI ... but then seemed to have relied entirely on Grose's report." [24]

But then, so did Roblin, and that is where the scandal began. In 1969, Schreyer's suspicions were of the politicians, not of the civil servants. It was inconceivable to him that his government was being betrayed by persons on the public payroll.

And so it was with Roblin. He later wrote that he had cautioned his colleagues in 1965 that "this project is not without risks", but, "I was referring to the feasibility of the project. I had no idea the risk was [from] a principal actor, Rex Grose. That came as an unbelievable shock and surprise." [25]

The NDP government did not "halt the deal" sooner because its lawyers advised that the deal made by the previous government was binding, that "there is no evidence of fraud", and that halting funds or seizing the project without proper legal grounds would cause a legal nightmare. Also, by removing $25 million of public money from Manitoba, Kasser created a Catch-22 situation; if Manitoba stopped loan advances, that $25 million remained in Switzerland; if it moved to receivership it invited a blizzard of lawsuits. The rapid payout process the MDC had agreed to on June 22, 1969, left the government the hostage of either Kasser or the courts.

In June 1970, the legal team advised that if funding was stopped, "The probability is that most of the $73.1 million already advanced by the MDC would have to be written off (*ICR*, p.1490)."

Stothert Engineering advised that receivership is "A step to be taken as a last resort, and after all attempts to reason with the officers [of CFI] had failed [*ICR*, p.1487]."

[22] *Ibid.*, October 5, 1974.
[23] *Ibid.*
[24] Roblin, *Speaking for Myself*, p. 143.
[25] *Ibid.*, p. 142.

Leifur Hallgrimson of the Attorney General's Office testified, "To close down the project in June [1970] or take it over ... would have been horrendous because construction was at its peak. It was difficult enough in January 1971 [*ICR*, p. 1487]."

The government moved slowly through the maze because it was playing a cat-and-mouse game—with partial success—to negotiate back the money from Zurich, because it desperately wanted the plant completed, and because there had been an incident.

On February 27, 1970, Alistair Stewart, disgusted by his study of the CFI deal, sent the premier a memo. It stated that those operating the MDC had less intelligence "than the chipmunk that chatters at me every morning". He proposed that the government should fire the directors and officers of the MDC, expose the entire CFI deal, blame it all on the preceding government, call an immediate election "and appeal to the people to justify you [and] you would probably come back with 35 to 40 seats" for the NDP.

The premier was furious. This suggested precisely the opposite of government policy, which was "trying to dampen down passions", and ensure the completion of the project.

But the damage was done. The memo immediately got into the hands of Rex Grose who, rather than being caught in his deceptions, used it as his reason for resigning. Grose gave it to Spivak who chose to cite this, rather than government statements to the legislature, as actual government policy. After Stewart's memo any move to seize the plant or stop funding it would have appeared crassly political. After all, what was the business climate in 1969-70?

The fear of opposition politicians, MDC bureaucrats, opinion makers and the business community was not that the government would not clean up the mess, but that it *would*. They feared that the "socialists" were itching to take over the complex.

The meeting on July 22, 1969, in New Jersey, which included MDC representatives, was not held because the government was moving too slowly, but because of fear it would move too fast. This led to $25 million being moved to Zurich beyond government reach.

On April 1, 1970, the day after Grose resigned, Donald Craik, deputy leader of the PC Party, spoke passionately in the legislature, blaming the government and stating that this was like superstar Gordie Howe resigning from the Detroit Red Wings. "This is what happened to a top civil servant yesterday ... Rex Grose was the Gordie Howe of industrial development."[26]

In mid-May 1970, when MLA and PC Party president Sidney Spivak visited Kasser at his home in New Jersey, did he do so because the government was moving too slowly or because he feared it would move *too fast*? Spivak told the inquiry commission he visited Kasser to find out where the money for the CFI plant was coming from. He had shown little interest in this while he was

[26] *Hansard*, April 1, 1970.

minister for the MDC prior to 1969, and on March 18, 1968, he had assured the legislature all was well at CFI (*ICR*, p. 1964). In any case, six weeks before his trip to New Jersey, his friend Rex Grose had stated the money came from the Manitoba taxpayers.

In June 1970, the government had temporarily suspended loan advances "To (a) ensure all further advances were made under satisfactory controls and (b) to secure return of the surplus money then in Swiss banks." Walter Newman later told the inquiry commission this damaged the complex and, instead, the government should have "taken over the project at the time [ICR p. 1491-6].

But the inquiry commission reported that in October 1969, "Walter Newman was retained by the son-in-law of Mr. Kasser, on behalf of CFI [p. 1542]." He "wished to combat the policies of the government by advising Kasser and Reiser on the strategy they should follow [p. 1571]."

In July 1970, "Walter Newman arranged for Reiser to tell his story to the press (Richard Malone and Peter McLintock of the *Winnipeg Free Press*; Harry Mardon and Tom Green of the *Tribune*)" to get more favourable treatment for CFI. [p. 1571]. "Kasser and Reiser were seeking money [from MDC] ... without certification [and] Mr. Newman's intervention, if successful, would have assisted them in their objective [p.1573]."

Soon after the receiver was appointed on January 7, 1971, "Newman was asked to come to Montclair for a meeting at Kasser's home [and] he assisted in retaining counsel for them to fight the government takeover [p. 1579].[27]

In July 1970, Reiser also met with George Doerksen, publisher of *Manitoba Business*. With George Litton, VP of Technopulp (Kasser's company) of Montclair, Doerksen toured the plant at The Pas and wrote rapturously:

> Former Premier Roblin's ability to put together a high finance deal is shown here. He assembled one of the most outstanding deals this province has ever seen. [As for financing] the MDC insisted on security more onerous than normal ... with strict supervision of purchases and disbursements ... Arthur D. Little certified payouts by the MDC to [CFI] ... Why did the NDP government bring Stothert Engineering to do a study? Harassment is so extreme that CFI operators fear they may not be able to complete the project ... Is it possible [the NDP] wants to provoke [CFI] into default so it could [nationalize] the plant?[28]

It was precisely this self-deluding ideology in the business community that the NDP government sought to overcome by toning down the rhetoric and by Schreyer (who was seen as a moderate) appointing himself minister of Industry

---

[27] Newman justified his actions to the inquiry with: "My view was that the government was trying to destroy the MDC .. And me .. I saw the letter of Alistair Stewart." ICR, p. 1570.

[28] *Manitoba Business*, August 1970.

and Commerce. The government feared that, in the climate of the time, stopping funding or seeking receivership of CFI without express legal advice that these were the only option, would damage the credit reputation of the province and raise the cry of "Communism", not only by those who later argued the government should have moved sooner, but internationally.

John Chamberlain, columnist for the *Los Angeles Herald*, in an article entitled 'Arabs Of The North', compared the Manitoba government with Cuba's Castro, Libya's Kaddafi and Chile's Allende, "Socialist ... Premier Schreyer [like Allende] ... ousted Churchill Forest Industries ... a US-owned company ... without paying a nickel. The money [CFI] spent on [the plant] is for naught ... Manitoba ... said CFI is not entitled to compensation [on a deal made] by an ousted Conservative government with 'mongrel' capitalists."

While this can be dismissed as a jolting reminder of American Cold War paranoia, it was significant because we needed American money to develop the Manitoba economy. Even more significant, in the context of the government's freedom to act, was the political climate in Manitoba after the election of the NDP government.

This was illustrated by the *Winnipeg Free Press*. On December 6, 1973, *two years* after the inquiry commission began revealing the CFI fraud, the paper reprinted Chamberlain's article.

ON OCTOBER 1, 1973, the courts awarded ownership of the CFI complex to the Province of Manitoba. At that time CFI owed the Government of Manitoba about $160 million. It became a crown corporation and was renamed Manitoba Forest Products (MANFOR). By March 1975, the debt, including costs of completing the plant, unpaid interest, and losses, totalled $177,542,373.[29]

The plant's debt position and almost continual annual losses did not trouble its union. In November 1977, seven secretaries struck for a sixteen per cent wage increase and the pulp and paper operation of some 500 employees walked out in support, costing the plant $150,000 a day. In 1984, a glossy annual report, costing $25,000, announced losses of almost $25 million the previous year.

In 1988, the complex was sold to Repap, which sold it to Tolko in 1997. "It had cost successive governments of Manitoba $307 million."[30] The government recovered about $30 million from the sale. An analyst estimated that the operation was worth $125 million.[31]

What did the people of Manitoba get for their investment? Former Premier Duff Roblin has written that, while accepting responsibility for whatever may have

---

[29] *Return to Order of the House*, May 29, 1975.
[30] *Winnipeg Free Press*, March 12, 1997.
[31] *Ibid.*, March 27, 1997.

gone wrong during his administration, something might be said for the final outcome, "Without minimizing difficulties in the situation, for the last 20 years 600 to 800 northerners have had jobs, millions of dollars worth of product has been sold, and a contribution has been made to the welfare of the people of The Pas."[32]

It is a sentiment to which the premiers succeeding him—Weir, Schreyer, Lyon, Pawley and Filmon—who were burdened by the complex can readily relate; the social side of this courageous but tarnished investment can be considered a qualified success.

BUT WHY DID THE ECONOMIC SIDE go so terribly wrong? As the besieged and bewildered King Arthur asked in *Camelot*, "How did we stumble into this agonizing absurdity?" One can conjecture it being a series of ghastly misunderstandings; the Roblin government accepted the Monoca proposal but expected the MDC to scrutinize the principals and protect the loan; Grose believed Roblin's cabinet had handed him a *fait accompli* to accommodate and so informed the MDC board; the directors believed this "done deal" was "foisted" on them to rubber-stamp without normal checks; after the election of the NDP, Grose agreed with Kasser to safeguard the project by quickly moving the money beyond the government's reach; Grose depended on Arthur D. Little to monitor the loan; ADL accepted Kasser's assurance the money was going to where it should, and Kasser was banking it in Zurich instead.

The inquiry commission summarized problems that had developed during this "darkest moment in Manitoba's economic history", and drew on its lessons to recommend, "Don't lend money to strangers; always keep a vigilant eye on borrowers; never allow the economics of an account be fudged by social goals." Then the commission spread the blame for the CFI fiasco among the participants. And the participants blamed each other.

Roblin and Newman defended themselves vigorously. Newman wrote angrily and unapologetically, expressing respect for Roblin and naming Schreyer as the villain.[33] He wrote of "hard-headed businessman" Rex Grose's "epic struggle to get the project launched"[34] ... "which made manifest Kasser's practical genius"[35]... "the MDC had the means to enforce compliance" of the lending rules upon Kasser and all went well under the PC government and while he controlled the MDC funds.[36]

The "collosal waste" as Newman put it, was due to the ill-advised reaction

[32] *Speaking for Myself,* p. 143.
[33] *Newman, What Happened when Kasser Came to Northern Manitoba.*
[34] *Ibid.,* p. 23.
[35] *Ibid.,* p. 43
[36] *Ibid.,* p. 33.

of the NDP government on discovering, in March 1970, that government was financing 100 per cent of the project. [37],[38]

Roblin wrote in more moderate terms, but agreed with Newman:

> Walter Newman was in charge of the money. He was the MDC's legal advisor ... and presided over disbursement of MDC funds ... the chokehold the MDC exercised in supervising the operation. So long as he was in charge, the CFI agreement gave him the powers to keep an unprincipled borrower in line ... When Grose dropped Newman [39] he opened the door to Kasser ... Grose became paymaster and relied on ADL for certification ... The nefarious plans of Kasser would not have worked without the laxity of ADL.[40]
>
> Grose sidestepped the MDC Directors, disposed of financial controller Walter Newman, and presided over the improvident payment of $60 million to ... a crook.[41]

The inquiry commission had special censure for Grose and ADL, "The new government was taken in by the [CFI] principals who were aided in their deception by Grose [p. 1444]. The racketeers were legitimized by an internationally recognized consultant [ADL] and the public was milked of many millions [p. 1507]."

This collaboration of MDC and ADL at the Montclair meeting on July 22, 1969, one week after the election of the NDP government, speeded payments and allowed $25 million of Manitoba taxpayer's money to be banked in Switzerland before the government realized what was happening. The inquiry commission wrote, "Of all the many deleterious actions taken by the MDC ... this was the worst and potentially most disastrous [p. 1446]."

So the answer to Preston's question about how was it possible for one man to fool so many people, appears clear. All it took was one overeager government, another feeling itself trapped, and a smart operator ... who had considerable inside help.

---

[37] *Ibid.* The late Walter Newman's book is written in the third person, from his perspective, and is a worthy addition to this complex and fascinating history. Aside from self-justification, he shows fierce loyalty to Roblin, genuine respect for the 'genius' of Kasser, great admiration followed by muted disillusionment for Grose, determination to see the CFI project completed, contempt for the inquiry commission and visceral disgust for the NDP government. It is not clear whether this is because of the way they handled the CFI file or because of the unseemly act of being elected.

[38] Columnist Fred Cleverley, taking his cue from Newman, wrote of the CFI debacle, "The failure comes when, upon discovering it was providing the bulk of the financing, a government decides it must have managerial control. That path invariably leads to disaster." *Winnipeg Free Press*, November 9, 1977. Apparently the government providing 100 per cent of the financing, while the borrower has 100 per cent of ownership and management is what is known as "free enterprise" in the Tory lexicon.

[39] So it was Grose, not Schreyer, who dropped Newman.

[40] *Speaking for Myself,* Chapter 7.

[41] *Ibid.*, p. 142.

Was government not sufficiently vigilant? Thirty years later, Roblin speculated that perhaps his uncritical acceptance of Grose's assurances, "had something to do with the nature of the project".[42] Similarly, the Schreyer government was fixated on development of the North, and perhaps also allowed itself to be seduced by "the nature of the project".

In this melancholy saga it is difficult to separate heroes from villains. If there were heroes it was a group of politicians who took a chance on developing the neglected North, a second group who sweated blood to release the government from the tar baby of a flawed project, a third group charged with the impossible task of disposing of this flea-bitten dog at a politically acceptable price, and the media that helped expose the fraud. If there were villains it was those who confused their loyalties to the project with their responsibilities to government, or who, perhaps, simply did not accept the legitimacy of the NDP government.

Could the project have been rescued after the money was spent and the plant built, or did we have the wrong plant in the wrong place at the wrong time making unprofitable products from trees maturing too slowly? Or must we leave the last word to Kasser?

By late 1970 the government was torn between seizing the plant or providing Kasser with further funds to complete it. But how much more would he ask for? Sidney Green, who had developed a grudging respect for Kasser's intellect and technical competence, called Kasser, discussed the situation, and then added, "I am interested in getting this project completed for the least amount of money possible. There are people here who do not want you on the job because they feel you are a crook. I don't know whether you are a crook or not. What I also don't know is whether the next person will be a crook."

To which Kasser replied, "Mr. Green, the next person may be worse than a crook. He may be an incompetent."[43]

---

[42] *Ibid.*, p. 137.
[43] *Green, Rise and Fall of a Political Animal*, p. 131.

XXXIII

Manitoba Hydro I

And there was light.
        —Genesis

The spillways had been closed and the water had piled up behind the enormous dam. Now the intake gates were opened and the great river catapulted ninety-eight feet to the riverbed below, rotating the giant turbines and spinning the generators in Manitoba's largest hydro-electric plant. It was June 1973. A twenty-five-year-old dream had been realized. A switch was thrown; the province's power production was doubled. And there was light.

When the great glaciers covering most of Western Canada for millennia receded, they left Manitoba with a remarkable gift—a depressed basin fed by rivers that drained a quarter of Canada. The Red, Winnipeg, Assiniboine and Saskatchewan Rivers turned Lake Winnipeg into an inland sea, a massive reservoir that eventually drained into Hudson Bay via the Nelson River. This became the cynosure of hydro-electric engineers and caused a decades-long game of passionate political one-upmanship.[1]

On February 15, 1966, Premier Duff Roblin had dramatically treated the legislature to a breathtaking revelation of how the wonders of Manitoba could be harnessed for the benefit of its people:

> The citizens of Manitoba are blessed with one of the greatest
> natural and continuing resources in the nation—the mighty Nelson River
> … fed by a 410,000-square-mile watershed extending 1,200 miles from
> the Rockies to Lake Superior and 900 miles north from a height of land
> separating us from the Mississippi.

---

[1] "Emotion and Politics Cloud Issue", Frances Russell, *Winnipeg Tribune*, February 3, 1972.

It flows from one of the world's largest lakes—Lake Winnipeg—
one of the world's great natural power reservoirs ... In its 400 miles into
Hudson Bay the Nelson falls 712 feet through a series of rapids, giving it
a power potential of more than four million kilowatts. Its flow exceeds
that of the Columbia or the Missouri ... Nearby is the Churchill, also flowing into Hudson Bay, draining a watershed of 90,000 square miles ... The
two rivers jointly have a watershed of over half a million square miles and
a power potential of more than five million kilowatts ... We had to decide
whether to proceed with small, costly thermal [coal] generating plants or
to tackle this giant in the North.[2]

The Nelson River Programming Board had recommended development of
the power potential because of the benefits: use of renewable resources in power
production; a source of power better suited to Manitoba's needs than thermal
plants; opportunity to advance technology by using the new direct current transmission of electric power; a large power source near Manitoba's mineral deposits
and forest resources and provision of power to southern Manitoba and for export.
Consequently the government had decided to proceed with a large power plant
at Kettle Rapids; the diversion of a portion of the Churchill River through South
Indian Lake into the Nelson; control works to enable the great natural storage
reservoir of Lake Winnipeg to be used for hydro-electric power purposes and a
double-line direct current transmission line to run 580 miles from Kettle Rapids
to Winnipeg.

On May 31, 1967, the Government of Manitoba signed an agreement with
the Government of Canada, which hired Atomic Energy of Canada to build the
580-mile, $180 million transmission line, the costs to be repaid by Manitoba over
fifty years.

In August 1967, Roblin resigned and Premier Walter Weir continued the
project. In December 1968, several university professors warned of damage to the
Cree settlement at South Indian Lake. In January 1969, Manitoba Hydro applied
for a license and the government, pursuant to the Water Powers Act, announced
a series of public hearings. They quickly became stormy and the government
adjourned them. In February, lawyers got an injunction to stop Hydro until the
quasi-judicial hearings were completed.

In March, to circumvent the injunction, Resources Minister Harry Enns
tabled Bill 15 to implement the grand scheme. But there was a startling omission
from the original proposal: Lake Winnipeg would not be used as a hydro reservoir.
Instead, South Indian Lake would be raised twenty-nine feet to serve as a substitute reservoir. The entire village on the lake, and 650 families would have to be
relocated; 55,000 cubic feet per second of water would be forced down the Rat-
Burntwood River system, and 900,000 acres of land and resources would be

---

[2] *Hansard*, February 15, 1966, pp. 233-7.

drowned. Working without a license, Hydro began work to divert the Churchill River. Manitoba was in an uproar. The NDP and several citizen's groups fought vigorously. Weir called a snap election and Bill 15 died when the Conservatives lost the election. On July 15th, 1969, the NDP took office and the work on the Churchill Diversion was stopped.

During the campaign, Ed Schreyer had stated that he believed a low level diversion of the Churchill River would be just as effective, less costly, and would make it unnecessary to move the native villages. On the day after the election Premier-elect Schreyer stated: "On South Indian Lake, because of the secrecy involved, we feel committed to no course of policy until we get full disclosure." [3]

Having committed itself to a review, the new government needed an expert to do the reviewing. David Cass-Beggs was tall, lean, austere, soft-spoken, black-suited, white-haired and arguably the foremost hydraulic engineer in Canada. As chairman, he had virtually created the Saskatchewan Power Corporation by building thermal plants on top of coal mines. He was fired by Premier Ross Thatcher when Thatcher replaced the NDP in 1964, and in 1969 Cass-Beggs was teaching at the University of Toronto.

He was hired on term to review all information available and "define problem areas and indicate directions in which solutions may lie". On September 9th, he reported that "time still permits revision of the program to omit high level diversion. The best alternative would be to control the Nelson River at the outlet of Lake Winnipeg and a more acceptable diversion from the Churchill."

In January 1970, he was appointed chairman of Manitoba Hydro and instructed to study all alternatives. The resultant studies, which were all made public, were the Underwood McLellan Report on the Churchill River Diversion; the Manitoba Hydro Task Force Report; the Crippen Report on the "effects of regulation of Lake Winnipeg as a multi-purpose reservoir and effects of regulation on (a) Nelson River flows (b) Lake Winnipeg water levels (c) resources.

On September 16, 1970, Cass Booey, chairman of the Manitoba Water Commission, wrote to Mines and Resources Minister Green, agreeing to the regulation of Lake Winnipeg for hydro-electric purposes and to the Hydro-proposed lake levels in the range of 711 to 715 feet above sea level.

Nine days later, Premier Schreyer said, "We must plan for enough power for the darkest, coldest day of winter." The government would build plants on the Nelson River, complete the transmission line from the Nelson to Winnipeg, regulate Lake Winnipeg, and divert part of the Churchill River into the Nelson. This would allow development of hydro-electric sites with up to eight million kilowatts of power, and create the largest power complex in Canada. [4]

It was essentially a return to the concept announced by Roblin in 1966, though with changes from the Weir government's proposals. The most significant

---

[3] *The Winnipeg Tribune*, June 27, 1969.

[4] It was later exceeded by the James Bay Project.

of these were that South Indian Lake would be raised ten feet instead of twenty-nine; only 30,000 cubic feet of water per second would flow down the Rat-Burntwood system, instead of 55,000 cfs; 180,000 acres of land would be flooded instead of 900,000, meaning that the village at South Indian Lake would not need to be relocated, and Lake Winnipeg would be regulated between 711 and 715 feet above datum, as opposed to natural levels of from 709 to 717, providing both hydro reservoir and flood control. Lake Winnipeg regulation would proceed first, allowing time to find the least damaging mode of diverting the Churchill River.

The reaction was Kafkaesque; for the next seven years, the government was like his mouse caught between being crushed by the closing walls or being eaten by the cat. Hydro became a political football and never ceased being tossed around. And neither did the government. The development became a virulent issue in the 1977 election and, twenty-nine years later, when it was rumoured that Winnipeg Mayor Glen Murray might seek advice from Schreyer about Winnipeg Hydro, the *Winnipeg Free Press* sought to refight the elections of 1969 and 1973 by editorially attacking Schreyer's record on Manitoba Hydro. It's interesting to note that in that year—1998—eighty per cent of Manitoba's power came from the Nelson and Hydro earned $250 million from exports.[5]

The Schreyer government was attacked by politicians, environmentalists, editors, ecologists, canoeists, columnists, fly fishermen, bird-watchers, commercial fishermen, poets, students, writers, miners, professors, hunters, historians, tree-huggers, trappers, Indians, engineers, churches, necromancers, and Jean Chrétien. Concerns were expressed about aquatic ecosystems, wildlife, ice scouring, eagle nests, whales in Hudson Bay, geese in the Nelson estuary, salt from Hudson Bay into the Churchill River, water flows, wildlife habitats, animals including moose, elk, reindeer, coyotes, foxes, mink, lynx, ermine, timber wolves, black bears, beavers, vegetation, wild rice, sports fishing, commercial fishing, river mouth erosion, aesthetic changes, migratory fowl, permafrost, marine animals, tidal zone plants, heritage sites, water chemistry, road damage, silting, sedimentation, turbidity, fish net fouling, tourism, recreation, socioeconomic factors, lack of native participation, native land claims, river transportation, historical routes, financing, radiation from power lines, danger of inter-lake biota transfer, fear by some that the National Energy Board would not permit foreign sales of electricity, fear by others that it would, and a suggestion by the Manitoba Naturalists Society that a six-mile detour of the transmission line to the United States, at $500,000 per mile, be considered to circumvent a field of crocuses.

Energy sources included human and animal power, wood, coal, wind, solar, geothermal, cesium, biomass, methane, alcohol, propane, water, nuclear ... and hydro-electric power. New fossil fuel sources included oil discovered in the North Sea, natural gas in the Arctic, heavy oil in Lloydminster and the Athabaska Tar

---

[5] *Winnipeg Free Press*, December 30, 1998.

Sands, but fossil fuels were non-renewable and becoming expensive. Electricity could be generated with biomass, gassified coal, photovoltaic cells, hydrogen fuel cells, windmills, and Bay of Fundy tides, but these were either supplementary sources or damaging to the environment. The genie of nuclear power had emerged from the crucible of war, and Canada had the world's largest uranium deposits, but this was in its first generation and largely untried, and no way had been found (nor has yet been found) to safely dispose of the plutonium waste.[6]

A century earlier, George Bernard Shaw had written that science creates two problems for each one it solves. That caveat had to be kept in mind when standing on the powerhouse at Kettle Rapids, sensing the movement of history and feeling the surging turbines like "the roar and thunder of the Odyssey", converting energy from flowing water into electricity and transmitting it over a slender wire to population centres 500 miles away. One needed to guard against becoming lost in technological euphoria—the naive belief that science can solve anything. Yet with allowance made for that, no matter the preferences, or how passionately the issues were debated, or how often the social and environmental conse-quences were reviewed, the logic of need, availability and comparative costs drove the government ineluctably to the harnessing of the Lake Winnipeg-Nelson-Churchill River System.

But this was a massive project with large, permanent, unpredictable con-sequences, with room for honest——and political—differences of opinion. The government saw Lake Winnipeg regulation as a dual hydro-reservoir/flood-control program, but others saw it as high water-level storage in the autumn when winds drove water south. The government saw low-level diversion reducing the level of South Indian Lake nineteen feet from what the Conservatives had wanted, but others saw it as raising the lake ten feet above its natural level The government saw its program reducing the potential flooding from more than 900,000 acres to 200,000, but others saw it as flooding 200,000 acres and all the attendant resources. The government saw the forcing of 55,000 cfs of water down the Rat-Burnwood River system, really vestigial creeks, as madness, but others saw reduction to 30,000 cfs as a waste of water that could spin turbines on the Nelson.

The government saw its $2 million Underwood McLellan study as crucial to mitigating damages from the diversion, but others saw it a waste of money and lack of political will. The government saw its program as one that would provide Manitoba's northern First Nations with opportunities to enter the social and eco-nomic mainstream, but others saw it as destroying their traditional lifestyle. The government saw itself as being sensitive to the cultural integrity of the Aboriginal people, while not allowing that to stop economic development, but others

[6] Despite its awesome potential, the *wunderkind* of energy has proved deceptive. In 1979, the nuclear electricity producing plant at Three Mile Island almost melted down, and in 1986, the Chernobyl plant in the Ukraine blew up. In 1997 Ontario Hydro, with a $31 billion debt, spent $6 billion closing down plants when piping material burned out much faster than expected.

saw refusal to stop the development as evidence the government was deaf to the concerns of native Manitobans.

It was a classic Catch-22 situation. If the government regulated Lake Winnipeg, they angered the Conservative opposition, which needed to protect its political decision to not do so, and the Lake Winnipeg Cottage Owners Association, which needed to fix blame for future lawsuits in the event of damage. If the government—like its predecessor—waived Lake Winnipeg regulation and opted for high-level diversion, they would infuriate the Friends of the Churchill, the Canadian Wildlife Federation, the Churchill Basin Group,[7] the Canadian Nature Federation, the Northern Flood Committee, the Canadian Council of Churches, the Manitoba Inter-Church Task Force on Northern Flooding, and the Canadian Association in Support of Native Peoples. If the government hesitated to go simultaneously with Churchill River diversion plus Lake Winnipeg regulation, they were accused of giving too much value to resources lost by flooding, which would invite brownouts, and failing to take the maximum advantage of hydro-electric power—"Manitoba's oil".[8] If the government proceeded with both simultaneously, they were accused of bankrupting Manitoba to sell cheap power to the United States.[9]

There were inconsistencies. Liberal leader Izzy Asper threatened an injunction[10] to stop flooding of South Indian Lake, but former Liberal leader Douglas Campbell supported flooding. Jack Murta, a federal Conservative cabinet minister from Manitoba, opposed flooding, but Harry Enns, the former PC minister of Resources supported flooding.

The PCs, in an example of "false memory syndrome" suddenly "remembered" they had intended raising South Indian Lake only fourteen feet rather than the twenty-nine feet specified in Bill 15, which had been presented to the legislature in early 1969. All these contrasting groups should have cancelled each other out, but only added to the cacophony.

Among the first to feel the wrath of the opposition and of the *Winnipeg Free Press* was Cass-Beggs. He was damned as a political prostitute who had given the NDP government the report it wanted, based not on science but politics. The paper wrote, "Since the advent of the NDP government and the appointment of

---

[7] The Churchill Basin Group found an essay, entitled "Love Among Cabbages", that purported to show that plants have senses and, in March 1973, did an essay, "What Do Trees Think" of their suffering in the north.

[8] "The fully developed Nelson River scheme will, over its lifetime, produce power equivalent to 10 billion barrels of oil. This is more than the entire reserves of Western Canada." *Winnipeg Free Press*, January 23, 1974.

[9] In 1973, an American utility offered to pay the cost of building the Long Spruce Power Plant, on condition that the province commit the total production to the U.S. for fifteen years, after which ownership would revert to Manitoba. The government reluctantly declined the offer on Manitoba Hydro's advice that we would need the power; in any case, it would have been political suicide to accept.

[10] Asper had stated that the 1973 election would be a plebiscite on the diversion, but went mute when the NDP won all five northern seats.

David Cass-Beggs as head of Manitoba Hydro, that body's activities and operations have been marked by confusion, suspicion and a lack of public confidence." [11] PC deputy leader Don Craik demanded that Cass-Beggs be fired, and the attack continued long after he left in late 1972 to become chairman of British Columbia Hydro.

A second line of attack was that the government was proceeding blindly without studying the implications. One evening, during the supper adjournment of the legislature, I went to the premier, "Tonight you are speaking on Hydro. I am collecting all the studies done to date and placing them under your desk. When the opposition begins interrupting with shouts about the need for studies, reach down and place them one by one on your desk and ask these hypocritical bastards how many of them they have read."

It worked as though scripted. He played his role like a pro and with uncharacteristic drama. He began his detailed explanation of what the government was doing and why, in his usual monotone until, as though on cue, the opposition began calling in chorus, like dogs in heat howling at the moon, for "more studies". One by one, he placed them on his desk, on top of each other, asking with each, "Have you read this one?"

There were twenty-six thick volumes of studies costing $32 million. The pile got so high it crashed, with a gratifying clatter, to the floor between the government and opposition seats. I had some added satisfaction when, on the way down the stairs from the visitor's gallery, I was accosted by two environmentalists, who complained bitterly, "It was unfair of your brother-in-law to use those studies that way."

Then we got them again. One day the PCs vociferously argued that regulating Lake Winnipeg at 715 feet was too high and would cause flooding. MLA John Gottfried asked the minister what the level of the lake was that day. The Conservatives recognized the 'planted' question and howled that it was out of order. But Speaker Peter Fox allowed it and the minister replied that the level of Lake Winnipeg, on the day in question—May 16, 1972—was sixteen feet six inches, eighteen inches higher than it would have been if regulated.

But our victories were few. Former Premier Campbell, respected by friend and foe for his personal integrity and fiscal prudence, was appointed to the Hydro board by the NDP government. In May 1971, he resigned. He conceded that people living near Lake Winnipeg had asked for flood control since the 1920s, that this was given impetus by the high water levels of 1950, '54, '55, '56 and 1966 (when it reached 718 feet) and that flood control had been rejected because of cost, but could be done in tandem with regulation of the lake as a hydro reservoir. But, he argued, Manitoba Hydro could get enough water from South Indian Lake.

---

[11] *Winnipeg Free Press*, January 19, 1972. The loathing of the Conservatives in the legislature for Cass-Beggs was such that after he left Manitoba, they repeatedly attacked his pension. Awarded to him by the Manitoba Civil Service Superannuation Board, the pension was $136 per month.

Lake Winnipeg [12] might be needed but not now; simultaneously proceeding with both projects was too expensive. He agreed there would be damage at South Indian Lake, but frugality trumped concern for the people who lived there, the environment and need for flood control of Lake Winnipeg.

Kris Kristjanson, assistant general manager of Manitoba Hydro, resigned a month later. In February 1967, he had signed the final report of the Nelson River Programming Board, which called for Lake Winnipeg regulation, but switched to the Conservative decision to waive that in favour of High Level flooding of South Indian Lake. His family was highly esteemed and his resignation hurt. [13]

In November 1970, the government licensed Manitoba Hydro to regulate Lake Winnipeg. The opposition demanded quasi-judicial public hearings by the Manitoba Water Commission. The government, fearing brownouts unless it proceeded immediately with either the Nelson River program or coal-burning thermal plants, and believing in the past four years all of value had been said, refused. They argued that hearings applied to the private sector, not to a publicly-owned utility; the decision to proceed was made by the government, so hearings would be a sham providing lawyers with a bonanza and the various political parties, each with their experts, the opportunity to confuse. Like the six blind men examining the elephant, the opinion given would depend on who was asked.

Sidney Green, the minister responsible for the Water Commission announced: "The Nelson River program must be decided upon by the government through reliance on hydro-electric and other departmental expertise." This was a highly complex technical issue, he stressed, that could not be resolved in public fora, but there would be meetings at which the public could obtain information on the program, ask questions, and offer advice on how to best attain desired ends.

The logic was impeccable, but the optics bad. The *Winnipeg Free Press* ran editorials entitled "Embarrassing", [14] and "Something To Hide", [15] and the PCs claimed the commission was "maimed" by the government. It also heightened, especially in the academic community, the belief that the government was on a one-dimensional course based on economics to the exclusion of all other concerns.

Cass Booey, hydrology professor at the University of Manitoba, had fought

---

[12] Campbell initially advised the minister that proceeding with the Lake Winnipeg reservoir would arouse the opposition of the cottage owners and damage the government politically. When informed he should not concern himself with the politics of the situation, he switched to the cost argument and said Hydro should first proceed with the Churchill River diversion. He resigned when he was outvoted 6 to 1 by his colleagues on the Hydro Board, but blamed the government.

[13] In the 1973 election campaign, Kristjanson spoke at the nominating meeting of Don Craik, deputy leader of the PCs. "If I lived in Riel [constituency], I would vote for Don Craik. In St. Boniface, I would vote for [Liberal candidate] Paul Marion." *Winnipeg Tribune*, May 18, 1973. Ironically, PC policy was to flood South Indian Lake to any level needed for power purposes, while the Liberals had threatened a court injunction to stop any flooding of the lake. The glaring inconsistency was ignored for the sake of defeating the NDP.

[14] January 2, 1972.

[15] January 19, 1972.

High Level Diversion of South Indian Lake in 1968-69. In November 1969, the NDP government appointed him chairman of the Manitoba Water Commission. In September 1970, he gave the commission's approval for regulation of Lake Winnipeg between 711 and 715 feet. Later, he argued that Lake Winnipeg could be held down to 714 feet instead of the 715 he had agreed to and became concerned more with the low level of Lake Winnipeg than with the high level of South Indian Lake. When he went public, Green dismissed him.

Dr. Robert Newbury, professor of Civil Engineering and Earth Sciences at the University of Manitoba, was commissioned to do a study of the environmental impact of Churchill River diversion. In January 1973, he and George Malaher, former director of the Manitoba Wildlife Branch, co-authored *Destruction of Manitoba's Last Great River*. Since he had prejudged his conclusions and compromised his impartiality, his contract was terminated.[16]

The Manitoba Environmental Council, created by the NDP as a citizen's committee to give layman's advice on matters referred to it by the government, made itself a lobby group to publicly fight the government on Churchill Diversion. In January 1973, the council asked the government to stop the diversion development and seek other sources of electricity. When the government disagreed, the council asked Jack Davis, federal minister of the Environment, to stop the program.[17]

The government wanted the most power at the least cost, but did not see this a trade-off between virgin environment and cheap power. Nor was regulation of Lake Winnipeg seen as a compromise to the high level flooding of South Indian Lake. Lake Winnipeg, as a hydro-electric power reservoir, was too obvious to be ignored, and diverting the Churchill into the Nelson was obvious for both augmenting the flow that propelled the turbines and ensuring that water from the north would be available if the south was dry. Even allowing for a loss of resources and damages to the region, the integrated program made sense. On December 21, 1972, two years after licensing the Lake Winnipeg regulation, and after studying ten different proposals for mitigating damages to people and environment, Manitoba Hydro was licensed to proceed with the Churchill River Diversion.

The licensing, along with the disaffection of Kristjanson, Booey and Newbury, inflamed the university community. Many of its faculty members were a product of the Sixties, driven by what American black activist and author James Baldwin called "over-compensatory liberalism".

In their zeal to save the environment they labelled all development "bad". In their desire to preserve the "traditional way of life" of Canada's Aboriginal people, they sometimes fenced them off and excluded them from the social and economic mainstream. Their sincerity was indisputable, but they were prepared to do all necessary to improve the world they inherited, except sacrifice inherited

---

[16] On an open-line radio program, Newbury stated that the Churchill River diversion would "kill the soul of the North and the body will soon follow", raising the question of whether he was an engineer or a poet.

[17] Council vice-president Ken Arenson was a Liberal candidate in 1973.

creature comforts. But these academics were our natural constituency, caught in the moral dilemma of wanting to continue support of the NDP government but disagreeing with its policy, and they must be treated with respect.

I spoke, on behalf of the premier, at the University of Manitoba. The walls of the Student Union building were papered with photos of "romantic" native tipis and shacks—as though Aboriginal Manitobans loved living in tarpaper shacks— pictographs and suspected sites of cemeteries (at times it seemed that seventy-five per cent of Manitoba was native burial grounds). All demanded preservation. I had been a student at the university four years earlier and knew how exercised young people can become, but I had also seen their attempt to ambush Green earlier. As I walked to the podium, I determined they would not do that to me.

> You say the government is influenced by economics alone, but if that was true we would adopt the Conservative plan for high level flooding of South Indian Lake and ignore Lake Winnipeg. Most criticism is that we are not concerned with economics. You say the government has hidden issues from public scrutiny. This issue has been debated in eight sessions of the legislature, four meetings of the Public Utilities Committee, six meetings of the Water Commission, many public meetings, and has had more ink spilled on it than any issue in Manitoba's history. You say the government is not concerned with the environment. The NDP has long argued that man cannot forever improve his economy by destroying his world, but it is ironic to hear comfortable inhabitants of urban areas, built by raping the ecology, telling us not to rape the ecology.
>
> You say we should use less electricity. That's a great idea. There must be 4,000 cars in your parking lot. I suspect most are plugged in to keep them warm and most have warmers so you don't freeze your butts when you leave here. This hall has more lights than I can count and you have electric heat. I note you have music piped into your washroom. All these use electricity. If you people are serious about saving electricity so we won't ruin virgin lands and the Indian lifestyle to build more power dams, I suggest you begin by turning off the muzak in your shithouse.

The churches sent the premier a book proposing that all northern development be stopped pending resolution of ecology issues and native land claims. They referred to the Mackenzie Valley Pipeline Inquiry, the message of which is "to honour the needs of people … and restore the harmony God saw when He looked on His Creation and found it good."[18] The inquiry was writing about a $10 billion, 2,600-mile, four-foot wide, pipeline owned by foreign multinationals seeking profit by carrying non-renewable natural gas from the Arctic to the American market. Somehow they confused that with a publicly owned utility

---

[18] *Moratorium*, Hugh and Karmel McCullum and John Olthius, Anglican Book Centre, Toronto.

reaping energy from water, which continued to the sea, to provide power to all Manitobans, including our native people.

I wondered if they were seeking absolution for actions implied in Chief Dan George's witticism: "When the white man came he had the Bible and we had the land; now we have the Bible and he has the land."

Critics offered everything but practical alternatives. Some said nothing must be done without agreement by First Nations, which would have paralyzed government and leave it unable to build projects like the Winnipeg Floodway, which required expropriation of 525 properties. Some suggested thermal plants, but that angered those concerned that CO_2 from coal would damage the ozone layer or cause acid rain, or that the flooding would cause a greenhouse effect.

Some said we should go nuclear, which would have made sense had we not been blessed with renewable hydro-electricity. Some proposed pumping water from South Indian Lake, rather than raising it, for gravity flow, but that would have used as much electricity as it gained. Some said more revenue could be gained by leaving the Churchill River as a recreational area like the Winnipeg River, but they forgot that the Winnipeg River became a recreational Mecca only after being raised as much as twenty-six feet for hydro-electric purposes.

Letters arrived offering to pay more for electricity if it saved South Indian Lake, but they largely came from outside Manitoba. Some said "Stop Everything". True, there would be no damage, but no electricity either. Farmers, developers, householders, miners, all wanted more power, not less. Most letters and calls came from those who wanted more power, faster and cheaper.[19] Some of those came from South Indian Lake. Many NDP supporters argued that power was being wasted; street lights on automatic timers went on too early and remained on too late, and public buildings had many lights on during the night. When Hydro spent $250,000 to encourage people to put electric heat in new homes, they argued that this proved more power plants were not needed. In late 1972, I went to the premier. "Hydro is advertising to put electric heat in people's homes and offices, but we know gas heat is cheaper. Why are we trying to convince people to use more expensive heat? If Hydro succeeds, we will use more power, build more plants, cause more social and environmental disruption, and cause more political problems for ourselves. Those who want power know where to get it without it being advertised."

"Good point. Perhaps you should discuss it with Cass-Beggs."

The chairman of Manitoba Hydro peered unblinkingly through his spectacles. "Very well. We will stop advertising. But if Manitobans install gas instead of electric furnaces, what will it cost if world oil prices rise and Alberta doubles natural gas prices?" A year later the world oil price quadrupled and by 1979 it was

---

[19] The *Winnipeg Free Press* editorialized (May 27, 1972): "The real issue is whether Manitoba Hydro, by this program, is fulfilling its mission to provide adequate supplies of low-cost power." The author should be pleased; more than thirty years later, Manitoba has the lowest power rates in North America, and exports great quantities of surplus electric power.

up 1300 per cent. By 1977, natural gas prices had increased 125 per cent, and Manitobans feared not only price increases, but rationing.

BY MID-1977, the Churchill River Diversion was complete with control works at Missi Falls to raise the water level of South Indian Lake, an eight-mile channel for outflow, and control works at Notigi to regulate flow into the Rat-Burntwood-Nelson river system. Lake Winnipeg regulation was complete with a channel to allow increased water flow and construction of control works at Jenpeg, including a 126,000 kilowatt power plant to regulate flow into the Nelson River. The 1,272,000 kW Kettle Rapids station was complete. The Long Spruce plant, fourteen miles downstream from Kettle, designed to produce 980,000 kW, was in operation, and the Limestone power plant, a further fourteen miles downstream, was begun. [20]

The permanent town of Gillam, with all amenities, had been built for Hydro's permanent maintenance staff. Two high voltage direct current 2,000 kilovolt transmission lines had been built to bring power 580 miles from Gillam to Winnipeg. Two converter stations, the Radisson at Gillam to convert power to direct current for transmission and the Dorsey at Winnipeg to convert to alternating current for use, had been built. Two 230 kV lines had been built to exchange power with Ontario and Saskatchewan. Two 230 kV transmission lines had been built to exchange power with the United States. Approval to build a 500 kV line to Minneapolis (completed in May 1980) to open the market as far south as Nebraska had been wrestled through the National Energy Board. [21]

A campsite for the 800-person crew to build Limestone, [22] had been built at Sundance. A 2,000-foot airstrip, a road from Gillam to Sundance and another from Leaf Rapids to South Indian Lake had been built. Diesel generators had been replaced by hydro-electric power in a number of native villages, including South Indian Lake. Mitigation works had been built at Churchill and Nelson House. And sites to add five million kW of electricity had been identified.

All this meant provision of Manitoba's energy needs indefinitely, while exporting power to keep rates low and pay for construction. And all this contributed to the destruction of the government.

The government had had to decide on the least damaging mode of providing electricity for Manitobans, as well as how to compensate for damages done. Consequently Manitoba Hydro was instructed to develop the most economical program, *while taking into account resource losses*—ecological, natural and human—

---

[20] That year, 1977, had the worst drought in ninety-two years; we had no brownouts.

[21] Ironically, the NEB seemed less reluctant to license increasing sales of non-renewable fossil fuels from Alberta to the U.S., than to allow Manitoba to export renewable energy.

[22] Designed to produce 1,330,000 kW of power, Limestone, the third plant on the Nelson, was postponed in 1977, restarted by the Pawley government in 1985 and completed in 1991 by the Filmon government.

in the North. This single caveat became labelled "political interference" by the opposition, and was fixed like an incubus on the government.

It became a battle of engineers. Tall, gaunt, bespectacled Leonard Bateman came up through the ranks to become systems planning engineer with the Manitoba Hydro-Electric Board in 1956; director of production in 1961; director of systems planning in 1967; assistant chief engineer in 1970 and assistant general manager and chief engineer in 1971 (in 1977 he won the Merit Award from the Manitoba Association of Professional Engineers). In 1972 he succeeded David Cass-Beggs as chairman and CEO of Manitoba Hydro, and became the point man at the annual examinations of Hydro by the Public Utilities Committee.

His chief inquisitor, an unlikely Torquemada, was Donald Craik.[23] He too was an engineer and had taught that subject at the University of Manitoba before election to the legislature in 1966, but was now deputy leader of the official opposition. Of medium height, impeccably dressed, quiet of demeanor, appearing bookish in dark-rimmed spectacles and dark hair parted neatly on one side, he was as soft-spoken as Bateman … but relentless.

They clashed in the spring of 1976. The issue was the sequence of construction. The PCs argued that it would have cost less had Hydro proceeded with the Churchill River diversion, several small power plants, some coal-burning plants, imported power from the United States, and left Lake Winnipeg regulation for the future. Hydro and the NDP government claimed that would require higher flooding of South Indian Lake than was environmentally and socially acceptable, that LWR was needed to assure security of power, and that the cost of the PC program would have been just as high.

On April 13th Craik challenged Bateman. "An awful lot of calls are being received from people who put in electric heat [by 1977, thirty-two per cent of houses with hydro were electrically heated] and are concerned with high cost."

"In my house," Bateman responded, "for $500 last year I have electric heat, hot water, car heaters, and all household conveniences."[24]

A week earlier, Craik had said, "Most callers [wish] they [had waited] for natural gas."

Bateman responded, "When we complete the plants we will know the cost of power for the next sixty-five years [the life expectancy of a hydro plant]. We have no control over the cost of oil, gas and coal."

Harry Enns, PC, MLA, added: "It would have been cheaper by going with Churchill Diversion alone and four smaller plants."

"We could not risk going into a system not secure," said Bateman.

---

[23] After the PC victory in October 1977, Craik became Hydro minister and fired Bateman, replacing him with Kristjansson so, as Hydro AGM, had signed the Nelson River Programming Board Report (in 1967), endorsing the LWR plan. He switched to the PC government's decision to waive that for the high level flooding of South Indian Lake, and resigned his position in 1970 to attack the NDP government politically.

[24] *Hansard*, p. 71.

"Could you have supplied [the necessary] power with only High Level Churchill Diversion?" Johansson, an NDP MLA asked Bateman.

"No. Impossible." [25]

The lengthy exchanges brought a *cri d'coeur* from Bateman. "Development of the Nelson River stands on the basis of many professional engineers with integrity having put their work on paper ...In 1966, the decision was made and we are proceeding. Let's, for Heaven's sake, realize what an asset this is." [26]

But it was just one dam thing after another. In January 1974, Manitoba Hydro had called for tenders for converters to double the capacity of the transmission lines from Gillam to Winnipeg. Canadian General Electric, largest supplier of electrical equipment for Manitoba Hydro, bid $102 million. Brown-Boveri (Canada) Ltd. bid $16 million less. CGE was ninety-two per cent owned by General Electric of New York. Brown-Boveri (Canada) was a subsidiary of a Swiss firm. CGE promised to do eighty per cent of its work in Canada, but much was merely assembling. Brown-Boveri promised to have more than thirty per cent of its work done by Federal Pioneer of Winnipeg.

Then things became complicated. Hugh Faulkner, federal minister of State (and a former CGE executive with a plant in his Peterborough riding) predicted that CGE would get the contract. Donald McDonald, federal minister of Industry, added that "the federal government ... would opt for the CGE bid." CGE offered to build a $5.5 million plant in Brandon if it got the contract. Hydro rejected that "blackmail" by boycotting CGE. McDonald said that giving the contract to Brown-Boveri "would not conform to federal objectives for developing technological opportunities." Schreyer replied if Manitoba had been informed earlier that this contract "was of national importance", we may have given it to CGE without tender, but now it was too late. McDonald hinted that if CGE did not get the contract, Manitoba might not get a $43 million low-interest, thirty-year loan. Schreyer said independent consultants had found Brown-Boveri's technology was the most advanced and that "the bids were evaluated by an independent engineering firm, which had always been acceptable to Ottawa as a requirement for a federal loan".

CGE cancelled the Brandon plant. Craik accused the government of risking Canadian jobs just to save money. Schreyer replied that if the government had ignored the tendering process and given the contract to CGE, the opposition would have accused the government of a political decision to ignore the engineering evaluation and buy "equipment not technically superior but costing $16 million more". [27]

A similar debate erupted when tenders were called for a new type of turbine for the Jenpeg plant. Four bids ranged from about $24 million to $31 million. The fifth was for $16 million. Hydro chose the lowest, from a Soviet firm. Opposition

---

[25] *Hansard*, April 6, 1976

[26] *Hansard*, June 1, 1976, p. 131

[27] *Winnipeg Tribune*, April 21, 1975. By contrast, Prime Minister Mulroney gave a billion-plus dollar contract to a Québec firm, despite the fact that a Winnipeg firm had won it one the basis of both price and technical competence.

criticism was fierce, implying this was giving aid and comfort to the enemy.

The PCs argued that the government should interfere politically to stop the Jenpeg purchase. Conversely, they had argued that the NDP government's instruction to Hydro to "take into account resource losses from high-level flooding" was unacceptable political interference. [28]

The opposition claimed that Manitoba would be bankrupted by going with both Lake Winnipeg Regulation and Churchill River Diversion simultaneously. And the government was painfully aware of the increasing Hydro debt, as well as of both its economic and political consequences, but was motivated to proceed not only by Hydro's projection of a seven per cent demand growth, but also by fear of future cost escalation. [29] Then it happened. World events conspired to force the pace of construction ... and to mire the government more deeply in debt.

By 1960, Canada was a net oil exporter and future supply seemed secure. In 1972, Imperial Oil's annual report stated: "Canada's present oil reserves, using present technology, are sufficient for *several hundred years*." [30]

In June 1973, the federal Department of Energy stated Canada had oil to at least 2050, *at below seven dollars a barrel*.[31] Premier Peter Lougheed stated that Alberta could supply Canada indefinitely and needed permits to export oil. Four months later, the Arab-Israeli War exploded; OPEC emerged and by January 1974, world oil prices had quadrupled from $3 to $12 a barrel.

Ottawa froze Canadian oil prices at $5.50 a barrel. The petroleum industry despaired that, without the incentive of world prices ($39 US by 1979), Canada would suffer oil shortages by 1980. The Department of Energy suddenly lost a zero; its eighty-year supply shrank to eight years. [32] It seemed that the Devonian Basin had sprung a leak and allowed the fossil fuels to escape.

There was global panic! U.S. Transport Minister Brock Adams warned Americans "to prepare for when the gas runs out" and enacted a fifty-five mph speed limit. In January 1977, Ohio, New Jersey and New York declared energy emergencies and some 4,000 U.S industrial plants closed to conserve natural gas supplies. [33] Papers reported irate drivers shooting each other at service station lineups, or shooting attendants who lacked the foresight to keep their storage tanks full. Independent fuel stations closed by the hundreds as the majors supplied only their chain stations. Gurus predicted $100-a-barrel oil and natural gas prices, up by 600 per cent. By 1976, Canada was a net oil importer and the president of Imperial Oil predicted a $5 billion oil trade deficit by 1985. [34]

---

[28] *Hansard,* April 13, 1976, pp. 69-70.

[29] The 580-mile transmission line from Gillam to Winnipeg cost $180 million in 1969, but would have cost $422 million in 1976.

[30] *The Big, Tough, Expensive Job: Imperial Oil and the Canadian Economy,* James Laxer, and Anne Martin, Toronto, Musson Book Company, 1976. p. 25

[31] *Ibid.,* p. 26.

[32] *Ibid.,* p. 27.

[33] *Winnipeg Tribune,* January 28, 1977.

[34] *Ibid.,* January 21, 1977.

Someone had goofed, or deliberately misled, but by how much? The government was totally dependent on the industry for information on oil reserves and the industry now became suspect.[35] Heightened by the fact that about seventy-five per cent of the Canadian petroleum industry and ninety-five per cent of refining capacity was foreign owned. Ottawa created PetroCanada, "a window on the oil industry", as the price of NDP support for the Trudeau government, which had been re-elected with a minority in 1972.

The ensuing inflation[36] had an enormous impact. The Kettle plant, completed in 1974, cost $324 million. Long Spruce, twenty per cent smaller and completed in 1978, cost $502 million. Limestone, only slightly larger than Kettle, was completed in 1992—at $1.73 billion.

Rising costs and possible rationing of natural gas made it logical to proceed apace with the massive construction program. But logic could not shake the PCs determination to charge the government with political interference, mismanagement and waste.

Manitoba Hydro is mandated to meet Manitoba's peak demand on the coldest day of the winter at normal water conditions. Surplus power is exported. From 1969–70 to 1977–78 capacity increased from 1,670,000 to 3,202,000 kW, domestic demand from 1,420,000 to 2,444,000 kW, revenue from $64 million to $243 million and export revenue from less than $100,000 to $35 million. In the eight-year period, export sales totalled about $120 million. By 1978, sixty per cent of Manitoba's power was coming from the Nelson River. Despite huge expenditures, Manitoba Hydro rates had actually relatively improved. In 1969, Manitoba had the third-lowest power rates in North America; by 1976 we had the second-lowest, behind only the newly nationalized Hydro-Québec. And because of the dual project (LWR and CRD) program running the same water through multiple power plants, the future promised to be even better.

Manitoba Hydro was so well managed that when its bonds went on sale in 1975, Moody's Investors Services of New York, considered the toughest bond rating agency in North America, gave Manitoba an AA credit rating for the first time in its history.[37] But the government was in big trouble. Building power plants is highly capital-intensive. From 1970 to the end of 1977 Manitoba Hydro assets increased from $500 million to $2.4 billion. But the long-term debt also increased—from $682 million to $2.1 billion and with this the critics played like dogs with a bone.

The PCs saw Manitoba Hydro as the instrument for avenging their 1969

---

[35] Oil prices became a function not of supply and demand, but of the intentions of the industry and its handmaiden governments. In 1973, they wanted export permits so needed a surplus; in 1974, they wanted to crank up prices, so needed a shortage.

[36] Inflation was at eleven per cent in 1977 and rose to thirteen per cent before being snuffed out by the Bank of Canada with seventeen per cent interest rates.

[37] "[Manitoba] pursues prudent fiscal policies, with relatively small financing requirements. Net direct debt is moderate and the bulk of guaranteed debt is for well-managed self-supporting crown companies [like Hydro]." *Moody's Bond Survey*, September 23, 1975.

humiliation. They would show Manitobans "political interference" had forced Hydro to proceed with LWR and CRD in tandem and "waste $604 million." [38] They would persuade people to ignore Hydro's value and see only its debt. Sterling Lyon, elected PC party leader in 1976, trumpeted the accusation and Craik stated if his party was elected he would consider stopping construction on the Nelson River and substitute small plants. [39]

Charges of "waste" gained credibility with the public when electricity costs, like everything in the mid-Seventies, began rising. The *Winnipeg Free Press* gave the premier space to explain what Hydro had done, and why, but paralleled it the same day with an editorial repeating the PC critique and that the average Manitoban "is paying two-thirds more for power than a few years ago." [40]

Free Press reporter Wally Dennison did several articles on rate increases and *Free Press* reporter Mike Ward wrote that these had induced Moody's Investors Services to review Manitoba's AA credit rating. [41] This became the yoke on the neck of the government in the 1977 election and led to a judicial inquiry afterward. [42]

Early 1977 was a bad time for the government, as seen in news headlines: "Lyon Laments 'Tragic' Increase In Hydro Rates"; [43] "Poor Paying More of Hydro Rise: Lyon". [44]

Former Premier Douglas Campbell had claimed that regulation of Lake Winnipeg as a Hydro reservoir "incurred debt taking forty-one cents of every revenue dollar". [45] He neglected to mention that in 1967, before a bulldozer had moved, Hydro's interest cost was thirty-nine cents of the dollar; by 1976, the interest cost was down to forty-one cents from forty-three cents in 1974; in 1976, the interest cost for privately owned Calgary Power was forty-nine cents. Campbell and the PCs had wanted coal plants and imported fuel instead of the LWR, but from 1967 to 1977 coal costs increased 330 per cent, and from 1973 to 1977 natural gas went up 110 per cent and heating oil 100 per cent. Yet Manitoba Hydro was expected to be inflation exempt.

There was some good news. The premier announced Manitoba's AA credit rating remained, despite attacks in the newspapers. And the same day Green "bet his political life", announcing he would resign from the government "if the charge [of wasting $600 million] was shown as having a scintilla of support by people trained in hydro-electric engineering", and went on to predict that "if Lyon

---

[38] The figure was seemingly arrived at by comparing 1970 estimates with final costs, but ignorning inflation, additions, and modifications.

[39] *Winnipeg Tribune*, December 6, 1976. In October 1977, Craik became minister for Manitoba Hydro and continued the NDP program.

[40] March 19, 1977.

[41] *Winnipeg Free Press*, February 18, 1977.

[42] Commission of Inquiry into Manitoba Hydro, December 1979.

[43] *Winnipeg Free Press*, January 25, 1977.

[44] *Winnipeg Tribune*, January 25, 1977.

[45] *Winnipeg Free Press*, December 18, 1976.

forms the next government there is nothing he will change". [46] Lyon's charge that millions were wasted by not building the Churchill River diversion before the Lake Winnipeg reservoir was damaged when Gordon Spafford, the engineer who had proposed that sequence admitted, "I don't know if my plan was practical." [47]

Manitoba Hydro's efficiency showed in the figures. From 1966 to 1976, the consumer price index doubled and the industrial wage index rose 260 per cent but Hydro went up sixty-nine per cent—less than the CPI increase. Manitobans paid a lower percentage of income for power in 1976 than ten years earlier. And surplus power was being sold to the U.S. for up to five times the production costs. [48]

Power costs in Manitoba were rising less than they would have without the massive increase in Manitoba Hydro output ... But they were rising. Inflation was a relentless corkscrew, pushing costs up and rate increases that in 1976 and '77 came at the worst time, politically speaking. Perceptions of Manitoba Hydro, and of the government, became a political Rorschach test in which people saw what they wanted to see or their imaginations contrived. By 1977, legislative reporter Robert Matas predicted the denouement of what should have been the brightest star in the firmament of the government's works in an article entitled: "Hydro Issue No Longer NDP's Strong Suit". [49] Liberal Leader Charles Huband charged, "the debt load of Hydro is so enormous it can only be paid off by tripling rates." [50] He failed to say that the government was made vulnerable by deciding to consider resource values and to save the native villages—a major Liberal election demand in 1973. The PC attack continued unequivocally, charging the NDP with "political interference" by assigning values to resources in the North caused "a tragic waste of $604 million". That was their story and they were sticking with it.

While critics were firm in their position, groups that should have supported the government vociferously were muted. Those who benefitted from the government's "political intereference" to mitigate damages in the North would not defend it. The Liberals had wanted no flooding of South Indian Lake, while the PCs wanted to flood higher and sooner, and by proceeding with both LWR and CRD, we had offended most of the vocal groups, including those who wanted more power, cheaper. Those who might have supported the government were more concerned with crocuses, fly-fishing, promoting the nuclear option [51] and causing a whole new set of problems costing the people of Manitoba, through electricity rates, multi-millions for questionable compensation.

---

[46] No one accepted Green's challenge, and when Lyon formed the government, the Conservatives completed the NDP Manitoba Hydro program.

[47] *Winnipeg Tribune*, April 13, 1977.

[48] In December 1976, production costs were .seven cents per kWh, while selling prices was up to four cents per kWh.

[49] *Winnipeg Tribune*, March 15, 1977.

[50] *Winnipeg Free Press*, December 6, 1976.

[51] "Criticism of the nuclear option has been negligible in Manitoba," wrote Steve Riley in the *Winnipeg Tribune*, December 6, 1976. Yet twenty years later, Ontario was abandoning its nuclear plants ("Meltdown. A $6 Nillion Shock", *Maclean's*, August 25, 1997) and the research facility at Pinawa, MB was closed. ("A Nuclear Shrine to the Sixties", *Winnipeg Free Press*, March 12, 1999).

Along the route of the hydro-electric development, houses were moved and new ones built, docks raised or rebuilt, cemeteries relocated or protected, tugboats provided to keep channels free of debris, weirs built to control water flow, works to mitigate damage, new trails built to traplines. Commitments were made to raise float plane bases, bridges, pump houses and sewage outfalls. Migratory bird nesting and staging areas were redeveloped, new spawning grounds for fish and new feeding and breeding grounds for waterfowl, deer and fur bearing animals were developed.

Potential damages to each village were assessed in a $2 million study and the results, with diagrams, communicated to residents, with "compensation claim" forms attached. Written notice was given that any community or individual adversely affected would be compensated and disputed claims resolved by an arbitration tribunal. The government was determined that no community or person damaged for the benefit of the general public would be left worse off than before the development began. However, the government was also determined to not give away the key to the treasury.

Since 1977, Manitoba Hydro receipts from exported power have been more than $2 billion, and Manitoba's rates among the lowest in North America. In 1999, Hydro's capital assets were $7,866 million and long-term debt $5,863 million. Peak demand was 3,560 million kW and capacity 5,140 million kW, eighty per cent on the Nelson River. Revenue from exports (sixty per cent to the U.S.) was $326 million, thirty per cent of the total. Gross revenue was $1,081 million, net profit $100 million, and water rental fees to the province were $55 million. [52]

The Government of Manitoba, by selling Manitoba Hydro Bonds, reduced its dependence on foreign funds and created a huge new capital market for Manitobans. By 2003, there had been no increase in residential power rates for seven years and in industrial rates for ten years, and Manitoba Hydro had integrated energy sources by purchasing Centra Gas. [53] The political decisions of 1970, which had contributed as much as any single factor to the defeat of the NDP government, proved fortuitous. Manitoba Hydro entered the new millennium as a billion dollar corporation.

In fact, it did so well that right-wing ideologues began speaking of privatizing it. The heavy lifting had been done by Manitobans and the most efficient hydro-electric system in North America had been built, so presumably the private sector could operate it—perhaps even without subsidies. The ultimate accolade, came twenty years later, from right-wing columnist Fred Cleverley: "Hydro's Nelson River plants are not dinosaurs [but] investments in the future, and will pay dividends for the next 100 years." [54] And it had become a honey pot!

---

[52] There are dangers in making long-term predictions with a beast as unruly as the weather. In 1997, Manitoba Hydro estimated that in the next nineteen years, power valued at $1.5 billion would be exported on long-term contracts along. The 2003-4 year was exceptionally dry, however, requiring Manitoba Hydro to buy power and incur a deficit. In 2004-5, Hydro had a profit of $136 million and projected a profit of $250 million for 2005-6. (*Winnipeg Free Press*, August 10, 2005).

[53] Manitoba Hydro bought Centra Gas in 1999 and Winnipeg Hydro in 2002, giving it a monopoly on electric and natural gas sales and distribution in Manitoba.

[54] *Winnipeg Free Press*, October 26, 1997.

XXXIV

Manitoba Hydro II

Show me the money.
　　　　　　　—Cuba Gooding

Ⅰhe **Government of Manitoba** had decided upon the most rational way of providing secure power for Manitobans ... and paid a political price. It now had to decide how to compensate those damaged by the first decision, which would exact a political price.

At the 1976 legislative committee meetings the government, besieged by accusations that its efforts to mitigate damages along the diversion channel was a "$604 million waste", received a taste of the problems it had hatched by touching the diversion channel at all. Premier Schreyer asked Leonard Bateman, CEO of Manitoba Hydro, "Is the alternative [to LWR and large power plants on the Nelson] to build smaller plants on the Burntwood?"

Bateman responded, "The environmental and social considerations are more overwhelming for Burntwood sites than the engineering problems." [1]

They also proved to be enormously expensive. The government saw Hydro as an instrument of social as well as economic development, for moving northern First Nations from welfare to wages and into the economic mainstream. It brought electricity, education and health services, airstrips, roads and reduced costs. It gave isolated communities access to the world and individuals ways to leave a life romanticized by those who had never lived there. Many of these saw it as destroying "self-sustaining communities" and the Aboriginal lifestyle.[2]

---

[1] *Hansard*, April 20, 1976

[2] In November 1974, *The Manitoban*, the University of Manitoba newspaper, published what was purported to be "Confidential Government Notes Detailing the Extent of Damage".(Con't on next page)

Realistically, the native lifestyle had been destroyed a century earlier when Europeans staked out land, built railroads, replaced natural grasses with wheat, and bison with domesticated livestock. Letters came to the Premier's Office pleading that we not disturb the native communities "by tearing up the permafrost to sell electricity to America". But how did that differ from tearing up the tall grass prairies to sell wheat to Russia and China?

The idea of "self-sustaining" native communities was a myth. South Indian Lake was extolled as one such "self-sustaining" community, but on enquiring, I received a list of forty-five families; only two were not receiving welfare assistance. And that was 1972, before the "pristine" conditions were defiled. Visiting South Indian Lake in mid-1973, I saw that we had brought electricity, roads and moved the village to the east side of the lake where residents wanted it. I concluded that Hydro was the best thing that had happened to them in a long time. And so did they.

Northern reporter Bob Lowery wrote of South Indian Lake in 1975:

> There is a buoyancy in the atmosphere in this community, the first to feel the effects of the Churchill River Diversion and Manitoba Hydro's program of restoration for resulting damage and relocation ... A new $3 million community complex [and] 95% employment rate gave lift to the 500 local residents ... This week the first two families received keys to new homes provided by Manitoba Hydro ... [which] will supply 58 units. The consensus is these are the best homes this community has ever seen. Each has three good-sized bedrooms, a large kitchen, dining-living room area, bathroom, clothes closet, both electric baseboard and wood stove heating and is insulated. Large windows look out on the black spruce forest and [the new resident] said in Cree, 'This is a wonderful home'. The second said, 'Never in my life did I ever expect to live in a home like this'.
>
> A 14-room school with a science lab and large gymnasium [is being built] for the community. It has shower rooms, library, sauna, and is available to the community after school. [Another resident], who will move into his new home Thursday, said, 'I never went to school a day in my life. I grew up on traplines and in fishing camps. I'm glad our children are getting this chance.'
>
> The centre has a new nursing home, mini-hospital, large store, laundromat and motel ... all to be operated by a locally-elected development board ... All will be serviced by the community's first sewer and water treatment plant. The high employment is largely due to

---

[2] (Con't.) Intent on detailing the socioeconomic ravages of Hydro, it instead exposed the myth of "self-sufficiency", detailing the numbers, employment and earnings of about 7,000 people with a total income of about $250,000 ... or about $35 per person. The article's authors may have spent more in one day on beer and sandwiches.

416

good-paying jobs in the community centre and on home construction programs and nearby Hydro sites. If there is a loss in production, compensation will be paid to fishermen.[3]

The Government of Manitoba intended to apply this South Indian Lake formula to all communities affected by Hydro development. But South Indian Lake was different. It was not a reserve.

During the 1974 federal election Indian Affairs Minister Jean Chrétien apparently discovered that Aboriginal Canadians have votes. Five reserves (Norway House, Nelson House, York Landing, Split Lake, Cross Lake) formed the Northern Flood Committee. Chrétien funded it and told Manitoba he would not agree to flooding of native land without prior consent by the NFC.[4] NFC lawyer D'Arcy McCaffrey informed us he was filing an injunction to stop the Churchill River Diversion.[5]

In Canada, private land is held by Torren's Title: land is vested in the Queen (the State), which can exercise "eminent domain" to expropriate land needed for public use, with compensation determined by negotiation or arbitration. Now Ottawa decided that natives could not be treated like whites. Instead of the normal process, we got a prescription for permanent race-based welfare, with the recipients defining the amount.

Premier Schreyer wrote to Prime Minister Trudeau, stating that by signing the federal-provincial agreement in 1966 to develop the North and build the Gillam-Winnipeg transmission line, Ottawa had committed itself to the program, and Ottawa must arrange with the First Nations for reserve lands needed on the route of the Hydro development. Ottawa had not objected in 1969 when the PC government announced it was planning to raise South Indian Lake by twenty-nine feet, nor in 1973 when Hydro was licensed to proceed with CRD; now that millions had been spent it was too late to object. Manitoba would pay for damages (as at South Indian Lake) and submit unsatisfied claims to an Ottawa-appointed arbitrator. "Manitoba will respect the rights of Indians as with other citizens," but insisted on its right to proceed as in other communities; it would not be stopped by NFC blackmail, and expected Ottawa to honour its obligations.[6]

Trudeau replied the matter should be left to the ministers.[7] So Sidney Green, Manitoba minister of Mines, Resources and Environmental Management wrote to his federal counterpart that Manitoba long ago agreed to give legal assistance to any person claiming compensation, but will not fund a committee

---

[3] *Winnipeg Tribune*, March 20, 1975. In 1996, Lowery received the Order of Canada for community involvement. In 1997, he was awarded the Silver Eagle Outstanding Citizen Award by the Indigenous Women's Collective of Manitoba. (*Winnipeg Free Press*, December 1, 2000)

[4] Chrétien to Schreyer, May 29, 1974.

[5] McCaffrey to Schreyer, July 5, 1974.

[6] Schreyer to Trudeau, July 31, 1974

[7] Trudeau to Schreyer, August 23, 1974.

engaged in a political campaign against the government and "attempting to deny the right of Manitoba to proceed with a program [which is] part of the Federal-Provincial Agreement of 1966." [8] The reply came from the new Indian Affairs minister, Judd Buchanan. Funding the NFC was to warn Manitoba to deal with damage to native lands and "Cabinet consent depends on Manitoba satisfying the NFC." [9]

Thus the Torrens Title met the Indian Act. While Manitoba intended to treat the affected persons like any other citizens, Ottawa considered them "Indians", and believed its obligations to them superceded any obligations to Manitoba under the 1966 agreement.

Ottawa was reversing the normal process of acquiring private land for public use by demanding compensation be agreed to before expropriation—with the landowners deciding the amount. In other words, Ottawa was funding the Northern Flood Committee to veto Manitoba's entire hydro-electric program. Our erstwhile partner was now our adversary.

Schreyer wrote to Trudeau: "I suggest we get together as soon as possible [to avoid] becoming involved in litigation where there is no real issue between us." [10] A $2 million federal-provincial study had assessed possible damages to each affected community. On January 31, 1975, a bundle of diagrams and maps was sent to every resident of these communities with a letter stating this was "a summary of what might occur when the diversion goes into operation." A "Claim For Compensation" form was enclosed.

NFC solicitor D'Arcy McCaffery responded that no negotiations would occur until "the Government of Manitoba recognizes the NFC as sole bargaining agent for the communities." Also, the government must provide a statement of remedies including: land transfers to natives; environmental safeguards; protection of hunting, fishing and trapping rights; tax exemptions, adoption of social and economic programs; participation of native people in development; cash and royalties compensation on the project; recognition of collective rights and claims of native peoples; no violation of native lands and rights; creation of development corporations; full disclosure of Hydro's past, present and future activities in the North and the right of native peoples to be heard on Hydro developments. The letter ended with some humour: "This list is not exhaustive. You may add to it." [11]

The NFC wanted not only compensation but the right to make government policy in the North in perpetuity, and to be arbiter of all future developments as related to First Nations.

The premier wrote to "Residents of Northern Manitoba", stating the NFC claims "the Government of Manitoba cannot proceed with hydro-electric development of Manitoba without prior NFC approval and negotiating with them the

---

[8] Green to Buchanan, October 15, 1974.
[9] Buchanan to Green, December 4, 1974.
[10] Schreyer to Trudeau, December 27, 1974.
[11] McCaffrey to Manitoba government solicitor W.S. Martin, April 25, 1975.

political, social and economic rights of the citizens of Manitoba. The government will not proceed with phases held illegal by courts and will compensate for disputed claims left to third-party arbitration—BUT WILL NOT ABDICATE its responsibility for social and economic programs."[12]

Buchanan sent Green an ultimatum: "I have provided more than $800,000 [13] to the NFC ... and will support court action ... the 1966 Agreement imposes no obligation on me."[14]

Checkmate! The native people of northern Mantioba had found a sovereign protector. And diversion of the Churchill River was on hold.

The premier responded with an ultimatum. He informed the prime minister he was releasing all correspondence and studies to the public and to Manitoba MPs. Manitoba would compensate and accept an Ottawa-appointed arbitrator but "will not negotiate the right to proceed with CRD. That was done eight years ago [by] the two signatory governments."[15] Then he announced that Manitoba would counter any legal action by Ottawa or the NFC by naming the Government of Canada as a co-defendant, and stop payment on the $178 million it owed Ottawa for the Gillam-Winnipeg power line.[16]

Warren Allmand, the third minister of Indian Affairs in three years argued: "It's [native] land and it can't be taken without agreement for compensation. Manitoba must realize that."[17] Then began the agonizing descent into disillusionment and defeat.

Three days later a Hydro road surveying crew was expelled from the Nelson House reserve. While Manitoba had been assuming we were dealing with Canadians subject to Canadian laws, the NFC and Ottawa was claiming that First Nations had all the rights of Canadians plus. Premier Schreyer stated that this opened the way to blackmail: "The concept of eminent domain is an essential aspect of public policy ... Under Ottawa's pernicious doctrine of consent ... construction of the St. Lawrence Seaway and the Winnipeg Floodway could have been held up in similar fashion."[18]

Manitoba's opposition parties got into the act. PC Leader Sterling Lyon demanded action: "There is no excuse for delaying a project vital to the future." Conversely, Liberal Leader Charles Huband demanded caution: Manitoba must not proceed without native consent.[19] Manitoba Indian Brotherhood president Lawrence Whitehead demanded "half the land in Manitoba for the 42,000 Treaty

---

[12] Schreyer to all residents, May 13, 1975.
[13] Manitoba had refused Ottawa's demand that we pay $1.7 million in Northern Flood Committee costs.
[14] Buchanan to Green, July 22, 1975.
[15] Schreyer to Trudeau, July 22, 1977.
[16] August 7, 1977.
[17] *Winnipeg Tribune*, July 20, 1977.
[18] *Winnipeg Free Press*, July 25, 1977. Even Justice Thomas Berger, who recommended a ten-year delay in the Mackenzie Valley gas pipeline from the North did not claim an Inuit or Dene veto.
[19] *Ibid.*, July 23, 1977.

Indians; I want to be a capitalist ... a millionaire and drive a Cadillac ... That's why I want more land." [20] The Manitoba Metis Federation claimed much of the remaining half. They demanded ten per cent of city properties in Winnipeg, Brandon and Portage la Prairie; title to Riding Mountain National Park; twenty-five per cent of Hudson's Bay Company assets in Manitoba; five per cent of numerous other communities; an unconditional grant of 1.4 million acres of land; $1 billion in cash to a Métis trust fund with proceeds tax exempt; ten to twenty-five per cent of all railway holdings and senior directorships on major Manitoba corporations. [21]

Schreyer repeated that he would settle native land claims that were subject to the right of expropriation for public purposes—just like any other expropriated land. Allmand replied Ottawa would not agree "without prior consent of the Indians". *The Winnipeg Tribune* editorialized:

> Indian Affairs Minister Warren Allmand speaks with a forked tongue ... compensation pledges to Indian communities were made by the Schreyer government seven years ago ... information on how much land will be flooded has been available for three years ... The Manitoba government keeps making clear proposals for compensation but rightly rejects the suggestion that a group of citizens has the right to veto a major public project. [22]

In 1976, Winnipeg lawyer Leon Mitchell became the joint Ottawa-Manitoba appointed mediator to resolve the conundrum. On August 2, 1977, he announced a tentative Northern Flood Agreement:

> A legally binding contract which, among other benefits and entitlements, establishes as actionable rights and adverse effects on the lands, pursuits, activities, interests, opportunities, lifestyles, and assets of those residing in the impact zone of the Lake Winnipeg Regulation and Churchill River Diversion Projects [and] also establishes a requirement of consultation in respect of future Hydro developments. [23]

Residents of affected communities would receive: transfer to native ownership of four acres for each of some 1,800 acres used by Hydro, which they could select and trade for more valuable land within five years; substantial rights to use land around lands selected; a $5 million development corporation funded by government; compensation for water level changes and for adverse affects to them-

---

[20] *Winnipeg Tribune*, July 29, 1977.

[21] *Ibid.*, May 21, 1977. The Métis land claims research was reportedly assisted by an $800,000 grant from Ottawa. (*Winnipeg Free Press*, August 2, 1977).

[22] July 22, 1977.

[23] Overview Planning Institute, February 1986.

selves in circumstances not applicable to other citizens affected by public projects; group disability, life and accident insurance policies. And the government was required to commit to "eradication of mass unemployment and poverty." [24]

There was a "reverse onus" clause: "The onus will be on Hydro to prove that the projects did not contribute to an adverse effect where any claim arises by virtue of actual or purported adverse effect of the Project." [25] Claims would be decided by an arbitrator, whose ruling would be final. "This Agreement ... shall be ... for the lifetime of the project ... and shall be binding upon successors, heirs, executors, and successors of any claimant." [26]

Any development as massive as the Nelson River hydro-electric project causes damage for which compensation must be paid, but this was a charge against Manitoba taxpayers and hydro users *in perpetuity*. Treaty rights had become a potent bargaining tool. Huband warned that whites must not expect so generous a deal if their lands were expropriated. [27]

McCaffrey was pleased. He stated that the $5 million from Hydro and the two governments for an economic development fund would be added to what is paid for individual or community losses and such loss claims could include deterioration in hunting and fishing areas and loss of access to traditional waterways. There could be up to $15 million of work for the five bands (bush-clearing, boat landings, shoreline reconstruction, dock works). The development fund secured by the agreement might mean 1,000 new jobs for native Manitobans and be used as "seed money" to bring $20 to $30 million in public money to the communities through government programs.[28]

Manitoba Hydro was pleased. Finally it could complete the work halted a year earlier. In late August, water began flowing through the $130 million Churchill River Diversion.

But not everyone was pleased. Ken Young, vice-president of the NFC, said the bands would seek ongoing compensation up to $1 million a year from Hydro. [29] Chief Francis Ross of Cross Lake said "my people are not happy [and] it must be the money." Chief Nelson Linklater of Nelson House said, "It's not over. I never signed." [30]

The Government of Manitoba was not pleased. On August 16th, Allmand and the chiefs of the five reserves, representing 7,000 Cree, met at the Winnipeg Airport and signed the agreement.

---

[24] In 1945, the Canadian government published a Green Paper promising full employment. It could not keep that promise either.

[25] Clause 23.2. In 1994, the arbitrator awarded damages to the family of a man when Hydro could not prove they did not cause the debris that swamped his boat. (*Winnipeg Free Press*, April 9, 1998.)

[26] Section 25.1.

[27] *The Winnipeg Tribune*, August 3, 1977.

[28] *Ibid.*, August 5, 1977.

[29] *Ibid.*, August 2, 1977.

[30] *Ibid.*, August 3, 1977.

Finalization needed only ratification by band members—and Manitoba. But the Government of Manitoba did not attend. Allmand was miffed: "Manitoba agreed [in principle]. I don't know why they didn't come today. Maybe they're on holidays."[31]

They were not. They were having the most gut-wrenching meeting of their tenure; they were analyzing what many would consider esoteric—interpretation of a single clause in a bulky document. The critical question was: *What would the arbitrator arbitrate?*

The premier wanted to ensure that arbitration would not pertain to future government policies for northern development "that have nothing to do with flooding". His letter to Allmand asking for clarification received the reply that point was "academic".[32]

Winnipeg Tribune staffer Pat McKinley analyzed the reasons for the Manitoba government's reluctance to sign:

> The agreement commits the province to economic, environmental and natural resource programs not normally contemplated when the government compensates individuals for land needed for public purposes ... Manitoba Hydro is now required to enter the field of social services by serving on a task force to find employment for northern natives. The province must pay the full cost of a wildlife planning board with majority representation from the bands, though need for wildlife planning did not arise solely from flooding ... It commits Manitoba to work with Ottawa and the bands to devise a development plan for the communities—again despite the fact that planned development has little to do with the flooding ... The province is justified in viewing it as a dangerous precedent: that long-standing problems are being handled in what is supposed to be agreement for compensation.
>
> The federal government has seized on Hydro's need to get the diversion into use [to get] Manitoba to pay for programs Ottawa wants on northern reserves. If other groups follow the Indians' example, the resulting 'me-too-ism' would create costly delays every time the province needs land for a public project.[33]

Huband was incensed. He claimed Schreyer's refusal to sign because of fear of future arbitration on issues not related to flooding proved that Green was really in charge of the government.[34] Green, his legal antennae alerted to future pitfalls, sent a memo, exuding melancholy and frustration, to his leader. "[Ottawa's] posi-

---

[31] *Winnipeg Free Press*, August 17, 1977.
[32] Schreyer to Allmand, August 12, 1977. Reply August 19, 1977.
[33] *Winnipeg Tribune*, August 20, 1977.
[34] *Winnipeg Free Press*, August 5, 1977.

tion makes it impossible to deal in a rational way ... The question of policy is fundamental. The agreement cannot be proceeded with in its present form ... Provincial policy [can not] be subject to determination by a [non-elected] third-party adjudicator ... If we abandon this principle in this case, we have no argument to refuse such contracts with the next group believing it can intimidate the government.[35]

A tense discussion ensued among members of the government. "We are being told to hand over our responsibilities as a government and enter into a permanent agreement to negotiate with the Indians. We will pay compensation as we would to whites. That is all. We will not enter into an agreement with the NFC which will give them the right to sue us in the future."

But there were saving words in it, such as "reasonable", but it would be a judge who would decide what is "reasonable" and cabinet members were afraid that if the government signed, they would make "the Indians captives of the NFC."[36]

Premier Schreyer desperately wanted to sign the agreement and get this all-consuming file off his desk. He wanted to give tangible expression to his abiding sympathy for Manitoba's First Nations and to his interest in the economic development of their communities. And he needed time to engage in was clearly going to be a hard-fought election. The document lay on the desk in front of him. It would be so easy to sign it and end this agony. But ...

He sent Allmand a letter, carefully worded, detailing concerns:

> While all the specific undertakings and obligations incurred in the agreement are acceptable to Manitoba ... we cannot regard the ambiguity of the wording of the Arbitration section i.e. Section 24, as 'academic' ... (as stated in your recent telex).
>
> Accordingly ... I am signing the agreement with respect to the economic development program ... I am also signing [the general agreement] ... with elaboration attached to make it clear that arbitration shall deal with matters that can in nature and quantum be considered appropriate to compensate for adverse effects that are attributable to the project. I assume that is acceptable, since it simply seeks to guard against awards being made for matters not attributable to the project.

His signature on the agreement was conditional on Ottawa accepting one

---

[35] Green to Schreyer, August 5, 1977

[36] On July 24, 1977, Hydro workers were ordered off the Nelson House Reserve, closing down road building and the construction of community facilities, pending acceptance of NFC terms. Jimmy Spence, the band's economic development officer reacted this way: "Our people are going to be damn mad when they find out they've lost their jobs ... While this project has been going on there hasn't been an unemployed guy in Nelson House ... We're getting damned fed up with the NFC ... These people in Winnipeg, especially the NFC who is supposed to represent us, never consult us." *Winnipeg Free Press*, July 25, 1977.

tiny 'clarification hereby being proposed to be included in the agreement as Section 24-38' i.e:

> Notwithstanding anything bearing contrary interpretation, it is agreed by all parties hereto that in any adjudication arising herefrom before the arbitrator or otherwise whereby damages may be awarded *such awards of damages shall be limited to such amount as would compensate that person or persons making claim for such adverse effects suffered that are directly and reasonably attributable to the project.* [37]

Schreyer added that, since Allmand had already described this clause as "academic", he should not mind agreeing to it. But Allmand did mind. The next day a furious McCaffrey burst into the premier's press conference shouting that the NFC and Ottawa had signed the agreement and "You must sign." The modified section sent to Ottawa was NOT acceptable. There would be court action.

The premier replied that when Ottawa and the chiefs signed on August 16th, they knew Manitoba would not sign because the clause in question "impinges on legislative autonomy and policy". There was no agreement until cabinet signed, and "Cabinet is not a rubber stamp." Government has no authority to abdicate policy-making responsibilities to a third-party veto. He stated that his government had faced the threat of a doctors' strike rather than give them a veto over health policy and rejected proposals giving the Manitoba Federation of Labour a veto over industrial policy. "Such matters are the exclusive jurisdiction of the democratic process which should not be abrogated by any government." [38]

Schreyer gave the media an eleven-page statement reviewing the history of the compensation negotiations, concluding with:

> The [Ottawa proposed] agreement provides for a four-to-one land exchange, total compensation to those affected, a $3.2 million development corporation, plus a blank cheque. Manitoba agrees to the first three, but no blank cheque …[Manitoba] has signed … the agreement with modification of one section to clarify future arbitration will be on matters directly attributable to the project … If this is not accepted because of some intention to have provincial policies and actions subject to arbitration even on matters not attributable to the project … then no agreement exists.

The Winnipeg Tribune editorialized: "[Manitoba] has refused to sign the formal agreement because of a clause which, they claim, would give the arbitrator power to make policy decisions. This reluctance by the province appears in the best interests of all the people rather than just a single group. It does not ignore

---

[37] Schreyer to Allmand, September 1, 1977.

[38] *Winnipeg Tribune*, September 3, 1977.

the special status of the Indians. Mr. Allmand is making a nuisance of himself." [39]

By then we were in the throes of a provincial election campaign. On September 15th McCaffrey (a Liberal candidate in a 1975 by-election) made headlines by sending the premier a list of twenty-two questions. Allmand threatened to take Manitoba to court. Huband and Lyon saw nothing offensive in the agreement. [40]

A great pall was enveloping the government. But,

> Wenn mann wirklich denkt es geht nicht mehr,
> Dann kommt von irgendwo ein lichtlein her. [41]

The light appeared in the form of the NFC chairman, Walter Monias. He invited the premier to meet with the five chiefs to explain why he had refused to sign the agreement. After the meeting, Monias said of the modification that Manitoba had proposed, "You have to respect that an arbitrator cannot take over the rights of government. The new clause protects both federal and provincial governments."

There had been much misunderstanding because the native people had been told Manitoba's clause endangered their hunting and fishing rights, but, "Its clear these rights have been ours for generations because of our treaties with the crown and this agreement cannot change that." Monias added, "We did not want lawyers present. They would have started another argument. We thought we understood what the premier meant by his new clause and we wanted to get his interpretation direct from him. We had a damn good time with Schreyer." [42]

Schreyer responded, "There is every reason to be optimistic." The next day his government was defeated in the election.

ON DECEMBER 16, 1977, Deputy Premier Don Craik, on behalf of Manitoba, signed the Northern Flood Agreement. For Ottawa it was signed by Hugh Faulkner, the fourth minister of Indian Affairs in three-and-a-half years. On March 15, 1978, it was ratified by the five native reserves. And then the money began to flow.

The NDP government had tentatively estimated, based on what would be paid to white communities, compensation to the five Indian communities should be about $7 million. The agreement signed by the Lyon government left Manitoba Hydro in the position of either paying in perpetuity or buying its way out. By March 31, 2002, $471 million had been paid for mitigation/ remedial works and

---

[39] *Ibid.*, September 15, 1977.

[40] *Winnipeg Free Press*, September 16, 1977.

[41] From the German: "When one truly fears the task is beyond one's might, then from somewhere strange there comes a light."

[42] *Op. cit.*, October 11, 1977.

lump-sum compensation, and 172,985 acres of land had been transferred to reserve ownership. For that, buyouts had been concluded with four (Split Lake, Norway House, Nelson House, York Landing) of the NFC represented communities. Of this amount, some $58 million was spent on the fifth community, Cross Lake. [43]

But Cross Lake refused to sign. It rejected Manitoba Hydro's buy-out offer of $110 million, [44] claiming the Northern Flood Agreement is a treaty that cannot be renegotiated and gives them authority to hold the Province of Manitoba and the Government of Canada responsible for their welfare *in perpetuity*. This argument is based on the strength of a single sentence in the Agreement, Article 16, Schedule E, committing the government to "eradication of mass poverty and unemployment".

Cross Lake complains of "85 per cent unemployment" and its main occupation seems to be blockading Hydro from doing work in the North, petitioning the United Nations, travelling to Europe to seek sympathy, and lobbying American utility companies to stop purchases of power from Manitoba Hydro until its community has been compensated for alleged damages. [45]

What has been the degree of damage? In 1999, Warren Allmand, then president of International Centre for Human Rights and Democratic Government, claimed "the [Manitoba Hydro] dams irreparably damaged aboriginal fishing and hunting." [46]

However, "Commercial fishers on Lake Winnipeg have hauled in the best catch in years," the *Free Press* had stated the summer before. And in early June 1999, the paper reported, "The annual commercial fish harvest in the Cross Lake area has reached the highest levels in this decade." In 1999, the manager of public affairs for Manitoba Hydro reported, "In the 1990s incomes for commercial fishermen from Cross Lake have been comparable or better than incomes over the more than 50 years for which data is available." [47]

Concerning hunting, provincial records show that, before they began to drop off for various reasons, the highest numbers ever in terms of both pelts sold and dollars to trappers were reported in 1980–81, three years after the entire Lake Winnipeg-Nelson River-Churchill Diversion program became operative. [48]

And what of the social effects of Hydro. Under the headline, "Shamattawa Docket Jammed: Court Sees 264 Charges in Community of Just 500", staffers Bob Lowery and Randy Turner reported: "Shamattawa, with a population of 500 on the reserve, has two sittings a month. Norway House with 10 times the population—

[43] Manitoba Hydro Annual Report to March 31, 2002.

[44] *Winnipeg Free Press*, August 15, 2002.

[45] In 2000, the arbitrator ordered Manitoba Hydro to pay $9.1 million into the Cross Lake Trust Fund, the proceeds of $315,000 annually to be used to operate the arena, which was built by Hydro and provided with free electricity.

[46] *Winnipeg Free Press*, June 22, 1999.

[47] *Ibid.*, July 9, 1999.

[48] Department of Natural Resources and Fur Council Report, 1985.

more than 5,000—has the same number of court dates."[49]

Yet Norway House is directly on the channel from Lake Winnipeg into the Nelson, while Shamattawa is some 100 miles away from it.

But where has the money gone? *Calgary Herald* editor Donald Campbell wrote, "As *Winnipeg Free Press* legislative reporter 1990 to 1993, I wrote ... a 10-part series on the dysfunctional Northern Flood Agreement, that prompted the federal Auditor General's Office to declare it had become 'a black hole' benefiting lawyers and advisors, but not the parties it was meant to serve."[50]

Three years later, this condemnation was emphasized under the glaring headline, "Disgraced Lawyer Jailed". Donald Neil MacIver's "troubles began after he successfully settled a land claim for the South Indian Lake community. He took $3 million more than the $1 million he billed, put it in a Swiss bank account and evaded taxes on the money."[51]

And two years later, the *Winnipeg Free Press*, commenting on the holdout by Cross Lake, editorialized: "The [Northern Flood Agreement] ... is often a sinkhole for money for lawyers, experts and consultants in quarrels over the terms of the Agreement."[52]

[49] *Winnipeg Free Press*, April 29, 1993.

[50] *Winnipeg Free Press*, September 24, 1997.

[51] *Ibid.*, July 11, 2000.

[52] April 22, 2002.

XXXV

The Griffin Steel Strike

We enacted legislation giving labour the right to strike without government or court interference. Now they want a law to guarantee every strike will be a success.
—Sidney Green

"**Y**ou sure as hell** will never get such legislation from me, said Premier Schreyer as he looked determinedly across the table.

Griffin Steel Foundries of Winnipeg, subsidiary of an American steel company, produced specialized products for the Canadian and American transportation industry. Established in 1959, by 1976 it employed 140 persons. In 1964, it was the first plant unionized by the Canadian Association of Industrial, Mechanical and Allied Workers (CAIMAW), becoming the home base of this new "Canadian", union and the focus for a "model" collective bargaining contract.

In 1973, the union signed its first, three-year agreement. Then, as often in the 1970s, the employer-employee relationship was disrupted by inflation. In the next two years, under union pressure, the company agreed to extra-contractual cost-of-living increases of fifteen and seventeen cents an hour. A third demand was rejected. The union leaders ordered their members to refuse overtime work.

When a foundry employee does not arrive for his shift, the company is faced with having a kettle of useless molten metal—or having standby workers available at substantial cost. To accommodate this, the company and employees had agreed to asking the man on the line to remain on overtime, while calling the next man in early. For seventeen years, this worked; the furnaces got serviced, the consumers got the product, and the employees got overtime wages.

In 1975, that accommodation was ended. A later study concluded: "Union leaders sensed that overtime was the perfect instrument to pressure management. By not allowing overtime, they believed they could achieve a wage increase outside their contract. They could also establish a slogan for their national organizing drive and gain support for union members in Manitoba."[1]

The company fired several workers. The union appealed. A board of arbitration ruled that the company could not, under the current agreement, fire employees for refusing overtime work. In June 1976, bargaining began on a new contract and the company inserted a "mandatory overtime" clause. On September 19, 1976, CAIMAW struck the plant. After four months the union realized it had miscalculated its economic strength and demanded government help. By then the demand for an extra-contractual wage increase had escalated into a crusade against "compulsory overtime".

In February 1977, the company wrote to all former employees: "Those wishing to return to work must contact their supervisors by February 24th. We will hire new permanent employees to replace striking employees who do not contact the company by this date. Strikers who decide to return later must apply for jobs on a first-come basis with new applicants."

On March 1st, Griffin reopened the plant to anyone wanting work. CAIMAW members had to choose between their job and their union.[2] The first day about thirty people, including nine union members, went to work. Strikers brought their wives and children to stiffen the picket line by lying down on the driveway to prevent anyone entering. Violent confrontations ensued. The City of Winnipeg sent in some sixty policemen to drag the bodies off the street and form a protective phalanx to allow workers through. Forty people were detained by police on the first day, and 250 in the first week. The union charged the police with brutality.

"It's a war zone out there. The strikers need our help," shouted emotionally-moved MLA Harry Shafransky, on returning to the caucus room after observing the picket line one morning.

But Attorney General Howard Pawley, equally sympathetic to the strikers (he almost resigned), but responsible for administering the law, reluctantly announced he would charge picketers who defied the law: "Neither we nor the police enjoy being 'used' in a labour dispute ... but access to property can't be obstructed."

To the union demand to abolish compulsory overtime, he replied, "This strike does not threaten life or health or involve an essential industry so it needs no government intervention." He was supported by former CNR upholsterer and union shop steward but now Minister of Labour Russell Paulley, who stated, "This government came to power on a platform of free collective bargaining. Overtime should be left to the bargaining process."

---

[1] "An Industrial Relations System Breaks Down: Lessons From A Strike", Terry Hercus and Diane Oades, University of MB Department of Labour Relations Study Paper, 1982, p. 12.

[2] Employers do not reopen on whim. In 1968, the author's company had half built an apartment block when the bricklayers' union, in a wage dispute, pulled its members out on "vacation". If we defied the union and hired other labour, we risked the building never being completed. The strike lasted three weeks. Thirty-five years later, that "vacation" is still marked by the white line, partway up the wall where the uncovered lime leached into the bricks.

Nevertheless, Paulley leaned on the company, which agreed to return to the bargaining table on condition that the union allow those who had crossed the picket lines to continue working. The union refused. The minister leaned on the company again. On March 24th, the company made a new offer: a maximum compulsory overtime of four hours a day or twenty hours per month, sixty strikers to return immediately based on seniority and others as vacancies arise, and the union to vote on the proposal by secret ballot.

During a heated debate at a union meeting a member insisted peer pressure was needed to keep possible recalcitrants in line. "If a secret ballot is held the union will be broken … Those with most to lose will vote to return and leave the rest of us in the cold … all decisions should be made by show of hands."[3] In an open vote the company proposal was rejected.

On April 26th the union counter-proposed that compulsory overtime be limited to sixteen hours a month and all strikers be recalled immediately, and replacements fired. The company agreed to the first condition, but not the second; it had hired replacement workers in good faith and would not sacrifice them.

The same day, Griffin won a court injunction prohibiting further obstruction at the plant entrance. The union was broken.[4] Some strikers returned to Griffin. About forty had already gone elsewhere.

In early 1977, the government sought to satisfy both sides by amending the Employment Standards Act; overtime was left to free collective bargaining but "compulsory" overtime hours must be paid at 1.75 per cent of regular time instead of 1.5 per cent. It infuriated the business community because it meant extra costs. It infuriated the union, which wanted government intervention, not bargaining.

From then on CAIMAW hostility was directed against the government. The union left a man on the picket line to embarrass the NDP throughout the 1977 election campaign. Said one striker, "We had the company beaten economically but with the assistance of the police, the courts and the government, they were able to reopen. The blame for the outcome of the strike lies with the provincial government … If they had banned overtime the company would have reached a settlement because they could not abandon the $25 million investment they had in this province."[5]

CAIMAW lost its fight for a wage increase and voluntary overtime, but succeeded in carving a new and potent issue into the labour relations and politics of Manitoba. At a political meeting on March 16, 1977, an exasperated Premier Schreyer, heckled by calls of "Are you on the side of the workers or the corporations?" and "Help us," from a room full of Griffin srikers, responded, "Manitoba and Saskatchewan are the only provinces requiring time-and-a-half pay after forty

---

[3] Hercus and Oades, *op.cit.*

[4] CAIMAW at Griffin was replaced by the Candaian Auto Workers (CAW). In 1995, the CAW struck Griffin over compulsory overtime.

[5] Hercus and Oades, *op. cit.*

hours. In Ontario and British Columbia it is forty-four and forty-eight hours respectively. We gave you the best labour law in Canada. What more do you want?"

Muriel Smith, former NDP president, who a few minutes earlier had been nominated as NDP candidate for Cresentwood, replied, "They want anti-scab legislation."

She gave a name to the issue the Griffin Strike had, unexpectedly, made into a cause célèbre. A minor squabble over extra-contractual pay had escalated into a fight about overtime, and then been elevated to a new, more dangerous, plateau.

The Griffin Strike created a symbol: "Remember Griffin" became an emotional slogan rivalling "Remember the Alamo" and "Remember *The Maine*". The search for public support worked its way through anti-Americanism, anti-unionism, anti-socialism, free collective bargaining, union-busting, union shop, overtime, and arrived at a principle with a wider focus—the demand for a law prohibiting workers from crossing a picket line into a struck plant.

The issue crossed party lines. Conservative MLA Bud Sherman walked the picket line. It grew and became manned by striker's families, members of other unions, ordinary citizens who became emotionally involved, politicians, clerics, university students, teachers, and civil servants who left their offices to picket.

The Premier's Office received a copy of a letter to the city police chief, stating that the writer's glasses had been broken in a scuffle with police on the Griffin picket line, and demanding compensation. I recognized the signature of a civil servant and replied, with a copy to the police chief, that if he had been at his job instead of picketing his glasses would not have been broken.

One morning about 150 people, mostly Griffin strikers, invaded The Ledge, persuaded someone on the custodial staff to unlock the Cabinet Room door, burst in, and loudly demanded to see the premier. I went to the Premier's Office. "You stay here," I told him. "This is my job."

I walked into the Cabinet Room, and someone shouted at me, "When is the premier coming to meet with us?"

"The premier is not coming. This is not a public circus. If you people want to meet with the premier, you make an appointment like anyone else. You do not burst in like a herd of animals. By the way, I notice some civil servants here. If they have time to be here they are not needed on the public payroll. Any civil servant here in two minutes will be summarily fired."

A number of people almost broke their legs getting out. The others, disheartened, began moving slowly out of the room, along the marble corridor and down the grand staircase. In the huge, ornate foyer they stopped for a while to wave anti-government placards and shout in chorus "One, two, three. One, two, three. We've been screwed by the NDP."

I looked down from the balcony and there among the seething, shouting, critical crowd stood our newly-nominated NDP candidate, Muriel Smith. [6]

---

[6] In 1981, she became deputy premier in the Pawley government.

As the nature of the "Griffin" issue changed, it placed strains on caucus, some of whose members saw the government's lack of action a betrayal of the party's heritage. And it strained the relationship between the government and its labour partner.

The "nationalist" CAIMAW was not a member of the Manitoba Federation of Labour, which had no moral obligation to assist the Griffin strikers. Indeed, CAIMAW was disliked by most unions affiliated with the NDP, so the MFL was willing to leave it to twist in the wind. However, as the issue of compulsory overtime, which most union leaders agreed should be left to free collective bargaining, metamorphosed into that of "anti-scab" legislation, it could not be ignored by self-respecting unionists.

Since the bloody confrontations at the Ford plants in the United States in 1935, labour had sought to establish the principle that the worker owns the job, that violence is not caused by strikers, but by those attempting to cross the picket lines to steal the striker's job, and that there was no authentic "free collective bargaining" so long as "scabs" were allowed to work in a struck plant.

"Anti-scab legislation" against "strikebreakers" had become a bedrock principle for organized labour. That posed a conundrum for the government, and a cluster of questions. Was it reasonable to believe workers would use the strike weapon to deliberately ruin an employer who provided them with income? Would such legislation not simply balance the employee's right to protect his job with the employer's right to close his plant, take his money and run? Do not management-employee relations involve a fundamental conflict over the division of the economic pie between investment and consumption and require empowerment of labour as a countervailing force?

Conversely, was such legislation not an unacceptable affront to the businessman who had contributed his time, sweat and house mortgage to his enterprise? Was not the modern strikebreaker (unlike past Pinkerton-hired goons) often simply an employee wanting to return to work, so the union's problem was its own failure to persuade its members to stay out? Was not labour seeking a law giving employees the prerogatives of ownership without the responsibilities, which was tantamount to expropriation without compensation? Could government enact legislation prohibiting people from working when jobs were available? Would legislation publicly perceived as too favourable to workers create a precedent for a later government to reverse it in favour of management?

If an "anti-scab" law applied to the private sector, must it not also apply to the public sector? If so, did that allow the civil service to close down the operations of the elected government? Could government sit idly while the ill lay helpless in struck hospitals and the apparatus of civil government ground to a halt? Would not "anti-scab" legislation result in legislation forcing people back to work?[7] If so, since the NDP government did not approve of the latter, could it

---

[7] In 1977, the Québec government of Premier René Levesque, sympathetic to organized labour, enacted.

enact the former? Unions already had the legal right to shut down a business, and a government, by persuading workers to respect their picket lines, but was it reasonable to allow that simply by invoking a law? Did too much law not negate the whole principle of free collective bargaining?

Nevertheless, the government appreciated labour's dilemma. And it was painfully aware that this legislation was desired by its ideological and political friends—the union half of the NDP—that the picket lines at Griffin were being manned mostly by NDP members, supporters and sympathizers, and that an election loomed. So the government desperately sought accommodation.

To this end, a three-hour meeting in April 1977 was attended by the government caucus, the party executive, and representatives of the MFL led by its vice-president, Wilf Hudson. The anti-scab issue was thoroughly dissected. The MFL's basic position was that strikes are a part of the normal bargaining process in a market economy, but leave employees without a paycheque. An anti-scab law would exert equivalent economic pressure on the employer.

About 10 P.M. the premier summed up the discussion. He added there was some sympathy for labour's position in caucus, which would meet soon to reach a decision on the issue. Then, as though his mind had suddenly moved from the abstract to the concrete, he said, "Your point that strikes would be more expeditiously resolved if both sides were deprived of their income is well taken. You realize, of course, that if we enact legislation prohibiting anyone from working in a struck plant we must also enact parallel legislation prohibiting anyone on strike from getting a job elsewhere while they are officially on strike."

"No, no, that's not what we want," said Hudson.

"Just a moment. Are you saying you want a law which will permit workers to strike a plant but obtain jobs elsewhere while no one will be allowed to go to work in the struck plant?"

"That's right."

The premier was sitting back in a corner of the large caucus room. A quizzical expression crossed his face. "Let me get this clear. Are you telling me that you want a law which will permit 140 employees to walk out of the Griffin Steel plant, and that you could leave one person on the picket line to keep the plant closed in perpetuity while the other 139 can go and get jobs elsewhere?"

"Yes," said Hudson.

The premier hunched forward, pulled the cigarette from his mouth, and pronounced with portentous deliberation, "Gentlemen, let me make this as clear as I know how. You sure as hell will never get such legislation from me."

---

[7] (Cont'd.) anti-scab legislation. In 1979, it legislated 250,000 public servants back to work. In 1980, cooks at Québec Hydro's James Bay site struck and picketed. Construction workers pushed them aside and cooked their own meals. They were charged with violating the province's anti-scab law, but acquitted - the court recognized that hungry men will eat, regardless of the law.

THE ANTI-SCAB issue drove a wedge between the government and labour, convulsed the party, followed the NDP government like a black dog in the 1977 election campaign, and remained a running sore in party-labour relations.[8] But no Manitoba government has yet enacted a law to guarantee that every labour strike, any more than every businessman's investment, will be a success.[9]

---

[8]   At the 1979 annual convention, with CAIMAW's token picket still at Griffin, a resolution was introduced: "be it resolved an NDP government would enact legislation to NOT allow hiring of new employees in an industrial dispute." I moved an amendment: "except where, and to the extent that, striking employees have found jobs elsewhere." I stated that only four of the twenty-two member caucus supplrted anti-scab laws. MLA Jay Cowan replied that anyone not supporting it should not be in the NDP caucus. At the next caucus meeting, when Cowan refused to apologize, Bud Boyce and Ben Hanuschak, former ministers in the Schreyer government, left the NDP and joined Sid Green to form the Progressive Party.

[9]   In 2004, Manitoba Premier Gary Doer, who had been president of the Manitoba Government Employees Association in 1977, told his convention that his government would NOT enact anti-scab laws. Nor was there any guarantee that an anti-scab law would be labour's "last territorial demand". In 1991, Premier Rae's NDP government of Ontario, to please the unions, enacted such legislation. Rae later wrote, "My thanks from the Auto Workers for this law was a gratuitous speech by President Buzz Hargrove dumping on our government at the CAW council meeting." *From Protest to Power*, Bob Rae, Penguin, Toronto, 1997, p. 234.

XXXVI

Party vs. Government

When a party becomes government there is a threat to the democratic process in the party.
—Anonymous NDP supporter

The election of a government marks a sea change in its relationship with the political party that gave it life. No matter how populist the party or how intensely it intends to maintain control over the members it elects to the legislature, it is axiomatic that the moment it forms a government the energy and the public spotlight move from the party to the government; the party becomes the victim of its own success.

But those who had spent years in smoke-filled halls or home basements promoting the party, and wearily walked streets distributing leaflets, having doors slammed in their faces and being chased out of yards by dogs, are not always pleased to be superceded by some Johnny-come-lately who, to the surprise of many, including the candidate, was elected. The faceless persons who bring the party to power have their fleeting moment of triumph on election night and fade again into the shadows to be neither consulted nor advised, but they want to ensure that the principles for which they campaigned and sacrificed are not diluted.

This is particularly true of a democratic populist party like the NDP. During its first term most members were satisfied to bask in the reflected glory of the elected members, but after the 1973 election, with the influx of those who had won their spurs in the campaign and were filled with revolutionary fervour and youthful zeal, a split developed between those focusing on ideology and those faced with the reality of governing. At times, at conventions or party council meetings, there were audible groans when cabinet ministers went to the floor microphone. To some NDPers the title "minister" became synonymous with "reactionary".

Muriel Smith came from a middle class family, taught school, and married the Oxford-educated son of the chief justice of Manitoba; the senior Smith had almost become leader of the Liberal Party and premier of the province in 1948. She was fortyish, slim, blonde, attractive, soft-spoken, intelligent, articulate and displayed a beguiling innocence when she joined the NDP "to become part of the solution instead of part of the problem." I saw it as a political coup.

We became acquainted through party activities. She had always been active on behalf of oppressed groups or individuals, but occasionally I found her indiscriminate sympathy somewhat irksome. Once, at a party council meeting she passed around a hat to collect funds to defend a man who was being deported to Jamaica. I had had enough of causes. "Mr. Chairman," I interjected, "is not this Rosie guy the one who smashed about $2 million worth of computer equipment at a Canadian university several years ago?"[1] The hat stopped in mid-passage.

Muriel and those working with her cared genuinely about the problems of the world, but the facility with which they could solve social and economic problems appeared to be in direct relation to their distance from them. They had quick cures for the phantasmagoria of problems in Guatemala, Nicaragua or Peru, but ask them how to effectively manage a crown corporation without offending the unions, or how to take the bums (both individual and corporate) off welfare without Draconian measures, or how to raise taxes on multinational corporations without risking their departure, or how to stop municipalities from bankrupting themselves by giving tax concesssions to corporations in return for promised jobs, or what to do if civil servants went on strike, or what to do with the minimum security prisoners who filled the jails to overflowing, and they would lapse into a low mumble—or worse, ideology.

But Muriel Smith paid her dues as an activist in the back rooms of both the party and the second wave of feminism. Her political determination and talents were revealed when she ran a solid campaign in the 1973 election against the leaders of both the Liberal and Conservative parties in a South Winnipeg constituency not known for its NDP supporters. And she quickly became a leader and spokeswoman in the feminist movement that was determined to open the doors for women into business, the professions and politics. In 1972, she became a founding member of the National Action Committee on the Status of Women.[2]

In 1975, she was elected president of the New Democratic Party of Manitoba and became the representative of those who considered themselves the keepers of the ideological flame, particularly in the area of social policy. They

---

[1] In 1969, Roosevelt Douglas was in a riot that destroyed the computer centre at Sir George Williams University (now Concordia) in Montreal. He was jailed and deported. In 2000 he returned to visit Canada, as president of the Republic of Dominica.

[2] NAC, founded in 1972 to force Ottawa to adopt the recommendations of the Royal Commission on the Status of Women, at one point spoke for up to 700 women's organizations. By 2001, however, it was collapsing because of lack of funding. (*Winnipeg Free Press*, March 8, 2004). In 2001 Muriel Smith was awarded the UNIFEM Canada Award for her work through the United Nations.

believed that government should bend to the will of the party.[3] Her election coincided with the tensions developing between the government and the MFL over the issue of anti-inflation controls. Her determination to make the government a "model employer" and her need for allies to support women's causes led to a relationship with the MFL that was at times almost incestuous. Hence, when the government was not amenable to labour's demands, the party office could be used to 'persuade'.

The NDP constitution of 1961 had brought labour into the party, not as individual members, but as an organized entity. From the beginning, there was a struggle for control of the party. At the founding convention of the New Democratic Party of Manitoba in 1962, "Old Socialist" Magnus Eliason, a life-long CCFer and strong supporter of its reincarnation as the NDP, waved a document, "Mr. Chairman, this is a list of names proposed for election to the executive. It is headed 'Steelworkers Slate'. This is an NDP, not a union, convention and I move that there be only one slate circulated and that is the one authorized by the executive."

The motion was seconded by Howard Pawley and passed. But it made no difference. At every convention a Steelworkers Slate or an MFL slate was circulated. Over time, it assumed sophistication, including several women, Aboriginal candidates, and the token farmer. Twenty years later, I rose at the annual convention, "Mr. Chairman, let us put an end to this travesty. I move that this convention resolves this will be the last time there will be any slate of names for the executive except the official one."

My resolution passed. The following year an MFL slate was again boldly circulated. I drew the attention of the convention to the fact that the previous year's resolution was being defied. Chairman Charles Bigelow dealt with the issue expeditiously. "We know," he said, and went on to the next subject.

I envied their fabled organization, honed at meetings held to educate members on labour history and discuss goals, and their vaunted discipline nurtured on picket lines when picketing was their only weapon. They never had a majority of delegates at party conventions, but their leaders could articulate their positions with a passion developed persuading reluctant workers to join unions and exhorting strikers to hold fast when they had mortgage payments to meet and children to feed. It gave them influence far beyond their numbers, and they knew how to use it.[4]

At every convention the MFL had the equivalent of its own caucus whip to keep delegates in line. At one convention the 'major-domo' was a young woman in

---

[3] Her successor as party president, Victor Schroeder, was to say of her, "I think Muriel Smith reasserted the role of the party in governmental affairs." (*Winnipeg Tribune*, January 31, 1977).

[4] Robert White, energetic union organizer and longtime president of the Canadian Auto Workers Union and of the Canadian Labour Congress, explains in his autobiography, *Hard Bargains: My Life on the Line*, the rigours of union organizing, the internal workings of unions and the iron will, discipline and persuasiveness needed in industrial bargaining.

a tweed suit with slighly flaring skirt and knee-high boots, erect and alert, striding with military precision along the aisles between the seats, walkie-talkie in hand, instructing her charges on how to vote. An image flashed into my mind: Bertha, the Beast of Belsen. The next year, Lewis Udall of the Canadian Union of Postal Workers, an easy-going, corpulent figure, puffing expansively on an eight-inch pipe and reminding me of a corvette laying a smoke screen, ambled back and forth in the aisles giving delegates the signal. During 'priorization', the process of moving significant resolutions forward, a delegate went to the floor microphone and moved that, "resolution number seventeen be moved up to number one". Labour delegates glanced at Udall, who nodded, and their hands shot up. After half a dozen such exercises, it appeared things were under control so Udall sat down. A delegate went to the microphone: "I move that number thirteen be moved up to number seven". The hands, accustomed by precedent, went up. Udall jumped to his feet so fast that his pipe fell out of his mouth amd scattered sparks on the table. "Wait a minute, wait a minute," he shouted, "that's the anti-abortion resolution." The labour delegates' hands, *auf befehl*, fell. It would have been a major *faux pas* for labour to vote to give preference to a resolution that its Voice of Women allies, who sought legalization of abortion on demand, considered anathema. How I envied their organized structure and iron discipline!

On January 30, 1976, the morning of the annual convention, I walked from my office at The Ledge to the Convention Centre. Once a year the NDP government was required, by the party constitution, to submit itself to the judgment of the annual convention, comprising delegates from all constituencies. Granted, since the NDP had formed the government, convention resolutions had been modified from commands to guidelines, but a resolution contradicting a major government policy would be politically damaging and generate editorial comments that the government was disliked even by its party members.

Manitoba's acceptance of the federal anti-inflation package had caused deep tensions in the party, particularly with its Labour component and their supporters on the party executive. Sid Green was aware of the discontent with the government's position and was himself unhappy with it, but he believed it to be the only rational option. As a member of the pre-convention resolutions committee, he sought to avoid a rupture between government and party by drafting a compromise resolution:

> Be it resolved this convention concurs in the reservations the provincial government has expressed concerning the federal program [and] questions its efficacy in dealing with the problem of inflation [but] recognizes that the provincial government is making a reasonable effort to cooperate with the national program. The NDP affirms its position ... that fundamental changes in our economic system are necesssary to deal with these problems in a long-term and definitive sense.

The resolution was delicately crafted to cover the bases: to agree with the federal government that action was needed to control inflation; to acknowledge that many considered the program both unfair and ineffective, and to avoid the embarrassment of having the NDP convention vote against a policy already agreed to by Manitoba's NDP government.

The resolution was adopted almost unanimously by the resolutions committee. Three days later—and three days before the convention—in the absence of Green who was in Ottawa at a federal NDP council meeting, and with only eight of the fifteen members present, the committee rescinded the resolution and quietly substituted the MFL position:

> Whereas the federal anti-inflation program will only freeze wages, not prices [and] the federal legislation will require the Manitoba government to implement wage controls in the civil service and public sector, be it resolved the government of Manitoba reject the federal anti-inflation program.

This was no mere disagreement; this was *Realpolitik*. I quickly scanned the convention agenda. The price-control resolution would be discussed early. I was scanning the agenda a second time, sensing something amiss, when Sid Green approached.

"Have you noticed anything peculiar about the agenda?" he asked me.

"Yes, but I don't know what it is."

"The premier will not be speaking."

Normally the premier spoke twice, on the first day to report on government activities during the past year, and again at the end of the convention when accepting re-nomination as party leader. Green pointed out that this time the premier was scheduled to speak only once—at the end of the convention.

"It must be a misprint. I'll point it out to Muriel."

I found her at a doorway, with Provincial Secretary Rick Taves.

"Muriel, there appears to be a problem with the agenda. The premier does not get to speak."

"Oh yes, he is on the agenda."

"Yes, but right at the end when many delegates will have gone home. He is not on to speak about the government's activities nor on the anti-inflation program, which will be an issue here."

Rick Taves interrupted, "Frankly, I don't give a fuck if the premier never speaks."

Suddenly, the pattern fell into place. "Rick, you are a party employee. I want to speak with my president." Rick left and I turned to Muriel. "Muriel, when I came over here I thought this was a misprint. I now know it is deliberate manipulation to embarrass the government. Look at the lineup of speakers. Len Stevens brings greetings from the MFL and he will speak against the anti-inflation program, followed by Grace Hartman bringing greetings from CUPE and she will speak against the anti-inflation program, followed by Ed Broadbent bringing greetings from the federal NDP and he will speak against the anti-inflation program. He is followed by the resolution opposing the position the government has already committed itself to without the premier ever having the opportunity to explain why the government did what it did."

"The premier can speak from the floor like other delegates."

"Muriel, you have high-powered speakers on the platform speaking against the government's policy and you expect the premier to defend the government from a floor microphone? Now this is what you are going to do. Schreyer is upstairs. You are going up there right now and explain to him there has been a misprint on the agenda and that he will be speaking right after Broadbent and just before the price and wage control resolution."

"I can't do that. The agenda has already been distributed."

"Muriel, if you don't immediately insert Schreyer between Broadbent and the resolution, I'm going up on that platform to explain to the delegates what you are doing to their premier and they will lynch you right here under this arch."

That afternoon, following Stevens, Hartman and Broadbent, and with the tension in the hall palpable, Schreyer spoke at length, perspiration dripping from his face, explaining that the guidelines for inflation restraint might be flawed and might fail, but they should be given a chance because the only other option was to turn the economy loose without management.

> I would hope we in this party keep an open mind on the major challenges of the day ... and avoid the Pavlovian response ... The free market economy can work equitably and effectively only if substantially modified by rational human decision-making and restraint ... There can be no sane response to the problem we face but some determined effort to check inflation ... Some say the guidelines are inequitable [and] that those in the lower income will be better off without them ... yet there has long been a great concern with inequity ... which suggests the old system without guidelines was worse ... We are engaging in rent control ... in curbing land speculation ... the rural stay option ... control of city sprawl ... full employment ... all of which are interventions in the free market ... [But] we cannot have full employment and avoid inflation in the absence of rational restraints.
>
> Inflation transfers wealth to those who already have it ... and to quote Franklin D. Roosevelt. 'The test of our progress is not in whether we add to the abundance of those who already have much, but in whether we provide for those who have little.'

It was a bravura performance. While the premier was speaking I asked a delegate, John Ryan, to reintroduce, at the appropriate moment, Green's original

resolution as a substitute, which by Robert's Rules, took precedence over the resolution on the agenda. After some passionate debate, Green's resolution was passed
by 324 to 225. The anti-government manoeuvre was defeated.

I was never forgiven by labour, nor by some party members. I had inadvertently challenged both labour and the party executive, which led to a struggle for
control of the party machinery and policy. But losing the argument at the convention did not deter those who could use the NDP Party office to make their point
and, one way or another, to break the anti-inflation guidelines.

Richard Taves was a sturdy, intense young man of medium height, with
a quiet demeanor and sudden flashes of anger. A school teacher, he had cut his
political teeth as an organizer for the Alberta NDP, which worked very closely with
the unions, and as executive assistant to the Alberta NDP's passionate leader, Grant
Notley. In April 1974, Taves was appointed provincial secretary of the Manitoba
NDP. He visualized the party influencing the government and imagined it as a
force for greater social change in the province. In Muriel Smith, who was elected
president a year later, he had an ally.

For whatever reason, things did not go well, and Taves' position as a
rallying figure gradually deteriorated. Despite having hired four organizers,
membership had dropped from 17,000 in 1973 to less than 7,000 in early 1976
(the Conservative Party boasted 21,000 at the same time). Eighteen months from
the next election the party was almost $80,000 in debt,[5] and was having little suc-
cess in raising funds or controlling spending. Constituencies threatened to stop
financial contributions to the provincial office until they saw improvements. In
January 1976, vice president Allan Cooper resigned to protest "the way finances
are being handled".

Because of my position in the Premier's Office, and as a regular attendee at
party council meetings, I became the focus of unhappy party members. Volunteers
at the party office brought me information on what they considered excessive
wages and bills being paid. Members leaned on their constituency executives,
who leaned on me to do something. I raised the issue at a council meeting in
late 1975, but Taves was safe behind a palace guard of MFL and Voice of Women
members.

At the conclusion of the annual convention on February 1, 1976, council
met briefly for the specific purpose of renewing Rick Taves' contract as provincial
secretary. I moved that it not be renewed pending a review of his work. The vote
split 18-18. Party president Muriel Smith was forced to break the tie. It was not an
easy decision. She hesitated momentarily, then said, "I will vote to maintain the
status quo. But with the condition that reappointment of the provincial secretary
be deferred for review at the next council meeting."

The item was not on the agenda when council met on March 13th and 14th
at the Norvilla Hotel. When I asked about it, Muriel Smith replied this had been

---

[5] This included the costs of the 1973 election recounts, over which Taves had no control.

decided at the last council meeting. Reminded of her pledge to discuss this at the current meeting, she pointed out that the minutes showed a vote of 19-18 in favor of reappointing Taves as provincial secretary, and announced his contract had been renewed by the executive.

I pointed out that the party constitution required that the appointment of the provincial secretary be ratified, post-facto, by council. Someone moved that council express confidence in the secretary, but others too, had heard Muriel's earlier commitment. As though a bomb had exploded, a minor argument over the activities of the party office became a vicious fight for control of the party.

Muriel Smith quickly lost control of the meeting. First VP Bob Mayer took the chair, stonewalled, lost control of the meeting, and relinquished the chair to second VP Vic Schroeder. Both Taves and the executive were now under attack. A fierce knock-down, drag-out debate ensued and "it all hung out". Costs were up, but revenue and membership down. The contract with the organizers initiated an exotic regime of benefits, severance pay and paid vacations. Taves' own contract exceeded the anti-inflation guidelines, which limited increases to $2,400 a year, by using the device of increasing per diem allowances.

It seemed that the provincial secretary and the party organizers were being used to break the wage guidlelines and to set new and unique standards for severance and vacation pay.[6]

Taves defended himself with a revealing statement: "If I am being accused of mismanaging the party office, I deny that. If I am being accused of opposing government policy [on price and wage controls], I am guilty as hell."

The motion of confidence in Rick Taves was carried 39 to 23. The uproar was tumultuous as people shouted that, by attempting to destroy Rick Taves I had destroyed myself. I responded, "It is not I, but Rick, who has been destroyed. But not by me. He has been destroyed by the clique ... that has formed around him, and by people who have encouraged him to believe he is working for the MFL instead of for the NDP. And the real tragedy is that they don't even realize what has happened. But there is one person here who does know, and that is Rick. He knows he cannot continue with almost forty per cent of council against him."

I had lost the vote. But the Fates move in mysterious ways. A month later, on April 13, 1976, the three members of the secretarial staff at the NDP provincial office struck for increased wages, a thirty-two-hour work week (down from thirty-five) and two additional annual holidays. They brought in MFL rent-a-pickets and paraded in front of the NDP office. When asked by reporters what they were striking for, they looked embarrassed and said they didn't know; that the media must ask Jean Durack, secretary of Local 342 of the Office and Professional Employees International Union.

I began receiving calls from people preparing their income tax statements who had not received receipts for their tax deductible contributions to the party

---

[6] At the 1977 NDP convention, the steelworkers proposed a paid-holidays schedule very much like that negotiated by Taves.

They had phoned the NDP office, got no answer, so they phoned me. I phoned the NDP office several times, with no answer. Then at noon on April 16th, Rick Taves answered.

"Rick, what's the problem there? I've received a number of calls from people wanting tax receipts and I have phoned your office several times in the last two days with no answer."

"Well, the girls at the office are on strike."

"I know that, but what has that to do with you? Surely you are there to keep the office operating."

"No, I've vacated the office and I'm working out of the MFL building. The only reason I'm here now is because the union gave me permission to cross the picket line to pick up my briefcase."

"What! You are the manager and you won't cross a picket line created by employees you're negotiating with? Is this your idea of office management? Rick, you're fired."

Three days later, on Monday, April 19th, the party executive, including representatives from cabinet, met and almost unanimously agreed to a "final offer" to the staff. It offered increased wages but no reduction of the thirty-five-hour week and no added holidays. On the morning of April 21st, I heard on the radio that the strike was settled and the NDP clerical staff was back at work.

Once a month the ministerial assistants met to disuss current issues and government responses to them. The party table officers had a standing invitation. Fatefully, a meeting was scheduled for the morning of April 21st. On the way, I stopped to see the premier. He was not in, but as I left a file on his desk I saw a hand-written letter. The writing was familiar. I picked it up. "The clerial staff turned down our offer ... Bob Mayer and I talked to Jean Durak and Len Stevens and the women on the picket line. Stevens found he could sell them on 34 hours.[7] They are going back to work Wed morning. We polled the Exec Tuesday night— were not able to reach several, yourself included, but had a majority." The note was signed "Muriel Smith".

I pocketed the letter, returned to my office, and quickly called five executive members. None had been polled. I was not surprised. I had learned that different party, even executive, members had different agendas. Walking to the meeting I thought to myself, Dammit! They've done it. The MFL will use the contract with the party organizers to set new standards for severance and vacations pay and they will use this contract with the three-member secretarial staff to ratchet more holidays and a shorter work week into all labour-management agreements.

At the end of the hour-long assistants meeting someone asked if it was true the NDP office clerical staff was back at work. Muriel Smith assured us they were. It gave me an opening. "Muriel, I assume the secretaries went back to work on the

---

[7] The Memorandum of Agreement, dated April 20th, agreeing to a thirty-four-hour week and two extra holidays, was signed by Jean Durack for the OPEIU and for the NDP by VP Bob Mayer, treasurer Keith Davis and by Len Stevens, who was not on the NDP executive.

basis of the final offer made by the executive Monday evening?"

"Oh yes, they accepted our offer."

"And there were no additional concessions made to them?"

"No, they went back on the basis of the executive's offer."

I took her letter from my pocket. It was a conversation stopper.

The fat was in the fire! The government caucus called a joint meeting with the party executive on the evening of April 29th. It was a gut-wrenching example of Murphy's Law and demonstrated a poignant attempt to undo the Gordian Knot tied by clashing interests within the party. In the end, we agreed that we needed better commmunication between party and caucus and resolved to appoint a joint committee, to report back within thirty days, and tabled the staff contract issue pending that report. The committee later recommended a constitutional amendment to remove the provincial secretary from the executive.

On May 14th, Jean Durack issued an intriguing statement. "We decided to give in," it stated, "for the good of the party. There is a political fight going on and the union and the girls felt we were being used … Most people are not aware of what happened and have blamed the wrong party—the union and its members."

It seemed that the staff at the NDP provincial office was being used to establish a whole new set of benefits which, presumably, would then be used as the norm in labour negotiations. By design or inadvertence, the NDP provincial council was being misled for the purpose of making the party office into a "model employer".

Several days later an emissary came to ask if Rick Taves could have three months to arrange his departure. He was a decent man torn by conflicting loyalties. He resigned on September 25, 1976, leaving the party organization in tatters and a deep well of suspicion and distrust among the various factions within the NDP, and between party and government. The unavoidable date with the sovereign electorate was approaching. But before it arrived there was to be one more catalysmic exercise in self-immolation.

XXXVII

Labours Lost

The fastest way to destroy a country's economy is to debauch its currency.
—Vladimir Lenin, 1914

Len Stevens would have agreed with Oscar Wilde—had he read Oscar Wilde—that "work is the curse of the drinking classes". He was convivial, loquacious, ready to share a drink, an anecdote, a laugh, a joke, while relaxing at a beer-laden table at the Union Centre. He was also steel-hard, alert, intelligent, profane and physical, with a tough "take no prisoners" attitude, and always bargained from strength. The sight of his lean, 5'9", whipcord-tough body, whether in dress suit or leather jacket, and handsome, eagle-eyed face in a crowd, invariably signalled something exciting was happening.

His father had been blooded during the epochal Winnipeg General Strike in 1919 (for better wages, a shorter work week, and the right to organize) and their home became a virtual union hall in Len's youth. He received his education about life—and death—in the Canadian Army overseas in World War II, and then at Manitoba Bridge in Winnipeg as a union organizer. He engaged in the wars between the Communist-dominated Mine, Mill and Smelter Workers Union and the United Steel Workers of America in the Manitoba nickel boom town of Thompson, and in the strike there against INCO. From 1968 to 1976, he was president of the Manitoba Federation of Labour, and then for ten years, until partially paralyzed, first director of the USWA Prairie Region.[1] In 1990, at a New Democratic Party convention, he was named "Mr. Labour" by former Premier of Manitoba, former Governor General of Canada, former Canadian High Commissioner to Australia, and his friend, Edward Schreyer.

---

[1]   Len Stevens died in August 2001.

The Winnipeg General Strike was a watershed in the political life of Manitoba and in the political thinking of Len Stevens. For him it marked the 'classes'; there was 'labour' and there were 'the others'. As a school trustee, city alderman and labour leader, his life was dedicated to what were once called 'radical' social values: better wages, safer working conditions, improved education and public health care. He worked with his hands to feed his family, and with his heart to organize his fellow workers into collective bargaining units to share in the growing wealth of the country, because he knew such sharing would not result from accident or altruism. On the fiftieth anniversary of the USWA he sent his fellows a message, "The same challenges face members today as … 50 years ago … There is nothing about the future that is fated. Workers must take their future into their own hands."

He recognized the power of the state to do long-term planning. "Shit," he said, "even that primitive Pharoah Ramses, whoever the hell he was, understood the basics of using the state for the collective welfare when he ordered grain stored against future drought."

He understood, with a knowledge deeper than the bastardized Keynesianism of academia, the need for the modern industrial state to modify the cyclical patterns endemic in a market economy, by injecting purchasing power into the income stream. "What's new and frightening about that? Roosevelt and Hitler applied the principles of debt financing before Keynes made it popular. And the wartime expenditures and the prosperity that followed after the bloodshed and destruction showed it is not the having but the building that creates prosperity."

He accepted capitalists, with their organizational talents and aspirations, as essential to a market economy, but had no patience with their inability—or refusal —to see the role of consumption in fuelling economic growth. He knew that in an industrial economy there could be no producers without consumers. There could be workers without capitalists, but no capitalists without workers. "That ignorant old crud, Henry Ford, knew that to become a billionaire he had to pay his wage slaves enough not to just keep them alive, but to buy cars. Yet two generations later his college-educated successors fear any increase in their employees' wages will rob them of their BMWs and three-martini lunches."

In 1972, he chided the Winnipeg Chamber of Commerce: "Chamber members and organized worker-customers should be natural allies [but] instead of being the voice of retailers and professionals, you are little Sir Echo for Big Industry. Your class solidarity has overcome your economic self-interest."

On the use of labour's ultimate weapon, the strike (though doctor's strikes are called a withdrawal of services), he was adamant.

> The only bargaining tool the labourer has is the work of his hands.
> Why must he work no matter what the conditions? Economic progress
> combines capital and labour so why when the entrepreneur withdraws
> his capital is it seen as a smart business decision, but when the worker

withholds his labour it is damned as criminal? When a capitalist is paid a million bucks he is a hero and given honorary university degrees, but when we want a living wage we are seen as killing the economy. Where in hell did this idea start that higher pay makes the rich industrious and the poor lazy?

He believed technological change and labour-saving devices not only would but should come, "otherwise we would still be living in caves", but benefits must be shared. Not only industrialists, but those who work for them, are affected by such change and if they have no voice in its application "efficiency" would be synonymous with job loss and reduced spending power for workers. "As Reuther told Ford, the computers replacing his employees won't strike but they sure as hell won't buy cars either. And the damned idiots never learn anything. They get new machinery not to improve the economy and reduce drudgery but to get rid of their workers and they expect us to accept it without protest."

But by what mechanism could eonomic benefits best be shared? A century earlier, Eugene Debs, president of the American Railway Union and founder of and perennial presidential candidate for the Socialist Party of America, and Samuel Gompers, founder and president of the American Federation of Labor, debated the role of unions. Should they be an integral part of a political party or an economic pressure group; should they demand a role in the country's decision-making institutions or be content with immediate material benefits—i.e. a shorter work week and higher wages?

"You want more money, but what do you want if you get it?" asked Debs.

"More," responded Gompers.

"And after you get more, what will you ask for?"

"More," said Gompers.

This debate between two movers and shakers at the formative stages of the modern social democratic and labour union structures illustrated the chasm between those who believed working people must speak through their own political party to shape the future of the economy, and those who wanted workers' unions to lobby for a share of it. Three decades later, in the United States, "socialism" was a four-letter word,[2] while labor unions had become a powerful force for civilized social values, and were legitimized in 1935 as an integral part of the redistributive mechanism of FDR's New Deal.

In Canada, some unionists were attracted to the Keynesian philosophy of the Depression-created Co-operative Commonwealth Federation, but most were caught up in the long post-war prosperity presided over by the Liberals. Having tasted the power of the ballot, they voted strategically, for the party that offered them most. In 1958, they voted for the Conservative Party led by John Diefenbaker, who offered "more".

---

[2] "American workers discarded Utopia for two dollars a day and roast beef," wrote S.E. Morrison in *History of the American People*, p. 574.

In 1961 that changed, theoretically. For the first time in North America, organized labour became an organic part of a political party when the Canadian Labour Congress merged with the twitching remnants of the CCF (which had been decimated in the 1958 election) to form the New Democratic Party. There were reservations among "old CCFers" who feared the "conservatism" of unions would drain the party of its social purpose, but to most it was a marriage made in heaven. It would bring together the political experience of the CCF—the government of Saskatchewan for seventeen years—with the mass votes, funding capacity and fabled organizing expertise, of labour.

It didn't work out quite that way. There was no monolith; the political commitment of the union leadership did not necessarily transmit to the membership, and even less to unorganized workers. The merger did not bring the expected bonanza of money[3] or votes and the union's superb organizing ability came at a price. It debilitated the vital core of the NDP by allowing it to relax in the belief that labour's electoral support was secure. Conversely, it gave unions the double advantage of voicing policies through the party while threatening the government at the polls, or with with job action. Labour adopted Debsian means to Gomperistic ends. In other words, they came to dominate the NDP policymaking apparatus, but continued to vote strategically. To labour's historical posture of voting to punish its enemies and support its friends was added a third reason for voting—to punish its political partners.[4]

Furthermore, unions were becoming less international and more insular, dragging the NDP with them. They were seeing the nation state not as an instrument to improve the lives of all citizens, but to create a "sheltered workshop" for themselves. This increased consumer prices and threatened to create a siege-model economy, selling fewer and fewer goods to a smaller and smaller market at higher and higher prices. And they saw public ownership not as instrument of public policy and an experiment in social democracy, but as a 'soft touch', offering above average pay, good working conditions, a lifetime job, and assured pensions. 'Crown corporation' became synonymous with 'bloated payroll'.

Like Gompers, they wanted "more". And they wanted it now: more statutory holidays; higher wages; shorter work weeks with the same take-home pay; extra-contract cost of living allowances (COLA); superior pensions; expanding health benefits; flexible working hours; paid educational leave to learn what they were supposed to know when hired; merit pay whether deserved or not; paid personal holidays, remoteness pay; payment for unused sick leave; 'catch up' wage increases for real or imagined past disadvantages or specious comparisons with other

---

[3] Union contributions of money and manpower were generous in elections, but otherwise minimal. Of NDP budgets of $419,865 (1975) and $390,000 (1976) about $6,430 and $6,500 came from unions. Only about ten per cent of union members were members of the NDP.

[4] In 1995, labour killed Bob Rae's NDP government in Ontario. In 1999, union-dominated Oshawa voted for anti-union Mike Harris.

jusrisdictions.[5] They wanted compulsory union dues checkoff, union (closed) shops, the right to refuse to handle 'hot' goods from a struck plant, the unconditional right to strike, free collective bargaining but government intervention if it failed, and easier rules for unionization.

And, of course, why not? If they could not get these from a 'friendly' government, who would they get it from?

Despite the political commitment of Stevens and other powerful labour leaders, there were periodic, if usually muted, suggestions for reevaluation of the labour-NDP relationship. And despite pride felt in the NDP that we were the chosen instrument of the working people of Canada, there were disillusionments.

Manitoba Hydro was engaged in a massive development on the Nelson River and the premier was the minister for Hydro. I received calls from men working there, complaining about food and facilities—while simultaneously receiving calls from their wives complaining that we were treating their men so well they did not come home on weekends. So I flew to Gillam, the permanent town that housed the work crews. The housing facilities were neat, clean, roomy, comfortable trailers complete with television. The mess hall seemed the size of a football field and down its middle stretched an endless table laden with food to please every palate or whim: beef, fowl, pork, mutton, fish, fresh vegetables flown in from California that morning, followed by ambrosial desserts. It was a banquet at which one could gorge and go back for more.

No one eats like that at home. And these guys were complaining!

Twenty years earlier, I had spent the winter with three other men at a logging camp in the Duck Mountains in a ten-by-fourteen-foot trailer in which we lived, ate and slept. Our bread and meat was stored in snowbanks and we cooked our meals on a tin stove, which also served to heat the shack and invariably went out during the night, leaving icicles dangling from the ceiling in the morning. It was unfair to make such comparisons perhaps, but such were my perceptions. I was the wrong person to complain to.

ART COULTER, the soft-spoken, courtly, long-time executive secretary of the MFL, phoned one day. "I want to speak with the premier."

"He's out of town but can I help you?"

"I just got a complaint from Gillam. Hydro moved 200 men from there to the site at Long Spruce in open trucks in the rain."

"I'll call Hydro to inquire and get back to you."

"There is no need to call Hydro. I've just told you what they did. I want to know what you are going to do about it?"

---

[5]   There was no consideration for the fact that house prices in Toronto and Vancouver were three times those of Winnipeg, and everything (car insurance, utilities, groceries) cost more.

"I'm going to call Hydro to get their version." I called Hydro, "Mr. Bateman, I have a complaint that you moved 200 men from one site to another on the Nelson in the rain in open trucks."

"No. We moved the men, but they were in buses."

I phoned Coulter, "Art. Bateman tells me the men were moved in buses."

"Well, yes, but they moved the luggage in open trucks."

For the past twenty years I had farmed and built apartment blocks, occupations in which, when something was broke, one fixed it. "Art. Are you telling me you had 200 men up there and no one had the brains or the energy to throw a tarp over the damned luggage?

"I don't like your attitude. I'm going to report you to the minister of Labour."

GEORGE SMITH was business agent for the International Union of Operating Engineers, which represented maintenance workers who struck the Health Sciences Centre in February 1976. Smith responded to the hospital's offer with "Obviously officials at the HSC are not concerned with patient care or they wouldn't have made such a ridiculous offer."[6] Since the HSC was under anti-inflation strictures, I saw it as a gratuitous insult.[7] We were colleagues on the Riel NDP constituency executive committee and at a meeting I told him I thought his position was unfair. "George, what is going to happen to patients in the hospital?"

"The government and administration will take care of them."

"You have a happy situation. You can walk off the job and blackmail the government into giving you what you want and know the government will look after the patients when you abandon them. I'm fed up with government being forced to assume other people's responsibilites. I have news for you. Next time you people walk out we will too and leave the patients to cope as best they can."

"But someone may die!"

"That's right. And one of them might be your mother."

"That's not fair."

THE CANADIAN ASSOCIATION of Industrial, Mechanical and Allied Workers Union (CAIMAW) was of the new genre of the 'national' Canadian unions that had broken with international unionism. It was part of the 1970s movement that demanded enhanced Canadian (as opposed to foreign) ownership of industry, more worker control, and employee input in management decisions, particularly

[6] *Winnipeg Tribune*, February 14, 1976.

[7] The Anti-Inflation Board rolled a twenty-three per cent increase back to eight per cent.

in crown corporations. Since the Schreyer government was favourable to all this, we believed we had earned the support of CAIMAW.

Flyer Bus became a publicly owned company when a local bus manufacturer borrowed money from the Manitoba Development Corporation and could not repay. The MDC took possession of it to protect the taxpayer's investment, just as a private lender would have done. It appointed a board of directors, which appointed the management of the firm. Electric trolley and diesel transit buses continued to be built and Flyer developed a continent-wide market. In October 1974, the union at Flyer struck.

That union was CAIMAW, which immediately began presssuring the government for a settlement. We explained that, just as in a private corporation, the union must negotiate with the management and the board of directors. Instead, CAIMAW decided to embarrass the government; its members picketed the homes of Premier Schreyer, Labour Minister Russell Paulley and Sidney Green, the minister responsible for the MDC, and they demonstrated in front of The Ledge carrying anti-NDP signs. [8]

A month after the strike began, I was visited by CAIMAW regional representative, Pat McEvoy, and three of his men. "We want to settle this," they told me. "It is embarrassing to strike a public plant. There are several issues we can fight out with the board, but there are two imperatives we must have before we can go farther and these can be decided only by the government."

"Well, I'm glad you came. This is an embarrassment for us also. The plant is not only publicly owned but is in the constituency of the minister of Labour, which really does not look good politically. So what are your two imperatives?"

"First, we want one of our people to attend board meetings."

"Done. We have always believed workers in publicly owned plants should have some voice in management. [9] Name your man and we will appoint him to the board. [10]

"We-e-ell, we just want someone to attend board meetings."

"Okay. Name your representative and we'll put him on the board."

"No. We don't want our person on the board. We want someone at the board meetings."

---

[8] Twenty years later, at a meeting, I related our problems with the unions. Allan Blakeney, former NDP premier of Saskatchewan, said his government had little trouble with private sector unions, who had experience at bargaining and knew there was a bottom line beyond which the plant was not viable. But public sector unions "think the Treasury is bottomless. And when they do not get what they want, they do not attack the board of the public corporation that employs them, or the government, they attack the NDP."

[9] Productivity depends not only on the workers, but on how the work is organized for them. We wanted employees of publicly owned enterprises to consider it their plant, and believed that any improvement in productivity redounds to their benefit.

[10] In 1974, Premier Dave Barrett's NDP government in BC acquired Kootenay Forest Products and appointed two members of the IWA to the board. Two years later, company president Jack Sigalet praised the experiment in industrial democracy. "It's the man on the job who can tell you how to run it. Unless he's being listened to, you haven't got a team." *Winnipeg Tribune*, November 3, 1976.

It took a moment to comprehend. "Oh! I see. You want a spy at the board meetings so he can run to the *Free Press* next day and have some fun at our expense. That won't work. When you are ready to take responsibility for management decisions, name your man and we will put him on the board. Until then there is nothing further to disusss on that subject. What is your other imperative?"

"We want a profit-sharing plan."

"Good. We have always believed workers in publicly owned plants should share in profits. There is one problem. Flyer lost about $4 million last year. Do you also want to share in the losses?"

They quietly demurred. A moment passed. "Let me make a counter-proposal. We will pay you a production bonus. We set a norm and pay extra for additional output. If the norm is five buses a week and you produce six, we pay a bonus."

"No! We don't want anyone telling us how hard to work."

"But I am not telling you how hard to work. You people decide that. I am just saying if you produce more you get paid more."

"No!"

There was a long, embarrassed silence while we all stared at the floor and shuffled our feet. Then, I said, "Gentlemen, I have a solution. It seems to me you came here to tell us we don't know how to operate that plant. You may have a point. I infer that means you do. I've always believed a business is operated best by its owners. So here is a proposition. We will sell the plant to the employees and you operate it."

"Oh, that would be wonderful. But we can't afford to buy it."

"We will make it affordable. We will sell you the plant for a dollar. And so you won't suffer from our bad management, we will throw in a subsidy of the amount we lost last year, about $4 million, for the next two years."

They put on their coats and left without a word.[11] I did not see them again but they tried one more ploy; they went political. NDP candidate Laurent Desjardins had been defeated in St. Boniface in the 1973 election. The election was controverted and the by-election was set for December 20, 1974. CAIMAW sent a letter to Premier Schreyer and to Opposition Leader Sidney Spivak stating that their members in St. Boniface would vote for the party that gave them "more". They circulated the letter to every household in the constituency. Spivak replied that he would suppport their demands. Schreyer replied that he believed the board offer was fair, but if they wanted the key to the Treasury, "You should vote for Mr. Spivak." We won the by-election. CAIMAW ended its strike.

IN MID-1974, Labour Minister Russ Paulley came to cabinet with an unusual request. Costs had increased more rapidly than anyone had expected during the

---

[11] In 1991, helped by Bob Rae's NDP government in Ontario, the employees became the major shareholders of ailing Algoma Steel in Sault Ste. Marie—and then reduced their own wages by $3 an hour.

three-year term of the current contract and would cabinet agree to give each civil servant increased pay, extra-contractual, of $25 a month, for a cost to the government of $2.7 million? Cabinet agreed and the word was sent. The president of the Manitoba Government Employees Association replied that this was not enough; they wanted $53 a month.

In his first five years as minister of Labour, Paulley worked tirelessly to improve the lot of working people. He doubled the minimum wage, improved procedures for collecting unpaid wages, provided for seven paid holidays, reduced the work week to forty hours, created a Women's Bureau, provided maternity leave and job protection during leave, provided for three weeks vacation after five years, extended the period of notice of termination, enacted a new Tradesman's Qualificaton Act, provided more inspectors to enforce labor laws, enacted provisions to reopen negotiations during the term of an agreement, where technological changes had a significant impact. He improved the Workers Compensation Act to double widows' allowances, increase orphaned children's allowances, doubled minimum compensation for permanent disability, and increased the wage ceiling for compensation claims. In 1972, he had amended the Labour Relations Act to include professional employees and to greatly facilitate unionization. Also, true to a long-time personal conviction, he freed civil servants to engage in political activities like any other citizen.

He gained nothing. When the 1972 wage offer did not please the MGEA, they demanded an arbitration board, whose ruling would be final, and imported an Alberta negotiator. When they were unhappy with the unanimous award, they demonstrated at The Ledge. In 1974, when the government gave them a bonus, gratis, they wanted more. Paulley replied, "If you are unhappy with it, please return it. The taxpayers will enjoy keeping it."

He suggested their demonstrations should not be at The Ledge, but at the office of their hand-picked negotiator, who had agreed to the award.

IN 1975, they got their revenge. The MGEA, the largest union in Manitoba, demanded astronomical wage increases—as though public-sector employees should be allowed to ignore economic reality and the relationship of wages to productivity—and threatened strikes,[12] arguing that while the Act did not allow strikes, it did not disallow strikes. Paulley, a former union steward, was in a schizoid position; he was both a friend of labour who firmly believed in their right to withhold their work, and 'chairman of the board', required to keep a vital plant—the government—operating.

[12] In 1976, the MGEA demanded, depending on the unit, a fifteen per cent pay increase, a 36-hour week, education leave with pay, flexible work hours, clothing for non-uniformed persons, a $4 shift premium, a $4-a-day weekend bonus, a tool allowance, sabbatical leave, career development, and a full day's pay for any part worked. In 1977, they threatened to vote against the government unless given the right to strike. That year, Alberta outlawed civil service strikes.

The spectre of a civil service strike creates a conundrum for any government, but a nightmare for one that is worker-oriented. So what to do? We could get a court to order them back to work, but what if they defied it, even in the face of being jailed? The time-honoured response to such situations was to have the legislature enact a law forcing them back to work. But we did not want to do that, not just because we sympathized with working people, but because we considered it ineffective.

Sidney Green explained, "Freedom breeds excellence but compulsion breeds mediocrity. If we legislate people back to work, productivity will collapse and we will be passing legislation forcing people to work harder."

We could let them walk out and shut down the government. But party president Muriel Smith demurred, "No, we can't do that. The welfare cheques must go out."

That left one option; in the event of a civil service strike we would hire substitute labour. The civil servants could walk off their jobs, but they could not shut down the government.

The MGEA demands were settled by negotiation, but the government had given notice it would, if necessary, take a stand inimical to what labour saw as a core issue; if government could hire strike-breakers, why not private employers? We were to pay a price in the 1977 election. Meanwhile, there was another hurdle. Something had gone wrong in the economy.

Historically, employment and inflation moved in tandem; rising prices accompany full employment. Now we had increasing costs but decreasing employment. We had both price inflation and economic stagnation—a unique phenomenon not previously experienced. Swedish economist Gunnar Myrdal named it "stagflation".[13]

Wages rose with no commensurate productivity increase. Prices were driven up by buyers fearing higher costs tomorrow. Those with bargaining strength kept their relative positions with more income. The 13,000-member MGEA demanded a one-year wage increase averaging fifty-three per cent. Nurses wanted thirty-two to thirty-six per cent plus signing bonuses. The building trades demanded a two-year increase of eighty per cent. University of Manitoba administrative staff demanded a twenty-five per cent increase or threatened to strike during spring exams. Strikes became a contagion, fuelling inflation by reducing supply, which increased prices, which increased production costs, which increased unemployment.

Inflation hurts the helpless: pensioners; those on fixed incomes; the frugal who saw the value of their savings depreciate daily. Inflation increases the income gap by moving wealth from the poor to the rich. Lenin had remarked sixty years earlier, "No economy is so bad that someone does not benefit from it," and the

---

[13] From 1974 to 1978 unemployment doubled, and so did inflation. From 1969 to 1977 inclusive, inflation increased sixty-five points, equal to the increase in the fifty-five years between 1914 and 1969.

beneficiaries of inflation were those able to take advantage of it. Scandalous profits were ripped off, with no contribution to the economy, by those flipping properties to others who aspired to flip them again.[14] Like a fire fed by oxygen drawn into its vortex, inflation fuelled an inflationary psychology, which fuelled more inflation.[15]

On Thanksgiving evening in 1975, Prime Minister Trudeau delivered his "turkey". In the 1974 federal election Conservative Leader Robert Stanfield had proposed anti-inflation price and wage controls. Trudeau had vigorously opposed them, and won the election. Eighteen months later, he reversed his position. He explained:

> There were two different sets of circumstances. In 1974, our inflation was externally caused by the OPEC oil price shocks, but then it became created internally by our own expectations. People said: 'Prices are going to go up so I must increase my prices before I sell my goods,' or 'I must demand higher wages before I sign my contract.' Labour, business, and private savers were all doing it: 'Interest is going up so I'll hold my money for higher rates.' When people expect higher prices, wages and interest, you get inflation … We asked labour and business leaders for voluntary restraint but didn't get far.
>
> By the fall of 1975, we had three options. One was to continue exhorting business and labour to reduce expectations voluntarily, but inflation had leaped to 10.8 per cent and could get out of control. The second was to induce a recession by imposing draconian monetary measures, but unemployment was already at seven per cent and costs of a policy-induced recession would be too high. The third alternative was wage-price controls."[16]

Ottawa announced the program and an anti-inflation board to roll back prices and wages if they went beyond acceptable limits. This applied to federal employees, companies with more than 500 employees, and construction firms with more than twenty employees.

A year earlier, the provinces had jointly petitioned Trudeau to do something about inflation. He now invited them to join the program and apply the anti-inflation guidelines to the provincial sector, particularly provincial employees and rents. All did except Saskatchewan, which established its own program.[17]

To join or not to join, that was the question! The Manitoba caucus and

---

[14] "Gonzo capitalists" was what Peter Newman called them. *The Canadian Establishment.*

[15] Inflation has both economic and political consequences. Before 1919, the German currency was valued at about four marks to the US dollar. The post-WWI demand for reparations by the Allies caused the German government to crank up the printing presses. By October 1924, the Reichsmark was about four billion to the US dollar, literally not worth the paper it was printed on. The frugal German middle class was destroyed and became easy prey for the Nazis.

[16] P.E. Trudeau, *Memoirs.*

[17] It did not help them economically or politically. In 1982, the Saskatchewan NDP government was humiliatingly defeated.

cabinet agonized, but the options were stark; they could ignore reality, impose their own controls, or cooperate with Ottawa. There were no illusions—but no alternatives either. Premier Schreyer denounced the "lunacy" of inflation and announced Manitoba would join the price and wage control program so long as these were "fairly and equitably administered".

Criticism from his labour partners was fierce and sustained. Labour again, in the interests of the general economy, was asked to swallow the bitter gall. In the past half-century workers had, with great expenditures of money and energy, and even blood, formed unions. They no longer came to the bargaining table as mendicants but as a powerful social, economic and political force. Ironically, it was their power that condemned them. As Trudeau explained, "Enforcement of the controls will be concentrated on those who, until tonight, have the power to get what they want."

One could weep for workers! Instead of holding down prices and allowing wages to adjust, the government was holding down wages and hoping prices would adjust. Labour had organized to make themselves immune to the vagaries of marketplace and government, but were now told they must not use their power, and by one of their own yet. To them the cure was too strong for the disease.

Len Stevens was a founding member of the NDP and a good friend of the Schreyer government. He had worked prodigiously to get it elected, was active at both local and executive levels, and used his influence with the unions to protect and defend it, while maintaining friendly pressure to respond to labour interests. But in the crunch, when views differed, he expected government to accept those of labour who, after all, were its friends. His mind strained for accommodation with his friends in government but his heart was with the worker's movement. He was a union man.

And now he was livid. "They are going to apply the law fairly and equitably? Bullshit! It might look that way on paper, but it won't be in practice.[18] Like some frigging Frenchman said, the law is equitable in allowing both rich and poor to sleep under bridges, but how bloody many rich do we find there."[19]

The MFL made its adamant opposition clear to the Manitoba government in a brief replete with incendiary terms: "political expediency"; "totalitarian government"; "destruction of civil liberties"; "pursuit of power"; "nefarious scheme". In August 1976, the MGEA asked the MFL to divorce itself from the NDP.

The Government of Manitoba saw the inflation control program as an instrument for "economic management", long at the core of democratic socialism. Government was the only force capable of standing guard when inflation came like a thief in the night to rob the weakest members of society of their hard-won gains. And they feared the alternative—demands that inflation be controlled by

---

[18] In January 1977, federal Finance Minister Donald Macdonald told a Canadian Club audience that profit restraints should be loosened.

[19] "The law, in its equitable majesty, forbids the nobleman and the beggarman to sleep under bridges." Anatole France, 1896.

the twin barbarities of high interest and high unemployment.

The fear proved real. In the 1980s, Bank of Canada Governor John Crowe, inspired by "monetarist" Milton Friedman, pushed the bank rate to twenty per cent and unemployment soared to the highest it had been since the 1930s.

Meanwhile labour, the other half of the NDP, firmly believed that, even with the best will and most rigorous application, it would prove much easier to control wages than prices and profits. And, of course, they were right. CAW President Bob White later estimated that "wage controls cost the Canada's labour force about $20 billion [over the three-year period] while corporate profits rose 58.3 per cent in 1978." [20]

The Vancouver Sun reported that "Edgar Kaiser took a pay increase of $60,363 while employees at his Sparwood mine were limited [by the price and wage control program] to a six-percent increase on their $7 hourly wage." [21]

The Manitoba government's action was fiercely opposed by all major provincial and national unions, [22] by the federal NDP, and by the executive of the Manitoba NDP. On November 18, 1975, Manitoba NDP President Muriel Smith wrote to caucus members, "Trudeau's guidelines [show] the difference between the Liberals and the NDP ... Corporation profits increased from $2,622 million in 1972 to $4,848 million in 1974, but average income earner's share of the GNP is decreasing ... If profits and prices are controlled, wages and salaries will follow."

The government held its course. Organized labour responded with a spate of walkouts, illegal strikes, "study sessions", "holidays" and "days of protest". It also made an insidious attempt to embarrass its political partner, the NDP government, by manipulating the Manitoba NDP party convention.

On September 6, 1977, Premier Schreyer called an election for October 11th. During the campaign, every morning, CUPE President Grace Hartman phoned to say she had eight organizers for us, but she would not give them to us until Schreyer promised to take Manitoba out of the control program the day after the election.

Labour wanted to be an organic part of a political party, but was not prepared to think politically or to subject itself to the discipline inherent in governing. Protesting was easier. [23]

In 1930, German Chancellor Heinrich Bruening, wrestling with the Depression and having to choose between lower benefits for workers or no benefits at all, reduced unemployment payments. The trade unions withdrew their support from his administration. In the ensuing election the Nazi Party surged

---

[20] *Hard Bargains, My Life on the Line*, p. 187.

[21] Reprinted in the *Winnipeg Free Press*, May 16, 1977.

[22] In 1979, CUPE president Grace Hartman told her annual convention delgates, "Government is the enemy."

[23] Former Ontario Premier Bob Rae wrote that in 1993, when he decided to reduce public sector wages to meet the projected $17 billion deficit, CLC President Bob White argued that "Why can't Ontario just do like the Reichmans do and declare bankruptcy?" *From Protest to Power*, p. 242.

upward and two years later Hitler was Chancellor of Germany. In 1979, the British trade union leadership destroyed the Labour government of James Callaghan and Britain got Margaret Thatcher. In Canada, labour turned against the NDP governments of Dave Barrett, Ed Schreyer, Allan Blakeney and Bob Rae. In their place, they got the Conservative governments of Bill Bennett, Sterling Lyon, Grant Devine and Mike Harris.

In addition to Manitoba's plethora of internal problems and programs, Premier Schreyer was also the province's point man on interprovincial issues. As did his predecessors and successors, he met annually with his provincial counterparts to discuss common goals and settle interprovincial disputes. In 1972, the meeting was in Halifax, where this portrait was taken. Seated on either side of Nova Scotia's Lieutenant Governor Dr. Clarence Gosse, are (from left) Alberta's Peter Lougheed, Alexander Campbell of P.E.I., Newfoundland's Frank Moores, Nova Scotia's Gerald Regan, Bill Davis of Ontario, Dr. Gosse, Robert Bourassa of Québec, New Brunswick's Richard Hatfield, Manitoba's Ed Schreyer, Allan Blakeney of Saskatchewan and, on the far right, representing British Columbia, where W.A.C Bennett's Social Credit Party had just lost to Dave Barrett's NDP, Lawrie Wallace, B.C. deputy minister of Intergovernmental Affairs.

Nova Scotia Communications & Information Centre

XXXVIII

Taxation and Turmoil

Taxes are not just a way of raising revenue, they are an instrument of social policy.
—Baron de Montesqieu, 1748

Progressive Conservatives and Liberals on one hand, and New Democrats on the other, had common goals: economic prosperity and quality of life. But their paths to them were quite different.

The capitalist philosophy of economics holds that those with surplus capital will invest it in building factories, which will create jobs, produce goods and make more profits, which will be reinvested, which will grow the gross domestic product and produce more capital for investment and jobs. Therefore the taxation system should be biased toward providing concessions to entrepreneurs so they can accumulate more capital to invest.

In 1986, Michael Wilson, minister of Finance in the Progressive Conservative government of Prime Minister Brian Mulroney, blamed the lack of growth in the Canadian economy on "an acute shortage of wealthy" Canadians. Conversely, Harvard Economics philosopher John Kenneth Galbraith described that as "Reaganesque" economics, which assumed that "if you feed enough oats to the horses, some will pass through for the sparrows."

The social democratic philosophy of the NDP was influenced by its forebear, the Depression-created Co-operative Commonwealth Federation, and by the preeminent economist of the twentieth century, John Maynard Keynes, who had written in 1936 that "The outstanding faults of our economic society are its failure to provide for full employment and its arbitrary and inequitable distribution of wealth and income." [1]

---

[1] *The General Theory of Employment, Interest and Money,* 1936.

Manitoba's NDP government believed that a prosperous economy is created by people buying goods, but felt that a growing GDP is not a good barometer of prosperity unless it is distributed throughout the economy.[2] The NDP believed that in a modern economy capital is the lifeblood of the system, that it must flow or the economy would die, and that it flows best if fed in at the bottom to serve the twin objectives of economic growth and social equity.

A hoary question in university Economics 101 asks: "If you want to establish an industry but have limited funds, would you use it to build a factory in the middle of the forest or to build a road to where the factory would be?" The conventional answer is that, if a factory is built and produces something consumers want, they will cut a road to the factory. The NDP believed that, in a mature economy, if the consumer has purchasing power, some enterprising individual will find a way to build a factory to satisfy the market. This meant a judicious mix of income transfers to maintain consumer purchasing power, while leaving enough capital to the producers to build the factory.

Experience showed that tax concessions to industry meant demands for more tax concessions, and consequent subsidy wars, until workers were paying taxes to buy their own jobs.[3] The NDP knew that in a federal political system like Canada's, these demands would be accompanied by threats to move elsewhere, and that some jurisdiction would always be rich enough—or desperate enough—to offer more no matter what the cost. The experience of the Minnedosa Distillery and the CFI plant at The Pas, where towns almost bankrupted themselves in that process, impelled the NDP government to enact laws in 1970 prohibiting municipalities from waiving taxes to attract industry. They knew that an entrepreneur made wealthy by tax concessions and subsidies did not necessarily reinvest in productive enterprise, at least not where it was most needed. And they knew the wealthier an entrepreneur became the more independent and mobile he became and the more likely he was to move his money to an offshore tax haven.

In 1973, federal Finance Minister John Turner enacted tax cuts, adjuring companies to use the extra money to expand and create jobs. Six months later he noted: "Corporation profits are up 30% and dividends are 12% ahead of 1972 ... [We are] wondering if manufacturers and processors are properly using the tax concessions."[4]

When President George W. Bush proposed massive across-the-board tax cuts to stimulate the American economy, a senior economist at the Brookings Institute, William Gale, wrote that this would benefit mostly the rich with little benefit to the economy:

---

[2] In 1976, Kuwait has the world's highest per capita GNP—$11,365, vs. second-place Sweden at $8,420 and ninth-place Canada at $6,060, but how did that distribute as personal income?

[3] In Mexico, with low taxes and huge concessions to industry, many tourist industry workers buy their jobs to get the tips.

[4] *Winnipeg Free Press,* August 21, 1973.

Tax cuts in general are not the best way to fight economic downturns ... To stimulate the economy the tax cuts should go to low- and middle-income households. These are more likely to spend the funds and to be the people who lose their jobs in a downturn. In contrast, every reasonable analysis shows that the vast part of the benefits from the president's proposal would go to the highest-income households, [which] are more likely to hoard them ... A tax cut for lower- and middle-income households [would be] more effective at stimulating the economy in the short run, fairer and more fiscally responsible, and leave resources available for other policy initiatives.[5]

Twenty-five years earlier, John Bulloch, president of the Canadian Federation of Independent Business, told a press conference that encouraging business investment through tax writeoffs cannot stimulate the economy, because plants are operating at three-quarter speed due to low demand for goods, and personal tax cuts are useless because the resulting increase in personal income would be saved or spent on imported goods. "The emphasis on capital incentives has been wrong and the Canadian people have been had ... I'm astounded by businessmen asking for more capital incentives. It makes one feel the dinosaurs are planning the animal kingdom in this country."[6]

Five years before that the Schreyer government's Planning and Priorities Committee 'think tank' had written in a major study,

Tax concessions to the well-off are paid for by lower-income earners, with no appreciable benefits. Incentives ... are biased to favour capital intensive industries and accelerate the rate of technological unemployment,[7] lead to increased foreign ownership, and exploitation and exportation of our natural resources. Raw material exports have lower labour content than manufactured exports and their increased exportation pushes up our exchange rate, depresses aggregate demand, hurts manufacturing industries, and creates instability in an already erratic investment cycle ... A more equitable tax system would transfer income from the well off, individual or corporate, to lower-income groups. This would provide steady stimulus to consumer spending, which should enable firms to invest.[8]

A society consists of more than just an economy dedicated to the production of material goods. The NDP believed the economy was made for man, not

[5] Ibid., March 20, 2001.
[6] Ibid., September 22, 1977.
[7] In 1982, Remi de Roo, of the Conference of Catholic Bishops, referred to this phenomenon as the creation of "techno-peasants".
[8] Province of Manitoba, Guidelines for the Seventies, March 1973.

man for the economy, and that it must be accompanied by social policy, which must be financed by a system of progressive taxation based on the ability to pay.

Any mention of "social policy" invariably raises the accusation that the NDP is promoting the "welfare state". In fact, the opposite was true.[9] The modern welfare system began when the people of France guillotined their establishment and the members of the British establishment feared they might be next. Therefore, in 1797, they devised the "Speenhamland System" requiring government to pay workers the difference between wages received and what they needed so they need not starve or steal. Employers immediately reduced wages and let the taxpayers pay the difference between wages and needs. In 1975, federal Postmaster—General Bryce Mackasey told the Canadian Daily Newspaper Publishers Association: "The defenders of the [capitalist] faith forget that the modern welfare system grew on corporate refusal to pay the social costs of its growth."

Manitoba's NDP government sought to shrink the "welfare state" by requiring the economy to pay its way. That needed a shift of taxation from property to income, and from low-income to high-income earners. The underlying philosophy was that no one becomes wealthy without the help of many others, that the costs of a society should be paid by those using most of its resources, and that the greater the gap between rich and poor the less secure the society. Ninety years earlier, when German Chancellor Bismarck introduced Europe's first social program, he argued that this was needed "to give all Germans a stake in the state".

The first step toward shifting the costs of society from welfare to wages was to increase the minimum wage. This went from $1.25 per hour in 1969 to $2.95 in 1977.

Abolition of the Medicare premium transferred approximately $54 million annually from an individual premium tax to general revenues. This shifted a major social cost to one's ability to pay, and left more money with low-income groups, which they could use to could bolster the economy with spending at the cash register. This transfer principle was continued with the introduction, in 1974, of a universal pharmacare program with eighty per cent of the costs of prescription drugs in excess of $50 per person paid out of general revenues.

The Property Tax Credit Plan signified the NDP government's determination to shift the tax load from property to income, and to maintain the ability-to-pay principle. It was introduced in the 1974 budget (the sixth balanced budget), which was increased each year as revenue permitted. In the 1976–1977 fiscal year it reached a range of up to $375, for a total property tax rebate of approximately $100 million. This relieved seventy-eighty per cent of pensioners of school taxes and removed thirty per cent from the tax rolls entirely. Conservative Don Craik damned the program as "a flimsy piece of tax tinkering" and Liberal Paul Marion

---

[9] In a 1975 interview, Premier Schreyer stated, "It has never been the socialist philosophy that welfare is a one-way street. It is an ad hoc expediency of the old line parties. To me, receipt of welfare carries the reciprocal obligation to work."

called it "a very cheap vote-buying technique", but the *Winnipeg Free Press* editorialized that "The NDP government's policy of giving property tax rebates to Manitobans ... is nice for the individual citizens."[10]

Municipalities are responsible for local improvements, which are paid from property taxes, but the government reduced this burden, and shifted it to general revenues, by increasing unconditional grants to municipalities from $3 per capita in 1970 to $22 per capita in 1977; giving municipalities a portion of growth taxes; paying half the capital cost of transit buses; providing loans to municipalities for public works and forgiving the labour portion, and increasing school foundation grants by another $23 million.[11] This meant the province was paying about seventy-five per cent of education costs compared with fifty per cent in 1969. In 1976, the chairman of the Manitoba Association of School Trustees objected to any further increase on the grounds that would rob local school boards of their rationale for pronouncing on education policy.

"Taxes are the price of civilization," wrote poet and chief justice of the United States Supreme Court, Oliver Wendell Holmes. The state must have revenue to provide the services a civilized society requires, and the level and mix of these sources of revenue are reflected in the annual budget. But the budget must also deal with things that go bump in the night.

In 1975-76, Premier Schreyer was his own minister of Finance and faced the quadruple and interrelated scourges of prospective energy shortages, rising unemployment, inflation created increases in program costs, and decreasing revenue to government.

His spending estimates showed sixty-two per cent earmarked for education, health and social services (hospital bed costs had risen twenty per cent in the past year), and spending for agriculture, (in trouble again), up by $16.7 million. The new money needed led to increases in 'sin' taxes (such as liquor and tobacco), a new surtax of two per cent on family income in excess of $25,000 (affecting three per cent of Manitobans, the increase worked out to $1 on an income of $25,000 and $2,655 on $100,000) and on the taxable profits of corporations.

Associate editor Harry Mardon of *The Winnipeg Tribune* objected to the increased spending, though he admitted that "Manitoba will continue to be the second-lowest province in terms of per capita government expenditures."[12] Conservative leader Sterling Lyon said that, instead of increasing taxes, the government should "cut out the fat". A third critic of increased spending was Great West Life Assurance president James Burns, who had earlier asked the Government of Manitoba to spend money on the Jets.

To deal with corporations escaping taxes by paying out larger than normal

---

[10] March 29, 1974.

[11] This allowed Winnipeg City Council to actually reduce property taxes in one-third of the city's school divisions—preparatory to the 1977 city council elections.

[12] *Winnipeg Tribune*, April 15, 1976

shareholder dividends, a new tax was introduced, not on profits but on worth. This was one-fifth of one per cent on the paid-up capital in excess of $100,000 and affected about twenty per cent or 1,200 corporations in Manitoba. Harry Mardon called this an "abhorrent tax",[13] though it was only half that imposed by Ontario.

To encourage conservation of non-renewable energy, the tax on motive fuels was increased and car registration changed from wheel-base to weight. This reduced the fee on a 1968 six-cylinder Plymouth but quadrupled that on a 1974 Lincoln. The president of Ford Canada strongly objected to the "big car" tax.[14]

Despite estimated new revenues of $39 million, there was a gap between revenue and expenditures. To maintain programs while not risking dampening the economy or inviting a backlash with still higher taxes, the government estimated budgetary overspending of $12.8 million—its first budgeted deficit. A deficit always gives a minister of Finance heart palpitations, but it was accepted. The *Winnipeg Free Press* editorialized, "The premier appears to have taken a middle course [between tax increases and spending reductions]. The average Manitoba taxpayer will probably experience some relief that taxes did not go as high as he felt they might."[15]

The Winnipeg Tribune editorialized, "We have to say this province is in generally good economic health compared to some other jurisdictions, that the premier as Finance minister appears to be genuinely seeking restraint, and that his proposals won't generate much anger among realists. And that, these days, is quite a feat."[16]

Manitoba Federation of Labour executive secretary Art Coulter proclaimed, "We can't expect much better, given the restraints."

Columnist Val Werier showed that a Manitoba family of four with an income of $8,225, paid taxes (federal and provincial income taxes and Medicare premiums) of $56 compared with $598 in Ontario.[17]

The *Toronto Globe and Mail* reported that the average income earner was paying less "unavoidable" taxes and payments to the government in Manitoba than in any other province.[18]

The Financial Times published a survey showing that for those on lower incomes, Manitoba taxes—considering all forms of taxation—were the lowest in Canada.[19]

Half of budget making consists of raising revenue, and the other half of

---

[13] *Ibid.*

[14] *Ibid.*, April 29, 1976. We discovered that the auto makers had shrunk the wheel base, but maintained the weight and horse power.

[15] *Winnipeg Free Press*, April 14, 1976.

[16] *Winnipeg Tribune*, April 14, 1976.

[17] *Ibid.*, April 28, 1976.

[18] April 23, 1976.

[19] August 23, 1976.

controlling spending. For seven years, the lines showing revenue and expenditure paralleled each other on the graphs, tending slowly upward, but in tandem. In 1976, they began to diverge. The expenditure line continued its easy upward curve but the revenue line began to fall off. Something unanticipated was happening out there. Inflation was driving up costs, but growth taxes were slowing down. The red lights were flashing.

Cabinet wrestled with the problem and the premier sent a memo to all departments; initial budgetary spending estimates (not counting inflation or new programs) must be cut and the civil service reduced. Spending was trimmed and in four months the civil service was reduced[20] by 410 persons solely by attrition, with no layoffs. Then a minister insisted he must hire a man whose talents were unique to Manitoba and crucial to his department. The dam was broken. Other departments followed.

Budget making is not a black art but at times it seems that budget makers, rather than relying on charts and tables, would be better served reverting to the ancient soothsayers' way of foretelling the future by reading the entrails of sheep. The aphorism that a budget is an orderly way of learning that one cannot live on one's income, applies to a political jurisdiction as well as to a household. But while a household budget needs to match spending to income, the state must under take the additional, and delicate, high-wire balancing of the conflicting needs of a host of social and economic groups, of maintaining social policy[21], and of attempting to satisfy unlimited and varying demands with limited resources, in a socially acceptable way. After 1974, the sudden advent of the worst inflation in a half-century made fiscal calculations that much more tentative and speculative.

President Harry S. Truman's cryptic comment, "What I need is a one-armed economist," famously demonstrated the frustrations known by every budget maker who has listened to his economic advisors, who observe that if he pursues a particular fiscal course it will have a particular result, but "on the other hand" something very different might occur.[22] That makes the budgeting process as much intuitive as rational, and as much an art as a science.

But even with the best of will, statistics and intuition, the "best laid plans of mice and man" can be scrambled by developments that are as aggravating as they are unpredictable.

There is the danger of being sideswiped by events. Normally the Department of Finance, based on past experience and future trends, can make a reasonable estimate of both revenue and expenditure for the coming year—but not necessarily.

---

[20] "Schreyer's Knife Busy Cutting Down Estimates", ran the headline in *The Winnipeg Tribune* on December 9, 1976.

[21] When Nortel CEO John Roth walked away with his $134 million in stock options after laying off 30,000 employees, it meant more government spending to re-employ, or retrain, some of these.

[22] Economists are people who earn a living by predicting it will be hot in August and cold in February but not necessarily." (Orben's Current Comedy) Another wag stated that an economist, if he does not know your telephone number, will estimate it.

The beef producers invaded the Legislative Building, threatened to get their guns unless the government gave them money, and left with an unbudgeted $18 million bailout package. The government, tired of micro-managing hospital budgets, finally gave them each a "global budget", adjusted for inflation and added services, and told the hospital administrations: "Here is your money, you decide how to spend it, but don't come back for more."

But, of course, they did. The union at the Health Sciences Centre, feeling the pressure of price inflation on their household budgets, demanded higher pay. The hospital administrators agreed with their employees that they deserved better wages, but lamented that it was not in their global budget, and directed them to the government. The union struck and demanded binding arbitration. The arbitrator awarded them an eight per cent increase and said, in effect: "You are entitled. Let the government find the money."

There was the problem of being sideswiped by the bureaucracy. The budget review process could run from early December to mid-March, when it was "frozen" and prepared for presentation to the legislature, usually in April. It was ritual for salesmen and firms doing public sector business to approach the government in February and March. That is when sales are made. That is when departments spend surplus money, or overspend, to show the need for more. "Beware the Ides of March" should be heeded by governments. Department follows department into the cabinet room. Each is led by its officers, accompanied by support staff carrying boxes of graphs, tables, charts and projections, designed to show that the funding received the previous year had been wisely spent, and that they needed more for the coming year. And more staff.

It was the turn of the massive and complex Department of Health, responsible for a third of total government expenditures and staff. The minister and deputy minister sat at the huge polished oak table, flanked by several associate and assistant deputy ministers, and behind sat a dozen support staff at the ready with documents that might be needed to prove a point, and to answer any question that might be asked by other ministers.

Across the table, in the great leather-upholstered chair, sat the premier. He was clearly weary. In addition to his other duties, he had been sitting in that chair up to ten hours a day for the past month, going line by line over the expenditures and minutae of a billion dollar-plus budget. He was bent over, squinting at a thick document, while the deputy minister droned on, explaining past spending and projecting future needs in money and staff. Suddenly the premier interrupted, "I note you are asking for an additional ninety-two SMYs."

The deputy minister confirmed that, indeed, his department needed funding for an additional ninety-two employees (Staff Man Years).

The premier ran his finger down the page. "I note we gave you an additional 106 new SMYs last year."

The deputy minister confirmed that was true. The premier looked up from the document, and across the table. "I note that eighty-four of those positions have not yet been filled."

The room went suddenly silent. Everything seemed to stop in mid-motion, like a video tape stopped with the remote control. Not a paper rustled; not a lip moved. After a long, embarrassing silence, the deputy minister's rattled voice filled the void, "We-e-e-l-l-l. If we had known you were going to notice that and ask about it, we would have filled them."[23]

A province could be sideswiped by the senior government. By the mid-1970s, Ottawa, beset by its own problems, began unilaterally reducing transfers to the provinces for shared cost programs (including Medicare). The provinces were left to cancel programs or find money to fill the gap. That gap created by Ottawa amounted to many millions of dollars. And the shift was insidious because the provinces did not know in advance what those reductions—and their shortfalls—would be.

Or a province could be side-swiped by another province. The estates tax applied when someone inherited an estate valued in excess of a threshold amount. It became a federal tax in 1939, but in the 1960s Alberta, wallowing in petro-dollars, began rebating to its own estate heirs the amount they had been taxed by Ottawa. Politicians in Ottawa were in the odious position of collecting the tax only to have their Alberta counterparts reap a vote harvest by rebating it. In 1971, Ottawa vacated the field and left the ten provinces free to adopt or abolish it. Manitoba's NDP government adopted it, less for revenue[24] than to serve the highly-prized principle of equity. It seemed incongruous in terms of public policy that government should be promoting a new feudal class by allowing tax-free roll-overs of large estates. Other provinces agreed— except Alberta.

It was not a new tax, but one transferred from Ottawa to the provinces, and Manitoba's tax was much less onerous than that which had been charged by Ottawa. But some considered it unfair.

A farmer wrote to complain that his brother and sister-in-law had died, leaving an estate that their three sons could not inherit because of the estates tax, which was based on "phoney" values, and they might be forced to go on welfare. He was sent the following reply:

> Your letter states your three nephews may be forced on welfare
> because they inherited an estate of 1,120 acres of land valued at $436,800
> ... If the subject farm lands have been assessed at $390 an acre for estates
> tax purposes, it is because that price has been established by the free
> market. Phoney as it may be, it is the price your neighbours are paying
> for land in that area and must therefore be considered a fair assessment.
> When your brother died two years ago the exemption on inter-

---

[23] He was dismissed.

[24] From 1971 to the end of 1976, about two per cent of estates were taxed. In 1977, with an exemption of about $250,000 net value, the estates tax yielded about $1.4 million (the highest ever) from 148 estates of a total of 7,779 deaths. Of these, three estates exceeded $1 million in net value. (Budget papers, 1977).

spousal transfer of estates was $200,000 net, so your sister-in-law would
have paid an estates tax on only the portion in excess of that amount after
deduction of all mortgages and other charges. If your sister-in-law died this
summer and the exemption on estates to family members is $250,000 net,
so your nephews will pay estates tax on only the portion in excess of that
amount. Furthermore, they can pay the tax over a five-year period. That
hardly makes them candidates for welfare.

The farmer's nephews were captive. They had to pay or lose their estate.
This did not apply universally. Others were more mobile.

Richard Bowles had been lieutenant governor of Manitoba between 1967
and 1970 and had returned to his legal practice. We had a nodding acquaintance
and in 1975, at a luncheon with a mutual friend, he took me aside. "We are not
of the same political persuasion," he said, "but I have considerable admiration for
your brother-in-law and I would like to get a message to him. Tell him I am getting rich transferring estates to Alberta because of his Inheritance Tax here."

If taxation is to be an instrument of social policy, an estates tax is essential.
The 1960s Report of the Carter Commission on Taxation had pronounced the
famous dictum: "A buck is a buck is a buck and should be taxed no matter what
its source." It made no sense in terms of equity that those earning income by the
sweat of their brow must pay income tax on it while those receiving unearned
gain in the form of an inheritance need not.

But society does not consist exclusively of consumers, but also of producers,
and at what point do the taxes imposed upon producers and investors to redis-
tribute income become so onerous that entrepreneurs leave the province? That is
a question that cannot be answered in theory—only in practice.

In an interview shortly after the 1969 election, premier-elect Schreyer was
asked: "Is there a point of diminishing returns when people will no longer come
here because of high income or other taxes and the people who are here will
leave?"

He replied:

> I don't deny that there is a breaking point to individual initiative,
> but I believe we are far from that, and that the energy and drive of our
> businessmen and executive people put into their work today far exceeds
> that by their counterparts a century ago, when there was virtually no taxa-
> tion. I believe in the existence of a human creative spirit and if a person
> has it they will apply it whether they are taxed 5% or 25%.[25]

It was a pretty thought, but wishful thinking. Even if true in principle, it
could not be sustained in a country where people—or at least money—were as

---

[25] *Winnipeg Tribune*, July 5, 1969.

mobile as in Canada, and where competing jurisdictions offered more. And now lawyer Richard Bowles, a closet friend, was informing us that while the theory of equity might be noble in principle, it had costs.

Someone has written, "In the long reach of history there is no right or wrong; there are only consequences." The government wrestled with the conundrum. The consequence was too costly to sustain the principle. The exemption on net value of inherited estates was gradually reworked to $500,000 for a couple. And government revenue decreased by the equivalent amount. [26]

In April 1977, Finance Minister Saul "The Fixer" Miller brought down the budget, the ninth for the NDP government. Again there was the delicate balancing of spending cuts against social and employment program maintenance, and of selective tax increases against a gap between spending and revenue. Spending was projected at $1,183 million—and the deficit at $27 million.

Total taxes were reduced by $44 million, averaging $120 per family. The property tax credit, increased to a maximum of $375, plus the cost-of-living credit, provided $126 million in direct tax relief and removed 75,000 people from the tax rolls. Adding together "unavoidable" fees (provincial income tax, property tax, health premiums) showed that a Manitoba taxpayer, married and with two children under sixteen, and an income of $15,000, paid $616. This compared with $876 in Alberta, $1,004 in Saskatchewan, and $1,053 in Ontario. Even at an income of 25,000, Manitobans paid $25 less than in British Columbia and $99 less than in Ontario.

The Edmonton Journal examined the budget tables and informed Albertans with the headline: "Overtaxed? Move to Manitoba."[27]

Despite the deficit, the praise for Miller's work was effusive. *The Winnipeg Tribune* editorialized that the budget was "responsible and prudent". Its legislative reporter, Jenni Mortin, wrote, "Mr. Miller produced the nearest thing … to a balanced budget, demonstrating financial responsibility … [and] has shown a common sense straightforward approach as Finance Minister." [28]

The headline in the *Manitoba Cooperator* read: "Provincial Budget Holds Line On Tax Increases".[29] The job creation component of the budget won business support. "Manitoba labour and business leaders hailed the province's new $33 million job creation program as an innovative shot in the arm for the economy … Norman Coughlan, president of the Winnipeg Chamber of Commerce, praised the government's move saying 'there's not a lot to be criticized in the program'." [30]

Not only were taxes held in check, but social services were maintained. "Manitoba Fares Well In Education Report", was the headline on a report by the

---

[26] The PC government of Sterling Lyon abolished the estates tax in 1978. Capitalist United States still had an estates tax when George W. Bush took office in 2001.

[27] June 2, 1977.

[28] April 22, 1977.

[29] April 28, 1977.

[30] Columnists John Sullivan and Mary Ann Fitzgerald, *Winnipeg Free Press*, May 5, 1977.

Paris-based Organization for Economic Cooperation and Development, exempting Manitoba from criticisms levelled at the Western provinces and Ontario.[31] The *Winnipeg Free Press* noted further that: "Manitoba towers above the rest of Canada in its progressive pension legislation."[32]

Despite opposition accusations that the government was hiring anyone able to walk and chew gum, figures showed that Manitoba, at fifteen per 1,000 population, had the third-lowest number of civil servants per capita in Canada.[33] Nor did opposition charges of spending extravagance reflect reality. Per capita spending ranged from $1,900 in Newfoundland to $1,400 in Nova Scotia. Manitoba, at $1,540, was third-lowest and only $8 higher than Ontario.

But the real measurement of comparative prudence lay in administrative costs. Manitoba, at 4.3 per cent of total government expenditures, was second-lowest in Canada. Ontario was highest at 7.6 per cent, and the national average for the ten provinces at 6.3. per cent.

The opposition's favourite game, which could terrify the public, was playing with the figures on provincial debt. Throughout 1976 and 1977, the PCs trumpeted that Manitoba's provincial debt was "$3,400 per person". They simply added the direct debt to that of the utilities (Manitoba Hydro and the Manitoba Telephone System) which were guaranteed by the Government of Manitoba but were self-sustaining. When they were in office, the Conservatives zealously separated the two forms of debt. Premier Roblin's 1966 budget speech noted:

> In addition to the net direct debt, which is supported by tax
> funds, [there is] the self-sustaining investment guaranteed by Manitoba ...
> These ... represent no charge on the consolidated fund. In some jurisdic-
> tions, these items do not enter into the public accounts, as the services are
> operated by private enterprise ... Owing to the needs of the Nelson River
> program and the Manitoba Telephone System expansion, the volume of
> investment guaranteed by the province will continue to grow. However,
> this represents not a tax burden but a gain from economic investment.[34]

Based on Roblin's earlier reasoning, the *Winnipeg Free Press* wrote, "Manitoba's net debt for every man woman and child ... is $382, according to statistics released Friday by Standard and Poors, the New York investment and credit rating agency."[35]

The opposition attacked Miller's projected $27 million deficit, citing Alberta as an example of fiscal responsibility. But *The Financial Times* showed New Brunswick, of similar size, had an $88 million deficit. Mighty Ontario had budgeted

---

[31] August 17, 1976.
[32] June 10, 1977.
[33] Alberta had 20.3 per 1,000, while Nova Scotia had 24.9 per 1,000.
[34] *Hansard*
[35] *Winnipeg Free Press*, March 5, 1977.

for a $977 million deficit. Only Alberta had a surplus. The wellhead price of oil had doubled since 1973 and every dollar of increase brought about $500 million into the Alberta economy.

It seemed we had hit a speed bump when the *Tribune* quoted an accountant as stating that Manitoba's "exorbitant income tax" made it the worst province to die in, under the headline: "Manitoba a Bad Place to Die".[36] But an earlier headline in the *Winnipeg Free Press*[37] read, "Move to Ontario If You're Rich, Stay in Manitoba If You're Not". Manitoba, under an NDP government, may have been a bad place to die, but it was a good place to live.

In Manitoba every man, woman and child now had access to an entire cluster of essential services including medical care, nursing home care, pharmacare, education in schools and universities, highways and public transit, work training, campgrounds and parks, courts, environmental protection, flood control and farm price stabilization, for provincial income taxes equivalent to the price of a new television set.

The fulsome praise was almost embarrassing. Things could not possibly get any better. Then they did. Someone found a *Winnipeg Free Press* news clipping with a huge, full-page headline, "Manitoba's economic stagnation getting steadily worse".

It reported that H.C. Pentland, professor of Economics at the University of Manitoba had told the Manitoba Conference on Technological Change: "Manitoba's economy is not only stagnant—it is the only province whose position is steadily worsening … Winnipeg has the smallest growth rate in the country … Average per capita income is 8% below the national average." Our hair rose on end, until we noted when the report was published. It was dated March 8, 1968—when the Conservatives were in office.

> There is a Divinity shapes our ends,
> Rough-hew them as we will.[38]

All was going so well; what could possibly go wrong? But we had forgotten what is quaintly referred to as Maslow's Law: "The greater the degree of comfort attained, the greater the increments of comfort needed to satisfy people."

Manitobans, particularly the members of the business community, had done well under the NDP government, but the mythology bred by ideology is potent. British Columbia Premier Dave Barrett had said of his 1975 election defeat: The whining of the establishment about being hard done by was overdone. They were not drying into their beer, they were crying into their cocktail glasses." The same phenomenon prevailed in Manitoba; those who had gained much wanted more. They needed an instrument through which to get it.

---

[36] *Winnipeg Tribune*, January 28, 1977.
[37] *Op. cit.*, March 22, 1976.
[38] Shakespeare, *Hamlet*.

XXXIX

Enter Lyon

Whether or not it is clear to you, no doubt the universe is unfolding as it should.
—Max Ehrman, *Disiderata*

Lyon's roar announced his intention to become king of the political jungle. The Progressive Conservatives had shown surprising strength in the 1973 election and subsequent by-elections, but needed a leader tough enough to attack the NDP government without apology, reactionary enough to inspire the right wing of the voting spectrum, experienced enough to not need to prove himself, and confident enough to look like a winner. Sterling Rufus Lyon, Q.C., was known as "Red", not just because of his middle name, reddish hair and ruddy complexion, but because of his temperament. Had he been a foot taller, his broad shoulders, stocky body and pugnacious demeanor [1] would have made him a valuable, and dangerous, football player. His undisputed and aggressive intelligence made him a good politician—and a dangerous opponent.

He came of a family that had owned the same farm since 1876 and he was raised in Portage la Prairie, a city of some 10,000 about seventy kilometres west of Winnipeg, which was famous for breeding politicians, including Prime Minister Arthur Meighen and Premier Douglas Campbell, as well as a chief justice of Manitoba, and a host of cabinet ministers and civil servants. He graduated from high school, where he was known as "a scrappy little bugger", with a gold medal, worked on survey crews and as a press reporter to earn money to attend law school. There he distinguished himself, cut his teeth as a crown attorney, and was elected to the legislature in November 1958.

---

[1] After Lyon became premier, some NDP wag, borrowing from seventeenth-century English political philosopher Thomas Hobbs, made up a placard: "Sterling Lyon is nasty, brutish and short."

He entered Premier Duff Roblin's cabinet to be, at thirty-one, the youngest attorney general in Canadian history and was recognized as, other than Roblin, the government's most able debater. During the next decade, he also served as minister of Natural Resources, minister of Public Utilities, minister of Tourism and Recreation, commissioner of Northern Affairs, minister of Municipal Affairs, and on Treasury Board. He became government house leader and Roblin's "enforcer", which made him enemies among both the opposition and his colleagues. When Roblin resigned in 1967, Lyon contested the party leadership as a "progressive Progressive Conservative", but lost to "conservative Progressive Conservative" Walter Weir. He did not run in 1969 when the Weir government was defeated by the NDP.

He became general counsel for General Distributors of Canada Ltd., a major Winnipeg firm, but did not lose his interest in politics. He ran federally in 1974, but was defeated by Liberal James Richardson. He was elected leader of the Progressive Conservative party in December 1975, and on November 2, 1976, at age forty-eight, in a surprisingly large by-election voter turnout of seventy-three per cent, was elected to the legislature by the very rural/conservative southwest Manitoba constituency of Souris-Killarney.

Lyon's "government is fat, sloppy and socialist"[2] approach delighted the rural audiences. NDP candidate Howard Nixon, master farmer from a family farming the same land since 1881, school trustee, RCAF veteran, chairman of the regional school division, Manitoba Pool Elevator director, chairman of both local and area hospital boards, reeve of the municipality, vice-president of the Westman Regional Development Board and elder of the United Church, ran third with fifteen per cent of the votes cast. Lyon, the parachute candidate who had lived in Winnipeg for twenty-five years, received sixty-five per cent.[3]

Lyon had been a prominent figure in the Roblin government, which had changed the province by a magnitude, but the "Red Tory", and. "progressive" image ascribed to him was, in terms of social policy, belied by his public positions.[4] He defended the introduction of the Manitoba Sales Tax in 1967 as nothing more than an attempt to remain in accord with other provinces. He vigorously opposed NDP proposals for premium-free Medicare and expressed incredulity at their suggestion this be paid out of income tax.[5] He argued in the legislature that the mining companies were paying as much royalties as could be extracted [despite it costing the province more to service them than the revenue received] without impairing development of the industry in Manitoba. He accused the NDP of "inventing" deprived persons in support of new social programs, and stated that

[2] It was reminiscent of, and as effective as, Lenin's 1917 reduction of a philosophy into: "peace, bread and land".

[3] The *Winnipeg Free Press* editorialized, "In Souris-Killarney the antagonism toward the present government and its socialistic policies solidified behind the Tories." November 3, 1977.

[4] "Liberals viewed Lyon as right of Barry Goldwater, who would polarize the right," Susan Hoeschen, *Financial Post*, March 20, 1976.

[5] *Hansard*, March 15, 1969.

socialist doctrines fail because "you don't understand human nature".[6]

While out of government, he kept his reputation for pungent political commentary. In a 1971 interview with columnist Frances Russell he referred to Prime Minister Trudeau as "a mid-Atlantic Gallic mind ... alien to the thinking and aspirations of his countrymen, English or French", and to Schreyer's government as "that bunch of amateurs on Broadway". He argued, "We don't need more government, but less, and we don't need Trudeau-style tax reform."

He pronounced, "If anyone redistributes my income it better be me. I and everyone else in Canada is better able to look after himself than government." The worst thing about Autopac, he said, is that "it robs people of freedom of choice". He felt "progressivism" meant that "The individual should have as much freedom as possible to make his own social and economic decisions. I am not for government intervention unless it assists in this."[7]

Ironically, this philosophy precisely mirrored that of Sidney Green, whom Lyon once honoured with "if he ever got on this side of the house he would make an outstanding minister".[8] Lyon and Green had been classmates at law school and had surprising mutual respect, but Lyon lost no opportunity to portray Green as the evil face of the NDP. Like Green, he instantly recognized the politics of any situation and attacked with a killer instinct. But Lyon had a quality Green had not: a ruthless vindictiveness born of total conviction that the political world was divided into "us" and "them".

Lyon's predecessor, the long-suffering Sidney Spivak, was opaque by comparison. Dante may have had someone like him in mind when he reserved the hottest place in his *Inferno* for those who, in times of crisis, could not decide which side they were on. His head was on the right, with business leaders who wanted cheap money from government and cheap labor from the Phillipines, but his heart vectored him toward the left in terms of social policy. Columnist Frances Russell wrote of his "fuzzy and indistinct image". "The major problem Conservative leader Sidney Spivak faces in maintaining his leadership and drawing the party on to power is the simple fact that he lacks cutting edge."[9]

Not so his successor. Spivak's defeat at a bitterly-contested convention in December 1975, when he billed himself "a watchdog against a right-wing establishment move to control the party"[10] and at which nineteen of his twenty-three caucus members voted against him, left the party in the hands of a "True Believer" who looked on socialists as the Crusaders had on Muslims.

Privately genial, and a devoted family man, his public life seemed dedicated to expunging socialists and their works. He spiced the language of politics with: "Socialism has not worked since the dawn of Christianity;" "socialists are the

---

[6] *Hansard*, April 3, 1969.

[7] *Winnipeg Free Press*, December 18, 1971.

[8] *Hansard*, March 15, 1968.

[9] *Winnipeg Free Press*, September 30, 1974.

[10] *Ibid.*, December 8, 1975.

anti-Christ" who "view the world through the wrong end of a sewer pipe" and are "handmaidens" for communists who, on taking over a country governed by social democrats, immediately shoot them "because they are so dumb". NDP policies were "low-brow nonsense of egalitarianism" and "social and economic regimentation", forcing Manitobans "to walk in lockstep into an envy-ridden future". "Before these strange people with an alien ideology, we never had to explain the value of private ownership—we just knew it." "Social welfare is not a right ... universality [in Medicare] is nonsense ... some don't want medical insurance so why force it." [11]

Lyon was a man with a mission. [12]

Before Lyon returned to the legislature, acting PC Leader Don Craik had paved the way for him with a powerful attack on the government in his reply to the speech from the throne, which was six times as long as the Throne Speech itself —on February 16, 1976. Craik, a soft-spoken engineer and former head of the Manitoba Research Council at the University of Manitoba, had been a respected MLA since 1966 and had served in Premier Weir's cabinet. He delivered an embryonic enunciation of what was later given legislative form by Margaret Thatcher, Ronald Reagan and Brian Mulroney, and embroidered into Premier Mike Harris's "Common Sense Revolution".

> Your idea of the kind of society you want for yourselves and your children is very different from ours ... You believe the ability of government to tax and spend is unlimited. You have little faith in the free and random decisions of the marketplace. You prefer the planned and controlled decisions of the state. You believe that government can dispose of money better than the men and women who work to earn it ...
>
> We believe the individual Manitoban is a better and more prudent manager of his or her own decisions and income than government can ever be ... that the private enterprise system works ... We believe in the kind of society where hard work and ability are rewarded ... that extra work and extra ability should receive extra rewards ... that members of our society, who through their efforts and sacrifice add to our total wealth, have a claim to a greater share of the total wealth we produce.

He went through a litany of charges, replete with artfully inserted and choreographed code words:

---

[11] *Brandon Sun*, October 2, 1976.

[12] Lyon was not mellowed by becoming premier. Saul Miller, the normally polite former NDP cabinet minister later raged in the legislature: "The premier poisoned the atmosphere of this house ... I have never heard in my 25 years in public life ... the kind of vicious, arrogant, ugly, mean, petty, personal vindictiveness one heard from the First Minister ... He lowers himself and politics to a gutter level." *Hansard*, May 18, 1978.

Government control of the economy and state ownership … gross
negligence and waste … mismanagement … Autopac monopoly … need
for common sense restraints … politicization of the civil service … the
destruction of the merit system … excessive spending[13] and taxation …
nationalization of farm land … expensive buildings for more civil servants[14]
… morass of Unicity … waste of $400 million on hydro … frightening
away mining companies[15] … disastrous rent controls … Flyer bus …
Saunders aircraft … education abandoning our children … hostility to
private ownership … unworkable socialist doctrines … damage to
public interest.

Craik concluded by tossing down the gauntlet:

I have spelled out where my party, and where the NDP, stand on
crucial issues facing Manitobans today … We have a fundamental disagreement with the government. We believe in private enterprise, private initiative,
private ownership and a healthy mixed economy. You believe in government
control of the economy and state ownership … I believe that when the
election comes the [NDP] will find Manitobans have had enough of them.[16]

Craik's *tour de force* made it clear the election would be fought on philosophy—poll taxes versus income taxes; production vs. distribution; subsidizing the
private sector vs. using the public sector. It remained to Lyon to fill in the blanks
with speeches short on policy alternatives, other than reducing taxes and the role
of government in decision making, but long on denunciation of socialists and rich
with imagery and "fighting words", which brought his audience to its feet, hungry
for blood and the perks of office denied them eight years earlier.

Of his approach and direction columnist Frances Russell wrote, "Sterling
Lyon is, above all, an astute, practical politician who takes his cue from the public
mood … He sensed the growing public movement to the right and against interventionist government, and articulated it."[17]

Lyon made two strategic decisions; he swung his party sharply to the right;[18]
and he deliberately targeted Ed Schreyer. His speeches were heavily laden with

---

[13] The Roblin and Weir governments (1958-69) had quadrupled government spending and Roblin argued
that the government should have a debt rather than a surplus.

[14] The Roblin and Weir governments more than doubled the civil service from 4,000 to 8,822. The NDP
increased it to 12,376 but that included transfers from private to public with Autopac and new programs
such as Pharmacare, Home Care, Nursing Care and so on.

[15] Green had published a list of twenty-six private companies that elected to partner with the public
Manitoba Mining Corporation.

[16] *Hansard*, February 16, 1976

[17] *Winnipeg Free Press*, November 2, 1977.

[18] Winnipeg city councillor Ken Wong left the PC party after fifteen years, because of Lyon's "ultra right-wing"
platform. "His leadership suggests that he is following the worst elements of the Nixon campaign."
(*Winnipeg Free Press*, April 14, 1977).

references to Schreyer as "a radical in moderate clothing", a "socialist tinkerer" and "a friend of Trudeau who craves the same restricted individual freedom and is on the road to ruining our national economy in pursuit of a strange new society." He attacked Schreyer's 1976 budget with palpable contempt. "Manitoba has led the pack in provincial taxes since this incompetent bunch came to office," he said, "expecting a socialist to be fiscally responsible is like expecting a vulture to say grace."

In his first major speech as leader, he predicted, to the wild applause of a crowd of 1,400 at a fund-raising dinner, that Manitobans were looking to the Progressive Conservatives to oust the Schreyer government. "If we do not it will be a disaster," he predicted.

He appealed to aspirations by predicting Schreyer's proposal for a two-and-a-half to one income formula[19] would be rejected by Manitobans because "they want the chance to better themselves not by reducing neighbours' incomes but by improving their own." Continuation of the NDP in office would "rob you of your economic freedom and destroy your political freedom," he said, adding that the NDP "land-lease" policy was undertaken "in blind obedience to a 19th century doctrine alien to all the traditions of this country ... which will reduce farmers to tenants of the state." [20]

By contrast, he promised, a government led by him would launch Manitoba on "a path of optimism" by abolishing the estates tax and hopefully the federal capital gains tax, and by replacing land leases with government loans. It would offer "a philosophy of renewed hope" instead of Schreyer's "income restrictions".

Lyon informed the meeting that party membership had increased from 9,000 to 21,000 during the past year and added "it will be 30,000 by election day".

"We'll beat the NDP machine because of the thousands of Manitobans who have looked at what the NDP has done and have decided to ensure that it and its discredited management are banished from office for a long, long time." [21]

Lyon soon moved from rural Souris-Killarney to the urban Charleswood constituency, with its combination of "old money" and upwardly mobile popula-tion. At his nominating meeting, he stated that his government would bring back sanity to government and Manitobans would be rewarded with reduced business taxes to generate jobs, a freeze on civil service hiring, a zero-based budgeting system, savings from better government management, and reduced income taxes. And his government would have the right attitude. "Don't listen to promises. Look at attitudes. Ascertain the drift the government will take."

Then he revealed the core of his political philosophy. "Most of all the

[19] In April 1976, Schreyer spoke at the Riel constituency meeting, lamenting the prevailing enormous income gaps and stated that "Sweden and Israel have reduced differentials in TAKE-HOME pay between two component groups, a captain of industry and a worker in the plant, in the order of two-and-a-half to one." The opposition and the media immediately interpreted this to mean a differential of two-and-a-half to one of MINIMUM WAGE, which was about half the take-home pay.

[20] *Winnipeg Tribune*, April 29, 1976. At this point, some 3,500 Manitoba farmers, including two Conservative MLAs, one a former minister of Agriculture, had accepted the opportunity to be "tenants of the state".

[21] *Winnipeg Free Press*, October 1, 1977.

Conservative government would try to reward individuals with 'more than their fair share'."[22]

It was a potent message for Manitobans whose income had soared during the preceding eight years to bring them into the "middle class", allowing them to contemplate reaching for the brass ring. By contrast, Schreyer's appeal for income equity and references to Franklin D. Roosevelt's incantation that "the test of our progress as a society is not in whether we add to the abundance of those who already have much, but in whether we provide for those who have little," was not what they wanted to hear.

The Conservative campaign appeared flawless. Full-page ads featured former NDP or Liberal supporters who were voting Progressive Conservative this time. Six months before the election was even called, Swan River Valley agricultural representative Douglas Gourlay attacked the Department of Agriculture, his employer, as a "welfare agency", demanded the resignation of its minister, his boss, for "mismanagement", and announced he would be a PC candidate.[23]

A card-sized foldover showed a smiling Lyon stating "Let's Make Manitoba Better", and hit three hot-button issues: "Manitoba Hydro—have you looked at your bill lately?"; "Saunders Aircraft—you're paying off its bills"and "Flyer Bus—other people are riding on your money". These issues had received great exposure in the legislature and the media and needed no explanation.

A spectacular four-page pamphlet displayed the red, white and blue party colours, and showed a serious-looking Lyon leaning on a podium and saying: "Let me tell you why I believe the coming election will be the most important in Manitoba history." It invited Manitobans to make "A Critical Choice For The Future" in which there would be more "individual opportunity and responsibility".

Suggestions by the NDP that Manitobans might lose some NDP-legislated social services if they elected a PC government, were denounced as "the politics of fear"—and almost turned the Tories into "socialists". A leaflet showed a friendly Lyon telling an elderly woman, "there must be—there will be—a continuation of premium-free medicare, pharmacare, home repair programs, lower income taxes, more nursing homes for needy older residents, and no school taxes on lower-and middle-income senior citizens."

The Conservatives' most effective propaganda device was an imaginative and professional TV commercial showing a cash register which rang intermittently, synchronized with a voiceover commentary:

> When we elected the NDP we signed a blank cheque. *Ka-ching,*
> *ka-ching.* For 40 million dollars for airplanes nobody bought. *Ka-ching, ka-*

---

[22] Brian Cole, *Winnipeg Free Press*, April 29, 1977. This philosophy was later immortalized in the movie Wall Street, with stockbroker Gordon Gekko's unforgettable comment, "Greed is good."

[23] Gourlay was mayor of the town of Swan River. The premier and I had a luncheon meeting with his council in 1976. He asked me who would pay for the lunch. We knew where we stood with him.

ching. For 50 million dollars of new government buildings. *Ka-ching, ka-ching*. For four million dollars worth of Columbia Forest Products with no market. *Ka-ching, ka-ching*.If we don't want a government wasting our money like this, then let's take the pen away. We just can't afford another NDP government. Vote Progressive Conservative.

It was devastating. There was just one little problem; the blank cheque to Columbia Forest Products at Sprague had been signed by the Conservative government in which Lyon was attorney general. When the NDP government challenged the deal and stopped payment, the court penalized the government for refusing to pay.

Schreyer called the ad "a sterling example of the Big Lie". A protest to the Advertising Council of Canada got the ad withdrawn and an apology issued— by the TV station, not the Conservatives. But the accusation was much more effective than the retraction. The theme of "plunder and blunder" by the NDP, and "lower taxes, less government, end waste" by a PC government, was paralleled with a singing jingle about "free Manitoba". Ten days before election day, before a cheering crowd of 300 in the tiny village of Dugald, Lyon again pledged to abolish the land-lease program and succession duties to ensure that "the long clammy hand" of government is removed from the people's pockets and "There will be a new way and a free Manitoba after October 11th."

Lyon's attack on Schreyer was also pressed with vigour, and he had short, pithy, popular solutions for every problem. Schreyer's two-and-a-half to one income formula was "class warfare" and the miniscule tax increases in the 1976 budget were not necessary because "all he's got to do is cut the fat".

But in case the incessant direct charges were deflected by Schreyer's obvious popularity, Lyon developed a second line of attack: "The NDP is a one-man band," he claimed. "[I]f Schreyer left what have you got? There would be Sidney Green, René Toupin, Len Evans, and all that bunch that aren't fit to run a peanut stand." [24]

Lyon's self-confidence was categorical—and aggravating. By September 21st, instead of showering promises of tax cuts and programs, he was warning Manitobans, "Don't expect too much from the Progressive Conservatives because the NDP has left the cupboard bare." He said that he would pursue a program of "acute protracted restraint". Shortly after becoming leader, he had asked Premier Schreyer's executive assistant, René Chartier, for an office larger than that assigned to him. When Chartier replied space was in short supply, Lyon retorted: "Just leave it alone. After the election I'll give myself a larger office."

One incident was almost uncanny. A letter went to "Jean-Pierre Frobert, 33 Blvd Republique, 1800 Bourges, France." It read,

Thank you for your letter of June 10th. I am pleased to advise there

---

[24] *Winnipeg Free Press*, October 1, 1977.

is a position for you as a Research Assistant with the Department of
Industry and Commerce of Manitoba ... at a biweekly salary of $384.79 ...
You would be reporting to Mr. G. Backeland who is French and English
speaking ... Documentation for you to gain entry to Canada will be
prepared.

The letter was dated July 7, 1977, four months before the election. It was
signed, Sterling Lyon. It was as though he was already Premier of Manitoba.

Nineteenth-century German military strategist, Karl von Clausewitz, had
written that the advantage lies with the attacker; he can concentrate his forces at a
particular point while the defender, not knowing where that point would be, must
disperse his along the entire perimeter. The government was on the defensive and
Lyon attacked like German General Guderian, unexpectedly and unstoppably
crashing his Panzers through the Ardennes in 1940.

PREMIER SCHREYER had a predilection for June elections. June was a good
month; the fields are green and the water sparkles in the sunlight, life is in the
renewal stage and people feel good about the future. And June had been a good
month for his government, which had won elections on June 25, 1969 and on
June 28, 1973. We hoped that the spell would hold. Also, without making it formal, this would be in line with his belief that, as in the United States, elections
should be fixed for four years without it being left to the discretion of the head
of government.

Setting an election date is not just a matter of statistics, but of intuition.
The government was down in the public opinion polls, but the economic statistics
were good. In 1976, the farmers had suffered the worst drought in ninety years,
but perhaps it would rain. The Liberals were down but might recover and bleed
off some Conservative votes. Inflation was savaging the economy, but it appeared
to be past its peak. The premier awaited the "feel" of the political stars being in the
right juxtaposition.

While he pondered, Premier Bill Davis of Ontario called an election for
June 9th. There was nothing except courtesy to prevent coincident elections, but
the experienced election workers who moved from province to province, like war
horses, at the call of an election, would be in Ontario, where the NDP had almost
become the official opposition four years earlier and was now believed to be within striking distance of the ultimate prize. Also, the government decides when the
legislature begins but the opposition decides when it ends. So the session continued, and Schreyer would not prorogue it in mid-session as Weir had done in 1969.

At 3:15 on the morning of June 18, 1977, Lieutenant Governor Bud Jobin
gave royal assent to fifty-three bills and prorogued the house. The truculent,
quarrelsome final session of the Thirtieth Legislature of Manitoba came to an

ill-tempered close. Aside from the media, who looked to it for news material, and the business community, who believed Jacquin's Postulate that, "No man's life, liberty or property is safe while the legislature is in session", few noticed, but it put the politicians on election alert.

But the June election 'window' had closed. And people do not like elections in mid-summer when they are soaking up sun or vacationing with their children. That meant a fall election and allowed the opposition to taunt the government, saying that it feared facing the electorate.

However, while Lyon did not allow his charges to be deflected by "irrele-vancies", his claim that the only certainties in socialist Manitoba were "debt and taxes", and that the NDP government was caught *en flagrante delicto* with the people of Manitoba, was refuted by statistics and less biased observers.

Manitoba's NDP government had won the stamp of approval of the most stringent, and impartial, assessor of all—the international bond rating agencies. On September 19, 1975, Moody's Investors Service Incorporated of New York, which advised world financial markets on the health of a borrower's economy, had awarded Manitoba—for the first time in its history—a AA bond rating "in recognition of the province's strong financial position supported by a steady and diversified economy".

> Manitoba has experienced above-average growth ... Provincial authorities have realistic expectations and good prospects of realizing them. They have demonstrated political sensitivity and pragmatic business acumen ... The province pursues prudent fiscal policies and has relatively small direct financing requirements ... Net direct debt is moderate and the guaranteed debt is for well-managed, self-supporting crown companies.
>
> Significant expansion in nearly all sectors resulted in the gross provincial product growing at a faster pace than for the nation, while inflation remained below the national average. Manitoba's financial operations have been extremely well conducted for several years ... Net direct debt of the province has declined steadily in relation to total personal income and in relation to general revenues to service that debt.

Winnipeg columnist Mike Ward, no lover of socialists, wrote that, "Manitoba has managed to get through 1975's worldwide economic problems better than most and actually came out on top in agriculture and factory shipments."[25]

A year later, vitriolic *Tribune* business editor Harry Mardon, who figuratively ate socialists for breakfast, wrote

> Manitoba last year enjoyed almost full employment ... Another

---

[25] *Ibid*, December 19, 1975.

bright feature was the pace of new construction. In Winnipeg alone, construction permits increased 74% over 1975 .... Sherritt-Gordon intends to go ahead with an underground mine at Ruttan Lake ... Winnipeg-based financial institutions all enjoyed excellent years during 1976 and anticipate 1977 will be even better ... Total retail sales were up over 11.5%, compared with Vancouver's 7.2% and Toronto's 6.1% ... It appears we had a good year in 1976 and the outlook for 1977 is for solid growth.[26]

Dedicated enemies were making sounds joyful to our ears.[27] *Saturday Night* added: "Manitoba is a good solid province with a good centrist administration. It's the mean in almost every economic index that banks and governments can churn out."[28] *Winnipeg Tribune* columnist Val Werier wrote: "It is astonishing that with all its wealth, Alberta's taxes (income tax, medicare fees, tax credits) on a family of four, are $349, compared with only $83 in Manitoba in an income bracket of $11,000."[29]

Business analyst Roger Newman wrote, "Most businessmen were appalled and shocked to the point of near hysteria when Manitobans unexpectedly elected the first NDP administration in 1969, [but] Manitoba's economy has performed much better in the 1970s than it did in the 1960s under the Conservative administrations of Roblin and Weir."[30]

The Globe and Mail marvelled that: "The heavily populated provinces of Ontario and Quebec have had large deficits ... [but] Manitoba ... [has a] virtually balanced budget ... most of the public debt is self-liquidating and has been incurred for electric power ... The provincial utilities have succeeded in supplying relatively cheap power."[31]

The NDP government had risked its political future with its decision to proceed with the multi-billion dollar hydro-electric development on the Nelson River and Lake Winnipeg.

Now it was paying off. Hydro-electric rates had doubled in the past decade, but natural gas was up 290 per cent and coal 325 per cent.

On employment, the *Winnipeg Free Press* reported: "In Ontario the unemployment rate is up ... In Alberta the rate rose ... In B.C. the rate was up ... In Manitoba the unemployment rate is down."[32]

And then there was the "Schreyer Factor". Lyon had taken the *grande risqué* in attacking the NDP's—and Manitoba's—golden boy, but it was a calculated risk.

---

[26] *Winnipeg Tribune*, January 20, 1977.

[27] By contrast, the day after the 1977 election, Mardon wrote, "A dark cloud has been lifted. Manitobans now can see a future of hope ... [after] the harm done by the NDP rule." *Winnipeg Tribune*, October 13, 1977.

[28] May 1977.

[29] May 7, 1977.

[30] *Toronto Globe and Mail*, July 23, 1977.

[31] September 8, 1977.

[32] September 13, 1977.

A delegate to a Liberal convention had analyzed, "The NDP is not the NDP; the NDP is Schreyer." Lyon knew that, as with Hannibal, "throwing Schreyer on the scales" would make the difference between victory and defeat. And he knew that to drive the stake through the heart of the NDP government he must destroy Schreyer. That, and his naturally combative nature, informed his strategy.

But Schreyer would not be that easy to destroy. Essentially, the premier was a moderate and a pragmatist. For this he made no apologies either to those who believed grants other than to business were welfare, which tinted him pink among the establishment, nor to those who would to burn down the world and start again from an Eden without a serpent, which made him suspect among the party's left wing. Nor did he hesitate to challenge his party. In 1972, as a result of both a commitment to Laurent Desjardins and his own personal convictions, he went to the wall for legislation providing public aid to private schools. He failed when a third of his own caucus voted against him but he emerged with his integrity and popularity intact. In 1976, he again confronted the party, particularly its powerful trade union component, by stating excessive wage demands were "slitting the throat of the economy" and supporting Prime Minister Trudeau's Price and Wage Control package, but he retained their respect. Few considered it inappropriate when the planners of the 1977 election campaign chose the motto: LEADERSHIP YOU CAN TRUST.

In its edition of July 15, 1974, *Time Magazine* named Schreyer as one of the world's leaders. In 1975, Schreyer received an award as an Outstanding Young Canadian.

The *Beausejour Beaver*, published in Schreyer's home town, confounded the proverb, "a prophet has no honour in his own country" by editorializing, "The personal popularity and admiration Premier Schreyer has built up since his party's surprising formation of the government in 1969, has been considerable." [33]

When Premier Schreyer refused to be intimidated by General Electric into changing a tender for hydro generators, despite promises of jobs in NDP-held Brandon East, *Tribune* business editor Harry Mardon wrote: "Premier Ed Schreyer … displayed great integrity and political courage." [34]

Columnist Susan Hoeschen wrote in *The Financial Post*, "Schreyer is clearly the single most popular figure in Manitoba politics today … [and] has managed with his soft-sell liberalism to make friends in many unlikely places—the kind of friends who will vote for him." [35]

In 1977, this was followed by her article with the headline: "Manitoba Has Problems But Schreyer Will Be Hard to Beat". [36]

Mel Michener, president of the Winnipeg Chamber of Commerce, pointed

---

[33] January 22, 1975.

[34] *Winnipeg Tribune*, May 3, 1975.

[35] March 20, 1976.

[36] *The Financial Post*, February 12, 1977.

to Manitoba's double-A credit rating, and stated: "That says something for Schreyer's economic management." [37]

The Toronto Star, in a front-page editorial, rhapsodized, "Canada is in mortal danger ... To save itself Canada must get a government to match the occasion ... The best way to do this is to add to the cabinet distinguished and trustworthy Canadians ... of the calibre of Premier Schreyer of Manitoba." [38]

When it was announced that Manitoba would support Ottawa's anti-inflation program, the *Winnipeg Free Press* editorialized: "Premier Schreyer and his government get full marks for courage ... it should have the support of Manitobans who believe Ottawa's program must be given a chance to prove itself." [39]

Saturday Night reported, "There is no questioning [Schreyer's] earnest, progressive intentions, or their inspiration. On the wall behind his desk in his legislative office ... there is a photograph of J.S. Woodsworth, the saintly founder of the CCF ... Winnipeg, under Schreyer, may obtain a new destiny as a model metropolis." [40]

From an area of Manitoba where "NDP" and "communism" were synonymous, came a letter for Premier Schreyer: "On behalf of the Mayor and Council of the Town of Steinbach, and its citizens, I thank you for the grants. Your efforts to reduce the education tax burden are greatly appreciated." [41]

And in an endorsement that could not be repaid in the coin of the realm, iconic Mayor Steve Juba of Winnipeg signed Schreyer's nomination papers, Main-streeted with him in his own constituency of Rossmere and, a week before E-Day, told the press, "I think the world of him." [42]

On September 6th, Schreyer set the election for October 11th. An election is a massive, complex operation consisting of more than party leaders making speeches. It is called a "campaign", is organized along military lines, and has a hierarchy. The premier decides when to ask the lieutenant governor for dissolution of the government and sets the date of the election, and the government then becomes a care-taker until the electorate chooses a new one.

The party leaders are the chief campaigners and field generals who give direction, set the tone, and encourage the troops. They are the focus of media attention, live on a knife's edge, and for them the campaign is an almost dehuman-izing endurance test and a wonderful opportunity to say something wrong—a misstep they fear worse than roasting in hell. Aside from them, for five weeks the real action is at the level of two entities who operate the electoral machinery, one on behalf of the political parties and the other on behalf of the electorate.

---

[37] *Toronto Star*, April 29, 1976.

[38] November 26, 1976.

[39] January 12, 1977.

[40] May 1977.

[41] Mayor Penner to Schreyer, April 21, 1977.

[42] *East Kildonan Examiner*, October 5, 1977.

The first is the provincial office of each party. The party's secretary and executive officers select the campaign chairman who, in conjunction with the election planning committee, develops the grand plan for the physical conduct of the campaign, determines the mottos, posters and literature to be used, categorizes the constituencies in terms of attention needed, and plans who goes where, when, and by what means. The campaign office determines the literature, posters and mottos to be used, prepares policy manuals, speaker's notes, candidates handbooks, newsletters, and conducts candidate's seminars on organizing, speechmaking, and scheduling news releases for maximum impact. It works with the constituency executives to organize candidate nominating meetings in optimum sequence, provide theme speakers, and assists the constituency executives responsible for organizing the voluntary troops at the grassroots level. These work out of spartan, noisy, paper-draped committee rooms rife with excitement and smelling of sweat and adrenalin. They distribute literature, identify supporters, placing election signs at strategic locations and on the property of supporters, and arranging to get them to the polls on E-Day—on time. It is these unheralded foot soldiers, whom Edmund Burke called "the small battalions", who often make the difference between victory and defeat.

The other is the office of the province's chief electoral officer, an employee of the legislature. The moment the election is announced, he begins appointing enumerators to canvas every address in the province and list all eligible voters. He appoints a returning officer for each electoral division, who selects the venue of the polling booths, appoints an officer to supervise each poll, and distributes ballot boxes and lists of voters.

On election night, as the work of the political machinery abruptly ends, the most significant work of the electoral office begins. Ironically, after all the sweat and striving, the final decision about who shall occupy the seats of the mighty is taken out of the hands of humans and reduced to the purely mechanical.

Things Fall Apart

Do not let me die bewildered.
                    —King Arthur in *Camelot*

They lined the walls, the small gray boxes with the paleolithic faces, stacked tier upon tier along the interminable marble and Tyndall-stone basement corridors, galvanized metal boxes ten by fourteen inches and fifteen inches high, with a slot in the top, a lock suspended from a hasp at the front, and each labelled with the name of an electoral constituency. They sat, inanimate and mute, but endowed by sentient, intelligent humans with the power to decide the destiny of men and nations. And they were being prepared to pronounce the fate of the Government of Manitoba.

I always felt a vague unease, an indefinable apprehension, when I saw them while walking along these basement corridors that were reminiscent of Carl Sandberg's "cool tombs", hurrying to a committee meeting carrying an armload of briefing papers, or to the cafeteria for a fast lunch, my feet automatically picking their way as I scanned the newspapers. But no matter how studiously my eyes were focused on the papers, my mind sensed the radiated malevolence as I realized my future and that of the government I served would be irrevocably decreed by the boxes stacked deep in the bowels of The Ledge.

It offended my sense of history that the democratic system of government based on individual decision making had been reduced to a childlike act as though, after a century of public education consuming enormous funds, the electors were illiterate. It seemed incongruous that, after millennia of striving by people to govern themselves, the decisions of rational persons had found their ultimate expression in the mechanical act of marking an X on a prescribed paper ballot and dropping it into a metal box.

But these were the receptacles that would contain the tangible consequences of an electoral process that had begun in the dim and distant past. From
the ancient Greeks, who came to the marketplace to shout the names of their candidates, through Oliver Cromwell and his Roundheads, who executed a king in
the mid-seventeenth century, to assert their right to choose their government and
limit its powers, to the "universal suffrage" revolutions of 1848 that rent Western
Europe (though only four per cent of the populace actually had the right to vote),
the path to today's electoral systems was long and slow.

Vox populi, vox dei—the voice of the people is the voice of God—said the
ancient Romans, but their bard, Horace, had discovered that "the people are a
many-headed beast". So what were they were saying? Jean-Jacques Rousseau, the
pre-revolutionary French political philosopher whose concept of the "sovereign
people" laid the foundation for both the American and French Revolutions and
subsequent constitutions, detected the popular voice in his semi-mystical General
Will. The concrete expression of that "Will", the most significant action a society
can take—the choosing of its government—would be registered by electors marking a symbol on paper and dropping it into a box. And what, on this pleasant
October day, would be the verdict of those dumb, gray, metal boxes with the
paleolithic faces?

The auguries were not encouraging. There had been a perceptible change
since those heady days of late 1973 when the *Toronto Star* had carried such headlines as: "The NDP Shows How The Tail Wags The Dog In National Politics";[1]
"Socialist Premiers Are Changing The Face Of The West",[2] and "Stephen Lewis
Says Ontario Preparing To Go NDP".[3]

In 1974, the federal NDP, which had become a power and had forced
through parliament such radical measures as Petro-Canada and the Foreign
Investment Review Board, had been reduced from thirty-two seats, the most
ever, to sixteen. National leader David Lewis, long a powerful voice for social and
economic equity, who had replaced the revered Tommy Douglas as leader, had
been defeated in his own seat. So had Premier Schreyer's friend, Douglas Rowland,
after only two years, by the emerging "religious right". In December 1975, after
little more than three years, the government of ebullient Dave Barrett had been
defeated in British Columbia. In June 1977, in Ontario, articulate Stephen
Lewis, having come tantalizing close to becoming the official opposition fell to a
shattering third-place finish and resigned as leader.

It seemed that everywhere in the Western World, democratic socialism, and
even liberalism, were under attack as the pendulum of public opinion swung
from a post-war moderate left back to the right. In November 1975, the Labour
government of New Zealand was defeated, as was the Labour government of

---

[1] December 8, 1973.
[2] December 10, 1973.
[3] December 11, 1973.

Australia the following month. Our *annus horribilis* was 1976. In September, the socialist government of Sweden, forty years in office and the fount of ideas and encouragement for others, was defeated by a four-party coalition. In Saskatchewan, where Premier Allan Blakeney had taken back the sacred ground, the Tories established a base from which leader Grant Devine reduced the NDP to a corporal's guard in 1981. In the United States, former California Governor Ronald Reagan made the speech which, in 1980, made him the Republican candidate who defeated liberal Democratic President Jimmy Carter.

In Canada, Joe Clark won the National Progressive Conservative leadership, defeated the Trudeau government in early 1979, and laid the base for the nine-year Mulroney regime (1984–93). In Britain, Margaret Thatcher became the "iron lady" of the Conservative party for the next fourteen years and prime minister in March 1979, when James Callaghan's Labour government was defeated on a confidence motion by a single vote. She attributed Labour's defeat to its "inability to control its trade union allies".

That, too, was a problem in Manitoba. Organized labour demanded things its political partner could not give. Furthermore labour, using its organizational clout in an expanding economy, had become the new middle class and was restive and ready to vote its aspirations. The Manitoba Federation of Labour asked its members to vote NDP and Premier Schreyer received a hero's welcome at the MFL convention on September 23, 1977,[4] but the Manitoba Government Employees Association, the largest union, threatened to vote against the government and asked the MFL to end its organic relationship with the NDP.

Nor had the NDP government made many friends in the business community, especially among the Chamber of Commerce types, who felt hard done by no matter how well they were doing. In addition to their historical antipathy to "socialists", they feared the NDP's determination to use government as an instrument of both societal democratization and economic development, and they blamed the NDP for insisting that Ottawa's Anti-Inflation Program limits profits as well as wages. In September 1976, Eric Kierans, former president of the Montreal and Canadian Stock Exchange told the Conference Board of Canada that Canadian business was receiving "the most handsome package of subsidies,[5] tax write-offs, allowances, deductions, cheap loans, export credits and other giveaways than anywhere outside Britain", that profits of Canada's 1,000 largest corporations had increased from $7.7 billion in 1970 to $17.8 billion in 1975, and that some of Canada's major corporations had more profit in the past five years than in their entire previous history. But it changed nothing; the business community (then as now) did not want government intervention, except to ameliorate problems

---

[4] A year later, in October 1978, the MFL convention defied its own executive and voted to make labour's traditional support for the NDP conditional on support of the NDP government for labour.

[5] Even clients of Canadian corporations milk Canadian taxpayers. "Bombardier is pursuing a $1.65 billion deal with Northwest Airlines of St. Paul, Minnesota … [which] warned this could hinge on Ottawa's financing." *Winnipeg Free Press*, May 29, 2001.

business created, so they could survive their own mistakes.[6]

Premier Schreyer added in an interview, "Despite the moaning about taxes and government spending, the recent Economic Council of Canada report notes that in the last 12 years, the top income percentiles have taken an even larger percentage of the total income than the bottom percentiles."[7]

But the NDP was mercilessly pilloried by those constantly demanding help from government, while simultaneously describing it as a tax-hungry incubus bleeding people white. In late 1977, INCO vice-president Walter Curlock revealed the tragi-comic fact that the Government of Canada gave INCO $79 million to open mines in Indonesia and Guatemala while 3,400 workers at Sudbury and Thompson were laid off. He explained they could do this in Canada but "third world countries would act against INCO if we took measures affecting their social or economic development."[8]

Other requests for help were merely comical. When independent Esso dealers were told to accept lower commissions or Esso would build its own retail outlets, they asked government to "legislate the oil companies out of the retail business immediately ... Esso dealers believe the only way to preserve free enterprise and competition in gasoline retailing is by government action."[9] Another special pleader! There must be no government intervention in the economy—except on their behalf.

IN MID-AFTERNOON on election day, I went to my office to act as a listening post and trouble-shooter for those having problems with the E-Day intricacies. Between phone calls, I assessed the campaign and future prospects of the government. Lyon had fought with the ferocity of a crusader while, at times, the government had acted like a tired boxer who had taken too many punches to the head. It had certainly taken too many defeats in its efforts to give "power to the people", many of whom seemed confused about what to do with it—or if they even wanted it. Lyon had detected that the public mood was shifting away from the post-war mixed economy, with publicly owned corporations filling the void left by the private sector, to a market economy that saw public enterprise as a barrier to private profit.

The Tories had been devilishly clever in combining the operating and utility debts, increasing Manitoba's "debt" from $382 per person, as stated by the bond rating agencies, to $3,400. The money borrowed by Manitoba Hydro, which

---

[6] When the micro-technology industry implodes because of its own excesses and lays off thousands, or privatized Air Canada downsizes to avoid bankruptcy, or banks tighten operations to improve share value, government must find funds for job retraining, unemployment insurance and welfare.

[7] *Winnipeg Tribune*, January 7, 1977.

[8] *Ibid.*, October 29, 1977.

[9] Telegram, Western Esso Dealers Committee to Premier Schreyer, May 27, 1975.

Roblin had deemed an "investment" to be repaid from future earnings of the self-sustaining utility, Lyon converted into a "debt" to be repaid from taxes. But the public did not see the difference; a debt is a debt. Also, Saul Miller's projected deficit had swelled ominously,[10] because of reduced revenues, higher costs flowing from the recession and reduced transfer payments from Ottawa. But again the public did not differentiate: a deficit is a deficit. It gave credence to Lyon's charge of NDP "waste and mismanagement".[11]

The Tories' master stroke had been the ringing cash register. The intricacies of Columbia Forest Products no longer mattered. Attempting to tie the can of CFP at Sprague and CFI at The Pas to the tail of the Tories proved futile. Manitobans no longer cared whose fault it was; they heard only the ringing of that damnable cash register tolling losses. The music had stopped with the withdrawal of the ad, but the memory and images lingered on.

About 150,000 Manitobans between the ages of eighteen and twenty-one, one-quarter of the electorate, had reached voting age since 1969 and knew nothing of the fierce fight for Medicare and Autopac. These policies were so successful that they had become enculturated and were taken for granted, as though they had always existed. Indeed, often a government does not get the benefit of the good it has done but suffers the opprobrium for its failures:

> The evil that men do lives after them,
> The good is often interred with their bones.[12]

Nor was Manitoba Hydro,[13] the NDP government's most significant long-term achievement, the political plus it should have been. The debate had become as metaphysical as the scholastic's argument over how many angels could dance on the head of a pin. The tired repetitions about dates, megawatts, acre-feet of water, cubic-feet-per-second flows, who said what when, sequences of development, diversion versus regulation, future power needs, and whether hydro chairman David Cass-Beggs was a hydraulic or a political engineer, had become as tedious as picking pepper out of birdseed and the public tuned out. Manitoba Hydro was transformed from a utility into a political football. The Tories blanketed the province with full-page ads: "Engineers state that the NDP wasted $605 million playing politics with Manitoba Hydro". Most hydraulic engineers agreed with the

---

[10] Miller had projected a $25 million deficit. The perils of budget-making in a volatile economy emerged when the industrialized world suffered an unexpected recession, causing a total of $54 million in reduced tax revenues and increased government costs, as well as reduced transfers from Ottawa to the tune of $50 million, for a total Manitoba deficit of $129 million. Don Craik, the new PC Finance minister, mischievously added $96 million in capital expenditures, historically amortized, allowing the new government to claim that the NDP had left a deficit of $225 million.

[11] At his defeat in 1981, Lyon left Howard Pawley NDP government a deficit of $251 million. (Budget, March 31, 1982).

[12] *Shakespeare*, Julius Caesar.

[13] The first of ten turbines at Long Spruce, the second Hydro site on the Nelson River, went into operation on October 7, 1977.

government, but the fact that forty per cent of Hydro revenues were being used to pay interest charges created suspicions that the Tories' engineers were right.

Two decades later, in 1999, Statscan reported that Manitoba Hydro had the lowest rates and highest profit of any Canadian utility, their $209 million surplus representing sixeen per cent of operating revenues.[14] Like Premier Duff Roblin's Winnipeg Floodway, the NDP's hydro-electric project was a triumph of vision and engineering. However, just as the significance of Duff's Ditch was not fully appreciated until the "Flood of the Century" thirty years later, so the significance of Manitoba's hydro-electric potential was not recognized until the energy price spike in 2000.

Meanwhile, maddeningly, the NDP was being out-manoeuvred and out-campaigned by opponents free to say whatever was to their advantage, and who knew that a government in office for eight years carried a load of baggage it had to defend.

And there WAS baggage.

Installation of the Russian-built turbines at Jenpeg, delayed by different measurement standards, allowed the Tories to attack the NDP for not buying turbines from General Electric (despite the multi-million dollar price difference), hinting, by implication, that during the Cold War, Manitoba should not be buying from communists. It also gave the Tories a *gratis* opportunity to charge the government with "waste and incompetence", and the increasing cost to those who had installed electric heating—including many NDP supporters—lent weight to their argument in the public mind.

Ventures financed by the Manitoba Development Corporation had fallen like tenpins. Many had been initiated by the previous government, but it was the NDP-initiated disasters of Flyer Bus and Saunders Aircraft that received media attention and gave credence to Lyon's charge that the NDP "can't run a peanut stand". The NDP government was hoisted on the Tories' petard, but also on its own.

A fire at a residence for the mentally disadvantaged in Portage la Prairie had caused the death of eight residents and brought a hurricane of media and political attacks, despite the government having spent $7 million to improve the facilities. It was a classical example of how governments are pinned to a Procrustean bed; if they spend they are criticized and if they do not, they are criticized.

What was termed the "Pilutical Affair" had also carried a whiff of scandal and government malfeasance. Judge Pilutik was the NDP government's first judicial appointment. In 1976, he was under investigation for misconduct. His resignation three days before an inquiry was to begin cast a hint of suspicion on the Office of the Attorney General.

Legislation increasing overtime pay from 1.5 per cent to 1.75 per cent, to reduce company demands for compulsory overtime, had been seen as a concession to the MFL, and enraged the business community. Sunday closing legislation,

---

[14] And then the mouthpieces for the profiteers began claiming that the public "can not run a peanut stand" and demanded that Manitoba Hydro be privatized—just like the Manitoba Telephone System was in 1996, when we had, arguably, the lowest rates in the world.

seen as a concession to the Retail Clerks Union, whose members did not want to work on Sundays, enraged those wanting to shop at Mom and Pop stores.

Business was angered by the NDP's Corporation Capital Tax of one-fifth of one percent (half the Ontario rate) on capital investment, which was designed for corporations that escaped income tax by ballooning their expenses and dividends. Labour was angered by the anti-inflation controls and the government's refusal to enact an anti-scab law. Landlords were angered by rent controls, which saved tenants $4 million in the first year, but cost landlords the equivalent amount. Farmers were angered by the inheritance tax, the government's reluctance to lend them more money to buy each other's overpriced land, and the mineral acreage tax of ten cents an acre imposed to encourage owners to develop potential mineral deposits instead of sitting on them. The tax was minuscule tax, but thousands of property owners gave up their mineral rights rather than pay ten cents an acre.

In the Interlake, a seat crucial to the NDP, people had been angered by the government's expropriation of properties on Hecla Island, a century-old Icelandic settlement, to turn it into a resort. The NDP government had proceeded reluctantly, but it was seen as an example of socialist insensitivity.[15] People forgot—or ignored —that the deal was negotiated with Ottawa, and the expropriation order signed by the preceding Weir government.

Aboriginal Manitobans, who had traditionally voted NDP and whose votes were crucial in the Northern constituencies, were angry. Ottawa and the lawyers for the Northern Flood Committee representing native communities affected by flooding along the route of the hydro-electric development, had drawn up an agreement and demanded that Manitoba sign it without changing a comma. The NDP government, concluding that the agreement took policy decisions about northern development out of the hands of the government, refused to sign.[16]

Francophones, whose votes were crucial in at least one constituency, were not wholly pleased. The NDP government reintroduced French as a language of instruction,[17] established the Bureau d'education Française in the Department of Education, and contributed about $1 million to their cultural centre in St. Boniface. But, mindful that Manitoba was not the habitation of English and French but of several score linguistic groups, it had refused to enact legislation making Manitoba officially bilingual.[18]

---

[15] Thirty years later, columnist Catherine Mitchell wrote, "In 1970, the population stood at 70. News reports noted that many older residents were happy to see the government move in, build the $1.3 million bridge and spend money to turn the area into a tourist resort." (*Winnipeg Free Press*, September 27, 2001) In 1997, the Conservative government of Gary Filmon began selling the land back.

[16] The NDP stated that native communities would be compensated on the same basis as property expropriated in other parts of the province and estimated a cost of perhaps $7 million. A month after being elected, the Lyon government signed the agreement including the clause the NDP found unacceptable. Since then, four of the five affected communities have been paid about $400 million. The fifth, Cross Lake, has refused to sign on the grounds that Lyon's signature entitles them to perpetual care.

[17] In March 1977, when the Norwood School Board offered half-French, half-English programs, 200 francophones marched on the legislature demanding that the government offer French-only programs.

[18] A Supreme Court decision provided for French-language services, but did not go so far as to declare Manitoba officially bilingual.

Day care had angered those who believed that parents should care for their own children, but also annoyed those, mostly NDPers, who felt that the government had not gone far enough, and it therefore cost the NDP campaign workers. The strike at the Griffin Steel plant and the wrenching issue of compulsory overtime had damaged the government with labour and cost the NDP more campaign workers.

Some had been angered into concluding that the NDP was good at redistributing wealth—which had been earned by others—but not at creating it. Roland Grandpré, director of the Manitoba Institute of Management commented, "I have no quarrel with wealth redistribution ... but what can be distributed in the future, if you are not improving the production of wealth now?"[19]

In fact, during the Schreyer administration, whether by good luck or good management, the economy DID grow enormously. That, ironically, had some negative political consequences. Personal income went up fast—and the tax on it became perceptible. Long-time NDP supporters brought their statements to the Premier's Office and pointed to the income tax box. Was their government's tax system robbing them?[20] Was Lyon right?

Limiting land purchases by foreigners had pleased those wanting to buy land without price competition, but angered those wanting to sell land to wealthy foreigners. Much worse was the land-lease option. It was a limited program to rescue farmers from their creditors, and keep land in the hands of Canadians, and for many it was the last chance they would have to farm. But the program was demonized as "communism" and had become a venomous political issue. It was a farsighted policy but a political disaster.

More politically disastrous was the premier's musing about reducing the income gap; upper-income groups saw it as proof that "Schreyer is a communist." The premier had forgotten Aristotle's analysis that, "In democracies, the Notables revolt because they are not equal, but are offered only an equal share." Ironically, he also offended those whose future he sought to secure—the young. These products of the Revolution of Rising Expectations had much but wanted more. The emerging "Me" generation viewed the world with the optimism of youth, seeing their future not in security but in opportunity, and the proposal not as a springboard but as a barrier to their reach for the brass ring.[21]

And the government had lost some support among older voters by

---

[19] *Winnipeg Free Press*, September 28, 1977. Twenty-four years later, Eric Kierans, former president of the Canadian Stock Exchange, former cabinet minister in both the Lesage and Trudeau governments, a closet NDPer who coauthored *The Corporate Welfare Bums* (1971) with NDP national leader David Lewis, stated that he no longer supported the NDP because "they have done much in terms of social policy, but they have no policy on how to make the economy grow." CBC interview, April 26, 2001

[20] In the TV series 'West Wing', when the president's chief-of-staff was asked why the black caucus opposed the proposed estates tax, he summarized, "Because the first generation of black millionaires is about to die." October 24, 2001.

[21] In a post-election interview with columnist Frances Russell, Schreyer agreed that his proposal for shrinking the income gap may well have cost him votes among those "fearing the unknown or yearning to be upwardly mobile." *Winnipeg Tribune*, October 31, 1977.

Schreyer playing Hamlet and musing about leaving for other fields of endeavor. After 1974, he was frequently reported being on the verge of leaving to become Trudeau's minister of Trade and Commerce, or to be appointed chairman of the National Energy Board, or to join the American James Schlesinger Group to negotiate native land claims along the proposed northern pipeline route. A year before the election he offered to resign and was prevailed upon by the party caucus to stay, but it loosened the ties of those drawn to the NDP because of Schreyer, and concerned about the nature and direction of a government without him.

There was a lassitude in the caucus. The "Big Things" had been done and there was nothing new to excite them and inspire them with a sense of mission. They were like soldiers prepared for battle but could not find a war.

And there was a lassitude in the party. While membership in the Progresssive Conservative Party mushroomed, NDP membership had dropped from 17,200 in 1973 to 12,600. The enthusiasm was not what it had been in 1969 and 1973. Some of the imported campaign organizers, like Hessian mercenaries, seemed to be in Manitoba simply because they were unhappy at home.

There was also a querulousness in the party. Two millennia earlier, Tacitus had written of Roman society, "War silences all debate," but this did not apply to the NDP. It seemed the more critical our electoral position became, the more party members forgot their role as defenders of the government, and instead, attacked the government for sins of omission or commission.

And the party was fragmenting itself by renting out its podium to disparate single-interest lobby groups,[22] who tended to vote strategically—for whoever offered them most. They were very active at party conventions but less so on the hustings. The party membership list was becoming illusory as a guide to campaign contributions and election-day workers.

The stench of political death was particularly acute among the government's appointees to boards and commissions. Such positions were the gift of the government and usually went to persons who had some common sense, took their jobs seriously ... and were NDP supporters. Now calls to them to solicit election contributions often got the response: "I'm a government employee now, and non-political." Pointing out that they were political appointees and would be fired if the government changed was answered with, "There is no reason for that. I'm a good public servant."[23]

Worst of all, I myself had lost my nerve! In 1976, the premier told me: "I'm going to run a small deficit this year. When people ask for more programs I want to be able to say we have no money."

---

[22] In 1994, Peter Fenwick, Newfoundland NDP leader, mused, "The NDP has become a party of interest lobbies—gays, abortionists, lesbians—and we must break free of their bondage." Three years later, former NDP Premier Bob Rae wrote, "In opposition it was easy for the party to become allied with groups preoccupied with one issue on another ... [but] a political party has to be more than a rag-bag of complaints and grievances if it wants to govern." *From Protest to Power*, p. 327.

[23] Most were summarily replaced with Conservatives.

I had heartily concurred. We had learned the difficulty of practicing the "saving" side of Keynesianism when we had a surplus. The constant demands for more spending as though government was a candy store, and for more programs that threatened to put half the people of Manitoba on the public payroll to look after the other half, had made us skeptical of new programs. But the lust for power, like ambition, "doth make cowards of us all".

In mid-campaign I approached the premier, "My ears are red from listening to young mothers pleading for a Denticare program like Medicare. Perhaps we should announce it now. It is not very expensive and will get us some votes we might need to snatch victory from the jaws of possible defeat."[24]

"No!" The premier slammed shut the door to the candy store.

Then I had attempted another ruse. The Government Information Services office provided the public with factual information about government programs. To save the party money, I wrote a news release favourable to the government and sent it to GIS for distribution. It was returned with a note that it did not conform to their mandate. I carefully rewrote it and submitted it again. Soft-spoken GIS director Norman Donough personally brought it back and handed it to me with the gentle but firm reproof, "This is not government information. It is party propaganda."

I had not even learned to cheat successfully!

SO I SAT IN MY OFFICE, in the gathering gloom of the October evening, a myriad images flashing through my mind. The New Democratic Party approached E-Day with an outer show of quiet confidence, but with inner apprehension. But surely Manitoba was eight years better and the electorate would respond.

Tory MLA Wally McKenzie had predicted the election would "rid Manitoba of the worst, cantankerous disease known in this province in 107 years—NDP socialism." But why? Surely the electorate would understand that, if nothing else, that "NDP socialism" had made Manitoba safe for capitalism by bringing an entire new tier of people into the middle class and helping to provide them with money to spend. Had we misread the economic climate and its impact on politics?

Had the generation that survived the world's worst depression and the world's most savage war, which had developed a community spirit and saw value in collective social programs, been replaced by the atomism of a younger generation that knew nothing of those twin terrors and just wanted to be left alone?

Was this new post-Depression generation so confident of its place in the future that, as Lyon was implying, they wanted social programs replaced with tax cuts and considered deficits bad when they were incurred to provide basic services

---

[24] Twenty-five years later this was still an issue. A study revealed that "A quarter of Canadians surveyed said they needed dental care in the past year, but didn't go to a dentist because of cost." *Winnipeg Free Press*, May 14, 2002.

for the general society, but acceptable if they were used to make the rich richer because they intended to be rich?

Our public spending programs, such as those used by Roblin to build the economy while repaying their costs from future growth, were now creating inflation instead of growth. We were caught in a bind; the more we spent on job creation programs the higher the inflation rate, and the less the value. Inflation was now an enemy, not a form of economic leverage as it had been a decade earlier.

Had we gone too far in ignoring Adam Smith's thesis that, in the Western World, it is the prospect of ever-increasing pay and profit that drives the engine of production, and that in our zeal for social security we had turned off the engine and failed to replace it with another motive force?

But we had established crown corporations to substitute for the 'movers and shakers' who would not come unless guaranteed, via subsidies and tax concessions, more than their fair share. And crown corporations would also keep Canada Canadian, so Canadians could benefit from its wealth, instead of allowing ourselves to become a "branch plant" economy reduced to expressing the sentiment of Mexican President Cardenas who, on his deathbed, muttered: "Poor Mexico, so far from God and so near to the United States."

Yet many saw crown corporations as an extension of government rather than of themselves, and they were seeing government as Oz-like, dissolving into a contraption of ropes, pulleys, bells and whistles when the veil is removed. It seemed one of the great ironies of politics that the more democratic the electoral system the less faith its people have in the government they have chosen. Here, in the most democratic of countries, many seemed to see the entrepreneur the essential ingredient in an enterprise economy, being replaced by stratum upon stratum of civil servants devising means of spending other people's money, being paid whether they did anything useful or not, and reducing the public service to a system of subsidized philandering.

The new, university-educated generation appeared to consider it an article of their status to regard civil servants and politicians as people to be despised. They tended to forget that those men and women, fallible as those who voted for them, venal as they sometimes are, and incompetent as they might sometimes prove to be, are all that stand between civilized society and chaos. They had missed the message of the American Declaration of Independence, which saw democratic government as an instrument to secure a people's freedoms, not to take them away. [25]

Indeed, as someone with more prescience than he probably appreciated he had, said, if government did not exist it would have to be invented. And on this fateful day the people of Manitoba were deciding the nature of the government they wanted to have.

---

[25] "We hold these truths to be self-evident, that all men are born free and equal, and that they are endowed by their Creator with certain inalienable rights, that among these are life, liberty and the pursuit of happiness. *That to secure these rights governments are instituted among men.*" (Author's italics)

The party was betting on Schreyer's personal popularity. In 1969, he was billed as "The Man for All Reasons", in 1973, Manitobans had been asked to "Re-elect Ed Schreyer's New Democrats" and in 1977, the focus was on "Leadership You Can Trust". Some party members objected to what they saw as promotion of a leadership cult rather than party policies. However, some polls showed the NDP as much as ten points behind the Tories, while Schreyers poll was up from sixty per cent in 1973 to sixty-five per cent in 1977, he consistently out-polled the other party leaders, and at least one poll showed Schreyer sixteen points ahead of Lyon. Indeed, the major complaint about him by those who would not vote for him seemed to be that "he is in the wrong party". Columnist Nicholas Hills expressed what appeared a consensus in an article headlined "Schreyer Key To NDP Fortunes".[26] In a world in which politics is not always rational, people were turning against Schreyer's government though they trusted Schreyer; indeed it seemed at times he might be the only thing we had going for us.

Schreyer, aware that elections are more than a personality contest, was betting on the eight-year record of his government. In the spring, the polls had shown we would be defeated but our rating was improving and the Tories seemed to be losing some of their early momentum. The Gross Provincial Product had almost tripled so the provincial direct debt as a percentage of GPP had actually shrunk from 8.5 per cent to 6.6 per cent (it was 7.6 per cent by the end of the Tory term in 1982 and 23.5 per cent by the end of the Pawley period in 1988). The percentage of revenue needed to finance the provincial debt had shrunk from 9.2 per cent to 4.2 per cent.

It was true that the economy was slowing down, but no more than elsewhere. GNP growth had dropped from 4.5 per cent in 1975 to a projected 3.5 per cent for 1977 and this was seen as fatal, but in fact this was so only by comparison with the growth of the past seven years. Two years later the Manitoba government would have been deliriously happy to have economic growth of 3.5 per cent.

In November 1976, a private consortium announced development of an $80-million office complex on Portage Avenue. A year later, *Financial Times* business reporter Roger Newman wrote:

> In the past year, multi-national companies have developed a sudden affection for Manitoba ... In spite of troubles that may lie ahead, Winnipeg this fall became the home of substantial new manufacturing plants that were opened by Winpak Ltd., Sperry Univac Defence Systems Ltd., and GWG Garments Ltd ... Potential investors from Germany and Japan have toured the province ... fostering hopes that more manufacturing development may be on the horizon ... [Provincial officials] say the province has no apparent blemishes on its record, such as Saskatchewan's nationalization of the potash industry, British Columbia's reputation for strikes and poor

---

[26] *Op cit.*, May 13, 1977.

labour relations, Quebec's unstable political climate … or high wage rates … in Alberta.[27]

We were doing better than we ourselves sometimes believed. There was no way the people of Manitoba would vote against us … It was time to go to election headquarters at the Union Centre, to savour victory or suffer *Götterdämerung*. The tension was palpable. Some poet wrote that in any contest "there are two pleasures for the choosing: the one is winning; the other, losing." Perhaps, but it was nicer to win …

Out in the darkness of that October night the Fates wove, and measured, and cut …

At 8 P.M. the polling places were closed and the ballot boxes opened. In contrast to the boisterous, hot-stove activities of the political people, this is a silent, almost subterranean operation, but it lies at the heart of the democratic system of choosing a government. The ballots are tabulated by the deputy returning officers in the presence of party agents and the results communicated to the chief electoral officer, who notifies the headquarters of each party. In less than ninety minutes the hyperactivity of the past six weeks was brought to a screeching halt.

The ugly, small, grey, metal boxes with the paleolithic faces rendered their verdict. The results were in. The NDP was out.[28] I thought of Shakespeare's *King Lear*: "Ingratitude, thou marble-hearted beast."

The Liberals had collapsed, the voters had polarized, and Lyon had pulled the sword from the stone. Like Phoebus Apollo forsaking beleaguered Hector at Troy, the *Zeitgeist* had moved from Schreyer to Lyon.

So, on that October night, we hunkered down, contemplating the detritus of the past eight plus years, and reminiscing about another time. What gaiety there was seemed contrived and the klink of beer bottles downright irksome. The NDP members and (now former) ministers gathered to commiserate with their leader. How young they had all looked on another evening, those eager neophytes of 1969 when they were young and their hearts were filled with fire. And how worn they now appeared after more than eight years of guiding Leviathan. A cruel irony was to be revealed by analysis of the voting pattern. Of the 623,575 Manitobans eligible to vote, an historically high seventy-eight per cent had done so. A shift of 510 votes from Progressive Conservative to NDP, spread over six constituencies, might have saved the government. But, as Tory guru Dalton Camp had observed, "Politics is a cruel business."

Lyon had won the largest popular vote in Manitoba in half a century. Later analysis showed that the NDP won fifty-two per cent of the seats in Winnipeg but only forty per cent of the votes. Ironically, during the NDP years the economy had

---

[27] *The Winnipeg Tribune*, November 1, 1977.
[28] Election results were: PC—33 seats (from 21); NDP—23 seats (from 31); Liberals—1 seat (from 3). The popular vote was PC—49% (from 37%); NDP—38% (from 42%); Liberals—12% (from 19%).

done so well that many families moved from the city to the suburbs—and voted PC. The native reserves remained largely with the NDP but there was a slight shift to the Liberals (D'Arcy McCaffrey had done his work well). The rural areas had been given new life by the NDP but they voted overwhelmingly PC. The francophone community had been assiduously courted, yet there was some slippage. The Ukrainian vote for the NDP dropped from sixty per cent in 1973 to fifty per cent.

That was politics! Granted, certain groups would vote against the NDP as a matter of principle, but the incomprehensible and unacceptable humiliation lay in the report by voting analyst Michael Kinnear: "Nearly every identifiable group, whether ethnic, economic, regional or whatever, tended to vote against the government."[29]

What had gone so terribly wrong? Had we done too little? Or had we done too much, and created too many disturbances.? Was it as Alexis de Tocqueville had stated 150 years earlier in his epic study *Democracy in America,* "People grow tired of confusion whose end is not in sight"? Or did the real reason for our defeat lie in the comment of an anonymous worker at the PC election headquarters: "I worked hard, but it was worth it; we got our freedom back"

No matter the reason, it was finished. Eight members of the NDP caucus, including three ministers, had gone down to defeat. Tomorrow Charon would ferry the fallen across the Styx. Tonight,

> The captains and the kings depart,
> The tumult and the shouting dies.[30]

---

[29] *Winnipeg Free Press,* December 2, 1977.
[30] Rudyard Kipling, *Recessional.*

Epilogue

Sic transit gloria.[1]

For ten days after the gray metal boxes had their way with us, we went about our work as though in a trance. The constitution demands there be a government and until the newly-elected one was sworn in, we were it.

On October 20, 1977, the NDP government of Manitoba held its last cabinet meeting, a desultory affair through which we moved like automatons. The young lions of 1969 were now seasoned, tired veterans (though after more than eight years the NDP caucus still had a larger percentage of MLAs below the age of fifty than the PCs).

The day after the 1969 election, Premier-elect Schreyer had mused that two terms should be enough for any government because by then it would be tired, and he was more right than he knew.[2] But once in office no one wants to leave, not just because of the status and perks, but because they want to try again, and apply experience to to do things better. However, the Big Things—Hydro and Medicare—were done and there was less on the political horizon to stir men's souls and cause the adrenalin to flow. Satisfying multiple, varied and unlimited demands with limited resources, redistributing the loaves and fishes, and maintaining economic growth while controlling inflation, had proved more difficult

---

[1] "Thus fame passes."

[2] For Premier Schreyer, the pervading pall was further darkened by the death of his father a week before election day. His father had entered Canada in his mother's womb in 1897, the son of an authentic sheepskin-clad immigrant from the Austrian Empire, to become a pioneer—a good farmer and a committed community activist. At eighty, still a lean, active six-footer with a purposeful look on his craggy face, he died suddenly of a heart attack. Like Montcalm at Québec two centuries earlier, he was spared the pain of witnessing the surrender of the Shining City on the Hill.

500

than imagined, and "betterment of the human condition" had become a moving target. But we had had our rendezvous with Destiny, which brought triumphs as well as tears, and the political history of Manitoba would be forever changed.

Derek Bedson, the unlikely survivor, came like a black, bent crone, wordlessly, without making eye contact, handing letters to the Premier's Office staff, instructing us to vacate by the end of Friday, October 21st, to make room for the new personnel. At the stroke of noon, October 24, 1977, the fifteen-cannon salute heralded the changing of the guard. The Progressive Conservative Government of Premier Sterling Lyon was in place.

Bedson showed the royal blood to which he occasionally alluded. When the new premier called in the NDP deputy minister of Public Works, Marvin Nordman, to dismiss him, Bedson was there. Nordman, wanting to be friendly in his misery, said: "Well, Derek, you're back in the saddle again," and Bedson shot back, "I never left it."

Premier-elect Lyon pronounced economic growth his top priority, and the *Winnipeg Free Press* (apparently without comprehending the internal contradiction) editorialized: "Lyon promised less government intervention in the private sector and more assistance to private enterprise which can be expected to lead to an expanding economy."[3] He abolished the inheritance tax, mineral acreage tax and windfall mining tax, reduced personal and corporate income taxes, and called on the private sector for advice and participation in the "new economy". The blossoming of Lincoln Town Cars on Winnipeg streets within weeks after the election, and the sounds of Happy Days Are Here Again, testified to the expectation among some that what Lyon called Manitoba's "sour economy" would sweeten with the expulsion of the "socialists".

But economic growth did not come. In 1978, Manitoba had the lowest growth rate and investment-increase rate of any province, the highest unemployment rate since the Depression, and a population decrease—the first since 1967—in 1979 and 1980. As a reminder of 1970, when it was predicted sensible people and businesses would flee Manitoba as though it had the plague if Autopac was established, *Winnipeg Tribune* cartoonist Jan Kamienski did a reprise depicting a wagon train leaving Manitoba over the caption: "Will the last Manitoban please turn out the lights."[4]

During 1978, the mining sector, in which Lyon had promised to spur activity, drastically reduced its operations. In Thompson, Manitoba's premier mining town, unemployment insurance payouts increased eighty per cent over 1977. The construction industry, Manitoba's largest employer, collapsed, mortgage foreclosures were up seventy per cent over 1977, and the joke of choice became that the major sign of Tory rule was the surfeit of "For Sale" signs on Winnipeg properties. *Manitoba Business* magazine editorialized, "The question to be

---

3 *Winnipeg Free Press*, October 12, 1977.
4 January 13, 1979.

answered is if income and corporate tax reductions are a fair exchange for loss of substantial amounts of business generated by the public treasury. The question is more pressing as hopes for new projects remain unrealized."[5]

By the end of 1979, Winnipeg had the lowest weekly earnings of twenty-five cities. College fees, university tuition, Pharmacare deductibles and urban transit fees were up, and Manitoba was the only province to suffer a decrease in the number of doctors since 1945. In early 1980, the head of the Department of Pathology at the University of Manitoba and five of his research staff announced they were leaving Manitoba, blaming the government for a shortage of ambulances and hospital beds. Some taxes had gone down, but so had the services that Manitobans expected.

In 1977, Premier Lyon had announced a program of "acute protracted restraint", and was cheered to the rafters by the business community and congratulated by the media. Programs were shredded and spending slashed. The City of Winnipeg, which had always demanded more from the NDP government no matter how much they got, was told provincial grants would not be increased. But public and editorial opinion had taken a 180-degree turn; those who had excoriated the NDP government for spending too much now instructed the Tory government to spend more. In early 1980, a *Winnipeg Free Press* editorial entitled "A Message For Mr. Lyon", warned of "slow growth" and "gloom" in the economy and continued by saying that a public opinion poll showed the government's

> awesome complacency in economic matters does not reassure Manitobans; it convinces them their government either does not notice the problems around them or is determined to pretend they do not exist. Winnipeg and the province face real problems of slow economic growth, declining population, inadequate housing and urban decay. Native people need to find a better life. The province's cultural institutions need money and the enthusiasm to preserve its great and valuable assets.[6]

In February 1980, when the Speech from the Throne was read, Jim Cartlidge, president of the usually fiercely anti-spending Winnipeg Chamber of Commerce, uncharacteristically began beating the drum for more spending.[7] The same day, in editorials entitled "A Change Of Direction"[8], and "Setting A New Direction"[9] both Winnipeg dailies congratulated the government on its more "activist" approach to the economy. Surely this would spur economic growth and inspire private investment.

But Manitoba's economy did not improve. Taxes went up and so did the deficits and debt that had formed so large a part of the PC attack on the NDP

---

[5] January/February 1979.
[6] January 23, 1980.
[7] *Winnipeg Tribune*, February 22, 1980.
[8] *Ibid.*
[9] *Winnipeg Free Press*, February 22, 1980.

government in 1977, and by March 31, 1979, Manitoba had the highest per capita debt of all the provinces except Newfoundland. In its four years, the Lyon government had four successive large deficts, total debt went up $900 million and moved from 6.6 per cent to 7.6 per cent of Gross Provincial Product. And in its last budget, in 1981, it admitted having negative economic growth during the past year.

To be fair, the Lyon government had the misfortune of hitting a bad patch in the general economy. To conform to its ideology, the Conservatives reduced public expenditure and expected private-sector investment to fill the gap. But the private sector did not respond. It was to cost the government both economically and politically.

One of Lyon's first actions was appointment of a one-man commission[10] to investigate Manitoba Hydro development projects that Tories variously labelled "the largest error in Manitoba history" and the "$604 million waste", purportedly engineered by the NDP government. It cost Manitoba taxpayers about $3 million for the momentous conclusion that had things been done differently there might have been a different cost. Ironically, by the time the report was tabled it seemed that Manitoba Hydro, because of its rapid expansion for which the NDP had paid a political price, was the only promising spot in the Manitoba economy. *The Winnipeg Tribune* announced prominently, "Hydro Future Looks Bright".[11]

The other revolutionary *bête noir* the Tories were determined to expunge was also put under the investigative microscope. The Burns Commission was appointed, did its ritual dance, and recommended termination of Autopac. But by then, the people of Manitoba had experienced its benefits and Premier Lyon, appearing unusually strained on the television screen, announced that "the eggs cannot be unscrambled", and Autopac would remain. Later, his minister of Agriculture, Harry Enns, stated at a "Schreyer Roast" that "Autopac is the best thing the Schreyer government did."

Ironically, with Hydro and Autopac secure, a vicious, long-term fight developed over the iconic program of which the NDP was most proud—Medicare. The attack, which continues today, comes less from the medical profession, which has learned to appreciate the benefits of Medicare to both their patients and themselves, but from many who benefit most from the health care system for which their parents sacrificed. Their entire experience has been with near-miraculous medical services provided with no cost barriers, so the complaints are largely about waiting lists. But as Edmund Burke, the ultimate political realist, observed, "Those who feed on the government's bread will, at the first scarcity, bite the hand that fed them."

A half-century ago, the "miracle" medications were Watkin's Medicated Ointment and Iodine, the ill were put to bed and fed chicken soup, and they either recovered … or died. In either case, there was no waiting list. Since then,

[10] Mr. Justice G.E. Tritschler. This was widely seen as an act of revenge for the CFI investigation launched by the NDP.
[11] *Winnipeg Tribune*, October 27, 1979.

medical science has developed PET scans, CAT scans, MRIs, laser knives, laparo-scopic cameras, angioplasty bubbles, cobalt bombs, liposuction to remove fat and cosmetic surgery to make sagging faces look better than new; we not only do not want to die, we do not even want to age. Hearts, lungs, kidneys, livers, are being transplanted, plugged blood vessels bypassed, tired joints replaced (the $6 million bionic man of TV fantasy is living among us), and drugs have made surgery less painful than watching our tech stocks. Abortions are performed on demand, wombs are transplanted, obviating the need for a rent-a-womb, ultrasound allows us to peek into the pregnant womb and abort the imperfect fetus, and gene splicing allows the creation of the designer baby.

Medical technology has subverted nature; the future of humanity no longer depends on the random conjunction of egg and sperm. Not long ago, it was obvious when a person was dead; now medical technology allows us to live until someone pulls the plug. And we wonder why waiting lists are long!

We have ritual criticism of the cost of "socialized medicine" and, ergo, high taxes. Life expectancy is seven years longer than before Medicare, commer-cials about "wonder" drugs make us feel deprived if we have no pain that would allow us to get a prescription, and we have facilities, procedures, diagnostics, pharmaceuticals, undreamed of a generation ago. The original insured package under Medicare covered hospitals, doctors and nurses, but we have added nursing care, home care, pharmacare, palliative care, optometric care, chiropractic care, children's denticare, alcohol and drug addictions care, urine leakage care and-physiotherapy—and that's the short list. And we wonder why costs increase!

Why has Medicare expanded so much? The Sixties witnessed our first mass graduation of women from universities. As women have always done, they estab-lished households and had children, but they also did something else; they went out and got jobs. That was good for them, but it created a social problem; there was no one at home to take care of grandma. Hospitals paid for by Medicare became a place to store her. In 1971, the Manitoba government was informed that about thirty per cent of those in hospitals were there only because no one was at home to care for them; their children were away making money. So we built nursing homes and when we told people this would cost them taxes, they replied, "We don't care. We need a life of our own, you take care of it."

A man I knew slightly phoned. "I've looked after my mother long enough, it's the government's turn, find her a nursing home." But the more nursing homes we built, the faster they filled. Then we were informed that about thirty per cent of those in nursing homes were there only because no one was at home to care for them; their children were away making money. So we established Home Care and when we told people it would cost them tax money, they replied, "We don't care, we have other things to do, we have children to raise, and by the way, we need day care."

In fiscal 2003–04 the Manitoba government spent $415 million for nursing care, $200 million for home care, and $65 million for day care, for a total of $680 million. If the government did not need to pay those costs we could abolish the corporate income tax, the corporate capital tax, the motive fuel tax, the gasoline tax, the mining tax and the land transfer tax. What would that do for our Tax Freedom Day! Or if spent only on core health services, how much would that shorten waiting lists! To achieve those ends, all we need to do is persuade Manitobans to care for their families.

And there is Pharmacare, established because "drugs" were no longer a seventy-five-cent bottle of Aspirin. In 2003–04 Pharmacare—just prescription drugs, not including those provided in hospitals—cost more than Duff Roblin's total provincial budget forty years earlier. In the three-year period from 2001 to 2003, the budget of Manitoba Health increased thirty per cent, but the amount it spent on drugs increased ninety per cent. So why not blame the drug companies instead of Medicare?

The attack on "socialized medicine" comes from several groups. First, the hyenas: those interested in dividends, not health. In 2004, Canadian public health care spending was about $90 billion and some salivate to get their teeth into that prize—people like those who lobbied the American government for deregulation of the financial sector and created the savings and loans scandal that cost taxpayers about $200 billion. Or people like those who lobbied for deregulation of the energy sector and created Enron, for which bills may be coming in for the next two generations.

Second, from the young and well-to-do. Their parents—who established Medicare—bought them an excellent education that has been parlayed into excellent incomes; many young men earn more in a month than their fathers did in a year and many young women earn more in a year than their mothers knew existed. They have found they can borrow money at less interest, and buy savings instruments for higher rates, than their neighbours, and when they buy an SUV they get an enormous discount, because the agency knows they will be back for another as soon as the ashtray is full. In brief, their positions have bought privileges. Then their doctor suggests elective surgery—and they must stand in line behind people with less income and education. So they demand a private hospital so they can jump the queue; they even offer to pay for it themselves! That is a tempting offer, but currently private hospitals draw all their staff from the public system, which does not shorten waiting lists and when the volunteer patients receive their bill, they will squeal like stuck pigs and demand release from paying taxes for the public system. Unfortunately, if Medicare cannot keep those who have money, it cannot afford those who don't.

A third group wants to square the circle with a system of public payment and private delivery of services, allowing competition to reduce costs and shorten waiting lists. But if "competition" reduces costs of medical services, why does the United States not have the lowest costs instead of the highest? And why does this group blithely ignore the fact that one can get fast services in the U.S. only because millions of Americans cannot even buy their way onto the waiting lists!

"Socialized medicine" provides every Canadian with the best medical services money can buy, but we are told we cannot afford it. We allow a wealthy Canadian family to escape taxes on as much as $2.5 billion, and we subsidize some of our richest corporations, but we have no money for Medicare. A doctor from B.C. comes to Winnipeg and establishes a $3 million state-of-the-art clinic, but he may be the only one who can afford to be treated there. If we had private care we would either pay for it ... or not get it. In other words, it would be available only to those who could pay.

Despite the enormous load placed on Medicare and the 'horror' stories about costs, in the past twenty years spending by Manitoba Health has increased so little as a percentage of GPP that one wonders if they are using the same accountants as Enron. But the attack continues: by those who covet that money, by those who believe nothing is of value unless it can be used to rip off the public, by those seduced by before-tax-supported "think tanks", and by the generation spoiled rotten by Medicare. They have had no opportunity to learn that the longest waiting list, and highest cost, is when one is ill and has no money.

IN JULY 1977, I had given the premier a memo:

> Like Aeschylus, drop by drop, we learn our wisdom with our blood. After eight years, we are exhausted by our efforts and disillusioned by our inability to reshape the world, and getting sloppy. As a result, the Tories may be elected. That might be the best thing that can happen to us. Those now in charge of the Tory party are not the young, fresh-faced activists of the Roblin era. They are relics of a day past: vindictive, middle-aged, cynical people, more interested in revenge for their defeat in 1969 by 'socialists' than in governing in the interests of the general populace; political troglodytes who are—even if inadvertently—stalking horses for privilege and instruments of a business community who have not read Adam Smith much less Keynes, and who still believe their own wealth would result from making everyone else poor; who believe if unions are abolished and wages reduced to 50 cents an hour, all would be rich. They will create a crisis that will give us an opportunity at the polls in four years and we will become heroes even if we do nothing more than reestablish the programs the Tories will destroy.

> Best of all, four years in Opposition will toughen us and we will return as a government rather than as starry-eyed operators of a gigantic candy store. Only one thing can ruin this lovely scenario; we might have the unmitigated misfortune to be re-elected.

We were not. But four years later, the NDP was back in office under the leadership of former Attorney General and Municipal Affairs minister, Howard Pawley (in the age of Thatcher and Reagan, Manitoba returned the Social Democrats). The Liberals, and the Progressives, formed by three NDP defectors, were wiped off the electoral map and the NDP won thirty-four seats to twenty-three for the PCs, giving Pawley the secure majority that had eluded Schreyer. But it was essentially a new group who had to learn their own lessons. They determined to compensate for Lyon's under-spending and their bastardized "Keynesianism" (spending money one year because that was needed and another year because it was there) ran amok. The required borrowing—just as interest rates suddenly jumped to record levels—in six-and-a-half years increased total debt from 7.6 per cent to 23.5 per cent of the GPP. On March 8, 1988, less than two years into its second mandate, the Pawley government was brought down on the budget vote, by one of its own backbenchers.[12]

Surprisingly, with a resurgent economy, they left their successors an unexpected surplus of $58 million, which the Filmon government cleverly "disappeared" into its newly-created $200 million Rainy Day Fund and then claimed it had been left a $142 million deficit.[13] And the NDP left the Filmon government another gift—the Limestone hydro-electric generating plant. In the teeth of criticism almost as vicious as that suffered by the Schreyer government, Pawley's administration had built the province's largest hydro plant, which brought millions into the Manitoba economy.

Ed Schreyer, who fitted the role of premier as though he had been made for it, was uncomfortable as leader of the opposition. He had been premier and knew a government has more information than its critics, that a government cannot always publicly reveal everything it knows, that not everything a government proposes should be automatically opposed, and that a government is not always wrong. In brief, he did not have the requisite taste for blood and told his caucus he did not see himself as an adequate opposition leader. For a year, like Hamlet, he wrestled with the question of "to be or not to be". Then he made a decision.

In November 1978, he mounted the platform at the annual NDP convention and, in a tough, knock-down drag-out speech, announced he would be leading the NDP in the next election because, "I like to fight Tories." The delegates cheered themselves hoarse; like the legendary once-and-future King Arthur who would return to lead his people in times of crisis, Schreyer would again take them to victory as he had, unexpected and unpredicted, in 1969.

One week later, the Schreyer's home phone rang. Jason, aged eleven, picked it up, listened, and turned wide-eyed: "Mom, it's the prime minister." Lily, half-annoyed at being interrupted while preparing breakfast, muttered: "Oh, what does he want?"

---

[12] Sixteen-year legislative veteran James Walding.

[13] *Winnipeg Free Press*, April 7, 1995; April 3, 1996 and November 17, 1999.

Ed, with shaving lather on his face, came to the phone and Prime Minister Trudeau intoned: "Eddie, the day after tomorrow I'm going to London to see the Queen, so if you want to be governor general, get on a plane and get to Ottawa *toute suite*."

The offer was unexpected, but not to be refused. His five-year tenure at Rideau Hall was followed by four years as High Commissioner to Australia. If, as some suspected, it was Trudeau's way of removing Schreyer from active politics so he would not become a threat to the national Liberals, it worked. When he returned to Manitoba, he felt that Canadians would not appreciate what would be perceived as such high-profile appointments being used as political stepping stones and he believed that he needed to do penance, so he spent several years teaching at foreign universities. Also, in the nine years he had been away, a new generation had taken control of the party and, while he remained a committed member, his political activity was to be confined to the edges, on minor boards and commissions.

His time for decision-making with political consequences, in which he engaged since he was barely old enough to vote, had passed. His most visible appointment, though not made by an NDP government, was as chancellor of University of Brandon in 2002.

Sterling Lyon, defeated in 1981 to become Manitoba's only one-term premier in the twentieth century, ended his political career and became a respected member of the Manitoba Appeals Court, serving until he retired in 2002. He had taken an early and keen interest in politics, was a genuine power in the activist and progressive government of Premier Roblin, and honed his political skills to win a sweeping victory and become premier of Manitoba. It must have been galling to suffer ignominious defeat for doing what he believed the ideological constituency that had elected him, wanted him to do. But an electorate can be fickle. And things change.

Howard Pawley's NDP government, swept into office on waves of high hopes in 1981, in three years saw its popularity reduced to a nadir of fourteen per cent by its ham-handed handling of an Autopac rate increase, and by its abortive effort to make French an official language of Manitoba. It experienced some recovery, but in the 1986 election its majority was reduced to two seats. The resignation of Laurent Desjardins in late 1987, partly because he could no longer abide the constant harping of party feminists for abortion-on-demand, left the government's fate to veteran James Walding, who had been humiliatingly reduced to the back benches in 1984 when, as Speaker, he had refused to bail out the government. In March 1988, he exercised his accidental but lethal power to bring it down.

Pawley resigned as premier. In November 1988, he ran for a federal seat, but was defeated. He moved to Ontario to become a very popular professor at the University of Windsor, but except as an occasional commentator, his political life, to which he had assiduously devoted himself since he ran as a sacrifice candidate in an impossible seat at the age of twenty-one, was over.

He was followed as premier of Manitoba by Gary Filmon, who had succeeded Lyon as leader of the PC Party. After gaining strength and popularity through three successive election victories, as thought in a Greek tragedy, in 1999 Filmon paid the ultimate political price following the public exposé of a vote-rigging scandal that had been illicitly undertaken by one of his staff members. The Conservatives were defeated by Gary Doer, who had succeeded Pawley as leader of the NDP. Doer's victory made it clear that the pioneers of 1969 had made the NDP a permanent feature of Manitoba electoral politics.

Following the 1977 election, some members of the old NDP caucus moved to the opposition benches, while others went back to the relative obscurity of their private lives. For some, the transition back to civilian life was more difficult than adjusting to power had been, for they suffered the curse of many defeated politicians. 'Normal' life had been severely disrupted. Nine years had passed and the world had changed. Those in professions, such as teaching, had missed out on salary classifications, promotions and the enormous changes in curricula and approaches, and virtually had to start over.[14] They had risked all in one game of pitch and toss, and were briefly triumphant, but now were forced to start again at the beginning, and they dared not breathe a word about their loss. Most people see the position of member of the legislature as one of power and perks and complaining about it being a long-term dead end would appear churlish and ungrateful.

And personal relationships among the "band of brothers" of 1969 were permanently changed. Individuals had been irretrievably categorized by eight years of positions held, authority wielded, and exposure to publicity. No matter our degree of sophistication about such matters or how dismissive we may be of the trappings of power, the elevation of persons to executive positions, be it in the public or private sector, confers on them an inexplicable mystique. It is not just that they have wielded power, but that it is viscerally assumed they were given that power because of some innate quality to which lesser mortals should defer.

FOR ME, the music had stopped but memories lingered on. There was a reluctance to let go. It was difficult to leave the scene of so many momentous encounters so there was a tendency to haunt the corridors of The Ledge in hopes of being able to occasionally advise our new MLAs, so they would not make the same mistakes we had. But it soon became clear that the last people the New Heroes wanted advice from were those who preceded them; after all, if they were so smart, why had they allowed themselves to be defeated?

---

[14] The same thing happened elsewhere. Conservative MLA and cabinet minister Don Orchard, retiring in 1995 after eighteen years, reported, "I gave up expanding a commercial farm operation and I'm still trying to catch up." *Winnipeg Sun*, September 30, 1997.

But there are recollections: of finding that politics is more than endless repetitions of innocuous *ad hominems*; of engaging in the relentless combat of ideas: of finding that, because the essence of government is action, ideas must be converted from rhetoric to practicalities; of observing how a democratic society makes rules for itself to live by; of learning an alert opposition is crucial to the democratic process. I had worked with those chosen by their fellows to administer institutions generations of men and women had laboured and sacrificed to create as a thin and tenuous barrier between civilized society and chaos. For a moment in time, I had seen and heard and felt and smelled the atmosphere of the political process in the raw, witnessing soaring ambitions and the imposition of self-restraints, in the struggle toward self actualization as individuals and as a society, by those giving substance to the idea, enunciated by King Arthur in the musical, *Camelot*, that men and women can govern themselves.

And there are the poignant memories which, after thirty years, haunt me still. Len Evans, the former Economics professor who became the affable, cherubic, workaholic minister of Industry and Commerce, was always alert to possibilities for improving the Manitoba economy. One project proposed (which remained sterile) under the rubric of our Stay Option, which entailed assisting people to remain in the rural areas by supporting agriculture and related industries, was a proposal to construct a rapeseed (as canola was then called) crushing plant at Dauphin. That required assessing market potential, estimating yields per acre, contracting with farmers for the necessary acreage, determining the size of the plant, and finding prospective markets for the product—canola oil.

The department advertised through the media and the embassies, inviting inquiries. A delegation came from Bangladesh. During the discussion, while assessing our production capacity, departmental civil servants provided educated guesses. Attending as an observer, I noticed a member of the delegation appeared somewhat disappointed so I said, half-facetiously, "Gentlemen, we have another variety of rapeseed, which produces considerably more oil. However, it also has a considerably higher content of uricic acid, which apparently has a tendency to cause heart disease and I don't suppose you want to import that."

The delegate from Bangladesh turned to me, "Mr. Schulz, we have a small country, one of the poorest in the world, and a large population that needs to be fed. Those living along the sea coast are more fortunate because they have access to fish but those in the interior sustain themselves with little but bread. We need oil for them to dip their dry crusts into. As for what ailments we might import, most of our people are dead by age thirty-five, so heart disease would be the very least of our concerns."

And then I felt that involuntary catch in my throat, and marvelled anew at my great good fortune that my parents had had the wisdom to bring me to this golden land. I often think of that incident when everything in Canada appears to be going wrong and there is a tendency to lapse into myriad complaints. I was particularly reminded of it, twenty years later, when reading Mordecai Richler's assessment of the problems of Canadians: "Canada is a cloud cuckoo land governed by idiots, its self-made problems comic relief to the real world where famine, racial strife and vandals in office are the unhappy rule." [15]

Regrets? I have a few and they are well remembered, but:

> The moving finger writes, and having writ, moves on.
> Not all your piety or wit will cancel half a line,
> Nor all your tears wash out a word of it. [16]

---

[15] *Barney's Version*, p. 386.
[16] The *Rubaiyat* of Omar Khayyam.

BIBLIOGRAPHY

Books

Allard, Jean. *The Rebirth of Big Bear's People: the Treaties: a New Foundation for Status Indian Rights in the 21ˢᵗ Century.* Winnipeg, unpublished manuscript

Beaulieu, Paul (ed). *Ed Schreyer: A Social Democrat in Power*, Winnipeg, Queenston House Publishers, 1977.

Becker, Carl L. *The Heavenly City of the Eighteenth Century Philosphers*, Yale University Press, 1932.

Blau, Peter. *Bureaucracy in Modern Society*, N.Y., Random House, 1956.

Bliss, Michael. *Right Honorable Men: the Descent of Canadian Politics from Macdonald to Mulroney*, Toronto, Harper-Collins Publishers, 1995.

Borins, Sandford F. and Brown, Lee. *Investments in Failure: Five Government Corporations That Cost the Canadian Taxpayers Millions,* Toronto, Methuen Publications, 1986.

Burke, James. *Paper Tomahawks: From Red Tape to Red Power*, Winnipeg, Queenston House, 1976.

Cardinal, Harold. *The Unjust Society*, Edmonton, Hurtig Publishers, 1969.

Cardinal, Harold. *The Rebirth of Canada's Indians,* Edmonton, Hurtig Publishers, 1977.

Carstairs, Sharon. *Not One of the Boys*, Toronto, McMillan, 1993.

Clark, Joe (Rt. Hon.). *A Nation Too Good to Lose: Renewing the Purpose of Canada*, Toronto, Key Porter Books, 1994.

Clarkson, Stephen, and McCall, Christina. *Trudeau and Our Times: the Magnificent Obsession* (Vol.1), Toronto, M&S, 1991.

Commoner, Barry. *The Poverty of Power: Energy And The Economic Crisis*, New York, Knopf, 1976.

Crossman, Richard (ed). *The God That Failed*, N.Y. Harper and Rowe, 1949.

Crosbie, John. *No Holds Barred: My Life in Politics*, Toronto, M&S, 1997.

Doern, Russell. *Wednesdays Are Cabinet Days*, Winnipeg, Queenston House, 1981.

Doern, Russell. *The Battle Over Bilingualism*, Winnipeg, Cambridge House, 1985.

Fromm, Erich. *Escape From Freedom*, N.Y. Avon Books, 1941.

Galbraith, John K. *The Culture of Contentment*, N.Y. Houghton Miflin Company, 1992.

George, Henry. *Progress and Poverty*, N.Y. Robert Schalkenbach Foundation, 1992 (first published 1879).

Grant, George P. *Lament for a Nation: the Defeat of Canadian Nationalism*, Toronto, M&S, 1965.

Gray, James H. *The Winter Years: The Depression on The Prairies*, Toronto, MacMillan, 1966.

Green, Sidney. *Rise And Fall of a Political Animal.* Winnipeg, Great Plains Publications, 2003.

Hardin, Hershel. *A Nation Unaware*, Vancouver, J.J. Douglas, 1974.

Hofstadter, Richard. *The Age of Reform: From Bryan to FDR.* N.Y., Vintage Books, 1955.

Hutchison, Bruce. *The Far Side of The Street*, Toronto, MacMillan of Canada, 1976.

Jones-Morrison, Sheila. *Rotten to the Core: the Politics of the Manitoba Metis Federation*, Winnipeg, 101060-an imprint of Gordon Shillingford Publishing Inc., 1995.

Keynes, J.M. *The Economic Consequences of The Peace: The Carthaginian Peace*, N.Y., Harcourt, Brace and Howe, 1920.

Laxer, James and Martin, Anne. *The Big, Tough, Expensive Job: Imperial Oil and the Canadian Economy*, Toronto, Musson Book Company, 1976.

Lewis, David. *Louder Voices: The Corporate Welfare Bums.* Toronto, James Lewis and Samuel, 1972.

Lipset, Seymor. *Agrarian Socialism: The Cooperative Commonwealth Federation in Saskatchewan*, N.Y. Doubleday Co, Anchor Books, 1959.

Mathias, Phillip. *Forced Growth: Five Studies of Government Involvement in The Development of Canada*, Toronto, James Lewis and Samuel Publishers, 1971.

Machiavelli, Niccolo. *The Prince*, Toronto, Encyclopaedia Britannica Inc., 1952. First published in 1513.

McAllister, James. *The Government of Edward Schreyer*, Toronto, Queen's University Press, 1984.

McCullum, Hugh. McCullum, Karmel, and Olthius, John. *Moratorium: Justice, Energy, the North, and the Native People*, The Berger Commission and the Mackenzie Valley Pipeline. Toronto, The Anglican Book Centre, 1977.

McKnight, John. *The Careless Society*, New York, Basic Books, 1995.

McLennan, Hugh. *Two Solitudes*, Toronto. McMillan of Canada, 1972 (first published 1946).

Myrdal, Gunnar. *The Challenge of Affluence*, N.Y. Random House (Vintage), 1965.

Nash, Knowlton. *Trivia Pursuit: How Showbiz Values Are Corrupting the News*, Toronto, M&S, 1998.

Newman, Peter C. *The Canadian Revolution 1985-1995: From Deference to Defiance*, Toronto, Penguin Books, 1995.

Newman, Peter C. *The Distemper of Our Times: Canadian Politics in Transition--1963–68*, Toronto, M&S, 1968.

Newman, Peter C. *The Canadian Establishment*, Toronto, M&S, 1975.

Newman, Walter C. *What Happened When Dr. Kasser Came to Northern Manitoba*, Winnipeg, Newmac Publishing Company, 1976.

Nielsen, Eric. *The House Is Not a Home*, Toronto, McMillan, 1989.

Noonan, Peggy. *What I Saw at The Revolution*, N.Y. Random House, 1990.

Orwell, George *Animal Farm*, London, Harcourt Brace, 1946.

Pakosh, Jarrod. *Versatile Tractors: A Farm Boy's Dream*, Toronto, Boston Mills Press, 2003.

Rae, Robert. *From Protest to Power: Personal Reflections on a Life in Politics*, Toronto, Penguin Books, 1996.

Reimer, Al. *My Harp Is Turned* to Mourning. Winnipeg, Hyperion Press, 1985.

Reston, James. *Deadline*, New York, Random House, 1991.

Richler Mordecai. *Barney's Version*, Toronto. Alfred Knopf, 199.7

Richler, Mordecai. *Home Sweet Home: My Canadian Album*, Toronto, M&S, 1984.

Riesman, David. *The Lonely Crowd,* Yale University Press, 1961.

Roblin, Duff. *Speaking For Myself: Politics And Other Pursuits*, Winnipeg, Great Plains Publications, 1999.

Safer, Morley. *Flashback,*. New York, Random House, 1990.

Silver, Jim. *Thin Ice: Politics And The Demise of an NHL Franchise*, Halifax, Fern Publishing, 1996.

Simpson, Jeffrey. *Faultlines: Struggling For a Canadian Vision*, Toronto, Harper Collins, 1993.

Sinclair, Upton. *The Jungle*, N.Y. Bantam Books, 1906.

Smith, Adam. *An Inquiry Into The Causes of The Wealth of Nations*, Toronto, William Benton, 1952 (first published 1776).

Steinbeck, John. *The Grapes of Wrath*, New York, Viking, 1939.

Stephanopoulos, George. *All Too Human: The Clinton White House*, New York, Little Brown, 1997

Stephens, Lincoln. *Autobiography of Lincoln Stephens*, New York, Harcourt, Brace & Co., 1931.

Stinson, Lloyd. *Political Warriors: Recollections of a Social Democrat*, Winnipeg, Queenston House, 1975.

Thomas, Lewis (ed). *The Making of a Socialist: The Recollections of T.C. Douglas*, Edmonton, University of Alberta Press, 1982.

Trudeau, Pierre-Elliot. *Memoirs*, Toronto, M&S, 1993.

Veblen, Thorstein. *The Theory of The Leisure Class*, N.Y., A.M. Kelley Booksellers, 1965 (first published 1899).

White, Theodore. *In Search of History*, New York, Harper and Rowe, 1978.

White, Robert. *Hard Bargains: My Life on The Line*, Toronto, M&S, 1987.

Wiseman, Nelson. *Social Democracy in Manitoba*, Winnipeg, University of Manitoba Press, 1983

Woodward, Robert. *Agenda: In The Clinton White House*, New York, Simon and Shuster, 1995

Young, Walter, D. *Anatomy of a Party: The National CCF 1932-61*. Toronto, University of Toronto Press, 1969.

Zimbalist, Andrew. *Baseball and Billions: the Economic Impact of Sports Teams and Stadiums*, N.Y. Basic Books, 1992.

Newspapers and Magazines

East Kildonan Examiner.
Hansard. Government of Manitoba
Macleans Magazine
Manitoba Business Journal
Manitoba Co-operator
Manitoba Real Estate News
North Kildonan Herald
Spotlight, University of Manitoba Dept. of Agriculture. (Winter, 1975)
Toronto Globe and Mail
Toronto Star
Winnipeg Free Press
Winnipeg Sun
Winnipeg Tribune

Government of Canada Publications:

White Paper on Indian Policy, 1969 Statistics Canada

Government of Manitoba Publications:

Guidelines For The Seventies, 1973.

Report of the Commission of Inquiry into the Pas Forestry and Industrial Complex, 1974.

Report of Commission of Inquiry into Manitoba Hydro (Tritschler Commission), 1979

Report on Targets for Economic Development, 1969.

INDEX